# INTIMATE RELATIONSHIPS

## SKILLS AND STRATEGIES THAT LEAD TO SUCCESS

# INTIMATE RELATIONSHIPS

## SKILLS AND STRATEGIES THAT LEAD TO SUCCESS

Veronica Johnson, Kimberly Parrow, and Sara Polanchek, Editors

University of Montana

cognella®

SAN DIEGO

Bassim Hamadeh, CEO and Publisher

Amy Smith, Senior Project Editor

Alia Bales, Production Editor

Jess Estrella, Senior Graphic Designer

Natalie Piccotti, Director of Marketing

Kassie Graves, Senior Vice President of Editorial

Jamie Giganti, Director of Academic Publishing

3970 Sorrento Valley Blvd., Ste. 500, San Diego, CA 92121

*I dedicate this book to my husband, Eric—you teach me every day about what it means to love someone and how to do it really well. To my dad, Walt—you've always taught me that my partner should be a bonus in my life. To my mom, Berni—you taught me how to be a strong, independent woman. To my stepmom, Stace—you have always been my model of self-confidence, love, and beauty. To my children, Marley and Magnus—you teach me every day about the kind of person I want to be in the world. Finally, to my coauthors, Kim and Sara—you two are the best. I couldn't have done this project without your wisdom, laughter, and commitment to the relationship success of every person who reads this anthology.*

—VIJ

*I dedicate this book to the students who attended the intimate relationships course, devoting invaluable time and effort in learning how to love well; to the graduate student counselors who devoted their full-throttled energy to providing care to the students in the intimate relationships lab; to the individuals and couples who have honored me with the privilege of supporting them through the struggles and triumphs of their intimate relationships; to my treasured coauthors Roni and Sara, for continued leadership and steadfast commitment to deliver high-quality relationship education and support to the students of the intimate relationships course at the University of Montana. Finally, to my family, thank you for providing the learning ground for understanding how the thread of divorce and remarriage shapes us and that it is our intimate relationships that make us whole.*

—KKP

*I have so much to be grateful for, but far and away (not counting my two scrumptious boys) is that I can declare with full honesty that I feel more love for my husband at the end of a pandemic than I did at the beginning. Yes Murph, you chew too loud, and yes, you get sappy too readily, but you always listen to me and in a year when my anxiety might have gotten the best of me, you helped me stay grounded and focused on what's most important. There is no one else I would have wanted to be trapped in a house with. Keep making me laugh and I think we will have this marriage thing in the bag. Also, a big shout out to Clayton, Atticus (C and A, I'd like your friendship to be studied in a lab someday), Wes, Pete, Abe, Carter, Joe, Leo, Max, Nick, Ian, Neto, and Elijah. I marvel at all of you relationship masters, and I know that the world would be such a better place if everyone experienced the gift of friendship that you've given to each other. Roni and Kim—what a privilege it has been to learn from you, feel supported by you, and laugh with you. I look forward to more.*

—SAP

# Contents

# Preface

This book is a long time in the making. In 2008, Roni developed and taught the first intimate relationships (IR) class to a group of 19 students. Over the years, our IR program has grown to attract over 100 students per semester, and we deliver over 1,600 hours of relationship counseling associated with the course each academic year. Sara taught IR as a doctoral student and now serves as the IR clinic director. She has supervised over 3,000 hours of relationship counseling. Kim has taught IR eight times and has counseled and supervised countless hours in the IR clinic. We've collected data from nearly 1,400 students over the years that explores students' self-esteem, self-efficacy, decision-making in relationships, endorsement of rape myths, and how these factors change over the course of completing IR, and our data collection is ongoing. What we've found when we've explored the results of our data is that, overall, students report significant increases in self-esteem, increased confidence in their decision-making in relationships, increased self-efficacy in their relationships, and a decrease in their endorsement of rape myths. What we bring to this anthology are the voices of the many students and clients we have engaged with over the years, in an attempt to fill some of the gaps we've observed in our curriculum. We also bring 50-plus years of collective experience in counseling, supervising, and teaching about intimate relationships.

The fact is, whether we are aware of it or not, we need relationships to survive. We don't come equipped with a manual that helps us to know how to achieve satisfying and successful intimate relationships. Our goal in constructing this anthology is to bring together a variety of voices, including our own, from different fields and perspectives, to offer the most comprehensive and practical guide to success in intimate relationships. We acknowledge the developmental nature of people and their relationships and how each life stage influences the establishment and main-tenance of relationships. We will begin each chapter with some pre-chapter primer questions for reflection, and at the end of the chapter we include some activities and recommendations for further reading on these topics and others.

When we speak of intimate relationships, we aren't only referring to romantic relationships. We want you, the reader, to approach this text with openness and curiosity so that you might consider all varieties of intimate relationships: familial relationships, friendships, romantic relationships, and sexual relationships. We want you to consider the many identities that we each bring to our relationships, such as varying sexual, gender, and cultural identities. We hope to provide a better understanding of the value of inclusivity and how understanding differences can enhance intimacy. We won't speak of relationship normality or abnormality. Each reading that we selected for this anthology spoke to a piece of what we hope you will learn about intimate relationships, and we know it's not perfect. We will offer context, questions for reflection, and activities that will help you put the content into perspective, and more importantly into action, in your own life. We also know that we have not and could not offer all perspectives in one anthology, so when we are aware of that, we will acknowledge it, and when we aren't, we hope you will offer your own perspective as you contextualize your own learning.

At the time of this writing we are in the midst of a global pandemic: COVID-19. For months we have stayed apart from loved ones outside of our households, and we mask up every time we leave the home. We spend hours upon hours on Zoom to work, to play, and to connect. Some struggle to stay connected and feel isolated. Some fight to make ends meet amidst lay-offs and school closures. Families grapple with remote learning and children miss their teachers and friends. Many have lost and will lose loved ones to the virus and will not have the chance to say goodbye. The political climate is such that our country is divided, and differences in belief, color, privilege, and value are not serving to bring us together but to drive us apart. We don't yet know how we will recover from the wounds that the virus and our political system have created, but we do have hope. We hope that when you are reading this book that you have hope and optimism for your future and the many relationships you will have. We hope that you learn some skills and strategies that you can use right away to make your hope a reality. Relationships are hard sometimes, and we hope to offer you some skills that will make the hard times a bit more manageable. Above all, we hope for your happiness and success in your relationships.

*"Hope is being able to see that there is light despite all of the darkness."*
—Desmond Tutu

# PART I

# Introduction to Intimate Relationships

# Chapter 1

# Forming Intimate Relationships

*"Follow your heart, but take your brain with you."*
—Alfred Adler

## EDITORS' INTRODUCTION

This chapter serves as an introduction to many of the topics we will present throughout the text. We know that repetition aids in remembering things, so we hope that the topics in this chapter serve as a primer to what lies ahead. We chose this reading in particular because, above all else, we want you to know what contributes to positive, satisfying intimate relationships. It's important to know about unhelpful communication strategies, red flags to watch out for, and how to effectively manage conflict. We will address managing challenges in relationships plenty, trust us! We begin with a reading from the positive psychology area, as we believe that being healthy, well-balanced, and grounded human beings makes us better able to establish and maintain all kinds of satisfying relationships. In fact, a 75-year-long study shows that one of the number-one predictors of physical, mental, and emotional health is maintaining connection through healthy relationships (Arnold, 2019).

John Gottman, renowned relationship researcher and counselor, developed a theory about healthy relationships he calls the sound relationship house (Gottman & Silver, 1999). We will refer to Gottman's work in many of the chapters to come, and we introduce it here so you can keep the following image in your mind as you read on. The sound relationship house (Figure 1.1) is built with supporting walls of trust and commitment. Each level of the house symbolically supports the structure of the relationship, just as a foundation, floor, and rooms

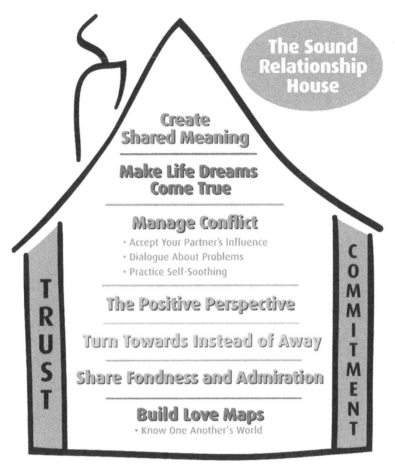

| Figure 1.1  The sound relationship house.

of a house do. We refer you to the Gottman Institute for more in-depth descriptions of each level of the house, and we encourage you to think about how you will build and reinforce each level of your current or future sound relationship house.

In "Building Positive Relationships," Frederick Brown and Cynthia LaJambe discuss some of the key features of positive relationships, how we meet and establish relationships, attraction in relationships, and how who we are as individuals influences who we are in relationships with others.

As you read, keep in mind the following primer questions for reflection. If you feel so inclined, take a few minutes and consider your responses to the following questions before you read, and then again after you've read the chapter.

## PRIMERS

1.  What are the top five most important things in your life? Really take a moment and think about this.

2.  Make a list of some of your most valued and important identities. This could take the form of a Venn diagram, with your name in the large circle in the middle and each of your identities making up the circles that surround your name and perhaps overlap each other. Your identity might include things like your ethnicity and culture, gender, sexual orientation, or perhaps your spiritual orientation, or the many roles that you play in your life such as friend, daughter, father. You might also include activities or work roles that are important to you, like hiker, artist, or student. Include as many as are important to you and know that you won't be able to capture all of your identities in one diagram.

## CREDIT

Fig. 1.1: Copyright © 2011 by Gottman Institute.

**READING 1.1**

# Building Positive Relationships

*By Frederick Brown and Cynthia LaJambe*

## FEATURES OF POSITIVE PERSONAL RELATIONSHIPS

### Preview

#### 1. New Technology

Do you have a cell phone or computer for your use? In less than a generation, the near universal use of these two devices for **communication**, and how people give and get information from each other, is well on the way to completely revolutionizing our relationships with one another worldwide. Anthropologists tell us that for thousands of generations, humans have always had close personal relationships with each other and communicated in physical person-to-person interactions. Sometimes it was making meaningful sounds with the breath from their lungs through their vocal cords and out their mouths that turned into all of the spoken languages of humankind, called **verbal** communication. Sometimes it was using hand motions, meaning "stop," or "come here," or "give me some." Also, people would look at each other's faces or body postures for any additional **nonverbal** information about how the speaker was feeling or what their intentions were. These are basic forms of communication.

**communication**—exchange of information by speaking, writing, and other signaling

**verbal**—using words either spoken or written in symbols

**nonverbal**—signaling using face, hand, arm, and body motions

## 2. New Challenges

Whether we are aware of it or not, we are pioneers in a new world of interpersonal relationships, using remote communication when we don't have to make any sound or hand or body motions or even see the other person. All we need are some abstract symbols that we now interpret as words or visual signals to communicate with others. The traditional limits of what was said and how it was said may no longer always apply. Back then, you could not be an unseen person when you communicated with someone. But when you think about it, this has not been the first time for remote contact. As humans began actually making weapons of warfare, from original face-to-face fighting, then across further and further distances, now we kill both enemies and innocent people alike from thousands of miles away, and not see people's faces as they are dying. Similarly, with our modern communications we can be anonymous and downright nasty and insulting on blog posts, Internet comments, or unidentified voice recording—and not get caught. What can the recipient of such verbal abuse do?

To discount and disregard such "trash talk" requires a new mind-set with which most humans simply do not have any historical experience, especially for those in the older generations who did not grow up with computers and cellphones. Today's world seems to have a constant stream of such nonpersonal abusive verbal communication, as well as crude and coarse everyday language. Simply read the comments section of most newspaper articles, blogs, or personal statements, and you will find many of them. How many unsolicited recorded telephone messages and three-rings-then-hang-up "phishing expeditions" do you respond to, as well as junk postal and electronic mail, and the constant onslaught of radio and television advertising? Considering the thousands of years of human face-to-face communication, most of these unwanted forms of communication are products of less than the last 25 years of human history. Generations ago, our ancestors knew that "it's a jungle out there," and it actually was! They had to protect themselves physically in order for humanity to survive. Today, the jungle is in the electronic mass media, the hackers, the identity thieves, the computer spy bots, and the "con jobs" that exploit the way humans have communicated personally with each other for countless generations. Yet, we humans are very resilient. New adaptive responses are being developed for the modern dangers of the technical jungles that include computer and phone password changes, secure e-mail and Web sites, e-mail filters, antivirus and antispyware software, telephone caller ID, government-mandated do-not-call lists, even television remote-control "mute" buttons for obnoxious ads, and much, much more. We now are having to adapt psychologically to the new predators, and most likely, we will survive. On the positive side, the electronic media have allowed us instantly to communicate with each other over vast distances: from the earth to the orbiting space station, from business offices around the globe to the main office in Sydney, Australia, from Grandma in San Francisco wishing happy birthday to her granddaughter in Miami, from Riley calling Mom after soccer practice to get a ride home.

## 3. Fundamental Relationship Needs

We will survive because we absolutely still need the company of other people. Why? It is because in relationship with other people we discover and develop our own personal meaning (Myers, 2000). Recall that humanistic psychologist Carl Rogers (1959) emphasized this clearly over a generation ago in his description of the "fully functioning person" [...] as did other psychologists. When students were asked across several semesters while taking a positive psychology class, what are the top five of their most important things in life, they always list some **relationship** with one or more people (Brown & LaJambe, 2015). What we mean by *relationship* is something that we have in common with another person. This "something" can be many things, large or small, formal or casual, like belonging to the same family, members of the same soccer team, liking the same hobby, having the same tastes in clothing, or enjoying the same flavored ice cream. It is these relationships with others, called **interpersonal relationships**, which apparently make life worthwhile for most of us. When we think back to the three pillars of positive psychology [...] , the three positive institutions, the *six positive traits* and 24 *strengths,* and the four *positive emotions*, it is the first one that emphasizes interpersonal relationships, i.e., a *strong family institution* with its caring and support of its members. If these family relationships are good, it is because they are built upon good interpersonal relationships. And what are these good interpersonal relationships based upon? Aren't they clear *communication* with one another and a *respect* for one another as persons, what Dr. Carl Rogers (1959) called *unconditional positive regard* [...] ?

**Viewing Relationships**

Individual in relation to the group
Basis of the interactions
Necessary components of relationships
Steps in developing relationships
Role of good communication

To understand the various ways of viewing relationships, we will explore these five aspects:

1. *Relationship* of the *individual to the group* as an independent or interdependent person.
2. The *basis of the interaction*: Four descriptive models will be discussed, based upon our biological, psychological, social, and economic needs.
3. The *necessary components* of satisfying relationships.
4. The steps involved in making good relationships.
5. The importance of communication, both verbal and nonverbal.

Each will be developed and discussed in separate sections of this [reading].

## Viewing Different Relationships

## 1. Each of Us in Our Culture

We are born into a world over which we have absolutely no control. We are born as the product of two different persons' biological characteristics, their physical strengths, and their weaknesses, over which we have no control. We are born into a culture that usually has a definite set of values that can be quite different from other cultures. At least one specific language will be used for verbal communication, which we will unconsciously learn in order to make our needs known to our caretakers. How we first unconsciously see ourselves acting in relationships with others has been determined by what our culture teaches us to expect. This is where we start to see some of the separation of viewpoints between different cultures.

**a. Attitude of independence.** In Western industrial societies, most of us are expected to develop into the mythical separate, or *independent*, self. According to this idea, with the right upbringing, we should be able finally to stand alone separately from others in what we do and in the way we do it. This idealized view is called **individualism**. It emphasizes personal priority to reach our own goals and to define our own self-esteem in terms of the personal characteristics that we develop for ourselves, rather than those for our group. As of now, societies that emphasize individualism are economically better off, their citizens have greater mobility, and they can choose to change where they want to live. They are more centered around the convenient services that are provided by large cities and have enough mass transportation that they are able to get around quite rapidly (Myers, 2002).

**individualism**—a separate or independent outlook on life; emphasizes one's own goals and defines one's self-esteem by personal successes

**b. Attitude of interdependence.** In contrast to *individualism* is the emphasis of cultures in Asia, Africa, and Central and South America that stress the needs and goals of the society over the individual. These societies value group **collectivism** more and are dependent upon each other, called *interdependence*, more than in the individualism societies. The emphasis is not as much upon individual self-esteem as it is upon the welfare of the group (Meyers, 2002b).

**collectivism**—an interdependent outlook on life; emphasizes the welfare of a group over that of an individual

These two categories, *individualism* and *collectivism*, are oversimplifications of cultures. All persons are both separate individuals, but also very interdependent on others, for no humans can survive completely independent of other humans. Without attachments to others, no relationships can be built, and without relationships, no individual can become fully human or can come to understand who they are as a person.

## 2. Descriptive Models of Human Relationships

Since there is not yet a complete theory of human behavior, all theoretical models in psychology try to answer a piece of the total puzzle. Each of the following theories of human relationships has a piece of that puzzle to help us better understand why we form and develop relationships. We shall look at Dr. Abraham Maslow's (1943) classic biological need theory for *belongingness and love*, Dr. Eric Berne's psychological *PAC* model, the *social* role model, and the economic *social balance* model. Each may help us become more aware of just why we enter into the social relationships we have, and why we stay in them or choose to leave them.

**a. Biological model—need for human contact.** One of the earliest positive human relationship theories came from humanistic psychologist Dr. Abraham Maslow (1954), who studied mentally healthy people to understand what healthy human needs are. He was opposed to theories of human personality and well-being that had developed from studies on the activities and personalities of people with mental problems and limitations. In essence, those studies said very little about what healthy personalities and relationships ought to have. He stated that certain normal human needs must be filled, from the three most basic deficiency or survival needs, to the highest two "meta," or psycho/spiritual needs. [A] hierarchical diagram of these needs [...] , starting at its base with

1. *physiological*, for food and water, air to breathe, sleep, clothing, and shelter from heat and cold, freedom from pain, reproduction of the species;
2. *safety*, from fear of harm, injury, or cruelty;
3. *belonging and love*, to be connected to others in caring and supportive ways;
4. *esteem*, a belief of being valued as a person and also of being respected by others, as reasons for living;
5. *self-actualization*, freedom to develop our potentials to become all that we are able to do, along with a sense of *transcendence* (thankfulness, forgiveness, and a zest for living), the sixth of the positive psychology virtues [...] .

For understanding the theoretical social need for **belongingness and love**, we will focus on item 3), belonging and love. Dr. Maslow clearly knew that humans are very social and need others in order to survive (Maslow, 1943). In fact, without other humans, no one learns a human language because human language is not built into us. We only learn languages through interactions with other humans in order to communicate our needs and wants. We humans socialize in all kinds of relationships, based upon many different factors. Obviously, some relationships can and do change over time, based upon a person's needs for *belongingness and love*. Babies and young children develop relationships with their caretakers in order to survive, school-age children and adolescents develop relationships with friends to play with, help each other, and share stories and secrets. Adults develop relationships for work support, to join with others in mutual hobbies and interests, to share ethical and religious beliefs, and professional, career, and civic group concerns. Finally, most humans at some time in their life develop extended sexual relationships with other humans, often in order to reproduce and care for their offspring to maintain the human species. What the social relationship is depends upon the age of the person, their needs at that time, and what they want to share socially.

**b. Psychological model—Parent-Adult-Child.** Although the **PAC model** is included as a theoretical model, it is not really a psychological theory. Rather, it is really a simple descriptive idea of levels of relatedness (Kececi & Tasocak, 2009). The PAC model was developed back in the 1960s by psychiatrist Dr. Eric Berne, who was attempting to explain in simple terms the basic components of our personality that interacted with other people in different ways. PAC stands for *parent*, *adult*, and *child*. Our emotions come from our biological "Child" part. Our values, like right and wrong that we learn from others, come from our "Parent" and other authority figures, like teachers and spiritual guides. Our thinking and reasoning abilities about our world and our needs come from our "Adult." He further divided our "Child" component into our "Natural Child," who is happy and smiley and feeling good, and our compromised or "Hurt Child," who is sad, lonely, and feeling hurt. Our "Parent" is divided into our "Nurturing Parent," who helps and supports and cares for others, and our "Judgmental Parent," who is critical and punishing of others when things go wrong. This Parent-Adult-Child (PAC) model is diagrammed in the adjacent Figure 1.1.1 Any of these components of our PAC model can interact with any of those of another person in either *complemental* or *crossed social* transactions. A very important feature we must keep in mind is that these components have nothing at all to do with our age, as we shall see.

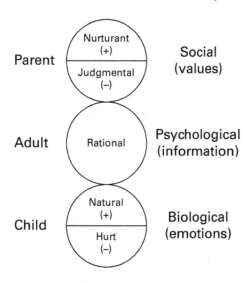

Figure 1.1.1 Dr. Eric Berne's model of the Parent-Adult-Child relationship within each person.

Adapted from: Dr. Eric Berne, "Dr. Eric Berne's model of the Parent-Adult-Child relationship within each person," Transactional analysis in psychotherapy: a systematic individual and social psychiatry.

**1) Complemental social transaction.** A *complemental social transaction* would be one in which two children, teenagers, or adults, are laughing and enjoying each other like emotionally happy children (Natural Children) or are acting like "compromised " mad children and upset with each other and feeling hurt (Hurt Child). A mother and child can be worried over a sick pet (Nurturing Parents), wondering what is the best thing to do to help their pet back to health, or two parents can be worried over a sick child and plan to go to the nearest emergency medical clinic. Or a social transaction between a student and a professor (Adults) can involve questions and answers about an academic subject, or a businessperson and customer (Adults) can be negotiating a sale, giving and getting information to solve a problem or reach a solution. Figure 1.1.2 shows complemental

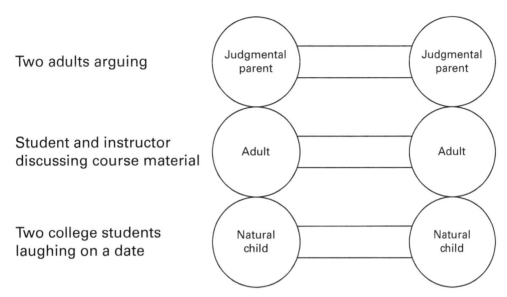

Two adults arguing — Judgmental parent ═══ Judgmental parent

Student and instructor discussing course material — Adult ═══ Adult

Two college students laughing on a date — Natural child ═══ Natural child

Figure 1.1.2 Examples of selected pair-wise complemental interactions between personality components of the PAC model.

transactions between the same PAC components of two different individuals. Examples of the PAC components by themselves could be a pet cared for by its young human pack mate (Nurturing Parent), a cook looking at a recipe to find the right ingredients (Adult), a parent deciding for how long to "ground" a child (Judgmental Parent) for deliberately breaking another child's toy (Hurt Child).

**2) Crossed transactions.** Examples of *crossed social transactions* would be a "Hurt Child" refusing to go to bed when asked to and beginning to cry, while the "Judgmental Parent" is reminding their child that they must go to bed now and will not take "no" for an answer. How about a person returning to their parked car and finding a meter officer writing up an overtime parking ticket? No amount of talking (Adult) by the driver explaining a reasonable delay will convince the officer to take back the ticket. Handing the ticket to the upset driver (Hurt Child), the officer states that the time on the meter has expired, and "rules are rules" (Judgmental Parent). A different example would be a grieving adult (Hurt Child) being comforted by another adult (Nurturing Parent). These social transactions can rapidly change several times during meetings, depending upon their changing natures. For example, a person with a new kitchen toaster that has broken may at first feel angry and upset (Hurt Child), but takes it back to a store and explains to someone in customer service exactly what happened (Adult), expecting to receive a replacement toaster. If refused, the customer may get upset again (Hurt Child) and demand (Judgmental Parent) the replacement. The store associate may feel attacked (Hurt Child) and call the manager, who then asks the customer what is wrong (Adult). Upon hearing the explanation given by the upset customer (Hurt Child), the manager agrees that a replacement is appropriate (Adult). The customer, realizing the manager is reasonable, then shifts into their

Adult with the good news, thanks the manager and leaves with the replacement, feeling happy again (Natural Child)! In complex interpersonal interactions, the roles can rapidly change as situations change and the social transactions switch rapidly among PAC states.

To summarize the PAC model, according to Dr. Berne, we carry our PAC components around all our life in our social transactions. The importance of this model is for each person to become consciously aware in which personality component they are functioning for most effective understanding of their transactions. As Dr. Berne observed, it is quite easy to slip into the emotional Hurt Child mode and then engage in emotional outbursts like anger or resentment in our social transactions, or rapidly switch into hostile Judgmental Parent social transactions to "pay back," which usually does not solve problems. To function most effectively, we need to stay in our Adult and "keep our cool." In that way, we can analyze what the situation is so that we can reasonably figure out what is best for us. In many ways, this is similar to Dr. Richard Lazarus's *three-stage transactional model* that is used for stress reduction. Once we know our own Child, Parent, and Adult, we can analyze our own moment-by-moment PAC changes and those of others for most effective social transactions.

**c. Social model—roles and expectations.** Consciously or unconsciously, most of us take on different behaviors and attitudes, depending upon who we are with. As young children, we were the child and our mom and dad were the parents. If we had brothers or sisters, our relationship was different with them than with Mom or Dad. As we grew older, we developed different relationships with our school or music teachers, our soccer or gym coaches, our acquaintances and friends, our coworkers and bosses, and perhaps even with romantic partners. In many of these different relationships, we learned that there were different social expectations for what we did with these people. So we adjusted our talk and behaved one way with one person, but talked and acted a different way with another person. In other words, we were taking on different roles. One time we acted like a child, another time like a student; the next time like a teammate, another time like a professional. In each case, we took on the **social role** of acting like how that person is expected to act, also "code switching" the way we talk.

The term *social role* is different from the idea of playacting like in plays or movies. In those cases, actors take on parts to act like people who they are not. In the *social role model* relationships, each person can function in ways that are appropriate for what their culture expects them to play (Myers, 2002). Some grown-ups live some of the time as a parent or as a teacher, as a businessperson or as a customer, repairperson or as a factory worker, and so on, or even several of these roles at different times. Sometimes children live their lives as a daughter or a son, a student, friend, athlete, performer, and combinations of several of these, all at the same time. The term *role* might seem to carry a sense of fakeness or dishonesty, of not being genuine in a relationship. However, the concept of *social role* is useful in that it points out that most of us genuinely function in different ways in relationship with others. Is it difficult to act like a college student if you are in college and taking college classes? No. A spouse who believes in faithfulness and lives that role is not play-acting. People who are "faking it" often do that in order to make us believe they are someone different, usually for some reason that only serves them and may actually harm us. The *social role model* describes the usual functions we often take on in our relationships with others.

There is a negative aspect to playing social roles when they put people into unfair positions, based upon false assumptions for that social role. For example, cultures mainly run by men often have made wrong judgments of what women can, in fact, do. Here in the United States, it was not until recently that women were finally accepted as being as capable and responsible as men as leaders in science, engineering, finance, politics, and business (Eagly, Wood, & Diekman, 2000; Peters, Kinsey, & Malloy, 2004). Apparently, those gender-difference misperceptions of social role capabilities are now decreasing (Diekman, Goodfriend, & Goodwin, 2004), along with development of new roles in gender relationships—combat-ready women in the military, male nurses, female engineers, stay-at-home dads.

**d. Economic model—fair exchange.** The object of this relationship model is to maximize efficiency (profit) with minimal effort (cost) to meet people's needs (Myers, 2002). Simply speaking, we often unconsciously check out how things are going in our relationships, whether they are at home, at work, or at play. Is it good (more pluses) or bad (more minuses), or both, and which do we have more of? If there are more pluses, we keep the relationship; if more minuses, we think of alternatives for finding a better relationship. This model is based on the science of *economics* (Homans, 1961), the study of the production, distribution, and use of goods that are exchanged between individuals, companies, or nations. In this case, the "goods" are what we are getting or giving to our relationship partner (Emerson, 1976). If we are getting at least as much as we are giving, if not getting even more, then it's a good relationship, and we are "profiting" from it and are happy with it. But if we are constantly giving more than what we are receiving, then we are suffering from an exchange "cost" and may feel upset (Lawler, 2001). Since this is a relationship, each partner needs to know what it is being exchanged: mutual sharing, care, money, work, ideas, interest, or help. Keep in mind that our relationship partner probably is also checking our relationship for how good it is for them. Then, too, if we have had similar relationships in the past, we may be checking out how our current relationship compares with our former ones.

To summarize, although none of these four social interaction models is complete by itself, each gives us a piece of the puzzle to understand how we interact in the personal relationships of our life. Our personal relationship needs will change over our life as we grow, change, and become more conscious of who we are as a person. What we want to be sure of is to develop positive relationships with others who fulfill our needs and maintain the relationships with those whom we are already in relationships.

# Social Transactions—Meetings

## 1. Types of Meetings

Conversations that take place at meetings depend entirely upon the reasons for the meetings. We can look at the three theoretical models that we discussed earlier for clues as to what might be wanted in the meetings. Is it to solidify a sense of *belongingness* with a friend, like informally talking with them about a movie that you saw together the night before? Is it gaining information in a *social exchange*, like being in a classroom situation discussing with your teacher the best way to study for an upcoming exam? Is it in a *social role* situation in which you are talking with your manager of your part-time job about your work schedule during final exam week? Is it a couple of friends, or coworkers, or committee members, or scattered family members getting together? To repeat, the *settings*, that is, the situations and people involved, in which the exchanges take place, pretty much set up what is talked about, and how it is talked about. Similarly, most of us learn most of what we know from interacting with others, which determines our future behavior in similar situations. Types of meetings vary, depending upon many factors, but each type proceeds following several typical steps.

People can find their first intentional meeting making them anxious or nervous, or they might feel excited and optimistic. Sometimes it depends on if they are the one who initiated it or the one who is responding to it. Similarly, a fear of being rejected may cause people to feel awkward. Regardless, most of us are willing to respond to people who begin a conversation with us if they are not seen as weird or a threat to us.

**a.  Implied meeting "rules."** To make first conversations easier between people who are strangers to each other, many societies provide "rules" or guidelines for how they begin. In Japan, when two strangers meet, they usually first exchange name cards. This is so that each knows the social ranking of the other so that the appropriate language for the person's ranking is used, as well as how deeply to bow to show proper respect for the person's rank, and so on. In North America, most conversation starts on a much less formal basis. Structure usually develops as the relationship progresses, and each person learns more about the position, status, and other relevant characteristics of the other. Yet, there are often unwritten "rules" for encounters, even though such rules may be vague and subject to different interpretations. For example, in North America, when two strangers meet formally, it is customary to say something like "hello, how are you?" If it is in a more relaxed environment, the conversation can start with a "hi," "hey," "how goes it?" or "wazzup?" A pretty standard response can be "okay," or "not much." Only the most socially unaware person begins to lay out their current life history, personal detail by detail to tell you exactly how they are. You may be entirely unprepared to hear those details, because your thinking is probably, "you're not following the rules!" Similarly, a common response today to "thank you" is not "you're welcome," or "I'm happy to do it," but instead, "no problem." Yet, its meaning does not actually mean that a problem might have been involved.

The early stages of meetings can include much uncertainty. In the second stage, people usually begin conversations talking about safe topics like external things until their respective roles in the relationship become clear. Then, topics can begin to shift as the members of the relationship start to become more comfortable with the other as the transactions received from the other are accepted as reasonable and pleasant.

Once a conversation has begun, how a person fits into it depends upon how they see their role in it and their relationship with the other person. How trusting they are of the other person usually determines how much they are willing to share of their private self. This has serious implication in today's remote mass media interactions with unknown persons, who claim to be what they are not. Examples include fake bank or credit company messages, trying to get you to tell them your bank or credit card number along with your social security number; fake college or university computer centers warning you that your e-mail account is full and you need to click on the following link or else your account will be deleted, and so on. How about the fake government official from another country, claiming to have money for you from a deceased relative if only you will pay a small processing fee to claim your inheritance? The purposes of these "conversations" may involve online "phishing" schemes to steal financial information, offering too-good-to-be-true "deals" if you buy using your credit card immediately, or for sexual stalking. In any case, the shared information is used against the person, and the betrayed person feels bad for being so naive. In summary, what the type of conversational exchange is, whether person to person or by Internet, will depend upon what a person expects to get out of the exchange.

**b. The first meeting.** Any meeting between people happens when one signals that they would like a response from us. This signal is called the *transactional stimulus*, and how we act is the *transactional response*. Some people are very socially skilled in their approaches to starting conversations. Others have some rehearsed lines that they have tried before with some apparent success. Here is where the "come-on" or "line" enters the interaction in "romantic" encounters. The most-used transactional stimulus line was "haven't we met before?" There are three possible transactional responses: "no," "yes," or "get lost!" Students in the author's class rated the three following examples of lines by men toward women in casual situations, like a meeting after a class or at a party. The best line was, "Your father must have been a thief, for he stole the stars from heaven and put them in your eyes." In the middle was, "You owe me a drink because I dropped mine when you walked in." The worst line was "I am not sure if I am gay or not—perhaps you can help me decide?"

## 2. Seeing the Person

How we make sense of other people when we meet them for the first time is a very basic process and is usually done automatically. We do it as a part of our self-survival, probably as old as human existence itself (Bargh, Chen, & Burrows, 1996). Like Dr. Richard Lazarus's *transactional analysis*, we immediately try to answer the questions "is this person harmless, or potentially harmful?" In other words, we are trying to reduce uncertainty about what meeting a new person might involve for us. We do this by attempting to predict on the basis of often very little information who and what that person is about. What information do we use—whatever is available to us at the time, usually incomplete and possibly very wrong?

**a. Stereotypes.** These are fixed beliefs that we have often applied to a new situation by first impressions, narrow past experiences that we remembered, or incomplete information. For example, it was long thought that babies bond with their mothers only because mothers give them milk. We know that is not completely true because research has clearly demonstrated that babies will bond with anyone who cares for them, holds them, talks and smiles at them, as well as protects and feeds them. Otherwise, fathers, grandparents, and adoptive parents could never bond with their babies. Another example, used earlier, was the long-held and long-fought incorrect stereotypical belief that women are not born as intelligent as men, and should not be in certain professions or be the heads of important businesses. Similar stereotypical beliefs that other people hold often are used to boost incorrect stereotypes that we already have developed. The thinking goes this way: if they believe that too, then it's probably not wrong.

**stereotype**—a long-time general belief of people that is a very rigid and overly simple idea about a person or thing and not necessarily true

The problem with stereotypes is that they bias our meeting with new people without allowing us better information on which to judge them. The fact is that we tend to want to feel comfortable with our beliefs more than spend the energy to correct our thinking. That often makes it extremely difficult to replace our incorrect ideas with better information. This self-serving refusal to replace wrong information is called a **confirmation bias.** In other words, we tend to select only the information that supports our position and try to ignore or disregard the rest. For example, women have demonstrated their competencies in many fields repeatedly in the last generation. Nevertheless, because of the biasing stereotype, images of memories "back when" are more likely to be recalled. This resulted in keeping the types of biased social roles we had mentioned earlier, such as when more women were stay-at-home moms raising the children and did not have a college education or professional degrees. In both cases, as more and more accurate instances replaced the old inaccurate beliefs, it became more difficult to hang on to the old inaccurate *confirmation bias.*

**b. Primacy effect.** "You never get a second chance to make a first impression," says an old quotation some credit to 19th-century American writer and humorist Mark Twain and used in more recent TV advertising for Head and Shoulders shampoo. Regardless, the impression made of a person at a first meeting, called the **primacy effect**, can directly influence our acceptance or rejection of them. This is whether the meeting could be for dating, developing a friendship, or hiring someone for a job. Positive first impressions have a great impact and may have a very lasting valuable "payoff." Overcoming a negative *primacy effect* may be extremely difficult because it usually leaves an emotional negativity that outweighs all the positive information (Lount, 2010). Initially, a person may make a very positive first impression. However, as an example, if photos posted on Facebook show them in a compromising or embarrassing situation, the lasting effect about that person can quickly become negative. If a job interview candidate dresses inappropriately for the position, knows little or nothing about the company, or has poor manners and speaks poorly, these are strong impressions that are difficult to ignore. More will be discussed about the *primacy effect* [...] when discussing personal factors and job interviewing.

> **primacy effect**—basing all judgments of a person off an initial first impression

**c. "Halo" and recency effects.** Perceptions of others can also be influenced by what is generally called *a halo effect*. That is, an expectation that a person, business, or group will perform in a given way depending upon some factor not at all related to their past performance (Nisbett & Wilson, 1977; Rosenzweig, 2007). For example, when a person's intelligence is based upon whether they are handsome or plain-looking, smiling or frowning, these are mistaken **halo effects**. Similarly, if a company is very successful, the assumption that therefore its workers are treated fairly is not necessarily a valid assumption. The object of making a good first impression in a job interview is to leave the observer with a positive *halo effect*, the expectation that the job competency of the person matches the personal impression they made at their first meeting. When the Facebook image that has nothing to do with job qualifications emerges under an entirely different context than a job interview, it can produce a lingering *recency effect* on job competency, resulting in a *negative halo* effect.

> **halo effect**—a person's future performance based on something not at all related to their present performance

A major accuracy problem in first-interview person perception is when people are deliberately misleading in attempts to bolster weak credentials. For their *primacy effect*, they claim advanced accomplishments that are not true. But as they become better known and their performance is less than what their ability claims were, less attractive characteristics now emerge. This newly changed impression of the person is called a **recency effect**. The

recency effect—
the newly changed
impression of a
person, based on the
most recent meeting

negative aspects of dishonesty, or "spinning" the truth, hold much weight. When they happen during a first meeting, the lasting impression can end any more meetings because of the *recency effect*.

## 3. Terminating the Meeting

The end of a meeting, like its beginning, usually follows a set of rules, depending upon what happened in the meeting. If the meeting's purpose was quite clear and its goals have been met, then usually clear indications are given so that all are aware of that, and no more meetings will be needed. If people want to meet again, various information will be shared, like e-mail addresses or phone numbers taken down to use later. When definite times or dates are stated for scheduling the next conversation or meeting, people usually are fairly convinced that it will happen. However, if the all-too-often used and indefinitely meant "See you later!" is said, this may indicate that there is some question about resuming the conversation. Most conversations between people meeting for the first time do not progress past the first few layers of the "onion" [...] , although it can be satisfying in that moment. Those that do reach deeper levels often involve some sort of problem-solving requirements like for business, or a personal attraction with a hope to learn more about the other.

## THE RELATIONSHIP PROCESS

Relationships usually develop in an organized step-wise manner, beginning with the first meeting. After that, where and how far the relationship goes is dependent upon every next step, and will end if the expectations of the relationship at that point are not met. Two questions need to be answered: First is, why do we want the meeting, and second, what are we expecting to get out of it? Why would we want to get to know this person? Obviously, there must be something positive that we see in the results of our meeting. What attracts us to them? Could they be a team member for work or at play? Do they seem to be fun, conscientious, gentle, highly analytic, or sexy? What have you heard about them that seems interesting to you? This is known as *personal attraction*. Other aspects that are involved include how each person sees the other fulfilling what they want in the relationship, known as *personal perception*. How willing are we to *accommodate*, that is, make room for the needs of the other person if we have a relationship? And finally, perhaps most importantly, what is our level of *communication*, the sharing of ideas, information, wants, and needs? Each of us in a good relationship clearly needs to know what the other expects so that there is *openness* and *honesty* for settling differences or misunderstandings, which are always bound to happen if the relationship has a life to it. We shall take up each of these factors in turn.

# From "Small Talk" to Intimacy—Onion Model

## 1. Peeling Back the Layers

Levels of relationship are like the layers of an onion—peeling each person's protective outermost superficial layer to the deepest most meaningful level of intimate self disclosure at the very living core (see Figure 1.1.3). The onion metaphor was developed from Social Penetration Theory over a generation ago (Altman & Taylor, 1973). The idea is that involvement and commitment deepen, usually in mutually occurring steps. Analysis of the transaction steps and their message content usually proceeds by moving gradually from safe public topics on to more vulnerable private ones. On the first layer, first comments are standard and mechanical *social phrases*, like talking about the weather, the time of day, or bus or plane schedules. Yet, this "small talk" appears useful in that it can show how willing another person is to talk, whether they are open to sharing information, and how comfortable they are in this conversation (Cassell & Bickmore, 2003).

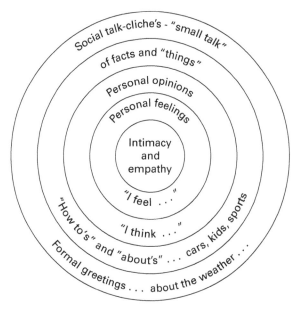

Figure 1.1.3 Onion-layer model of levels of communication, from outermost shallow to innermost intense contact and communication.

Irwin Altman and Dalmas Arnold Taylor, "Onion-Layer Model of Levels of Communication," Social Penetration: The Development of Interpersonal Relationships.

If an encounter continues to a second level, it usually involves talking about "*things*" while exploring common or mutual safe interests "out there." These include information about favorite music, movies, video stars, foods, colors, cars, sports, vacation spots, types of work, and so on. Young adults often segregate into same-gender groups to talk about fashions, sports, music, TV or movie stars, their jobs, and diet and workout schedules if they are weight and fitness conscious. Women often are found talking about child-care or PTA (Parent-Teacher Association) if they have children. Men often are talking sports, cars, power tools, or jobs.

## 2. The Self-Other Overlap

An interesting model of positive interpersonal relating was developed about a generation ago, called *self-expansion theory* (Aron & Aron, 1986). If we are in a good relationship with another person, we want to share some of ourselves with them, and they with us. In this way, we both expand our knowing about each other. In turn, this was expanded by Dr. Barbara Fredrickson into the *broaden-and-build theory* (1998, 2001) of close relationships. Essentially, it is this: If the relationship we are in is a positive one that makes us feel comfortable and happy, we are more likely to share more of our personal information with another and feel a closer "oneness" with the other. In other words, we begin to "overlap" in our feelings, interests, and activities with the other person. These positive emotions and moods result in positive activities, which, in turn, produce more positive emotions and moods. Furthermore, a greater inclusiveness happens with the other person so that there is a greater amount of thinking of "we," rather than just "me." This then becomes a **self-other overlap** (Waugh & Fredrickson, 2006). This happens when our sharing continues at deeper levels, especially when we might be thinking of developing a strong interpersonal relationship. It is also interesting that the individuals involved also develop a greater attitude of *interdependence,* rather than continue one of separate *independence.*

**self-other overlap**— the increase in "we" thinking as a relationship deepens

## 3. Developing Mutual Support with Increasing Vulnerability

As a relationship continues to develop, a third level may progress by daring to express a *personal opinion*: "I think," "I like, or don't like," "if you ask me," and so on. At any of these levels, the encounter can be terminated by one person or both, if topics are no longer of mutual interest. The whole process of dating, going out, or old-fashioned terms of "courting" or "keeping company" involves gradually getting to know someone well at ever-increasing depths. If the relationship continues, mutual vulnerability and mutual support develop in this increasing *self-other overlap* for caring, loyalty, and protection of the other person.

## 4. Reaching Intimacy

When a relationship has progressed to the point where persons trust each other, *emotional sharing* may begin. Phrases now include, "I feel this way," "I care about that," "I love or I hate these things," and "the thing that freaks me out the most is," and "I hurt for someone or something." By this time, each knows something personal about the other, mutually sharing as the trust grows in the relationship. As it further deepens, a more intense mutual sharing develops with the most private emotions or innermost portions of each person's life. Who are these people to us? While we were children, most often these involved our immediate family members. As we grew older, it was our best friends in school, certain trusted relatives and adult friends, or perhaps a caring teacher. As adults, our significant others may be loyal friends, trusted coworkers, live-in companions or spouses, perhaps eventually our own children. **Intimacy** has now developed, the final step in a caring, supportive, committed, and loyal relationship.

**intimacy**—a deep emotional relationship based upon caring and trust, of family members, close friends, and/or sexual partners

# Personal Attraction

Although the attractiveness of someone for us is a very personal matter, whether as a friend, a coworker, or a pair-bonded sexual partner, researchers have identified five core factors that influence our perception of who is attractive to us. These are known by various terms as *physical attractiveness*, *availability*, *propinquity*, *similarity*, and *complementarity*. Others listed by some researchers include social and cultural background, personality, interests and activities, social skills, and reciprocal liking. However, as we shall see, most of those can be classified under *similarity*.

## 1. Physical Attractiveness

According to researchers on college dating (Peretti & Abplanalp, 2004), the first and most important immediate factor is physical attractiveness, both for women and men (Regan & Berscheid, 1997). Regardless of a meeting's purpose, without knowing someone, the first impression of the person is what we see, either face-to-face or projected on some viewer, such as a picture, a cellphone image, or the Internet. The importance of physical attractiveness has been known for a very long time, but has been very much underestimated (Krebs & Adinolfi, 1975, p. 245). In general, we are unconsciously attracted to people who we see as physically attractive (Zuckerman, Miyake, & Elkin, 1995). Furthermore, who we are attracted to often involves how attractive we think ourselves to be (Alvarez & Jaffe, 2004). It is interesting to realize that after the first meetings, physical attractiveness decreases the more we get to know someone. In fact, as a relationship matures, physical attractiveness often is replaced by some personality characteristics a person has that might have been suspicious at first because they seemed so different, or "opposite" (see *complemental* below).

## 2. Availability

A second factor in personal attraction is whether a person is **available**. In some way, it is easier to define *unavailability*. If you call a friend to go to a movie, but they are out of town, then they are *unavailable* to you. If you want to start a personal relationship with someone, but for whatever reason they do not want a relationship with you, then they are not *available* as a possible companion. If you apply for a job, but it has already been filled, then the job is no longer *available* to you. In other words, to make any connection with anything or anybody, that possibility must exist so that it can be tried. If a person is wearing a symbol of connectedness to another person, like an engagement or wedding ring, those are symbols of *unavailability* for a long-term pair-bonded relationship. However, that same person could be *available* for something else, like being a member of an activity committee or as a coworker on a business project. Depending upon the type of

**available**—ready or free to take part in something, like a relationship

relationship we wish to start with another person, the issue of their psychosocial *availability* to us is a limiting factor.

## 3. Propinquity

The word **propinquity** (pro-**pink**-wit-**tee**) is a rarely used word now, although it is a useful old concept in the study of attractiveness. It refers to "nearness" or similarity and can take many forms. It can include similar social and cultural background in personality, having common interests and activities, or the same type of social skills. It also includes *proximity*, or physically being in the same area, next door, on the same building floor or same neighborhood. The closer physically we are to someone, the greater is the possibility of starting a conversation with them. If we want a permanent relationship with a hometown person, we ought to stay at home! If we want a relationship with a particular sort of person, we need to be where that type of person is in order to increase our chances of meeting them. They could be taking the same college class, or are business or professional coworkers, club members, or now on dating sites or chat rooms on the internet. This idea of propinquity is reflected in the words of the old 1970 love song by Crosby, Stills, and Nash from long before the cell phone and Internet: "*And if you can't be with the one you love, honey, love the one you're with.*"

**propinquity—** nearness, which can include being physically in the same location, or nearness in thinking, attitudes, goals, and interests.

Although the process of checking out the *propinquity* of a person we are having a relationship with may seem obvious, its effects on behavior can be significant. Some psychologists even consider this preference for the familiar faces that we see around us as a genetically determined survival feature. This is because people with whom we feel familiar are perceived as more predictable and safe (Devine, 1995; Zajonc, 1998).

A final word on the concept of *propinquity* (*similarity*). An often-quoted old expression is that "familiarity breeds contempt." However, the reality is that familiarity usually breeds *contentment*. In other words, what we like of ourselves, we usually also like in others. The greater the similarity, the less is the question about what to expect (Dijkstra & Barelds, 2008). For example, later in their lives, people often associate more often with others who have had similar lifetime experiences than they do with those whose experiences have been very different from their own.

## 4. Complementarity

Do opposites really attract each other? This idea is known as the *principle of complementarity*. Apparently, this not the case for those who have nothing in common because there would be little reason for those types of people to meet. Rather, **complementarity** is viewed as a balancing of needs or talents between partners who have a relationship in which together their different features fulfill each other (Dryer & Horowitz, 1997). For example, one partner may act very dominant, while the other is content to submit to the other in a way that is satisfying to both of them. One person in a relationship may be very creative, while the other is very practical and can turn novel ideas into well-worked-out actions; together they accomplish more than each could do on their own. Although most people tend to prefer partners similar in personality so that there is a comfortable predictability, they also like partners who have different characteristics than their own (Dijkstra & Barelds, 2008). Difference can be exciting, in that it can add a new dimension to explore, as long as the person also shares personality features with us.

**complementarity**—differences that join together and make a unit even better, like a balance between creativity and practicality

## Personal Respect

Without relationships with other humans, none of us can become all of those positive things that we think we humans are capable of, some of which we actually share with nonhuman animals in their basic forms. As examples, many two- and four-limbed (legs and fins) warm-blooded land and sea animals have genetic mechanisms to care for their young and each other so that they survive. These include forms of cooperation for food gathering, nursing, protecting young, and protection of the groups. Sociobiologist Dr. Edward Wilson (1975) has shown how some groups of animals are divided up by their genetics into guards to signal danger and soldiers to defend groups, or live together in large groups to surround the young for protection. Not only are humans able to do these things, but in much more complex and creative ways. However, this requires living in groups where creativity can develop and complex ideas can be shared. Our development of complex verbal languages, both spoken and written, extends far beyond any other animal language forms. They have allowed us to share with each other and to record information to share in the future with others. We now share systems of knowledge, such as arts and humanities, science and mathematics, engineering and medicine, business and law, cultural traditions of beliefs, and so on. These have come about from respect for others' ideas, based upon personal respect, and a willingness to try out ideas to see if they, in fact, do work.

As Dr. Maslow's *hierarchy of needs* (1943) indicates, we must receive certain required things we don't have, both physiologically and psychologically, if we are going to survive as well as *flourish*, that is, become *self-actualized* persons. This is only possible by means of personal relationships with others, which require building lasting relationships that are healthy for all involved. Developing healthy personal relationships is one of the guiding principles of positive psychology's approaches to personality and psychotherapy. The principle is illustrated in a universal rule respected across time in all of the great civilizations of the world, known as the "Golden Rule." It declares that we should treat others the same way we would want them to treat us, or not to treat others in ways that we would not want to be treated. In other words, relationships have to be worked on through personal respect of others if they are to last and become a foundation for personal growth.

## Making Room for Individual Differences

Since each of us is in some way like no other person, according to Drs. Kluckhohn and Murray (1953, [...] ), this difference must be considered in our relationships. To consider differences and be sensitive to them, this is what is known as **accommodation**. [P]eople can come to agreement in various ways when there are differences between their needs and desires, including *concession*, *compromise*, and *bargaining*. This is the process of give-and-take between people in a relationship so that all members can end up relatively satisfied with what they get. What has to exist is what has been discussed earlier, a relationship that includes *openness* and *honesty*. In that way, any dissatisfactions with the accommodated arrangements can be adjusted later for better satisfaction between partners. Without deliberate mutual attempts to restructure the *accommodations*, they may take on a life of their own and become difficult to change.

**accommodation**— the process of compromise so that results are mutually satisfying to both partners

## Control

We have been discussing the features that make up healthy personal relationships, those that result in each person thinking that they are getting enough positive out of their relationship that they want it to continue. An expectation of all healthy relationships is the belief that each person has some **control** over what goes on in the relationship. In any relationship, there is often an unspoken, and often not clearly understood, question of who has control of what parts of the relationship. Whether they are openly stated or not in a relationship, what guides the development of positive lasting relationships are two major factors: *openness* and *honesty*.

**control**—freedom or ability to direct events or conditions

In opposition are relationship patterns that directly challenge the structure of healthy relationships and what is acceptable in most modern societies. What separates unhealthy relationship patterns from positive healthy ones is that somewhere, somehow, *control* has gone wrong, with someone feeling powerless, taken advantage of, or discounted. These relationships are considered as potentially *destructive*. Often, one person is manipulating the relationship, attempting to gain as much as possible for themselves, even though they are destroying the relationship itself. It is very important to understand that what all of these unhealthy patterns have in common is the issue of *control*. More will be discussed below, under the topic of *violence* in relationships.

## Openness

The concept of **openness** relates to the directness and clearness of communications between individuals, so that each knows what the other is about with little confusion or misunderstanding. In that way, each person has the sense that the relationship environment they are in has an orderliness to it, because they know what to expect. However, not being told everything that needs to be known or having important information left out to mislead another, can cause lack of *openness*. How much to share and why is a topic to be discussed shortly. Lack of fully knowing may lead to a sense of not being able to control the relationship environment, or worse still, being intentionally deceived, another topic to be taken up in the next section. In this way, lack of openness is closely related to *lack of honesty*.

There are two other sides to the issue of openness. The first is the issue of someone demanding that another "tell all," at one time referred to as the "tyranny of openness" (Altman & Taylor, 1973). Recent research on the topic indicates that when such a demand is placed on someone, questions may arise about what the demander intends to do with this information if the private information has nothing to do with the current relationship. A need to protect one's own survival may also develop (Paul, Wenzel, & Harvey, 2008). That would have the effect of shutting down openness.

### 1. Self-Disclosure

To get to an intimate relationship means that the people in it will probably have gotten to know quite a bit about each other through information sharing. Any personal self-information voluntarily shared with another person might be defined as **self-disclosure** of what had been unknown information to the listener, including "sharing secrets." As recalled from earlier discussion of the Johari window [...]  (Luft & Ingham, 1950), when any private information about oneself is shared with others, then it becomes public information. Do others need to know it, and if so, how will it benefit them or our relationship?

As relationships progress and people begin to trust each other more, they tend to share personal aspects of themselves, as long as they trust the others. What they share and when it occurs depends upon the information and the level of the relationship. Early in the formative stages of a relationship, persons who share personal experiences with others ("I-sharing") are usually seen as more attractive for developing relationships than those who do not share (Pinel, Long, et al., 2006). This also gives the others confidence that, by being trusted with this personal information, the one who did the sharing can be trusted. Obviously, if this is a relationship expecting to become an intimate one, then the question arises about what information is important for the other to know for an open and honest relationship.

## 2. How Much Is Too Much?

If non-shared private information is uncovered later in a relationship, a major question to answer is what effect would it have on the current relationship? For examples, a law court conviction for driving while under age and intoxicated years ago may have little effect now on the relationship, if no signs of uncontrolled drinking have been observed over an extended time. A question of older generations was whether someone ought to disclose past sexual experiences to a prospective spouse. Data from more than a decade ago indicates that, for the present generation it is a "non-question," that by age 19, at least 70 percent of females and 65 percent of males have already engaged in sexual activity (Terry-Humen, Manlove, & Cottingham, 2006). However, sexual history can give information about the risk of exposure to sexually transmitted diseases. Also, having to pay child support to someone else as a continuing financial obligation is an important piece of information if one intends to have a committed intimate relationship.

To tell or not are personal judgments that an individual has to decide. At some point, the person who decides to share their private information must get a sense from the one with whom they are sharing that they are going to be understood and will be cared for (Reis & Patrick, 1996). Regardless, in a work situation or a strictly social one, the necessity of sharing deeply personal information may never come up as an issue, because it is not relevant to those situations.

## 3. "Dumping the Load"

A second issue with openness is what has been called "dumping the load." With full disclosure of information, persons may attempt to relieve themselves of any guilt over personal wrongdoing. Depending upon the seriousness of the information and whether it has broken social laws, the recipient may have a difficult time processing the information. Or a compromised situation may involve others in which the listener may not know what to do with the revealed information. This would be especially true about information revealing that crimes have been committed, or that people will be hurt in some way. No one wants to be put in that difficult situation. In fact, in some cases not reporting certain activities, like known child abuse, can have serious legal and/or moral implications for those who have been told the information, if they do not report it to law services

## Honesty

Being **honest** is defined as saying what is *true* or the way things actually are and acting in the way things are accepted by society. If a person says something that they know is not true, they are lying and are dishonest. They are deliberately engaging in behavior that tricks another person to gain some advantage over them and challenges what is accepted by society. What happens when a good relationship goes bad?

[...]

## Positive Growth-Producing Relationships

The information we learned in the prior chapters of using *mindfulness* for coping with stressors can be a help to us here. We can use that information to help us become ever more *mindful* of who we are, how we see life, what our expectations are, and what satisfies us to make us happy in a fulfilled sense. These, in turn, will make us more sensitive to the world in which we live and more aware of the meaningfulness of our relationship. It can help to synchronize us with the realities we live with, both with a mindfulness that is "tough-minded" (James, 1890) and with *resiliency*. To use Dr. Carl Rogers's (1959) term *congruence*, what we are doing in our relationships will be more congruent with what we are expecting for our life. With a tough-minded view, our measure of who we are and how we see the people in our relationships will have a higher chance of being accurate.

### 1. Who Am I?

[T]he starting point for self-awareness involves an as-accurate-as-possible Johari window (Luft & Ingham, 1950) view of ourselves, "known to self" and "known to others." As we recall, parts of us known to others as well as ourselves are considered "public." This is either obvious information about us that can be seen physically and publicly shared with others or is generally known. However, parts of us are known socially to others, but not to us. These are our "blind spots," like unconsciously wrinkling our nose to move our eyeglasses, or tugging on an ear stud or earring when we are nervous, or muttering to ourselves when trying to work out a problem. Parts of us we may keep hidden from others on purpose because it does not help them in any way to know it, or we just don't want others to know that about us. This is the part we call "private" and that we only disclose to others when we think they can be trusted. Then there is that part of us in the lower-right-hand pane of the Johari window that is unknown to others and unknown to us as well. This is our "unknown" or unconscious, the part of us that we can slowly get to know over time if we are reflective. We can become more aware of ourselves as we mature, gaining the strength and wisdom to accept all that we are.

Also important is to become mindful of our unique style of communicating with others. Most of us are sensitive enough to know that we probably *code-switch* our way of talking, depending upon whom we are talking with, and the situation in which our conversation is taking place. Talking with our best friend is done in a way that is probably different from talking with a child. Talking with someone who has knowledge about a topic we know is different from talking with someone who does not have that same knowledge. Becoming aware of ourselves is necessary, not only of our

**code-switching**—adjusting our words to the listener, like simple words for a child, informal words with a friend, soothing words for somebody who is hurting

personal style, but also of the reasons why we do what we do, the assumptions we make, and our coping patterns on which they are based. This is also a part of becoming more conscious than we were in the past. Knowing who we are can help us to understand the types of relationships we might want and how to keep them.

## 2. Who Are We?

A relationship is a joint effort of at least two people and will remain so as long as they are involved in some way, good or bad. What we get out of it depends, first of all, on why we are in it. For the relationship to remain requires that all involved in it are accepting of each other and work to reduce or eliminate those divisive aspects that may conflict with its goals. Not all relationships are the same, as the onion model shows. An acquaintance, a friend, a coworker, a family member, or an intimate partner, all are possible relationships we may have over our lifetime. Issues of openness, honesty, respect, and accommodation will have to be worked out with the type of relationship we want.

## 3. Positive Affect and Flourishing

In the final analysis, we have to agree with social psychologist Dr. David Myers (2002): "*close relationships predict health*" (p. 552). If we are to enhance our life, it means we must admit others into ours, just as they can admit us into theirs. Not only that, if our relationships are to continue and grow, there must be positive feelings we have for members in our relationship and in the growth-producing activities and outcomes we have together. This increases the *self-other overlap* that was discussed earlier. Apparently, this is true across our lifetime, not only for romantic relationships, but also for child-parent relationships and long-term friendships. In an extensive review of the positive psychology literature, Dr. Amy Gentzler and her student, Meaghan Ramsey (Ramsey & Gentzler, 2015), reported that the positive relationships between affect (emotions, moods, and attitude) and positive aspects of relationships interact directly with each other in a continuing dance across our life. What this means is that the positive affect that is felt from the partners in relationships influences their behaviors and outcomes positively. These outcomes, in turn, help to maintain the positive moods and attitudes in the relationship. In their review of the literature, they listed several, but not all, of the positive emotions that already have been studied extensively. They are no surprise to us because most have already been discussed in the first two chapters of this book, and include the following:

1. *love*—although more of an attitude, it promotes other positive feelings toward another
2. *gratitude*—promotes prosocial behavior, a desire to continue the relationship, and strengthens the relationship bonds by not taking the other person for granted

3. *joy*—the intense positive feeling often involves wanting to share, thus increasing the positive bond

4. *pride*—a positive feeling from an actual success that may cause the person to share with another, also increasing the positive bond

5. *interest*—a positive desire to learn more about, become more involved with, and do more with the other

6. *amusement and laughter*—sharing social experiences in an atmosphere that can develop trust and relative intimacy can increase positive emotional bonds.

Together, we become more than what we are by ourselves. How much we get out of our relationships depends upon how well we know ourselves, how well we try to get to know the others, and how mindful we are of this process of knowing who we are in relationships with others. After all, isn't the process of *flourishing*, with the help of others, the reason we make relationships in the first place? If so, then we need to do all of the positive things possible that are life giving with them, and with all others with whom we will have life-giving relationships across our lifetime.

## CHAPTER SUMMARY

- Persons can belong to groups that are either *individualistic*, with emphasis upon fulfilling personal needs, or *collectivistic*, with emphasis upon fulfilling the needs of the group.

- Four models of personal relationships are discussed: Maslow's needs relationships, Berne's PAC transactions, the social exchange theory, and the social roles theory.

- The *social exchange model* emphasizes an "economic" ratio of rewards-to-costs for those in the relationship to measure the *satisfaction* outcome.

- Maslow's belongingness need says we need other humans in order to survive.

- The PAC *transactional model* analyzes the interactions among each individual's *parent*, *adult*, and *child* aspects in the relationship.

- The *social role model* involves each person fulfilling social *role expectations* of their culture.

- Relationships with others begin with initiating an *encounter*, following the social rules, and then terminating it according to accepted unwritten social rules.

- *Personal perception* often involves *stereotyping*, that is, predicting outcomes based upon too little information.

- Personal perception often involves a first impression *primacy* effect, a residual *halo* effect, and a last impression *recency* effect.

- *Attraction* includes physical attractiveness, proximity, availability, similarity, and complementarity.

- Poor relationships can involve *intentional deception*, *divisiveness*, and even *violence*, including sexual assault.

- *Verbal communication* transmits factual information, while *nonverbal communication* can transmit emotional information by voice tone, facial expressions, and body positions.

- Effective communication requires attention to verbal and nonverbal messages, clarity and consistency of communication, and sensitivity to the needs of the other person.

- Positive growth-producing relationships are built from mindfulness of who we are in relationships with others that results from positive affect and actions of a "self-you overlap."

## REFERENCES

Altman, I., & Taylor, D. A. (1973). *Social penetration: The development of interpersonal relationships.* New York: Holt.

Alvarez, L., & Jaffe, K. (2004). Narcissism guides mate selection: Humans mate assortively, as revealed by facial resemblance, following an algorithm of "self" seeking like. *Evolutionary Psychology, human-nature.com/ep, 2*, 177–194.

Aron, A., & Aron, E. N. (1986). *Love as expansion of the self: Understanding attraction and satisfaction.* New York: Hemisphere.

Bargh, J. A., Chen, M., & Burrows, L. (1996). Automaticity of social behavior: Direct effects of trait construct and stereotype activation on action. *Journal of Personality and Social Psychology, 71*, 230–244.

Berne, E. (1961). *Transactional analysis in psychotherapy: A systematic individual and social psychiatry.* New York: Ballantine Books.

Cassell, J., & Bickmore, T. (2003). Negotiated collusion: Modeling social language and its relationship effects in intelligent agents. *User Modeling and User-Adapted Interaction, 13* (1–2), 89–132.

Devine, P. G. (1995). Prejudice and out-group perception. In A. Tesser (Ed.), *Advanced social psychology.* New York: McGraw-Hill.

Diekman, A. B., Goodfriend, W., & Goodwin, S. (2004). Dynamic stereotypes of power: Perceived change and stability in gender hierarchies. *Sex Roles, 50*, 201–215.

Dryer, D. C., & Horowitz, L. M. (1997). When do opposites attract? Interpersonal complementarity versus similarity. *Journal of Personality and Social Psychology, 72* (3), 592–603.

Eagly, A. H., Wood, W., & Diekman, A. B. (2000). Social role theory of sex differences and similarities: A current appraisal. In T. Eckes & H. M. Trautner (Eds.), *The developmental social psychology of gender* (pp. 123–174). Mahwah, NJ: Erlbaum.

Emerson, R. M. (1976). Social exchange theory. *Annual Review of Sociology 2*: 335.

Fredrickson, B. L. (1998). What good are positive emotions? *Review of General Psychology, 2*, 300–319.

Fredrickson, B. L. (2001). The role of positive emotions in positive psychology: The broaden-and-build theory of positive emotions. *American Psychologist, 56*, 218–226.

Homans, G. (1961). *Social behavior: Its elementary forms.* New York: Harcourt Brace Jovanovich.

James, W. (1890). *The principles of psychology.* New York: Holt.

Kececi, A., & Tasocak, G. (2009). Nurse faculty members' ego states: Transactional analysis approach. *Nurse Education Today, 29* (7), 746–752.

Krebs, D., & Adinolfi, A. A. (1975). Physical attractiveness, social relations, and personality style. *Journal of Personality Psychology, 31*, 245–263.

Lawler, E. J. (2001). An affect theory of social exchange. *American Journal of Sociology 107* (2), 321.

Lount, R. B. (2010). The impact of positive mood on trust in interpersonal and intergroup interactions. *Journal of Personality and Social Psychology, 98*(3), 420–433.

Luft, J., & Ingham, H. (1950). The Johari window: A graphic model of interpersonal awareness. *Proceedings of the western training laboratory in group development.* (Los Angeles: UCLA).

Maslow, A. H. (1943). A theory of human motivation. *Psychological Review, 50* (4), 370–396.

Maslow, A. (1954). *Motivation and personality.* New York: Harper.

Myers, D. G. (2000). The funds, friends, and faith of happy people. *American Psychologist, 55* (1), 56–57.

Myers, D. G. (2002). *Social psychology* (5th ed.). New York: McGraw-Hill.

Nisbett, R. E., & Wilson, T. D. (1977). The halo effect: Evidence for unconscious alteration of judgments. *Journal of Personality and Social Psychology, 35* (4), 250–256.

Paul, E., Wenzel, A., & Harvey, J. (2008). Hookups: A facilitator or a barrier to relationship initiation and intimacy development? Pp. 371–390. In S. Sprecher, A. Wenzel, & J. Harvey (Eds.), *Handbook of relationship initiation.* New York: Taylor & Francis.

Peters, S., Kinsey, P., & Malloy, T. E. (2004). Gender and leadership perceptions among African Americans. *Basic and Applied Social Psychology, 26*, 93–101.

Pinel, E. C., Long, A. E., Landau, M. J., Alexander, K., & Pyszczynski, T. (2006). *Journal of Personality and Social Psychology, 90* (2), 243–257.

Regan, P. C., & Berscheid, E. (1997). Gender differences in characteristics desired in potential sexual and marriage partners. *Journal of Psychology and Human Sexuality,* 9 (10), 25–37.

Rogers, C. R. (1959). A theory of therapy, personality, and interpersonal relationships, as developed in the client-centered framework. In S. Koch (Ed.), *Psychology: A study of a science, 1*, pp. 184–256. New York: McGraw-Hill.

Rosenzweig, P. (2007). *The halo effect: And the eight other business delusions that deceive managers.* New York: Free Press.

Terry-Humen, W., Manlove, J., & Cottingham, S. (2006). Trends and recent estimates: Sexual activity among U.S. teens. *Child trends.* Publication no. 2006-08. http://www.childtrends.org/?publications= trends-and-recent-estimates-sexual-activity-among-u-s-teens

Waugh, C. E., & Fredrickson, B. L. (2006). Nice to know you: Positive emotions, self-other overlap, and complex understanding in the formation of a new relationship. *Journal of Positive Psychology, 1* (2), 93–106.

Wilson, E. O. (1975*). Sociobiology: The New Synthesis.* Cambridge, MA: Harvard University Press.

Zajonc, R. B. (1998). Emotions. In D. Gilbert, S. T. Fiske, & G. Lindzey (Eds.), *Handbook of social psychology* (4th ed.). New York: McGraw-Hill.

Zuckerman, M., Miyake, K., & Elkin, C. S. (1995). Effects of attractiveness and maturity of face and voice on interpersonal impression. *Journal of Research in Personality, 29,* 253–272.

## END-OF-CHAPTER REFLECTIONS

Reflect on the multiple identities that you listed at the beginning of this chapter.

1. How do your multiple identities influence your relationships?
2. Are there some identities that are more visible in some relationships than others?
3. Where do you feel most seen and understood?
4. Which parts of yourself might you want to share more of in your relationships?
5. Choose one or two people in your life that you might share more of yourself with and consider how you might do this sometime in the next week.
6. What is it like to consider opening up more?

## REFERENCES

Arnold, L. (2019, April 21). *75-year Harvard study: what makes us happy?* AP News. https://apnews.com/article/6dab1e79c34e4514af8d184d951f5733

Gottman, J., & Silver, N. (1999). *The seven principles for making marriage work.* Crown.

## RECOMMENDATIONS FOR FURTHER READING

Matthes, R. (2018, November 6). Your relationship bill of rights. *Psychology Today,* 72–79. https://www.psychologytoday.com/us/articles/201811/your-relationship-bill-rights

Seligman, M. E. P., & Csikszentmihalyi, M. (2000). Positive psychology: An introduction. *The American Psychologist, 55*(1), 5–14. https://psycnet.apa.org/doi/10.1037/0003-066X.55.1.5

# Chapter 2

# Technology and Modern Relationships

*with Arianna Vokos*

Imagine this scenario for a moment: You wake up and notice the sun coming in your window and you hear your partner breathing quietly next to you. As you both begin to wake up you connect with some physical touch and shared grumbling about what lies ahead with work and shared tasks. You take a few moments to quietly forecast your day, stretch, and head to the bathroom for your morning shower.

Now imagine a contrasting scenario: You wake in the morning to the light coming from your partner's screen. You offer a brief "good morning" and reach for your phone. That one TikTok song that was all over your "For You Page" last night is still stuck in your head. All across the world things happened while you were sleeping. A glance at your phone reveals all the notifications that popped up overnight. You have 14 work emails and 45 text messages from two different group chats. Your friend sent you 15 TikTok's to watch, and you have a low balance alert on Mint. You take a few minutes and scan through and respond to everything before even putting your feet on the floor for the day. A quick snap to your friend ensures that your 155-day snap streak stays alive, and you go about your day.

In an ideal world, which morning might feel most restorative? Which might better prepare you for what lies ahead? Most importantly, which might lead to more connection between you and your partner?

The latter scenario may be a reality for many people, who seek and anticipate these types of interactions all day, every day. In modern Western society, and in many other places around the globe, the expectation that we are available and connected through technology is growing more and more each day. Scholars have coined this anywhere-anytime connectivity a "gratification niche" (Chan, 2015), and some are concerned that our excessive use of devices such as smartphones and tablets is addictive. Edward Tufte, statistician and professor emeritus of political science, statistics, and computer science at Yale University, says, "There are only two industries that call their customers 'users': illegal drugs and software" (Oriowski, 2020). There is no arguing the usefulness of technology to aid in nearly every part of life. It is worth considering, however, the impact that technology can have (both positive and negative) on our developing selves, and especially our relationships. This chapter will provide some insight into what we know, from what perspective, and what is yet to be discovered about technology as it relates to interpersonal relationships and overall well-being.

Think about how you might move through your day without the use of technology. As I (Roni) type, I wonder how I would write this anthology without the internet and a resource, a computer as my tool, and email to communicate. With the integration of technology into daily life comes societal change that we have never seen before. Today, much of popular culture largely exists online; most people get their news online, and people are connecting and communicating online like never before. We create a reality based on what we read and watch online, but what we don't know is that what we see is tailored very specifically to us. Facts can be distorted with a few key words, and there are now many versions of a "fact" that are intentionally provided to people who are already primed to hear a particular story. According to Tristan Harris, former design ethicist for Google, and cofounder of the Center for Humane Technology, "Facebook may be the greatest tool of social persuasion ever created" (Oriowski, 2020).

You can probably easily recall a time that you observed (or maybe participated in) a debate over a Facebook post that voiced a controversial political opinion or stance. Perhaps you unfriended or blocked someone because of their stance. Being able to talk about differences with others is an important skill, but when we're doing it behind a screen, do we become so bold as to alienate ourselves from others? Perhaps what results from becoming "known" by the internet is that we're directed toward others, and toward content, that supports our beliefs. What (and who) might we miss out on if all we see is content that is consistent with our own perspectives?

There are many invaluable gifts that technology has offered us—connection with distant family members, online dating, and the endless entertainment that we enjoy through our many technological media. On the flip side, the potential impact of technology, namely social media, on our mental health, communication skills, and overall human development calls to question whether what we think of as advancement is perhaps serving to further distance us from reality and human connection.

We acknowledge that some readers may consider themselves fully up-to-date on recent trends in technology, and others may feel like you're learning a new language. We also acknowledge that we aren't fully schooled in all aspects of technology, though we try to stay informed. Wherever you are in your comfort and familiarity with technology, we invite you to consider how technology impacts you and your relationships and what you want to do about it.

In this chapter we will explore the following:

- Social media
- Online dating
- Texting and "sexting"
- Pornography
- Prioritizing face-to-face connection

As you read, keep in mind the following primer questions for reflection. If you feel so inclined, take a few minutes and consider your responses to the following questions before you read, and then again after you've read the chapter.

## PRIMERS

1. How do you use technology to connect with people in your life?

2. Imagine what it would be like if, for 1 day, you had no access to technology (phone, email, social media, television, radio, etc.). Consider this a regular day, not a vacation day, or a day when you plan to intentionally disconnect. How would you feel? How would you go about your day? What adaptations would you need to make to accommodate being unplugged?

3. Right now, before reading on, turn off your phone, close your email and any other applications or programs you have open on your computer or device. Notice how it feels. As you read, allow any thoughts you have to enter your mind and then set them aside to refocus on your reading.

## SOCIAL MEDIA

Let's first rewind to a time long ago, when the # wasn't a #hashtag and nobody took photos of their meals (or if they did, it was on a camera that wasn't their smartphone); tweets were something that birds did; selfie was not a word; and in order to provide a status update, you had to make a phone call or write a letter and take it to the post office. Only 2 decades ago, social media barely existed, and our communities were limited to the people we saw, emailed, and called on the phone. Technology has impacted all aspects of society (Rosenfeld & Thomas, 2012). Figure 2.1 is a basic timeline of social media developments over time, beginning with the first social media platform, Six Degrees, in 1997.

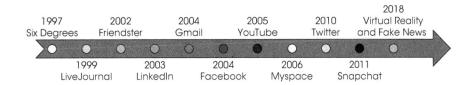

| Figure 2.1  Social media timeline.

Social media platforms allow a plethora of options for connection; we can now document nearly every aspect of our lives and broadcast it to as many people as are interested—the more the better. We can document through text (a status update on Facebook); we can post a photo or video on Snapchat or Instagram; we can hear from elected officials on Twitter; we can create, watch, and discover millions of videos through TikTok and share them with #Twitter. We can "go live" on Facebook, YouTube, and TikTok; Facetime with friends; and group text or chat through Google. This represents only a sampling of what we are capable of with technology. With so many options, are we ever really alone?

## Loneliness

One relational aspect that researchers have been especially curious about is how social media and internet use relate to loneliness. Historically, in order to connect with someone, you needed to call them and arrange a meeting place and time. Using apps like Skype, WhatsApp, Facebook, and Facetime (among many others), it is now easy to see and talk to people without requiring much planning, or even leaving the home. This is known as *access* to others (Finkel et al., 2012). Practically, it is much easier to connect with others through many different internet platforms. That said, with increased access and ease, fewer young adults are meeting face-to-face and going on dates. One outcome of this is that adolescents are waiting longer to get their driver's licenses. Ironically, for some, *more* access to online "connection" is leaving individuals physically disconnected.

When first examined, studies showed that increased access to and modalities of internet use were associated with greater self-esteem and lower levels of depression and loneliness. The picture has changed somewhat since 2010, where the expectation of always being available and the quantity of social connections have exceeded our ability to manage our access and usage (Chan, 2015). Tristan Harris acknowledges that we are evolved to care what people in our social circles and communities think about us; it serves an important function in our society and supports our human need to belong. Humans are not, however, evolved to care what 10,000 people think of us (Oriowski, 2020).

For some, when we engage on social media, we attempt to portray an image of perfection, happiness, prosperity, and adventure. Anything less than a utopian lifestyle is boring and won't yield enough likes to support a fragile self-esteem. The consequences of trying to uphold a utopian lifestyle are significant for many young people, who may experience what is now named "Snapchat dysmorphia"—seeking plastic surgery so one can look more like their social media filter (Oriowski, 2020). Dr. Anna Lembke, Stanford University School of Medicine medication director of addiction medicine, states that "social media is a drug. We have a basic biological imperative to connect with other people, that directly affects the release of dopamine in the neural pathway" (Oriowski, 2020). Humans are social beings, and connection with others is a biological need. What do you think happens when our primary method of connection is through technology as opposed to face-to-face? When it comes to social media, how much is too much? Is it possible that social media is literally leaving us alone?

The research is mixed on how social media use relates to loneliness. Consider the following statements for a moment. How can it be that the following contradicting statements are all true?

- For older adults who have limited capacity to engage with others face-to-face, social internet use may reduce feelings of loneliness. After all, some interaction, even if not in person, is better than no interaction at all.
- Among young adults (under age 34), perceptions of loneliness and social internet use appear unrelated (Nowland et al., 2018).
- Rates of depression and anxiety in youth and young adults rose sharply around the rise of Facebook, and suicide rates in middle- and high school–aged girls have risen 150% since 2010 (Oriowski, 2020).

We have to remember that while there appears to be a relationship (correlation) between mental health problems (depression, anxiety, suicide) and the rise of Facebook, we can't conclude that Facebook, or social media in general, is the cause. We are curious, however, about how connection from behind a screen contributes to our mental health. What do you think?

One would think that ease of access might enable people to interact *more* with others, and thus reduce feelings of loneliness, but what seems important about social interaction, whether face-to-face or online, is the depth of the interaction. "When the Internet is used as a way station on the route to enhancing existing relationships and forging new social connections, it is a useful tool for reducing loneliness. But when social technologies are used to escape the social world and withdraw from the 'social pain' of interaction, feelings of loneliness are increased" (Nowland et al., 2018, p. 70).

Young adults today have grown up with technology all around them; many of you reading this anthology may not be able to remember a time without the internet. Connecting via technology may seem like the best (and perhaps only) way to establish a relationship that may eventually transition to face-to-face. Perhaps the perception of loneliness as linked to social internet use is completely foreign to those who have always been connected online. It is possible that, for some, pursuing face-to-face connection may seem outdated, odd, or even lead to greater isolation. Consider for a moment the impact of primarily engaging with others from behind a screen. What do you imagine is missing from our ability to connect when we can't fully see, hear, and touch the people we feel closest to?

The messages we communicate here seem contradictory; for some, social internet use can lead to greater feelings of loneliness, while for others it allows a social network that isn't possible in a face-to-face setting, perhaps due to geography, ability, social anxiety, and/ or access to others, among other factors. Our concern about social internet use is when people of any age are capable of engaging in face-to-face relationships and choose instead to engage online. Giles Slade (2012) puts this in perspective in his book *Big Disconnect: The Story of Technology and Loneliness*. Slade proposes that we are sacrificing the depth of our connection with others (and the subsequent release of the bonding hormone oxytocin) when we elect to engage online as opposed to face-to-face. Clearly there are both benefits and drawbacks when we discuss technology use. We encourage you to think about the time you spend engaging with others face-to-face versus online—how would you rate the quality and depth of your relationships?

The way we use the internet also matters when considering the depth of our connection to others, and specifically loneliness (Nowland et al., 2018). In the 18–34 age group, a lot of "weak ties"—varied media connections with many friends and acquaintances—often are associated with greater levels of overall well-being. Those in the 35–70-plus age group, however, typically enjoy fewer associations and strong ties (established relationships). Further, the 35–70-plus age group generally experiences a greater sense of well-being when they practice *media multiplexity*—using multiple media methods for maintaining established relationships (Chan, 2015).

The take-home message from this research suggests that when adults ages 35–70-plus use technology to keep them connected with people they're already in strong tie relationships, their overall well-being improves. For youth and young adults, well-being seems to increase as the number of associations goes up. This information leads us to question if/how youth and young adults will transition from people with hundreds of weak ties to people with established and meaningful relationships? As you reflect on your own internet use, do you see any connection between how you feel and how much, or in what ways you're using the internet and social media?

## Connectedness

As humans, we're all trying to live our best lives under the circumstances we're provided. Abraham Maslow calls this concept self-actualization. Others consider psychological well-being to be comprised of living a purposeful life, being optimistic, and gaining the respect of others (Diener et al., 2009, as cited in Chan, 2015). Healthy relationships and a sense of connection with others as you'll recall from Chapter 1, are at the heart of well-being. We need communication to establish and maintain emotional bonds with others. Especially given the challenges of the recent COVID-19 pandemic, technology has been essential in keeping us connected to people whom we couldn't safely see in person. We each have our own level of multimodal connectedness—a personal communication system in which people use various forms of media to connect with other people in their daily lives (text, email, chat, etc.; Chan, 2015). There is no doubt that technology helps us stay connected with people we don't see every day. Our challenge for you is to consider how technology affects the relationships you have with people you *do* see and interact with on a daily basis.

At this point, research indicates that studying the connection between internet use and relationship outcomes can offer interesting data, though we can't yet predict a relationship's success or failure (e.g., divorce) based on each partner's use of technology (Cacioppo et al., 2013). So, as you're reading, if you are concerned about your own internet use, it's important to self-reflect on how, how much, and when you use it. Careful self-reflection and accurate self-assessment will help you determine whether your use of the internet is beneficial or harmful to your relational health and well-being. We'll offer some suggestions for managing your technology use, for your own well-being and that of your relationships, at the end of this chapter. In the meantime, choose one important person in your life to discuss these concepts with; how does technology use affect your relationship?

For those seeking a potential romantic partner, what we do know is that social media, and the internet in general, are significantly influencing where and how people are meeting. Due to the accessibility and (for some demographics) universality of online connections, many new relationships are beginning online (Rosenfeld & Thomas, 2012). While this is true for young, heterosexual individuals, it is especially true for those who have fewer desirable relational options to choose from (e.g., LGBTQ+ individuals, middle-aged and older adults, those living in rural communities, etc.; Rosenfeld & Thomas, 2012). In fact, for LGBTQ+ individuals, meeting potential romantic partners online is rapidly and decidedly overtaking every other way of meeting (e.g., friends, at work, at school, in a bar, etc.; Rosenfeld & Thomas, 2012). This increased accessibility of potential partners has opened doors for many people who felt bound by geographical location and is also influencing diversity and freedom to choose a mate.

## ONLINE DATING

Online dating has changed the way that many people in society approach getting to know one another and establish new relationships. With its recent rise in popularity, the online dating community has significantly impacted the way many people meet and interact as well as approach and pursue potential partners (Finkel et al., 2012).

There are three main considerations around the differences between online dating and dating in person: (a) access, (b) expectations for communication, and (c) relational knowledge. First, online dating has significantly increased our access to potential relationship partners (Finkel et al., 2012). For most of 2020, amidst a global pandemic, the internet was the only way for many to seek and access potential partners. Most people who were looking for a partner had easy access to the internet and had the resources and skills to be able to download an app or quickly create an online dating profile. Setting up and using online dating apps or websites could be done from almost anywhere, from most devices. Historically, most of these services required some financial investment, though today many applications are free. In an age where most Americans check their phones an average of 46 times per day (74 for young adults), having a giant database of potential partners with very little regulation or oversight at our fingertips is unprecedented (Eadicicco, 2015). This means that we don't know how society will change in the long term as a result of online dating.

For some, what can happen when there are so many choices is that potential partners are ruled out due to characteristics or preferences that, if we had met them in person, wouldn't be deal breakers. For example, imagine for a moment that you view a person's profile online and they endorse a particular religion or political affiliation that you don't share. You quickly dismiss that person and move on. Now imagine this scenario: You meet someone at a yoga class who you immediately connect with; would you first ask them about their religious/political affiliation before asking them to coffee? While we believe that sharing values in a relationship is very important, there may be forces at play when we meet someone in person that we miss out on in an online setting. Some would argue that online dating takes a lot of the time and guesswork out of choosing a suitable mate. Others would argue that perhaps it is the differences that can make a relationship complementary and that we don't have to be the same in every aspect of our beings to experience a fulfilling and satisfying intimate relationship. What do you think?

With so many choices, how can we know that we've picked the right person? Having access to so many choices can actually reduce our relationship satisfaction once we establish one. Barry Schwartz (2004) calls this the *paradox of choice*. He first warns us that having endless choices produces paralysis instead of liberation—it feels impossible to choose. Once we do choose, we are less satisfied with the choice we made than if we had fewer choices. Our expectations become so high that even when we make a good choice, we feel worse, wondering if there was another option that might have been just a little bit better. We don't believe, nor is there any evidence to support, that there is only one person out there for each of us. That said, as a culture we are persistently concerned with more and better. How does this cultural norm play out in our relationships, specifically in online dating when access to hundreds of potential partners doesn't go away once a tie is established? The reduction in relationship satisfaction initially in online relationships could be due to the stress of having too many choices or could be due to the fact that there are more romantic alternatives than we could possibly hope to meet in a lifetime (Houdek et al., 2018).

Another way that dating apps and websites have changed the way we approach relationships is that many people expect constant communication with potential romantic partners (Finkel et al., 2012). Much of the romantic communication happens even before we have met potential partners face-to-face (Finkel et al., 2012). There is ongoing debate about whether having the expectation of constant communication and openness is healthy for new relationships. This trend is also mirrored in the professional world, with many jobs expecting constant access to work email or phone calls. The expectation for constant communication leaves little time to be alone or unplug.

The last major difference between online and face-to-face dating is the amount of relational knowledge that we have access to before meeting. After all, isn't getting to know each other half the fun? Once a relationship is established, this knowledge can even include knowing where another person is at all times. Many apps offer the ability to locate or track someone (with their consent) and many people use this tool in their relationships. There is a roaring conversation on social media and in magazine articles debating whether using these location trackers is relationship enhancing or not. Some people report that the use of location services indicates a lack of trust in the relationship and increases unhealthy habits like spying or snooping. Others state that it's a convenient tool that reduces the need for mundane communication like "Where are you?" or "Will you stop at the store?" It can focus intentional communication on deeper subjects rather than constantly discussing logistics and estimated times of arrival. At this point, there is little research indicating the impact that these specific services can have on relationships, and users are expected to self-analyze their own relational motivations for using it. What do you think? Consider discussing this with someone you're close with.

Many dating apps and sites have the capacity to match their users with potential romantic partners (Finkel et al., 2012). The popular dating site Match.com (n.d.a.) boasts that "Match. com has led to more dates, relationships, and marriages than any other site." While some online dating apps attempt to use algorithms to match consumers based on data that they've collected, there is no evidence to support relational outcomes using this method (Finkel et al., 2012). On other platforms, like Tinder, Grindr, and Bumble, users match themselves with other profile pictures, which then gives way for communication reciprocity. This strategy puts a lot of weight on the images associated with profiles, neglecting personality characteristics, thoughts, and values that accompany the profile (Chappetta & Barth, 2016).

While initial attraction is often based on physical appearance, there are many other characteristics that more reliably establish compatibility between partners, and that can lead to lasting relationships. Making decisions primarily based on the physical appearance of someone else can make it more challenging to build relational foundations without missing a more holistic view of who a person is (Chappetta & Barth, 2016). We propose an online dating app where people choose potential dating partners based on profile alone, sans photo, just like on the reality singing competition *The Voice*! How do you think choosing a partner based on their interests, values, and preferences would influence relationship success, as opposed to swiping right based on physical appearance?

The many ways that online dating will continue to shape our society remain to be seen. Though there is some research about how our collective online presence is impacting our society, no one can really know the greater picture of the impact of online dating on relationship success until more research is done. Current projections vary from a general feeling of concern that the internet will destroy relationships as we know them to the feeling that the internet can help people of all ages, genders, races, sexual orientations, faith affiliations, and so on find happiness that they wouldn't have found otherwise.

If you find yourself in the population of people using dating apps, remember to ensure that you're using them thoughtfully, safely, and with intent so that they can enhance your relational experience rather than detract from it. Following are some online dating safety tips that will help you on your journey, courtesy of Match.com (n.d.b.).

## Online Dating Safety Tips

1. Never send money or disclose financial information online.

2. Protect your personal information—address, details about your life, Social Security number, and so on, in early communications online.

3. Keep your conversations on the dating platform; don't move to phone, text, or email communication too soon.

4. Be wary of long-distance and overseas relationships; some scammers will ask for help to "move home" or will be hesitant to meet in person or talk on the phone. These people may not be who they say they are. Trust your gut; if you are uncomfortable with any aspect of your communication, say so.

5. Report suspicious information to the dating site. Some examples of violations of online dating site behavior (specific to Match.com) are as follows:
   a. Requests for money or donations
   b. Underage users
   c. Harassment, threats, and offensive messages
   d. Inappropriate or harmful behavior during or after meeting in person
   e. Fraudulent profiles

    f.  Spam or solicitation, including links to commercial website or attempts to sell products or services.

6.  Protect your account with a strong password and never provide information to someone who contacts you from the site asking for personal information.

Once you've established a dating relationship online and feel ready to move the relationship face-to-face, Match.com (n.d.b.) offers some useful safety guidance for extending the relationship "offline."

Meeting in Person Safety Tips:

1.  Don't be in a rush.
2.  Meet in a public place and stay public.
3.  Tell friends and family about your plans.
4.  Use your own form of transportation.
5.  Know your limits, especially as it pertains to drugs or alcohol.
6.  Don't leave drinks or other personal items unattended.
7.  If you feel uncomfortable, leave.
8.  Be careful while traveling. Specific to LGBTQ+, know the laws regulating relationships by sexuality and don't log into your dating app while there. You can visit ILGA World to see the latest sexual orientation laws by country.

Match (n.d.b.) provides additional safety measures regarding sexual health and consent, and resources for help, support, or advice.

## SEXTING

Sexting is another way technology is affecting romantic relationships. We aren't just talking about sending your partner the run-of-the-mill heart emoji. Sexting is defined as sending sexually explicit messages or images to another person through a text messaging application. Due to increased access to others via the internet, the social norm of always being connected, and the prevalence of devices (smartphones, tablets, etc.) that connect to the internet, sexting has become commonplace, especially among young adults aged 18–24 (Walker & Seath, 2017). It is estimated that, internationally, between 18 and 68% of young adults sext (Dir & Cyders, 2015).

What impact does sexting have on relationships? The short answer is, it depends. Most people who engage in sexting behavior report doing so in the context of some sort of existing relationship. This includes people who are dating casually, seriously dating, cohabitating, or pursuing a romantic relationship. On one hand, sexting can be used as a tool to enhance relationships through increased communication and consensual sexual exploration (Dir & Cyders, 2015). On the other hand, nonconsensual sexting is in the realm of intimate partner violence. "Aggravated sexting involves adults or elements of abusive behavior, such as the nonconsensual distribution of sexual images, sexual abuse, extortion, or threats, whereas experimental sexting does not involve adults or abusive elements" (Symons et al., 2018, p. 3837). As is true with any sexual behavior or practice, consent is key. If you're wondering if your partner is comfortable with and would enjoy receiving an explicit text message, it's always best to ask first. Before you give consent to send or receive explicit images consider any future harm that could come from the permanence of explicit images. Those pictures don't necessarily go away even if the relationship does.

While there is some support for the idea that sexting can be relationship enhancing, there is also a discussion around the indirect impact that sexting can have on our larger culture around relationships. Some suggest that, while consensual sexting itself doesn't appear to be the cause of negative relational behavior, it could indirectly contribute to social attitudes that perpetuate norms that are antimonogamous and more self-focused (Dir & Cyder, 2015). This could include societal trends like hook-up culture or the rising prevalence of cheating when a relationship isn't living up to the immediate expectations of one partner. Society has generally viewed sexting as a sexually and socially deviant behavior. Due to its rising prevalence, some studies suggest that this mentality is changing. Often, individuals who sext are viewed as being more likely to engage in risky behavior (relationally, sexually, and otherwise), though some studies show that this concern may be overstated (Dir & Cyders, 2015).

There appears to be documented differences in the ways that men and women view and experience sexting (Dir & Cyders, 2015). As is the case with many studies in relationship research, this study views this data from the perspective of a gender binary society. While this data is by no means representative of how every person experiences the gender spectrum, it can pose some interesting perspectives on how many people in our society view the act of sending and receiving sexually explicit content.

Generally, those who identify as women state that they have had negative experiences and expectations associated with sexting (Dir & Cyders, 2015). Interestingly, many women also report that they are the recipients of unsolicited sexts and images at much higher rates than most men receive these messages. This could be one of the reasons some women report having a much more negative perspective on sexting than most men. Many men, on the other hand, report that they have a positive perspective on sexting and view it as an enjoyable activity that enhances their relationships with others (Dir & Cyders, 2015). Men are also much more likely to send unsolicited messages to people that they don't know (Dir & Cyders, 2015). The differences between men and women appears to be distilled down to the issue of consent. **People who don't give consent to receive sexts don't like to receive sexts.** The act of sending illicit images to nonconsenting others is generally viewed in the literature as a form of sexual or intimate partner violence (Dekker et al., 2019). What do you think? If you received a sext from someone without your consent, how might you feel?

Sexting trends are also found among young people who have had sexual experiences before or who expect a sexual experience to happen very soon. Young men are generally viewed as the initiators of sexts, either by sending or asking for pictures, and young women appear to put limits on that type of interaction (Symons et al., 2018). At the same time, young people are equally likely to send photos to people with whom they are in face-to-face relationships as they are with whom they have only interacted with online (Symons et al., 2018). Sending photos to someone you have never met before in person could lead to unwanted consequences, like that person misrepresenting themselves as someone else or the dispersal of your photos in ways you may not want them dispersed. Use caution because things that are sent or posted online can be difficult to delete or recover.

The effects of sexting have largely been studied without emphasis on whether the recipient has given their consent. As a result, all sexting often gets viewed through the lens of sexual assault. While it is vital to discuss the harmful effects of nonconsensual sexting, we would be remiss if we didn't give credence to the potential benefits of appropriate and consensual sexting in relationships. Many sex education programs only highlight the dangers of sexting rather than also discussing how it could be helpful and positive, when used in a prosocial way within a healthy relationship. Rather than simply preaching sexual abstinence (both physical and technological), it is more accurate to educate others on the importance of getting consent if they feel that a sexting relationship might be a tool to benefit an in-person relationship (Dekker et al., 2019). "Hence, from a normalcy discourse, (consensual) sexting is seen as an activity that can support young people in their sexual development and thus in terms of sexual agency, sexual expression, and exploration of their sexuality" (Symons et al., 2018, p. 3838). While it is good to highlight the positive, it is important to emphasize the need for consent in any sexual act, especially for something like sending and receiving sexts, because people may not consider sexting in the same category as other sexual acts.

In Chapter 5, we emphasize the importance of communication, communication, communication when it comes to achieving good sex. Now that you've considered the many ways, and the many forms of media that we can use to communicate, we add a caveat—consent, consent, consent!

# PORNOGRAPHY

Perhaps the most provocative topic in the realm of technology and relationships is the increasing use of pornography among youth and adults worldwide (Hald et al., 2013). One study on heterosexual couples estimates that 72% of men and 56% of women report using pornography at some point in their lives (Muusses et al., 2015). Undeniably, pornography has become largely consumed and produced by a huge percentage of the world's population.

We present some data here from the internet's biggest video library of pornography: Pornhub. Though not the only place on the internet where pornography is readily available, it is by far the biggest resource. In 2019, they had 42 billion visits to the site, with 39 billion searches performed. Though many people watch pornography on this site, many also use the upload feature on the site as well. In 2019, 6.83 million videos were uploaded, which continues a significant trend of growth over the past few years. This translates to 169 years' worth of new content uploaded in 2019 alone. Every minute, there were an average of 219,985 views and 80,032 unique visits to the site (Pornhub, 2019).

Much pornographic content available on the internet is provided free of charge, and there are minimal security checks in place to ensure that users (and uploaders) are over 18. Worldwide, 83.7% of Pornhub's (2019) traffic was viewed on a cell phone or other mobile device, making it accessible almost anywhere in the world. Fifty-two percent of content is viewed on Apple mobile devices, though 75.5 % of desktop views were running a Windows operating system. Google pointed 94.06% of users to Pornhub while other search engines made up the other 6% (Pornhub, 2019). Clearly, the consumption of pornography is a global phenomenon with users signing in all over the world.

While Pornhub tracks descriptive statistics, it also tracks comments, likes, messages, and other qualitative interactions that users can have on the site. Interestingly, one of the most mentioned words in comments and messages across the site is the word "love" (Pornhub, 2019). Though there is no explanation of this on the site, it does incite the question, "Are porn users looking to love and feel loved?"

In 2016, the most searched video keyword was *stepmom*, which insinuates that users enjoy watching relationships between people who already are somewhat maternally related, though not biologically (Pornhub, 2019). As counselors, we have some curiosity regarding the psychology behind the sexual gratification that might emerge from a maternal adjacent relationship, but we will leave that discussion for another book. In 2019, preference shifted to the keyword *amateur*, and the hypothesis is that people are interested in a more real experience than watching something clearly scripted with a high production value. *Transgender* is another search term that was more popular recently than in years past (Pornhub, 2019). Another search term that skyrocketed up the rankings (besides *alien*, which was in second place), was *POV*

(Pornhub, 2019). POV refers to "point of view," which depicts sex from the point of view of one of the participants. Pornhub advertises this new trend with the statements such as "Users looking for a more realistic porn-viewing experience could tune-in and unzip, getting everything they needed without all the real-world troubles. Who needs an IRL (in real life) partner when you have POV Pornhub videos on your side?" (Pornhub, 2019).

The increasing use of pornography is a global trend, with the United States and Japan topping the list (Pornhub, 2019). Additionally, the average amount of time that users spent on the site grew to over 10 minutes in 2019. The most popular time to view porn is on Sunday evenings at 11:00 p.m., while the least popular time is on Monday mornings at 5:00 a.m., though there are users on the site at all times (Pornhub, 2019).

Demographically, there are some differences in how men and women use pornography. In 2019 there was a 3% increase in users who identify as female, which raises the proportion of female (32%) to male users (68%; Pornhub). Again, these numbers are viewed through a gender binary lens and don't represent all gender identities. Pornhub reports that in 2019 the average age of its users was 36, which rose from 35.5 in 2018. Sixty one percent of Pornhub's users ranged between 18 and 34, though the age of its users is self-reported by each user. There are minimal internet safety strategies in place to ensure that users accessing this content are over 18, so it would follow that the real average age might be much younger. Most scholars estimate that the average age that children who identify as boys are exposed to porn is 11 years old. Some websites that target concerned parents report that users under 10 years old account for a fifth of the underage users (Fight the New Drug, 2020).

How does pornography influence society at large, and our intimate relationships? There are several hypotheses associated with this question and several different ways researchers study pornography. While there are some trends that are beginning to emerge, there is an overwhelming narrative that pornography and its effects should continue to be researched so that we can learn more.

There are several ways that regular pornography users differ from those who do not use it consistently. One study suggests that people who use internet pornography regularly are more likely to pay for, or be paid for sex, have sex with multiple partners, and have extramarital sex (Wright & Randall, 2012). Another study reports that the exposure of people to internet pornography increases "notions of women as sex objects" and is associated with less egalitarian views of gender roles and instances of hostile sexism (Hald et al., 2013). Yet another stated that internet pornography users were more likely to display narcissistic characteristics, both generally and sexually (Kasper et al., 2015).

One particular concern over youth accessing pornography is that they may use it to answer questions they have about sex. Asking parents and other trusted adults about sex can be awkward and embarrassing, and youth will often seek alternative resources (e.g., friends and the internet) to learn more. With few restrictions in place to prevent underage users from accessing pornographic material online, we worry that youth may use pornography as a form of sex education—a how-to manual, which may be grossly inaccurate in terms of what a sexual partner may actually enjoy. Be careful not to mistake enthusiastic acting with what an authentic sexual experience might entail. Pornography largely contributes to the objectification of women, endorsing rape culture—the normalization of rape due to societal attitudes about gender and sexuality. (More on this in Chapter 12.)

Viewing pornography with a partner can be an enjoyable part of a healthy sexual relationship; however, using it to fill in the gaps of sexual education can lead to misinformation and less satisfaction in a sexual partnership. The best way to know what a partner enjoys sexually is to ask, experiment, and respond to your partner's cues. If you have questions about sex, the internet can be a useful resource, but be sure to seek reputable resources. We offer some reputable resources to answer all sex questions in Chapter 5.

There appear to be gender differences in pornography use; men were more likely to use pornography as an aid in masturbation, while women were more likely to use it as a sexual tool with their partners. Several studies have suggested that using internet pornography alone (without a partner) is associated with lower relationship quality and sexual satisfaction (Muusses et al., 2015). Muusses et al. (2015) reported that when pornography was used as a supplement to sex in heterosexual relationships there was a positive relationship between a woman's use of sexually explicit internet materials and her partner's perception of their relationship quality and sexual satisfaction. It appeared that men's use of sexually explicit internet materials was negatively associated with women's view of relationship quality and sexual satisfaction (Muusses et al., 2015).

It is possible that individuals predisposed to earlier and more sexual engagement may also be the ones to increasingly seek sexual content online. Could pornography use be both a symptom of and the cause of relational tension at the same time? Though much of the research illustrates a negative view of pornography use both alone and in relationships, a critical thinker would examine these ideas. Like sexting, could pornography have a relationship-enhancing component, or are the negative impacts too large to overcome? What do you think?

Most researchers suggest that we can't know if pornography use is the cause of some of what we observe in users (endorsement of rape culture, objectification, and violence against women) or a symptom of some other relational trend like attachment style, personal history, culture, or relationship quality (Hald et al., 2013). Undoubtedly, a combination of factors, including pornography use, contribute to relationship quality and satisfaction, but we can't ignore the potential influence that such easy, unrestricted access to massive amounts of explicit material can have on intimacy within modern romantic relationships.

## Revenge Pornography

Revenge pornography is a category of pornography that is distributed to others without consent. Often times, it is also filmed without consent (Walker & Sleath, 2017). This has become an increasingly big problem, because research has shown that viewing the victim's sex acts without their consent can lead to many negative consequences, including "debilitating loss of self-esteem, anxiety, panic attacks, crippling feelings of humiliation and shame, discharge from employment, verbal and physical harassment, and even stalking" (Walker & Sleath, 2017, p. 9). The general consensus, also regarding sexting, is that nonconsensual sharing of images and videos should be viewed from the perspective of intimate partner violence and sexual assault, though many people haven't thought about it in that way before (Walker & Sleath, 2017). Revenge pornography can be used to control, threaten, or punish current or ex partners, and many states are developing legislation around the distribution of revenge pornography (Walker & Sleath, 2017).

Technology can be used as a tool to enhance relationship connection and satisfaction, *and* it can broaden the number of ways people can hurt each other in relationships. Before taking images and videos of yourself or your partner, consider this: Will it enhance your relationship, or are the risks of using it too high? What we hope you take away from these discussions about sexting and pornography is this: Really think about what you want in your relationships and use technology (if you choose to) as a supplement to a healthy sexual relationship. Talk with your partner about how you want to use technology to enhance your partnership, communicate often, and always, *always*, make consent a priority before introducing sexting or pornography into your relationship.

## PRIORITIZING FACE-TO-FACE CONNECTION

*"Love lurks in the lulls, in the unstructured moments of just being together –
the times we are now* most *likely to turn to our devices"*
—(Marano, 2016, p. 54)

Now that we've discussed the myriad ways that we use technology to connect with significant others in our lives, let's turn back to the importance of face-to-face interaction. Touch, eye contact, and turning toward our partners and loved ones are essential elements of relational health. Imagine that you had a bad day and you meet with a friend for dinner. As you begin to share your experiences of the day, your friend's phone vibrates and they immediately turn to respond to a text message. Imagine how you feel in that moment. Are you feeling heard? Valued? Attended to? Research has demonstrated that merely the presence of a mobile device during a conversation between strangers can negatively affect feelings of closeness, connection, and ratings of conversation quality (Przybylski & Weinstein, 2012). Following are some simple suggestions to help you establish healthy boundaries around the use of technology, for your own health and well-being and that of your relationships.

1. Turn off all notifications on your smartphone.
2. Agree to keep devices out of your bedroom (or shut off all apps) at a specific time.
3. Limit time spent on social media; what do you think is a reasonable time to spend? Track it and see how close you are to your budget.
4. Intentionally set aside relationship time. When you're with a friend, give them your full attention. If you're in a romantic relationship, make time each day to be unplugged together.

Our challenge to you after reading this chapter is to reflect on the many interpersonal skills you already know and have yet to learn (there are more to come!), and set aside your phone for specific periods of time when you're with the people you care about face-to-face. Listen, share, touch, smile, and remember that often what matters most is right in front of you.

## CONCLUSION

Undeniably, the way we view and experience relationships is changing as rapidly as technology advances. The trends described in this chapter may evolve as swiftly as they initially came about, and we undoubtedly will be faced with new developments and challenges as our world fluctuates around us. With the need for more and quicker research to understand the societal trends that are happening before our eyes, we are left with no clear path on what technological rules we should follow to have the healthiest relationships. Do we ban pornography? Do we require cell phones to restrict image sending? Do we crack down on pornography usage by people under 18? Do we monitor or discontinue online dating? Do we exclusively use app-based dating services? How much time is too much time in front of a screen? There are no clear answers, and more questions are uncovered as the body of research grows. What we are left with is the hope that we have the skills to critically consider how our actions on and consumption of the internet affect us and others.

What we do know about relationships is that it is vital that we clearly and respectfully communicate our thoughts, feelings, and needs with our partners and potential partners. At the same time, we need to allow space and time for our partners and potential partners to express their thoughts, feelings, and needs to us so that we can collectively decide what is best for our relationships. It is up to us, within our relationships, to decide how communication and partner exploration are affected by technology.

## END-OF-CHAPTER REFLECTIONS
_____

Next time you are in a waiting room, a restaurant, or standing in line, choose *not* to reach for your phone to pass the time. Notice what's happening around you and check in with yourself. How are you feeling? What's it like to be present in the moment without your phone? Allow yourself to experience whatever comes up for you and challenge yourself to be present in the moment more often!

# REFERENCES

Cacioppo, J., Cacioppo, S., Gonzaga, G., Ogburn, E., & Vanderweele, T. (2013). Marital satisfaction and break-ups differ across on-line and off-line meeting venues. *Proceedings of the National Academy of Sciences of the United States of America, 110*(25), 10135. https://doi.org/10.1073/pnas.1222447110

Chan, M. (2015). Multi-modal connectedness and quality of life: Examining the influences of technology adoption and interpersonal communication on well-being across the life span. *Journal of Computer-Mediated Communication, 20*, 3–18. https://doi.org/10.1111/jcc4.12089

Chappetta, K., & Barth, J. (2016). How gender role stereotypes affect attraction in an online dating scenario. *Computers in Human Behavior, 63*, 738–746. https://doi.org/10.1016/j.chb.2016.06.006

Dekker, A., Wenzlaff, F., Daubmann, A., Pinnschmidt, H., & Briken, P. (2019). (Don't) look at me! How the assumed consensual or non-consensual distribution affects perception and evaluation of sexting images. *Journal of Clinical Medicine, 8*(5), 706. https://doi.org/10.3390/jcm8050706

Dir, A. L., & Cyders, M. A. (2015). Risks, risk factors, and outcomes associated with phone and internet sexting among university students in the united states. *Archives of Sexual Behavior, 44*(6), 1675–1684. https://doi.org/10.1007/s10508-014-0370-7

Eadicicco, L. (2015, December 15). Americans check their phones 8 billion times per day. *Time.* from https://time.com/4147614/smartphone-usage-us-2015/

Fight the New Drug. (2020, November 23). *What's the average age of a child's first exposure to porn?* https://fightthenewdrug.org/real-average-age-of-first-exposure/

Finkel, E., Eastwick, P., Karney, B., Reis, H., & Sprecher, S. (2012). Online dating: A critical analysis from the perspective of psychological science. *Psychological Science in the Public Interest, 13*(1), 3–66. https://doi.org/10.1177/1529100612436522

Hald, G., Malamuth, N., & Lange, T. (2013). Pornography and sexist attitudes among heterosexuals. *Journal of Communication, 63*(4), 638–660. https://doi.org/10.1111/jcom.12037

Houdek, P., Koblovský, P., Šťastný, D., & Vranka, M. (2018). Consumer decision making in the information age. *Society*, *55*(5), 422–429. https://doi.org/10.1007/s12115-018-0283-5

Kasper, T., Short, M. B., & Milam, A. (2015). Narcissism and internet pornography use. *Journal of Sex & Marital Therapy*, *41*(5), 481–486. https://doi.org/10.1080/0092623X.2014.931313

Marano, H. E. (2016, July/August). Love interrupts. *Psychology Today*, *49*(4), 50.

Match.com. (n.d.a.). *Home page*. www.match.com

Match.com. (n.d.b.). *Dating safety tips*. https://www.match.com/help/safetytips.aspx?lid=4

Muusses, L., Kerkhof, P., & Finkenauer, C. (2015). Internet pornography and relationship quality: A longitudinal study of within and between partner effects of adjustment, sexual satisfaction and sexually explicit internet material among newly-weds. *Computers in Human Behavior*, *45*, 77–84. https://doi.org/10.1016/j.chb.2014.11.077

Nowland, R., Necka, E., & Cacioppo, J. (2018). Loneliness and social internet use: Pathways to reconnection in a digital world? *Perspectives on Psychological Science*, *13*(1), 70–87. https://doi.org/10.1177/1745691617713052

Oriowski, J. (Director). (2020). *The social dilemma* [Film]. Netflix.

Pornhub. (2019). *The 2019 year in review*. https://www.pornhub.com/insights/2019-year-in-review#2019

Przybylski, A. K. & Weinstein, N. (2012). Can you connect with me now? How the presence of mobile communication technology influences face-to-face conversation quality. *Journal of Social and Personal Relationships*, *30*(3). 237–246. https://doi.org/10.1177/0265407512453827

Rosenfeld, M., & Thomas, R. (2012). Searching for a mate: The rise of the internet as a social intermediary. *American Sociological Review*, *77*(4), 523–547. https://doi.org/10.1177/0003122412448050

Schwartz, B. (2004). *The paradox of choice: Why more is less*. HarperCollins.

Slade, G. (2012). *Big disconnect: The story of technology and loneliness*. Prometheus.

Symons, K., Ponnet, K., Walrave, M., & Heirman, W. (2018). Sexting scripts in adolescent relationships: Is sexting becoming the norm? *New Media & Society*, *20*(10), 3836–3857. https://doi.org/10.1177/1461444818761869

Walker, K., & Sleath, E. (2017). A systematic review of the current knowledge regarding revenge pornography and non-consensual sharing of sexually explicit media. *Aggression and Violent Behavior*, *36*, 9–24. https://doi.org/10.1016/j.avb.2017.06.010

Wright, P., & Randall, A. (2012). Internet pornography exposure and risky sexual behavior among adult males in the united states. *Computers in Human Behavior*, *28*(4), 1410–1416. https://doi.org/10.1016/j.chb.2012.03.003

## RECOMMENDATIONS FOR FURTHER READING

Ansari, A. (2015). In Klinenberg E. (Ed.), *Modern romance*. Penguin.

Buren, J., & Lunde, C. (2018). Sexting among adolescents: A nuanced and gendered online challenge for young people. *Computers in Human Behavior*, *85*, 210–217. https://doi.org/10.1016/j.chb.2018.02.003

Marano, H. E. (2016, July/August). Love interrupts. *Psychology Today*, *49*(4), 50.

Renoe, E. (2017). *The new lonely: Intimacy in the age of isolation*. CreateSpace.

Schwartz, B. (2004). *The paradox of choice: Why more is less*. HarperCollins.

Steiner-Adair, C., & Barker, T. H. (2014). *The big disconnect: Protecting childhood and family relationships in the digital age*. HarperCollins.

## RECOMMENDED FILM

Oriowski, J. (Director). (2020). *The social dilemma* [Film]. Netflix.

# Chapter 3

# The Self in Relationship

## EDITORS' INTRODUCTION

This may come as a surprise, but your ability to be successful in your interpersonal relationships begins with the relationship you have with yourself. You read that right, the way you feel about yourself—your worthiness of love, your value as a human being, your self-efficacy, or your belief in your ability to be successful—all contribute to your success and satisfaction in your interpersonal relationships. There is remarkable truth to the phrase, "You have to love yourself first before you can love someone else." Equally as important as cultivating your self-worth in relationships is managing your expectations that your relationship (and your partner) will be perfect (Marano, 2010). After all, happiness and contentment begin with you! While having high expectations for a romantic partner is important, expectations for perfection can lead to dissatisfaction and a hyper focus on what's wrong, instead of what's right.

In "Learning to Love Yourself," Daniel Beaver describes how you might work toward a healthy self-concept, which involves at its core becoming in touch with your feelings, establishing healthy boundaries in your relationships, letting go a little, and listening to your intuition. We offer two caveats for this reading: (a) Beaver speaks to cultural norms around boundary-setting in families. We acknowledge that families are different in different cultures, so we encourage you to consider all varieties of family cultures that may disagree with Beaver's perspective on appropriate boundaries; and (b) While Beaver says that a healthy gauge in relationships is comfort, we encourage you to think about it in two ways; on one hand, it's very appropriate and reasonable to check in with yourself about what you're comfortable with in your relationships, and, on the other hand, sometimes venturing outside of your comfort zone with someone you trust is a worthy venture and an opportunity for personal growth.

As you read, keep in mind the following primer questions for reflection. If you feel so inclined, take a few minutes and consider your responses to the following questions before you read, and then again after you've finished each reading.

## PRIMER

1.  How often are you aware of how you're feeling? Can you put words to your emotions? Refer to Gloria Wilcox's (1982) feeling wheel to help you identify some feelings that you may not have the words for yet. The feeling wheel can help us specify and understand our feelings as we work from the center of the wheel outward. At the center of the wheel

# The Feeling Wheel

| Figure 3.1 The feeling wheel.

are our core feelings—mad, scared, peaceful, sad, joyful, and powerful. Notice as you move to the next circle of the wheel that feelings related to each of the six core feelings are more specific experiences relating to the core feeling, and we get even more specific as we move to the outermost circle. If you can begin by identifying the core feeling you're experiencing, you have so many more options to consider! Being able to clearly identify and express your feelings is a great skill to practice—both for better understanding yourself and for expressing yourself to those you care about. As you consider your feelings, try to suspend judgment of yourself; as Beaver will tell you, there is no such thing as a "bad" or a "good" feeling.

## CREDIT

Fig. 3.1: Copyright © 2020 by Gottman Institute.

# Learning to Love Yourself

*By Daniel Beaver*

*"But if nobody loves you*
*and you feel like dust*
*on an empty shelve*
*just remember*
*you can love yourself"*
—Keb Moe

When I first heard the phrase "learning to love yourself," it sounded like psychobabble. This saying is so vague. If I ask a client, "How do you love yourself?" I usually get a response that is just as vague. I intend to take this concept and make it very clear how to love yourself on both a cognitive and behavioral level. Just as I teach couples how to create emotional intimacy, I have the same goal of teaching individuals self-intimacy.

Does loving yourself mean saying, "Dan, I love you, you are so great." Not really, it's not that simple. Loving yourself in this context doesn't necessarily refer to masturbation, although that can be a part of the experience. The first major cognitive concept in learning to love yourself is that you need to respect and validate your own emotions. Whatever you feel emotionally is a fact for you. You don't question the validity of your emotions. You don't tell yourself not to feel what you feel.

To respect and validate one's own emotions, a person needs to know what emotions actually are. As a therapist, I ask my patients what they feel emotionally all the time, but for many of them, it's hard to identify what they actually feel. We live in a culture that encourages emotional repression; as a result, people find it difficult to know what they feel emotionally. When I ask my patients what they feel, they usually respond with what they *think*, not what they *feel*. I might ask a patient, "So when your wife talks to you that way when you forget what she told you, how does that affect you emotionally?" Usually the patient will respond with some type of statement about what he thinks, such as, "I feel that she shouldn't talk to me that way. I feel like she is talking to me like a child." In both of these responses, the patient believes he is communicating his emotions, but there is no mention of any emotion. He uses the phrase "I feel," but no emotional words follow. What he is really expressing is his thoughts or judgments, but not emotion.

When trying to identify your emotions, it's best to try to use only one-word descriptions, such as angry, hurt, sad, pleased, happy, or scared. These are a few words that can describe a person's emotional experience. As a therapist, I am looking for these words when I ask the question, "How does that make you feel?" Learning to identify these emotional words is a process of awareness that anyone can follow if they so desire, regardless of gender or age. I have had experience with people who had only about a three-word emotional vocabulary, but who developed a more extensive list of words to describe their emotions over time.

I often ask clients how they feel emotionally, and they will answer that they feel bad or good. It is so common for people to view the terms *bad* or *good* as if they are human emotions. The truth is that these words are value judgments, not human emotions. For example, when someone says they feel bad, I will ask them again if they feel "bad," what do they really feel? This may irritate them a little bit, but then they will usually express a real emotion like sadness or guilt. The goal is to be as accurate as you can about what you truly feel emotionally.

Once individuals identify what they feel emotionally, then the next step is to give that emotion validity. What this means is that individuals believe that how they feel emotionally is a fact, that is, that there is no question or debate as to the validity of what they feel. They don't believe that they need to defend or justify why they feel the way they do, it's just how they feel emotionally. When individuals are able to validate their own emotional truth, they won't tolerate being intimately involved with someone who doesn't share their same belief or respect of emotions.

When I hear the saying, "You have to love yourself before you can love someone else," it sounds great. But what does it mean? In practical terms, when a person respects and validates their own emotions, they will be involved only with someone who thinks the same way. However, if someone doesn't respect their own emotions, then most likely they will allow themselves to be treated with emotional disrespect by another person, which I don't consider a very loving relationship. It is critical that a person respects their own emotions if they want to have a healthy, successful, loving relationship.

# PSYCHOLOGICAL BOUNDARIES: ONE KEY TO ALL THREE INTIMACIES

The use of the term boundaries is a relatively new concept. It's one of those psychological buzzwords that are used in popular culture. For the layperson, it's a rather vague concept. Having boundaries in the physical world is not new: neighbors have fences separating their property; countries have borders separating their land. When these boundaries are respected, people usually live in peace; but when these boundaries aren't respected, people and countries go to war. In the same way, people have boundaries separating their psychological space. These boundaries are invisible, but they exist nonetheless. When these boundaries are respected, people get along a lot better in relationships.

The issue for individuals is their ability to establish these boundaries in their daily interactions with others. This becomes especially important in the context of an intimate relationship. Having the confidence that you can establish boundaries in your personal life is the key to falling in love. This confidence allows a person to have that sense of abandon and vulnerability that is so essential to experiencing both emotional and sexual intimacy to the fullest.

In explaining the concept of establishing psychological boundaries in relationships, I like to use the metaphor of what it's like to ski. One of the most crucial abilities in skiing is having the confidence that you know how to stop, preferably on a dime. When skiers point their skis down the mountain and gravity starts to pull them down faster and faster, they are experiencing the rush of skiing. They are "letting go to the mountain" as opposed to resisting and fighting the pull of gravity. Resistance is stressful, exhausting, and not a lot fun. What allows skiers to let go is the confidence that when they become uncomfortable with their experience, they can put the edges of their skis into the hill to slow down or stop if that's what they choose. They are in control the whole time. They choose to let go to the thrill of abandon or to stop to feel comfortable if they are starting to get out of control.

In a relationship, the equivalent of letting go to the hill when skiing is that sense of falling in love. Letting go emotionally in a relationship is very scary if a person doesn't have that sense of having control over what happens to them; that is, they don't have the sense they can set a boundary when they are feeling uncomfortable, or if they do set a boundary that it will be respected. This inability to set boundaries becomes a major block to forming an intimate relationship.

Some people create physical boundaries because they can't establish psychological ones. An example of this is a couple who have a long distant relationship. They put a lot of mileage between themselves, and when they get together, it's incredibly passionate and intimate. They can only tolerate this high level of togetherness for a short time. Boundaries that chronically fail to keep people separated enough are typically described as enmeshed, which means they begin to lose their sense of self in the relationship. This occurs because they are unable to set psychological boundaries and generally are afraid of creating conflicts in the relationship. The way they reestablish their sense of self is to return to their respective homes many miles away from each other. On the surface, this type of relationship might seem difficult and painful, but it keeps the people involved psychologically safe.

Many times this same thing is going on with a single person who has a long-term affair with someone who is married. They complain about how painful it is to be alone so much of the time, and that the person they're involved with says they are going to get a divorce, but doesn't seem to be in a big hurry to do so. On the surface, why would this single person stay in this type of relationship given that they experience so much frustration and loneliness at not being able to spend more time with their lover? The answer lies in understanding the concept of boundaries. The fact that their lover is married and not available provides a certain boundary that keeps them apart, which in turn provides a certain protection against losing their true sense of self. Usually the individual isn't conscious of this safety reason, but it is the only psychological reward I can see for paying such a high price for remaining in this type of relationship.

This pattern can sometimes be seen with the kind of relationships women form with gay men. Gay men represent no threat to the women's sexual boundary so they can relax around them and open up and have greater emotional intimacy because there is no chance that this intimacy will develop into anything sexual, which they might find threatening or conflicting.

The daughter or son who hasn't psychologically cut the cord with their parents also has boundary problems. If the parents believe that they have unhampered access to their adult child's life, the married child's relationship with their spouse will be affected. The spouse will feel as if they are married to two people: one is the adult spouse, and the other is a child who still hasn't psychologically broken away from their parents' control and influence. This isn't a true commitment to the marriage. A choice has to be made in setting boundaries with your parents. They may become upset with any boundaries to their relationship with their adult child; but they have to respect that their child is now an adult and they no longer have any control over how their child leads their life.

## SETTING PSYCHOLOGICAL BOUNDARIES

Now that you understand the importance of setting psychological boundaries the question remains, how do you set boundaries in the reality of daily life? I teach this skill every day to my clients and students; but our culture doesn't really teach how to set boundaries except when it comes to our sexual lives. We are encouraged to set all the boundaries we want when it comes to sexual activity, but outside our sex lives, little is said or encouraged. In fact, I think setting boundaries is discouraged in our society.

I try to make psychological concepts such as setting boundaries simple, so people will have an easier time implementing the new skill or behavior into their everyday lives. Simplifying the application of psychological concepts doesn't mean that they will be easy to apply. Some emotional issues may still inhibit their application, but simplifying the process definitely helps.

The basic boundary application process deals with the emotions of comfortable versus uncomfortable. These two emotions can be the basis of how to set a psychological boundary. Just ask yourself the question, "Are you comfortable or not with whatever is being proposed?" These two emotions are your guides in life. They will tell you what is true and right for you. This may not be the same for someone else; but that's okay, because you are learning to love yourself and take care of yourself in a world where others may not care about how you feel emotionally. But you do—at least I hope so.

People are always asking me what I want. Do I want Chinese food or Mexican food for dinner? Do I want to go camping or to stay in a hotel? Which table do I want in a restaurant? On and on it goes. When I hear these questions, the first thing I ask myself is how I feel. If I am not comfortable, I don't move forward. That's how I set a boundary. Listening to and accepting my emotion of comfort gives me the power to set the boundary between others and myself. My emotions are a fact; I don't have to debate their validity, and I don't even have to know why I feel the way I do to give them validity.

If you love another adult, would you want them to do something that they are not comfortable doing? I wouldn't. The price tag for deciding to move forward and not listening to their own emotions is too high. The usual price is resentment, which will later manifest itself in the relationship in some unhealthy way. This also doesn't take into account the unhealthy effect repressed resentment has on the individual, both physically and psychologically.

How many women have sex with a partner when they aren't comfortable participating? Way too many, unfortunately. They participate for all kinds of reasons: "It's just not worth the hassle if I say no and stick to my boundary;" "If I don't participate, he will get upset and pout for days"; "If I say no, he might find someone else and leave me." For these kinds of reasons, the woman does something that she doesn't really want to do, but she sets it up as if she doesn't have a choice. The consequence is that she ends up with a lot of resentment, which is directed at the sexual experience. Eventually, she will lose her sexual desire and most likely, her partner will judge her negatively for her lack of interest—all because she didn't set a sexual boundary within her relationship in the beginning.

# EDITORS' INTRODUCTION

Part of learning to love yourself involves learning how to take care of yourself and achieve balance in your life. In the next reading, "What Is Self-Care?", Daniel Testa and Varunee Faii Sangganjanavanich discuss what it looks like to take good care of yourself under stressful circumstances and how to strive for optimal wellness. The reading is directed specifically to college students, which you all are; however, we encourage you to consider what self-care and wellness look like regardless of your life stage. We must care for ourselves at all stages of life, and in all types of relationships, in order to be our best selves for ourselves and for those we care about.

## PRIMER

1.  How do you take care of yourself? Self-care can look very different for different people. Make a list of the ways that you practice self-care. Are there additional ways of practicing self-care that you'd like to add to the list? How might you go about making more space in your life to practice self-care? Keep these questions in mind as you read. Daniel Testa and Varunee Faii Sangganjanavanich will guide you through additional activities in the reading that will help you evaluate and hone your self-care practice.

## READING 3.2

# What Is Self-Care?

*By Daniel S. Testa and Varunee Faii Sangganjanavanich*

There is no question that college experience can be fun and exciting. Being in a different environment, meeting new people, and pursuing your dreams are positive aspects of entering college. However, college experience can also be challenging at times. Being away from home, trying to do well in classes, and getting along with a roommate can create stress. As you deal with the reality that college is stressful and challenging at times, you are faced with an important question: So what can I do about it? There is hope, and the answer rests with a few words: self-care. This [reading] will help you gain a better understanding of what self-care is and why it is critical as you begin your college experience.

## WHAT IT IS VS. WHAT IT IS NOT

When you think of *self-care*, what comes to mind? What does it mean to care for yourself? At the heart of self-care is a focus on tending to the needs of your mind, body, and for some individuals, your spirit. But what does that really mean? Let's break down the meaning of "care" a bit more.

*Care* as a noun means "the provision of what is necessary for the health, welfare, maintenance, and protection of someone or something" or "serious attention or consideration applied to doing something correctly or to avoid damage or risk." What stands out to you with both of those definitions? When we apply those definitions to ourselves, we see that self-care involves doing what is necessary to improve, maintain, and protect our health. You will inevitably have challenging moments in college, and self-care can help boost your well-being. You may feel like you are on an even keel and self-care can help you stay at that desired level. Finally, we have talked about the stressful moments that are guaranteed to be headed your way. While you do not have a crystal ball to see what those moments will be and when they will occur, self-care can help soften the blow when it arrives.

Now, let's look at the definition of care as a verb. To care means to "feel concern or interest or attach importance to something" or to "look after and provide for the needs of." Again, what stands out to you in those definitions? You may have noticed that self-care is not just something you do for yourself. Rather, it is an attitude you can have toward yourself. It is an attitude of intentionality, meaning that there is a purpose to your actions. For example, you don't listen to music to just listen to "something." Rather, you purposefully listen to music to clear your mind when you have a difficult day. It is a way for you to decompress and deal with your internal struggles. This action is called "self-care."

So what is the purpose exactly? Well, you might just say self-care, right? While this might be true, it is important to introduce a new term that is similar to self-care—*wellness*. While taking care of yourself does serve a purpose, it leads to a greater goal of achieving wellness. So what is wellness exactly and how does it relate to self-care? Wellness is defined as "a way of life oriented toward optimal health and well-being, in which body, mind, and spirit are integrated by the individual to live life more fully within the human and natural community. Ideally, it is the optimum state of health and well-being that each individual is capable of achieving." Phew! That is a long definition. Let's break it down.

The first part of the definition states that wellness is focused on optimal health and well-being. This means that you are going about your days as best as you possibly can. And this differs for each person. The important point is to ask yourself, "Am I functioning as best as I possibly can?"

The second piece of the definition highlights that wellness involves attending to not just your body, but to your mind and your spirit as well. This means that wellness takes on a more holistic approach—meaning that all parts interact with one another. As you will learn in the next chapters, you will see a connection between all the different parts of yourself. As you attend to one part, it will affect others. So your mind, body, and spirit are all interconnected. Wellness involves an understanding of these interconnections. The goal is to achieve balance between these interconnections.

To give you a visual depiction of how wellness involves many different environmental and biological factors which are interconnected between your mind, body, and spirit, we have included the *Wheel of Wellness*. This model was the first of its kind to identify the multiple connections that impact your overall health and longevity. Take a look at the wheel and notice what stands out to you. There are a few points which we will highlight. You will notice that spirituality is at the center indicating that it is the most important characteristic of your well-being. […] For now, we will mention that spirituality refers to having a sense of meaning and purpose in life.

You will notice 12 spokes in the wheel that promote a sense of self-direction. These spokes aim to direct you in a positive direction as you respond to demands of work and leisure activities, developing friendships, and having romantic relationships. On the outside of the wheel, you

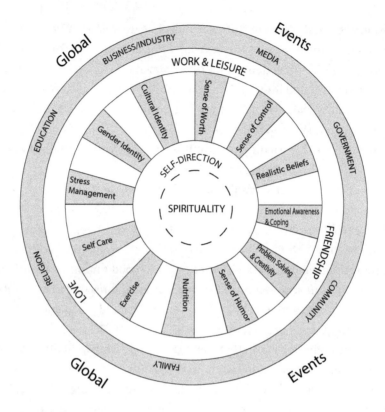

| Figure 3.2.1

will see different forces in life such as media and government that affect your wellness. Finally, this model highlights that all the components are interactive. So as you make adjustments to one area, changes will be experienced in other areas.

You must learn how to live and interact with the world around you. It would be great if we could all live healthy, happy lives in a little bubble and not have to deal with others, right? Wrong! Part of living in this world means dealing with your natural surroundings. We can discourage ourselves when we are afraid to meet the tasks that life presents. This discouragement usually takes the form of avoidance. When we avoid what is uncomfortable, we tend to engage in unhealthy and self-destructive behaviors. You will come to understand that to achieve your wellness goals you will most likely have to involve other people. Acknowledging and embracing this interdependence with others will be key to your welfare and success in college.

The final piece of the definition talks about achieving a state of *optimum* health and well-being, which means that you achieve the best or most favorable state possible. It is important to remember that your optimum health and well-being might look very different from someone else's. Your physical optimum might be running 10 miles, while someone else can only run 3 miles. As you engage in self-care, you will see that it is more about quality than quantity.

---

## BOX 3.2.1 YOUR TURN

### Where I am vs. Where I want to be

**Directions:** Take some time to reflect on the following prompts and rate yourself on where you feel you are currently. Then, think about where you want to be and how you will get there.

1. I would rate my current physical condition as a _____.

    | 1 | 2 | 3 | 4 | 5 | 6 | 7 | 8 | 9 | 10 |
    |---|---|---|---|---|---|---|---|---|---|
    | Very Poor | | Poor | | Okay | | Good | | Excellent | |

2. I would ideally like it to be a _____.

    | 1 | 2 | 3 | 4 | 5 | 6 | 7 | 8 | 9 | 10 |
    |---|---|---|---|---|---|---|---|---|---|
    | Very Poor | | Poor | | Okay | | Good | | Excellent | |

3. I would rate my current state of mental health as a _____.

    | 1 | 2 | 3 | 4 | 5 | 6 | 7 | 8 | 9 | 10 |
    |---|---|---|---|---|---|---|---|---|---|
    | Very Poor | | Poor | | Okay | | Good | | Excellent | |

4. I would ideally like it to be a _____.

    | 1 | 2 | 3 | 4 | 5 | 6 | 7 | 8 | 9 | 10 |
    |---|---|---|---|---|---|---|---|---|---|
    | Very Poor | | Poor | | Okay | | Good | | Excellent | |

5. I would rate my connection to the world around me as a _____.

    | 1 | 2 | 3 | 4 | 5 | 6 | 7 | 8 | 9 | 10 |
    |---|---|---|---|---|---|---|---|---|---|
    | Very Poor | | Poor | | Okay | | Good | | Excellent | |

6. I would ideally like it to be a _____.

    | 1 | 2 | 3 | 4 | 5 | 6 | 7 | 8 | 9 | 10 |
    |---|---|---|---|---|---|---|---|---|---|
    | Very Poor | | Poor | | Okay | | Good | | Excellent | |

## GUILT FOR PRACTICING SELF-CARE

One of the first hurdles with practicing self-care is getting over the myth that self-care is a selfish act. Overcoming this feeling can be very difficult since taking care of oneself typically brings guilt to people. All our lives we are told that we should be there for others—that it is our responsibility to put others before ourselves. When we try to take of ourselves, we may be told or made to feel that we have been selfish. For example, your friends may want you to listen to their problems, but you have to study for the final exam. You may experience feelings of guilt because you feel like you somehow let them down when they need you. So when the next opportunity arrives to engage in self-care, we remember these feelings of guilt which override our logic. The end result is we forget the importance of caring for ourselves. However, it is important to keep in mind that you have to be well before trying to help others.

Our culture seems preoccupied with constantly staying busy whether that is to earn money so you can put food on the table, study a lot so you get good grades, go to class so you can earn your degree, or work hard so you can land that next promotion. When you wake up in the morning, do you ever consider what you are going to do that day to take care of yourself? Probably not! You are most likely thinking about how you will have enough time to get everything done that you need to accomplish for the day. What is the saying? "Work now—play later," right? The point is that we have created a culture that puts self-care at the bottom of the list. We have also taught ourselves that to practice self-care is an act of selfishness and we could be doing "better" things with our time. We also seem to have this belief that we can just keep giving and serving others without any repercussions. We do not seem to realize that our energy is limited.

Do not misunderstand—it is a wonderful trait if you enjoy doing things for others and taking care of those around you. However, if you do not learn to take care of yourself, you put your mind and body at risk for additional harm. Without self-care, you will lose energy. If you do not stop to take the time to refuel, you will find yourself constantly struggling and running on empty. Consequently, you may experience feelings of resentment and feeling like a burden to others. Most importantly, those relationships you enjoy so much will begin to suffer. Remember the following saying: "You cannot give what you do not have."

---

### BOX 3.2.4 **YOUR TURN**

**Tending to My Mind, Body, and Spirit**

**Directions:** Now that we have talked about self-care and wellness as focused on a mind–body–spirit connection, take a moment to reflect on how you have been tending to each aspect. Identify and list ways in which you have currently been either taking care of each piece or neglecting them.

I have been taking care of my body by:

_____

_____

_____

I have been neglecting my body by:

_____

_____

_____

I have been taking care of my mind by:

_____

_____

_____

I have been neglecting my mind by:

_____

_____

_____

I have been taking care of my spirit by:

_____

_____

_____

I have been neglecting my spirit by:

_____

_____

_____

# BOX 3.2.5 TOOL

- Sometimes we can feel guilt and selfishness for wanting to take time out to help ourselves.
- The energy we use to care for ourselves and others is finite.
- Lack of self-care can lead to negative health consequences such as burnout and resentment.

- About two-thirds of college students engage in self-care practices before visiting a student health service center for symptoms that led to their visit.

- Popular sources of self-care information include family members or friends, previous encounters with a healthcare provider, or medication advertisements.

- College students most often cite their college's website as the primary source of mental health services and support. Helpful website tools include availability to make online appointments, completing online mental health screening, information on accessing accommodations and free mental health services, and a frequently asked questions page.

## RECOVERY, HEALING, AND SELF-PRESERVATION

[T]he next years of your life will present challenges that you probably do not realize are even possible at this point. It is essential that you accept these moments as being inevitable. Doing so will allow you to put more attention into being proactive and coming up with ways to take care of yourself when these moments arrive. We want to drive this point home to you because this [reading] is not designed to stop unfortunate events from occurring. Rather, this [reading] is designed to educate you on how self-care can be a critical component of your success in college and beyond.

A simple analogy that resembles the concepts in this [reading] is when you become sick. You cannot predict when or how you will get sick, but the odds are high that you will become ill at some point in your life. Sure there are things you can do to lessen your chances of getting sick like washing your hands. And if by chance you do get a cold, you have options available to help ease the symptoms. You still have to ride out the illness, but you do not have to feel as miserable. By using this analogy, you can see how self-care and wellness is focused on recovery and healing.

Odds are you will be faced with difficult circumstances in college that test your mind and body. You can take proactive steps to prevent situations from occurring or becoming out of control. If a situation does occur, you can engage in activities to help ease the stress and suffering. They can be anything that helps you feel centered and recharges your battery. This is where self-preservation comes in.

Remember that self-care is not self-centeredness—it is self-compassion. Making an effort to love yourself will help you grow, heal, and become more resilient to the stress and obstacles that you will face in college. So take these small steps toward loving yourself. Listen to your mind and body when it is sending signals to you that it is in distress, needs to relax, or needs to be more active. This may sound cliché but as you put the concepts in this [reading] into practice, give yourself a pat on the back each moment you practice self-care. Acknowledge the effort you put into loving and caring for yourself. These small actions will help reinforce why you are engaging in wellness. Having a strong wellness routine will make your college experience that much more enjoyable and rewarding. So let's get started!

## BOX 3.2.7  YOUR TURN HOW DO I CARE FOR MYSELF?

**Directions:** Take some time now to review how you currently heal and recover from challenging situations.

1. Overall, how much time and effort do I put into caring for myself?

_____

_____

_____

2. When I become physically sick, how do I care for my body?

_____

_____

_____

3. When I am feeling anxious or depressed, how do I care for and tend to my mind and thoughts?

_____

_____

_____

4. When stressful events occur in my life, what do I do to get myself through these moments?

_____

_____

_____

## BOX 3.2.8 TOOL

- Self-care and wellness is about healing, recovering, and preserving your self during difficult life experiences.

- Self-care is an act of self-love.

- Self-care will lead to a more rewarding and enjoyable college experience.


## BOX 3.2.9 DID YOU KNOW?

- Most college students report their general health to be excellent, very good, or good.

- Health issues such as stress management, sleep, and anxiety are reported to negatively impact first-year college students.

- First-year college students often report struggling with nutrition as they transition to a more independent lifestyle.


## BOX 3.2.10 VOICES FROM CAMPUS

### Surviving

How do you learn to care for yourself when all you have known your entire life is taking care of others? When I look back on my childhood, if I can even say it was a childhood, I always had to care for my family. I basically had to learn how to be an adult by the age of 10. My father had early onset Alzheimer's disease and my mother struggled with both diabetes and breast cancer. It fell on me to take care of the cooking and day-to-day chores around the house. I was up at 4 a.m. prepping meals and organizing medications only to spend the rest of the day at school worrying about whether they took their medications correctly or whether there was an accident or crisis waiting for me when I got off the school bus. When I was old enough to drive, I was the one taking my parents to a seemingly endless number of doctor appointments and emergency room visits. I wish I could erase all the memories of countless hours spent on the phone arguing with insurance companies over medical bills.

It was almost impossible for me to think about having a single moment to myself. As I look back, it feels as though my entire youth was spent monitoring, checking, resolving, or preventing one problematic situation after the other. My life felt as though it was always in the future—there was no time to worry about the past, and the present moments could be used to take care of the unknown to come.

When my father passed away, I was going into my senior year of high school. During the first half of the school year, my mom's health quickly spiraled downhill. I think the loss of my dad was just too much for her on top of the illnesses she was battling. With my dad being gone, it gave me some more free time to spend with my mother. I am grateful for the last few months I had with her because it was the closest we had ever been our entire lives. I talked to her about my fears of going on alone, and she told me her regrets of not being a better mother and letting me enjoy my childhood. But she made me promise her that I would move on and go to college. She died the day after my high school graduation.

I still remember that summer before I left for college. I remember it for one particular reason—the silence. Before my parents died, there was always some sort of noise going on—either one of them yelling for me to help them with something, the sound of my father walking around late at night, or the endless noise of the television which my mother spent the last half of her life in front of. Now, there was just silence. It almost seemed deafening. And with the silence came an awkward and uncomfortable feeling—a feeling of stillness. I was used to being busy and occupied with taking care of my parents. Now that I had nothing to do, it was like I had no more sense of purpose. Just an irritating question that kept nagging at me like a splinter in my mind—"Now what do I do?"

I worked a couple summer jobs to make the time pass by. Eventually, the day came when I packed what little I had and left for college. I decided to attend out of state so it would give me a fresh start. I figured a new environment would be good for me and I could leave home behind me.

I remember the first semester being incredibly stressful, and I had a difficult time adjusting. You would think that being so organized and on top of things with my parents would be a strength going into college, but you would be wrong. My life became unmanageable. I remember feeling so ashamed and embarrassed. I wondered how I could let things fall apart this way when I was able to do everything for my parents. One of my instructors noticed that I was having difficulties in my class and suggested that I talk with a counselor.

Although I was reluctant to go, it was one of the most rewarding experiences I have had in my life. It took me some time to become comfortable and trust him, but my counselor was incredibly kind and supportive from beginning to end. He helped me realize that I was more lost than ever because I never learned how to take care of myself. Through our talks together, he helped me realize that my struggles were normal and that there was hope. We spent the first year working on various issues. He helped me work through the grief of my parents' death and the loss of my own childhood, while also figuring out my next steps forward. He helped me learn to turn the care that I gave to my parents onto myself. Looking back on it, my counselor helped me get to know me. Our talks about self-care and wellness opened up opportunities for me that I never thought were possible. I no longer felt like I was just surviving—I was finally living.

## CREDIT

- Fig. 3.2.1: Copyright © 1996 by Jane Myers, Thomas Sweeney, and Melvin Witmer.

# EDITORS' INTRODUCTION

Not surprisingly, our ability to live a healthy life and our self-concept and self-esteem are all affected to some extent by our families of origin. Our earliest relationships with our primary caregivers, most often our parents, shape our view of ourselves, others, and the world, according to Alfred Adler's individual psychology (Ansbacher & Ansbacher, 1956). There is evidence to suggest that the way we connect with romantic partners in adulthood is related to how we connected to or attached to our primary caregivers as children (Hazan & Shaver, 1987). A full review of attachment theory, as originally developed by John Bowlby in the 1940s, is beyond the scope of this book, but we provide a summary of adult attachment and recommendations for further reading on the topic.

Adult attachment, especially as it relates to childhood attachment styles, is a complex concept, but we hope to distill it here so that you can usefully apply it to your own life and perhaps identify areas that you might like to reflect on further. Brennan et al. (1998) define adult attachment in terms of attachment-related anxiety and attachment-related avoidance. Based on reports of current relationships, and considering past relationships with caregivers, adults classify themselves somewhere along a continuum of attachment-related anxiety (how concerned we are about abandonment) and attachment-related avoidance (how comfortable we feel with intimacy and closeness; see Figure 3.2).

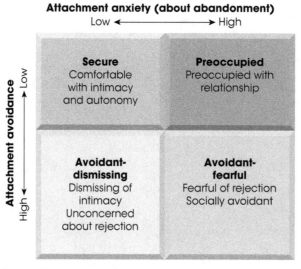

| Figure 3.2. Adult attachment styles.

*Secure*. Adults who report low anxiety related to intimacy and abandonment and low avoidance of intimacy consider themselves able to securely attach to a romantic partner. They are most often confident, self-assured, and relaxed in their relationships, able to express their needs to their partners, and able to achieve a healthy level of interdependence with their partners.

*Preoccupied*. Adults who report high levels of anxiety and low levels of avoidance related to intimacy and abandonment fall into the preoccupied attachment category. These individuals may feel especially concerned with the security of their relationship, concern that the partner does not value the relationship in the same way they do, while at the same time making concerted efforts to connect and achieve intimacy with the partner.

*Fearful-avoidant*. Adults who report high levels of anxiety about abandonment and high levels of avoidance related to intimacy, like adults who are preoccupied in their attachment style, are concerned about the stability and security of their relationship and the value their partner places on it, but unlike someone identifying as preoccupied, these adults are fearful and avoidant of experiencing intimacy and being vulnerable in their relationships.

*Dismissing-avoidant*. Adults who report low levels of anxiety about abandonment and low levels of avoidance of intimacy tend to be withdrawn in their relationships if they venture into relationships at all. They are hesitant to connect with others and are somewhat resolved in their solitude. They don't tend to desire intimacy with others and are not concerned with rejection, relationship stability, or security.

When considering your own attachment style, keep in mind a very important distinction: How we *make sense* of our childhood experiences (the story we tell ourselves) influences our attachment style in adulthood (Siegel, 2011). Said another way, strength and resiliency can come from difficult childhood experiences.

> People who were securely attached tended to acknowledge both positive and negative aspects of their family experiences, and they were able to show how these experiences related to their later development. They could give a *coherent* account of their pasts and how they came to be who they are as adults. (Siegel, 2011, p. 172)

In the final reading for this chapter, "Love: The Immutable Longing for Contact," Dr. Susan Johnson, a renowned couples therapist, author, and researcher, describes how attachment with our adult romantic partners is influenced by our needs for safety, security, and responsiveness, how we can better understand our own feelings and behaviors in relationships, and those of our partners. While the reading is a bit dated, current research and developments in couple therapy have shown that emotional connection and security form the foundation for lasting relationships. John Gottman (2015) refers to this concept as "building the emotional bank account," which is achieved by *turning toward* our partner's *bids for connection*. In fact, Gottman's research has shown that it takes at least five positive interactions to counteract one negative interaction. This is referred to as the "magic 5:1 ratio." As you read, think about how your needs for safety, security, and responsiveness influence your adult relationships. An important consideration, which we address in the end-of-chapter reflections, is how attachment style can change during the course of one's life and can look and feel different in different relationships. Unfortunately, we didn't all grow up with model parental figures, and we don't want you to be discouraged if you identify with one of the insecure attachment styles. We will address some things you can do to influence your attachment style in order to be healthy and happy in your relationships.

## PRIMER

1.  What did you learn about relationships from the family you grew up in? What happened when there was a conflict? What was it like when someone in the family had a bad day? What did family look like to you, and how do you think some of your family relationships have influenced the way you enter relationships today?

## CREDIT

Fig. 3.2: Source: https://slideplayer.com/slide/12682098/.

# Love

## The Immutable Longing for Contact

*By Susan Johnson and Hara Estroff Marano*

An illusion. An anesthetic. An irrational compulsion. A neurosis. An emotional storm. An immature ideal. These are the descriptions of love that have long populated the psychological literature. Let us not even consider the obvious fact that they are highly judgmental and dismissive. The question I want to pose is, does any one of them, or even all of them together, come close to capturing the extraordinary experience that for most people is an enormous part of the meaning of life—an experience that fosters well-being and growth?

As a marital therapist, my job is to help people experience love, to move from distance and alienation to contact and caring. But in order to help distressed couples change, I realized early on that I needed a model of what a good relationship is. For too long, the choices have been contained to two. There is the psychodynamic, or psychoanalytic, view, which holds that adult relationships arc more or less reflections of childhood relationships—replays of old conflicts. And there is the behaviorist view: Love is a rational exchange in which couples make deals based on their needs, and they succeed to the degree that they master the negotiation process. Love is then either a crazy compulsion or, after couples calm down, a kind of rational friendship where the partners make good deals.

I can assure you that if i tried to persuade the couples I see in therapy to leave with an understanding of their childhood or a rational friendship, they would not be satisfied. The truth is that these conventional descriptions do not adequately reflect the process of marital distress or the rekindling of love that I observe as a marital therapist. Possessing insights as to why you have certain sore spots or honing negotiation skills seems to somehow miss the mark. Neither addresses the intense emotional responses that consume distressed couples. As I watch couples, I see that raw emotion, hurt, longing, and fear are the most powerful things in the room. Couples seem to have a desperate need to connect emotionally—and a desperate fear of connecting.

There are, of course, many elements to a relationship. It is true that echoes of the past are present in relationships, but this focus does not capture enough of what goes on and ignores the power of present interactions. Couples do also make bargains. Rut the essence of their connection is not a bargain. It is, rather, a bond.

The bond between two people hinges on two things—their accessibility and responsiveness to each other. The notion that the tie between two people is created through accessibility and responsiveness is an outgrowth of attachment theory. First put forth by the late British psychiatrist John Bowlby 30 years ago and later elaborated both by him and psychologist Mary Ainsworth in America, attachment theory is only now gathering significant momentum. It promises to be one of the most significant psychological ideas put forth in the 20th century. As many researchers are now demonstrating, it is certainly the most viable way of making sense of the mother-infant (and father-infant) bond.

## VIEWING LOVE THROUGH A LENS

Over the past decade, a number of psychologists, including myself, have begun to see in attachment theory an understanding of adult relationships. In my experience attachment is the best lens for viewing adult love. When viewed through this lens, love relationships do not seem irrational at all; we do not have to pronounce them mysterious or outside our usual way of being. Nor do we have to shrink them to fit the laws of economic exchange. They make perfect—many would say intuitive—sense. And attachment theory goes a long way toward explaining what goes wrong in relationships and what to do about it.

John Bowlby observed that the need for physical closeness between a mother and child serves evolutionary goals; in a dangerous world, a responsive caregiver ensures survival of the infant. Attachment theory states that our primary motivation in life is to be connected with other people—because it is the only security we ever have. Maintaining closeness is a bona fide survival need.

Through the consistent and reliable responsiveness of a close adult, infants, particularly in the second six months of life, begin to trust that the world is a good place and come to believe they have some value in it. The deep sense of security that develops fosters in the infant enough confidence to begin exploring the surrounding world, making excursions into it, and developing relationships with others—though racing back to mom, being held by her, and perhaps even clinging to her whenever feeling threatened. In secure attachment lie the seeds for self-esteem, initiative, and eventual independence. We explore the world from a secure base.

Thanks to Mary Ainsworth, a large and growing body of research supports attachment theory. She devised a procedure to test human attachment. Called the "strange situation," it allows researchers to observe mothers and children during a carefully calibrated process of separation and reunion. Ainsworth found that whenever children feel threatened or can no longer easily reach their attachment figure, they engage in behavior designed to regain proximity—they call, they protest, they seek, they cry, they reach out. Closeness achieved, they do all they can to maintain it: They hug, they coo, they make eye contact, they cling—and, that all-time pleaser, they smile.

Ainsworth noticed that children differ in their attachment security and their patterns of behavior sort into three basic "attachment styles." Most children are securely attached: They show signs of distress when left with a stranger, seek their mother when she returns. hold her for a short time then go back to exploring and playing. These infants develop attachment security because they have mothers who are sensitive and responsive to their signals.

On the other hand, she found, 40 percent of kids are insecurely attached. Some are anxious/ambivalent. They show lots of distress separating, and on reunion, they approach and reject their mother. Their mothers usually respond inconsistently to them, sometimes unavailable, other times affectionate. So preoccupied are these infants with their care-giver's availability that they never get to explore their world.

The third group of children have an avoidant attachment style. They do not seem distressed during separation, and they don't even acknowledge their mother during reunion. These infants keep their distress well-hidden; though they appear to dismiss relationships entirely, internally they are in a state of physiological arousal. These children are usually reared by caregivers who rebuff their attempts at close bodily contact.

These responses are not arbitrary but universal. Evolution has seen to that because they serve survival needs. Some researchers are busy identifying the neurobiologial systems that underlie attachment behavior and mediate the response to attachment threats. They are finding specific patterns of changes in biochemistry and physiology during experimental separation experiences.

Attachment bonds are particularly durable, and once an infant is attached, separation—or the threat of it—is extremely stressful and anxiety-producing. In the absence of attachment danger, children explore the world around them. But if the accessibility of a caregiver is questionable or threatened, the attachment behavior system shifts into high gear. Facing the loss or unreliability of an attachment figure, infants typically are thrust into panic and they mount an angry protest. Eventually, however, the protest dies down and they succumb to a despair that looks like classic depression.

The implications of attachment theory are extraordinary and extend to the deepest corners of our psyche. Attachment impacts the way we process information, how we see the world, and the nature of our social experience. Our attachment experience influences whether we see ourselves as lovable. Research now shows that we carry attachment styles with us into life, where they serve as predispositions to later behavior in love relationships.

We seek close physical proximity to a partner, and rely on their continuing affections and availability, because it is a survival need. What satisfies the need for attachment in adults is what satisfies the need in the young: Eye contact, touching, stroking, and holding a partner deliver the same security and comfort. When threatened, or fearful, or experiencing loss, we turn to our partner for psychological comfort. Or try to.

The core elements of love are the same for children and adults—the need to feel that somebody is emotionally there for you, that you can make contact with another person who will respond to you, particularly if you are in need. The essence of love is a partner responding to a need, not because it's a good deal—but even when it's not. That allows you to sense the world as home rather than as a dangerous place. In this sense, we never grow up.

It is growing clear that the dynamics of attachment are similar across the life span. Implicit in the anger of a couple who are fighting over everything is the protest of the child who is trying to restore the closeness and responsiveness of a parent. In the grief of adults who have lost a partner is the despair of a child who has lost a parent and experiences helplessness and withdrawal.

## THE MUSICALITY OF EMOTION

Attachment theory makes sense of a matter that psychology has just begun to puzzle over—how we come to regulate our emotions. We regulate feelings, specifically negative one's—fear, sadness, anger—through the development of affectional bonds with others, and continuing contact with them. Through the lens of attachment we also come to understand that the expression of emotion is the primary communication system in relationships; it's how we adjust closeness and distance. Emotion is the music of the interpersonal dance. And when attachment is threatened—when we feel alienated from a partner or worry about our partner's availability—the music either gets turned way up, into the heavy metal of angry protest, or way down, shut off altogether.

The lens of attachment sharply illustrates the dangerous distortion personified in a popular icon of Western culture: the John Wayne image of the self-contained man, the man who is never dependent and never needs anyone else. Our need for attachment ensures that we become who we are as individuals because of our connection with other people. Our personality evolves in a context of contact with other people; it doesn't simply arise from within. Our attachment needs make dependence on another person an integral part of being human. Self-sufficiency is a lie.

# A PLACE FOR VULNERABILITY

The most basic message of attachment theory is that to be valid adults, we do not need to deny that we are also always, until the end of our life, vulnerable children. A good intimate adult relationship is a safe place where two people can experience feelings of vulnerability—being scared, feeling overwhelmed by life, being unsure of who they are. It is the place where we can deal with those things, not deny them, control them, or regulate them, the old John Wayne way. Relatedness is a core aspect of our selves.

Yet Western psychology and psychiatry have often labeled feelings of dependency as pathologic and banished them to childhood. Our mistaken beliefs about dependency and self-sufficiency lead us to define strength as the ability to process inner experience and regulate our emotions all by ourselves. Attachment theory suggests that, not only is that not functional, it is impossible. We are social beings not constituted for such physiological and emotional isolation. For those who attempt it, there are enormous costs. A great deal of literature in health and psychology shows that the cost of social isolation is physical and psychological breakdown. Under such conditions, we simply deteriorate.

There is nothing inherently demeaning or diminishing in allowing someone else to comfort you. We need other people to help us process our emotions and deal with the slings and arrows of being alive—especially the slings and arrows. In fact, the essence of making intimate contact is sharing hurts and vulnerability with someone else. You allow someone into a place where you are not defended. You put contact before self-protection. In marital distress the opposite happens, self-protection comes before contact. If you cannot share, then a part of your being is excluded from the relationship.

The couples I see have taught me that it is almost impossible to be accessible, responsive, emotionally engaged with someone if you are not able to experience and express your own vulnerabilities. If you cannot allow yourself to experience and show your vulnerability, you cannot tell others what you need and explicitly ask others to respond to you. But troubled couples naturally want to hide and protect their vulnerability, although that usually precludes any satisfying kind of emotional contact.

Like psychoanalytic theory, attachment theory sees early relationships as formative of personality and relationships later on. But unlike Freudian theory, it sees our view of ourselves and relationship styles as subject to revision as we integrate new experiences. This capacity makes growth possible. The past influences the present, but we are not condemned to repeat it.

The attachment system involves attachment behaviors, emotional responses, and internal representations, or models. In our psyches, we create working models of attachment figures, of ourselves, and of relationships. Built from our experience in the world, these internal working models are at the same time cognitive and affective, and they in turn guide how we organize our experience and how we respond to intimate others.

The reason our behavior in relationships is relatively stable is that, although they are susceptible to revision, we carry these internal working models into new social situations. They write the script by which we navigate the social world. Our internal working models of ourselves, our relationship, and our close ones create expectations of support and nurturance—and become the architects of the disappointments we feel. They are the creators of self-fulfilling prophecies.

But the existence of internal models also explains why you can have very different experiences in two different relationships. Essentially, you meet a new potential partner who brings a different behavioral repertoire. This allows you to engage in a different dance of proximity and distance—she is home to receive your phone calls, he doesn't react with veiled hostility when you call him at the office. Being accessible and responsive, your new partner doesn't ignite your anxiety and launch you into attachment panic. What's more, with a different set of internal working models, your new partner appraises your behavior differently and then offers a different response. From such new experience, a tarnished inner vision of relationships or of your sense of self can then begin to change.

## A NEW WAY OF CONTACT

That may be what passionate love really is—we find someone who connects with us and alleviates our attachment fears, which opens up a whole new possibility of acceptance and responsiveness. Love is transforming—not just of the world but of the self. We find a whole new way of contacting another human being, and this emotional engagement opens up new possibilities of becoming ourselves. That is the intoxicating thing about the relationship. It modifies how people experience themselves and how they see other people.

From my point of view, attachment theory also redefines the place of sexual behavior. For the past 40 years, we seem to have come to believe that sex is the essence of love relationships. That is not my experience in working with couples. Sex per sex is often but a small part of adult intimacy. Attachment theory tells us that the basic security in life is contact with other people. We need to be held, to be emotionally connected. I think that the most basic human experience of relatedness is two people—mother and child, father and child, two adults—seeing and holding each other, providing the safety, security, and feeling of human connectedness that for most, in the end, makes life meaningful. Many people use sex as a way to create or substitute for the sense of connection they are needing. I would guess that many a man or woman has engaged in sex just to meet a need for being held.

So perhaps now the mystery of love is becoming clear. We fall in love when an attachment bond is formed. We stay in love by maintaining the bond. We use our repertoire of emotions to signal the need for comfort through contact, the need for a little distance. We help each other process our inner and outer worlds and experience each other's pain, fear, joy.

What, then, goes wrong in couples? As I see it, healthy, normal attachment needs go unmet and attachment fears begin to I take over the relationship.

We know that distressed couples settle into rigid interaction patterns. Perhaps the most distressed pattern is that of the disappointed, angry, blaming wife demanding contact from a man who withdraws. Couples can stay stuck in this for years. We know from the research of John Gottman that this is a sure killer of marriages.

But it is only through the lens of attachment that we come to understand what makes such patterns of behavior so devastating. The answer is, they block emotional engagement; they stand in the way of contact and exacerbate attachment fears. As partners hurl anger and contempt at each other or withdraw, emotional engagement becomes more and more difficult. Patterns of attack-defend or attack-withdraw are highly corrosive to a relationship because they preclude a safe way for a couple to emotionally engage each other and create a secure bond.

What couples are really fighting about is rarely the issue they seem to be fighting about—the chores, the kids. It is always about separateness and connectedness, safety and trust, the risk of letting someone in to see the exposed, vulnerable self.

Marital distress, then, is not a product of personality flaws. Nor is anger in relationships irrational. It is often a natural part of a protest that follows the loss of accessibility and responsiveness to a partner. It is an adaptive reaction—anger motivates people to overcome barriers to reunion. Self-defeating as it may be, anger is an attempt to discourage a partner from further distancing.

## A COMPELLING EMOTION

But fear is the most compelling emotion in a distressed relationship. Hostility in a partner is usually a sign that the fear level has gone way up—the partner feels threatened. Attachment fears—of being unlovable, abandoned, rejected-are so tied to survival that they elicit strong fight or flee responses. In protecting ourselves, we often undermine ourselves as a secure base for our partner, who becomes alarmed. Our partner then confirms our fears and becomes the enemy, the betrayer.

Such fear sets off an alarm system. It heightens both the anger of those experiencing anxiety in attachment and the dismissal of emotional needs by those given to avoidance.

## A NEW FRAME FOR BEHAVIOR

The lens of attachment puts a whole new frame on our behavior in relationships. The angry, blaming wife who continues to pursue with blame, even though she understands this behavior may drive her husband away, is not acting irrationally. Nor do her actions necessarily reflect a lack of communication skill. She is engaged in a desperate intensification of attachment behaviors—hers is an entreaty for contact. She perceives her husband as inaccessible and emotionally unresponsive: a threat that engages the attachment behavioral system. Of course, the defensiveness and conflict make safe contact increasingly less likely, and the cycle of distress escalates. It keeps going because the person never gets the contact and the reassurance that will bring closure and allow the attachment fears to be dealt with.

In working with couples, my colleague Les Greenberg and I have elaborated a therapy, "Emotionally Focused Couples Therapy," that views marital distress in terms of attachment insecurities. It recognizes that relationship problems are created by how individuals react to, cope with, and disown their own attachment needs and those of their spouse. A major goal of therapy is owning and validating needs for contact and security, helping people to expand their emotional range, rather than shut their feelings down or constantly control them. It is not about ventilating feelings, but about allowing people to immerse themselves more deeply in their experience and process elements of it they usually protect against—the desperation and loneliness behind anger, the fear and helplessness behind silent withdrawal.

The most powerful change agent in a distressed relationship seems to be the expression of the tender, more disarming emotions, such as longing, fear, and sadness. It is the most powerful tool to evoke contact and responsiveness from a significant other. If I help couples create contact, couples can then solve their own problems.

Most couples begin by declaring how incredibly angry they are. They have good reason to be angry. As they come to feel more of their anger, not justify or contain it, they usually begin to explore and experience more of what it is about. The experience starts to include elements they don't usually focus on, which they may even as inappropriate. In fact one reason for feeling so angry is that they feel totally helpless and unlovable, which scares them.

Soon one partner begins talking to the other about what happened one second before lashing out—an incredible sense of helplessness, a voice that comes into the head and said, "I'm not going to feel this way. I refuse to feel so helpless and needy. This is unacceptable." And now the experience has been expanded beyond anger and partners start to contact hidden parts of themselves—in the presence of the other.

This is a new and compelling experience for them that enables one partner to turn to the spouse and confide, "Somehow, some part of me has given up the hope of ever feeling cherished, and instead I've become enraged because I am so sure that you could never really hold me and love me." This kind of dialogue redefines the relationship as one where a person can be vulnerable and confide what is most terrifying about him or herself or the world. And the partner, with the therapist's help, is there both for comfort and as a validating mirror of those experiences of the self.

## BUILDING A SECURE BASE

The relationship is then starting to be a secure base where people can be vulnerable, bring out the neediness or other elements of themselves that frighten them, and ask for their attachment needs to be met. In this safe context, the husband or wife doesn't see the partner as weak but as available—not dangerous. I may hear one say: "That's the part I fell in love with." In a sense, the language of love is the language of vulnerability. While Western psychology focuses on the value of self-sufficiency, in our personal lives we struggle to integrate our needs for contact and care into our adult experience.

Attachment theory is an idea whose time has finally come because it allows us to be whole people. It views behavior gone awry as a well-meaning adaptation to past or present experience. And it views the desire for contact as healthy. Secure attachments promote emotional health and buffer us against life's many stresses. Love then becomes the most powerful arena for healing and for growth, and from this secure base, both men and women can go out and explore, even create, the world.

## AFTER THE FIGHT

Anger and hostility in marital relationships are usually interpreted by a partner as rejection. They are felt as distancing behaviors, and set off attachment alarms; you respond as if your life is threatened. But hostility itself is often an outgrowth of feelings of fear; your partner is perhaps feeling threatened. It is important to recognize that it may be an attempt to bring you back into contact rather than to control you. In some sense, the appropriate response to hostility may be a a hug rather than a return of verbal barrage. But we fight for our life when threatened; we defend ourselves with anything that comes to mind.

It's after the fight that you have a real chance to reprocess the events more accurately, to enlarge the experience to include elements that were left out of the argument while you were trying to win. An attachment lens on relationships encourages us to look at aggression in intimate relationships as a common way of dealing with fear. It also implies there's nothing wrong with dependency needs; it gives us permission to have feelings of wanting to be cared for without feeling weak or judging ourselves as "dependent." After the fight, you need to recapitulate the events with the inclusion of these feelings.

After a fight, in non-distressed relationships, the immediate emotionally reactivity dies down. (The problem in distressed relationships is that it never quite dies down.) When it does die down, if you have a secure base in a relationship, then is the time to talk about fears and attachment concerns.

This creates the opportunity for real closeness. As in: "When I heard you saying that you wanted to go away with your friends for a golfing vacation, I just got scared all to hell. You're saying that you don't need to be with me as much as I need to be with you. I get totally terrified if I think I'm hearing that."

If I have a secure base, I'm much more likely to allow myself to access the feeling that I'm afraid. I'm much more likely to tell my partner I'm afraid. Hopefully, my partner will actually help me with that fear. My fear level will be reduced. My partner's response will help me see myself as lovable, and that exchange also then becomes a positive intimacy experience in the history of the relationship.

This kind of sharing is what adult intimacy is all about. You and your partner find each other as human beings who need comfort, contact, and caring.

## END-OF-CHAPTER REFLECTIONS

1. Keep a log of your emotions for the next few days. Challenge yourself to bring your attention to your emotions at least five times/day. Use Gloria Willcox's (1982) feeling wheel as a guide. Another way to track your mood is through the many mood tracking apps available for smartphones. Daylio is a free app available on Google Play and the Apple store that can help with mood tracking and provides opportunity for journal entries. Visit www.daylio.net for more information.

2. Do you know your attachment style? Visit the following link, take the free quiz, and learn more about your attachment style and how it might influence your intimate relationships: https://www.attachmentproject.com/

3. How can we become more secure in our relationships? One way, among many, is to reflect on how to increase your self-esteem and self-confidence through some of the strategies suggested in the first two readings of this chapter: self-compassion and self-care. Other ways are through supportive relationships with trusted others and/or with a counselor. If you have never considered counseling before, now may be the time!

## REFERENCES

Ansbacher, H. L., & Ansbacher, R. R. (Eds.). (1956). *The individual psychology of Alfred Adler.* Basic Books.

Brennan, K. A., Clark, C. L., & Shaver, P. R. (1998). Self-report measurement of adult attachment: An integrative overview. In J. A. Simpson & W. S. Rholes (Eds.), *Attachment theory and close relationships* (pp. 46–76). Guilford.

Gottman, J. M., & Silver, N. (2015). *The seven principles for making marriage work: A practical guide from the country's foremost relationship expert.* Harmony.

Hazan, C., & Shaver, P. (1987). Romantic love conceptualized as an attachment process. *Journal of Personality and Social Psychology, 52*(3), 511–524.

Marano, H. E. (2010, March/April). The expectations trap. *Psychology Today, 43*(2), 62.

Siegel, D. J. (2011). *Mindsight: The new science of personal transformation.* Bantam.

Wilcox, G. (1982). The feeling wheel. *Transactional Analysis Journal, 12*(4). 274–276. https://doi.org/10.1177/036215378201200411

# RECOMMENDATIONS FOR FURTHER READING

Fraley, R. C. (2018). *Adult attachment theory and research: A brief overview.* http://labs.psychology.illinois. edu/~rcfraley/attachment.htm

Johnson, S. (2008). *Hold me tight: Seven conversations for a lifetime of love.* Little, Brown & Company.

Johnson, S. (2004). *The practice of emotionally focused therapy* (2nd ed.). Brunner/Routledge.

Mikulincer, M., & Shaver, P. (2007). *Attachment in adulthood.* Guilford.

Simpson, J., & Rholes, S. W. (2015). *Attachment theory and research: New directions and emerging themes.* Guilford.

# Chapter 4

# Gender and Gender Socialization

## EDITORS' INTRODUCTION

We follow our discussion of the self in relationship with a discussion about gender—how we each identify and express our gender. Gender, like sexuality, is a complex social concept and should not be confused with biological sex, which refers to an individual's sexual organs. Our gender does not always match our anatomical sex or our gender assignment at birth as either "male," "female," or "intersex." We now know that gender identity consists of more than just identifying as a man or a woman, and our society is progressing to recognize the many gender identities that exist outside the gender binary. We also now know that gender identity is fluid and can change throughout one's life. Gender identity and gender expression are distinct from sexual orientation. The "genderbread person" provides us with a nice and simple visual of how to differentiate and understand the complexities of gender identity, gender expression, and anatomical sex.

We acknowledge that for some, concepts of gender identity and gender expression may be very new, and for some these concepts may be familiar. Wherever you are in your process of learning about and understanding gender, that's okay. We also acknowledge that we (Roni, Kim, and Sara) are also in a learning process, as we *all* are *all* the time. We encourage your curiosity and your questions as you read, and we challenge you to bring what you're learning here to your conversations with others so that we may all grow a bit in our understanding of the many variations of gender identity and gender expression.

**Gender identity** refers to how we understand ourselves in terms of gender: man, woman, both, neither, or a different gender identity (e.g., genderqueer/gender nonconforming/gender nonbinary; two-spirit; transgender; etc.). For more information on sexual orientation

The Genderbread person v4 by it's pronounced **METRO** Sexual.com

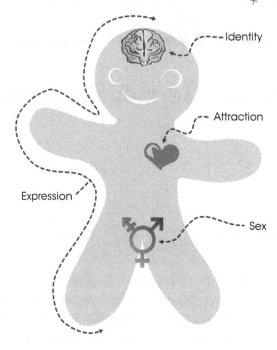

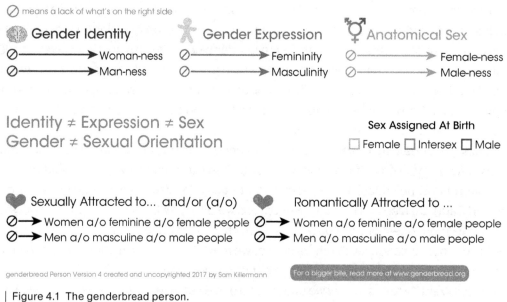

| Figure 4.1 The genderbread person.

and gender identities, as well as other resources to promote understanding and equality among marginalized groups, visit the Human Rights Campaign website (www.hrc.org) (specifically the definitions page: https://www.hrc.org/resources/sexual-orientation-and-gender-identity-terminology-and-definitions). **Gender expression** refers to how we publicly express our gender, our outward appearance through our aesthetic style, mannerisms, and voice. Gender is also expressed by chosen name (some will choose a name different from that given at birth to better reflect their gender identity) and gender pronouns (he/him/his; she/her/hers; they/them/theirs, etc.). (For more information about gender pronouns, visit https://transstudent.org/graphics/pronouns101/.)

An understanding of the many gender identities and ways of expressing gender helps us examine the gender roles that we play in each of our lives and in our relationships. Gender roles are how we engage with the world, related to our gender identity and gender expression. For example, I (Roni) identify as a cisgendered woman. I express my gender in more feminine ways; I wear makeup, jewelry, and clothing that is considered feminine. I learned many of the societal "shoulds" of being a woman from my mom. However, at times the messages I received about being a woman differed from what society says a woman should do, or should be. For example, I learned that a woman should care about her appearance, have good manners, and keep a tidy home. I also learned that a woman can be whatever she wants to be, that she doesn't need to depend on a man for her well-being. I was unaware of the many barriers that women face in the world of work and life until I became an adult. Throughout my adulthood, I learned about socially constructed views on gender and how those views shape how we see ourselves related to our gender. Sometimes those messages are affirming, and sometimes they are harmful and even dangerous. For individuals who do not identify or express their gender according to the binary, these messages have left many feeling isolated and nonexistent. We begin this chapter with a reading entitled "Gender: The Infinite Ocean" by Innis Sampson. Sampson shares their experience of identifying as gender queer, and they explore their spiritual experience of understanding and expressing their gender, likening their experience to growing gills—they could swim in the ocean, instead of drown.

As you read, keep in mind the following primer questions for reflection. If you feel so inclined, take a few minutes and consider your responses to the following questions before you read, and then again after you've finished each reading.

## PRIMERS

1. How do you identify in terms of gender? Is this something you've thought much about during your life? Why or why not?
2. How did you learn about gender?
3. How have familial and societal messages about gender shaped your behavior in your relationships?

## CREDIT
Fig. 4.1: Source: https://www.genderbread.org/resource/genderbread-person-v4-0.

# Gender

The Infinite Ocean

*By Innis Sampson*

## SELF-CREATED, SELF-DEFINED, SELF-SUSTAINED

When gender is seen as binary, any deviations from these polar extremes are rendered invisible. In this silenced state, diversity suffers, which in turn negatively impacts individuals and community. A person's identity and individuality are robbed from them when gender becomes a binary label. This binary labeling demonstrates a lack of sensitivity and respect for a person's background, experiences, skills, and knowledge. Variety within community diminishes when this valuable information is not shared and diversity isn't valued and prioritized amongst members.

When gender is self-created, self-defined, and self-sustained, existence within community becomes positive and allows people, as well as community, to flourish. Because one cannot exist without the other, it is the responsibility of both the individual and the community to maintain a healthy and safe environment for gender variant people. This ultimately creates a safe environment for everyone. Most people would not allow another to dictate their race, ability, sex, or other personal characteristics. Although sometimes these things may seem apparent, no one can truly know another person's realities or preferences. This ignorance often leads to the "isms" (ageism, racism, sexism, able-ism, etc.) and can become hurtful to individuals and community at large.

When speaking about the isms, genderism does not come up often. Genderism is the belief that gender is binary, and that only two genders-male and female-exist. Genderism marries gender and sex, concluding that they are one and the same. Many people make this mistake, but it's important, even crucial, to remember that "sex" refers to one's biological sex at birth: male, female, or intersex. Gender is a person's internal sense of self, role, expression, and behavior. Gender is also determined by society and others' perception. Misgendering can become very detrimental to the person who is being misidentified.

I have experienced genderism in many different types of communities. Even the most open communities which tout feminism, diversity, and queer inclusion have exhibited genderism towards me. These experiences have been in cities, towns, neighborhoods, intentional communities, group organizations, and friend circles. Often these experiences were due to a lack of information about gender politics and visibility of gender variant people within community. I do not believe that my gender and my sex are one and the same, and that has been difficult for many to understand and accept. For me, these experiences have been hurtful, awkward, scary, and painful. They have also been enlightening, positive, and have allowed me to work on my patience as well as develop my teaching skills.

> Gender is incredibly intimate, exceptional, and is often left unspoken until there is a safe space without judgment.

For the purposes of this [reading], I feel that examining my own "gender work" is more valuable than focusing on the gender-based interactions I have had with others. Although my experiences with others have helped shape my understanding of gender, most of my work has been done within my self. Communities can become sensitive to gender variant people but I think they can benefit most from becoming sensitive to everyone's realities and preferences, because this story could be anyone's. Gender is something that is incredibly intimate, exceptional, and is often left unspoken until there is a safe space without judgment. It is a community's responsibility to create these safe spaces.

For many years, the unfavorable gender-based experiences I have had within community affected my self-confidence negatively. When I found myself in a community that was understanding of gender issues, I valued that safe space and I made the decision to live my truth and let my true spirit show. I set off and embarked on a journey that has been perpetually changing the way I look at my life, relationships, and self as a whole.

## SPIRITUAL GENDER

I am a storyteller. I am a spiritual body. I am a gender warrior. During my time on this Earth, I have been a conscious and unconscious warrior: fighting politics, disassembling stereotypes, and constructing (dis)comfort all in the name of freedom—my own name. There is an innate personal freedom inside everyone, one which is often denied. It is often absent-mindedly given to other people, institutions, or structures to determine and label. This act of surrender compromises respect and responsibility, and therein, the true self is relinquished. When the self is given up, you can envision this act as the conforming masses of society moving quickly down a voracious river, advancing towards an unforgiving sea without question. Some find that their eyes fill with water, splashed from another's desperate attempt to stay afloat. The vision is skewed, creating blurred forms and grandiose ideas. It becomes a sink-or-swim game and many who drown never dream of growing gills. There is a comfort in the darkness of the depths and there is always company just as nearsighted and comfortable.

A few years ago, I went through the painful process of growing my own gills. My new breath allowed me to explore all parts of the ocean: the beautiful and the terrifying. Then I grew legs and walked upon the shore. All in due time, I returned to the Earth, and thus became the rocks, the soil, the plants, and the animals. My name is Innis. My name means "an island with two rivers flowing through it." I am an island in the sea. These rivers flow through me as sentient representations of the sacred feminine and the sacred masculine. The sea surrounds me, steady and safe in my comfort. My fluid nature is muted, influenced by quiet balance of the creator and the nurturer. Great energies undulate; the Earth and the sky form the great coalescence. I have built and sustained myself in this sea. I have accepted that the rivers are an innate part of me. I am a spiritual body and I do not deny my presence on this Earth.

When I was denying my presence in the past, I was denying my spirit. I define my own gender as the seamless interrelationship between my physical self—my body, my outward presentation and behaviors—and my internal sense of self: my spirit. Ultimately, my gender is a mirror of my spirit. It has taken me years to even begin entertaining that idea, and even more energy for me to live it. There is an innate spiritual connection between how I present myself as a human being and who I am as one of the innumerable souls navigating the sea of the universe. I certainly did not always feel this sense of spiritual connection to who I have become.

## A MIRROR OF THE SOUL

I have found, through my life experiences, that gender is not at all what it appears. It is in the presentation, expression, and actions of a person, so it is expressed internally and externally. It lives, grows, and sometimes hides within the heart. Sometimes it is swaddled and sometimes it is bare. Its appearance sometimes can feel like pure comfort; other times it is extremely raw.

My gender has been in a constant state of flux for my whole life. This fluidity has always been rooted in my being, and my journey has been about connecting to that base root. No matter how far I feel I have diverted off the path to understanding my true self, I always come back to center, pulled back in like the tides of the ocean. Sometimes this pull has been abrupt and painful, and sometimes it is nothing less than blissful.

I identify the ever-fluidity of my gender as genderqueer. For me, genderqueer is an umbrella term but it means that I am queering my relationships to gender and sexual orientation. For me they are intertwined. For me, queering is a deviation within the norm. Those who identify as queer as a sexuality often work beyond traditional labels to create space for those who are gender and sexually variant and who may have alternative views of sexual orientations. I also qualify my sexual orientation as "queer." My exploration of gender has certainly been a transition, but I am not trans-identified.

I think that some people who are unaware of gender politics perceive gender transitions, in whatever form they make take, to be a dualistic transition. It is seen as linear, beginning at one place and ending at another. In speaking about my journey, this can't be further from the truth. My ritual of identity and transition often feels akin to the cyclical energy of the moon, dictating the tides of the ocean and creating undulations and surges of self-discovery. My identity and transition are both conscious and unconscious. I exist as much as I live. I make conscious choices about how I present myself in certain communities. I try to examine and understand how that affects my self-confidence and others' understanding.

## DUALITY AND TRIALITY

My spiritual journey is not a linear experience where I began at one place and ended in another. It is an ongoing process that moves beyond the perceived duality of nature. Duality is a polar expression where only realms of opposites exist. In the quality of being dual, or being made up of two things, energy is focused on contrast and the differences between those two points. The values of those opposing points are not celebrated; they are only pitted against each other. Male and female, black and white, night and day are common examples of duality. Duality can be seen visually as a line with two points at each end of the line. As humans, we are bombarded with examples of duality every day, and have become accustomed to absolute polar extremes. In my exploration of gender, duality has reared its two ugly heads time and time again in opposition of my journey.

With inhuman amounts of strength, my fight against duality turned into a peaceful battle. My spirit evolved with truthfulness and love. I began listening to myself more. With my intuition I was able to become more in touch with my true needs. I began to live my truth. It was certainly uncomfortable, but the more I changed my life to become the one that I wanted, the more I became happy, grounded, and proud of myself.

Spiritually, I searched for something that could help put some perspective on the work that I had been doing. One day I came across the idea of triality. From my understanding, triality is moving beyond duality by adding another point, or perspective that is virtually infinite. This other vantage point allows one to recognize the balance between the dualistic nature of things. There is a state of observation that is separate from emotion, which allows us to consciously balance out perceived opposites. This act creates an internal and external transition that in turn births openness and infinite possibility.

Triality is a limitless spectrum of points not married by a line or lines but connected in a universal nature. Think about the stars and how they are all connected and part of a common form but each has its own place in space. This model of triality feels like a community to me. There is a collective force to this group that is unified because of its sharing of space and relationship to each other, and its celebration of diversity.

My gender became reaffirmed in the idea of triality. My identity was not one ( female) or the other (male) but something else. This something else is not entirely new, but birthed from these dualistic energies. I channel my masculinity through a feminine lens (specifically my body) to create a holistic otherness, a third gender that is infinite. It is everything those energies are, but everything they are not. It is in between and outside. It is a multi-colored spectrum. It is self-created, self-defined, and a true product of my soul's searching. The community sustains the self and allows for all to interact. It is that cosmic community and it is that ocean.

## EMPOWERMENT IN COMMUNITY

As a gender variant person I have realized that not only is my honesty my most powerful tool, but it allows me to create truthful relationships with those in community. To me, community is my most powerful support system. I cannot compare anything to the feelings that I have had being involved in my community, the queer community. Queer community has granted me the space (physically and mentally) to express my true self. There is an understanding of sensitivity towards everyone's identity and journey, and there is an emphasis on respecting that. Respect in queer community breeds empowerment within me.

Innis Sampson writes: "I have been living in and visiting a vast array of communities for the past four years. I am a co-facilitator and the Sustainability Director of Project Knomad, a youth-oriented community group dedicated to preserving the arts, creating safe spaces, and empowering underprivileged individuals. I am a poet and writer of queer life and spiritual exploration. I love cats."

I cannot always be in queer community though. An overwhelming majority of my time is spent outside of queer community. When there is not a lot of LBGTQIA (lesbian, bisexual, gay, trans, queer, intersex, asexual) and gender variant visibility in a particular community, I often feel hyper aware of my environment and the way that people react to my identity and appearance. I have created internal and external safety tactics for myself to ease navigating through non-queer communities, as well as worked on ways to stay constant, sure, and comfortable in my gender and self-expression. I have recognized that when I exhibit these tactics, people become aware that I am pushing away fear, conformity, and self-restriction. My presence does not become about gender anymore but living my truth in an effort to be a positive example to others to simply be themselves.

I believe there are universal and humanistic tools communities can use in an effort to work towards becoming sensitive and more understanding to gender variant people. The most powerful implements of compassion are listening, having empathy, becoming allies, and respecting everyone regardless of internal or external identity. We truly have no idea of each other's struggles until we open our hearts and shed all of our stereotypes, projections, and stubborn ideas of "this is the way it has always been."

When it comes to gender, I can only speak for myself and from my own experiences. I do not believe that everyone's gender journey is spiritual; mine just happened to be. I also believe that there is no such thing as coincidence, and I see all of my life's lessons as part of a bigger whole.

My journey is far from over but I have found myself grounded in that ocean I once feared. I remember that my transition is internal as well as external—and that it is as limitless as the communities that surround me. I remember that the best work that I can do in community is to simply be myself, watching the trickle-down theory form a vast ocean, ever wealthy with beautiful diversity.

# EDITORS' INTRODUCTION

Next, we offer Greta Christina's perspective on gender and gender pronouns in "Trans People and Basic Human Respect." Christina challenges us to embody an inclusive perspective when considering individual gender identities and expressions and encourages us to be curious instead of afraid when we encounter what is unknown to us. It is only through curiosity that we can develop greater understanding.

## PRIMER

1. What do you do, think, and feel when you encounter someone who is unfamiliar to you? How might you challenge some of your assumptions when faced with someone whose identity doesn't fit your assumptions?

# Trans People and Basic Human Respect

*By Greta Christina*

There's something that's been puzzling me. I've been thinking about cisgender people who get upset about transgender people. ("Cisgender," for those of you who aren't familiar with the term, is the opposite of "transgender"; it means someone whose gender identity corresponds with the sex they were assigned at birth.) Some cis people object to the new vocabulary many trans people are advocating for or are simply making use of changes in names, pronouns, and so on. Others object to the very existence of transgender people: they think gender is solely and entirely determined by the genitals we were born with and that any other perception of it is just nonsense.

Here's what's puzzling me: Why do these people care?

Let's assume, purely for the sake of disproving the assumption, that trans people are somehow mistaken—that they "really" are the gender they were assigned at birth based on their genitals, and it's silly for them to think otherwise. I obviously don't think that—I think it's a horrible opinion, deeply offensive, and out of touch with well-documented reality. But assuming that this opinion is true will help me demonstrate just how wrong it is. So for the sake of argument, let's assume it's true.

So what? How could it possibly affect you? What business is it of yours? If someone else is identifying with a gender that you personally think is "wrong," how does it harm you in any way?

In reality, I think there are a lot of answers to the question, "Why do people care?" I think accepting the existence of trans people makes everyone else rethink gender in ways that may be unsettling. If we're invested in the idea that gender roles are "natural" and inborn, it makes us rethink that. If we're invested in the idea that gender is 100 percent socially constructed, it makes us rethink *that*. It makes us rethink masculinity and femininity in ways that may undercut our sense of our own masculinity or femininity. Indeed, trans identity causes us to question the very idea of a gender binary—the idea that there are two and only two genders that are distinct and easy to identify. It makes us rethink what gender even is.

For years, the reasons I thought of myself as female (to the degree that I thought about it at all) were that (a) I was born with a vagina, and (b) I've been treated as female since birth and have absorbed my culture's opinions of what it means to be female. Even when I was defying those opinions, I was still accepting my basic femaleness. In other words, my defiance of sexist gender norms has been an attempt to redefine what it meant to be female, not an attempt to step away from it. But a trans woman identifies as female, not because of the genitals she was born with or how others see her, but for completely different reasons, based on her own understanding and experience of her gender. When I accept that trans people, you know, exist, and that they understand their own bodies and their own genders better than I do, it means I have to rethink why, exactly, I see myself as female, and whether that's even important to me.

So yeah, it can be difficult. I get that. But I still don't have any patience with those who can't deal with transgender identity.

The existence of transgendered people might make us question our assumptions. Since when is that a bad thing? We're humanists and skeptics. We're supposed to be willing to question our assumptions. If hanging onto our assumptions requires that we close our eyes to reality, that we ignore not only extensive research but also the lived experiences of millions of people, then there's something seriously wrong with our assumptions. That's true for people with traditional or conservative views on gender and sexuality, who are convinced that men are just men and women are just women and that the two are easy to distinguish and that's all there is to it. And it's true for a small but vocal subset of radical feminists who reject trans people's very existence, in hateful and harmful ways, because accepting them would undercut the specific feminist principles they're glued to. When our assumptions lead us to either internal contradictions or glaring ethical horrors, then those assumptions bloody well should be questioned.

Trans people aren't making you redefine your gender. You can identify as any gender you feel comfortable with. That's sort of the point. So why do you think it's up to you to decide for someone else how they self-identify? I keep talking about cis people accepting trans people's existence, but why should acceptance of other people's identity even be in cis people's hands?

As for the changes in language, yes, there are new rules to keep up with. Trans people often change their names, and some do it more than once. Some identify as male or female; others identify with blended gender identities, or with entirely different gender identities other than male or female. Others don't identify with any gender, or reject the idea of a gender binary. Some choose to be identified with the gendered pronouns "he" or "she," while others prefer new gender-neutral pronouns like "zie" or "hir" or use "they" as a singular pronoun. There are new words, new names, and new etiquettes.

So if you're having a hard time with the new rules, there's a very old, simple rule that covers the situation perfectly. To quote Miss Manners, "The polite thing to do has always been to address people as they wish to be addressed."

When people get married and change their names, when they get doctorates and change their honorifics, or when they stop wanting to be called by their childhood nicknames, we usually try to keep up. Is it really that much harder to try to keep track of trans people's preferred names and pronouns? Mis-gendering trans people isn't just a casual bit of poor manners; it reinforces, even if unintentionally, the oppressive weight of a culture that disrespects trans identities and tries to silence them with shame, ridicule, hatred, harassment, discrimination, denial of their very existence, and all too often with violence and death. Is it really such an imposition to try to get it right?

I can't speak for trans people, as I'm not one (and obviously, not all trans people are alike or think alike). But I do know that, in general, most people of any kind are fairly forgiving of honest mistakes. Now, when it comes to trans people even an honest mistake may be one more demoralizing drop in the bucket of being mis-gendered dozens or hundreds of times in a day, so even if trans people are forgiving of your slip ups, it's still important to work on getting it right. But if you clearly regret your mistakes and are clearly trying to get things right, most people of any kind will probably cut you some slack. "I'm genuinely trying but I sometimes screw up" is a valid reason for making a mistake. "Screw you for even asking me to get it right"... not so much.

And one last thing on the topic of language: some cisgender people object to the word "cisgender" on the very basis of self-definition. Even if they understand the word's origins (the Latin-derived prefix "cis-" means "on this side of" and the prefix "trans-" means "on the other side of"), and even if they understand that "cisgender" is simply a descriptive word and is not a slur, they still don't like it. Some dislike the word even if they understand that it doesn't imply any kind of acceptance of traditionally rigid gender norms and that it really just means "I identify as the gender I was assigned at birth, whatever that means to me." They argue that they didn't choose the word and that therefore they shouldn't be expected to use it or accept it being applied to them.

Fair enough. If we cisgender people had come up with another word to describe ourselves, that would be a fair critique. But we didn't. We were content to let ourselves be called—what? "Not-transgender"? "Normal"? Nothing at all? We were content to let ourselves be defined as the default assumption, as the thing that doesn't even have to have a name because it's just how people are. We were content to let our lack of a name mark trans people as other—as not like regular people.

So a word got chosen for us, by people who were sick of being disparaged, disrespected, and marked as other, and who needed parallel language that framed different gender experiences as equally valid. We cis people had the chance to choose our own language. We blew it. We need to suck it up.

Trans people in the United States have nearly double the unemployment rate of the general population. Forty-seven percent have been fired or denied a promotion for being transgender or gender non-conforming. Trans people in the United States are nearly four times more likely than the general population to live in extreme poverty. Nineteen percent have been refused a home or an apartment, and 11 percent have been evicted based on their gender identity. Among trans Americans, 29 percent have experienced police harassment or disrespect; 19 percent have been refused medical care; 57 percent have experienced significant rejection by their families; and 41 percent have attempted suicide (compared to 1.6 percent of the general population).

Violence against trans people is likewise epidemic. Seventy-two percent of all LGBT homicide victims are trans women. Over 50 percent of transgender people have experienced sexual violence at some point in their lives. In elementary and secondary school, 78 percent of trans Americans have experienced harassment; 35 percent have been physically assaulted; and 12 percent were sexually assaulted. (Not incidentally, these incidents disproportionately involve trans people of color.) These statistics from prominent LGBT advocacy groups are probably low; because of the trans stigma, violence against trans people is almost certainly underreported.

Given all this, are cis people really going to complain because we have to rethink our ideas about gender and remember some unfamiliar pronouns? Trans people are human beings. We're humanists. Let's act like it. Giving people the basic right to define themselves, and the basic acknowledgement that they know more about their bodies and their lives than we do, is not too much to ask.

# EDITORS' INTRODUCTION

Sampson's and Christina's discussions on concepts of gender guide us to think about how society and the media have shaped what we think we know about and expect from men and women, and how these expectations can be harmful to all genders and to our relationships. In "Men's Manifesto," Ben Atherton-Zeman challenges men (and women and gender nonconforming) to define masculinity differently, and to put the new "Men's Manifesto" into action. He acknowledges the harm that has come from gender socialization, specifically violence against women. Atherton-Zeman calls for men to embrace their *expressive qualities* (e.g., kindness, warmth, tenderness, affection), women to embrace their *instrumental qualities* (e.g., confidence, assertiveness, leadership, independence), and for all genders to strive for equality in their intimate relationships.

## PRIMER

1. Take a few moments and reflect on what society tells us it means to be a man, and what it means to be a woman. How do these messages influence your own gender identity and gender expression?

# Men's Manifesto

*By Ben Atherton-Zeman*

Reports of men's violence against women dominate our headlines. In Colorado high schools, in Pennsylvania Amish country, in homes in the United States and around the world, my gender is perpetrating violence against women in record numbers.

In 2001, eleven-year-old Nestor Nieves was stabbed to death outside a Springfield, Massachusetts, movie theatre by another boy his age. Subsequent news reports indicated that Nieves was going to the movie with a girl that the other boy wanted to date. "That other boy was jealous and got mad," said Nestor's stepfather, Angel Herrera.

In recent years, this kind of event has been described as "youth violence" rather than what it really is: male violence. Many of the highly publicized shootings of recent years have involved some kind of dating violence—usually a girl wouldn't go out with one of the boys. In each of these shootings, though, the attackers have all been men. Media analysis of these tragedies usually misses this important point.

When I read about Nestor Nieves' murder, it made me think about my own experiences going to middle school in Springfield. I learned many things there about what it means to be a man. There were some good lessons: Be strong about your opinions, stand up against injustice, take initiative rather than standing back, and so forth. But there were some lessons I could have done without: Always have a girlfriend, always have the biggest car or make the most money, don't show vulnerable feelings. If a girl doesn't want to kiss you, kiss her really well and she'll "melt." If your girlfriend doesn't do what she "should," it's all right to bring her into line. And if she's going out with someone else, you have the right to a jealous, even homicidal rage against that other person—or against her.

All the popular guys in the Springfield Middle School, as in the other schools I attended, embodied these qualities. They were the guys I wanted to be like, and I tried my hardest to embody what Jackson Katz calls the "Tough Guise." These same role models were on TV, the movies, and in our popular culture. Any guy who deviated from this got labeled a sissy, gay, or somehow girl-like (the worst thing to be called as a young boy, which is a problem in itself).

I, for one, am sick of it. One of the reasons our sons are killing is because we have encouraged it. One of the reasons our brothers and fathers have abused their wives, girlfriends, and partners is because we haven't said, with a unified voice, that this is not a "manly" thing to do. We need to do more work to change what it means to be a man, what it means to be one of the "cool" and popular guys. Toward this end, I propose a Men's Manifesto.

We will be our own role models, and the role models for other men and boys. Rejecting some of traditional masculinity, we will embrace what is useful to us and sometimes create new definitions of what it means to be a man.

We boys and men claim the right to define what's cool. It doesn't have to mean aloofness, toughness, unreasonable jealousy, and possessiveness. We declare that it's cool to be tough sometimes, and vulnerable some others. We declare it cool to support the women (or men) we date in their independence: Love isn't about control and sex isn't about coercion.

We will stand up against injustice. We will speak out against it, and we will listen without defensiveness when it is pointed out in us. Rather than hiding behind "I didn't mean to," we will listen to the effects of our actions, not just point out our good intentions. Strength as men will be measured not just by how many barbells we can lift, but by how well we can listen.

We will not use homophobic, sexist, racist, or other oppressive slurs to gain the upper hand with someone else. And when we're called sissy, fag, or girly, we will take it as a compliment. Strength as men will not be measured in opposition to women and things female, but in unity with those things.

We will be men in this way with determination—sometimes quietly, sometimes proudly, and always unapologetically. We will write country western, rap, and rock songs with these voices. We will raise our sons this way, and raise our daughters to be strong and articulate. We will refuse to accept it if others say this isn't the way to be a man. This is our way to be men, and we will not be denied our self-defined manhood.

We are sick of violence from intimate partners. Gay men, bisexuals, heterosexuals, lesbians, and transgender folks all have the rights to joyful relationships free of violence and control. Since most of this violence is males controlling females, we pledge to never commit, condone, or remain silent about this violence. We choose to respect, listen to, seek equality with, and share power with the women in our lives, and to encourage other men and boys to do the same.

Nestor Nieves didn't have to die. The other boy could have gone and talked to his friends about how jealous he felt, how frustrated he was that the girl went to the movies with someone else. Every murder is preventable, especially if we can change our culture of violent masculinity. We must stand with our boys before these things happen, and stand with each other as we boldly define a new form of manhood.

# EDITORS' INTRODUCTION

We further the discussion about gender socialization with a reading entitled "How We Enter: Men, Gender, and Sexual Assault" by B. Loewe. Loewe discusses how gender socialization often serves to perpetuate patriarchy instead of break it down. He addresses some of the myths around sexual assault (that women are the only victims) and shares his personal experience. Loewe introduces the concept of privilege and power, which we will expand on in Chapter 12. We include this reading here because Loewe discusses his experience of male gender socialization and the role it played in silencing and disconnecting him from himself. Loewe asks a very important question in this reading that we would like you to consider before you proceed.

## PRIMERS

1. "What does real, positive masculinity look like?" (Loewe, 2008, p. 102)
2. What does real, positive femininity look like?

# How We Enter

Men, Gender, and Sexual Assault

*By B. Loewe*

**M**y mother took me aside from my eighth birthday pool party to scold me. It was 1990, the summer after third grade, and we'd set up a big tent in our backyard. My sister wasn't allowed to sleep in it at night. My mom gave her the same reason she gave for Kate not being able to play in the woods, only this time the evening news agreed. All the mothers were talking about the "Silver Spring rapist." Pat McCall didn't know what rape was. So he and I snuck around to the soda machines and I explained in a whisper in his ear, "Rape is when a man forces a woman to have sex with him," and we ran out screaming toward the shallow end of the pool until I heard my mom call my name in mid-stride. She said that my friends and I were very young, and that I shouldn't share such things because their parents might not want them to know about it yet.

That summer my friends and I inherited our first lesson in sex education: rape mythology. We crafted a common imagery in hushed tones in each other's basements out of earshot of our parents who would be sure to censor us. There were dark men stalking alleys or, in our suburbanized version, the surrounding woods. And there were unsuspecting, helpless women who fell victim to their attack, as these men carried out their plot, pushing themselves on top of women and forcing them to have sex. For our young, uneducated, but highly imaginative minds, the story always stopped there. We had no concept of what sex actually was, other than that it was something dirty, wrong, and to be desired like grass stains on church clothes. It was something that women could give us and that some men took from them. We saw the potential power we, as man-boys, were to inherit; the manhood we were to adopt and avoid. We affirmed our own moral purity in knowing that we would never misuse that power. We learned that men are stronger than women, but that rapists are predator-types who abuse the power all men rightfully hold. As far as we knew, potential abusers remained relegated to alleys and bushes, living as a lurking threat. They were not people who played a role in any other part of our lives; not as mothers or fathers, not as neighbors, relatives, partners, or religious leaders. Surely we didn't know any rapists. And, surely, we could not be abused.

As we've grown up, so have many of our understandings about sexual assault. However, the way men respond to sexual assault is still often based on these lessons we first learned as children. And so these attempts at addressing sexual assault perpetuate patriarchy rather than breaking it down. Working with a framework of men-as-attackers and women-as-survivors, our conception of power can only rest in the hands of men. In dealing with sexual assault, this makes "good men" the protectors and avengers and in general makes women preyed upon and in need of prayers. If this is our story, then gender is determined not by our biology, but rather by which end of the knife we're on. If some of our earliest ideas of manhood depend upon having control over women, what does it mean to let go of that handle? Or even further, what does it mean when men feel the steel against their own throats?

Men's groups dedicated to anti-sexist work have done their darnedest to raise consciousness about these issues. Feminist men's groups I've been involved with focus on defying stereotypes by examining how we fit them. In these groups, we get emotional about not being in touch with our emotions. We patiently listen to each other talk about our impatience with our partners. With good reason, we focus on patriarchy as something we, as male-socialized people, do to others. We look at the outward effect of behavior we've internalized in order to be better organizers, better partners, better friends to the people in our lives. Whether we're describing scenarios that involve dominating conversations or dominating other people's bodies, from our position of masculinity, we analyze ourselves as potential perpetrators, always identifying with the person in power. We're willing to examine in depth our effect on a fairy-tale She-ra but we're unable to see ourselves as anything other than a He-Man, Master of the Universe. Examining our own moments of weakness is rarely a topic we talk about. Weakness would be too sharp a point to bring near our identities so inflated with masculinity. We are always strong, always the actor, never the acted upon. Thus, it is difficult to see ourselves as potential survivors, potentially vulnerable.

With patriarchy so pervasive, it's no wonder that men have to struggle so hard to unravel their myths of supremacy. In order to do so, men must confront the very basis of their identity, to acknowledge our own vulnerability, and to begin rethinking and rebuilding meanings of power. This self-examination requires the very tools that the process of becoming men convinces us to abandon. From the time we are young, boys are taught we should not cry or express hurt. As bell hooks explains in *All About Love*, boys "must be tough, they are learning how to mask true feelings. In worst-case scenarios they are learning how not to feel anything ever." At every point that we might imagine living without absolute control, without being masters of our destiny, there is another road sign rerouting us toward expressway erections.

But what happens when our lives and our lessons contradict? More specifically, what happens when men are the victims, rather than the perpetrators, of assault? For me, it took years before this possibility could be considered anything other than a joke.

I never classified my experience as sexual assault because it never fit my definition of abuse. It wasn't forced. It wasn't violent. It was inappropriately discreet; the epitome of "bad touch." Importantly, I was a man-boy and they were women. I knew that as a "red-blooded American teenage boy" I was supposed to want sex all the time and welcome any chance at it.

I believed that I held the social power in that room and I wasn't going to let these two women affect that. I wasn't going to let them affect me. I walked out of that room confused. In all my previous ideas about abusive sexuality, the powerful man overtook or ignored the will and desires of the less-powerful woman. If a woman could do this to me, what did that say about my power and my masculinity? Besides, wasn't this supposed to be kinky? Men are always supposed to want sex so this must be a joke. *Women could never have power over me.*

And thus, as long as I stayed in my manhead, this encounter when I was sixteen years old wasn't an assault. It was a funny story to tell friends because the idea that I could have been acted on instead of being the crafter of my own universe, Charles in Charge, unaffected by the world around me, was absurd.

As long as I relied upon these early lessons of masculinity, sexuality, and power for my self-definition of manhood, I could neither deal with the reality of my own world nor effectively act in solidarity with the women and gender variant people in my life. My desire to maintain my own sense of power debilitated my ability to participate in efforts to actually end sexual violence. Without a broader systemic analysis, activist men's groups deal with every assault case as another individual man gone wrong. For these groups, it's up to men to use our strength and rationale to either bring the perpetrator back into the fold of appropriate manhood or expel him from the circle. This approach perpetuates patriarchy rather than finding strategies to redraw the systems that shape our world.

It wasn't until I was in a men's discussion about sexual assault where, in go-around fashion, people could make comments like "I passed out drunk and when I woke up, someone was on top of me having sex," and then move on to the next person without any emotional content, that my male bonds began to break down. When we wrapped up the group, all I could say was how inadequate it was. The clock struck two hours and we were done. I walked to the nearby rocks and cried.

Later my partner at the time confronted me about the group's collective lack of emotion in the discussion. She asked, "How can you all expect to struggle against sexual violence when you don't let it affect you? When you don't feel it?" I defended the group and said that men deal with things intellectually and that it's a different, not a lesser, way of processing than emotional ways. I pointed to how I treated my own experience of being abused as an example.

Then things shifted. This conversation with my partner forced me to realize that I did not have a different experience or a different relationship to my body. I had a detached one, an absence of a relationship with my body. She said, "It's not a different experience, it's half an experience." I agreed. I wanted to be whole.

Most literature on male survivors of sexual assault describes a "feminization process" where men feel "less like a man" after being abused. Often, this state of being is described as standard but temporary, with multiple appeals to survivors to reclaim their traits of traditional masculinity: to be strong, to be courageous. Many resources available to male survivors assure men that they are still "real men" and explain that abuse causes most to question their sexuality and gender identity.

No one should have to survive abuse. But, at the same time, I don't think it's a bad thing for men to have to critically think through gender socialization. One of the effects of having social power, of having privilege, is the ability to live *without* questioning one's identity; to assume, in this case, that hegemonic manhood is natural, normal, and preferred.

The existence of male survivors actually interrupts these myths. Our existence creates a space for redefining or abandoning constructed male identity. Patriarchy may not be the knife whose handle men firmly grasp and wield, but, rather, a double-edged blade that targets some and cuts us all.

It is not in redirecting, but in redesigning, our relations that all of our wounds can heal. With this new framework, I could neither be the Superman hero with the shadowy stranger in the alley as my foil, nor could women remain hapless objects in a world that I, and other men, create.

While men must grapple with the privilege and responsibility that socialization allots us, we can also un-puff our chests and end the posturing. We can strive to be something other than the action figures of our collective imagination.

Having lived through a harsh denial of our invincibility, having our scripts interrupted, we have the chance to either deny our experience—as I did for half a decade—or we can reject the role we're expected to play and improvise a new place for ourselves. We can reinvent a world of sharp contrasts and create a space amongst the subtler tones, to dance in the hues between poles. We can stop viewing life in polar opposites and start becoming human as a way to own up to and fight against male privilege, and to end masculinist patterns of domination over others.

More often than not, discussions about male sexual assault are used by men to avoid responsibility for the power and privilege they maintain. The topic of men as victims, especially victims of the actions of women, is used to obscure the prevalence of male sexual violence. Worse yet, these are used as cloaked conversations coated with allegations of reverse sexism meant to maintain, not reexamine, men's power. Recognizing this dynamic creates an even bigger challenge to understanding that, according to the National Alliance to End Sexual

Violence, one out of six boys will experience sexual assault by the time they reach eighteen. By comparison, though, one in three women will be sexually assaulted in her lifetime. What this means is that we need to include men as victims in conversations about sexual assault without decentralizing women's experience and without taking away from the leadership of women and gender variant survivors. We must recognize that while sexual assault affects everyone, it is also a tool of patriarchy that specifically and disproportionately targets those assigned less social power.

Male socialization kept me from understanding that I had been molested, and women's support finally enabled me to identify as someone who was—five years after the fact.

I bring this up crying on a bus ride with a guy friend. I tell him that he doesn't know a thing about my past and I accuse him of assuming that I haven't been abused. In doing so, I assumed the same of him. I was wrong. But he says he never thinks about it. It never registers. But then what do men let register with them? Are we so out of touch with ourselves and so in touch with trying to maintain power that we must deny our vulnerability to everyone? With no space to talk about ourselves as victims, we maintain the tough-guy persona that patriarchy demands of us. As bell hooks writes (again in *All About Love*), "patriarchal masculinity requires of boys and men not only that they see themselves as more powerful and superior to women but that they do whatever it takes to maintain their controlling position." If this is true, what must men do if we are ever to play an effective role in challenging sexual assault in our communities? What is at the core of our identities if we remove superiority over women and moral purity compared to more abusive men? What will give us permission to express our own vulnerabilities? What does real, positive masculinity look like?

To be honest, I rarely feel emotionally equipped to deal with these questions or mentally prepared to write about them. I get a knot in my stomach every time I think about sexual abuse and I have spent days in an inexplicable fog after reading or hearing yet another survivor's account of assault. But I know that we can do better, that our conversations can become more inclusive, that our approach needs to change in order for all our attempts, from pummeling to processing, from ostracizing to education, to ever be effective. I write this because I want to get past the shock, the shock at my presence in survivors spaces and at my tears in men's groups, to get past the bravado and the bitter days, the binaries and the ghosts I bring to bed. In this society, everyone comes out damaged goods. In setting out to transform the world we must also be ready to transform ourselves. Toward a world of healing, tomorrow is ours.

## BIBLIOGRAPHY

hooks, bell. *All About Love: New Visions*. New York: Harper Paperbacks, 2001.

# END-OF-CHAPTER REFLECTIONS

To conclude our discussion on gender for now, we ask you to consider the ways that gender socialization helps and hinders us in different settings. Consider the student-athlete for a moment. Many stereotypically masculine, instrumental qualities (aggression, drive, leadership, etc.) serve the student-athlete well, but what about off of the proverbial field/court/track? Is it okay to admit and experience some of the stereotypically feminine, expressive qualities, like vulnerability? Weakness? Pain? We invite our colleague, and exercise science professor, Dr. Collin Fehr, to share his experience as an athlete, a coach, a teacher, and a researcher on the importance of relationship in supporting the optimum performance of athletes. Before you read Collin's excerpt, consider the following question.

## PRIMER

1. What motivates and inspires you to do better and perform better in your relationships, in your hobbies, in your work?

## Gender Socialization in Sport, by Dr. Collin Fehr

Pickleball is the fastest growing sport in America. Mixed doubles (men and women competing together) is the most popular division in tournaments across the country. Although men are generally bigger, faster, and stronger than women, this advantage is less pronounced in the sport of pickleball. Despite this, the primary tactical approach in mixed doubles is to "hit to the woman." The assumption here is that the woman is always the weaker player. As a certified pickleball professional, this view has always bothered me, because it is not true and is a result of gender socialization.

Examples of gender socialization are plenty in the sporting world. I once coached a female cross-country athlete to "be aggressive" when running uphill. She responded with resistance "because aggression is more of a masculine thing." Conversely, I consulted a male golfer who struggled to feel emotion or joy, even when things were going well in his sport ("because showing emotion is not very manly"). Student-athletes navigate situations like these every day. Although some aspects of gender socialization may be beneficial in sport, strict adherence to these prescribed norms may lead to unintended consequences outside the competition venue.

As a practicing mental performance consultant with athletes of all sports, I have learned that at the core of every sport psychology issue is an important relationship (e.g., self, parent, coach, romantic partner). Student-athletes often experience conflict in these relationships when their behavior is more "prescribed" (due to gender norms) than what they actually feel. For example, I once had a meeting with a male student-athlete who shared some sensitive information with me. His eyes began to well with tears, which he tried to hold back (because he did not want to appear weak in front of his coach). To his surprise, I told him I did not think he was weak. In fact, I told him that his willingness to be vulnerable with someone he respected was actually a sign of strength. At that point, he experienced an emotional catharsis, a complete expulsion of the pent-up emotion he had held for most of his athletic career. According to him, this moment became a "turning point" for him not only as an athlete, but as a person.

Ultimately, sport represents a convergence of both instrumental and expressive traits. All student-athletes must develop drive, assertiveness, and emotional management skills to be successful in sport. However, they must also submit to the inherent uncertainties of competition, which lead to feelings of vulnerability. This is what makes sport so interesting! Acknowledging this will help student-athletes overcome some of the negative aspects of gender socialization in sport and hopefully apply them in other important relationships off the playing field.

## RECOMMENDATIONS FOR FURTHER READING

Doyle, G. (2020). *Untamed*. Random House.

Ladin, J. (2015). The genesis of gender. *Tikkum, 30*(3), 39–43. https://doi.org/10.1215/08879982-3140164

Spence, J. T., & Buckner, C. E. (2000). Instrumental and expressive traits, trait stereotypes, and sexist attitudes: What do they signify? *Psychology of Women Quarterly, 24*, 44–62.

# PART II

# Applications

# Chapter 5

# Sex and Sexuality

## EDITORS' INTRODUCTION

You now have a basic knowledge of the many aspects that form a solid foundation for success-ful and satisfying intimate relationships: a knowledge of the self, a healthy self-esteem and sense of self-worth, a secure attachment style, healthy self-care practices, an understanding of gender and its role in intimate relationships, and many, many more factors! We now turn to developing and applying skills that will facilitate the establishment and maintenance of intimate relationships. It will not surprise you that a theme will emerge in the skills we emphasize: communication. Chapter 6 is devoted entirely to communication, but aspects of this critical skill will appear in each of the chapters in Part II. Communication is not just how we talk to each other, but how we process information, experience emotion, move our bodies, and choose our words to best express our needs, desires, and understanding of our intimate partners. To begin, let's talk about sex.

Many confuse the word *sex* with *intimacy*. When we refer to intimacy throughout this anthology, we are referring to much more than sex. Sex can be part of an intimate relationship but is not required in order for a relationship to be experienced as intimate by both or all parties. Sex is just one part of physical intimacy, which can also include touching, hugging, or just being physically close. Other types of intimacy (experts haven't settled on exactly how many types of intimacy there are) include emotional intimacy, intellectual intimacy, experiential intimacy, spiritual intimacy, and so on. In fact, we can experience sex as much more than physical intimacy; it can be an emotionally, intellectually, and spiritually intimate experience between consenting adults.

You may be reading this anthology with lots of experience with sex, none at all, or some-where in between. Much of the reading for this chapter will discuss how to navigate the complexities of sex when involved in a sexual relationship. The important thing to know before reading on is that wherever you are in your sexual development is okay! If you've never had sex before, we hope to offer some information that will be useful to you when you are ready to engage in a sexual relationship. If you have some (or a lot of) experience with sex, we hope to offer tools that will make sex better and more fulfilling. We approach our discussion about sex from the perspective that it is much more than an act that is meant for reproduction. It is a normal, intimate, fun, and exciting experience among consenting adults.

Our hope is that you experience all types of intimacy in your sexual life. That said, sometimes our expectations of what sex should be can get in the way of enjoying it for what it is. Our expectations for sex come from many places: our families, friends, religion, television, the internet, our own experiences. We learn what we should do, what we shouldn't do, what's normal, what's *not* normal, and so on. There really is no such thing as normal or abnormal when it comes to sex. As long as it's consensual and everybody's having fun, it's good and okay. Not every sexual experience you have will send fireworks exploding in the sky, and sometimes we just have to accept that sex is good enough. Barry McCarthy, writer, therapist, and expert in sex and sexuality introduced the *Good Enough Sex* model (Metz & McCarthy, 2007); in short, we have to accept our sexual experiences for what they are, and not expect every sexual experience to be perfect. When we become more accepting of our sexual experiences, we can better access and embrace the core of sexuality, desire, followed by pleasure, eroticism, and satisfaction (McCarthy & Ross, 2018).

While the readings in this chapter refer mostly to heterosexual, monogamous sexual relationships, we want you to consider that concepts in the readings can and do apply to sexual variations and diversities: consensual nonmonogamous relationships; gay, lesbian, and bisexual relationships; and so on. Healthline.com has an excellent list, with definitions, of the many types of sexual orientations, attractions, and behaviors. Visit https://www.healthline.com/health/different-types-of-sexuality#why-it-matters for more information.

The first reading in this chapter is entitled "A New Kind of Sex Education: Good Sex 101 and Critical Living Skills," by Donna Freitas. Freitas challenges hook-up culture—young adults engaging in casual sexual encounters with no interest in a romantic relationship or emotional ties (Garcia et al., 2012)—and encourages college students to apply the critical thinking skills they are learning in the classroom to their own personal development. She empowers students to express themselves authentically, embrace their developing sexuality, and not let society define what good sex looks like for them.

As you read, keep in mind the following primer questions for reflection. If you feel so inclined, take a few minutes and consider your responses to the following questions before you read, and then again after you've read the chapter.

## PRIMERS

We credit this activity to our colleague Dr. Kirsten Murray, who surprised and empowered us all during a workshop about love. Challenge yourself to complete this activity before you read and know that it's only for you; you don't have to share what you write unless you want to, and we hope that by the end of this chapter you do!

1. Grab a piece of paper (or open a blank document on your device) and write down your favorite meal. Include all the details, from the appetizer, to the main course, to dessert. What does it taste like? What time of day would you like to eat it? Are you eating with someone? What is the atmosphere like? Include as many details as you can.

2. Now, what is your ideal sexual experience? No one has to read this but you, so don't hold back! Answer the same questions here as you did when describing your favorite meal. What does it look like/feel like/taste like from beginning to end? Who are you with? Where are you? Include as many details as you can. Also know that this is just one example of "how you like your sex," and this scenario can change many times. You get to decide what good sex looks like for you!

3. Last, compare your experiences writing about your ideal meal and your ideal sex. How were they different? Similar? What do you think contributes to these processes of expression? Consider societal rules, family-of-origin rules and roles, and norms in your relationship(s). Consider how pieces of your identity like gender, sexual orientation, age, race, ethnicity, religious and/or spiritual beliefs, and the like play a role in how we talk (or write) about sex.

# A New Kind of Sex Education
## Good Sex 101 and Critical Living Skills

*By Donna Freitas*

Lately, every time I speak about my study and my book *Sex and the Soul*, people ask me if I have seen the HBO series *Girls*. The show has been hailed as this generation's *Sex and the City* because it's about sex and the single girl, and yet it lacks the glamour and sexiness that Carrie, Samantha, Charlotte, and Miranda brought to their adventures as best friends living it up in New York City.

In an op-ed column in the *New York Times*, journalist Frank Bruni expressed his perplexity about what the series seemed to be saying about the younger generation—in particular its women—and their relationship to sex. He described how, during sex scenes, the women characters seemed present more as "props," to be told dispassionately to move this way or that for the purpose of male pleasure, than as "partners." The women's roles were to be "largely a fleshy canvas" for male fantasies during sex. "You watch these scenes," Bruni wrote, "and other examples of the zeitgeist-y, early-20s heroines of 'Girls' engaging in, recoiling from, mulling and mourning sex, and you think: Gloria Steinem went to the barricades for *this*? Salaries may be better than in decades past and the cabinet and Congress less choked with testosterone. But in the bedroom? What's happening there remains something of a muddle, if not something of a mess."[1]

Watching the sex scenes of this series is like watching hookup culture come to life, as though the stories of the thousands of students with whom I have spoken over the past few years were pulled together and made into a television show. The pilot's sex scene has the main character heading to the apartment of what appears to be her serial hookup partner, who, after some jokes that she should be his sex slave, begins giving her directions in a monotone voice about what he wants her to do—lay face down on the couch, bend her knees, remove her skirt and stockings so she's naked from the waist down. When she becomes uneasy about his plans to have anal sex, he agrees to simply have sex with her from behind—at which point they make distracted small talk, until eventually he requests they shift to "quiet time." There is an element of humor built into everyone's ambivalence toward just about every aspect of their post-college lives, yet ultimately it is difficult to find such depressing ambivalence funny.

It has been difficult enough to listen to so much sadness about the state of college sex, but to see it on screen is a new level of disheartening. It fairly begs viewers to ask: is this what we want for the next generation with respect to sex? I've long wondered what the post-college, twenty-something, professional world would look like as the hookup generation graduated from college, and the HBO series *Girls* appears determined to portray exactly this. To compare the show to *Sex and the City* seems strange—not only does *Girls* lack the glamour and sexiness of this earlier HBO hit, but *Girls* also lacks the playfulness and camaraderie of the earlier show's four famous characters. This new series about "girls" seems to turn on the notion that everything about post-college life is ambivalent; that there is little to which anyone today might aspire. That the sex is depressing and boring, too, is par for the course.

Recently at a university lecture, a young woman in the audience asked me—in all sincerity—why sex was such a big deal. "Why does sex have to be any different than, say, taking a walk by myself?" she wondered. "What distinguishes sex from all the other things we do that *aren't* such a big deal?" A number of students began to speculate in answer. They definitely thought that sex was a big deal, though no one could articulate why they felt this way.

In response to their discussion, I suggested we consider the meaning of sex and talk about what they thought good sex was. It was soon clear that these students had never pondered such topics. Questions came up like the following: What would good sex feel like? Who would it be with? In what kind of setting? Would it be brief and casual? Would they want to have sex with some form of commitment, and if so, why? If not, why not? Such questions were foreign to their university experience. It was a struggle for them to imagine what good sex might entail. It was as though, until that moment, it had not occurred to anyone that they not only had the right to ask such questions, but owed it to themselves to do so if they were thinking of having or already having sex. Not only hookup culture, but American popular culture and the politics of the left and the right had taught these students that sex was something defined *for* them and not *by* them. Despite being at college—a place where critical thinking about the social and political spheres is expected to occur—these students had never weighed in on the meaning of sex, or been empowered to realize that, in fact, it is their *right* to define what they want out of sex.

The great irony of hookup culture—whether pre-, during, or post-college—is that it's ultimately a culture of repression. If the Victorian era represents the repression of sexual desire, then the era of the hookup is about the repression of romantic feeling, love, and sexual desire, too, in favor of greater access to sex—sex for the sake of sex. Women and men both learn to shove their desires deep down into a dark place, to be revealed to no one. They learn to be ashamed if they long for love, and embarrassed if they fail to uphold the social contract of hookup culture and do not happen to enjoy no-strings-attached sex that much.

The further irony of hookup culture is that, while being sexually active is the norm for students, the sex itself becomes mechanical as a result of so much repression of emotion. College, ideally, is supposed to function as a time in life when young people get to let go of repression; it's supposed to open them up to the world, not shut them down to it; it's supposed to encourage them to become who they are meant to become, not teach them to hide that self; and, most of all, college is supposed to empower them to find their voices and speak up, not learn that the voices bubbling up inside of them are shameful. That a culture that has come to dominate so many colleges and universities thwarts these ideals among its students—and within an aspect of their lives that is so central, intimate, and identity-shaping as sex—is unacceptable.

Another question I am often asked at lectures is some variation of "Who is to blame for hookup culture?" There are the obvious speculations that follow—the cultural obsession with celebrity and pop stars, television and the movies, technology, and the fact that today pornography is ubiquitous. While all of these have contributed to the existence of hookup culture, we also must consider the role that colleges themselves play in its perpetuation. Colleges are supposed to be centers of intellectual inquiry, of cultural critique and evaluation, places where community members—faculty, staff, administration, and students alike—enter into dialogue about the world around them. Therefore, colleges should be the very locations where something like hookup culture could not survive. Instead, colleges are producing all of the following:

- Women's studies majors to whom it does not occur that there might be a disconnect between their work in the history of the feminist movement and the fact that they attend theme parties on the weekend

- Male students who do not seem to know that they are struggling to live up to gendered expectations that may not suit them, or are afraid to admit they might be, since that somehow might cost them their masculinity

- Women and men who learn to hide their true opinions and any aspects of themselves that might mark them as outside the norm, despite the fact that their colleges boast communities of tolerance

- Students who learn to be ashamed of their politics

- Young men who engage in the stereotypical male bravado expected by college "guys" in American culture, while burying all emotion and vulnerability

- A generation that is more socially activist than ever, yet whose members have no idea how to apply the ideals of social justice to their own actions and immediate community or how to foster an awareness of human dignity at their parties and in their sexual decision-making

It is well known that much of a college education takes place outside the classroom, yet many colleges falter in their effort to empower students to apply what they learn in their courses to life beyond those four walls. Faculty members are trained in an academy that devalues the personal as a valid source of inquiry, reflection, and application; that teaches aspiring PhDs that to relate their own work or a classroom conversation to personal subjects (like sex and relationships) is to strip away the rigor required for research; that to open the subject one studies and teaches to the lives of the very real bodies that fill their classrooms is to somehow water everything down. Yet, to bracket the personal is to undermine a college community's ability to respond to the culture of hooking up in which their students live, socialize, and have sex. That students are rarely empowered to bring their critical-thinking skills to bear on their own lives within the college classroom should give everyone pause.

An effective response to hookup culture could be as simple as inviting students to apply critical-thinking skills to the task of evaluating their weekend activities; asking them to draw on their on-campus experiences as they discuss gender, politics, philosophy, literature, theology, education, and social justice inside the classroom; teaching them that their experiences are valid sources for evaluation; allowing the personal to be of value; and making sure students understand that the "I"—a personal pronoun many professors still teach does not belong in student papers—is imperative if they are to understand their role as subjects in relation to their studies. Helping students make this connection between critical thinking and critical living is the best method for tackling the negatives of hookup culture. Encouraging this kind of thinking (and living) recognizes that, at its root, hookup culture silences, shames, isolates, and dis-empowers students, quashing their ethics, desires, and differences, their need for respect and connection, and their need to be treated with bodily dignity, to express emotion, and to experience pleasure. To get beyond the "whateverism" that hookup culture breeds among those living within it, students must be empowered to put those critical-thinking skills to work, evaluating hookup culture itself as a college "text" in its own right, a text that is relevant to studies that consider gender, sexual orientation, politics, moral and religious commitments, and many of the other topics that so many of their classes examine.

The tools for addressing such issues are embedded in the loftiest texts of the Western canon itself, in classics like Plato's *The Symposium* and Aristotle's *Nicomachean Ethics*, in St. Augustine's *Confessions*, and in Shakespeare's plays and sonnets. A text like Descartes's *Meditations* could help communities raise questions about how new technologies affect our ideas of sex and our experience of the body. In the spirit of Socrates, many college administrations, faculty, and staff already love to challenge students to think about queries such as Who am I? What does it mean to be human? Do I have a purpose? What is the good? The true? as they navigate through a core curriculum and a variety of majors. All a university needs to do is expressly open up texts like these to classroom conversations about the meaning (or lack thereof) of sex within the college experience, about relationships, and about how students treat one another and behave on the weekends.

The good news about discussing good sex in the midst of hookup culture is that all the potential conditions exist in the courses already taught and in the structures already in place for programming on a college campus. Applying these resources to this particular conversation must be an intentional and coordinated effort, however, and it requires an awareness among faculty, staff, and college administrators about the issues surrounding sex and hooking up on campus. We need to acknowledge that the subject of "good sex" is important to the college experience, and in fact just as important as any other subject when it comes to preparing the students of today to make their way in the world as the confident, empowered, respectful citizens we hope they turn out to be. I would go so far as to say that colleges and universities need to think about where the topic of educating their students about good sex fits into those mission statements I spoke about in this book's Introduction, since the attitudes students develop about sex are a central part of who they become by the time they graduate.

For this dialogue to be successful, there must also be an openness about the fact that "good sex" may ultimately mean different things to different people. It could include hooking up, long-term love, romance, dating, saving sex for a later date (be that next semester or for marriage), or taking a "time-out" from sex for a while. Students need time for personal (and academic) reflection to figure out what this meaning is for them In this space for reflection, there is so much for students to consider: the circumstances in which sex occurs; the timing of sex; the type of relationship (if any) in place before sex occurs; the many kinds of sexual intimacy that are possible; whether they would like to be "in love," or "in like," or simply attracted to a partner; what role their emotions play, and what role their partner's emotions play; the ways in which they might experience pleasure and also give pleasure to their partner; what happens after the sex. The possibilities of how someone might decide what good sex looks like are vast. If colleges and universities include study and reflection on sex and relationship as part of their mission—given hookup culture on campus—they will be helping students open their eyes and see that the hookup is just one option among many for navigating sexuality and romantic relationship during their young-adult lives, and that, most of all, it is their right to choose which option is best. When they are ready.

# EDITORS' INTRODUCTION

Our next reading ventures into the realm of established romantic and sexual relationships. Talking about sex can be hard, and we want to acknowledge that while at the same time encouraging you to engage in conversations with your current (or future) partner(s) about sex so that it comes as close as it can to being your favorite meal.

In "Communicating Interpersonally About Sex," Valerie Peterson discusses the need to sometimes make desires explicit; we can't expect our partners to read our minds. She also considers the many factors that can affect a sexual experience and some tips for effective communication before, during, and after sex. Expressing what we need and want in a sexual relationship requires us to get in touch with ourselves, which sometimes calls for reflection and self-exploration.

## PRIMERS

1. Rate yourself on the following scale regarding your comfort in talking about sex.

| Very uncomfortable | Neither comfortable nor uncomfortable | Very comfortable |
|---|---|---|
| 1 | 5 | 10 |

Why did you place yourself where you did on the scale? Take some time and think about past experiences you've had (sexual or otherwise) that have influenced your comfort in talking about sex.

2. What would it take for you to move up one number on the scale?

# Communicating Interpersonally About Sex

*By Valerie V. Peterson*

M ost people think of successful sexual intimacy as involving not only their own sexual pleasure, but the sexual pleasure of a partner. From this perspective, some sort of communication ( from simple expression to detailed direction) is an important part of sexual experience. It is important for people to be aware of—and honest about—their own likes and dislikes, and also to share what they know of those things, as well as matters of body, mind, and situation, with their intimate partners. It is also important to listen. Giving off body language and paying attention to a partner's body language is one way to convey and pick up on what is preferred, but sometimes a more direct and descriptive approach is needed. That is, sometimes people need to more explicitly *say* something, or use visual symbols that stand for words to convey something about what they like and don't like, how they feel, what they want, and even what's going on in their larger world, if they want to steer sexual activities toward desired actions and reactions.

In this way, humans are not like (other) animals. As self-reflexive creatures, we think not only in terms of "now," but in terms of our "selves," past actions, histories, meanings, and possible futures.[2] We communicate not only *with* our sexual actions, but *about* sex and sexuality. Intimate acts, expressions, and performances are not only potentially meaningful actions of the moment, they are also past actions subject to inquiry, and future possibilities subject to changes we might make or choose. When intimacy feels transparent, participants are not especially aware of themselves or their bodies or their "performance"; that is, they're not thinking too much *about* what's being done *in* the moment, they're just in the moment (what some people call "flow"). But in order for intimacy to feel or be transparent, some sort of common ground of meaning or understanding may be needed, and instances of happy transparent states will most likely require at least some communication about what is, has been, or will be going on.

Some people object to talking about sex. They think the best sex is sex without words—sex that needn't be talked about or include talk at all. This way of thinking is supported by myths, two of which relate directly to communication: "the myth of the mind-reading lover" (who understands a lover's need at every moment) and "the myth of the context-free sexual encounter" (for instance, no potential pregnancy, no sexual history to negotiate, no distracting cares of the world). These myths are pervasive in popular culture: We see them in TV shows, music, stories in popular magazines, Hollywood films, and pornography.

Life seldom mirrors these myths. This is not to deny the reality of sexual chemistry. Nor is it to deny the thrill that some people get from one-night stands. But the thrill of one-night stands may have as much or more to do with the taboos of behaviors engaged in, the satisfaction of pent-up desires, the thrill of conquest, and the temporary relief from not being alone, as it does with the quality of these temporary intimate encounters themselves. Ironically, feelings of liberation from social and cultural norms, fostered by temporary liaisons, and the " freedom of sexual speech" that can be experienced in such contexts, may make one-night-stand participants *more* inclined to communicate about their sexual needs than they would in more socially sanctioned relationships.[3] This may help explain the appeal of one-night stands for people who find sexual communication challenging, or whose conventional relationships suffer or have suffered from " communication breakdown," sexual or otherwise.

Nobody knows automatically what feels good to another person; what feels good to one person may not feel good to someone else. Heterosexuals face the added challenge of their partner having some body parts that are different from those with which they are more familiar (though it should be noted that having a same-sex partner does not remove the challenges of difference, "otherness," or unique and individual tastes). Because sexual intimacy can be rather complicated, rules of sex are oft en unhelpful. There are some things that we can say we know, in general, about men and women and pleasure, but these facts may have nothing to do with any individual person. And even when there is relative certainty about some sexual "fact," general knowledge is nothing until it is applied. This means that instead of searching for the "foolproof sexual technique" or "magic series of moves," people need to communicate before, during, and/or after sexual intimacy to fill in the gaps of understanding that science, sexual maxims, technique books, popular media, hearsay, and other sources of information will never fully address.

Early on, a person should probably try to find out how their sexual partner feels about *communication about* sex. For example, does the partner feel comfortable with talk (their own and/or the other person's) during sex? If so, can this talk take the form of direction, or should it be mostly sounds only, or words of encouragement? Is the partner willing to talk about sex afterward? Confidences may need to be built, and some verbal and nonverbal vocabularies established. Because of the sensitive nature of sexuality (e.g., its embodiment, its dangers, its significance to those involved), the *way* communication *about* sexual intimacy occurs is just as important as the information about sexual intimacy that is conveyed. Gentleness of tone, optimism and good humor, directness and clarity without crassness or hostility (including the careful use of terms and symbols), and a willingness to listen and respond to the concerns of others all help lead sexual partners toward what works and what is desired, not only early on in sexual intimacies, but across the span of intimate relations.

Fears of talking about sex are in some ways like fears of talking about a person's sense of humor. People don't want to talk about why they think a joke is or isn't funny because they fear it might ruin the pleasure of the joke, or future jokes. If we think of sexual intimacy as a "sense of humor," and if a person wants to enjoy "joking around" (sexual intimacy) with someone in the future, then it helps to know how particular kinds of jokes "work"—or don't—with that person (how intimate gestures are received by a partner), to get a feel for his or her sense of humor (sexual tastes). This critical analysis may take an occasional toll on a few particular jokes (sexual practices), at least until memory fades and the jokes can be told "fresh" again (and unlike jokes, welcome sexual techniques and practices take much longer to—or may never—get "old"). It would be unwise to spend too much time as a critic and not enough time as a jokester or appreciator—it's no fun if the joy of humor/sexuality is smothered by analysis. But discussing jokes would only undermine an entire sense of humor if there were only one joke to be had (only one way of doing intimacy), or if there were only one chance at getting a laugh (only one chance at sexual interaction), or if criticism was overdone or done poorly. In other words, discussing jokes doesn't necessarily undermine an entire sense of humor, and neither does discussing matters of sexual intimacy necessarily undermine sexual desire and the pleasures of intimacy. It is, however, a delicate matter.

One issue about which any sexual partner should feel entitled to comment is pain, and one word that should always be allowed during sex is "ouch."[4] Even though an expression indicating pain will likely be a turn-off to a partner, it is important that sex not become painful and one-sided. This is not simply because it is more likely that better sex (and thus perhaps *more* better sex) will happen in the future if things go well, but because it is important not to do harm to others. Sometimes there is a fine line between pleasure and pain, and in these instances it is not always clear what should be said or done. In general, however, a person knows when something hurts (or is becoming painful). In those instances, the person should say something, or clearly indicate as much, and their partner should respond in appropriate ways—that is, in ways that reduce or eliminate suffering. If pain distracts from a person's ability to become aroused or sustain arousal, or to act as a means to their partner's satisfaction, then it undermines intimacy. If there is something that could be done to alleviate the pain (e.g., a shift or change of position, use of a lubricant, lighter pressure/grip), this should be mentioned. In the long run, partners do each other no favor by bearing unpleasant sensations, nor is it good to ignore another person's discomfort. Such head-in-the-sand responses to pain can easily lead to resentment over past sexual encounters or trepidation regarding sexual encounters in the future, and this does little to promote intimacy and shared good feelings.

Another important focus of sexual communication is a partner's sexual tastes—a person's more predictable sexual likes and dislikes. Because sexual tastes are rooted in unique bodies, they are unique to individuals, but they also may be common to and shaped by cultures and social groups. Some sex and marriage manuals, for example, directly target particular social groups (for instance, gay, lesbian, Christian, Jewish, and so on), while broader cultural norms regarding sex and sexuality are conveyed in more diffuse and environmental ways. It is easier to have transparent sexual relations with someone if you share their sexual values, can read their intimate gestures, and enjoy the ways they communicate through touch and other verbal and nonverbal means. This doesn't require the complete sharing of sexual mores and tastes, or social group or culture, but it does point to the usefulness of exploring areas of shared sexual values, and catering (within reason) to the sexual tastes of intimate partners.

It is also worth mentioning that sexual tastes may vary, depending on the stage of arousal a person is in, and across a person's sexual life span. For instance, a man may become less sensitive to contact right after (first) orgasm, whereas contact that might be too intense to a woman at the outset of intimacy might be more welcome or desired at later stages of arousal.[5] Sexual tastes also may become more varied as a person becomes more sexually experienced. Pacing practices (teasing, variations of intensity, rhythm) are especially important in intimacy, because of the part they play in sexual momentum. These are all places where people need to be open to learning (and relearning) what works for themselves and for their partner(s).

Communicating about sexual likes and dislikes is important, especially when intimacy is new and unfamiliar, but it should be done in moderation. Too much talk during intimacy can be distracting and can undermine the flow of interaction (sex is no fun if the experience starts to feel like an experiment or exam). Too little direction during intimacy may make it hard for a partner to understand what is desired, because only in-the-moment direction could adequately convey such things clearly. In some cases, the coherence or momentum of a sexual encounter may have to be compromised, or even sacrificed, for the sake of communication that would benefit future encounters. In general, too much pre- or post-intimacy critical commentary about what is and isn't liked may curb enthusiasm for future interaction; not enough pre- or post-intimacy direction may leave a partner confused as to how to proceed next time. Humor is oft en an asset in sexual communication, but because taste is such a personal matter, humor about tastes should be used carefully and sparingly. As long as it is not seen as excessive or unseemly, positive commentary may be welcome.

Proper timing of commentary is also important. It helps to save constructive criticism for times that are close enough to an encounter for memory's sake, but far enough away in time from intimate acts that those acts can be considered while in a less physically and emotionally vulnerable state. Talking about sex a few hours or more after an encounter, for example, gives enough critical distance to speak about recent sexual activities while saving face. It also gives enough time to process the discussion and forget about the fact that matters were discussed, before the next encounter. If sexual partners are part of a relationship based on more than sex alone, they might remind themselves that they will have plenty of time to experiment and find things out about each other. If the relationship is mainly sexual and runs into sexual difficulties, it may be harder for the parties involved to take this long-term view.

Interpersonal semiotic systems (wholly invented signals and symbolic forms of communication) also may be used to communicate about bodies, needs, feelings, and the larger situation. These systems may be borrowed or original, simple or complex. Partners may agree, for example, to a few simple nonverbal cues, things like a twist of the torso or a squeeze of the hand on a shoulder. These cues would mean something that then would no longer need to be said verbally, during intimacy. For instance, a partner might say, "If I do this, ... it means move up a little. ... If I do this, ... it means slow down a bit" or "when I move this way while you're doing this, it means I want you to ..." or "if I do 'X,' then that means I'd like you to lighten up pressure or your grip a bit." Because symbolic, signal-like kinds of semiotic communication are learned (and not causally related to their referent, as are indexical signs), they need to be explained explicitly (preferably outside the sex act itself) so that partners know the "message" of any signs used.[6]

Beyond simple gestural cues, other signs and signals such as code words, colors, music, theatrical and contextual cues, book excerpts and illustrations, etc., also may be invented and/or used to communicate about states of mind and body. For example, women may wear a particular style of underwear to indicate the "visit" of a menstrual cycle. Partners might come up with a secret code phrase to share their sexual desires with each other, even while in public (perhaps "we have some laundry to do tonight"). Or they may refer to books (e.g., I'd like to try what's pictured on p. 37). Or they may agree upon a conventional or unconventional nonverbal sign of sexual interest (maybe a particular lamp or candle being lit, the drapes or blinds being pulled, a particular kind of music being played). Perhaps they may make up their own name for a sexual position (e.g., let's 46). Maybe one or the other wears a particular garment to indicate sexual interest, and so forth.

When symbols are ambiguous (when they may or may not necessarily "mean" something), they may provide interpretive "wiggle room" in ways that help reduce the risk of losing face, ease disappointment, and enhance social and interpersonal harmony. Playing a particular kind of music, say, may or may not signify sexual interest, so if a partner does not respond in a sexual way, the music can appear to be chosen simply for its enjoyment value. The same might be said for an ambiguous caress. If a partner does not respond with sexual interest, the caress can be seen as simply an expression of affection. In any event, symbolic means of communication expand the sexual vocabulary into a wider nonverbal/visual territory. They also make it easier for bashful, "artsy," and more visually inclined people to steer sexual behavior in desired ways.

Other matters relevant to sex that also may require communication include situational factors (stresses, duties, chores, pressures), psychological concerns (taboos, fantasies, body image issues, fears, ideologies, etc.), and bodily matters (reactions to prescription or other drugs, the time of the month in a woman's menstrual cycle, the time of day, weight, health, contraceptive use issues, gastrointestinal matters, and bathroom needs, for example). All these things are intimately related to the way a particular sexual encounter will go (or if it will "go" at all). For instance, a sexual technique may need to be avoided if it is associated with a previous bad experience or taboo; a short break may be called for if contraceptive preparations are needed; a full stomach may preclude a position that would be just fine on an empty stomach; and a pot on a hot stove or kids nearing the end of their video entertainment may recommend a shorter, rather than longer, encounter.

The complexity of sexual practice recommends *against* thinking of sex as something a person can master once and for all, and *for* thinking of sex as a wide range of possible actions that may or may not be appropriate with any particular partner, in any particular intimate scenario and sequence of events. It also recommends that cultural myths or "facts" about male and female bodies, scientific findings, expert testimony about arousal, and ideas about bodies learned from any previous intimate partners may be worth considering, but may not necessarily be worth employing, especially when a partner's responses show that his or her arousal or desire operates otherwise. Unlike ways of thinking about sex that try to identify typical practices or "sure-fire" techniques (which can get boring over time), interpersonal ways of understanding intimacy highlight the need for interaction, attentiveness, and communication. They are more likely to leave room for variety, change, and the demands of particular individuals and situations.

## ENDNOTES

1. Arthur Asa Berger, 1998.

2. Josiah Royce, 1967.

3. See, for example, John Gray's (1995) discussion of his post-monk, premarriage sexual investigations, in which he asked various female sexual partners quite frankly and openly about their sexual likes and dislikes—and his discovery that this had a positive effect on their libidos.

4. For an example of failure in advice on this matter, see John Gray (1995). His list of 10 sexual turn-offs for men includes "ouch, that hurts" (p. 55). Gray recommends women avoid saying this, for fear it will undermine a man's sexual enthusiasm. But responding to sex-related pain is more important than maintaining sexual momentum.

5. William Masters and Virginia E. Johnson, 1966.

6. Arthur Asa Berger, 1998.

## WORKS CITED

Berger, A. A. (1998). *Seeing Is Believing: An Introduction to Visual Communication* (2nd ed.). Mountain View, CA: Mayfield.

Gray, J. (1995). *Mars and Venus in the Bedroom: A Guide to Lasting Romance and Passion.* New York: Harper Collins.

Masters, W. H., and Johnson, V. E. (1966). *Human Sexual Response.* New York: Bantam Books.

Royce, J. (1967). *Perception, conception, and interpretation. In The Problem of Christianity* (pp. 109–163). New York: Archon Books.

# EDITORS' INTRODUCTION

It almost always helps to have some practical applications that bring content knowledge and learning to life. The next reading is directed toward couples. If you are not in a couple relationship at this point in time, think about past relationships you've had or things you want to file away for a future relationship. In "Sex and Intimacy," Krill and Bevan offer some exercises that couples can practice to enhance intimacy and sexual satisfaction. Whether you are in a romantic relationship right now or not, imagine what it might be like to engage in some of the activities presented in this reading. Chances are, you'll have an opportunity to try some of them out in the future.

Krill and Bevan offer several questions for reflection and suggested activities throughout the reading, so we hold off on offering you a prereading primer for now.

# Sex and Intimacy

*By William E. Krill and Lynda Bevan*

## PHYSICAL (NON-SEXUAL) INTIMACY

Following the Second World War, there were many orphans left in Europe, and these children were placed in large care giving facilities. It was discovered that despite being fed and kept warm and given needed medicines, the children lost weight. The missing ingredient for them to thrive, as any parent knows, is human touch. Physical touch is imperative to satisfaction in human life. In our busy lives, non-sexual touch may become just another chore, something we are too busy for, or something we withhold out of our resentments.

There is of course, casual, incidental physical intimacy all over the place, from bumping into folks on a crowded subway train to a business handshake to the light skin-to-skin contact while getting your change at the grocery store. But intentional, non-sexual touch is different and far more nurturing *because* of it being *intentional*.

How many times have we heard a person complain that their partner never seems to touch them much unless sex is involved? It is, perhaps, a cultural learning process for males that touch with their partner should or must always result in an orgasm. This is likely because in our culture, boys, as they get older, are touched less and less by their parents, while girls tend to get just as many hugs and affectionate touches as when they were small. Boys tend not to hug each other or hold hands in our culture as girls often do. Due to homophobia, even boys and fathers come to a point where they hug far less than girls and fathers. This translates into the only acceptable place for boys and men to be touched is during sex.

But we men need to grow and mature to a point where we can stop cheating ourselves (and out partners) out of non-sexual touch. We need to get the courage up to tolerate our emotional feelings of vulnerability and start touching not only our partners, but our kids and even friends. Touching others is not only good for our emotional health, but good for our physical health as well.

## Individual Questions to Answer and Then Share:

1. What is your favorite non-sexual way to be touched? What do you think is your partner's favorite way to be touched?

2. If you have children of both genders, do you think you touch the girls more than the boys?

3. Are you a good hugger? Do you think that there are different kinds of hugs?

4. What way of touching do you wish your partner would do more of?

5. Can you cuddle with your partner without becoming sexually aroused?

**Intimacy Maintenance Challenge:** Pick up the pace on non-sexual touch of your partner.

**Intimacy Enrichment Challenge:** Once you find out what kind of touch your partner wants more of, commit to doing that touch at least once a day for a week.

**Individual Activity:** Learn how to give a simple relaxation massage (book or video).

**Couple activity:** Since massages are most pleasant when there is no pressure for reciprocation, set aside (two different) times and give each other a massage. If you are the giver in the first time slot, you become the receiver in the second time slot. Remember that this is not about the massage leading to sex, unless that's the plan in the first place!

## SEXUAL INTIMACY

Most adults think that sexual intimacy is a fairly straightforward and simple thing, and when it works well, it can *appear* to be quite simple, but in reality, it is a very complex and elegant process in healthy relationships. Everyone who has been around the block a few times knows that a person can have sex without any intimacy, or a person can have sex with an intense level of intimacy that can surpass all expectations and enter the realm of the sublime.

Our culture is inundated with sexual images and concepts that often violate our sensibilities of sacredness of sex in our own lives. This constant press wears on us and can acculturate us into buying into a rather shallow and jaded view of sex. We can either come to the conclusion that we are not getting what we deserve, that we are inadequate, or sex is just a chore to be tolerated. Instead of getting the healthy and real facts about human sexuality and our own sexuality, we get taken in by fallacies.

For monogamous couples, sexual intimacy is the only one that should be exclusive to the relationship. One may be intellectually intimate with many people, even incidentally. Or, we can be emotionally intimate with friends and colleagues; physically intimate with our kids and friends, or, if we are in a career such as hairstyling, we may be physically intimate with relative strangers. Still yet, we can be spiritually intimate with others at worship, or even simply one on one with our Higher Power. And in many ways, sexual intimacy can include 'difficult intimacy' at various times in a long term relationship. A secret that few couples come to understand is that it is in sexual intimacy with our partner that we have the potential to experience *all* of the six-fold intimacies *at the same time*.

That sex is physical and emotional is fairly easy to understand, while sexual intimacy having aspects of intellectual, spiritual, and difficult intimacy are harder to grasp. Human sexual intimacy is an incredible, nuanced and sublime communication gift that can truly take a lifetime to master, extract the most from, and experience the very limits of human intimacy in and through. Reaching such mastery requires that the individual is able to engage in self growth as much as engaging in couple growth. It also requires self-discipline to seek out important sexual information from the fields of physiology, emotional health, spirituality, and relationship health.

## Individual Questions to Answer and Then Share:

1. Would you like your sexual experiences to be more intimate?

2. Are you able to identify aspects of your sex life that include all six intimacies?

3. When was the last time you have sought out high quality adult sex education to learn something new about sex?

4. Do you feel pressures from the culture giving you messages about your sexuality? What?

5. Do you have any ideas on where to start if you were to decide to learn more about healthy sexuality in relationship?

**Intimacy Maintenance Challenge:** The next time you invite or are invited to make love, be intentional about doubling the time you usually reserve for this; then use the time to extend your foreplay.

**Intimacy Enrichment Challenge:** Learn some basic massage techniques and then use them as part of a relaxing and de-stressing gift before you move on to more overtly sexual foreplay.

**Individual Activity:** Locate a solidly researched, non-pornographic article or book concerning adult sex education, and read it. Take notes, even.

**Couple Activity:** Set aside time to have an open and honest discussion about a fairly narrow sexual topic, such as which positions you would like to try that are outside of your "usual." Be sure to discuss why a position you would desire is so appealing to you, and likewise, if you reject a position proposed, why you find it unappealing.

# EROTICISM

'Eroticism' is the fusion of thinking, emotion, and behavior in our sexuality. It is the *'what'* of what turns us on sexually. What each person finds erotic is quite individualized while at the same time having a universal theme. It is important to note that there is a very wide variety of what even normal human beings find erotic. Each person develops a unique "erotic map" over the course of their lifetime, developing even from a very young age. This is because as human beings, we are gifted with five senses, and these senses make our lives *sensual*. Sight, sound, smells, tastes, and touch all play a role in our understanding and communicating in the world, and we develop preferences and attachments to particular sensory experiences along our way in life (grandma's oatmeal cookies, for one example). Sensuality, or enjoyment of the senses in a sexual way, is erotic.

It seems that eroticism should be just a natural progression and enjoyment of such a wonderful gift as sex, but for many, damage occurs along the way that creates wounds surrounding their eroticism. Things like abuse, or harsh parental or religious prohibitions against enjoying the five senses (or particularly those having to do with sex), can result in adult sex lives that are arid, stale, repressed and constricted, or even consistently painful, both emotionally and physically.

Yet, wounds can be healed (sometimes with the help of a workbook or good counselor), and a person's erotic map can begin to stir and grow again, both in detail and depth. Couples who have been together for decades may think they've explored everything erotic and sexual they are willing to. Even they may find hidden regions of sexual and erotic intimacy, just waiting to be awakened, unwrapped, and enjoyed.

Of course, since our eroticism contains wounds and anxieties, it is often difficult to approach discussing eroticism due to the inherent sensitivity of the topic. When we can create a safe space for ourselves and our partner to reveal our/them-selves, the rewards can be breathtaking.

## Individual Questions to Answer and Then Share:

1. Are you aware of your own wounds regarding eroticism?

2. Do you have a sense of when and where those erotic wounds happened?

3. Have you determined what is erotic to you? Do you know your 'erotic map?'

4. If you have unresolved erotic wounds, how might you go about healing them?

**Intimacy Maintenance:** Choose one of your erotic wounds, and then share them with your partner.

**Intimacy Enrichment:** Discover a facet of your 'erotic map' that has not been explored, and then share it with your partner. This is usually some erotic or sexual behavior that you have thought about/fantasized about, but have not shared verbally or in behavior with anyone else.

**Individual Activity:** Choose one of your erotic wounds to focus time, energy, and healing upon.

**Couple activity:** Determine an area of your erotic maps that overlap, choose an erotic/sexual behavior, create a safe emotional and physical space, and *do it*. Remember not to push your partner to do any behavior that they do not desire to engage in.

    *Realize that the above activities will produce anxiety, but follow through despite this.

## SEXUAL FUNCTIONING ISSUES

There can be many sources of sexual functioning issues, including the development of physical illness, history of sexual abuse, troubled relationships, impaired intimacy maintenance, or a lack of quality sex education. Interestingly, the last three reasons listed are the most common. In recent decades, the tendency to jump to medicines to help sexual issues gives rather false hopes of cures for them. The proof is when we see men take the 'little blue pill,' achieve a great erection, and still really do not want to have sex.

Common issues are: inability or failure during sex to remain physically aroused (maintain erection or lubrication), low sexual desire, physical pain during sex, and inability to achieve orgasm.

Effective treatment of such common issues requires a holistic approach that includes not just medical intervention, or even medical interventions as the primary choice of treatment, but often counseling and education, not to mention a larger view of human sexual potential beyond performance issues like erections and orgasms. Most couples, unfortunately, do not even *come close* to approaching the fullest potential for sexual *satisfaction* in their relationships.

Most sexual functioning problems are a result of relationship issues, and ideally need a couple therapy approach that casts a much wider net than identifying success as the firmness of an erection or the number of orgasms. For a good part of the population, there are unhealed issues of child sexual abuse, relationship problems, or unresolved wounds from coming out as a lesbian, gay, bisexual, or transgendered person that are the root causes for sexual functioning issues. Those seeking help for sexual functioning issues need to be very thorough in checking out the qualifications, therapeutic stance, and cultural awareness level of the counselor they intend to engage.

## Individual Questions to Answer and Then Share:

1. Are there sexual functioning issues in your life?
2. Have you seen a medical doctor to explore if medical issues are the cause?
3. Have you sought out a qualified counselor to address other approaches to the functioning issue?
4. What is your current strategy for coping with the sexual functioning issue you may have? Is it working?

**Intimacy Maintenance:** If you or your partner have a sexual functioning issue, slow down, and work at staying emotionally connected when the issue presents. For example, if one of you seems to lose desire/passion in the midst of foreplay, discuss when the disconnection began, and what you were both thinking and doing at the time. You might then decide to just hold each other, or eye gaze until you reconnect at the emotional level.

**Intimacy Enrichment:** The next time you have sex, plan to allow for *double* the time you usually set aside, and *slow down* the erotic/sexual process. For example: instead of proceeding linearly from the invitation to sex, rapidly through foreplay, and then on to orgasm, slow things down by 'anointing' your lover's body with fragrant oil, focusing on and enjoying the touch and textures you discover while doing so.

**Individual Activity:** Determine what you will choose to do if and when a sexual functioning issue presents in your relationship. Determine how you will verbally, emotionally, and behaviorally respond, either in a better way than you have been, or if you have not experienced a sexual functioning issue together, in preparation for the future possibility.

**Couple activity:** If the sexual functioning issue presents, offer reassurance to your partner by changing focus away from the issue, and engage in some other mutually pleasing activity. For example, if he loses his erection, he might begin to engage her in oral sex, or either of you might begin a backrub for the other.

## SPIRITUAL INTIMACY

Spiritual intimacy does not have to be 'religious' or based in dogma, though for most couples, there is likely a history of some religious-denominational experience. For many spiritual traditions, being a couple, being married, and being monogamous has spiritual underpinnings, and marriage is viewed as structure both representing and enriching the spirituality of the participants. At least in the United States, most marriages begin with church ceremonies. Even in coupling without legal or church marriage, the monogamous ideal is often held, which assumes or implies a 'spiritual bond' of some sort.

Spiritual intimacy may include church activity such as worship or service work, and this may be done individually, or as a couple or family. Such activities can serve very well to help build spiritual intimacy for a couple. Couple expressions of spiritual intimacy may be conjoint devotions or prayer, or meditation. Even time spent together in nature can be a shared spiritual experience. Certainly, the exercise of engaging regularly in the other five intimacies can produce couple spiritual intimacy, but this does not mean that spiritual intimacy should be neglected its fair share of attention.

All couples can benefit from the formulation of a 'mission statement' for their couple-hood. Why are you together? (While love is the usual answer, what is being asked here is: what is the mission?) For most couples this is a tough question to answer, and coming up with a mission statement is not an easy task. The mission statement is very valuable, because it can provide a 'beacon,' central point of reference, or core spiritual principle for everything that the couple decides to do in their life together. It can give purpose, measure, and to some degree, safeguard against a drifting away from what the couple has mutually agreed is important.

Here is the author's marriage/family mission statement:

"To create a community of life and love."

Make your mission statement one sentence, and make each word *count*.

## Individual Questions to Answer and Then Share:

1. Do you feel your couple relationship is spiritual? How?
2. What areas of spiritual intimacy could be improved upon?
3. Do you have a 'mission statement?'
4. What goes into your mission statement?

**Intimacy Maintenance:** If you already have a church tradition, keep going! If you do not, consider visiting churches or other spiritual resources to find a comfortable place that will enhance your own and your couple spiritual intimacy.

**Intimacy Enrichment:** Find a spiritual text to read and discuss together.

**Individual Activity:** Spend some time praying for/and or meditating on your couple relationship.
**Couple activity:** Together, craft a mission statement, then post it somewhere in the house that will keep the mission in front of you. Measure all you choose to do by the mission statement.

## DIFFICULT INTIMACY

There is a delightfully wise saying that goes: "No sex should ever be safe sex; if sex is safe, you are not doing it right!" The saying, of course, is not about sexually transmitted diseases or pregnancy, but that there needs to be a level of emotional vulnerability and risk to our sex lives that produces growth in overall intimacy in our relationship. Taking emotional risks and being vulnerable is difficult, because it makes us anxious. The same is true about all intimacy, not just sexual intimacy.

While sexual intimacy is usually quite pleasurable, not all intimacy is pleasant. A heated argument is often a very intimate exchange, as is delivering a baby, or shared grief. Some difficult intimacy comes our way uninvited and intrusive, like the intimate news from our doctor of a serious illness. But for our purposes, difficult intimacy is when we have something that is hard to share with someone we love. We may be, in fact, very anxious and worried about just how to word what is in our heart and what is on our mind, but we feel pressed to share the truth, in love. Feelings of intense anxiety arise as we anticipate how the other person will receive what we have to say.

When couples avoid difficult intimacy, they are actually avoiding what can result in great personal and couple growth. The courage and habit of dealing with difficult issues as they arise is how difficult intimacy can temper the metal of couple-hood into a resilient, hardened, and strong bond.

### Individual Questions to Answer and Then Share:

1. Most couples have a few things in their relationship that are difficult and ongoing, such as disagreements about finances, for example. What are the points in your relationship that have traditionally been difficult?

2. There is a level of risk and anxiety in speaking your heart and mind. What thoughts are in your head that keep you from speaking?

3. Are you aware of how you avoid the difficult issues? Simply not bring them up? Gloss them over, sweep them under the rug, or joke about them?

4. Do you think there is a way to enter discussion about difficult things so that argument and hurt feelings will not happen?

**Intimacy Maintenance:** Note the next time you become irritated with your partner and then consciously slow down the process, pay attention to your negative thoughts, take a deep breath, and try calming yourself.

**Intimacy Enrichment:** Discuss a past issue that has been resolved, and explore the positive results of whatever decisions or compromises that came from the resolution.

**Individual Activity:** Make a list of the 'difficult' topics that you tend to avoid discussing. Use this list later to methodically address each of the areas of difficult intimacy with your partner. Keep going until your list is cleared.

**Couple Activity:** Compare lists and choose to address one of the difficult issues.

[...]

# END-OF-CHAPTER REFLECTIONS

What questions do you still have about sex? Sometimes we think we should be expected to know everything there is to know about sex, but the fact is that we're all developing and learning about ourselves and others *all the time*. Following are some vetted resources that will provide you with reliable and valid answers to all your sex questions. If you do any internet searching on your own, be sure to check out who is offering the information on the website; we've made sure that a medical doctor and/or licensed mental health professional are authoring or contributing to the following websites.

- Everydayhealth.com has a great list of articles and resources related to all things "wellness" and a particularly robust list of articles about sex and sexual health. Visit www.everydayhealth.com/sexual-health for more information.

- Sexualbeing.org has some excellent resources related to sex education, protection from and treatment for STDs, and an especially interesting blog. Visit www.sexualbeing.org for more information.

- Planned Parenthood has a wealth of resources related to sexual health and wellness. Visit www.plannedparenthood.org for more information.

We're often asked how to keep passion alive in long-term romantic relationships. We offer some strategies, knowing that there are so many more strategies you can develop in your relationships. Keep these in mind and add to them with your own relationship experience.

1. Make your sexual relationship a priority and protect physical intimacy from anxiety and conflict.

2. Separate sexuality from sensuality. Sensuality restores emotional connection and makes partners feel closer and more interested in sex.

3. Communicate your sexual and sensual needs clearly to your partner.

4. *The platinum rule*: Do unto your partner as *they need*, not as you need.

# REFERENCES

Garcia, J. R., Reiber, C., Massey, S. G., & Merriwether, A. M. (2012). Sexual hookup culture: A review. *Review of General Psychology, 16*(2), 161-176. DOI: 10.1037/a0027911

McCarthy, B., & Ross, L. W. (2018). Maintaining sexual desire and satisfaction in securely bonded couples. *The Family Journal: Counseling and Therapy for Couples and Families, 26*(2), 217–222. https://doi.org/10.1177%2F1066480718775732

Metz, M. E. & McCarthy, B. W. (2007). The "good-enough sex" model for couple sexual satisfaction. *Sexual and Relationship Therapy, 22*(3), 351–362. https://doi.org/10.1080/14681990601013492

# RECOMMENDATIONS FOR FURTHER READING

Southern, S. (2019). Good enough sex: An interview with Barry McCarthy. *The Family Journal: Counseling and Therapy for Couples and Families, 27*(1), 5–10. https://doi.org/10.1177%2F1066480718804792

Metz, M. E., & McCarthy, B. W. (2011). *Enduring desire: Your guide to lifelong intimacy.* Routledge.

---

*Chapter 6* ————————

# Healthy Communication

## EDITORS' INTRODUCTION

This is the chapter you've all been waiting for, and probably one of the most important components of a successful intimate relationship, or any relationship for that matter: communication. We begin this chapter with an excerpt from the reading with which you began this anthology: "Building Positive Relationships," by Brown and LaJambe. In it, Brown and LaJambe discuss the many ways that animals and humans communicate—verbally, nonverbally, symbolically, and so on. You may never have thought too much about the many ways you use your voice, words, and body to communicate. Regardless, you are sending messages in your interpersonal interactions with every part of your being. Your messages may be accurately interpreted by others some of the time, and inaccurately interpreted some of the time. You can undoubtedly think of a time that your intended message was misunderstood, and likely some repair work was in order! We also must consider how we communicate when the added components of vocal inflection and body language aren't present: through text, email, instant messages, social media messaging, chatting, and so on. In fact, Shigetaka Kurita invented what we now know as the emoji in 1999 for the exact purpose of helping us to communicate accurately via text.

Brown and LaJambe will discuss personal space in this reading, and we think it's important to acknowledge how our concept of personal space has and will continue to change as a result of the COVID-19 pandemic. We can't yet know the full impact that COVID-19 will have on our social and psychological well-being. Only time (and research) will tell us. What we have come to practice—social distancing—will fade as more and more people are vaccinated, but we encourage you to think about how COVID-19 has changed our perceptions of and comfort with personal space; we now must concern ourselves with the *safety* of being close to others. Also consider how our communication mediums have been affected by wearing masks. Hopefully at the time of this reading we are all back together in the same room without masks, but COVID-19 has undoubtedly affected our perceptions of personal space and how we communicate and understand each other through a variety of verbal, nonverbal, and symbolic cues.

As you read, keep in mind the following primer questions for reflection. If you feel so inclined, take a few minutes and consider your responses to the following questions before you read, and then again after you've read the chapter.

## PRIMERS

1. How do you intentionally add to your words to ensure your messages are received the way you intend? Think of as many communication strategies as you can, for example vocal inflection, proximity, touch, body language, and emojis.

2. How effective are you in communicating the way you intend to? Are there adjustments you would like to make to your communication style in order to improve the way others understand your message?

# Building Positive Relationships

*By Frederick Brown and Cynthia LaJambe*

[...]

## KEEPING A STRONG RELATIONSHIP

## A. Social Structure

Establishing clear expectations for making relationships work under many different kinds of situations often requires some sort of outline for participants to follow. This is referred to as social structure and is an important topic in the science of sociology. What *social structure* usually results in is an orderliness among people in terms of how activities that require relationships work. The military service is a perfect example of a very large formal *social structure*, in which the duties are clearly spelled out for each person, from bottom to top. As a result, each person is expected to know what they are responsible for and to whom. The same thing is true for many institutions and business organizations. Highly detailed job descriptions are often provided that describe what is expected of each person in the organization. For orderly formal group decision making, one of the most widely used books in the English-speaking world is known informally as *Robert's Rules of Order* (Robert, 2011), recently revised into the 11th edition.

In personal or family relationships, *social structure* also is present, but often not in such formal ways. Yet, if relationships are to continue productively and not involve constant confusion and errors, some sort of agreement must finally be worked out in terms of who does what, when, and how. In informal relationships, some sort of social structure develops over time as people get to know each other. If people have had experiences before in a similar relationship, say working on a college homecoming committee, those experiences can be used to structure the duties of each member in order to complete the jobs that need to be done. In different cultures, customs may structure family life according to patterns that have been workable across generations. Regardless of the relationship, for a working social structure to continue, each member in it must know what is expected of them.

## B. Good Communication

An old joke asks the question: What are the three most important factors in a strong positive relationship? The answer: Communication, communication, communication! Back to where we started this [reading], we learned that relationships develop based upon the way its members relate to one another by making their needs and wants clear. That means openly sharing difficulties and concerns that need to be fixed and working together toward mutually satisfying problem solving. As we have learned throughout this [reading], we communicate with each other both *verbally* and *nonverbally*. Now we will look into the details of how each of these work.

### 1. Verbal Communication—Words Alone

Sounds that carry meanings are common among all sorts of animals. Our pets can signal us their needs by the noises they make with their mouths. Bird chirps warn others to stay away. Crickets rub their legs against their bodies to signal readiness for mating. Elephants rumble deep in their throats to send messages across miles to locate other herds. Fish and frogs croak, and whales sing long songs deep in the oceans. What is unique to humans, and perhaps some birds, are strings of specific sound combinations made by the lungs, throat, and mouth that represent complex messages carried between each other. Not only are these sounds used by humans, but also symbols that stand for these sounds are made by using visual (written words), auditory (Morse code), and pulsed electronic codes. Regardless of our cultural language and the symbols we use, when we give our name and address, recall childhood experiences, or give opinions about a book or movie, these verbal behaviors give information about us to others. It is important that the person we are communicating with can understand what we are saying. Listed in the adjacent *Perspective* are some of the common communication errors.

**Perspective**

**Common Errors in Communication**

**Different word meanings**—depends upon listener's experiences

**Selective attention**—listener motivated to hear what they want, not what speaker *intends*; receives only a partial message

**Insensitivity**—what is said causes different feelings and emotions for speaker and listener; incorrect sensing causes wrong interpretation by the listener

## 2. Nonverbal Communication—Adding to the Words

According to anthropologist Dr. Ray Birdwhistell, most verbal communication carries no more than 30 to 35 percent of the total information about a relationship in words alone (McDermott, 1980). The rest of the message is carried by *nonverbal* communication in order to help us understand better another person's emotions or feelings about the message. In fact, it may not be surprising to learn that *nonverbal* signals are involved in most of the information we share with others during social transactions (Onsager, 2014). All of us by now have probably heard a synthesized recording in which prerecorded alphabetical letters have been put together to make words and phrases. What is most evident is the artificial sound of it because often the words are not pronounced correctly, since all parts of the words have the same emphasis and no emotions are present. The addition of different emphasis and emotions adds much to our interpreting the meaning of a verbal message. One of the major challenges with e-mail and texting using our computers and phones is that only the words are seen on a screen. This problem gave rise to adding additional symbols to indicate emotions, called *emoticons*, in the form of happy, sad, surprised, and all kinds of facial expressions. In other words, we often need emotional signals along with the words to get messages right.

**a. Facial expressions.** Facial expressions are a major source of nonverbal communication. Originally, it was thought that people's emotional facial expressions were nearly identical anywhere in the world (Ekman, 1992, 1994) (a smiling face is a happy face, a tense face is not; a turned-up and turned-away nose indicates disgust, and wide-open eyes and mouth with raised eyebrows say that person is surprised). But current research indicates that like human languages, there can be cultural differences or regional "accents" in facial expressions (Elfenbein, 2013; Marsh, Elfenbein, & Ambady, 2003). Additional research, by Dr. Lisa Barrett and colleagues (2011), demonstrates that accurate interpretations of facial expressions of emotion depend upon the context in which they occur. For example, looking at a person's face whose mouth is wide open in a scream, with head tilted back and eyes looking upward, does not tell you whether the person is screaming in fear or in happiness after winning an important sports game! The point is, we can "read" other people's faces for information about their emotions, but more accurately if we know the context of their verbal messages.

**b. Head and hand movements.** How we move our head and hands often provides added signals of what a person is thinking or what they feel. As examples, in the United States, we nod our head up and down for "Yes," shake it sideways for "No," tilt it to one side as if to ask a question, raise our eyebrows to show skepticism, and roll our eyes in impatience or disbelief. We cross our fingers for good luck, bump fists for a greeting or pump them in the air as a sign of success, and flip up a middle finger in an age-old sign of insult and contempt. A raised and shaking clenched fist means "Watch out!" while an open, waving hand is a friendly greeting. We shrug our shoulders to signal "I don't know" or "whatever!" Our thumb can go down for a "no good" rejection and up for "everything's fine" acceptance. Yet in France, a thumbs-up means the number one. In the United States, using your thumb and forefinger to form a circle means "okay," but in Brazil it is a vulgar sign of complete contempt!

**c. Body postures.** Humans share with other animals using body posture or movements to send specific messages. A stiff-legged and stiff-tailed dog, or fox, or bear with lips drawn back and teeth showing is sending a clear hostile message of either attack or defense. A deer, buffalo, or ox with head lowered and stamping forefeet is signaling warnings before a charge. A skunk scratching the ground and turning its rump toward us is telling us to get away quickly or we'll be sprayed and stink like we'll never forget! These messages are quite clear. For humans, many of our body postures or movements can convey clear nonverbal information about intense emotions (Aviezer, Trope, & Todorov, 2012). However, for less tense emotions, apparently they are not as clear as culturally accepted hand and head movements or the animal postures described above. We may cross our arms or legs, sit back or lean forward, clasp and unclasp our hands, or let them hang loosely. What they mean will depend upon the context in which they are expressed.

Most single body gestures seen alone are not good indicators of any hidden meaning. Often, they must be in a special context or situation before they can be interpreted with some accuracy. A person standing alone while looking at flowers with arms folded across their chest may find that's just a relaxing position for their arms. However, stiffly standing sideways in front of a person without a smile and deliberately crossing the arms can communicate distrust and intentional psychological distance from them. On the positive side, we can stand near and directly in front of a person with legs slightly apart and fold our arms in a relaxed manner. Also, if we lean toward the other person while standing quietly, smiling and listening intently, and our eyes are on them while we both are smiling, indicates respect and interest in what they have to say. If we move near them, even touching them, and the other person accepts our touch, it indicates warmth, closeness, and accessibility. To summarize, attempting to interpret meanings from head, hands, and body movements is another method we try to use to increase accuracy in our judgments of others so that we can reduce uncertainly in understanding their communications with us.

**d. Needing Our Own Space.** According to anthropologist Dr. Edward Hall (1966), surrounding each of us is a very flexible privacy zone called our **personal space** that varies with our age, gender, cultural background, social status, relationship, and personality. These variables determine how physically *proximal*, or near, any person gets to us. Dr. Hall coined the term *proxemics* (prox-**ee**-mix) as the study of *nearness* of people to each other in different cultures.

Depending upon how formal and different two people are in social status, this distance can range from people actually touching us to standing *approximately* 12 feet away. However, most of our relationships with our general friends and coworkers take place approximately a handshake distance away from each other (Myers, 2002). Typically, once we are within four feet of another person, we are inside a person's *personal space*, where our family and close friends are usually allowed. Culturally, personal space can differ dramatically. North Americans and north Europeans maintain wider personal space than do southern Europeans, Mediterraneans, and Asians (Baron & Byrne, 2000). In Turkey, men approach women more closely than women do other men (Kaya & Erkip, 1999). As a gender, women approach other women more closely than men approach other men. In some Middle Eastern cultures, strangers communicate face-to-face close enough to smell the breath of the other person. How comfortable would this arrangement be to us? Look at the adjacent *Perspective* for an example of private space intrusion.

There are circumstances where unwanted closeness is unavoidable and personal space is violated. This happens to people all the time in crowded streets, elevators, buses, subway cars, and hallways. In circumstances with strangers, people usually can be observed to *act* as if they are alone, with eyes turned away or looking straight ahead or down. They will barely respond to the unknown person next to them, even though their bodies may be touching. If any casual comment is made, most often it is made in general or to someone separated from that person by the bodies of others. In these ways, in crowds, a person's *personal space* is maintained psychologically.

**e. Multiple communication channels.** By now, it ought to be clear to us that our conversations with others involve our whole body, from slight head nods or adjustments to total body movements. When we want our listener to hear with accuracy, we use anything available to us emotionally and physically to make certain that our message is received by them. Other than face-to-face personally or by video programs such as Skype, until we have means to add the richness of nonverbal signals when texting or e-mailing, we must understand that the meanings we want to share in our electronic messages may not be as complete as we might want them to be.

# REFERENCES

Aviezer, H., Trope, Y., & Todorov, A. (2012). Body cues, not facial expressions, discriminate between intense positive and negative emotions. *Science, 338* (6111), 1225–1229.

Baron, R. A., & Byrne, D. (2000). *Social psychology: Understanding human interaction* (9th ed.). Boston: Allyn & Bacon.

Barrett, L. F., Mesquita, B., & Gendron, M. (2011). Context in emotion perception. *Current Directions in Psychological Science, 30,* 286–290.

Ekman, P. (1992). An argument for basic emotions. *Cognition and Emotion, 6,* 169–200.

Ekman, P. (1994). Strong evidence for universals in facial expression: A reply to Russell's mistaken critique. *Psychological Bulletin, 115,* 268–287.

Elfenbein, H. A. (2013). Nonverbal dialects and accents in facial expressions of emotion. *Emotion Review, 5* 12, 90–96.

Hall, E. T. (1966). *The hidden dimension.* Garden City, NY: Doubleday.

Kaya, N., & Erkip, F. (1999). Invasion of personal space under the condition of short-term crowding: A case study on an automatic teller machine. *Journal of Environmental Psychology, 19* (2), 183–189.

Marsh, A. A., Elfenbein, H. A., & Ambady, N. (2003). Nonverbal "accents": Cultural differences in facial expressions of emotion. *Psychological Science, 14* (4), 373–375.

McDermott, R. (1980). Profile: Ray L. Birdwhistell. *Kinesics Report, 2* (3), 1–16.

Myers, D. G. (2002). *Social psychology* (5th ed.). New York: McGraw-Hill.

Onsager, M. (2014). Understanding the importance of non-verbal communication. *Body Language Dictionary.* New York.

Robert, H. M. (2011). *Robert's rules of order newly revised* (11th ed.). Cambridge, MA: Perseus Books Group.

# EDITORS' INTRODUCTION

As you now understand, communication is a layered process. In intimate relationships, we must consider an additional layer of communication: touch. In the next reading, "Louder Than Words," Rick Chillot discusses how we communicate via touch and how adept we are at interpreting messages communicated through touch, without even knowing it. As the famous family therapist Virginia Satir, stated, "We need 4 hugs a day for survival. We need 8 hugs a day for maintenance. We need 12 hugs a day for growth." In fact, a hug or touch that lasts at least 6 seconds activates the limbic system in our brain to release oxytocin (the cuddle hormone), and vasopressin (the bonding hormone). Touch literally and figuratively connects us with our world, and we're healthier because of it.

## PRIMER

1. How long do you think you hug your loved ones? Think about the last time you hugged a family member, friend, and/or romantic partner. Your challenge next time you hug a loved one is to hold on for 6 seconds. At first it may feel like a long time, but hold on! That hug will cause each of you to feel closer and could even make you laugh as it gets more awkward to hold on!

# Louder Than Words

*By Rick Chillot*

Touch is the first sense we acquire and the secret weapon in many a successful relationship. Here's how to regain fluency in your first language.

You're in a crowded subway car on a Tuesday morning, or perhaps on a city bus. Still-sleepy commuters, lulled by vibrations, remain hushed, yet silently broadcast their thoughts.

A toddler in his stroller looks warily at his fellow passengers, brows stitched with concern. He turns to Mom for reassurance, reaching out a small hand. She quietly takes it, squeezes, and releases. He relaxes, smiles, turns away—then back to Mom. She takes his hand again: squeeze and release. • A twenty-something in a skirt and blazer sits stiffly, a leather-bound portfolio on her lap. She repeatedly pushes a few blonde wisps off her face, then touches her neck, her subconscious movements both revealing and relieving her anxiety about her 9 a.m. interview. • A couple propped against a pole shares messages of affection; she rubs his arms with her hands, he nuzzles his face in her hair. • A middle-aged woman, squished into a corner, assuredly bumps the young man beside her with some elbow and hip. The message is clear; he instantly adjusts to make room.

Probing our ability to communicate nonverbally is hardly a new psychological tack; researchers have long documented the complex emotions and desires that our posture, motions, and expressions reveal. Yet until recently, the idea that people can impart and interpret emotional content via another nonverbal modality—touch—seemed iffy, even to researchers, such as DePauw University psychologist Matthew Hertenstein, who study it. In 2009, he demonstrated that we have an innate ability to decode emotions via touch alone. In a series of studies, Hertenstein had volunteers attempt to communicate a list of emotions to a blindfolded stranger solely through touch. Many participants were apprehensive about the experiment. "This is a touch-phobic society," he says. "We're not used to touching strangers, or even our friends, necessarily."

But touch they did—it was, after all, for science. The results suggest that for all our caution about touching, we come equipped with an ability to send and receive emotional signals solely by doing so. Participants communicated eight distinct emotions—anger, fear, disgust, love, gratitude, sympathy, happiness, and sadness—with accuracy rates as high as 78 percent. "I was surprised," Hertenstein admits. "I thought the accuracy would be at chance level," about 25 percent.

Previous studies by Hertenstein and others have produced similar findings abroad, including in Spain (where people were better at comminicating via touch than in America) and the U.K. Research has also been conducted in Pakistan and Turkey. "Everywhere we've studied this, people seem able to do it," he says.

| Figure 6.2.1

Indeed, we appear to be wired to interpret the touch of our fellow humans. A study providing evidence of this ability was published in 2012 by a team who used fMRI scans to measure brain activation in people being touched. The subjects, all heterosexual males, were shown a video of a man or a woman who was purportedly touching them on the leg. Unsurprisingly, subjects rated the experience of male touch as less pleasant. Brain scans revealed that a part of the brain called the primary somatosensory cortex responded more sharply to a woman's touch than to a man's. But here's the twist: The videos were fake. It was *always* a woman touching the subjects.

The results were startling, because the primary somatosensory cortex had been thought to encode only basic qualities of touch, such as smoothness or pressure. That its activity varied depending on whom subjects believed was touching them suggests that the emotional and social components of touch are all but inseparable from physical sensations. "When you're being touched by another person, your brain isn't set up to give you the objective qualities of that touch," says study coauthor Michael Spezio, a psychologist at Scripps College. "The entire experience is affected by your social evaluation of the person touching you."

If touch is a language, it seems we instinctively know how to use it. But apparently it's a skill we take for granted. When asked about it, the subjects in Hertenstein's studies consistently underestimated their ability to communicate via touch—even while their actions suggested that touch may in fact be more versatile than voice, facial expression, and other modalities for expressing emotion.

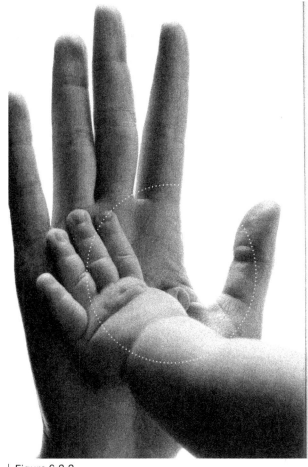

| Figure 6.2.2

A mother's touch can mitigate pain when babies are given a blood test. Infant massage has also been linked to better sleep and increased sociability—as well as increased growth of premature babies.

"With the face and voice, in general we can identify just one or two positive signals that are not confused with each other," says Hertenstein. For example, joy is the only positive emotion that has been reliably decoded in studies of the face. Meanwhile, his research shows that touch can communicate *multiple* positive emotions: joy, love, gratitude, and sympathy. Scientists used to believe touching was simply a means of enhancing messages signaled through speech or body language, "but it seems instead that touch is a much more nuanced, sophisticated, and precise way to communicate emotions," Hertenstein says.

It may also increase the speed of communication: "If you're close enough to touch, it's often the easiest way to signal something," says Laura Guerrero, coauthor of *Close Encounters: Communication in Relationships*, who researches nonverbal and emotional communication at

Arizona State University. This immediacy is particularly noteworthy when it comes to bonding. "We feel more connected to someone if they touch us," Guerrero notes.

There's no phrase book to translate the language of touch; if anything, experts have barely begun documenting its grammar and vocabulary. "We found that there are many different ways to indicate a given emotion through touch," Hertenstein notes. What's more, how a touch gets interpreted is very context dependent. "Whether we're at the doctor's office or in a nightclub plays a huge role in how the brain responds to the same type of contact," Spezio explains. Still, examining some of the notable ways that we communicate and bond through touch (and how we develop the capacity to do so) reveals the versatility of this tool and suggests ways to make better use of it. There's much to be gained from embracing our tactile sense—in particular, more positive interactions and a deeper sense of connection with others.

## LEARNING THE LANGUAGE OF TOUCH

We begin receiving tactile signals even before birth, as the vibration of our mother's heartbeat is amplified by amniotic fluid. No wonder then that touch plays a critical role in parent-child relationships from the start: "It's an essential channel of communication with caregivers for a child," says San Diego State University School of Communication emeritus professor Peter Andersen, author of *Nonverbal Communication: Forms and Functions.*

A mother's touch enhances attachment between mother and child; it can signify security ("You're safe; I'm here") and, depending on the type of touch, it can generate positive or negative emotions. (Playing pat-a-cake makes infants happy, while a sudden squeeze from Mom often signals a warning not to interact with a new object). Mom's touch even seems to mitigate pain when infants are given a blood test. University of Miami School of Medicine's Tiffany Field, director of the Touch Research Institute, has linked touch, in the form of massage, to a slew of benefits, including better sleep, reduced irritability, and increased sociability among infants—as well as improved growth of preemies.

We're never touched as much as when we're children, which is when our comfort level with physical contact, and with physical closeness in general (what scientists call proxemics), develops. "The fact that there's a lot of cultural variation in comfort with touch suggests it's predominantly learned," Andersen says.

Warm climates tend to produce cultures that are more liberal about touching than colder regions (think Greeks versus Germans, or Southern hospitality versus New England stoicism). There are a number of hypotheses as to why, including the fact that a higher ambient temperature increases the availability of skin ("It pays to touch somebody if there's skin showing or they're wearing light clothing through which they can feel the touch," Andersen says); the effect of

# SURFACE IMPACT

## The Physical Sensations of Objects We Touch Influence Our More Abstract Feelings.

IT'S NOT JUST the physical contact we make with other people that produces unexpected reverberations in our psyches. "How our physical body interacts with the world is fundamentally connected to our thinking," says Josh Ackerman, an evolutionary psychologist at MIT's Sloan School of Management. The idea that our physical selves shape our psychological selves, known as embodied cognition, has been a popular subject of research in recent years.

For example, a 2010 study by Ackerman and colleagues revealed that the physical qualities of objects people touched—their hardness or softness, heaviness or lightness, roughness or smoothness—tilted people's judgments toward those same abstract qualities. So folks holding a heavy clipboard were more likely to judge someone as serious; touching a rough texture was linked to judgments of harshness. Sitting in a hard wooden chair seemed to make people more rigid in a negotiation. A 2008 study by one of Ackerman's coauthors, Yale University psychologist John Bargh, found that holding a hot drink makes people rate strangers as warmer—more caring and generous—while another of his studies, published in 2011 in *Emotion*, revealed that the feeling of loneliness can be mitigated by an experience of physical warmth (holding a warm pack).

Such translation of touch sensations into abstract qualities offers a glimpse into how the physical sensations we experience early in life become a kind of mental scaffold that supports more metaphorical thinking as we grow older. We build abstract concepts on top of the physical ones (for example, our concept of a "rough" or "coarse" personality is based on our understanding of tactile roughness). That connection between physical sensation and abstract concept remains, so experiencing the former triggers the latter.

Does that mean that you should avoid sitting in a soft chair at the car dealership? Or use heavier stock for your business cards, or take a hot shower when you're home alone on a Saturday night and feeling low? Yes and no, says Ackerman. Like a magic trick, the phenomenon works only if you're not aware of what's really happening. "If you pay attention to the fact that you're touching something hard or heavy, your mind will overrule it," he explains. So taking note of the comfy chair as you settle down to negotiate your car loan should undo the tendency to become a softer negotiator. And your firm handshake might convince an interviewer that you're a strong, substantial candidate ... unless it occurs to him that you're trying to make a good impression with that strong grip. —*RC* sunlight on mood ("It increases affiliativeness and libidinousness—lack of sunlight can make us depressed, with fewer interactions"); and migratory patterns ("Our ancestors tended to migrate to the same climate zone they came from. The upper Midwest is heavily German and Scandinavian, while Spaniards and Italians went to Mexico and Brazil. That influences the brand of touch").

What goes on in your home also plays a role. Andersen notes that atheists and agnostics touch more than religious types, "probably because religions often teach that some kinds of touch are inappropriate or sinful." Tolerance for touch isn't set in stone, however. Spend time in a different culture, or even with touchyfeely friends, and your attitude toward touch can change.

By the time we're adults, most of us have learned that touching tends to raise the stakes, particularly when it comes to a sense of connectivity. Even fleeting contact with a stranger

## WHAT YOUR SKIN REVEALS

**The Skin is a Rich Source of Information About What We're Thinking and Feeling-No Touch Required. By Joe Navarro**

THE SKIN RESPONDS to emotions very quickly. When we lovingly care for someone, our skin, which is very vascular, responds through vasodilation, which makes the skin feel warm, soft, and pliable. The warmth can often be detected, even without touching, when we are in close proximity to those who truly care for us. This change is also why we can tell when a kiss is indifferent (cold, rigid) or heavenly (warm, soft, tender).

In social settings, the skin flushes when a person becomes flummoxed or embarrassed, or has been caught doing something he shouldn't. In a forensic setting, sweat communicates a great deal—it can tip off investigators that they have hit a hot issue during an interview. Though inconclusive evidence of deception, it may indicate guilty knowledge or worse. Similarly, a suspect may pull clothing away from the skin at the neck, shoulders, or front of the shirt when something is bothering her and her skin suddenly becomes warm from stress due to fear or apprehension.

In reaction to strong negative emotions, threats, or danger, the body sends blood to larger muscles in case they are needed for running or fighting. This withdrawal of blood causes the skin to feel cold—and may also cause goose bumps to appear. The skin can also drain of color (turn gray, ashen, and pale) when a person is in shock or suddenly receives bad news, which gives us immediate insight into what is going on inside his or her mind, often more accurately than the spoken word could.

can have a measurable effect, both fostering and enhancing cooperation. In research done back in 1976, clerks at a university library returned library cards to students either with or without briefly touching the student's hand. Student interviews revealed that those who'd been touched evaluated the clerk and the library more favorably. The effect held even when students hadn't noticed the touch.

More recent studies have found that seemingly insignificant touches yield bigger tips for waitresses, that people shop and buy more if they're touched by a store greeter, and that strangers are more likely to help someone if a touch accompanies the request. Call it the human touch, a brief reminder that we are, at our core, social animals. "Lots of times in these studies people don't even remember bein touched. They just feel there's a connection, they feel that they like that person more," Guerrero says.

Just how strong is touch's bonding benefit? To find out, a team led by University of Illinois at Urbana-Champaign psychologist Michael Kraus tracked physical contact between teammates during NBA games (consider all those chest bumps, high fives, and backslaps). The study revealed that the more oncourt touching there was early in the season, the more successful teams and individuals were by season's end. The effect of touch was independent of salary or performance, eliminating the possibility that players touch more if they're more skilled or better compensated.

"We were very surprised. Touch predicted performance across all the NBA teams," says Kraus. "Basketball players sometimes don't have time to say an encouraging word to a teammate; instead, they developed this incredible repertoire of touch to communicate

| Figure 6.2.3

quickly and accurately," he explains, adding that touch can likely improve performance across any cooperative context. As with our primate relatives, who strengthen social bonds by grooming each other, in humans, "touch strengthens relationships and is a marker of closeness," he says. "It increases cooperation but is also an indicator of how strong bonds are between people."

If a post-rebound slap on the back or the brush of a hand while delivering a bill can help us all get along a bit better, it maybe because "when you stimulate the pressure receptors in the skin, you lower stress hormones," says the Touch Research Institute's Field. At the same time, warm touch stimulates release of the "cuddle hormone," oxytocin, which enhances a sense of trust and attachment.

| Figure 6.2.4

The release also helps explain our propensity for self-caressing, which we do hundreds of times each day as a calming mechanism. "We do a lot of self-touching flipping our hair, hugging ourselves," Field notes. Other common behaviors include massaging our foreheads, rubbing our hands, or stroking our necks. Evidence supports the idea that it's effective: Self-massage has been shown to slow the heart rate and lower the level of the stress hormone cortisol.

## A TOUCH OF LOVE

Every evening at bedtime, DePauw's Hertenstein gives his young son a back rub. "It's a bonding opportunity for the two of us. Oxytocin levels go up, heart rates go down, all these wonderful things that you can't see." Moments like these also reveal the reciprocal nature of touch, he says: "You can't touch without being touched. A lot of those same beneficial physiological consequences happen to me, the person doing the touching."

In fact, when we're the ones initiating contact, we may reap all the same benefits as those we're touching. For example, Field's research has revealed that a person giving a massage experiences as great a reduction in stress hormones as the person on the receiving end. "Studies have shown that a person giving a hug gets just as much benefit as a person being hugged," she adds.

Moreover, touching another person isn't just a one-way street when it comes to signaling; aside from sending them a message, it reveals a great of deal information about their state of mind, Hertenstein notes. Are they open to touch or do they pull away? Are they relaxed or tense? Are they warm—or perhaps cold and clammy? "Sometimes I'll touch my wife and can tell instantly—even if my eyes are closed—that she's stressed," he says. "You can sense that through muscle tightness and contraction, and this kind of information can guide our behavior with that person—it influences what we think, how we perceive what they say."

Perhaps because touch affects both the person being touched and the one doing the touching, it is one of the most fundamental ways of fostering and communicating intimacy in a romantic relationship. One paper proposed a sequence of 12 behaviors of increasing intimacy that couples generally follow: After the first three (eye-to-body contact, eye-to-eye contact, and speaking), the remaining nine involve touching (starting with holding hands, then kissing, and eventually sexual intimacy). "Touch functions a bit differently depending on the stage of the relationship," says Guerrero. "In the beginning it's kind of exploratory. Will the other person reciprocate if I touch?" As the relationship progresses, touching begins to spike. "You see lots of public touch," she notes, "people holding hands the whole time they're together or with their arms around each other's shoulders. It signals they're intensifying the relationship."

But it would be a mistake to think that the amount of touching couples do continues to follow an escalating trajectory. Research involving observation of couples in public and analysis of their self-reports shows that the amount of touching rises at the beginning of a relationship, peaks somewhere early in a marriage, and then tapers off. Over time romantic partners adjust the amount of touching they do, up or downshifting their behavior to move closer to their significant other's habits. Inability to converge on a common comfort zone tends to derail a relationship early on, while among couples in long-term marriages, touching reaches an almost one-to-one ratio.

While couples who are satisfied with each other do tend to touch more, the true indicator of a healthy long-term bond is not how often your partner touches you but how often he or she touches you in *response* to your touch. "The stronger the reciprocity, the more likely someone is to report emotional intimacy and satisfaction with the relationship," Guerrero says. As with many things in relationships, satisfaction is as much about what we do for our partner as about what we're getting.

## THE LAWS OF SOCIAL CONTACT

The most important things we reveal through touch: "probably our degree of dominance and our degree of intimacy," Andersen says. Take, for example, the handshake, one of the few situations in which it's OK to make prolonged contact with a stranger. As such, it's an important opportunity for sending a message about yourself. "A limp handshake signifies uncertainty, low enthusiasm, introversion," Andersen says, while a viselike grip can be taken as a sign that you're trying to dominate. "You want to have a firm but not bone-crushing handshake," he advises, since it's better to be perceived as overly warm than as a cold fish. "We like people to have a kind of medium-high level of warmth," Andersen says. "A person who touches a lot says, 'I'm a friendly, intimate person.' More touch oriented doctors, teachers, and managers get higher ratings."

> Over time people adjust the amount of touching they do to move closer to their significant other's habits. Among couples in long-term marriages, touching reaches an almost one-to-one ratio.

Still, outside of close relationships, the consequences of sending the wrong message also increase. "Touchy people are taking some risk that they might be perceived as being over-the-top or harassing," says Andersen. "Physical contact can be creepy; it can be threatening." Context matters, which is why we have rules about whom we can touch, where, and when. "Generally, from the shoulder down to the hand are the only acceptable areas for touch," at least between casual acquaintances, according to Andersen. "The back is very low in nerve endings, so that's OK too."

Of course, there are other contextual considerations as well. Different cultures and individuals have different tolerance levels for touch. Same-sex and opposite-sex touches have different implications. Then there's the quality of the touch, the duration, the intensity, the circumstances. "It's a complex matrix," Andersen says. A quick touch and release—like a tap on a cubicle mate's shoulder to get her attention—no problem. But a stroke on the shoulder could be easily misinterpreted. ("Most cases of sexual harassment involve stroking touches," notes Andersen.)

A touch will naturally seem more intimate if it is accompanied by other signals, such as a prolonged gaze, or if it is held an instant too long. Meanwhile, a squeeze on the arm could be a sign of sympathy or support, but if it doesn't end quickly and is accompanied by intense eye contact, it can come across as a squeeze of aggression. Environment changes things too: On the playing field, a man might feel comfortable giving his teammate a pat on the butt for a job well done, but that congratulatory gesture wouldn't do too well in the office.

Really, the only rule that ensures communicating by touch won't get you into trouble is this: Don't do it. Which is likely what it says in the employee handbook for your workplace. Still, leaving your humanity behind every time you leave home isn't very appealing. Andersen's slightly less stringent guidelines for touch: Outside of your closest relationships, stick to the safe zones of shoulders and arms (handshakes, high fives, backslaps), and in the office, it's always better for a subordinate, rather than a superior or manager, to initiate.

If there's a *most* appropriate time to communicate via touch, it's probably when someone needs consoling. "Research shows that touch is the best way to comfort," says Guerrero. "If you ask people how they'd comfort someone in a given situation, they tend to list pats, hugs, and different kinds of touch behaviors more than anything else. Even opposite-sex friends, for example, who usually don't touch a lot so they won't send the wrong signals, won't worry about being misinterpreted," she says.

Maybe that's because there are times—during intense grief or fear, but also in ecstatic moments of joy or love—when only the language of touch can fully express what we feel.

# EDITORS' INTRODUCTION

Beyond the visible, audible, and tactile messages that we use to communicate are the emotional cues that we send and receive. Related to this method of communication are John Gottman's four horsemen of the apocalypse (Lisitsa, 2013). The four horsemen of the apocalypse (criticism, contempt, stonewalling, and defensiveness), said to be the best predictors of relationship distress and failure, are described. After each horseman, we've provided the antidote, or specific skill and practice that can protect a couple's relationship from ultimate dissolution. Practicing the antidotes regularly, and not just as an alternative to the horsemen, will significantly improve your communication.

**Horseman #1**—*Criticism*: Degrading your partner's actions as a reflection of their personality. For example, "You are such a slob!"

> **Antidote:** *Gentle (or softened) start-up.* Use an "I" statement to specifically identify the behavior that your partner exhibits and ask for a specific alternative. For example, "I am upset that you left your clothes on the floor. Will you please pick up your clothes and put them in the hamper?"

**Horseman #2**—*Contempt*: Using a tone of voice or actions that shame or denigrate your partner's character. The intent behind this form of communication is insult and injury. Contempt typically includes sarcasm and/or eye rolling and communicates that "I am better than you." For example, "What, did you just *forget* you had a boyfriend when you *decided* to miss our date?"

> **Antidote:** *Creating a culture of appreciation.* Give your partner the benefit of the doubt; consider a positive attribution for their behavior, and identify what you appreciate about them. Avoid sarcasm and make mutual respect an agreed-on requirement of your relationship.

**Horseman #3**—*Stonewalling*: Shutting down communication in order to avoid conflict. This often looks like leaving the room during a disagreement, ignoring the issue, or denying that there is a problem. The cause of stonewalling is usually "flooding," which happens when we are overwhelmed and dysregulated during a conflict or at the threat of conflict.

**Antidote:** *Self-soothing.* In order to stay present during a disagreement, take deep breaths to calm the nervous system, take breaks (with a commitment to return to the conversation), and/or communicate that you're feeling flooded and need to calm down so you can stay engaged. More on self-soothing will come in Chapter 7.

**Horseman #4**—*Defensiveness*: Denying your partner's position on an issue and turning the blame to them. For example, when your partner confronts you for being late, you respond, "Well, at least I didn't completely forget your birthday!"

**Antidote:** *Accepting responsibility.* Acknowledge your behavior, admit that you were wrong, and apologize. See the end-of-chapter reflections for a recipe for a good apology.

# THE FOUR HORSEMEN
## AND HOW TO STOP THEM WITH THEIR ANTIDOTES

| | |
|---|---|
| **Criticism**<br>Verbally attacking personality or character. | **Gentle start up**<br>Talk about your feelings using "I" statements and express a positive need. |
| **Contempt**<br>Attacking sense of self with an intent to insult or abuse. | **Build culture of appreciation**<br>Remind yourself of your partner's positive qualities and find gratitude for positive actions. |
| **Stonewalling**<br>Withdrawing to avoid conflict and convey disapproval, distance, and separation. | **Physiological self-soothing**<br>Take a break and spend that time doing something soothing and distracting. |
| **Defensiveness**<br>Victimizing yourself to ward off a perceived attack and reverse the blame. | **Take responsibility**<br>Accept your partner's perspective and offer an apology for any wrongdoing. |

| Figure 6.1  The four horsemen.

In the following reading, Daniel Beaver discusses how using "I messages" can help partners express their needs and wants and have a better chance of getting the response they want from their partners. Owning your perspective and giving your partner an opportunity to own theirs is an invaluable skill in effective communication. Keep the four horsemen in mind (Figure 6.1) as you read "Intimate Communications: Letting Your Mate Know Who You Are," by Daniel Beaver. Beaver writes to married couples, but keep in mind that the strategies he discusses are relevant to many forms of intimate relationships.

## PRIMER

1. Do you notice any of the four horsemen showing up in your relationships? Think of a specific time that you used criticism, contempt, stonewalling, or defensiveness in your relationship and make a plan to do something differently next time. Draw on the antidotes to the four horsemen to execute your plan.

## CREDITS

# Intimate Communications

Letting Your Mate Know Who You Are

*By Daniel Beaver*

As a marriage counselor, I'm in the business of helping people to improve their relationships with their mates. But just passing out psychological theory does not produce much change, I've found. Real change occurs only when people learn specific ways to integrate the concepts I discuss with them into their day-to-day experiences with their marriage partners.

*Intimate communication* is the term I use to describe what husbands and wives do when they tell each other about themselves—about their deepest emotions, their fears, and their most personal wants or needs. Many people come into counseling believing that they communicate well, but most of them say they don't. And even many of those who believe that they communicate well discover that their communications are not, in the final analysis, either personal or intimate. They have good conversations and they have intellectual discussions about their kids, their parents, their friends, or the political scene. But problems arise for them when they start talking about themselves. In the beginning of their relationships, these people may have been able to communicate intimately with their partners, expressing their feelings and personal secrets, their dreams and aspirations. But somewhere in the course of their marriage, perhaps as they had to confront the various personal conflicts normal to marriage, their intimate communication system broke down. As a result, they began to avoid personal subjects and talk about things outside of the intimate sphere.

Nowhere in our culture are we taught how to communicate intimately. Most people of our parents' generation talked together only when they were outside the range of their children's hearing. Or they yelled at each other. So a newly married couple often has little or no experience in effective and intimate communication. They certainly didn't have a class on communication in high school or college. Somehow we've all gotten the idea that if two people are in love, they will just naturally get along well with each other. "Why should you have to teach marriage partners how to talk to each other? They can work it out on their own. They don't need any help," the popular myth seems to say.

The communication of emotions is the primary way we let ourselves be vulnerable to our mates. The way an emotion is communicated and the degree to which it is expressed by a couple generally shows how vulnerable and intimate two people are with each other. But people are generally not comfortable with intimate communication. For example, what would probably happen if someone asked me how I was doing, and I replied, "I'm feeling lonely and afraid"? Most likely, the person who had asked how I was would be so surprised he or she wouldn't know what to say. This would not necessarily mean thati person was uncaring or indifferent to my feelings, but he or she is probably not accustomed to that level of intimacy in everyday communication. To be sure, I'm not advocating that people open themselves up to the point that they tell everyone they meet how they're really feeling. Most of the time social cordialities, though superficial, serve our needs very well. But in marriage, where feelings are so important, intimate communication is essential.

## ACTING OUT EMOTIONS

Often people try to communicate their feelings nonverbally. Examples of nonverbal communication are when a person slams a door, or mopes around the house, or paces back and forth, or sits in a chair and sighs a lot. This person is trying to communicate his or her emotions through behavior, through sounds and body language.

How do you know, for certain what people are thinking or feeling when they express themselves in these ways? The truth is that it is impossible to know exactly what another person is feeling unless he or she tells you. When your spouse slams a door and sits down in a chair with his or her back to you, refusing to speak, it would be reasonable to assume that he or she is angry, frustrated, or hurt. I use the word *assume* advisedly, because in nonverbal communication, the would-be listener must interpret the other person's behavior—and this can lead to real trouble.

Let us say that a husband assumes his wife is angry with him because she is acting grumpy and doesn't want to talk to him. Rather than deal with the matter now, he decides to leave her alone until she feels better. After leaving her alone all day, he discovers that she wasn't angry with him at all. Instead, she was angry at a friend of hers. But now she is mad at him, too, because he seemed indifferent to her troubles. When you act as if your assumptions are facts, you set yourself up to be an ass or a fool. An easy way to remember this concept is to take apart the word *assumes* and sees what it stands for: ASS-U-ME—that is, an ass out of you and me.

There's nothing wrong with two partners making assumptions during the *process* of intimate communication. You might guess at what's troubling your spouse and then ask if that's what he or she is feeling. But to avoid making an "ass" of yourself, you must check out the validity of your assumption with the person about whom you are making that assumption. For example:

> "I have the feeling that you are angry with me. Is that true?" "No, I'm not angry with you; I'm just feeling hurt and disappointed that my mother didn't call." Or the same person might have said, "Yes, I'm angry with you for leaving the house in such a mess."

In the first response, the assumption turned out to be false or invalid, so it should be thrown out. However, the second response indicates that the assumption is valid, and there is no misunderstanding. Assumptions in communication become a problem only when they are acted on automatically as if they were facts.

People who act out their emotions rather than communicating them verbally not only leave their communications open to wrong assumptions, but also prevent intimacy from developing in their relationships. When people act out their emotions, they are not being vulnerable or open to their spouses. How can they be vulnerable if they haven't opened up and taken the risk necessary to verbalize their emotions for their spouses to hear? To put it mildly, it is hard to be intimate with someone who is just sitting in a chair and *acting* angry or sad, but not saying a word.

## DUMPING EMOTIONS

Another way people project emotion without communicating is through a verbal style called "dumping." Although words are involved, dumping prevents intimacy just as acting out in the nonverbal style does. It goes something like this:

"John, how many times have I told you not to leave your clothes all over the place? You really shouldn't do that because you set such a poor example for the kids. You are so sloppy. I don't know how I live with you. I always have to tell you about it, and you never seem to understand. Please listen to me. I'm just trying to be honest with you and tell you how I feel."

Most likely this woman is feeling hurt, angry, maybe even frustrated, but we can only *assume* that these are her feelings. There is no way to tell, from what she said, how she is actually feeling. However, had you been on the receiving end of the above monologue, you would probably feel angry or hurt. Few adults like to be talked to in this manner, especially not by someone they love. How do people on the receiving end express their feelings of hurt and anger? Usually they take one of two paths. They may react defensively with anger and aggression. For example, John might say to his wife, "You are not so neat yourself. You leave clothes all over the place, too. So who are you to judge?" The person on the receiving end of this response will probably become defensive, too, and launch a counterattack. Generally, this form of Communication—attack/defend—escalate in volume and intensity until neither one can hear what the other is saying. Then they usually reach a certain point of frustration, quit yelling, and finally fall into sulking. Nothing is resolved. Neither of them has been able to communicate their feelings, and now both of them feel miserable. Have they become closer or more intimate? On the contrary, the gap between them has probably been widened. Some couples take hours to cool off after such encounters, some take days, and often there are residual feelings of anger, frustration, or pain that inhibit intimacy for months.

A second common way that people respond after receiving such an attack is by withdrawing completely from the interaction. They may just "clam up" or they may literally "stalk off" to get away from the situation. Whatever path of withdrawal the person takes, the message is the same: "I'm not listening to you when you talk like that!" The person who launched the original attack then becomes increasingly angry because his or her emotions are not being acknowledged, and because the person with whom they wished to communicate obviously isn't listening. Both partners end up feeling ignored and hurt, often unaware of the mechanism that precipitated their alienation from one another.

## YOU MESSAGES: CREATING AN ADVERSARY

Sentences that begin with the word *you* should tip a person off to the fact that he or she is being dumped on. For example, phrases such as "you should," or "you always," or "you never, you dummy," or any variation on this theme are *you* messages. Go back to the communication theme given earlier about the sloppy husband and see how many *you* messages there are. The entire example is a series of *you* messages. Many books that deal with parent-child communication talk about *you* messages as being a poor form of communication even when talking to children. Believe me; they are just as ineffective with adults.

The reason that *you* messages are not effective is that the people using them are not disclosing any of their emotions. They are not taking responsibility for their feelings. They are unable to express what it is that they feel. Instead, they "dump" their emotions in a barrage of accusations, orders, complaints, and judgments. The person who communicates through the use of *you* messages tells you all about yourself—what you should do, what you never do or always do, but they don't tell you about themselves, for that would make them vulnerable.

## "I" MESSAGE: THE ART OF INTIMATE VERBALIZATION

"I" messages are sentences that start with the pronoun I. Three types of "I" messages are of particular importance to us here: "I feel," "I want," and "I need." These are the key phrases in effective, intimate communication.

Using "I" messages, a person might say, "*I feel* angry when all these clothes are left on the floor," or "*I feel* disappointed and sad when you cancel out at the last minute," or "*I feel* excited when you invite me out to dinner," or "*I feel* hurt when you make cracks about the way I look." All these statements start with the phrase "I feel," followed by the words that describe your *emotion*. There can be variations, such as the addition of adverbs, or you might even leave out the word *feel* and just say, for example, "*I appreciates* it when you clean up after yourself."

When a husband communicates his emotions through "I" messages, he is opening up and becoming vulnerable. He is taking responsibility for how he feels by telling exactly the emotions he is feeling. His wife needn't *assume* how her husband feels because he has told her what he feels. He is giving her intimate information about himself, information that he probably doesn't share with many people. He is giving her a chance to know him in an intimate way—but he is also taking a risk. The feelings he makes known might be judged by her, or she might reject him when she learns about his feelings, and this, obviously, could hurt. This is the basic fear of becoming vulnerable. An example of a rejection response to an "I" message might be the following exchange between a husband and his wife.

"I'm feeling really afraid of going to that party tonight, honey."

"Well, you shouldn't be afraid. You're just acting silly. So get dressed and let's go!" If the husband who is afraid of going to the party gets this kind of response, he might not only feel afraid, he may also feel *hurt*. Following the hurt may come anger at being judged and put down about the way he feels. He will probably either become defensive or withdraw into silence from the interaction.

The fear of being hurt is the main reason people avoid putting themselves in a vulnerable position. The problem with people letting this fear run their lives is that it prevents their enjoying intimacy with their mates. Their relationships remain superficial However, when they choose to take a risk and become vulnerable, then they are giving their relationships a chance to become close and intimate. If a person continually gets hurt, then he or she may want to reconsider seriously whether or not he or she wants to stay in the relationship, or, at least, stay in it in any intimate way. When a spouse becomes vulnerable in a marriage, the worst that can happen is that he or she may find that intimacy has no chance. On the other hand, if neither partner takes the risk in becoming vulnerable, intimacy may never become possible.

Sometimes people misunderstand how to use "I" messages. Here are some examples you should try to avoid: "I just want to be open and honest with you and tell you how I feel I really feel you are inconsiderate of me and my feelings" or "I feel you should go to the store," or "I feel like the rules should change," or "I feel that you should call me when you go out." A close examination of these statements quickly reveals that they are not true "I" messages, but only sentences onto which the phrase, "I feel," has been tacked. In reality, they are *you* messages. Remember, an "I" message describes a feeling experienced by the speaker. Have you ever *experienced* the emotions "you," or "that," or "like"? Of course not. What the person in the first example is saying is, "I think you are inconsiderate of me." This person may—in fact, probably does—feels something (angry, sad, etc.) about the behavior he or she may feel shows inconsideration, but has not said yet how he or she feels. Expressing what they think, rather than what they feel, is a common way that people hide their emotions from their partners. It is a lot safer, emotionally, to stay "in your head" than to express the emotions that involves your entire being.

Another valuable "I" message for building intimate communication begins with the phrase, "I want." But what were most of us taught about stating what we wanted as children? Most people were told again and again how *selfish* they were when they asked for things for themselves. In essence, we were taught not to talk about what we *want*. Younger children who have not yet learned this lesson have no trouble taking responsibility for what they want. They will tell their parents, "I want an ice cream cone," or "I want to go home" or "I want to go outside." Their parents don't have to guess or make assumptions-the children themselves are very clear about what they want. If there is a problem in this, it is not in the asking but in the *expectation;* children fully expect to get what they want simply because they've asked for it. And when they don't get what they want they may feel angry or hurt, unable to understand why anything must stand in the way of their complete satisfaction.

What I am suggesting is that you express what you want in the same clear, direct manner you used as a child, but without the hook that most children put at the end—that is, without the expectation that just because you ask for something, you are going to get it. That expectation is selfish, aggressive, demanding, and inconsiderate of the wants or needs of the person you love. Expressing what you want in an intimate relationship without selfish expectation is a responsible way of taking care of yourself. You assert your wants *in hopes* that you will get them, putting them out on the table for negotiation.

In my work, I have heard people argue against communicating what they want in the clear, direct ways I advise. The argument is a common one that is based on myths embedded in our society's marriage fantasy. The argument runs something like this: "If I have to tell you what I want, then it just isn't worth it! If you don't know by now what I want, then who have you been living with anyway? Besides, if I tell you what I want, then you are just doing it because I asked. I want you to do things for me without me having to ask." This myth would work if we were all psychics with powerful abilities to read minds—but obviously we are not. People who insist that their partners develop mind-reading skills generally end up feeling misunderstood, frustrated, and hurt. They don't get what they want. They only get what their partners *assume*—there's that word again—they want.

If a person has expressed clearly what he or she wants, and that person's partner agrees to give what is asked for, then there should be no need for the want to be expressed over and over again. If he or she must keep asking for what he or she wants, then either that person's partner didn't understand the request or there is some other emotional problem that needs to be solved in this relationship.

Many married people are afraid to express what they want because they fear conflict. No matter how much they're in love, people are never carbon copies of each other. Because they are different, they are not always going to want the same things their partners want. For example, one may want to go out to dinner, while the other wants to eat at home. One may want to make love, while the other wants to go to sleep. Conflicts of this kind are normal in marriage, and learning to deal effectively with this fact can be as rewarding as it is difficult. One common but destructive belief is the notion that a couple that does not have conflicts has a good marriage. The truth of the matter is that I have seen hundreds of these couples, all of them seeking solutions to their "invisible" problems.

What I have learned is that the classic, smoothly running marriage—the "model" marriage—usually involves two very insecure people. All too often, one discovers in such marriages a man and a woman who are afraid of confrontation and their own feelings of anger. When potential conflicts arise between them, one or both may avoid the situation by "selling themselves out" and deferring to the other's wants rather than expressing their own wants. They are seldom aware that, in the long run, they are setting up their marriage for failure. Here's an example of an exchange between the two partners in such a marriage:

"What do you want to do tonight, dear?"
"Oh, whatever you want to do."
"Well, I want to do whatever you want to do!"

Here is a case where neither husband nor wife wants to take responsibility for what they want. Another exchange might run as follows: He says, "I want to go to the football game this weekend," and even though his wife hates football, she says, "Oh, sure, that sounds great. Whatever *you* would like, honey." This wife is "selling out." What does *she* really want? Perhaps she is hiding the fact that she wants to go to Carmel for the weekend. Only she doesn't express this want because she prefers to avoid a fight.

This lack of assertiveness is a major problem in many marriages. When people give in, when they try to be *nice* in an intimate relationship and don't tell each other what they really want, they're ultimately hurting themselves as well as the relationship. If they don't express what they want, they are not going to get it. And after a period of not getting what they want, they are going to feel hurt and resentful toward their spouses. This is the point when people begin to resent being married. For the moment, it may seem very nice to be living together without conflict or hassle, but in the long run, when one or both partners begin to cash in on their past-due resentments, the emotional price tag for all this "niceness" is revealed.

Everything described thus far has been based on the assumption that both people in the marriage have things they want. But what if they don't want anything? Or what if they really have no preference? Then none of this applies. Resentment will not develop because the person with no preferences is not selling out. Even if both people in a relationship express what they want, they may still have difficulty communicating their wants clearly. Many people express their wants in such vague, nebulous ways that only they themselves can understand what they want. Examples of this type of "I want" statement are: "I want you to be more romantic"; "I want to be understood"; "I want respect"; "I want more love." All these "I" messages sound good, but they are all much too broad, far too open to interpretation. The last of these example statements may be stereotypical, but it serves to illustrate a good point. The wife says to her husband, "I want more love. I don't feel you really care for me." The husband replies, "Here's my paycheck. Go buy yourself some new clothes." His wife retorts, "That's not what I want. I want you to love me." The husband reacts defensively: "Look, I worked hard to get you this big house and that swimming pool and your new car. If that's not love, then I don't know what you want." In a way, he's telling the truth: he really *doesn't* know what she wants. And there is no way for him to know unless she tells him *exactly* what he can do to demonstrate his love. He thinks he is expressing his love by giving her things. She doesn't see it that way, because, to her, love is expressed in another way. It is as if they're using two different languages, each foreign to the other. The longer they communicate, the more frustrated, hurt, and disappointed both people become. They may decide not to express what they want at all, because "It's just not worth it."

Another example of the same problem, but one with some possibility for resolution of the frustration, occurred during a marriage counseling session I had with a young couple. It went like this: The husband said to his wife "I want you to show me more respect." I interrupted and said, "What's one thing she could *do* that would show you her respect?" He turned to her and replied, "Stop putting me down in front of our children." The message was clear. The wife now had a specific line of action to take. In his first, rather unclear, request, the husband left much to the imagination. In the second request, there could be no room for assumption. His wife had been asked to show respect, and now she knew one sure way to show it.

When you express what you want, "paint a picture" so that the person who is in a position to fill that need can see exactly what you want. You greatly increase your chances of getting what you want when you're "I" message is clear and specific. A "1 want: message is like a verbal prescription for curing the ill that's troubling you. Many people communicate what they don't like about their partner's behavior, but seldom do they express what they *want*—that is, they never tell their spouses how to improve the situation. You are letting yourself be vulnerable to your partner when you allow him or her to understand what you want from the relationship and from life in general.

## "I NEED" IS DIFFERENT THAN "I WANT"

We should draw a distinction here between wants and *needs.* Needs are trust, sex, respect, companionship, and intimate communication. The difference between needs and wants is that *needs* are not negotiable. They have to be met. Wants, however, are negotiable. What I *need* never changes, but what I *want* may change from moment to moment.

The statement is often made, particularly in reference to marriage, that one person cannot meet all the needs of another person. This statement is true—but only up to a point. What it fails to mention is what *types* of needs are being discussed. People have certain core or "universal" needs that have to be met. Such needs are prerequisites for the continuance of any loving relationship. People generally feel resentment and pain when even one of these needs goes unmet, even for a relatively short period of time. But needs differ. One person may have a long list of needs, whereas another may have only one need—for example, emotional or financial security. That one need may suffice for that person, even when no other needs are being met.

Sometimes needs can, or even *must,* be met by some one outside the marriage. For example, in my own case, I need physical activities and certain intellectual pursuits. I has a need for tennis or skiing, but my wife doesn't have to participate in these activities in order for us to stay together. I go to professional workshops and programs to satisfy my need to stay intellectually stimulated in my field, but I don't need my wife to do these things with me. I can get these needs met with a friend or a colleague. It would be *nice* if she sometimes did these things with me, but it isn't necessary that she participate in these activities to make me happy with our marriage.

When people are unclear about their needs, I advise them to ask themselves this question: "If I were single again tomorrow, what would be my personal needs from an emotional point of view?" Once people become clear about their specific needs, their next step must be to communicate these needs and the ways in which they can be satisfied by their spouses.

## EXERCISE NO 2: "I" MESSAGES

**Purposes** To develop skills expressing and listening to "I" messages.

**Preparations** Make room for one hour of uninterrupted time with your mate. make room for one hour of uninterrupted time with your mate.

**Exercises** Sit facing each other. You will be taking turns expressing and listening. When you are the listener, do not interrupt your mate except to ask for clarification. While doing this exercise, do not argue, debate, or discuss any of the issues being raised. Listen as though you were an objective third person and do not have to do anything about the information you are receiving.

When you are the speaker, begin each of your statements with the pronoun I and express each of the following points to your mate:

1. *Appreciation:* Tell your mate one thing that you appreciate about him or her. Focus on a single feature of your mate's personality or behavior. It can be a small thing or a large one—that doesn't matter as much as being clear about what you feel and expressing your feelings in the I context.

2. *Resentment:* Tell your mate about one thing in his or her behavior that you resent. Be specific. Be clear. Be brief and focus on a single source of resentment. Begin each statement you make with the pronoun I.

3. *Want or Need:* Tell your mate about one thing you want or need from him or her. Describe a single specific action that he or she might take to satisfy this want or need.

Now reverse roles so that the listener becomes the speaker and the speaker becomes the listener.

You may repeat this exercise as many times as you wish, trading roles back and forth until one of you wants to stop.

After both partners have completed this exercise, do not further discuss the issues raised here. Although you may have strong feelings about some of the information communicated, bear in mind that you are not *required* to do anything about it, nor should you expect an immediate change in your mate's behavior because of what you have expressed here. You are not being ordered to change in the way that your parents or teachers may have done when you were not a child, nor are you assuming a parental role and ordering your spouse to change. Instead, you are exchanging information about what you and your mate feel you want from each other. What you finally choose to do with this information is entirely up to you.

Remember that asking does not guarantee that you will get what you want. Asking only *informs* the other person of your wants. Similarly, when others inform you of what they want, you are not obligated to fulfill their wants. There are no guarantees here.

## END-OF-CHAPTER REFLECTIONS

Learning how to accept responsibility and apologize in any relationship is hard. Knowing how to apologize when you've done something you regret is a skill in and of itself. Following is a recipe for a good apology (Lazare, 2004). Take a moment to think of something you need to apologize for and put the following steps into practice. Practice is the key here. Work through the steps a few times and then decide if/when/how you want to deliver your apology.

Recipe for a good apology:

1. Acknowledge what you did that was wrong.

2. Accept responsibility for your behavior.

3. Express genuine remorse.

4. Offer reparations (if possible).

5. Promise better behavior in the future.

## REFERENCES

Lazare, A. (2004). *On apology.* Oxford.

Lisitsa, E. (2013, April 23). *The four horsemen: Criticism, contempt, defensiveness, and stonewalling.* The Gottman Institute. https://www.gottman.com/blog/the-four-horsemen-recognizing-criticism-contempt-defensiveness-and-stonewalling/

## RECOMMENDATIONS FOR FURTHER READING

The Gottman Institute (www.gottman.com) has a variety of healthy relationship resources available, some for free, on their website. Some of our favorites are the free card deck apps, available through Google Play and iTunes. There are also a series of informative blogs available, as well as many other practical tools to add to your relationship toolkit.

Greenberg, M. (2016, March 30). The science of love and attachment. *Psychology Today.* https://www.psychologytoday.com/us/blog/the-mindful-self-express/201603/the-science-love-and-attachment

Haber, R. (2002). Virginia Satir: An integrated humanistic approach. *Contemporary Family Therapy, 24*(1), 23–34.

Wiley, A. R. (2007). Connecting as a couple: Communication skills for healthy relationships. *The Forum for Family and Consumer Issues, 12*(1), 1–10. https://www.theforumjournal.org/wp-content/uploads/2018/05/Connecting-as-a-couple.pdf

# Chapter 7

# Mastering Difficult Conversations

## EDITORS' INTRODUCTION

We've often had clients tell us, "I wish my partner was a better communicator," or "How can my relationship change if I'm the only one in counseling?" In an ideal world, couples would come to counseling together and both partners would learn and practice the skills we introduced in Chapter 6. Unfortunately, we don't live in an ideal world. What we do know is that the way that you enter a difficult conversation, or any conversation for that matter, influences the outcome. Are you wanting to be heard? To be understood? To reach an agreement? This chapter is intended to help you navigate and eventually master difficult conversations. We begin with "Basics of Emotional Intelligence," by Lynda McDermott. McDermott discusses emotional intelligence (EI) as it pertains to success in the world of business, but in fact emotional intelligence applies to all of the interpersonal interactions you will have throughout your life. Not only does EI help you navigate relationships, but it helps you recognize and manage your emotions so that you move through the world feeling grounded and self-aware.

The truth is, something actually happens in our brains when we're triggered by people, especially those we care about. Dan Siegel states that we literally "lose our minds" when this happens, preventing us from responding to an upsetting situation in a rational way. There are nine prefrontal (front of the brain, directly behind your forehead) functions that can become compromised when we're upset, and these are also considered key elements of emotional well-being (Siegel, 2011):

1. Bodily regulation
2. Attuned communication
3. Emotional balance

4. Response flexibility

5. Fear modulation

6. Empathy

7. Insight

8. Moral awareness

9. Intuition

It would be unreasonable to expect that we maintain all of these functions in all situations. That said, there are ways that we can learn to achieve balance and "mindsight" (Seigel, 2011) in our everyday interactions, so that our brain doesn't get high-jacked in stressful situations. McDermott discusses several of these strategies.

McDermott closes by discussing emotionally intelligent teams in a work environment. We encourage you to also think about the concept of an emotionally intelligent team as your relationship (friendship, romantic relationship, family, etc.). The analogy "the whole is greater than the sum of its parts" is relevant here; let's shift our focus to the success of our relationships, and not whether we are right or wrong. The goal—a solid relationship—is likely to be a greater gain than the result of one (or many) difficult conversation(s).

As you read, keep in mind the following "primer" questions for reflection. If you feel so inclined, take a few minutes and consider your responses to the following questions before you read, and then again after you've read the chapter.

## PRIMER

1. Think of a situation when you were overwhelmed by emotions and unable to respond the way you would have liked to. For example, maybe a friend said something that hurt your feelings, or a parent brought up an issue from the past that pushed your buttons. Make a list of what was actually happening in your body when this happened. For example, did you notice your heart beating faster? Did you feel tingling in your body? Did you start breathing faster? Did your palms get sweaty? These are just some examples of physiological responses we can have to stressful situations. Keep your list handy as you read and imagine what skills you could apply to calm your body so that your mind can do the work next time.

# Basics of Emotional Intelligence

*By Lynda C. McDermott*

## WHAT IS EI?

We all know a story about someone who was exceptionally intelligent, but who could not make big career strides because he or she lacked good "people skills." We probably also know of someone who is not particularly intellectually gifted but who progressively rose to top-level positions. How do you explain one person's failure and another's success? IQ? Past experiences? Expertise? Perseverance? Political skills? Research from the last two decades suggests that the most successful performers in organizations are alike in one critical way—they all have *emotional intelligence (EI)*.

It is a commonly held belief that employees should leave their emotions outside the workplace. "Don't be so emotional" and "Don't take it personally" are phrases often used by bosses or colleagues with a co-worker who is visibly upset over a situation at work. However, in the last 20 years there has been much research to suggest that emotions are a natural part of the brain's decision-making process and should not be disregarded.

In the early 1990s, psychologists Peter Salovey and Jack Mayer were the first to propose that individuals differ in their abilities to perceive, understand, and use their emotions. They labeled this ability *emotional intelligence.*

The concept of applying emotional intelligence in the workplace was later popularized by the work of Daniel Goleman in his books *Emotional Intelligence* (1995) and *Working with Emotional Intelligence* (1998). Goleman was interested in understanding the EI competencies that support superior work performance.

There continues to be some disagreement between academic researchers (such as John Mayer and Peter Salovey) and practitioners (such as Daniel Goleman and Reuven Bar-On) about what competencies should be included in a definition of emotional intelligence.

This *Infoline* does not focus on any one person's definition of emotional intelligence; rather it uses an amalgam of thoughts and ideas.

While there are varying emotional intelligence definitions and models that have been developed over the years, we are defining it as: *Our capacity to recognize our own feelings and those of others and to manage emotions in ourselves and others.*

Emotional intelligence competencies include

- self-awareness
- self-regulation
- motivation
- social awareness
- social skills.

For more detailed descriptions of the competencies, see the sidebar *Emotional Intelligence Competency Definitions.*

This *Infoline* is designed for anyone looking to understand the basics of emotional intelligence with an eye toward improving their abilities. It is also useful for a trainer or coach who wants to develop the emotional intelligence of others. You will learn how

- emotional intelligence is related to work performance
- our brains govern emotional intelligence
- to assess your own and others' emotional intelligence
- to develop emotional intelligence competencies
- to assess and develop a team's emotional intelligence.

## The Value of Emotional Intelligence

Many people believe emotional intelligence simply means "being nice" or employing "touchy-feely" management. This is a narrow view. Emotional intelligence is really about understanding yourself and relating to others.

Anyone who wants to ascend the ranks in their organization will have to deal with more and more people. When moving into a leadership position, managing relationships with others is easily as important as planning a budget. Emotional intelligence contributes to other managerial talents such as managing conflict and negotiating.

Even if you do not want to take on a managerial position, research from the last two decades suggests possessing and applying emotional intelligence competencies has a positive impact on job performance. Who doesn't want to work better with their colleagues?

## Important EI Findings

Daniel Goleman and countless other researchers have analyzed data from hundreds of organizations across a range of job positions. Here are some of the important findings:

- Emotional competencies are much more important in contributing to work excellence than pure intellect and expertise.

- Emotional intelligence competencies provide a competitive edge for those who want to climb the organizational ladder because they contribute 80 to 90 percent of the competencies that distinguish outstanding leaders from average ones.

- The most successful global companies are run by leaders who display attitudes that include self-confidence, self-control, achievement-orientation, empathy, and teamwork—all components of emotional intelligence.

- Higher degrees of emotional intelligence contribute to the "bottom-line," whether you are a partner in a multinational consulting firm or a cosmetics sales agent.

- Executives who "derail" are often seen as lacking *emotional strength*. They were unwilling to hear and see the reality of a situation and then move to constructively deal with it.

- When it comes to emotional intelligence, both genders appear to have it in relatively equal measurements, although women seem to have significantly stronger interpersonal skills and men appear to have a stronger sense of self.

The bad news is that our own current state of emotional intelligence has been hard-wired as a result of our brain's development and socialization. The good news is that emotional competencies can be developed.

## Why We Get Emotional

Our emotional intelligence is a function of the interconnections between the neural systems that are responsible for the intellect and those that are responsible for the emotions. Our emotional brain circuitry runs from the prefrontal area to the amygdala, located on either side of the mid-brain. This limbic area of the brain, in moments of high emotion such as anxiety, frustration, or fear is actually stronger than the rest of the brain and can, in fact, "hijack" our ability to reason and problem-solve.

While the amygdala is watching out for signs of danger, the prefrontal lobes have the ability to keep the amygdala's urges restrained so that our response in potentially threatening situations is more measured and skillful. The challenge is to "catch" the amygdala before it overrides the prefrontal lobes.

Being emotionally intelligent involves two sets of competencies: personal and social. Each competency has its own skills and behaviors. Knowing these competencies is crucial to understanding and building emotional intelligence.

## Personal Competence (Self)

These skills are focused on you and how well you know yourself.

- **Self-Awareness**

Knowing one's internal states, preferences, resources, and intuitions. This is the foundational skill of emotional intelligence.

- Emotional Awareness: Recognizing one's emotions and their effects.
- Accurate Self-Assessment: Knowing one's strengths and limits.
- Self-Confidence: Having a strong sense of one's self-worth and capabilities.

- **Self-Regulation**

Managing one's internal states, impulses, and resources.

- Self-Control: Keeping disruptive emotions and impulses in check.
- Trustworthiness: Maintaining standards of honesty and integrity.
- Conscientiousness: Taking responsibility for personal performance.
- Adaptability: Having flexibility in handling change.
- Innovation: Being comfortable with novel ideas, approaches, and new information.

- **Motivation**

Understanding emotional tendencies that guide or facilitate reaching goals.

- Achievement Drive: Striving to improve or meet a standard of excellence.
- Commitment: Aligning with the goals of the group or organization.
- Initiative: Being ready to act on opportunities.
- Optimism: Having persistence in pursuing goals despite obstacles and setbacks.

## Social Competence (Others)

These skills are focused on how well you interact with and understand other people.

■ **Social Awareness**

Being aware of others' feelings, needs, and concerns.

- Empathy: Having an active interest in others and demonstrating that you care.
- Understanding Others: Sensing others' feelings, perspectives, and concerns.
- Developing Others: Sensing others' development needs and bolstering their abilities.
- Service Orientation: Anticipating, recognizing, and meeting customers' needs.
- Leveraging Diversity: Cultivating opportunities through different kinds of people.
- Political Awareness: Reading a group's emotional currents and power relationships.

■ **Social Skills**

Being looked upon favorably by others.

- Influence: Wielding effective tactics for persuasion.
- Communication: Listening openly and sending convincing messages.
- Conflict Management: Negotiating and resolving disagreements.
- Leadership: Inspiring and guiding individuals or groups.
- Change Catalyst: Initiating or managing change.
- Building Bonds: Nurturing instrumental relationships.
- Collaboration and Cooperation: Working with others toward shared goals.
- Team Capabilities: Creating group synergy.

## Bruce's Emotional Outburst

Let's look at an example of how our emotions can overtake our brain and cause us to act irrationally.

Meet Bruce, a mid-level manager at a software company. Bruce was furious. His boss caught him off-guard in a meeting with high-level executives by questioning a decision about the product launch that was made several years earlier, when Bruce was a newly appointed team leader. His boss had not been with the company at that time.

Bruce's immediate reaction was to verbally "attack" his boss by angrily replying: "It's easy for people who weren't around then to second-guess things today. You don't have a clue about what the competition was doing to us back then." The rest of the people attending the meeting were shocked by Bruce's outburst.

Bruce was surprised by his boss's question and angry that he hadn't been asked about the product's history earlier instead of getting put on the spot. Bruce felt threatened by his boss's question, and his emotional brain undermined the workings of his intellectual brain. Bruce's amygdala, a limbic brain structure that is on constant alert for danger, commandeered the other parts of Bruce's brain, including rational centers in the neocortex, for an immediate reaction to the perceived threat.

In essence Bruce's amygdala "hijacked" the rest of his brain and caused him to "snap" instead of allowing the prefrontal area to veto his emotional impulse and respond more effectively.

If Bruce had a more well-developed capacity for self-control under stressful situations, he might have taken the spotlight off of himself and calmed down by asking his boss a question. For example, what part of the product launch decision was his boss most interested in hearing about. Then Bruce would have been able to more effectively respond to his boss's specific question with the facts and not with his emotions.

## Control Your Emotions

Learning to control our emotions at work or at home is important because:

- Negative emotions—especially chronic anger or deep-seated frustration erode your mental abilities and confidence.

- Emotional distress not only impedes work performance, but also interferes with your ability to read others' emotions accurately, and negatively influences your interpersonal and social skills.

Therefore, one of the first steps in building your overall EI competence is to become more aware of your emotions—being able to describe them at any point in time and to understand their source.

The next step is to move beyond understanding to being able to execute self-control in order to modify your responses to situations so they are more appropriate and effective.

For more information, see the sidebar *Manage Your Emotions*.

# MANAGE YOUR EMOTIONS

Learning to properly manage your emotions is one of the first steps to improving your emotional intelligence. Anger and anxiety are two of the most common emotions. Authors Jeff Feldman and Karl Mulle offer the following advice to cope with these powerful feelings.

## Manage Anger

- **Practice postponing your anger response for small increments of time**—Eventually, you will be able to postpone indefinitely and choose your response.

- **Find the triggers**—Identify the situations and circumstances that tend to trigger your anger response and manage those situations.

- **Mix pleasantness with anger**—Just as oil doesn't mix with water, anger doesn't mix with feelings of pleasantness. This is a behavioral strategy. To manage your anger, do something that makes you feel good.

- **Reframe your anger**—Anger is often a signal to ask yourself the question: What is actually beneath my anger? The primary emotions that tend to drive anger are fear, deep concern, worry, guilt, and hurt. When you use your self-awareness to connect with your primary emotions, you are actually managing your anger by *reframing* it as one of these primary emotions.

- **Choose your battles carefully**—There are things in life that are worth spending your anger energy on, but you have to separate them from the things that are trivial. When you feel angry, your amydgala is not always drawing a clear distinction between a real injustice and a trivial offense.

## Manage Anxiety

- **Ask anxiety inventory questions**—Anxiety is an emotion that will tend to narrow your field of perception by making it difficult for you to see what is going on and what your choices are. We often get paralyzed by anxiety because we can't come up with a good answer to a question like, "What do I do?" Instead, we can ask:

  — What is going on here?

  — What's the worst thing that could happen?

  — How likely is it?

  — Is it in or out of my control?

  — Is there anything I can do?

- **Recognize the irrationality of worry**—Much of the time we spend worrying is unproductive, because worry does not actually accomplish anything. It has been estimated that only 10 percent of what we spend our energy worrying about is actually within our control. Focus your worry energy on the things that you can control that are important.

- **Resist using worry as a tool to manipulate others**—Worry can be used as a way to get other people to do what you want them to do. Parents do this all the time with children. A child is expected not to climb a tree because the parent is worried about the potential for an injury. The child complies, not because of understanding the safety issues, but because the child does not want the parent to worry. The parent is unwittingly teaching the child to be manipulated by emotion instead of teaching the child to think about what is or isn't responsible behavior.

*From Jeff Feldman and Karl Mulle's,* Put Emotional Intelligence to Work, *ASTD Press, 2007.*

[...]

## Develop EI Competencies

It's true that some people are just born with more emotional intelligence than others. But everyone can build their EI competencies. If fact, there are some data that show emotional intelligence actually improves as we age—it's called *maturity*. But people often resist hearing that they may need to develop more emotional intelligence because emotional intelligence is linked so closely to identity. No one wants to be told that his or her behavior is wrong.

### Don't Take It Personally

The interactive habits we have developed over time have contributed to our own perceptions of our success, and we may expect others to just "live with it." When someone suggests that we need to learn to control our temper or to be less blunt in our feedback to others, they are calling into question habits and behaviors that not only define part of who we are, but also what others have come to expect from interacting with us.

To really improve emotional intelligence, you must first learn to not take feedback personally. No matter how exceptional someone's emotional intelligence, we all have faults that can be worked on.

### Find Motivation to Improve

Finding the proper motivation helps drive the desire to improve emotional intelligence. Your motivation may be to

- increase your effectiveness in working with others
- increase your potential for promotion
- achieve more fulfilling personal relationships
- improve a bad performance review.

If someone has been scalded by feedback from a boss or significant other or is motivated by threats or a fear of loss, the motivation to change will probably not be sustainable.

The key to motivation is appealing to a person's "hot buttons." The four primary motivators for change are

- money
- power
- status
- popularity.

What motivates you?

If you are looking to drive change in a group of others, find out what motivates each individual. Change motivated by what someone will gain has a much higher chance of being sustained.

## Rehearse Your Reactions

One important EI development strategy for overcoming old behavioral habits is to engage in mental rehearsals. This is a process imagining a better way of acting in real-life settings. By cueing up the situation and imagining behaving in a different and more productive way, the prefrontal cortex of the brain becomes acutely focused on these new patterns. Without that practiced new response, a person will act out old and potentially unproductive routines.

For example, before a meeting with colleagues or more senior executives, Bruce (the team leader who had a confrontation with his boss) could imagine someone saying something that might call into question his capabilities, which would lead to him feel upset. By mentally rehearsing for a confrontation, Bruce prepares himself to deliver a more measured response.

Rehearse your own reactions, and take the following steps when faced with a confrontation:

- Use active listening in order to understand the true nature of the statement or question being asked.
- Ask clarifying questions.
- Don't interrupt while the other person is talking.

- Try to be objective and not defensive by trying to understand the other person's point of view.

## Positive Visioning

Thinking through how to handle situations that have been problematic in the past greatly improves your ability to learn new skills. For years, sports coaches have used this strategy of "positive visioning" with athletes to help them imagine competing successfully. The brain cells used to mentally practice something are the same brain cells that are used during an actual situation, so the mental practice serves to strengthen the brain connections.

### Enlist a Buddy

You may enlist a coach or "buddy" at work to observe your behavior and provide real-time feedback. Regardless of the type of activity, if you are committing to experimentation with new behaviors, you need to find a way to get feedback from others about the progress you are making.

Your EI buddy doesn't have to be a friend. In fact, it is often better to have a buddy that you are not connected to emotionally. If you are too friendly with your chosen "coach," he or she may be reluctant to give constructive feedback and may just tell you what you want to hear. You should look for someone with whom you interact on a daily basis and whom you trust to give you honest, direct, and timely feedback.

### Overcome Relapses

Remember, working on your emotional intelligence is particularly difficult because it involves modifying your ingrained behaviors. Having a relapse is common. It's important to not get discouraged and to remain focused on your goals. Keep trying, and you will continually improve as relapses grow less and less common.

---

**AN EI SUCCESS STORY**

While attending an off-site leadership development program, Barbara received feedback from an EI coach that indicated that there was a significant "gap" between how she saw herself and how others perceived her behavior at work. More specifically, others saw her as "too opinionated" and "not a good listener." She was also seen as extremely competitive with her co-workers.

Understandably, Barbara was devastated by the assessment and initially reacted defensively. However, working with the coach, she began to understand how she had developed this leadership profile over the years and, frankly, how it had helped her move up the career ladder

---

in tough environments where that type of behavior was rewarded. What she came to understand, however, was that if she wanted to continue to advance she needed to develop her ability to empathize with others and develop her ability to influence and not just "command" others.

Barbara enlisted the help of her EI coach to develop a learning action plan to improve her skills. She knew she needed to practice paying attention to others' feelings and needs. She also needed to watch the impact of her own behavior on those around her. She took the opportunity to learn more about different ways to influence others.

In her role, Barbara was in constant contact with direct reports, peers, and customers so that she had many opportunities to practice new behaviors and ways of interacting. She also enlisted the help of a trusted colleague whom she could bounce ideas off of and who would give her straight feedback on how she was progressing.

In a three-month period, the EI coach solicited feedback for Barbara from her direct reports and peers, who reported that they had seen a real effort on Barbara's part to change her behavior—not, without "relapses." They appreciated her commitment and expected to see her continued progress. After six months, her boss gave her a performance review that favorably reflected her sustained progress.

Barbara, herself, reported that her interactions at work were considerably less stressful and that she was getting more projects completed with more cooperation from others. The positive results she was getting were reinforcing her work effort at building her emotional intelligence.

See the sidebar, *An EI Success Story,* which describes one woman's journey to improve her emotional intelligence.

## Why Training Fails

Unfortunately for those of us in the training and development field, training programs designed to teach a broad array of EI skills have a minimum amount of long-term impact. Some of the reasons why these general, one-size-fits-all EI training programs don't work are:

- The learners sent to these programs may not be motivated to learn and change.

- Most training programs appeal to the neocortex area of the brain, which is effective in learning technical or analytical skills or for comprehending concepts—not changing behavior.

- Emotional intelligence improvement requires reshaping behavioral habits learned early in one's life that have grown in strength over time. It is not sufficient to teach the rational definitions of emotional intelligence in a one-day program or even to give examples of how others use emotional intelligence successfully at work. Optimizing the limbic areas of the brain requires thoughtfulness, practice, and continuous feedback.

So then, how do you train and coach for emotional intelligence? As we indicated earlier, you have to start with finding a motivated learner. The most effective training and coaching methodologies for developing EI competencies rely on

- individuals deciding what and how they will change
- experiential learning that comes through role play, group discussion, and simulation
- continuous practice in order to reprogram neural circuits that lead to sustainable changes in habitual patterns of thinking, feeling, and behaving (this is not unlike what it takes to unlearn specific elements of a bad golf swing and replace them with minor changes in stance or hand placement that can make a difference in several golf strokes).

See the job aid, *Emotional Intelligence Development Plan,* at the end of this *Infoline* for help designing an emotional intelligence learning plan for yourself or others.

### EI As a Liability

Can you have too much emotional intelligence? Probably not. But there might be a danger in overdoing an EI asset to the point that it stops being an asset and becomes a liability.

For example, if you are too empathetic you may be hesitant to fire anyone. If you are too achievement focused you may constantly change strategies to beat the competition and lose focus. And interestingly enough, although self-awareness is seen as the foundation for emotional intelligence, an overly critical focus on one's self can lead to reduced self-esteem.

## Emotionally Intelligent Teams

In the last few decades organizations have placed a greater emphasis on creating teams to make decisions and collaborate on work projects. The assumption is that group synergy creates better decisions and work products than any one talented individual. However, this assumes that the team is truly able to elicit the best ideas of its members and coalesce around decisions and deliverables.

There is evidence throughout the workplace that some groups never achieve this vision of high performance because they cannot manage the dynamics of unproductive arguing, interpersonal competition, and power politics. Essentially, a team of people performs better than individuals only when they exhibit what we have come to define as *emotionally intelligent team behavior.*

While there has been extensive research on how emotional intelligence is directly critical to an individual's effectiveness at work, there has been less research on how the collective emotional intelligence of people who work together can actually improve team performance. We cannot assume that a collection of highly emotionally intelligent people will, by definition, become a highly effective team. Team dynamics, themselves, create an identity for a team that is unique and requires its own type of self-awareness and self-management.

The research of Vanessa Urch Druskat and Steve Wolff has identified that three conditions are essential for a team's effectiveness:

- trust among team members
- a sense of team identity
- a sense of team efficacy.

A team can still function and achieve results if any one of these is missing, but it will not be as effective, and its members will not be as fully engaged or motivated to perform at their highest levels.

Emotional intelligence, as defined by Goleman and others, has primarily focused on personal and social competence. A team is more complex. For a team to demonstrate emotional intelligence, the team needs to be aware of and act upon

- the emotions of all of its members

## INTELLIGENT TEAMWORK

One high-performing team adopted these team norms in order to establish a team culture that was conducive to meet both the team and the team members' needs.

- Share information openly within the team and with all key stakeholders.
- When a conflict or disagreement emerges, look first for areas of agreement.
- Faced with challenges, be optimistic and proactive problem-solvers. Don't blame.
- Be advocates for the team and its goals within and outside of the team.
- Heed the maxim: If you're uncomfortable with something, speak up. If you don't agree, silence is not golden. Make proposals, if possible.
- Debate ideas. Don't attack one another.

- Listen actively and without interruption to the contributions of others.

- Have fun and celebrate success.

- When problem-solving or making decisions, respect differences in perspectives.

- Ask quieter team members to speak up and ask those more vocal to give others "air time."

- Deal directly with team members with whom you have a problem. Don't talk "behind their backs."

- Be sensitive to and supportive of one another's needs.

- Periodically assess and give feedback to the team and individuals regarding their effectiveness.

- Validate team members' contributions. Let members know they are valued.

---

- the team's own culture and climate
- the emotions toward the team coming from its stakeholders, i.e., those groups and individuals who influence the team's success.

Truly emotionally intelligent teams recognize that emotions are best not suppressed or avoided. They consciously seek out an assessment of the team's and its stakeholders' emotional perceptions and work at building effective relationships within and outside of the team.

## Building Team EI

Emotionally intelligent teams take responsibility for defining what success looks like and for behaving in ways that will ensure their success. One way that teams can begin to build their emotional intelligence is by formally establishing team norms, which are explicit expectations of the team regarding the types of behaviors that they believe will create a high-performance team culture.

For some examples of emotionally intelligent team norms, see the sidebar *Intelligent Teamwork*.

Emotionally intelligent teams also continuously monitor individual and group behaviors, to ensure they continue to be in alignment with the norms, and confront the team and its members when they are not.

Highly emotionally intelligent teams also reach outside of the team to try to understand the concerns and needs of their stakeholders and the wider organizational culture and politics. They encourage cross-pollination of ideas with others and monitor whether they are meeting stakeholder expectations.

The team leader plays a critical role in setting the tone and culture for a team, but when a team establishes and holds itself accountable for this process of "self-management," it creates a shared leadership for the team's emotional intelligence. When these core values and norms are jointly owned by the team, the team leader does not even need to be present for these habits to be put into practice.

## The EI Journey

Is emotional intelligence sufficient for leading a successful organization, creating a successful relationship, or leading a successful life?

No. It is just one component. Success is determined by the integration of all different types of intelligence: cognitive intelligence, emotional intelligence, and strategic intelligence. The most successful people have developed these capabilities to their fullest and are able to understand which EI competencies are required to be effective.

Still, emotional intelligence is unique because it directly affects how we see ourselves and how we interact with those around us. Understanding and building your emotional intelligence not only enriches your working life but your life outside of the office as well.

## REFERENCES & RESOURCES

### Articles

Charan, Ram, and Geoffrey Calvin. "Why CEOs Fail." *Fortune,* June 1999, pp. 60–75.

Cherniss, Cary, et. al. "Bringing Emotional Intelligence to the Workplace." *The Consortium for Research on Emotional Intelligence in Organizations,* 1998. www.eiconsortium.org/reports/technical_report.html.

Druskat, Vanessa Urch, and Steven B. Wolf. "Building the Emotional Intelligence of Groups." *Harvard Business Review,* March 2001, pp. 81–90.

Goleman, Daniel. "Leadership that Gets Results." *Harvard Business Review,* March 2000, pp. 78–90.

———. "What Makes a Leader?" *Harvard Business Review,* January 2004, pp. 82–91.

Kahn, Jeremy. "The World's Most Admired Companies." *Fortune,* October 1999, pp. 206–226.

Mayer, John D., and Peter Salovey. "The Intelligence of Emotional Intelligence." *Intelligence,* October 1993, pp. 433–442.

Salovey, Peter, and John D. Mayer. "Emotional Intelligence." *Imagination, Cognition and Personality,* July 1990, pp. 185–211.

### Books

Bradberry, Travis, and Jean Greaves. *The Emotional Intelligence Quick Book.* New York: Simon & Schuster, 2005.

Cherniss, Cary, and Daniel Goleman, eds. *The Emotionally Intelligent Workplace: How to Select for, Measure, and Improve Emotional Intelligence in Individuals, Groups, and Organizations.* San Francisco: Jossey-Bass, 2001.

Cherniss, Cary, and Mitchel Adler. *Promoting Emotional Intelligence in Organizations.* Alexandria, VA: ASTD, 2000.

Druskat, Vanessa Urch, Gerald Mount, and Fabio Sala. *Linking Emotional Intelligence and Performance At Work.* Mahwah, NJ: Lawrence Erlbaum Associates, 2006.

Feldman, Jeff, and Karl Mulle. *Put Emotional Intelligence to Work.* Alexandria, VA: ASTD Press, 2007.

Goleman, Daniel. *Emotional Intelligence.* New York: Bantam, 1995.

———. *Working with Emotional Intelligence.* New York: Bantam, 1998.

Goleman, Daniel, and Annie McKee Boyatzis. *Primal Leadership: Learning to Lead with Emotional Intelligence.* Boston: Harvard Business School Press, 2004.

Hughes, Marcia M., Bonita L. Patterson, and James Bradford Terrell. *Emotional Intelligence In Action: Training and Coaching Activities for Leaders and Managers.* San Francisco: Pfeiffer, 2005.

Lynn, Adele B. *The Emotional Intelligence Activity Book: 50 Activities for Promoting EQ at Work.* New York: AMACOM, 2002.

McDermott, Lynda, William Waite, and Nolan Brawley. *World Class Teams.* New York: Wiley, 1998.

## Websites

www.6seconds.org

www.eiconsortium.org

www.haygroup.com

www.mrgconsulting.com

www.talentsmart.com

Emotional intelligence measurement sites:

www.cjwolfe.com

www.eqi.mhs.com

www.essisystems.com
www.haygroup.com/TL

## JOB AID

## Select Your EI Buddy

The journey to improving your emotional intelligence (EI) can be long and frustrating. It always helps to have an informal coach or buddy to help you through difficult moments and provide you with objective feedback and pointers. This job aid is designed to help you choose who is best suited to help you along the way.

Candidate 1: _____

1. Is this person willing to help me?

   Yes        No

2. Is this person familiar with emotional intelligence competencies?

   Very Much        Somewhat        Not Much

3. Does this person have time to help me?

   Very Much        Somewhat        Not Much

4. Does this person work closely with me on a daily basis?

   Very Often        Somewhat        Not Often

5. Can this person be trusted to give me honest, candid feedback?

   Very Much        Somewhat        Not Much

Additional Comments: _____

_____

Candidate 2: _____

1. Is this person willing to help me?

   Yes        No

2. Is this person familiar with emotional intelligence competencies?

   Very Much        Somewhat        Not Much

3. Does this person have time to help me?

Very Much          Somewhat          Not Much

4. Does this person work closely with me on a daily basis?

Very Often          Somewhat          Not Often

5. Can this person be trusted to give me honest, candid feedback?

Very Much          Somewhat          Not Much

Additional Comments: _____

_____

Candidate 3: _____

1. Is this person willing to help me?

Yes          No

2. Is this person familiar with emotional intelligence competencies?

Very Much          Somewhat          Not Much

3. Does this person have time to help me?

Very Much          Somewhat          Not Much

4. Does this person work closely with me on a daily basis?

Very Often          Somewhat          Not Often

5. Can this person be trusted to give me honest, candid feedback?

Very Much          Somewhat          Not Much

Additional Comments: _____

_____

Review your choices carefully. Your ideal buddy is someone who is very familiar with emotional intelligence, works with you often and knows your behavior, has time to help, and will offer you objective feedback.

# JOB AID

## Emotional Intelligence Development Plan

This job aid outlines the steps you should take if you want to strengthen your emotional intelligence (EI). Because each individual is different, customize this plan to help you achieve your specific emotional intelligence goals. This job aid also can be used by an EI coach to help someone else develop their emotional intelligence competencies.

| Step | Description | Action | Your Plan |
|------|-------------|--------|-----------|
| Step 1 | Assess your motive and values for change. | Identify the "what's in it for me" motivator for you to commit to a change process that would improve your emotional intelligence, as well as your job performance or relationships with others. | |
| Step 2 | Obtain EI feedback. | Through some form of EI assessment (such as interviews, observation, multirater surveys, and so on), objectively identify how you are viewed by others with whom you interact. | |
| Step 3 | Balance goals of preservation and adaptation. | Identify your EI strengths and where the gaps are between how you would like to be perceived and how others observe you to be behaving today. | |
| Step 4 | Develop an EI action learning plan. | For each EI competency to be developed, identify specific behavioral goals and strategies for improvement, such as reading, formal training, coaching, and so on. | |
| Step 5 | Execute the plan. | Engage in learning and practicing activities to help you achieve your EI goals. | |
| Step 6 | Seek feedback and positive reinforcement. | Enlist the support of people who will give you feedback on your progress. | |

# EDITORS' INTRODUCTION

Ironically, one of the most important tools to effective communication, and to mastering difficult conversations, is not talking at all; it's listening. The late and great Carl Rogers (1961) taught us that the greatest gifts we can give another person are the core relationship conditions of genuineness, unconditional positive regard, and empathy (the kind of listening that communicates understanding). Rogers revolutionized the counseling and psychology fields by proposing that these core conditions were both necessary and sufficient for client growth and healing. We propose that the same is true for intimate relationships. If we hold our partners in high regard (remember the antidote to contempt from Chapter 6?), are authentic in our interactions, and listen to understand and build relationship (as opposed to respond or rebut), we are much more likely to receive what we hope for in return from our partners and also to successfully navigate a difficult conversation. John Gottman claims that more than 69% of our conflicts in an intimate relationship are unresolvable (Fulwiler, 2012), meaning that the same conflict (over money, sex, leisure time, parenting, etc.) will happen time and again in our relationships. Perpetual versus solvable problems will be covered in more detail in Chapter 8. For now, we offer some listening strategies for managing these recurring issues now, so you're better prepared to handle them later. Let's retrain our brains to listen, be curious, and seek understanding in the following reading, "Listening," by Martin Davidson.

## PRIMER

1. Think back to the last conversation you had. It could have been today, or yesterday, but make sure it's recent enough that you can recall it well. What was the purpose of the conversation? Did you have any goals that you were trying to achieve? How well do you think you listened to your partner's perspective? How well do you think they listened to you?

# Listening

*By Martin N. Davidson*

O ne of the most important skills for attaining interpersonal competence is listening. Most people think of effective listening as "active listening" in which the listener uses a series of proactive behavioral techniques to encourage another to speak. While active listening is an important technique, it is but a portion of the full listening skill set. Drawing on the work of Carl Rogers, I propose a more comprehensive model of listening that, if mastered and incorporated into one's interpersonal toolkit, leads to greater interpersonal competence and more rewarding relationships, both professional and personal.

## GOALS OF EFFECTIVE LISTENING

The specific goals of listening are best broken into short-term and long-term goals. The short-term goal, *listening to understand*, conveys a focus on the interpersonal episode in which the listening actually occurs. In this context the goal of listening is make sense of what the other person is trying to communicate. A secondary objective is to elicit the maximum amount of relevant information during that episode. In contrast, *listening to build relationship* focuses on longer-term objectives of a given interaction. Here, the goals are to encourage the exchange of information in the future, to motivate people to work effectively with us, and to lay a foundation for trust and respect in future engagements. Typically, people think of listening primarily in terms of its short-term goals. However, the greatest benefits of effective listening accrue over time.

# THE LISTENING CONTINUUM

Organizational scholars, psychologists, and counselors have developed and refined a useful model of the range of behaviors that constitute listening.[1] The model, reproduced in **Figure 7.2.1**, suggests that listening behavior ranges from highly non-engaging behaviors (labeled speaker-centered behaviors) to highly engaging behaviors (labeled listener-centered behaviors). The extremes of the continuum are so labeled because they reflect how much the listener influences and controls what is discussed, relative to the speaker. For example, when we listen in silence and simply allow the speaker to speak (an extremely speaker-centered behavior), she or he determines the topic to be "discussed." As a listener, we have no say in what issues are raised, thus the speaker controls the discourse. In contrast, when we engage in commands and threats (not an uncommon scenario in many professional settings), we are engaging in highly listener-centered behaviors. Indeed, we would hardly even consider these interactions as ones involving listening.

| | Speaker-Centered Responses |
|---|---|
| Reflective Responses | Silence |
| | Affirmations of contact (e.g., "Hm-mm") |
| | Paraphrase or Restatement |
| | Clarification |
| | Reflection of core feelings (surfacing) |
| Middle Range Responses | Interpretation |
| | Encouragement, assurance |
| | Question |
| | Confrontation |
| Directive Responses | Challenge |
| | Advice |
| | Entreatment (urge, "sell," cajole, moralize) |
| | Commands or threats |
| | Listener-Centered Response |

| Figure 7.2.1.

---

1    See A.G. Athos and J.J. Gabarro, *Interpersonal Behavior* (Englewood Cliffs, NJ: Prentice-Hall, 1978) and A. Benjamin, *The Helping Interview* (Boston: Houghton Mifflin, 1969) for examples of this line of thought.

The model groups the set of listening behaviors into three categories, each reflecting the relative level of engagement by the listener. Reflective responses are the most speaker-centered and require the least active behavior (though considerable skill is required to execute these responses). Middle-range responses require moderate levels of active engagement, and as such, limit the amount of control the speaker maintains over the topic of conversation. Finally, directive responses allow the listener to control the topic of conversation very explicitly.

## REFLECTIVE REPONSES

*Silence.* Using silence means simply not speaking. As a listening skill, this is clearly an extreme example of speaker-centered responses and must be used carefully. It is easy to cause embarrassment, confusion, or fear in the speaker when the listener uses silence exclusively. Silence is more commonly useful in conjunction with other reflective skills.

*Affirmations of Contact.* Affirmations are useful in communicating to the speaker that the listener is engaged, yet is not trying to alter the topic of conversation. In U.S. society, affirmations are typically the most reflective response that we use. It is much more socially acceptable and comfortable than complete silence. However, note that the listener can influence topics by affirming only what she or he wants to hear. Subtly, the speaker will tend to shy away from topics that are not affirmed by the listener.

*Paraphrase and Restatement.* In paraphrasing and restating the speaker's points, we use words for the first time. Here, the listener uses identical or similar language and repeats back to the speaker what the listener hears. The listener should not introduce new ideas or concepts into the exchange. Rather she or he should be a "parrot." The purpose of using paraphrasing and restating is to communicate to the speaker that he or she is being heard and understood verbally.

*Clarification.* Clarification responses are statements that reflect or reveal what is in the speaker's awareness, but are not explicitly stated. Consider a speaker who tells you a series of stories describing unsuccessful job interviews he has had:

> My first interview was with Bain and I was so nervous and answered questions so tentatively, I knew I didn't have a chance. But I figured, "Hey, it's good practice." When I interviewed with Anderson, I was more poised and I thought I did a pretty good job. But I still didn't get an offer. I interviewed with a few boutique shops and I really liked one of them, but I came up empty there, too. Finally, I had my McKinsey interview, which is the position I really wanted. I got a call back on that one, but apparently, I just missed the cut.

Upon hearing these stories, the listener might try to clarify by saying, "It seems like you've been involved in a lot of tough interview situations." The speaker never stated, "I've been in a lot of difficult interview situations," so the listener's remark is more than a simple paraphrase. The speaker might say in response to a useful clarifying remark: "I wouldn't have thought to describe it that way, but yes, you're right on target." Yet the response makes plain the reality of the situation. Clarifying remarks tend to occur earlier in the exchange and tend to be helpful in surfacing facts and events.

*Reflection of Core Feelings.* Reflection of core feelings is a sister skill to clarification. Like clarification, reflection of core feelings involves identifying what is fully or partially in the speaker's awareness and making it explicit. The difference between the two is that in clarification, the listener is making explicit facts or events. In core-feeling reflection, the listener is making explicit feelings and emotions that the speaker is communicating, *especially when the speaker is not identifying those feelings.* Consider the interview monologue above. A possible core-feeling reflection might be, "It sounds like experiencing these unsuccessful interviews was really discouraging for you." Again, note that the speaker said nothing about being discouraged. In this case, the listener interpreted what the speaker might have been feeling, and offered it as feedback to the speaker. Reflections of core feelings typically are offered in the later stages of an exchange or with people who are more familiar with one another. These are the points at which empathy and trust are likely to be greatest between the listener and the speaker.

## MIDDLE RANGE RESPONSES

*Interpretation.* Interpretation reflects what the listener thinks is at the core of what the speaker is expressing, but in a way that reconfigures it so that it is presented to the speaker in a new light. Usually, interpretation responds to aspects of what the speaker is experiencing that are not in her awareness.

Interpretation is usually most effective (1) when a good relationship has already developed, (2) when the listener has a fairly complete sense of what the speaker is experiencing, and (3) when the listener feels fairly certain that the interpretation will be helpful to the speaker and that she is "ready" to hear it. Thus, interpretation tends to be more appropriate during later stages of an encounter, when these conditions have developed, than in earlier stages. Its greatest usefulness is in helping the speaker see the connections or aspects of her situation that she was not aware of, thereby facilitating better self-understanding.

*Encouragement and Assurance.* These responses openly encourage the speaker to pursue a line of thought that he may be hesitant to explore but that the listener thinks would be fruitful.

Here, as in interpretation, the listener's own thoughts and feelings become more important, although his or her reaction is in response to what the speaker has expressed.

Encouragement can be useful if the listener thinks that the speaker is reluctant to go on because he is afraid of disapproval of what he is about to say. When this is the case, encouragement or assurance can be a way of verbally affirming that the listener is willing to accept the speaker's thoughts and feelings, regardless of what they might be. Encouragement can be a very powerful response in enabling the speaker to explore a conflict or problem more deeply.

*Question.* Questioning is an extremely powerful listening tool and has aspects that are both reflective and directive. Hence, questioning rests at the midpoint of the continuum. In its more reflective form, the listener asks a direct question, but the question is in response to what the speaker has previously expressed. The purpose of the question is to clarify the speaker's own thoughts and feelings. When a question is asked in response to the speaker's meanings, it can be especially helpful if it is asked in the true interest of understanding the speaker. This interest may be conveyed by gesture, tone of voice, or by phrasing. Reflective questions are best phrased as "open" questions that elicit extensive responses. For example, "What made you consider that job as an option?" offers the speaker the opportunity to discuss her thinking about job choice. In contrast, a "closed" question such as "Did you choose the consulting job or the I-banking job?" only leaves room for one of two responses. Open, reflective questions can be very useful in helping a speaker clarify her own thoughts by directing her to an aspect of what she has said that needs further exploration.

Alternatively, questions can be used in a more directive manner. The listener may ask the speaker a question from the listener's frame of reference that leads the speaker to an area the listener wants to explore and away from what the speaker has been previously expressing.

This type of question can be useful for obtaining specifically needed information (which may be necessary for understanding what the speaker is saying). It can also be useful for directing the speaker's attention to more fruitful areas of exploration, especially where the going may be difficult. Questions of this nature are usually best asked in the middle or later stages of an encounter, when trust and rapport are more firmly rooted. Questions directed to content inevitably result in disrupting the flow of the speaker's exploration.

*Confrontation.* With this response, the listener confronts the speaker with inconsistencies or contradictions in what the speaker has expressed (at least as the listener sees it), or confronts the speaker with gaps in what he has said. Although this is clearly a directive response and from the listener's frame of reference, it is directed to and works off material the speaker has already expressed.

Confrontation can be especially effective in helping the speaker recognize inconsistencies either in his assumptions or when he is evading an important aspect of what he is discussing. However, great risks are involved in using confrontation as a response, and it should not be used unless trust and acceptance have already developed. It should not be used unless the listener is fairly certain that the confrontation will be beneficial in helping the speaker better understand himself. Otherwise, the confrontation can be destructive and can serve to put the speaker on the defensive.

## DIRECTIVE RESPONSES

These responses are essentially directive in nature and come from the listener's frame of reference. In all these responses, the listener is reacting from her own point of view of what the speaker has said; further, she is implicitly or explicitly passing judgment on the truth, usefulness, or importance of what the speaker has expressed.

*Challenge.* Here, the listener challenges the veracity of the speaker's statement or the degree to which it is consistent with the listener's view of the situation. This type of response can be useful in questioning assumptions the speaker holds that may impair his ability to fully understand the situation. They can also enable the speaker to see where important assumptions or feelings do not check with reality (or at least with the listener's view of reality). A challenge can also help the speaker gain a broader perspective on his situation, and therefore give him a better understanding of it. It can also be useful, as a last resort, to get the speaker out of superficiality in which he is avoiding important aspects of his problem.

However, this kind of response or lead is risky, in that it is implicitly judgmental and comes from an external frame of reference, and it may leave the speaker feeling threatened and attacked. It should not be used unless a great deal of trust, empathy, and acceptance has already developed in the relationship; otherwise, the speaker's reaction will surely be defensive. It tends to be more appropriate and useful in later stages of an encounter.

*Advice or Suggestion.* The listener gives advice or counsel from the listener's point of view on the speaker's problem or situation. This lead or response (depending on the context) is most useful toward the end of an encounter in which the other person has asked us for our advice. It is least useful in the early exploratory stages of an encounter and can actively impede further exploration. It is especially appropriate when the speaker has explicitly sought advice and we feel we know enough about him and his situation to give it. Any explanation from our point of view of why a speaker is experiencing difficulties can be also considered part of this category, since we are telling him how and why we think he is having a problem or conflict.

*Entreatment (urging, "selling," cajoling, moralizing, etc).* Entreatment is stronger than advice, in that the listener truly wishes to convince the speaker of what the listener thinks the speaker ought to do. Entreatment includes attempts to convince the speaker to take a certain course of action or to think a certain way, based on the listener's own interpretation of the situation. (This also includes, of course, situations in which the listener feels his suggestion is in the speaker's best interest.)

Entreatment is appropriate (at least as the listener would see it) when the listener feels that the consequences are serious if the speaker does not act on the recommended advice. Although skillful "selling," cajoling, and moralizing can often get a speaker to change his behavior for the moment (and perhaps even change his mind temporarily), they are seldom effective responses in helping the speaker surface the underlying reasons for his initial resistance to the advice.

*Commands or Threats.* These are implied or expressed threats on the part of the listener to punish the speaker unless the speaker acts as the listener wishes him to act. When commands or threats are needed among adults, it is a sign that all attempts at communicating, helping, and understanding have failed. Its use is obvious: to prevent the speaker from acting in a way that the listener sees as highly undesirable or self-destructive. Its appropriateness is limited to those situations in which all else has failed and the listener believes it is critically important to impose her or his will on the speaker.

## FINAL THOUGHTS ON EFFECTIVE LISTENING

To be an effective listener, you will find it is helpful to have a command of the entire listening continuum, even if you tend to use some of the skills more than others. As is always the case in building interpersonal competence, having a particular skill does not mean you have to use it all the time. Rather, consider the skill a part of your "interpersonal toolkit," available for any occasion when you might need it.

That said, there is no substitute for practice in building listening competence. Like learning to ride a bicycle, using the listening continuum may feel awkward at first, and you may feel unskilled in what you may think should be a natural skill. But as you practice, being an effective listener becomes considerably easier. Mastery is experienced not only as having technical command of the listening skills, but also as having a genuine sense of empathy and connectedness to your speaker, whomever she may be.

Finally, even as you come to master all of the skills along the continuum, keep in mind that no one can be an effective listener all the time. Effective listening is a challenging skill that requires the listener's attention and energy. When you are tired or feeling stressed, you may not be able to listen well, even if you really want to. In other cases, you may have the energy to listen effectively, but you may have a difficult relationship with the speaker, or the content of the speaker's communication may be too painful for you stay focused. All of us encounter such situations from time to time. Thus, the final skill in being an effective listener is knowing when to say, "I'm sorry, but I can't be a helpful listener for you."

# EDITORS' INTRODUCTION

We've now discussed some very specific skills for effective communication and conversation mastery. The next reading is entitled "In Your Relationships" by Karen Sherman. In it, Sherman provides some examples of real couples that show us how to engage the skills you've learned thus far—listening to understand, self-soothing (the antidote to stonewalling), and being open and transparent about your feelings. You'll recall from Chapter 3 that we bring experiences from our families of origin into our adult relationships, and sometimes old patterns are reenacted in adulthood. Sherman refers to reactions that are triggered by old patterns as "small self" reactions, a response to a present situation that unconsciously reminds us of something that happened in the past.

We are not destined to repeat old patterns in our current relationships. Notice in the examples that Sherman provides how each partner notices themselves caught in an old relationship pattern and makes a conscious choice to do something different.

## PRIMERS

1.  John Gottman uses pulse oximeters in his research to signal to couples (and counselors) that a person's heart rate has risen above 100 beats/minute. One hundred heartbeats per minute is the threshold at which we are no longer able to listen and engage with our partners; our limbic (regulatory) system has entered the "fight, flight, or freeze" mode signaling danger. When this happens, the counselor pauses the session and engages the couple in self-soothing activities to help them bring their heartrate down and reengage in counseling. There are free apps on both Google Play and the App Store that can help you monitor your heart rate. Try downloading a heart rate app and get an idea of how your heartrate fluctuates as you do different activities and engage in different situations.

2.  Work on incorporating some self-soothing techniques into your daily self-care practice. Mindfulness meditation can help to lower blood pressure and overall feelings of anxiety and depression, as well as provide many other physical and psychological benefits. Visit www.mindful.org for "getting started" instructions and sample exercises in practicing mindfulness.

# In Your Relationships

*By Karen H. Sherman*

S urely, life is more difficult when you are not free to respond to it in a clear, non-reactive way. And when you are reacting to something that is really an implicit memory from the past (or in lay terms, an "old button" getting triggered), you are not emotionally free. The work you have been doing in this book, thus far, has been for the purpose of allowing you to heal those old wounds so that you are no longer getting set off.

Perhaps the greatest vulnerability for your emotions will be when you are in a relationship with someone. It is such irony because being in a relationship is something we all desire. After all, it is through partnership that you hope to get your sense of worthiness, your sense that you matter. And when things are going well, there is nothing better.

But it is also in this situation that you are most likely to get hurt. You take a risk ... you open yourself up. But by putting your emotions on the line, so to speak, there's a greater chance that your needs won't be met.

One possible reason that this is true is because unknowingly, you have probably chosen to be with someone who is similar to a member of your family of origin where there are unresolved issues. The famous relationship therapist, Harville Hendrix (*Getting the Love You Want*, 2007), speaks about this phenomenon. This process occurs at a sub-awareness level; something about the person's energy feels comfortable and familiar to you; and so you are drawn to him or her in the hope of resolving the leftover concern.

Once the two of you get involved, these issues start to play out. Suddenly, there's a situation that upsets you. The reaction on your part is quick and automatic. Very often, the expressed emotion is one of frustration or anger. But these are reactive emotions; these are secondary emotions. Usually, underlying these are more basic emotions like hurt or a sense of unworthiness. And similar to other situations previously discussed in this book, it will *feel* like whatever has just taken place is what is upsetting you. In reality, something from the past has been "hooked into" and set off.

[This reading] is written to bring to your awareness the heightened vulnerability you have to these types of reactions when you are involved with someone romantically! Your emotions are more at stake. Furthermore ... because you are having these reactions, it does put the relationship at risk. Why? Well, let's be honest: a reaction on your part that gets targeted on to your partner when, in fact, there was no cause, isn't likely to be well-received. Additionally, if you still have many leftover wounds and therefore many reactions like this, it's really going to take a toll on your partner.

Let me give you an example of how this might actually "look." Years ago, I worked with a young couple where the woman had childhood issues of a father who was never present. He worked all the time and wasn't able to give her much attention. Her spouse was not only aware of this history but very sensitive to it. On one occasion, he had to go away on a business trip for several days. Then, it turned out that the company tacked on a second trip which would mean he would be gone an especially long time.

Knowing how distressing his wife would find this long absence, he spent the entire day at work trying to rearrange plans, find different flights, and figure out some way to alter the amount of days he'd be gone. But nothing was possible. He called me and asked what to do. We discussed how to present the situation to her, reassuring her how important she was to him, the extent to which he went to try to change things, the efforts he would make to stay in touch with her.

Nothing he said mattered—she went ballistic! Was she reacting to her spouse? No. She was, without realizing it, re-experiencing the old painful feelings she had when she felt like an abandoned little girl.

Here's another situation: I worked with a couple where the wife felt that the husband was very insensitive to her needs and that she just didn't matter to him. He worked very hard to be more aware of her. Things definitely did improve.

Then, in one session, they came in very upset and here is what he reported: he had gone to their son's basketball game without her because she had gone to the doctor, not feeling well. After the game, he called to inquire how the exam went and how she felt. I privately thought, "That was good." He also let her know he and another family would be going out to dinner with the kids so he'd be late in getting home and inquired if she'd want to come. I privately thought, "That was good."

Even she admitted, "So far, so good." But when he got home and went upstairs to check on her (more points for him), he said, "There was *that* expression on her face." She was extremely upset with him. Why? Because he hadn't asked if she wanted him to bring home a slice of pizza!

When we worked on this feeling, though she initially felt it really was because he didn't care about her, she was able to hook it back to an experience with her mother not paying attention to her. There were many such episodes, implicit memories, with stored energy that got triggered when her husband did something that felt similar.

Sometimes, things get even more complicated because each partner has issues from the past that get set off in the present by things their mate does or says.

Fortunately, I have found in my practice that these reactions can be worked with as a couple. When these reactions are dealt with, the couple weathers the storminess much better. Also, there is a healing that takes place that is very unique just by virtue of the fact that it is coming from such an emotionally significant person.

Before looking at the exercises, it is important that each partner be familiar with understanding why these reactions occur. Therefore, I recommend that each partner be familiar with the premises of this [reading]. Also, both partners should come to an agreement that they will try this exercise the next time one of the partners is having a reaction.

For the purposes of the exercise, the person having the reaction will be referred to as Person A and the partner being targeted will be referred to as Partner B.

## EXERCISE #1: IN YOUR RELATIONSHIPS—BEST CASE SCENARIO:

1. When it becomes obvious that Partner A is having a reaction (the reaction is quick and automatic and really seems to be an over-reaction to what has happened), Partner B should take a deep breath just to ground him or herself.

2. Partner B should gently state, "I can see this is really upsetting (frustrating, angering, saddening) you." This is an important first step. The small self needs to feel validated, understood. It does not matter if Partner B agrees with the reaction. At this point, it is the small self who is having the reaction; that is to say, it is the emotional part of the self. Therefore, logic will not work!

3. Once, the small self has calmed down, Partner B can gently inquire, "Is it possible that something upset your small self? Can you share it with me?" This then serves as a variation of the adult self experience in being loving and accepting.

4. It is really important that as Partner A shares whatever the experience is, Partner B is present. That means that Partner B is not distracted and doing anything else; rather, Partner B is making eye contact and perhaps gently making a physical gesture.

5. If Partner B thinks Partner A is done speaking, rather than ask, "Are you done?" say, "Tell me more." The latter is much more receptive and inviting and sends the message that, "I am here for you."

Certain adjustments may have to be made to suit your particular relationship. I have worked with couples where Partner B has, in fact, followed the basic model I have described, but Partner A doesn't feel comforted by it. It is always best to discuss how Partner B can be more responsive when things have calmed down. When someone is emotional, he or she cannot think logically.

Some people will want to be held. In fact, when emotions are stirred up and you are held tightly, it helps to calm the system down and help regulate it again. However, others do not want to be held and will find attempts to do so restrictive.

Perhaps Partner A might want to just sit in silence with Partner B in the room waiting for a period of time before anything is actually said. Should this be the case, the two of you might have to work out a signal where Partner A lets Partner B know it's okay to talk; or the arrangement might be that Partner B will periodically inquire if it's okay to talk.

Unfortunately, there is no way I can possibly imagine all the possible scenarios that might apply to you and your relationship. As with the rest of this [reading], I offer you a guideline for the process. In summary, use this last exercise but adapt it as it is appropriate for the needs of Partner A.

## EXERCISE #2: ALTERNATE TO IN YOUR RELATIONSHIPS— PARTNER B GETS GRABBED:

It is very likely that at least in the beginning of working with this model, Partner A will have a reaction and Partner B will respond with his or her own reaction. Nobody likes to be attacked and, therefore, responds defensively.

Very often, the common reaction to feeling attacked is to leave the room. If Partner B chooses to do this, it will be extremely helpful if it can be stated, "I am leaving only to calm down; I am *not* leaving you."

Of course, there is the possibility that Partner B will attack back as well.

The following is suggested should Partner B get grabbed:

1. Partner B recognizes that Partner A was having a small self reaction. After a while when Partner B has had a chance to calm down, if Partner B did attack Partner A, Partner B should first acknowledge that he/she got grabbed and apologize.

2. Partner B then says, "As I had a little while to think about things, I realized how upset you were. I do want to work on this with you. Can you tell me more about what you were experiencing?"

1. Proceed with Steps 3–5 as in Exercise #1.

## EXERCISE #3: ALTERNATE TO IN YOUR RELATIONSHIPS— PARTNER A ACKNOWLEDGES TRIGGERED REACTION:

If you are Partner A and realize that the reaction you have had was from your small self, that's great! It's still possible to have some healing work done with your partner.

1. Approach your partner (Partner B) and let him or her know that you've had a chance to think about the incident and you realize that you got grabbed, that your buttons got set off and that your small self was having a reaction.

2. Apologize and ask if he or she is willing to help you work through the process.

3. Explain what in the situation set you off; that is, what you perceived that was upsetting. For example: was it the way something was said?, was it a facial expression?, was it a gesture that was used?, was something not done that you had anticipated?

4. Share what feelings were aroused in you.

5. Relate what old situations this reminded you of.

6. If your partner is not offering you the type of nurturing you would like, ask for what you need. Remember, others are not mind readers; but if you ask for what you need and he or she is willing to give it to you, it is because you do matter to them. Also remember that the difference between your past experiences and now is that as a small child you did not have the ability to ask for what you needed. The very act of being able to do so now is part of the healing process.

## BIBLIOGRAPHY

Hendrix, H. (2007). *Getting the love you want.* New York, NY: Holt Paperbacks.

## END-OF-CHAPTER REFLECTIONS

1. Think back to the scenario you imagined at the beginning of the chapter, where your buttons were pushed and you felt overwhelmed. How would you have liked to respond? What might you have needed to do to calm yourself in the moment so you could have responded the way you would have liked to?

2. Walk through the scenario you just imagined with your new, better response. Practice your response to yourself and imagine calming yourself as you move through the scenario. McDermott discusses how mental imagery actually helps to retrain your brain to perform differently next time.

3. Next time you are in a conversation with someone you care about, make a point to listen only for understanding. Challenge yourself to abandon any agenda you might have to share your perspective, relate to a common experience, or shift the conversation. Try reflecting what you've heard and, even better, the feeling that your partner is communicating. Notice what happens—how your partner responds—to your very attentive listening.

4. Next time you are talking with a loved one, try out the heart rate monitor. If you notice your heart rate rising above 100 beats/minute, take a break and practice some self-soothing tools (deep breathing, positive self-talk, a walk, meditation, etc.) to bring your heart rate down and allow you to reenter the conversation. Reentry is key! Be sure to communicate that you need a break and commit to coming back to the conversation after a specific amount of time.

## REFERENCES

Fulwiler, M. (2012, July 2). *Managing conflict: Solvable vs. perpetual problems*. The Gottman Institute. https://www.gottman.com/blog/managing-conflict-solvable-vs-perpetual-problems/

Siegel, D. J. (2011). *Mindsight: The new science of personal transformation*. Bantam.

Rogers, C. R. (1961). *On becoming a person*. Houghton Mifflin.

## RECOMMENDATIONS FOR FURTHER READING

Daniel Goleman, the author of *Emotional Intelligence* and *Social Intelligence: The New Science of Human Relationships,* has a series of podcasts on emotional intelligence at https://www.keystepmedia.com/

Hanh, T. N. (2001). *You are here: Discovering the magic of the present moment.* Shambhala.

Hanh, T. N. (1975). *The miracle of mindfulness: An introduction to the practice of meditation.* Beacon.

# Chapter 8

# Conflict Management and Relationship Repair

## EDITORS' INTRODUCTION

Let's begin this chapter with a brief imagination activity. First, bring to mind someone you care about. Take a moment and visualize them sitting with you as you read this text. Now, think about the last time you were in conflict with that person. Depending on the outcome of that conflict, like many of us, you may notice an immediate sense of discomfort. The physiological reaction you are having is a normal and common response to the threat of engaging in conflict, especially with someone you love. Although conflict, even in healthy relationships, can be dysregulating and uncomfortable, it is manageable.

One of the greatest myths about intimate relationships is that the presence of conflict is a bad sign and the relationship is doomed to fail. In truth, conflict happens in all intimate relationships. The question of whether conflict is or isn't a bad sign depends on a multitude of other considerations. Conflict as a sign of an unhealthy intimate relationship is examined in Chapter 12. In the context of this chapter, we will view conflict as a naturally occurring byproduct of bringing the likes, dislikes, values, and ideologies of two individuals into a shared intimate relationship.

Most of us learned how to engage in conflict by what we observed as children and adolescents at home, at school, and in in the media. As a result, we often recreate what was modeled for us—even not so awesome behaviors. In the first reading of this chapter, "Conflict Chains, Patterns, and Styles," Marla Hall explores conflict engagement styles and then provides examples of common, harmful patterns partners use when addressing relational conflict. We hope you will learn to recognize conflict behaviors, why they endure, and how they erode intimacy. In short, what is gained in the moment (i.e. winning the argument, avoiding a confrontation) can come at the cost of what we want long-term—*a satisfying intimate partnership.*

As you read, keep in mind the following primer questions for reflection. If you feel so inclined, take a few minutes and consider your responses to the following questions before you read, and then again after you've finished each reading.

## PRIMERS

1. What is your conflict management style? You can take the Conflict Styles Assessment provided by the U.S. Institute of Peace here: https://www.usip.org/public-education/students/conflict-styles-assessment.

2. Bring to mind a recent conflict between two people you either observed or were engaged in. As you think about the interaction, what behaviors occurred? For example, did anyone raise their voice, use sarcasm, or walk out? What conflict management style(s) did you observe?

3. What is your go-to conflict style: Do you always have to have the last word, avoid conflict at all costs, accommodate every request in order to keep the peace, or make efforts toward a compromise?

# Conflict Chains, Patterns, and Styles

*By Maria I. Hall*

> *Our character is basically a composite of our habits. Because they are consistent, often unconscious patterns, they constantly, daily, express our character.*
> —Stephen Covey

## LEARNING OBJECTIVES

1. Explain what conflict chains are and how it can be beneficial to understand the links in your own conflict chains.

2. Explain how to identify your conflict chains as well as the discriminative stimuli that trigger them and the reinforcers that maintain them.

3. Describe the various interactive conflict patterns that involve one individual who can be viewed as the aggressor and one who can be viewed as nonassertive, or at least less overtly assertive than the aggressor.

4. Compare and contrast the five major conflict styles.

5. Explain how tactics differ from styles and under which conditions one is likely to use particular styles as their tactic of choice.

## SKILL DEVELOPMENT

- Identifying and breaking conflict chains
- Identifying and altering your conflict style

# CHAINS

In the context of human behavior, **chains** are sequences of events that occur in the same order repeatedly. Many of our behaviors occur in chains. And many of our conflicts, even though they involve another person, tend to occur in repeating and predictable chains.

## Behavioral Chains

**Behavioral chains** are series of behaviors that tend to occur together and in the same order. For example, your morning routine probably repeats in pretty much the same order day after day—your alarm goes off, perhaps you hit the snooze button a couple of times before struggling out of bed, you take a shower, brush your teeth, have coffee and breakfast, get ready for work or school, and off you go. Even within that chain there are several chains—for example, how you shower, brush your teeth, or get dressed. Your morning routine may have different chains or patterns for weekdays versus weekends, but there will likely be a great deal of consistency within those two patterns. Your patterns will also differ to some extent from the patterns of others, but there will likely be a great deal of similarity—most with family members, but also with others in your culture. Part of the reason so much of our behavior flows so smoothly is because it occurs in chains. Once a chain is set in motion, the following behaviors can occur habitually, without much thought. For the most part, this benefits us. We do not have to put a lot of conscious effort into every move we make; instead we "go with the flow." In fact, because chains are so beneficial, we often create chains when training others to perform complex tasks or when trying to create consistency. Alternatively, many chains develop naturally.

## Conflict Chains

**Conflict chains** most often develop without thought. Unless someone has actively tried to employ particular constructive strategies to their conflicts and practiced those same strategies, it is likely that whatever conflict chains emerged happened through contingency shaping. **Contingency shaping** means that behaviors that are reinforced or that pay off for the individual tend to be repeated, while behaviors that are punished or that do not pay off tend to not be repeated. This happens with behavior generally, and with conflict behaviors specifically. When behaviors occur in chains, the entire chain gets shaped and is maintained by the reinforcers that occur at the completion of the chain. The behaviors that occur during the actual conflict are a big part of the conflict chain, but we must not ignore the behaviors that occur leading up to the occurrence of the conflict. If these behaviors also happen repeatedly and in a relatively predictable sequence, they are also an important part of the conflict chain.

An example of a conflict chain might go something like this. Let's say that Brett has a habit of going to a particular bar on Fridays for happy hour. Brett tends to like to discuss his views on controversial topics once he has a few drinks in him, and he needs to be "right." His friends know this and just keep the peace by agreeing with him regardless of his rant. Sometimes, however, Brett will spot a new face and try to convert that individual to his way of thinking. If the person has a differing point of view and begins to engage in a back-and-forth with Brett, Brett will quickly escalate and start shouting at the person. Sometimes the person will just back off and leave once Brett starts yelling. In those cases, Brett considers that he has won and the fact that he is "right" is proven to him. If the person continues to engage, most often Brett's buddies will eventually step in and break up the argument by steering the other person away from Brett and redirecting Brett to a discussion with them in which they assure him that he is right. Again, the conflict ends with Brett feeling like he has won and is right. As can be seen in this example the conflict chain is not exactly the same in every circumstance, but certain factors are repeated. The SDs for the conflict chain are Fridays, happy hour, the bar, and being with friends. The actual conflict begins when the new person disagrees with Brett. The conflict chain, however, begins long before the actual conflict. Arguably, it begins when Brett leaves work and heads to that specific bar. The chain continues with Brett arriving at the bar, ordering a drink, drinking, talking with friends, ordering another drink, drinking while talking with friends (this repeats a varied number of times), Brett spotting a new person, engaging that person in conversation, responding to the person when he disagrees, responding again when the person disagrees again, repeat again and again with more alcohol perhaps added to the mix, and eventually the conflict ends in one of the two ways described earlier. There are a couple of things to note. Since Brett was the individual of focus, the behavioral chain of focus included only Brett's behaviors with reference to the interactions of others. The behaviors of the others serve as consequences and antecedents to Brett's individual behaviors—consequences for the individual behavior that he just acted out and antecedents to his next behavior in the chain. Brett's perceptions that he has won and that he was proven to be right are the main things reinforcing his conflict chain.

The oft-repeated behavioral chains leading up to conflict are set in motion by SDs. The SDs sometimes also elicit emotions, but sometimes the emotions occur later, such as in the beginning of the actual conflict or within the conflict chain. Sometimes it is the same SD that elicits the emotion and sets in motion the behavioral chain leading to the conflict; sometimes the chain is set in motion by the SDs and then something else that occurs later serves as the SD for the emotion. In the above example, the SDs of Friday happy hour at Brett's favorite bar are antecedent to the (voluntary, habitual) conflict behaviors, but they do not trigger the anger that is apparent when he argues. The alcohol certainly may be a factor in Brett's anger, but the real trigger to the emotion appears to be when another person disagrees with him.

Identifying chains in conflict situations is important because if you can identify a consistent chain, you also can potentially identify weak links in the chain. This means that you can possibly identify places in the chain where you can make a change and thus break the chain that leads to the destructive conflict. The earlier in the chain you can break a link, the easier it will be to make a change that leads to a different outcome—potentially a more constructive management of the conflict situation.

The only way to understand the relationship between SDs, conflict chains, and the consequences that maintain your conflict chains is to closely analyze repeated incidents that involve those components and actively look for the patterns that emerge. Although it will help your understanding of the conflict to look at how and where emotion is involved, your focus needs to be upon the voluntary behaviors and the SDs for the chains of those voluntary behaviors. As noted previously, voluntary behaviors are much easier to gain control over, and if we can identify weak links that occur prior to the actual conflict or ones that occur very early in the actual conflict we will be more likely to break the destructive cycle.

The most effective way to identify the discriminative stimuli that trigger conflict chains is to think about repeated conflicts you have had with a specific conflict partner and to work backwards through many instances of the conflict, beginning with the destructive conflict itself. Think of a specific instance of the (repeated) conflict:

1. Who said or did what that occurred at the onset of the conflict and that seemed to spark the conflict discussion?
2. Where, specifically, were each of you when the conflict began?
3. What, specifically, were each of you doing when the conflict began?
4. What were you thinking and feeling just before the conflict began?
5. When did the conflict actually begin (time of day, after doing a repeated task or activity, etc.)?

Next, mentally take a step backward in time and think through those same questions one step removed. What was being said/done just before doing/saying what sparked the conflict? Where were you just before you were where you were when the conflict began? What were you each doing just before you each were doing whatever you each were doing just before the conflict began? What were you thinking and feeling just before you were thinking and feeling whatever you were just before the conflict began? At this point you may want to repeat these questions taking another step back in time.

After doing this for your first instance, you may want to look at a few other similar instances of the "same" conflict. Doing this may very well reveal a chain that leads to the actual conflict scenario. Taking a close look at those early links and at the SDs may reveal places where the chain can be broken relatively easily.

For example, [...] a specific pathway in the park had become a trigger for an ongoing argument, walking that pathway might be identified as a "weak link." Avoiding that pathway and beginning an unemotional discussion on the topic while walking elsewhere in the park or while sitting on a bench in the park would break the link and potentially set the stage for a more constructive dialogue. It could also be that the park itself, and not the pathway, had become the trigger, and thus you might have to alter your pattern even more—walking in a completely different location or choosing a new location and doing some other activity instead of walking.

The point of identifying and looking closely at the (early) links in the conflict chains is to provide you with insight into potential options, to alternatives that will at least temporarily break the cycle and create an opportunity for something different. It is important to then employ other skills such as active listening or using constructive complaints instead of criticism to develop a more constructive, more productive resolution to the conflict.

An analytical tool that may help in identifying the links is to create a diagram of your conflict. A diagram may help illustrate a common relationship between the two conflict parties in a conflict chain. An example of how to diagram a conflict chain is provided below.

In this diagram, CP1 indicates conflict partner 1, CP2 indicates conflict partner 2, SD is a discriminative stimulus, B indicates a behavior, R indicates reinforcement, and numbers following Bs indicate the order of the behavior in the chain.

```
SD—CP1B1———CP1B2———CP1B3———CP1B4———CP1B5———CP1B6—R
SD———CP2B1———CP2B2———CP2B3———CP2B4———CB2B5———CB2B6—R
```

This diagram indicates that each person's chain is set in motion by one or more SDs and each person's chain proceeds in a (relatively) predictable fashion with an exchange between the two parties. This is a very simple diagram and does not reflect emotions or the many possible variations in the interactions between the two parties. For example, one person may dominate the actual verbal exchange while the other person's chain may consist of a lot of nonverbal behaviors that occur while the other person rants. Nevertheless, it can help to use this model to diagram your repeating conflicts in order to better identify the behaviors common to both of the conflict parties involved.

## CONFLICT PATTERNS

By their very definition, interpersonal conflicts occur between two or more individuals. Most commonly the conflict is between two people. Further, in close relationships between family members, friends, and intimate partners, a repeated pattern of interaction commonly occurs. Gunther (2018) identifies nine destructive interactive patterns common in close relationships. Most of these involve one individual who could be viewed as the aggressor and one who acts in a relatively nonassertive way—at least during the actual conflict. A review of these common patterns of interaction may help you to identify your role in your own conflicts. Note that the potential reinforcers identified for each participant in the scenarios below are speculation, but they illustrate why each person repeats their actions in the interactive patterns that have developed.

## Shouter Versus Silent Martyr

In this interaction the "shouter," or aggressor, escalates quickly into yelling at the non-assertive "silent martyr" after being triggered—often by something the martyr has said or done. The martyr sits in silence while the shouter explodes and quietly takes note of the shouter's aggressive tactics—perhaps feeling more and more like someone being wronged by a bully. The aggressive shouter eventually stops when unable to draw the silent martyr into the drama, but likely walks away with some satisfaction of having made his or her point and thinking he or she is right. There may also be a sense of relief at having released anger. The silent martyr has likely learned that responding to the accusations will not lead to a good outcome and quite probably experiences relief when the yelling subsides. The martyr may also feel a sense of accomplishment for not having been drawn into the fight and even a sense of satisfaction or superiority for not having come down to the aggressor's level.

## Snarky Versus Unflappable

The snarky aggressor is often one with sarcastic wit and a sharp tongue. This person weaponizes his or her sarcastic wit by attacking with snide, spiteful comments aimed directly at the unflappable receiver. The unflappable conflict partner appears to let the poisoned verbal arrows be deflected from their thick skin. The snarky individual typically escalates, coming at the unflappable with stronger, more hurtful shots, but they will eventually storm off as long as the nonassertive individual remains unflappable and does not appear to be affected by the tirade. What the snarky individual may be getting out of this repeating pattern is a sense of self-satisfaction with their ferocious wit, and it's likely that they do sometimes get a rise out of the person they hit with the snide remarks. This intermittent reinforcement has come to maintain the snarky behavior. The unflappable person may also feel a sense of self-satisfaction, but for a very different reason. For example, there could be a sense of winning and perhaps even a sense of pride in not letting the remarks get to them.

## Pursuer Versus Runner

The pattern in the "pursuer versus runner" scenario is somewhat different in that the runner does not play a nonassertive role in the interaction. Often the pattern begins with both people being combative and, in fact, the runner sometimes plays "hit and run" by being the initiator of the conflict and then fleeing when their verbal hit does not result in an immediate win. The pursuer follows the runner, both literally and figuratively, all the while trying to make points or have the runner answer their questions. Their goal in pursuing appears to be to bring the conflict to some resolution. At some point the runner will typically give up the running and fight back by responding in fury. This "fighting fire with fire" approach by the runner tends to work, because the pursuer will, at that point, usually stop. Both the pursuer and the runner gain at least a temporary resolution to the conflict as it is over at least for the moment. The runner probably also experiences some relief at ending the dispute and stopping the pursuit as well as getting in the final word. The pursuer gets a reaction out of the runner and, regardless of whether he or she wins the battle, may at least gain a sense of closure.

## Threat-Maker Versus Underdog

Threat-makers need to dominate, and they typically do this by creating fear in their conflict partner. Whether or not they have any intention of following through on their threats, they use them as a way of intimidating their conflict partner—keeping them in their place and keeping them from challenging their real or perceived authority. The underdogs tend not to challenge, but rather they may very well accommodate the threat-maker to try to keep the peace out of fear that the threat-maker may follow through with those threats. If the underdog has experienced situations in which the threat-maker has indeed followed through with the threats, he or she will be more likely to be "kept in line" with those threats. The underdog will not "rock the boat" until they have had enough (if ever). At that point they may physically leave the relationship. In the ongoing conflict prior to the underdog leaving, the threat-maker tends to get whatever she or he demands because it is impossible or at least highly unlikely for the underdog to not give in due to the fear the threat-maker creates and stokes. The underdog, by accommodating, is able to avoid whatever the threat-maker is threatening to do.

## Flipper Versus Self-Doubter

Flippers are experts at turning the subject of the conflict back on their conflict partner. When accused or criticized, the flipper will make the same accusation or criticism of the person who first launched the judgment. They will attack with the same weapon used to attack them. This tends to put the "self-doubter" on the defense. They go from playing offense to playing defense as if the conflict ball has been turned over. The flipper is often skilled not only in flipping or reversing the roles, but in verbally annihilating their conflict opponent. The flipper likely comes away from the conflict feeling like the victor and emboldened by not only his or her success, but by a sense of putting the other person in their place. The self-doubter may believe that at least they were heard and that the flipper might at least think about what was said. The self-doubter is also probably inclined to try different topics or different tactics in the future.

## Escalating Yellers

In this scenario, both conflict parties are aggressors. Both attack and retreat as they do a war dance around the topic. Both become more and more entrenched in their position as the temperature of the argument rises. Neither party tends to hear or even consider anything the other says beyond defending against whatever point the other has tried to make. The only agreement in this conflict tends to be an unspoken agreement that the conflict come to an end—typically when both are exhausted from the battle. In these situations neither party is seen as winning; however, both parties likely still believe they are right at the end of the fight. Both probably focus on the solid points they believe they made—disregarding the fact that the other person did not hear or at least did not value or respect those points. They both also probably feel good about not backing down and for standing up for what they believe is right.

## Answer-Seeker Versus Truth-Dodger

This conflict pattern typically begins with one partner asking questions that the other person does not want to answer. Those questions usually revolve around something the truth dodger has done. The more the answer seeker tries to gain an understanding of why the other person acted in the manner they did, the more the truth dodger avoids—both by what he or she says and by trying to distract or detract from the issue at hand. In a sense the truth dodger generally appears to win the confrontation, because the answer seeker typically gives up trying at some point. The truth dodger successfully avoids addressing the real issue and probably experiences some relief when the answer seeker stops probing. The answer seeker is left without full answers, but perhaps comes away satisfied that their doubts or concerns were confirmed. Over time each successive confirmation of doubt will cause a deterioration in the relationship.

## Drama Queen/King Versus Scoffer

Drama kings and queens tend to exaggerate; they tend to make a very big deal out of even small differences. Scoffers do not want to deal with the drama; they want to get directly at the issue—if only they can get through the dramatic costuming to find what that is. The more the scoffer tries to find or address the issue, the more the drama king or queen is incited to play the dramatic role of the offended. They focus more on the "woe is me" aspect than how or why they feel they have been offended. They continue to seek attention more than resolution right into the final act where they typically make a grand exit from the situation. While the drama king or queen exits likely feeling righteous in their indignation and pumped up by the belief that they are an unsung hero in their valiant fight of being misunderstood or trounced upon, the scoffer often feels satisfied in the belief that they were right that there was no substance to the drama expert's complaints.

## Bad Guy Versus Good Guy

In this conflict, the aggressor or the bad guy typically begins the conflict by challenging or criticizing the supposed good guy. The good guy then typically submits or gives in to the bad guy, which has two immediate effects. The bad guy feels an increased need to justify their demands, while the good guy feels even more unjustly accused—even more like the good guy being maligned by the bad guy. The bad guy is not completely immune to the good guy's feelings of being unjustly attacked and thus, after the conflict ends, they try to repair what they have broken. The good guy takes these efforts as evidence of the injustice since the remorse makes it appear as if even the bad guy realizes they were at fault. It is oddly possible that both parties come away from the conflict feeling like winners. The bad guy can perceive they won because the good guy gave in to the demands without even a struggle, while the good guy can perceive that they won because their suffering was unjustified as admitted by the bad guy aggressor.

There are certainly additional patterns that emerge between conflict partners, but the above represent the most common interactions between conflict partners that are familiar with one another and engage in relatively frequent conflict. The individual behaviors in the patterns discussed above can also be seen in typical conflict styles.

## CONFLICT STYLES AND TACTICS

There are five **conflict styles** discussed widely in the conflict management literature: competing, avoiding, accommodating, compromising, and collaborating. Styles tend to be enduring—meaning that individuals characteristically behave in character with a particular style. We don't, however, typically employ that style in all circumstances. Under specific conditions we may use a different style, and in those situations the style is seen as a tactic. **Tactics** are the strategies used in a given conflict scenario. For example, someone who has a competing style in conflict situations may use a compromising or cooperating tactic in some specific situations. Each of the five styles is characterized by particular behaviors, and each has advantages and disadvantages that can influence when the style could or should be used as a tactic for managing conflict.

### Competing

The competing style is sometimes also described as dominating, forcing, or standing your ground. The style embraces a "winners and losers" approach and because of this can be the most destructive conflict style. Individuals who compete in conflicts typically have little or no regard for the other person, the other person's goals, or the relationship—at least in the heat of the conflict. In conflict situations, those who compete with, dominate, or force others must be right; they must get their way; they must win. Extreme conflict competitors tend to confront, pressure, and coerce. They are aggressive and go after their goals at the expense of the other person in the conflict. It is not their concern if their actions cause harm to the other. Although those who use the competing style can be **assertive** rather than aggressive (i.e., strongly pursuing their goals without harming their conflict partner), in the thick of the conflict they may very well cross the line into aggressiveness. The competing style is also the conflict style associated with threats and bullying. Clearly not all competing involves threats and bullying, but a very real danger of this style is that individuals who routinely compete when in conflict scenarios could evolve their methods into these highly destructive behaviors.

The main advantage of the competing style is that it tends to be a quick way to resolve a situation. Little, if any, time is spent debating or looking for mutually beneficial solutions. The conflict is over quickly as the competitor demands their preferred resolution. It is a good style to use in situations where time is of the essence, where there is no ongoing relationship between the conflict partners, when you know with certainty that you are right, or in actual competitions where the victor is rewarded. This could even include situations where creativity is enhanced by competing to come up with the best resolution to a problem.

There are obvious disadvantages to the competing style as well. First and foremost, this style is highly destructive to relationships. If both individuals in the conflict are competitive, the win-lose approach tends to bring out strong emotions, and one or both individuals may resort to unethical tactics. If one of the partners is unwilling or unable to engage in the conflict directly, they may turn to indirect strategies that focus more on harming their conflict partner and less on reaching their goals. Because of the potential or even likely harm to a relationship, the competitive style should, in most situations, not be used when the relationship between the individuals is important and ongoing. Also, because the style tends to be off-putting, it should not be used if you want the other person to feel they can discuss issues openly or even disagree without feeling attacked.

## Avoiding

There are many ways that people avoid conflict. One way is to simply deny that any conflict exists. In this situation the individual may perceive any conflict as so painful and destructive that they, in essence, protect themselves by refusing to see the conflicts in their life that are inevitably occurring. Another way that people avoid is by simply not speaking in the conflict situation. This could include refusing to answer questions or physically leaving the situation. Deflecting to another topic or trying to change the mood by making light of the subject—even laughing, smiling, or joking about it—are additional avoidance tactics. Bluntly stating that they will not talk about the subject is a very overt avoidance tactic, while talking in the abstract not only is an avoidance tactic, but takes off some of the pressure of the situation. Asking questions can be an avoidance tactic but also can be used to gain insight into the other person's goals and interests.

There are definitely situations in which it would be advantageous to employ the avoiding style. For example, if the situation is dangerous or if one or both of the conflict parties are very angry, avoiding may be the best tactic in the moment. Avoiding in the moment may also serve to buy time to think about the situation more constructively. It may be good to avoid when the topic is relatively insignificant—not worth the attention and effort to address. The idea that you need to "pick your battles" acknowledges that some battles are just not worth fighting, and although the conflict scenario may not be perceived as a battle, it may be best to just choose to not engage in a particular conflict. Avoidance may also be the best choice when you perceive that there is not a way for you to win or achieve your goal or when you believe the other person actually is in a better position to solve the problem.

Avoiding also has several disadvantages. An important disadvantage is that a person who routinely avoids conflict can be perceived as not caring about the relationship. Also because an outcome of conflict is change, someone who typically avoids conflict can be perceived as being unwilling to change. Perhaps one of the most potentially problematic results of avoiding is that the conflict goes unresolved and over time may grow into a much larger issue. After festering, the issue may come to a head and result in a highly emotional, combative, destructive conflict. Lastly, because continuously avoiding conflict could lead to increased stress and the health risks that go with it, avoiding is not the most beneficial style to adopt long term.

## Accommodating

The accommodating style bears some similarity to avoiding in that both styles are characterized by a person not really engaging in the conflict. The difference is that those who accommodate or oblige don't ignore the conflict, but rather they give in to what the conflict partner wants. Individuals who regularly accommodate can be seen as being very cooperative, but instead of working *with* the other individual it is more like they are working *for* the other person. They want to please, even when pleasing the other person comes at their own expense. They prefer harmony even when some discord may be the impetus for positive change. Accommodating can also be viewed on a continuum from those who accommodate in character with their gentle, docile demeanor to those who accommodate begrudgingly, who comply perhaps out of fear or a sense of futility. Individuals in abusive relationships often adopt this style.

The main advantage of accommodating is that it can create or maintain harmony in a relationship. It is an appropriate tactic to use when the other person in the conflict is more important than the issue that is the topic of the conflict. It is also an effective tactic to use when you are or were wrong. Giving in on an issue about which you are wrong not only is more efficient and effective in the moment, but also communicates to the other person that you are willing to cooperate and will not simply stand your ground on all issues. Another situation in which accommodating might be the tactic to use is when the issue is clearly more important to the other person than to you. Accommodating may also be of value when one person in the conflict has considerably more knowledge, experience, or prestige than the other. Deferring to the person who is higher up in the hierarchy or who has more knowledge and experience not only shows respect to that person but may earn respect from that person.

A person who always accommodates rarely if ever gets—or perhaps even pursues—something he or she wants if it is different from what the other person wants. This is a real disadvantage of accommodating in that it stifles growth of both the individual and the relationship. In some relationships, the partners take turns accommodating. While on the surface this may seem like a great harmonizing strategy, since the relationship is never tested, one or both parties may become insecure in the relationship or not remain committed to the relationship. Because accommodating is such a passive strategy, many do not realize just how often they accommodate. Accommodating may keep things on an even keel, but is not likely to result in positive change or growth. It also may result in a relationship stagnating or the accommodating individual reaching a point of boredom or frustration that could lead to him or her leaving the relationship in some way.

## Compromising

Compromise is sometimes seen as a win-win strategy, but that is not entirely accurate. When individuals compromise they do win, but they also give up things. Parties who engage in conflict and compromise meet somewhere in the middle. Neither gets all that they want, but both get some of what they want. The strategy is a cooperative strategy in that the two individuals work together to find a solution that is acceptable to both, and they further cooperate by being willing to give in or give up on some of what they originally wanted. In order for parties to agree to compromise, generally both parties in the conflict need to have somewhat equivalent power [...]. If one person has considerably more power than the other, there is little or no motivation for the person of higher power to compromise. Compromise can take several forms. For example, partners may take turns in decision-making; they may find a solution that splits the difference or is different from what either really wanted; they may compromise on a temporary solution while working on something more beneficial to both.

Two advantages of compromising are that it saves time and both individuals get at least some of what they want. It is also a good strategy to use when other strategies have failed or are unsuitable. Because compromising is typically seen as a fair approach, both parties generally enjoy some level of satisfaction with how the conflict was resolved.

A clear disadvantage of compromising is that although many see it as a "win-win" strategy, others view it as a "lose-lose" strategy since neither party gets everything they want. In addition, because compromise often leads to quick solutions, it can become overused and in that way stifle more creative and beneficial outcomes.

## Collaborating

Collaborating is the true "win-win" style of conflict management. In this situation, both individuals work together to come up with novel and creative solutions that will satisfy both of their goals. Each person's goals are important to both, and the relationship between the two is also a high priority to both conflict partners. Collaborating does require some concessions—some give and take—but not at the goal level. The concessions occur on the path to the solution, and the solution sought is one that will allow both to have their interests met and goals accomplished.

Collaborating is a highly effective conflict management strategy and has additional advantages of building trust and rapport between the conflict partners. People who collaborate tend to be assertive (e.g., actively sharing their ideas and giving feedback) but not aggressive (e.g., harming their conflict partner or forcing their positions on the other).

The main disadvantage of the collaborating style is that it generally requires more time and effort than the other strategies. Because of this, it should not be the style of choice when the issue is not that important or when you simply don't have the time to invest. Another caution about the collaborating style is that some who have a lot of power will engage in pseudo-collaborating, which sounds and looks like collaborating but ultimately results in the more powerful person always getting his or her way.

An individual's predominant style is likely dictated by their history with conflict going back to early experiences in their families and continuing through their experiences with many other conflict partners over the years. Individuals may also have more than one style that they use frequently based upon their varying roles. For example, a woman who grew up observing the interactions between a competing or dominating father and an accommodating mother might be inclined to follow her mother's model in her relationships with boyfriends or a husband. That might not hold true, however, if she witnessed her mother experiencing a lot of emotional or physical pain—in that case she may be more inclined to avoid or perhaps even compete or fight back. Other female models will also have an influence.

She might have observed her female teachers or other women successfully collaborating with their colleagues and perhaps with their students, so she may try to emulate their actions. She may have been on the losing end of competitive conflicts with her father or siblings or others and learned to avoid conflict more generally. In her role as a sister, she could adopt any of the styles based upon the relationship she had and continues to have with her siblings, and she could even adopt different styles with specific siblings. In her role as a mother she will most likely emulate her mother unless her experiences as a child motivate her to behave differently.

How anyone acts in any specific conflict as an adult will likely vary to a large degree depending on what is likely to be gained in that scenario. If maintaining the relationship is what is most valuable to you with a particular person, you may very well accommodate. If you fear being put in an uncomfortable position, you are relatively likely to avoid. If you believe you have the skills to pursue a mutually desirable solution, you will likely lean toward collaborating. If you have a strong need to win in the situation, you will be motivated to compete. If you want to be viewed as fair and easy to work with, but not a pushover, you may be inclined to compromise.

When observing your own predominant conflict style or the dominant styles of others, it will always benefit you to understand how adopting that particular style is paying off for you or for that person. Remember that people repeat behaviors that pay off for them, and they do not repeat behaviors that either do not pay off or lead to undesirable, punitive consequences. The fact that the style predominates shows that it is repeated; therefore, behaving in that way is unquestionably paying off for you or your conflict partner. It may not be easy to figure out how that action is beneficial, but if you want to change your style or use other tactics more often, it is important to try to uncover what has been reinforcing and motivating the conflict behaviors you favor.

## BIBLIOGRAPHY

Gunther, Randi. 2018. "Nine Conflict Patterns that Damage Relationships: Changing the Roles You Play." *Psychology Today*. https://www.psychologytoday.com/us/blog/rediscovering-love/201806/nine-conflict-patterns-damage-relationships.

# EDITORS' INTRODUCTION

Dr. John Gottman offers this insight regarding intimate relationships: "Conflict is inevitable, combat is optional." In other words, you do not have to fight with your partner in order to address the differences that occur in your relationship. As couples counselors, one of the first things we focus on is "we-ness," that is, identifying that the main goal is a healthy "we" or relationship rather than figuring out who is right. As individuals, when a healthy relationship is the goal, we are able to focus more on managing the conflict rather than focusing on our partner's shortcomings.

Research has demonstrated that one of key factors in relationship satisfaction is how well a couple manages conflict (Gottman & Krokoff, 1989). Further, scholars have identified a number of behaviors successful couples use as they navigate conflict. With few exceptions, this research holds for all couples, including gay, lesbian, and heterosexual relationships (Gottman et al., 2003). One notable exception is that gay and lesbian couples are much more successful in entering difficult conversations than are heterosexual couples (Gottman et al., 2003). (For more information on power dynamics during conflict, see Chapter 12.)

The next reading is selected from the chapter "Managing Conflict" in Clunis and Green's book, *Lesbian Couples: A Guide to Creating Healthy Relationships*. Following the tradition of relationship scholars like John Gottman, Sue Johnson, Robert Levinson, and Nan Silver, the authors provide a comprehensive look at common conflict scenarios couples face. Several research-based conflict management skills are presented, along with ideas of how to address, navigate, and negotiate constructive conflict discussions. Although the examples Clunis and Green use are with lesbian couples, keep in mind that the depictions of the people and the content could also be presented in gay or heterosexual couple relationships. In other words, people are people, and when we love intimately conflict is inevitable *and* manageable.

## PRIMER

1. Consider what it would be like to be on the same side of the negotiating table as your partner when addressing conflict. What attitude might you need to hold in order to prioritize the health of your relationship over being right?

# Managing Conflict

*By D. Merilee Clunis and G. Dorsey Green*

For many people, conflict has negative associations. The word itself may conjure up images of an exhausting struggle in which there is a winner and a loser. At best, you may envision an unpleasant clash that is painful or uncomfortable and, therefore, to be avoided. Perhaps your parents fought frequently and unskillfully. You may believe that conflict is a signal that your relationship is in trouble, that you are mismatched or have failed somehow in reaching the goal of having a good relationship.

In fact, conflict is a normal and inevitable part of relationships. Because you and your partner are individuals, with different opinions, wants, experiences, perceptions, and values, you will be in conflict with each other about something at some point in your relationship. You cannot avoid disagreement altogether unless you raise denial to an art form. But how you manage conflict is another story.

> Elaine and Jean have been partners for almost a year and have always spent most of their free time together. Their friends kid them about being Siamese twins. Jean is very devoted to Elaine: She tries to guess what Elaine wants and then do it before she's even asked. She is a good mind reader most of the time. If Elaine feels good, Jean feels good. If Elaine is in a bad mood, Jean soon feels down. Jean can't stand for Elaine to be disappointed or upset with her. She is very uncomfortable if they disagree about anything. The idea of a verbal fight scares Jean to death. It is unthinkable.

Jean has a hard time knowing what *she* wants. She is very focused on her relationship and on what Elaine wants. Since she can't stand for Elaine to be upset with her, she avoids knowing or asking for what she wants, in case it's not what Elaine wants. She accommodates and sometimes even placates Elaine, at least on the surface. At the same time, Jean sometimes builds resentments. Or she may resist doing what Elaine wants, but in an indirect way. For example, when Jean doesn't want to do things, she often gets a headache. She frequently gets headaches when she and Elaine have planned to go dancing. The only place to go dancing in their area is at a local men's bar. Jean hates that bar, but she has never said this to Elaine. So she gets headaches. She doesn't do this on purpose, it just happens.

## ASKING FOR WHAT WE WANT

The conflict between Jean and Elaine highlights issues around "wanting." Because we are women, many of us were taught early in life that wanting is not acceptable; wanting is greedy, selfish, demanding, and not nice. Good little girls wait until something is offered, share what they have, and don't ask directly for what they want. Getting what we want means that someone else will be deprived. Since other people's needs are more important, we learn to put their needs first. Jean is a good example of that training—she only wants Elaine to be happy. Then she will be happy. Deep down, Jean is afraid that if she asks for what she wants, she won't get it; furthermore, no one will love her. So she resorts to indirect, and even manipulative, tactics to try to get at least some of what she wants. At other times, Jean convinces herself that she doesn't really want anything, she gets confused about what she wants, or she makes Elaine's desires her own. It's hard for many women to believe that we have the right to *have* wants and needs. It is a step further to become aware of what these wants are and to ask for them clearly and directly.

What does Jean do when she doesn't get what she wants? Though she may not be sure what she wants and does not ask clearly for it, she does react when she is not happy with what she is getting. She may feel any or all of the following: disappointed, hurt, deprived, angry, betrayed, or cheated. These feelings provide the motivation for conflict. They fuel Jean's struggle to try to get what she wants from Elaine, to punish Elaine for not giving her what she wants, or to resist Elaine's pressure to do what Elaine wants. Jean gets headaches when Elaine wants to go to the bar. Then they spend the evening at home, which is what Jean wanted all along but did not ask for directly. Each time Elaine suggests they go to the bar, they go through this ritual. Each feels frustrated with the other and bad about herself.

This kind of below-the-surface struggle happens because we are fearful of open conflict. There are many reasons for this. Some of us hold to the belief that truly happy couples never fight. Conflict means the relationship is (or soon could be) in trouble. Trained to be peacemakers and soothers, many of us are as uncomfortable with our own anger as we are with our partner's. Anger may have been very controlled and unexpressed in our families. Or we may have grown up with family violence. In any event, many of us may have learned to ignore or swallow our own angry feelings. We give in to our partner and try to smooth over any difficulties.

Whether parents follow the motto of "Never disagree in front of the children" like Jean's parents did, or they engage in brawls, children often do not learn how to deal effectively with conflict. The message they learn is that in intimate relationships there are either no disagreements or that disagreements lead to violence.

When conflicts are not addressed openly and directly, devious power plays and indirect attacks are more likely. Such strategies as "forgetting" something that is important to your partner, "just not being interested" in sex, apathy toward your partner, and exaggerated interest in work and other people by comparison may be signs of smoldering resentments that are not being addressed. Jean's indirect approaches include her headaches. She is also sometimes just too tired to do what Elaine wants. Elaine accuses Jean of pouting, but Jean would never acknowledge that—because she doesn't acknowledge that she's not getting what she wants.

Recognizing and expressing wants is linked to self-esteem and a healthy sense of being separate [...]. Jean needs to believe that "It's okay to want; I deserve to have my needs met; I have a right to ask directly for what I want." She also needs to learn that wanting and getting are different. Just because Jean asks does not mean that she will have her request granted. Since she so rarely asks for anything, but waits until it is important that she gets it, she is devastated if things don't go her way. Then she convinces herself that there is no point in asking for anything ever again. "I don't get what I want anyway, so why stick my neck out? I'll just be disappointed."

It is possible for conflict to change from being a "dirty word" for Jean and Elaine. If Jean gets clearer with herself about what she wants, if she expresses these desires to Elaine, and if the couple negotiates about meeting them, Jean's indirect methods will not be necessary.

## CONFLICT STYLES

There are three styles of fighting that describe how most couples try to resolve their differences. Some couples do whatever is required to avoid conflict, other couples fight a lot, and yet others are able to talk through their differences and work our solutions without arguing.

Research indicates that no one style is necessarily better than another.[1] Many relationships can work well even though the couple tends to shove things under the rug. Other couples can have loud arguments and still report being very satisfied in their relationship. The important thing is that the style works for *both* people. Couples run into trouble if partners have different styles. For example, one woman may want to talk through a conflict while the other wants to ignore it.

Lois believes in talking disagreements through—she calls it processing. In her previous relationship, she and her ex managed to work out their differences pretty successfully using this approach. She was taken aback when her new partner, Rene, complained that as far as she was concerned they were spending far too much time "processing things to death."

Difficulties can also occur if the style followed doesn't really work for the couple. For example, partners may both avoid conflict but not truly let the issue go.

Jackie and Lorraine both disliked conflict intensely. When they disagreed, they dropped the subject and avoided each other for a while. Eventually they didn't talk to each other about much at all because many topics had become off-limits. They had little real communication, and their sense of closeness was eroded.

If partners identify their styles and talk about what works and doesn't work for each of them, hopefully they can reach some agreements about how they want to handle their conflicts.

Bobbie and Muretta have a problem about how they fight. Bobbie comes from a family of "yellers," and when she gets angry, she raises her voice. This upsets Muretta, who gets very frightened when people yell. Bobbie maintains that she is just expressing her feelings and there is nothing wrong with what she does. Muretta insists she cannot stand it and inevitably they end up arguing about Bobbie yelling rather than about whatever started the disagreement.

These two have different emotional styles, which are unlikely to change since these styles are part of their personalities. Bobbie is passionate and emotionally expressive; Muretta prefers to talk things over calmly and rationally. When Bobbie yells, Muretta feels overwhelmed and unable to think clearly. They need to realize how their styles are different, be respectful of these differences, and find an approach that feels comfortable, or at least workable, to both. Perhaps Bobbie could time-limit her yelling, lower her voice a few decibels, or face the window rather than yelling directly toward Muretta. For her part, Muretta might take notes while Bobbie vents, make sure there is enough physical space between them to feel less overwhelmed, or only have these interactions outside. Another possibility is that Bobbie could yell for a certain amount of time, then they could take a short break and come back together when Muretta feels she can express herself clearly and Bobbie indicates that she can listen.

## PERPETUAL PROBLEMS

Whatever your styles, there are two kinds of conflicts in relationships—resolvable and perpetual problems.[2] [A]lmost 70 percent of all couple conflicts fall into the category of perpetual problems—the ones that keep coming up over and over again. These will be an ongoing part of your life in some form or another, because they are fueled by underlying and fundamental differences between you and your partner.

Success in a relationship depends, in part, on figuring out which problems are resolvable and which ones are perpetual. As we pointed out earlier, it is not possible to resolve all of your conflicts, nor is it necessary to do so in order to have a healthy relationship. It is necessary to resolve the problems you can and to learn to cope with those of the perpetual variety. You do this by avoiding situations that worsen them and by developing strategies and routines that help you deal with them.[3]

> Kiri and Ravella have very different ideas about what constitutes an acceptable level of order in the house they share. Kiri could have written the adage, "A place for everything and everything in its place." Ravella always has a number of projects going on, which means piles of papers and materials here and there. She also has a tendency to misplace things. Their frequent bickering about this issue sometimes flares into nasty arguments.

This couple needs to keep acknowledging their difference and continue talking about it because it is an ongoing and often daily occurrence. A sense of humor and a light touch on Kiri's part will go a long way toward smoothing the rough places with this perpetual problem. Similarly, Ravella's genuine attempts to contain her things and good-naturedly compromise with Kiri will be helpful. Undoubtedly, when one or both of them are stressed, they may have a blowup about something important like Ravella misplacing her wallet and causing them to be late to a party because she has to find it. Hopefully, Kiri can get over her fit of pique, and Ravella can be appropriately contrite, so they can carry on with their evening and have a good time.

## SOLVABLE PROBLEMS

Solvable problems are more likely situational, specific, and focused on a particular issue. They are usually less intense than perpetual problems because they are about what they seem to be about. Of course, the arguments may still be unpleasant and even painful. In addition, if solvable conflicts do not get resolved, they can deepen and become perpetual problems.

When they first started living together, Annie and Jan agreed on a system for household tasks. Grocery shopping is Jan's job. However, she has been working long hours, is under a lot of stress, and has not been keeping up with the food shopping. Annie has tried to be understanding, but it has been weeks now since Jan did a thorough shopping job and they are running out of things. This morning when there was no milk for her cereal, Annie hit the roof.

Ever since they brought their newborn baby home from the hospital, Diane has felt like she couldn't do anything right for him. Her partner, Mina, the birth mother, complains that Diane isn't doing enough, but every time she tries to diaper him or soothe his crying, Mina suggests that she do it differently. Diane is beginning to feel incompetent—and resentful.

Both of these situations began recently and appear solvable, assuming that they are not expressing deeper issues. Jan is under temporary stress, and she and Annie need to work out a different arrangement, at least for the time being. Mina and Diane are also in a stressful situation—happy, but stressful nonetheless. Assuming that Mina's critiquing of Diane's every move is a new behavior, these two need to talk through what is going on for each of them and resolve how they are going to be with each other, and with their baby.

## DO'S FOR ADDRESSING CONFLICTS

Here are a number of suggestions for dealing with conflict.[4] Many of these are useful for both perpetual and solvable problems.

- DO make sure your partner feels that you understand and accept her. It is hard, maybe even close to impossible, to accept advice or requests for change when we feel misunderstood, rejected, or judged and found lacking.

- DO treat your partner with the same respect you would show to a guest. Would you berate a guest for breaking a glass or blow up at company who arrived late for dinner? We already possess the skills required for behaving civilly and sensitively to guests— we usually don't require special training. We just don't always apply these skills in our intimate relationships.

- DO keep your language in the realm of complaints rather than criticism. Complaints address specific behavior; criticism is global and adds blame and general character assassination. For example, "I get nervous when you drive this fast. I thought we agreed that you would keep to the speed limit when I'm with you" is a complaint. "Here you go again, driving recklessly. You know how scared I get; you don't care about my feelings.

And you're going to get us both killed" is a criticism. Since you can turn any complaint into a criticism by adding, "What is wrong with you?" to it, delete this phrase from your vocabulary.

- DO avoid directing contempt, which includes sarcasm and cynicism, toward your partner. Sneering, eye rolling, and name calling are also in the contempt family. Contempt is poisonous to relationships because it conveys disgust and leads to more conflict. It is fueled by long-simmering negative thoughts, which you are more likely to have if your differences are not resolved. Work on resolving or relieving those conflicts, cultivate positive thoughts, and practice the strategy [...] of nurturing fondness and affection for your partner.

- DO try asking yourself, "How did I contribute to this conflict?" as a way of reducing your defensiveness. Defensiveness is really a way to blame your partner, and it merely escalates the conflict. The more you can hold on to yourself, avoid taking everything your partner says too personally, and take responsibility for your contribution to the problem, the more likely you will keep the discussion on track.

- DO "soften your start-up" when you bring up a complaint. If you go straight for the jugular, you'll get a lot of blood. It won't be a pretty sight and you will likely get a battle or withdrawal from your partner. The start-up is important because research indicates that discussions almost inevitably end on the same note they began.[5] So if it starts off badly, it will probably end up the same way—not to mention the in-between. There are various ways to soften your start-up. The next section, which outlines a structure for negotiating, elaborates on these suggestions: Be descriptive, clear, and specific, use "I" messages, and be polite and appreciative. An example of a harsh start-up is "You never pay any attention to me." You can soften your start-up with rephrasing: "I know that you have been really busy, but I miss having fun times with you. I'm feeling a little lonely."

- DO bring issues up sooner rather than later. Like mushrooms, resentments grow in the dark, and the intensity of negative feeling increases as well. It becomes harder to initiate a discussion with a gentler start-up.

- DO learn to put on the brakes when your discussion starts going badly. Gottman refers to this as "making and receiving repair attempts." He has even developed a long list of scripted phrases that you can use to try to de-escalate tension and keep the discussion from spiraling out of control.[6] Some examples are "I see your point," "Let's find our common ground," "I'm sorry. Please forgive me." "Can we take a break?" "I feel blamed. Can you rephrase that?" and "I need things to be calmer right now."

- DO develop your skills to calm the situation by soothing yourself and each other. Being able to soothe yourself keeps you from experiencing severe emotional distress even if your partner is criticizing you. Instead of feeling flooded, overwhelmed, and shell-shocked, you can listen and respond appropriately. You are also more able to hear your partner's repair attempts. To soothe·yourself in the midst of a conversation, you may need to breathe deeply, to "count to ten," or to really focus on listening rather than on rehearsing your own response. If you become overwhelmed and too distressed to think clearly—it's been described as "brain freeze"—you need to take a time-out to calm yourself. Your system has become flooded with adrenaline and it will take twenty minutes for it to physically recover. During this twenty-minute time-out, make sure that you monitor your self-talk. It won't calm you down to spend the time criticizing your partner, or yourself, in your mind. Hopefully you have had a previous conversation with your partner about what you can do to help calm and soothe each other. So when you return to the discussion, you can employ some of those approaches—as can she.

- DO allow yourself to be influenced by your partner [...]. While it is important to remain clear about your own wants and needs, you also need to listen to her about hers. This will allow the two of you to negotiate solutions that satisfy you both. By exploring your wants and preferences in a collaborative way, you increase the chances that you will develop creative solutions that truly address the issues and that you can both genuinely support.

- DO tolerate each other's faults. Until you accept your partner—warts and all—you will be on a mission to change her. Resolving conflict is not about one of you doing all of the changing. It is about negotiating, finding common ground, and searching for ways to accommodate each other without giving up yourself.

## A STRUCTURE FOR DEALING WITH CONFLICTS

For couples who could benefit from having a structure for working on negotiating solvable problems (and even working on perpetual problems), we offer an eight-step model of the negotiation process. This model has been adapted from *Self Care* by Yetta Bernhard and from *Parent Effectiveness Training* by Thomas Gordon.[7]

Sometimes you or your partner may be clear about what you want. Sometimes one or both of you may have identified a problem behavior or a problem issue, but do not yet have a specific idea about how to resolve the situation. This approach can be used in either case.

### Step One: Warm-Up

This is a solo part, where you need to ask yourself the following kinds of questions: Am I really angry or only mildly irritated? What do I want my partner to do, or not do, that is different from what she is or isn't doing? What specifically do I dislike? What do I want? Do I really want this change, or do I want to hurt my partner? Is this issue really important to me? Are my feelings in proportion?

## Step Two: Set the Time

Ask your partner for a definite time to talk. If you encounter some resistance, be persistent; tell her that the issue is important to you and that it hasn't gone away and won't until you discuss it. Try to set the time for as soon as possible, but also respect your partner's wants. If the topic is a hot one, set a limit on how much time you'll talk. Sometimes it is easier to get agreement on meeting for fifteen minutes or a half hour, rather than leaving the amount of time open-ended. If you do not finish in the time you agreed upon, arrange to extend the current discussion for another set amount of time or to continue at a specific later time.

## Step Three: State the Problem

If the situation is that there is something your partner does, or does not do, that you don't like, clearly describe what that is. Keep it to the point: simple, direct, and short. It is very important to stick to the facts, without blaming and adding your feelings about the behavior. If you have a hard time being clear or keeping your feelings out of it, you may need to practice this step in advance. Rehearse what you are going to say and your tone of voice.

If the situation is a more general issue, such as planning vacations, saving for retirement, or landscaping the back yard, both of you should give your perspective on the issue by stating all the information you have about it. Ask yourself, "What are the facts surrounding the topic of planning vacations?"

## Step Four: State Feelings

Use "I" messages to describe how you feel—"I feel angry, hurt, disappointed, confused." Avoid the blaming quality of "you" messages, such as "You make me feel so mad when you just sit there like a lump." Instead, take responsibility for your reactions and feelings and say, "I feel mad." Include the other feelings you may have underneath, or secondary to the anger, such as "I'm scared about feeling so angry and about talking with you about it. I'm really nervous right now." Resist the temptation to blame your partner for your feelings and to end by saying, "And it's all your fault that I feel the way I do." Blaming will likely make your partner defensive; after all, she has been attacked and blamed by you. Plus, the discussion is harder to keep on a constructive tack.

## Step Five: Make a Specific Request

Ask specifically for what you want. Make your request simple, clear, and direct. You want your partner to do, or not do, what? Avoid asking for changes in "attitudes" because these are not specific. For example, "I want you to be more considerate" is not specific enough. Exactly what is it that you want her to do, or not do, that would show you consideration? Asking her to "clean up her dishes" is also not specific enough. Is she showing the consideration you want if she brings them from the living room into the kitchen? Do you want her to pile them in the sink? Or wash them and leave them in the rack? Or dry them and put them away?

## Step Six: Respond and Negotiate

This is where the partner who has been on the listening end gets to talk. If this is you, hopefully you will really have been able to listen without getting defensive and will have checked already, or will check at this point, that you clearly understand the problem, your feelings, and the specific request your partner has made. You can make this check by summarizing; for example, "Let me make sure I understand. When I don't call and let you know that I will be late, you worry about what may have happened to me. You want me to call if I will be late, so that you won't worry."

You then respond to the change proposed by your partner—not to your feelings about the problem or to the questions of whether or not it is a real problem. Telling her that she should not feel the way she does, or that the problem is not a real one, is not an acceptable response. Appropriate responses to specific requests usually take one of five forms:

1. "Yes, I'll do it."

2. "Yes, I agree, with the following conditions." The conditions must relate directly to the proposal and not involve some other issue as a trade—the reason being that this introduces another issue, and may take the negotiations off track. The following is an example of appropriate conditions: "I am willing to schedule and take the car in for tune-ups as long as you are willing to pick it up if I am working out of town."

3. "No, I won't do it." This may indicate some hostility or some previously unshared strong feelings or wants.

4. "No, I don't want to do that, but I would be willing to do this." You make a counterproposal.

5. "How about a time-out? Let me think about this until [a specific time in the future]."

When the situation under discussion is an issue rather than one partner's specific request of the other, both of you toss out ideas for possible solutions. In this brainstorm, all ideas are shared—practical or not—without evaluation in order to encourage the fullest and most creative solutions to emerge. Avoid the "that won't work because" mentality. Wait until later to evaluate the ideas. Once all the ideas for a solution are out, you can negotiate the solution or combination of approaches that appeals to you.

## Step Seven: Reach Resolution

If you have come to an agreement, then the conflict is resolved. Set a trial period after which you can meet again to modify or continue the agreement. Agreements for changes to the solutions can be renegotiated whenever they stop serving either partner's needs.

If you have not been able to reach an agreement in the time allotted, set a time for another session and declare this one over.

## Step Eight: Clarify the Agreement

Repeat the agreement aloud, in turn, making sure you both have exactly the same understanding about it. It's a good idea to write the agreement down on paper, because our memories are often imperfect.

## TROUBLESHOOTING THE NEGOTIATIONS

*If you get too distressed or angry to continue negotiating or if the process is going off track:*
Use the "time-out" technique. Time-out means just that. It is a break in the action, much as it is used in sports, to give you and your partner a break to regroup, calm down, and plan your strategy. Both must agree to abide by the time-out; i.e., one person must not follow the other through the house trying to re-engage her in discussion before the time-out is over. The person who calls for a time-out needs to specify how long she wants. Take at least twenty minutes (because of the adrenaline issue we mentioned earlier). You can always approach your partner after one time-out and request another, if you need more time. We also recommend that you take no more of a break than twenty-four hours because longer than that usually means you are avoiding the issue and leaving your partner hanging.

*If you have a tendency to blame:*
Practice the "I" message technique. This involves describing your feelings *as* your feelings; i.e., "I feel hurt when you. …" It is important not to confuse "feel" with "think." "I feel that you are a jerk" is *not* an "I feel" message. Neither is "I feel that you are trying to manipulate me." These are "I think" statements. To tell the difference, look at the word that follows the word "feel." Is it a feeling or is it the word "that"? If it is "that," you know that "that" is *not* a feeling. […]

*If you have trouble listening, or if either of you feels unheard or not listened to:*
You might try repeating your partner's ideas back to her (or even in your own mind) to make sure that you didn't miss or misunderstand anything. The key thing is to check out your comprehension of what she has said before you respond with your ideas or point of view. Keep in mind that she is the expert on what she said, or at least on what she meant. Don't go on until *she* agrees that you heard her accurately and understood what she said. Often a misunderstanding in communication occurs very early in the process and the whole discussion gets off on the wrong foot.

*If you store up old resentments and then throw them into each argument:*
Make a grievance list that contains all the things that you ever resented or were hurt about. Don't leave anything out. Then go through the list. Cross off any grievances that you really can let go. Now look at the others to see which ones might be suitable for conflict resolution. Go through the eight steps outlined to address the items on your list.

*If you are getting nowhere in your attempts to negotiate:*
Consider the possibility that you are working with a perpetual problem (see below). Get some outside help: Go to a workshop, read a book [...], see a counselor, or use other interventions that are likely to improve your understanding of yourself and your partner, your skills, and your conflict styles.

## THE MOST COMMON COUPLE CONFLICTS

It is possible to predict what a couple fights about even without knowing anything about them. The most typical areas of marital conflict are money, sex, work stress, housework, "in-laws"/ family (biological and chosen), and children.[8] Look over the list. Do at least some of the hot buttons in your relationship appear?

Even though every relationship is different and a couple may be very happy in their relationship, these issues—and others—are likely candidates for conflict because they touch on the most important tasks involved in any relationship. The following outline of relationship tasks has been adapted from *The Seven Principles for Making Marriage Work*, by John Gottman and Nan Silver, and from *The Good Marriage* by Judith Wallerstein and Sandra Blakeslee.[9]

1. Building togetherness and creating autonomy. As a couple, you need to create a psychological "identity" for your relationship—what you want it to be—and also include a sense of individual autonomy in the "we-ness."
2. Separating from your family of origin (if you haven't already) and redefining your ties with family. Defining yourself as partner first, daughter second. (Done in concert with number one.)
3. Exploring sexual love and intimacy.
4. Making your relationship a haven of peace.
5. Making a safe place for conflict.
6. Coping with crises.
7. Providing emotional nurturance.

8. Sharing laughter and keeping interests alive.

9. Becoming and being parents (if there are children involved).

10. Dealing with money. You have to balance the freedom and empowerment that money represents with the security it also symbolizes.

You and your partner may have different ideas about these issues and tasks, how important they are, and how they should be accomplished.

> Stephanie always wanted to have children and thought that her partner, Ari, did too. At first there were obstacles such as needing to finish school and being able to afford a living space that was big enough. But now that they are in a position to actually go ahead and find a donor, Ari's enthusiasm seems to have faded.

> Cathy jokes that her Scottish ancestry is responsible for her approach to money. She credits her grandmother, who used to advise her to "Watch the pennies, and the dollars will take care of themselves." Her partner, Denise, is more of a spender who practices "shopping therapy" whenever she can. Every year at tax time they get into arguments about what to do with any refund.

> Greta is more interested in sex than her partner, Jen. If the frequency or intensity of their sex life slips a bit, Greta is convinced it is the beginning of "lesbian bed death." Jen's attitude is more casual and relaxed—which alarms Greta even more. She is convinced that Jen is not taking the issue seriously enough.

> Adrian is unhappy with the local public junior high school and wants to send her daughter, Shauna, to private school. The problem is the money. Both she and her partner, Melanie, would need to keep working full-time to afford the tuition. Melanie would have to postpone her dream of working only part-time and pursuing her writing.

The challenge for each of these couples is to work together as a team to devise a plan that both partners feel good about. [...]

## ADDRESSING PERPETUAL PROBLEMS: OVERCOMING GRIDLOCK

In our relationships—just like in traffic—we can be hopelessly stuck and frustrated. If you and your partner seem mired in an endless recycling of the same argument, it may be that you have become stuck in a gridlocked perpetual problem.[10] The goal in relationship gridlock is not to solve the problem but to move from being stuck to having dialogue, so you can learn to live with the problem. You need to do so because if it is a perpetual problem, it will likely be with you for the duration of your relationship.

Signs of gridlock include:

- making no headway in discussions—which can then turn ugly,
- getting more polarized in your positions,
- feeling hurt,
- feeling rejected, and
- emotionally disengaging from your partner.

In order to get beyond feeling stuck, first you must understand the underlying cause of the gridlock. Gridlock is a "sign that you have dreams for your life that are not being addressed or respected by each other. These dreams are the hopes, aspirations, and wishes that are part of your identity and give purpose and meaning to your life."[11]

> Daphne and Mickey have been together for ten years and have three children. One of the issues they argue about is vacations. Daphne wants to spend vacations with her extended family on the East Coast. They have a big house on the water where everybody gathers during the summer. The cousins get to meet each other and have a ball. The adults can visit and take turns cooking, lifeguarding, and lying in the hammock. Mickey would prefer to have some time alone with Daphne where they do something active—a skiing, backpacking, or bicycle trip—and then have some adventure as a family, just the two of them and the kids.

What dreams might be embedded in this conflict?

Daphne: Extended family is very important to me. My happiest memories of growing up are of times at my family summer place. I want my children to have those memories too. My dream is for us as a family to have the feeling of closeness and connection that I had with the community of my extended family.

Mickey: I have spent a lot of time and energy trying to get over the effects of growing up in a very dysfunctional family. I moved across the country to get some distance from my family—to escape actually. I am very cautious about getting too involved with Daphne's family. I see some dysfunctional patterns there as well and it scares me. My dream is to establish our own traditions with ourselves, our children, and our friends.

Once the dreams are uncovered, Daphne and Mickey can talk about them. One option is for them to take turns talking honestly about their dreams. One talks for fifteen minutes while the other listens, then they switch. The listener's job is to listen as a friend would, to ask supportive questions, and to understand why this dream is so important. If you try this yourself, remember that the purpose is not to resolve the conflict. It is to encourage a dialogue and to lessen the hurt so the problem becomes less painful.

Hopefully, once you each understand what hidden dreams underlie a perpetual problem, you can support your partner's dream. This does not mean that you will do whatever your partner wants or take on her dream as yours. The goal here is to be supportive. Listening, being interested, and understanding (not necessarily agreeing) is one level of support, and that may be as far as you can go. You may be willing to go further and support the dream in some tangible way—say financially. You may even be willing to join your partner in realizing her dream.

Ending the gridlock requires making peace with the issue. You need to clarify what aspects of the issue are nonnegotiable. These are the ones you cannot give up without violating your basic needs, core values, and sense of integrity. And you need to figure out what aspects you can be more flexible about. Try to make the first list short and the second long. Then share this information with your partner—perhaps using the eight-step negotiation process outlined earlier in this [reading]. Work toward a solution that honors and respects both of your dreams.

[...]

## NOTES

1. Gottman and Silver, *The Seven Principles*, 15.

2. Ibid., 129–155.

3. Ibid., 131.

4. Adapted from Gottman and Silver, *The Seven Principles*, 159–185; and Matthew McKay et al., *Couple Skills*, 117–128.

5. Gottman and Silver, *The Seven Principles*, 27.

6. Ibid., 170–176.

7. Yetta M. Bernhard, *Self Care* (Berkeley, CA: Celestial Arts, 1975); and Thomas Gordon, *P.E.T.: Parent Effectiveness Training* (New York: New American Library, 1970), 236–253.

8. Gottman and Silver, *The Seven Principles*, 187.

9. Gottman and Silver, *The Seven Principles*; and Wallerstein and Blakeslee, *The Good Marriage*, 27–29.

10. Gottman and Silver, *The Seven Principles*, 132–133.

11. Ibid., 217–218.

## BIBLIOGRAPHY

Bernhard, Yetta. *Self Care*. Berkeley, CA: Celestial Arts, 1975.

Gordon, Thomas. *P.E.T: Parent Effectiveness Training*. New York: New American Library, 1970.

Gottman, John M., and Nan Silver. *The Seven Principles for Making Marriage Work*. New York: Crown, 1999.

McKay, M., P. Fanning, and K. Paleg. *Couple Skills: Making Your Relationship Work*. Oakland, CA: New Harbinger, 1994.

Wallerstein, Judith S., and Sandra Blakeslee. *The Good Marriage: How and Why Love Lasts*. New York: Warner Books, 1995.

# RELATIONAL TRANSGRESSIONS AND REPAIR

Sometimes conflict occurs as the result of a relational transgression or relationship rupture. This type of conflict is somewhat different than common disagreements depicted in the reading from Clunis and Green. Relational transgressions are events, behaviors, or actions where one partner deliberately goes against established implicit or explicit rules or norms of the relationship (Metts & Cupach, 2007). Hurtful behaviors such as cruelty (i.e., avoidance, criticism), lying, or infidelity can cause ruptures in the relationship and force one or both partners into deciding whether to break up or repair the relationship and stay together. This "should I stay or should I go" state of mind can be confusing, emotionally taxing, and difficult to navigate. Self-care anyone?

There is extensive research on how couples and individuals address relational transgression—way beyond what we can offer here. Briefly, an individual's decision to leave an offending partner after a transgression is influenced by many factors, including their level of commitment, how satisfied they are in the relationship, the quality of alternatives (other partners or being single; Emmers-Sommer, 2003), the offender's perceived motivations, and the severity of the transgression (Metts & Copach, 2007). Thus, the state of the relationship, the severity of the transgression, and the couple's ability to engage in constructive conflict discussions set the stage for forgiveness and relational repair or breakup. (We discuss the process of breaking up in Chapter 13.)

One of the key factors in the decision to stay in the relationship is how the transgressor communicates about their offense. Offenders who accept responsibility and show remorse are more likely to be forgiven (Metts & Cupach, 2007). Because forgiveness is the precursor to relational repair, *how* we apologize to our partner matters! Apologizing well is one of the most useful relationship skills you will ever master. Please refer to Lazare's (2004) recipe for a good apology in the end-of-chapter reflections in Chapter 6.

Relational repair work will improve intimate relationships after any type of conflict and is a necessity after a transgression has occurred. The communication skills offered in prior chapters along with the conflict management skills offered in this chapter will help you and your partner navigate relational repair, and addressing the transgression directly and constructively is key. Couples who communicate about their relationship and problems directly rather than avoiding them or one another have a better chance of repair and continuing their relationship (Emmer-Sommer, 2003). In other words, if you hurt your partner or make a mistake in your relationship, apologize—and if your partner is willing to forgive, allow time for each of you to talk openly and honestly about what happened and the future of your relational "we-ness." Most importantly, as you have come to know in prior chapters, communicate, communicate, communicate!

## END-OF-CHAPTER REFLECTIONS

Now that you have had a chance to examine relational transgressions and negative behavior patterns people engage in during conflict, we hope that you become more purposeful and deliberate in how you behave when you are in a conflict with your intimate partner. The conflict management skills presented in this chapter are most helpful when both partners are aware of them. Finally, it is never too late to seek professional support for your intimate relationship. Seek couples counseling if you or your partner are feeling dissatisfied, are trying to repair after a transgression, or navigating a disruptive change. Remember, conflict happens in all intimate relationships; *how* well you manage conflict as a couple will reflect *how* well you love!

## REFERENCES

Emmers-Sommer, Tara M. (2003). When partners falter: Repair after a transgression. In D. J. Canary & M. Dainton (Eds.), *Maintaining relationships through communication* (pp. 185–206). Routledge.

Gottman, J. M., & Krokoff, L. J. (1989). The relationship between marital interaction and marital satisfaction—a longitudinal view. *Journal of Consulting and Clinical Psychology, 57*, 47–52.

Gottman, J. M., Levenson, R. W., Swanson, C., Swanson, K., Tyson, R., & Yoshimoto, D. (2003). Observing gay, lesbian and heterosexual couples' relationships. *Journal of Homosexuality, 45*(1), 65–91.

Metts, S., & Cupach, W. R. (2007). Responses to relational transgressions: Hurt, anger and sometimes forgiveness. In B. H. Spitzberg & W. R. Cupach (Eds.), *The dark side of interpersonal communication* (2nd ed.) (pp. 243–273). Erlbaum.

## RECOMMENDATIONS FOR FURTHER READING

Gottman, J., & Silver, N. (1999). *The seven principles for making marriage work*. Crown.

# PART III

# Variations on Intimate Relationships

# *Chapter 9*

# Friendship

## EDITORS' INTRODUCTION

For some of you, friendship comes easy. You've always been invited to birthday parties, had someone to shop with, or meet for some hoops. You've definitely had someone to call when you were bored. For others, the process of forging friendships has felt cumbersome, awkward, and maybe even painful. You may have watched others laughing together in groups and wished you had a group of your own. Regardless of where you fall on that continuum, it is likely that the friendship domain of your life has been challenged in the last year.

At the time of this writing, COVID-19 has touched most of us to some degree and has quite likely altered the way you interact with the friends you already have, and most certainly has made you think about the way you make new friends. If you are one of the lucky ones and friendship has always come easy, it's possible that even you have encountered difficulty since the term *social-distancing* interrupted the way we socialize and live. Think about some of the ways friendships have been affected by COVID-19. Kindergartners are at an age when they should be learning how to interpret social situations—a foundation for budding friendship skills—and instead they are spending a year of crucial development isolated or behind a mask without the benefit of facial expressions necessary to give and receive feedback. High school students have not been able to participate in activities (music, sports, science labs, prom, pep rallies, clubs, bus rides, carpools, parties, lunchroom shenanigans, etc.) that allow for more effortless connections with others and provide the sod for friendships to be maintained and for new friendships to emerge and grow. College freshmen—who've historically been able to rely on the buzz created by individuating from their parents—are now sequestered to their dorm rooms at a time when meeting others and forging new friendships should be rampant.

When you read "Friendship and Health" by Julianne Holt-Lunstad, and "Friendship and Mental Health Functioning" by Alan King, Tiffany Russell, and Amy Veith, you will see that constraints on friendship are not a small matter. Said simply, when our friendships are strong and meaningful, so are our physical and emotional health. When friendships are distant, filled with angst, or insecure, our physical and emotional health suffer. Most important is that regardless of the current state of your friendship circle—whether you are satisfied with the friends you have, you'd like to make new friends, or you'd like to resurrect past friendships that have faded away—acquiring friends is a skill that can be learned at any age.

At the end of this chapter, we will provide some resources that can get the friendship-acquisition ball rolling. For now, keep in mind the following primer questions for reflection. If you feel so inclined, take a few minutes and consider your responses to the following questions before you read, and then again after you've read the chapter.

## PRIMERS

1. Think about a friendship you've had, regardless of age, that felt the most strong and mutually supportive. If this friendship is current, congratulations! Read the excerpt on friendship maintenance to be sure you keep this important relationship going. If the friendship that comes to mind is from your past or even your childhood, try to conjure up how you felt about your overall wellness when this relationship was active. What comes to mind?

2. Make a list (either in your mind or on paper) of the friendships that are most important to you. How would you assess the overall health of your current friends? Are you satisfied with the quality and quantity of these relationships? Would you like more friends? Or perhaps you'd like to create distance with those relationships that might not be working well for you. Remember that friendships break up in similarly painful ways as romantic relationships; refer to Chapter 13 on breakups for more guidance.

## READING 9.1

# Friendship and Health

*By Julianne Holt-Lunstad*

## INTRODUCTION

> *Friendship is unnecessary, like philosophy, like art ... It has no survival value; rather it is one of those things that give value to survival.*
> —C. S. Lewis

Not only do close friendships give meaning to our lives and make us happier (Helliwell, Layard, & Sachs, 2013), but contrary to this statement by C.S. Lewis there is now substantial evidence that they have a powerful influence on physical health and even survival. Indeed, both the quantity and quality of social relationships may influence physical health and risk for early mortality. Research evidence indicates that having fewer and lower-quality social relationships is associated with poorer physical health and greater risk for early mortality, while having more and better relationships is associated with better physical health and greater odds of survival (De Vogli, Chandola, & Marmot, 2007; Holt-Lunstad, Smith, & Layton, 2010; Uchino, 2006). Social relationships can take many forms that include both familial and nonfamilial relationships. Much of the early research on social relationships and physical health has been focused on familial or kin relationships, however, a significant amount of time is spent interacting among friends (Hartup & Stevens, 1999). This has led to an increased focus on *friendship* as an important component of one's social network and source of social support, which subsequently may have important implications for health.

The aims of this [reading] are to (1) describe the multiple ways in which friendship has been defined and systematically studied; (2) review the historical and theoretical perspectives that may be applied to understanding the association between friendship and health; (3) provide an overview of the conceptual pathways by which friendships may influence health; (4) review the evidence that links friendship to better physical health outcomes; (5) address the potential

Julianne Holt-Lunstad, Selection from "Friendship and Health," *The Psychology of Friendship*, ed. Mahzad Hojjat and Anne Moyer, pp. 233-234, 238-248. Copyright © 2017 by Oxford University Press. Reprinted with permission.

detrimental influence of friends on health; and finally (6) address potential implications of changing trends in technology-mediated social interaction for understanding the association between friendship and health.

## Definition and Measurement Approaches

The terms "friendship," "peer relationships," and "social networks" are often used interchangeably but are distinct constructs. Friendship has been defined as a relationship based on mutual respect, appreciation, and liking (Bryan, Puckett, & Newman, 2013), whereas peer relationships are conceptualized as time spent with those of roughly the same age and maturity level. Although these may overlap, they are not necessarily the same construct given that peers may or may not be considered friends. Likewise, as will he discussed further later, the concept of "friendship" is evolving and broadening as Internet social networks advance.

Within the health literature, the influence of friendship has been measured in diverse ways—similar to the influence of social relationships more broadly. These can be broken down into two broad categories that examine the structure and functions of the relationship (Berkman, Glass, Brissette, & Seeman, 2000; Cohen & Wills, 1985; Uchino, 2006). Generally, these two approaches distinguish the aspects of social/friendship networks and the support that they provide. *Structural* aspects of relationships refer to the extent to which individuals are situated or integrated into social networks. A *social network* describes connections between individuals and their relationships or network ties. Measures of social networks typically assess the density, size, or number of relationships. *Social integration* is used to describe the extent of participation of an individual in a broad range of social relationships, including active engagement in a variety of social activities or relationships, and a sense of communality and identification with one's social roles. *Functional social support* and corresponding measures focus on the specific functions served by friends, and are measured by actual or perceived availability of support, aid, or resources from these friendships. For example, friendship can be an important source of social support, which can include *emotional support* (e.g., expressions of care and concern), *informational support* (e.g., information or advice to help one cope with stress), *tangible support* (e.g., direct material aid, also referred to as instrumental, practical, or financial support), and *belonging support* (e.g., others to engage in social activities; Cohen, Mermelstein, Kamarck, & Hoberman, 1985; Cutrona & Russell, 1990). These functions also can be differentiated in terms of whether social support is perceived or received (Dunkel-Schetter & Skokan, 1990). Perceived support refers to the perception that support is available and will be provided if needed, whereas received support refers to the actual support provided by others. Importantly, received and perceived support are only moderately correlated and thus should be viewed as distinct constructs (Wills & Shiner, 2000). Thus, the influence of friendships on physical health is generally evaluated in terms of (1) the extent of integration in social networks, (2) the quality of social interactions that are intended to be supportive (e.g., received social support), and (3) the beliefs and perceptions of support availability held by individuals (e.g., perceived social support).

[...]

## FRIENDSHIP AND PHYSICAL HEALTH OUTCOMES

Does friendship have a significant influence on physical health, or does one's physical health influence friendships? There is data to suggest the association between friendship and health may be bidirectional, such that friendship can influence health and health can influence friendship (Bryan et al., 2013). Importantly, however, there exists strong epidemiological evidence of a directional effect of relationships on health (Holt-Lunstad et al., 2010). Thus, the majority of this [reading] focuses on the directional effect of friendship on physical health. Likewise, the influence that friendships may have on physical health may be either positive or negative. While being socially connected can be protective, friendships may also have a deleterious effect on health via encouraging unhealthy and risky behaviors and/or by serving as sources of stress.

### Effects of Health on Friendship

There is evidence to suggest that health factors (e.g., smoking status, BMI, muscularity, depression, etc.) can influence the development, maintenance, and dissolution of friendships (O'Malley & Christakis, 2011). Adolescents in poor health are also more likely to form smaller social networks and occupy less prominence within their networks than their healthy peers (Haas, Schaefer, & Kornienko, 2010). However, in a review of youth with chronic pediatric conditions, evidence suggests that children and adolescents with chronic health conditions such as cancer, asthma, and diabetes generally do not have more problems with peer relations than do their healthy counterparts (La Greca, Bearman, & Moore, 2002). Moreover, this review found that friends often facilitated adaptation to their health condition. However, those with more stigmatizing conditions (e.g., HIV) and conditions of the central nervous system (CNS; e.g., cerebral palsy) were more likely to encounter social difficulties. Thus, it appears that the nature of the health condition may play an important role in whether it may impact friendships and peer relations.

### Effects of Friendship on Health

Overall, there is strong evidence for the protective effect of social relationships on health, with stronger evidence for perceived support than received support (see review by Uchino, 2009).

This evidence comes from laboratory, field, and epidemiological studies across morbidity and mortality outcomes. Most studies measure perceptions of social support in a broad way that includes perceptions of support from friends, family, and acquaintances; however, the majority of these studies do not break down results by relationship type. Thus, results include the effects of friendships, but few studies isolate the effects of friendship specifically. Evidence for effects of friendship on health behaviors, self-reported health and symptomatology, clinical health outcomes, and overall mortality are briefly highlighted in this section.

## Health Behaviors

In both youth and adults, friends and peers have a significant influence on the development and maintenance of positive and negative health habits. Friends may influence health by encouraging, modeling, or promoting norms of healthy behaviors (e.g., physical activity, fruit and vegetable consumption, adequate sleep) and deterring risky behaviors (e.g., smoking, binge drinking, drug use, risky sexual behaviors). For instance, even among adults, data shows that peers influence fruit and vegetable consumption (Buller et al., 1999). In older adult women, support from a friend was the most successful in predicting physical activity across the life span (Harvey & Alexander, 2012). Many health behaviors tend to also cluster together such that they co-occur (e.g., alcohol and substance abuse, nutrition and physical activity). One study found that descriptive norms of friends were associated with multiple behavior clusters (Dusseldorp et al., 2014). Thus, not only might friends influence health habits, but, given that these habits tend to cluster, this influence may be compounded.

Friends can also be sources of information relevant to health behaviors. For example, in a recent study of a random sample of 915 adolescents, participants completed an anonymous questionnaire that asked about their preferred source of health information (Baheiraei, Khoori, Foroushani, Ahmadi, & Ybarra, 2014). Results of this study indicated that the preferred source of this information was their mothers (51.11%) and same-sex friends (40.11%), with older adolescents preferring friends. In another study, older women were asked whom they were closest to and how they contributed to their health (Moremen, 2008). When it came to direct caregiving, most preferred family members to friends; however, some felt they would also call on their friends. Women described the ways in which confidants kept them healthy, which included "(1) offering advice and encouragement about diet and exercise, (2) providing meals and transportation, (3) laughing, talking, and joking with them, (4) keeping them happy and feeling good about themselves, and, on rare occasions, (5) offering spiritual guidance" (Moremen, 2008, p. 160).

## Self-Reported Health and Symptomology

The majority of studies that examine the health influence of friendship specifically measure self-reported health. A longitudinal study among a Scottish cohort found that the number of friends in childhood predicted self-rated health in adulthood (Almquist, 2012). There were gender differences in this association, such that for women it was a gradient effect (the fewer the number of friends the worse the health) whereas for men it was more of a threshold effect (only those without friends showed poorer health). In a national survey study of older adults, older people who had a close companion friend in the place where they worship had higher self-reported health and with fewer outpatient physician visits over time; however, these findings only held for the oldest-old study participants (Krause, 2010). This also appears to be consistent among adolescents. Examining the friendship data from the National Longitudinal Study of Adolescent Health, results show that having a larger number of friends improves physical and mental health (Ho, 2014). Specifically, each additional friend increases an individual's general health measure by 6.6%. Taken together these data suggest that the number of friends one has, across childhood, adolescence, adulthood, and old age, is beneficial to physical health.

Social support has been shown across a number of studies to buffer the negative effects of stress, but there may be some utility to support from friends specifically. For example, one study found that having a friend to confide in played a moderating role in the negative health effects associated with losing a spouse (widowhood, divorce, separation; Bookwala, Marshall, & Manning, 2014). This study found that those who had a friend as a confidante reported lower somatic depressive symptoms, better self-rated health, and fewer sick days in bed during the preceding year than those who reported not having a friend as confidante.

## Clinical Health Outcomes

There is substantial evidence linking social support to coronary heart disease (CHD), the leading cause of death in most industrialized countries. For example, in a prospective study examining perceived social support from family, friends, acquaintances, and significant others on mortality or recurrent event, found that perceived social support was associated with better recovery among patients with a recent acute myocardial infarction (Lett et al., 2007). Further, a 2010 systematic review and meta-analysis examined prospective studies that measured both structural and functional social support and cardiovascular outcomes at follow-up. These included studies of CHD etiology, development of CHD in previously healthy individuals, and CHD prognosis, which includes individuals with preexisting CHD (Barth, Schneider, & von Kanel, 2010). Across multiple studies, there is evidence for the beneficial effect of functional support. Perceived social support, or the perception of positive social resources, is important in CHD prognosis.

Another clinical outcome that is gaining interest is oral health, given that periodontal disease is also significantly associated with heart disease (Lockhart et al., 2012). In an intriguing study of oral health, various aspects of social relationships, including number of close friends, were examined to see whether these were associated with clinical measures of current disease, markers of good oral function, and subjective oral health (Tsakos et al., 2013). They found that those with four to six close friends had fewer decayed teeth and lower probability for root decay than those with fewer friends.

## Mortality

There is now substantial evidence for the protective effect of being socially connected on risk for mortality from all causes. Some of the first epidemiological evidence was highlighted in an influential review of five prospective studies (House, Landis, & Umberson, 1988). Since that time, the number of studies examining the influence of social relationships (both functional and structural aspects) and mortality has grown exponentially. In a meta-analysis of 148 independent prospective studies, results indicate that individuals with greater social connections (averaged across the different measurement approaches) have a 50% greater likelihood of survival compared with those low in social connections (Holt-Lunstad et al., 2010). The effect was consistent across gender, age, initial health status, and causes of mortality.

There is now evidence of the directional effect of relationships' influence on mortality (Holt-Lunstad et al., 2010). Most studies tracked initially healthy participants; however, regardless of initial health status, those who were more socially connected lived longer. Most notably, the overall magnitude of the effect on risk for mortality was comparable with and in many cases exceeded the effect of many well-established risk factors for mortality. For instance, lacking social connectedness carries a risk equivalent to smoking up to 15 cigarettes per day, and is greater than alcohol abuse, physical inactivity (sedentary lifestyle), obesity, and air pollution, among others.

The studies included in the meta-analytic review measured the influence of social relationships in diverse ways, including both functional (received support, perceived social support, and perceived loneliness) and structural aspects (marital status, social networks, social integration, complex measures of social integrations, living alone, social isolation). With the exception of marital status and perhaps living alone, each of these measurement approaches likely included the influence of friends. Assessments that took into account the multidimensional aspects of social relationships were associated with a 91% increased odds of survival. Such measures account for a diversity of relationships. Likewise, other research suggests that having a diversity (not just a large number) of relationships was associated with better immune functioning (Cohen, Doyle, Skoner, Rabin, & Gwaltney, 1997) and even white matter microstructural integrity in the brain (Molesworth, Sheu, Cohen, Gianaros, & Verstynen, 2015). Together, these data suggest that perhaps different relationships serve different functions and thus access to diversity would be adaptive. Further, these data suggest that both friendship networks and the social support they provide are important.

## Potentially Deleterious Health Effects of Friendship

While friends can exert a positive influence on health behaviors, evidence shows that friends can also exert a powerful negative influence as well.

## Unhealthy Behaviors

A unique approach to understanding the role of friendship on health behaviors comes from the work of Christakis and Fowler on *social contagion*. They review a series of studies that show the spread of various health indicators within social networks (Christakis & Fowler, 2013). For example, one's chances of becoming obese increased by 57% if he or she had a friend who became obese within a given time frame (Christakis & Fowler, 2007). Evidence from large datasets demonstrates the significant influence of social networks on alcohol consumption (Rosenquist, Murabito, Fowler, & Christakis, 2010), smoking (Christakis & Fowler, 2008), aspirin use and cardiac events (Strully et al., 2012), depression (Rosenquist, Fowler, & Christakis, 2011), and sleep loss and drug use in adolescents (Mednick, Christakis, & Fowler, 2010). They further argue that formation of friendships, relationships that are neither kin nor mate, tend to be formed with genetically similar others (Christakis & Fowler, 2014; Fowler, Settle, & Christakis, 2011).

### Sources of Stress

Friends can be rich sources of social support that can help us in times of stress, but friendships can also be sources of stress themselves. Much of the research has focused primarily on positive relationships, however many friendships are characterized by both positivity and negativity (Campo et al., 2009; Uchino, Holt-Lunstad, Uno, & Flinders, 2001). The assumption that friendships are solely supportive has overgeneralized many individuals' experiences—yet data shows that roughly half of peoples friendship networks are made up of ambivalent relationships (Bushman & Holt-Lunstad, 2009; Holt-Lunstad & Clark, 2014).

Several studies have examined the influence of interacting with an ambivalent friend relative to a supportive friend on cardiovascular reactivity (Gramer & Supp, 2014; Holt-Lunstad & Clark, 2014; Holt-Lunstad, Uchino, Smith, & Hicks, 2007; Uno, Uchino, & Smith, 2002). In these studies, participants were asked to bring in a friend to the lab as part of the study. Results from these studies have demonstrated greater cardiovascular reactivity when interacting with an ambivalent friend compared with a supportive friend. Several other studies using other research designs have shown consistent findings. This finding is consistent whether the target (ambivalent relationship) is physically present or not (Carlisle et al., 2012), whether one is interacting with an experimentally manipulated or existing relationship, and whether the effect is examined at the relationship level (examining a specific relationship dyad; Holt-Lunstad et al., 2007) or network level (number of ambivalent relationships in one's network; Uchino et al., 2001). Greater cardiovascular reactivity associated with ambivalent relationships was also seen across multiple types of laboratory tasks; and when examining young adult (mostly undergraduate) as well as middle to older adult samples (Uchino, Holt-Lunstad, Bloor, & Campo, 2005). Taken together, the evidence suggests a generalized negative influence of ambivalent relationships on acute cardiovascular functioning in a laboratory setting. These studies suggest that ambivalent relationships are linked to deleterious health-relevant processes. Importantly, there is also evidence to suggest that these effects may be chronic. Ambivalent friendships occupy roughly half of one's social network, involve a similar level of contact as supportive friends, and are maintained over the long term, suggesting that the influence of these relationships may not be isolated but rather may potentially have a pervasive impact (Bushman & Holt-Lunstad, 2009).

## LOOKING TO THE FUTURE

Recent advancements in technology have led to dramatic shifts in the way in which we interact socially and the way in which social support is communicated. The use of the Internet and mobile technology is widespread, even in developing and emerging nations (Pew Research, 2015), and is now the primary form of communication. Recent developments in technology are even changing the way in which many define what is considered a friend (see Ledbetter, [...]). For example, many do not consider a friend on Facebook to be true a friend. Technology is already currently involved in and influencing the development, maintenance, and even termination of friendships, and new developments (e.g., intelligent machines, wearable devices, immersive environments, etc.) arc happening at an exponentially rapid pace. The long-term consequences of these developments are yet unknown.

This raises an important question of whether friendship online has similar health effects as off-line friendships. Research is now exploring both equivalencies between technology-mediated and face-to-face communication, as well as the potential unique benefits of each approach to social support. There is some evidence to suggest that participation in a broader social network available online can promote well-being and provide a buffering effect during times of stress (Dutta-Bergman, 2004). For example, one study found that the number of Facebook friends was associated with stronger perceptions of social support, which was associated with reduced stress, and in turn less self-reported physical illness and greater well-being (Nabi, Prestin, & So, 2013). In an experimental study where subjects were randomly assigned to increase frequency of Facebook posts, results revealed experimentally induced reductions in loneliness relative to the control group and that these reductions in loneliness were due to increased feelings of connection to friends on a daily basis (Deters & Mehl, 2013). However, other studies point to potential pitfalls (Luxton, June, & Fairall, 2012; Steers, Wickham, & Acitelli, 2014). For instance, presence of a mobile phone in social settings may reduce closeness and quality of interactions interfering with social support (Przybylski & Weinstein, 2013). Likewise, usage of social media has been linked to greater depressive symptomology (Steers et al., 2014) and even suicide-related behavior (Luxton et al., 2012). Thus, we need to acknowledge and better understand both the positive and negative health implications associated with social technology.

## CONCLUSION

Friendship is an important and significant part of our daily social experience that has widespread implications for our health and well-being. There is currently a large and growing literature on the significant influence our social relationships have on physical health; however, relatively less is known about friendship specifically. While much is known about social networks and the social support associated with them, few studies specify the specific nature of the relationship type (e.g., friend, spouse, family, coworker, parent-child, etc.). Undoubtedly, friendships are a part of our social networks and are a frequent source of social support—both of which have been robustly linked to physical health outcomes. Further, meta-analytic data on mortality found the greatest effect among studies that used multidimensional measures of social integration—it was associated with a 91% increased odds of survival. Such measures account for a diversity of relationships (e.g., spouse, children, parents, other relatives, close friends, community involvement, coworkers, neighbors, etc.), suggesting that perhaps different relationships serve different functions and thus access to diversity would be adaptive. Given recent trends suggesting technology-mediated communication is now the dominant form of social interaction, friends may occupy a greater prominence among interaction partners via social technology. Importantly, while research suggests that friends and friendship networks may have a powerful influence on health, this influence may be positive or negative. Although more data is needed, it is possible that social technology may accelerate and accentuate this influence. Additionally, a life span perspective is needed to take into account distinct antecedent processes and mechanisms that are relevant to different sources of support over time (Uchino, 2009). Finally, because friendship is unique in being a voluntary/optional relationship, further research is needed to determine the potential particular pathways by which friendships influence health.

# REFERENCES

Almquist, Y. M. (2012). Childhood friendships and adult health: Findings from the Aberdeen Children of the 1950s cohort study. *European Journal of Public Health, 22,* 378–383. doi: 10.1093/eurpub/ckr045

Baheiraei, A., Khoori, E., Foroushani, A. R., Ahmadi, F., & Ybarra, M. L. (2014). What sources do adolescents turn to for information about their health concerns? *International Journal of Adolescent Medicine and Health, 26,* 61–68. doi: 10.1515/ijamh-2012-0112

Barnes, J. (1954). Class and committees in a Norwegian island parish. *Human Relations, 7,* 39–58.

Barth, J., Schneider, S., & von Kanel, R. (2010). Lack of social support in the etiology and the prognosis of coronary heart disease: A systematic review and meta-analysis. *Psychosomatic Medicine, 72,* 229–238. doi: 10.1097/PSY.0b0l3e3181d01611

Berkman, L. F., Glass, T., Brissette, I., & Seeman, T. E. (2000). From social integration to health: Durkheim in the new millennium. *Social Science and Medicine, 51,* 843–857.

Bookwala, J., Marshall, K. I., & Manning, S. W. (2014). Who needs a friend? Marital status transitions and physical health outcomes in later life. *Health Psychology, 33,* 505–515. doi: 10.1037/hea0000049

Bott, E. (1957). *Family and social network.* London, UK: Tavistock Press.

Bryan, K. S., Puckett, Y. N., & Newman, M. L. (2013). Peer relationships and health: From childhood through adulthood. In M. L. Newman, N. A. Roberts, M. L. Newman, & N. A. Roberts (Eds.), *Health and social relationships: The good, the bad, and the complicated* (pp. 167–188). Washington, DC: American Psychological Association. doi: 10.1037/14036-008

Buller, D. B., Morrill, C., Taren, D., Aickin, M., Sennott-Miller, L., Buller, M. K., ... Wentzel, T. M. (1999). Randomized trial testing the effect of peer education at increasing fruit and vegetable intake. *Journal of the National Cancer Institute, 91,* 1491–1500.

Bushman, B. B., & Holt-Lunstad, J. (2009). Understanding social relationship maintenance among friends: Why we don't end those frustrating friendships. *Journal of Social and Clinical Psychology, 28,* 749–778. doi:10.152l/jscp.2009.28.6.749

Campo, R. A., Uchino, B. N., Vaughn, A. A., Reblin, M., Smith, T. W., & Holt-Lunstad, J. (2009). The assessment of positivity and negativity in social networks: The reliability and validity of the Social Relationships Index. *Journal of Community Psychology, 37,* 471–486.

Carlisle, M., Uchino, B. N., Sanbonmatsu, D. M., Smith, T. W., Cribbet, M. R., Birmingham, W., ... Vaughn, A. A. (2012). Subliminal activation of social ties moderates cardiovascular reactivity during acute stress. *Health Psychology, 31,* 217–225. doi: 10.1037/a0025187

Cassell, J. (1976). The contribution of the social environment to host resistance. *American Journal of Epidemiology, 104,* 107–123.

Christakis, N. A., & Fowler, J. H. (2007). The spread of obesity in a large social network over 32 years. *New England Journal of Medicine, 357,* 370–379. doi: 10.1056/NEJMsa066082

Christakis, N. A., & Fowler, J. H. (2008). The collective dynamics of smoking in a large social network. *New England Journal of Medicine, 358,* 2249–2258. doi: 10.1056/NEJMsa0706154

Christakis, N. A., & Fowler, J. H. (2013). Social contagion theory': Examining dynamic social networks and human behavior. *Statistics in Medicine, 32,* 556–577. doi: 10.1002/sim.5408

Christakis, N. A., & Fowler, J. H. (2014). Friendship and natural selection. *Proceedings of the National Academies of Science USA, 111 Suppl 3,*10796–10801. doi: 10.1073/pnas.1400825111

Cobb, S. (1976). Social support as a moderator of life stress. *Psychosomatic Medicine, 38,* 300–314.

Cohen, S. (1988). Psychosocial models of the role of social support in the etiology of physical disease. *Health Psychology, 7,* 269–297.

Cohen, S., Doyle, W. J., Skoner, D. P., Rabin, B. S., & Gwaltney, J. M., Jr. (1997). Social ties and susceptibility to the common cold. *JAMA, 277,* 1940–1944.

Cohen, S., Mermelstein, R. J., Kamarck, T., & Hoberman, H. M. (1985). Measuring the functional components of social support. In I. G. Sarason & B. Sarason (Eds.), *Social support: Theory, research and applications* (pp.73–94). The Hague, Holland: Martines Niijhoff.

Cohen, S., & Wills, T. A. (1985). Stress, social support, and the buffering hypothesis. *Psychological Bulletin, 98,* 310–357.

Cutrona, C. E, & Russell, D. W. (1990). Type of social support and specific stress: Towards a theory of optimal matching. In B. R. Sarason, I. G. Sarason, & G. R. Pierce (Eds.), *Social support: An interactional view* (pp. 319–366). New York, NY: Wiley.

De Vogli, R., Chandola, T., & Marmot, M. G. (2007). Negative aspects of close relationships and heart disease. *Archives of Internal Medicine, 167,* 1951–1957. doi: 10.1001/archinte.167.18.1951

Deters, F. G., & Mehl, M. R. (2013). Does Posting Facebook status updates increase or decrease loneliness? An online social networking experiment. *Social Psychological and Personality Science, 4.* doi: 10.1177/1948550612469233

Dockray, S., & Steptoe, A. (2010). Positive affect and psychobiological processes. *Neuroscience And Biobehavioral Reviews, 35,* 69–75. doi: 10.1016/j.neubiorev.2010.01.006

Dunkel-Schetter, C., & Skokan, L. A. (1990). Determinants of social support provision in personal relationships. *Journal of Social and Personal Relationships, 7,* 437–450.

Dusseldorp, E., Klein Velderman, M., Paulussen, T. W., Junger, M., van Nieuwenhuijzen, M., & Reijneveld, S. A. (2014). Targets for primary prevention: Cultural, social and intrapersonal factors associated with co-occurring health-related behaviours. *Psychology and Health, 29,* 598–611. doi: 10.1080/08870446.2013.879137

Dutta-Bergman, M. J. (2004). Health attitudes, health cognitions, and health behaviors among Internet health information seekers: Population-based survey. *Journal of Medical Internet Research, 6,* el5. doi: 10.2196/jmir.6.2.el5

Fowler, J. H., Settle, J. E., & Christakis, N. A. (2011). Correlated genotypes in friendship networks. *Proceedings of the National Academies of Science USA, 108,* 1993–1997. doi: 10.1073/pnas.1011687108

Gable, S. L., Gosnell, C. L., Maisel, N. C., & Strachman, A. (2012). Safely testing the alarm: Close others' responses to personal positive events. *Journal of Personality and Social Psychology, 103,* 963–981. doi: 10.1037/a0029488

Gable, S. L., Reis, H. T., Impett, E. A., & Asher, E. R. (2004). What do you do when things go right? The intrapersonal and interpersonal benefits of sharing positive events. *Journal of Personality and Social Psychology, 87,* 228–245. doi: 10.1037/0022-3514.87.2.228

Gramer, M., & Supp, N. (2014). Social support and prolonged cardiovascular reactivity: The moderating influence of relationship quality and type of support. *Biological Psychology, 101,* 1–8. doi: 10.1016/j.biopsycho.2014.06.002

Haas, S. A., Schaefer, D. R., & Kornienko, O. (2010). Health and the structure of adolescent social networks. *Journal of Health and Social Behavior, 51,* 424–439. doi: 10.1177/0022146510386791

Hartup, W. W., & Stevens, N. (1999). Friendship and adaption across the life span. *Current Directions in Psychological Science, 8,* 76–79.

Harvey, I. S., & Alexander, K. (2012). Perceived social support and preventive health behavioral outcomes among older women. *Journal of Cross Cultural Gerontology, 27,* 275–290. doi: 10.1007/s10823-012-9172-3

Helliwell, J. F., Layard, R., & Sachs, J. (Eds.). 2013. *World happiness report 2013.* New York, NY: UN Sustainable Development Solutions Network.

Ho, C. Y. (2014). Better health with more friends: The role of social capital in producing health. *Health Economics, 25,* 91–100. doi: 10.1002/hec.313l

Holt-Lunstad, J., & Clark, B. D. (2014). Social stressors and cardiovascular response: influence of ambivalent relationships and behavioral ambivalence. *International Journal of Psychophysiology, 93,* 381–389. doi: 10.1016/j.ijpsycho.2014.05.014

Holt-Lunstad, J., Smith, T. B., & Layton, J. B. (2010). Social relationships and mortality risk: A meta-analytic review. *PLoS Medicine, 7,* el000316. doi: 10.1371/journal.pmed.1000316

Holt-Lunstad, J., Uchino, B. N., Smith, T. W., & Hicks, A. (2007). On the importance of relationship quality: The impact of ambivalence in friendships on cardiovascular functioning. *Annals of Behavioral Medicine, 33,* 278–290. doi: 10.1080/08836610701359795

House, J. S., Landis, K. R., & Umberson, D. (1988). Social relationships and health. *Science, 241,* 540–545.

Krause, N. (2010). Close companions at church, health, and health care use in late life. *Journal of Aging and Health, 22,* 434–453. doi: 10.1177/0898264309359537

La Greca, A. M., Bearman, K. J., & Moore, H. (2002). Peer relations of youth with pediatric conditions and health risks: Promoting social support and healthy lifestyles. *Journal of Developmental and Behavioral Pediatrics, 23,* 271–280.

Lakey, B., & Orehek, E. (2011). Relational regulation theory: A new approach to explain the link between perceived social support and mental health. *Psychological Review, 118,* 482–495. doi: 10.1037/a0023477

Lambert, N. M., Gwinn, A. M., Baumeister, R. F., Strachman, A., Washburn, I. J., Gable, S. L., & Fincham, F. D. (2013). A boost of positive affect: The perks of sharing positive experiences. *Journal of Social and Personal Relationships, 30,* 24–43. doi: 10.1177/0265407512449400

Lett, H. S., Blumenthal, J. A., Babyak, M. A., Catellier, D. J., Carney, R. M., Berkman, L. F., ... Schneiderman, N. (2007). Social support and prognosis in patients at increased psychosocial risk recovering from myocardial infarction. *Health Psychology, 26*, 418–427. doi: 10.1037/0278-6133.26.4.418

Lockhart, P. B., Bolger, A. F., Papapanou, P. N., Osinbowale, O., Trevisan, M., Levison, M. E., ... Baddour, L. M. (2012). Periodontal disease and atherosclerotic vascular disease: Does the evidence support an independent association? A scientific statement from the American Heart Association. *Circulation, 125*, 2520–2544. doi: 10.1161/CIR.0b013e31825719f3

Luxton, D. D., June, J. D., & Fairall, J. M. (2012). Social media and suicide: A public health perspective. *American Journal of Public Health, 102*(Suppl 2), S195–200. doi: 10.2105/AJPH.2011.300608

Mednick, S. C., Christakis, N. A., & Fowler, J. H. (2010). The spread of sleep loss influences drug use in adolescent social networks. *PLoS One, 5*, e9775. doi: 10.1371/journal.pone.0009775

Mitchell, J. C. (1969). *The concept and use of social networks.* Manchester, UK: Manchester University Press.

Molesworth, T., Sheu, L. K., Cohen, S., Gianaros, P. J., & Verstynen, T. D. (2015). Social network diversity and white matter microstructural integrity in humans. *Social Cognitive and Affective Neuroscience,* doi: 10.1093/scan/nsv001

Monroe, W. S. (1898). Social consciousness in children. *Psychological Review, 5*, 68–70.

Moremen, R. D. (2008). Best friends: the role of confidantes in older women's health. *Journal of Women and Aging, 20*, 149–167.

Nabi, R. L., Prestin, A., & So, J. (2013). Facebook friends with (health) benefits? Exploring social network site use and perceptions of social support, stress, and well-being. *Cyberpsychology, Behavior, and Social Networking, 16*, 721–727. doi: 10.1089/cyber.2012.0521

O'Malley, A. J., & Christakis, N. A. (2011). Longitudinal analysis of large social networks: Estimating the effect of health traits on changes in friendship tics. *Statistics in Medicine, 30*, 950–964. doi: 10.1002/sim.4190

Pew Research Center. (2015). *Internet seen as positive influence on education but negative influence on morality in emerging and developing nations.* Retrieved from http://www.pewglobal.org/tiles/2015/03/Pew-Research-Center-Technology-Report-FINAL-March-19-20151.pdf

Przybylski, A. K., & Weinstein, N. (2013). Can you connect with me now? How the presence of mobile communication technology influences face-to-face conversation quality. *Journal of Social and Personal Relationships, 30*, 237–246.

Rosenquist, J. N., Fowler, J. H., & Christakis, N. A. (2011). Social network determinants of depression. *Molecular Psychiatry, 16*, 273–281. doi: 10.1038/mp.2010.13

Rosenquist, J. N., Murabito, J., Fowler, J. H., & Christakis, N. A. (2010). The spread of alcohol consumption behavior in a large social network. *Annals of Internal Medicine, 152*, 426–433, W141. doi: 10.7326/0003-4819-152-7-201004060-00007

Steers, M. N., Wickham, R. E., & Acitelli, L. K. (2014). Seeing everyone else's highlight reels: How Facebook usage is linked to depressive symptoms. *Journal of Social and Clinical Psychology, 33*, 701–731. doi: 10.1521/jscp.2014.33.8.701

Stellar, J. E., John-Henderson, N., Anderson, C. L., Gordon, A. M., McNeil, G. D., & Keltner, D. (2015). Positive affect and markers of inflammation: Discrete positive emotions predict lower levels of inflammatory cytokines. *Emotion, 15,* 129–133. doi:10.1037/emo0000033

Strully, K. W., Fowler, J. H., Murabito, J. M., Benjamin, E. J., Levy, D., & Christakis, N. A. (2012). Aspirin use and cardiovascular events in social networks. *Social Science and Medicine, 74,* 1125–1129. doi: 10.1016/j.socscimed.2011.12.033

Thoits, P. A. (2011). Mechanisms linking social ties and support to physical and mental health. *Journal of Health and Social Behavior, 52,* 145–161. doi: 10.1177/0022146510395592

Tsakos, G., Sabbah, W., Chandola, T., Newton, T., Kawachi, I., Aida, J., ... Watt, R. G. (2013). Social relationships and oral health among adults aged 60 years or older. *Psychosomatic Medicine, 75,* 178–186. doi: 10.1097/PSY.0b013e31827d221b

Uchino, B. N. (2006). Social support and health: A review of physiological processes potentially underlying links to disease outcomes. *Journal of Behavioral Medicine, 29,* 377–387. doi: 10.1007/sl0865-006-9056-5

Uchino, B. N. (2009). What a lifespan approach might tell us about why distinct measures of social support have differential links to physical health. *Journal of Social and Personal Relationships, 26,* 53–62. doi: 10.1177/0265407509105521

Uchino, B. N., Holt-Lunstad, J., Bloor, L. E., & Campo, R. A. (2005). Aging and cardiovascular reactivity to stress: Longitudinal evidence for changes in stress reactivity. *Psychology of Aging, 20,* 134–143. doi: 10.1037/0882-7974.20.1.134

Uchino, B. N., Holt-Lunstad, J., Uno, D., & Flinders, J. B. (2001). Heterogeneity in the social networks of young and older adults: Prediction of mental health and cardiovascular reactivity during acute stress. *Journal of Behavioral Medicine, 24,* 361–382.

Umberson, D. (1987). Family status and health behaviors: Social control as a dimension of social integration. *Journal of Health and Social Behavior, 28,* 306–319.

Uno, D., Uchino, B. N., & Smith, T. W. (2002). Relationship quality moderates the effect of social support given by close friends on cardiovascular reactivity in women. *International Journal of Behavioral Medicine,* 9, 243–262.

Veenstra, A., Lakey, B., Cohen, J. C., Neely, L. C., Orehek, E., Barry, R., & Abeare, C. A. (2011). Forecasting the specific providers that recipients will perceive as unusually supportive. *Personal Relationships, 18,* 677–696.

Wills, T. A., & Shinar, O. (2000). Measuring perceived and received social support. In S. Cohen, L. Gordon, & B. Gottlieb (Eds.), *Social support measurement and intervention: A guide for health and social scientists* (pp. 86–135). New York, NY: Oxford University Press.

# Friendship and Mental Health Functioning

*By Alan R. King, Tiffany D. Russell, and Amy C. Veith*

S ias and Bartoo (2007) described friendships as a psychological "vaccine" against both physical and mental illness. They hypothesized that prophylactic benefits are often derived from the emotional, tangible, and informational support provided in close personal friendships.

Other clinical researchers have posited that broader forms of social support provide resiliency by "buffering" reactions to life stress (Turner & Brown, 2010). This [reading] reviews evidence in support of the contention that personal friendships and social support enhance resiliency to stressors such as trauma, losses, maltreatment, and other developmental adversities. This literature review will be followed by an analysis of original data that provides a test of the general hypothesis that close child and adult relationships portend better overall mental health.

Links between friendship and mental health indices are complex. First, friendship represents a complex construct without a uniform definition. Second, mental health symptom clusters extend across many relevant dimensions that vary in their sensitivity to interpersonal influences. Third, relationships between mental health and friendship variables, however measured, are inherently complicated by their bidirectional nature. While cause-effect relationships prove difficult to establish, collective correlational findings are useful in identifying the sorts of mental health symptom clusters that are most likely to emerge when critical social support and friendship circles have been destabilized.

## DEFINING QUALITIES OF FRIENDSHIP

Hayes (1988) defined friendship as a voluntary interdependence of two persons over time involving companionship, intimacy, affection, and mutual assistance intended to facilitate the socioemotional goals of both parties. Sullivan (1953) emphasized decades ago that friendships serve many purposes including companionship, assistance, affection, intimacy, alliance, emotional security, and self-validation. Friendships also convey a sense of mutual value, enhance communication and interpersonal skills, and buffer both partners against life stressors (Bukowski, Hoza, & Boivin, 1994).

## DEVELOPMENTAL CONTRIBUTORS TO FRIENDSHIP CAPACITY

Secure and affirming parent-child relationships have been predictive of close and sustainable young adult friendships (Wise & King, 2008). Conversely, childhood maltreatment and other forms of developmental adversity may have deleterious effects on the capacity of the child to develop healthy friendships and other interpersonal relationships. Childhood abuse victims appear to have greater difficulty in initiating and sustaining satisfying peer relationships (Smith, 1995). Parental physical abuse has been found to predict less rewarding adult best friendships (Mugge, King, & Klophaus, 2009). Children from abusive homes have reported that they feel more negative toward a greater portion of their best friendships than do children with nonremarkable histories (Salzinger, Feldman, Hammer, & Rosario, 1993). Abused girls tend to report higher levels of anxiety, depression, and avoidance in their adult relationships (Fletcher, 2009; Godbout, Sabourin, & Lusser, 2009). Peers of abused children have also reported that their abused counterparts are more aggressive and less cooperative (Egeland, Yates, Appleyard, & Dulmen, 2002). Studies have tended to find lower levels of peer support during adolescence (Doucent & Aseltine, 2003) and strained adult friendships among individuals exposed to domestic violence during upbringing (Green & King, 2009; Wise & King, 2008).

## FRIENDSHIP BENEFITS

Close friendships portend higher levels of self-esteem, psychosocial adjustment, and interpersonal sensitivity (Bagwell et al., 2005). Individuals who identify lifetime friendships have been found to be better adjusted than their friendless peers (Gupta & Korte, 1994). Adults who describe their friendships as more positive and satisfying also report lesser feelings of anxiety and hostility (Bagwell et al., 2005). Young adults who described a close friendship in preadolescence have been found to show greater enjoyment, assistance, intimacy, emotional support, sensitivity, loyalty, mutual affection, and overall higher quality of life than those who did not (Bagwell, Newcomb, & Bukowski, 1998). Close best friendships predict higher general interpersonal happiness (Demir, Özdemir, & Weitekamp, 2007). Best friendships also appear to reduce the chances of being victimized by peers and, if victimization occurs, buffer the negative effects (Cowie, 2000; Owens, Shute, & Slee, 2000). These protective benefits may extend to dampening the deleterious effects of problematic home environments (Schwartz, Dodge, Pettit, & Bates, 2000).

Theoretical and qualitative writings are available to posit the mechanisms by which friendship conveys so many benefits. Friendships often provide warmth, affection, nurturance, and intimacy (Bollmer, 2005) while contributing to self-esteem, positive family attitudes, and enhanced romantic relationships (Bagwell et al., 1998). Reciprocal friendships can supply cognitive and affective resources, foster a sense of well-being, socialize both parties, facilitate mastery of age-related tasks, and provide developmental advantages that can extend into old age (Hartup & Stevens, 1997). The sense of inclusion and belonging in childhood and adolescence can extend to participation in social organizations and a satisfying social life in adulthood (Furman & Robbins, 1985). Friendships also facilitate adaptive life transitions, including college and workforce entrance, marriage, having children, spousal death, and retirement (Magnusson, Stattin, & Allen, 1985).

While positive friendship effects appear numerous, the negative impact of peer rejection warrants equal attention. Deviant peer interactions appear to diminish feelings of well-being (Pagel, Erdly, & Becker, 1987) and contribute to delinquency among vulnerable adolescents (Hartup & Stevens, 1997). Peer rejection and early school dropout have been linked (Coie, Lochman, Terry, & Hyman, 1992). Peer rejection has also been associated with delinquency, criminality, lower school performance, vocational competence, aspiration level, less participation in social activities, and many mental health problems in preschool, middle school, and adolescence (Deater-Decker, 2001). Peer rejection can come in a variety of forms, including bullying, being ignored, and relational aggression (Bagwell et al., 1998; Salmivalli, Kaukiainen, & Lagerspetz, 2000). Children who are victimized by peers often express hostility, aggression, or withdrawal from social interactions. Social withdrawal after peer rejection has often been accompanied by depression (Rubin & Burgess, in press) and even suicidal ideation (Carlo & Raffaelli, 2000; DiFilippo & Overholser, 2000) among children and adolescents.

## FRIENDSHIPS AND MENTAL HEALTH

Adults whose friendships were characterized by frequent conflict, antagonism, and inequality have been shown to have higher rates of psychiatric symptoms than their positively relating peers (Bagwell et al., 2005). King and Terrance (2008) studied best friendship correlates with psychiatric symptomatology among college students using the Minnesota Multiphasic Personality Inventory (MMPI-2). They found 57 (31%) significant ($p < .05$) correlations between MMPI-2 and Acquaintance Description Form (ADF-F2; Wright, 1985, 1989) scale indicators of best friendship closeness, value, and durability (Cohen $d$ effect sizes ranging from .28 to .72). Four of the ADF-F2 scales (security, social regulation, personal, and situational maintenance difficulty) were strongly related to the selected MMPI-2 features. Higher Depression (D), Psychathenia (Pt), and Hypochondriasis (Hs) scores predicted lower levels of best friendship security along with higher situational maintenance difficulty.

While close friendships often serve positive, protective, and healthy functions, relationships high in antagonism, conflict, and inequality can just as predictably trigger internalized or externalized symptoms of psychological distress (Bagwell et al., 2005). In this regard, destabilized "friendships" appear to be detrimental to mental health. Nezlek, Imbrie, and Shean (1994) found that individuals with low levels of intimacy (i.e., low quality) with their best friends had higher levels of depression. Friendships appear to have an even more direct impact on self-esteem. As with depression, the more positive features in a friendship dyad, the greater the self-esteem and the lower the symptomology of the individuals (Bagwell et al., 2005). Further, King and Terrance (2005) relied on the Millon Clinical Multiaxial Inventory (MCM1-II; Millon, 1987) and the ADF-F2 to examine associations between personality disorder attributes and best friendship qualities. Passive-aggressive, avoidant, schizotypal, sadistic-aggressive, antisocial, borderline, and/or self-defeating personality disorder attributes were linked to best friendships that were less secure (effect sizes ranging from.67 to.78). Passive-aggressive, self-defeating and borderline attributes also predicted best friendships that were more strongly influenced by the pressures and expectations of outsiders.

## SOCIAL SUPPORT AND MENTAL HEALTH

Friendships contribute greatly to the broader resiliency factor of "social support." Social support has been defined as the perceived level of emotional, informational, or practical assistance collectively provided, or made available, by significant others (Thoits, 2010). Emotional support includes providing love, empathy, and nurturance to another person. Informational support may come in the form of advice or suggestions to deal with a problem or stressful event. Instrumental (practical) social support is represented by tangible aid or services that directly help someone in need. The perception of social support can be even more effective than tangible support itself (Taylor, 2011). While an individual who lost their job may be comforted by their spouse, just knowledge of the availability of partner support is effective comfort in its own right. Perceived, rather than demonstrable, social support has been most strongly linked with stress resistance and well-being (Turner & Brown, 2010). The subjective experience of having a network of caring individuals when needed constitutes social support (House, 1981).

The "buffering hypothesis" proposes that social support enhances resiliency in responding to life stressors (Turner & Brown, 2010). The diathesis-stress model of psychopathology posits that stressors interact with a genetic predisposition to produce the expression of a disorder (Holmes, 2004). Social support is an important consideration in this model since it serves as a protective factor against the deleterious effects of both stressors and genetic predispositions (Buchanan, 1994). Social support appears to have positive effects on mental health prior to onset, at onset, and during stressor exposure. Social support also reduces the risk of onset and relapse after successful treatment (Gayer-Anderson & Morgan, 2013).

In one 3-year follow-up study of first episode psychotic patients, higher levels of social support predicted lower levels of positive symptoms (e.g., auditory or visual hallucinations) and fewer hospitalizations (Norman et al., 2005). Social support and stress have been found to account for 40% of the variance in depression symptoms among single mothers (Cairney, Boyle, Offord, & Racine, 2003). Depression also appears to erode peer social support during later adolescence (Stice, Ragan, & Randall, 2004). Beyond depression, social support also has an effect on anger and other emotions. Social support was inversely related to anger, impulsivity, and suicide risk within one PTSD sample (Kotler, Iancu, Efroni, & Amir, 2001).

[...]

# REFERENCES

Bagwell, C. L., Bender, S. E., Andreassi, C. L., Kinoshita, T. L., Montarello, S. A., & Muller, J. G. (2005). Friendship quality and perceived relationship changes predict psychosocial adjustment in early adulthood. *Journal of Social and Personal Relationships, 22,* 235–254. doi: 10.1177/0265407505050945

Bagwell, C., Newcomb, A., & Bukowski, W. (1998). Preadolescent friendship and peer rejection as predictors of adult adjustment. *Child Development, 69,* 140–140. doi: 10.2307/1132076

Bollmer, J. (2005). A friend in need: The role of friendship quality as a protective factor in peer victimization and bullying. *Journal of Interpersonal Violence, 20,* 701–712. doi: 10.11 77/0886260504272897

Bradshaw, T., & Haddock, G. (1998). Is befriending by trained volunteers of value to people suffering from long-term mental illness? *Journal of Advanced Nursing, 27,* 713–720. doi:10. 1046/j.1365-2648.1998.00618.x

Bukowski, W. M., Hoza, B., & Boivin, M. (1994). Measuring friendship quality during pre- and early adolescence: The development and psychometric properties of the Friendship Qualities Scale. *Journal of Social and Personal Relationships, 11,* 471–484. doi: 10.1177/0265407594113011

Buss, A. H., & Perry, M. (1992). The aggression questionnaire. *Personality Processes and Individual Differences, 63,* 452–459. doi: 10.1037/0022-3514.63.3.452

Cairney, J., Boyle, M., Offord, D. R., & Racine, Y. (2003). Stress, social support and depression in single and married mothers. *Social Psychiatry and Psychiatric Epidemiology, 38,* 442–449. doi: 10.1007/s00127-003-0661-0

Coie, J. D., Lochman, J. E., Terry, R., & Hyman, C. (1992). Predicting early adolescent disorder from childhood aggression and peer rejection. *Journal of Consulting and Clinical Psychology, 60,* 783–792. doi: 10.1037//0022-006x.60.5.783

Cowie, H. (2000). Bystanding or standing by: Gender issues in coping with bullying in English schools. *Aggressive Behavior, 26,* 85–97, doi:10.1002/(SICI)l098-2337(2000)26:l&lt;85:: AID-AB7&gt;3.0.CO;2–5

Davidson, L., Haglund, K. E., Stayner, D. A., Rakfeldt, J., Chinman, M. J., & Tebes, J. K. (2001). "It was just realizing … that life isn't one big honor": A qualitative study of supported socialization. *Psychiatric Rehabilitation Journal, 24,* 275–292. doi:10.1037/h0095084

Davidson, L., Stayner, D. A., Nickou, C., Styron, T. H., Rowe, M., & Chinman, M. J. (2001). "Simply to be let in": Inclusion as a basis for recovery. *Psychiatric Rehabilitation Journal, 24,* 375–388. doi:10.1037/h0095067

Deater-Deckard, K. (2001). Annotation: Recent research examining the role of peer relationships in the development of psychopathology. *Journal of Child Psychology and Psychiatry, 42*(5), 565–579. doi: 10.1111/1469-7610.00753

Demir, M., Özdemir, M., & Weitekamp, L. (2007). Looking to happy tomorrows with friends: Best and close friendships as they predict happiness. *Journal of Happiness Studies, 8,* 243–271. doi: 10.1007/s10902-006-9025-2

Diener, E., Emmons, R. A., Larsen, R. J., & Griffin, S. (1985). The Satisfaction with Life Scale. *Journal of Personality Assessment, 49,* 71–75. doi: 10.1207/sl5327752jpa4901_13

DiFilippo, J. M., & Overholser, J. C. (2000). Suicidal ideation in adolescent psychiatric inpatients as associated with depression and attachment relationships. *Journal of Clinical Child Psychology, 29,* 155–166. doi:10.1207/s15374424jccp2902_2

Doucent, J., & Aseltine, R. H. (2003). Childhood family adversity and the quality of marital relationships in young adulthood. *Journal of Social and Personal Relationships, 20,* 818–842. doi: 10.1177/0265407503206006

Eckenrode, J., & Hamilton, S. (2000). One-to-one support interventions: Home visitation and mentoring. In S. Cohen, L. G. Underwood, & B. H. Gottlieb (Eds.), *Social support measurement, and intervention: A guide for health and social scientists* (pp. 246–277). New York, NY: Oxford University Press.

Egeland, B., Yates, T., Appleyard, K., & van Dulmen, M. (2002). The long-term consequences of maltreatment in the early years: A developmental pathway model to antisocial behavior. *Children's Services: Social Policy, Research, and Practice, 5,* 249–260. doi: 10.1207/S15326918CS0504_2

Ferguson, G. A. (1981). *Statistical analysis in psychology and education* (5th ed.). New York, NY: McGraw-Hill.

Fletcher, J. M. (2009). Childhood mistreatment and adolescent and young adult depression. *Social Science and Medicine, 68,* 199–806. doi:10.1016/j.socscimed.2008.12.005

Furman, W., & Robbins, P. (1985). What's the point? Selection of treatment objectives. In B. Schneider M, K. H. Rubin, & J. E. Ledingham (Eds.), *Childrens peer relations: Issues in assessment and intervention* (pp. 41–54). New York, NY: Spring-Verlag. doi:10.1007/978-1-4684-6325-5_3

Godbout, N., Sabourin, S., & Lusser, Y. (2009). Child sexual abuse and adult romantic adjustment: Comparison of single- and multiple-indicator measures. *Journal of Interpersonal Violence, 24,* 693–706. doi: 10.1177/0886260508317179

Goldfarb, L. A., Dynens, E. M., & Garrard, M. (1985). The Goldfarb Fear of Fat Scale. *Journal of Personality Assessment, 49,* 329–332. doi: 10.l207/sl5327752jpa4903_21

Green, J. S., & King, A. R. (2009). Domestic violence and parental divorce as predictors of best friendship qualities among college students. *Journal of Divorce and Remarriage, 50,* 100–118. doi: 10.1080/10502550802365805

Gupta, V., & Korte, C. (1994). The effects of a confidant and a peer group on the well-being of single elders. *International Journal of Aging and Human Development, 39,* 293–302. doi: 10.2190/4yyh-9xau-wqf9-apvt

Harris, T., Brown, G. W., & Robinson, R. (1999). Befriending as an intervention for chronic depressions among women in an inner city: Role of fresh-start experiences and baseline psychosocial factors in remission from depression. *British Journal of Psychiatry, 174,* 225–232. doi: 10.1192/bjp.174.3.225

Hartup, W., & Stevens, N. (1997). Friendships and adaptation in the life course. *Psychological Bulletin, 121,* 355–370. doi:10.1037//0033-2909.121.3.355

Hartup, W., & Stevens, N. (1999). Friendships and adaptation across the life span. *Current Directions in Psychological Science, 8,* 76–79. doi: 10.1111/1467-8721-00018

Hayes, R., 1988. Friendship. In: Duck, S. (Ed.), *Handbook of personal relationships: theory, research, interventions* (pp. 391–408). Chichester, NY: Wiley.

House, J. S. (1981). *Work stress and social support,* Reading, MA: Addison-Wesley.

Kamarck, T. W. (2005). *Hostility: Buss-Perry Aggression Questionnaire.* http://pmbcii.psy.cmu.edu/core_c/Buss_Perry_Aggression_Questionnaire.html

Kotler, M., Iancu, I., Efroni, R., & Amir, M. (2001). Anger, impulsivity, social support, and suicide risk in patients with posttraumatic stress disorder. *Journal of Nervous and Mental Disease, 189,* 162–167. doi: 10.1097/00005053-200103000-00004

LOGSCAN, (1998). *Peer Relationships, http://www.unc.edu/depts/sph/longscan/pages/measures/Ages12to14/writeups/Age%2012%20and%2014%20Peer%20Relationships.pdf*

Magnusson, D., Stattin, H., & Allen, V. L. (1985). Biological maturation and social development; A longitudinal study of some adjustment processes from mid-adolescence to adulthood. *Journal of Youth and Adolescence, 14,* 267–283. doi:10.1007/bf02089234

McCorkle, B., Rogers, E., Dunn, E., Lyass, A., & Wan, Y. (2009). Increasing social support for individuals with serious mental illness: Evaluating the compeer model of intentional friendship. *Community Mental Health Journal, 44,* 359–366. doi:10.1007/sl0597-008-9137-8

Millon, T. (1987). *Manual for the MCMI-II.* Minneapolis, MN: National Computer Systems.

Mitchell, G., & Pistrang, N. (2011). Befriending for mental health problems: Processes of helping. *Psychology and Psychotherapy: Theory, Research and Practice, 84,* 151–169. doi: 10.1348/147608310x508566

Mugge, J. R., King, A. R., & Klophaus, V. (2009). The quality of young adult best friendships after exposure to childhood physical abuse, domestic violence or parental alcoholism. In F. Columbus (Ed.), *Friendships: Types, cultural variations, and psychological and social aspects.* Hauppauge, NY: Nova Science.

Nezlek, J. B., Imbrie, M., & Shean, G. D. (1994). Depression and everyday social interaction. *Journal of Personality and Social Psychology, 67,* 1101–1111. doi: 10.1037//0022-3514.67.6.1101

Norman, R. M., Malla, A. K., Manchanda, R., Harricharan, R., Takhar, J., & Northcott, S. (2005). Social support and three-year symptom and admission outcomes for first episode psychosis. *Schizophrenia Research, 80,* 227–234. doi: 10.10l6/j.schres.2005.05.006

Owens, L., Shute, R., & Slee, P. (2000). "Guess what I just heard!": Indirect aggression among teenage girls in Australia. *Aggressive Behavior, 26,* 67–83. doi: 10.1002/(sici) 1098–2337

Pagel, M. D., Erdly, W. W., & Becker, J. (1987). Social networks: We get by with (and in spite of) a little help from our friends. *Journal of Personality and Social Psychology, 53,* 793–804. doi: 10.1037//0022-3514.53.4.793

Pavot, W., & Diener, E. (1993). Review of the Satisfaction with Life Scale. *Psychological Assessment, 5,* 164–172. doi: 10.1037/1040-3590.5.2.164

Pavot, W., & Diener, E. (2008). The Satisfaction with Life Scale and the emerging construct of life satisfaction. *Journal of Positive Psychology, 3,* 137–152. doi: 10.1080/17439760 701756946

Pavot, W. G., Diener, E., Colvin, C. R., & Sandvik, E. (1991). Further validation of the Satisfaction with Life Scale: Evidence for the cross-method convergence of well-being measures. *Journal of Personality Assessment,* 57, 149–161. doi: 10.1207/s15327752jpa 5701_17

Rubin, K. H., & Burgess, K. (in press). Social withdrawal. In M. W. Vasey & M. R. Dadds (Eds.), *The developmental psychopathology of anxiety.* Oxford, UK: Oxford University Press.

Salmivalli, C., Kaukiainen, A., & Lagerspetz, K. (2000). Aggression and sociometric status among peers: Do gender and type of aggression matter? *Scandinavian Journal of Psychology, 41,* 17–24. doi: 10.1111/1467-9450.00166

Salzinger, S., Feldman, R. S., Hammer, M., & Rosario, M. (1993). The effects of physical abuse on children's social relationships. *Child Development, 64,* 169–187. doi: 10.2307/1131444

Schwartz, D., Dodge, K. A., Pettit, G. S., & Bates, J. E.; the Conduct Problems Prevention Research Group. (2000). Friendship as a moderating factor in the pathway between early harsh home environment and later victimization in the peer group. *Developmental Psychology, 36,* 646–662. doi.org/10.1037//0012-1649.36.5.646

Selzer, M. L. (1971). The Michigan Alcoholism Screening Test: A quest for a new diagnostic instrument. *American Journal of Psychiatry, 127,* 1653–1658.

Shields, A. L., Howell, R. T., Potter, J. S., & Weiss, R. D. (2007). The Michigan Alcoholism Screening Test and its shortened form: A meta-analytic inquiry into score reliability. *Substance Use and Misuse, 42,* 1783–1800. doi: 10.1080/10826080701212295

Sias, P.M., & Bartoo, H. (2007). Friendship, social support, and health. In L. L'Abate (Ed.), *Low-cost approaches to promote physical and mental health: Theory, research, and practice.* New York, NY: Springer Science.

Smith, M.C. (1995). A preliminary description of nonschool-based friendship in young high-risk children. *Child Abuse & Neglect, 19,* 1497–1511, doi:10.1016/0145-2134(95)00108-6

Staeheli, M., Stayner, D., & Davidson, L. (2004). Pathways to friendship in the lives of people with psychosis: Incorporating narrative into experimental research. *Journal of Phenomenological Psychology,* 35, 233–252. doi:10.1163/1569162042652209

Stice, E., Ragan, J., & Randall, P. (2004). Prospective relations between social support and depression: Differential direction of effects for parent and peer support? *Journal of Abnormal Psychology, 113,* 155–159. doi: 10.1037/0021-843X.113.1.155

Storgaard, H., Nielsen, S. D., & Gluud, C. (1994). The validity of the Michigan Alcoholism Screening Test (MAST). *Alcohol and Alcoholism, 29,* 493–502.

Sullivan, H. S. (1953). *The interpersonal theory of psychiatry.* New York, NY: Norton, doi: 10.10 37/h0050700

Taylor, S. E. (2011). Social support: A review. In H. S. Friedman (Ed), *The handbook of health psychology* (pp. 189–214). New York, NY: Oxford University Press.

Teitelbaum, L. M., & Mullen, K. B. (2000). The validity of the MAST in psychiatric settings: A meta-analytic integration. *Journal of Studies on Alcohol, 61,* 254–261.

Thoits, P. A. (2010). Stress and health major findings and policy implications. *Journal of Health and Social Behavior, 51,* S41–S53. doi: 10.1177/0022146510383499

Turner, R. J., & Brown, R. L. (2010). *Social support and mental health: A handbook for the study of mental health; Social contexts, theories, and systems* (2nd ed). New York, NY: Cambridge University Press.

Walter, N., & King, A. R. (2013). Childhood physical abuse and mindfulness as predictors of young adult friendship maintenance difficulty. In C. Mohiyeddini (Ed.), *Emotional relationships: Types, challenges and physical/mental health impacts* (pp. 77–94) Hauppauge, NY: Nova Science.

Wise, R. A., & King, A. R. (2008). Family environment as a predictor of the quality of college students' friendships. *Journal of Family Issues, 29,* 828–848. doi:10.1177/0192513 X07309461

Wright, P. H. (1985). The Acquaintance Description Form. In S. Duck & D. Perlman (Eds.), *Understanding personal relationships: An interdisciplinary approach.* (pp. 39–62) London, UK: Sage.

Wright, P. H. (1989). The essence of personal relationships and their value for the individual (pp. 1–22). In G. Graham & H. LaFollette (Eds.), *Person to person.* Philadelphia, PA: Temple Press.

Wright, P. H., & Conneran, P.J. (1989). Measuring strain in personal relationships: A refinement. *Psychological Reports, 64,* 1321–1322.

# EDITORS' INTRODUCTION

You now understand that friendships have many (very important) rewards beyond the good feelings they may bring in moments of togetherness. Now it's time to put in the work required to keep these friendships going; yes, the best relationships require skills and effort, even friendships, so be sure to read the next reading, "Maintaining Long-Lasting Friendships," by Deborah Oswald. Again, take a few moments to ponder the following questions before, during, and/or after, your read.

## PRIMERS

1. Think about the friendships you have or have had that you enjoy the most. What are the elements of this friendship that stand out to you? After you read the next excerpt you will know the top four friendship maintenance behaviors, so compare what these are with the elements you've identified in your rewarding platonic relationships.

2. In the next excerpt you will learn about the ways that technological platforms (Snapchat, Facebook, texting, Instagram, etc.) can benefit or hinder the maintenance of friendships. Compare what you learn with what you notice in your own use of these platforms.

# Maintaining Long-Lasting Friendships

*By Debra L. Oswald*

Friendships play a significant role in peoples social lives. Friendships provide significant social support and opportunities for social connection, and having friendships is connected with mental well-being (e.g., Baumeister & Leary, 1995), happiness (e.g., Demir, Ozdeir, & Marum, 2011), and decreased social loneliness (e.g., Binder, Roberts, & Sutcliffe, 2012). Given the importance of friendships, it is essential to understand not only how friendships are initiated and formed but also how people maintain these friendships over time. In this [reading], I will provide an overview of the research on the importance of engaging in maintenance behaviors to sustain long-lasting, quality friendships. The first part of the [reading], reviews the types of behaviors used to maintain friendships with a focus on understanding the variability of behaviors, friendship developmental aspects, and the frequency of use and effectiveness of these maintenance behaviors. The final part of this [reading] provides an overview of theoretical frameworks for understanding the process of friendship maintenance. Specifically, we consider how maintenance behaviors function within the context of interdependence theory and interpersonal styles.

Unlike other types of relationships, such as marital and familial relationships, friendships are purely voluntary (Wiseman, 1986). As such, they have a unique vulnerability to relationship deterioration and termination. Indeed it has been suggested that friendships have the "weakest of any close bond in social life, because if it loses the qualities which make for the extraordinary closeness combined with the voluntariness it encourages, it chances loss of all" (Wiseman, p. 192). For example, Roberts and Dunbar (2011) found that both close and intimate friendships, compared with kin relations, experienced greater decrease in emotional intensity of the relationships when there was a decrease in contact or joint activities. "The researchers note that their study "reveals that even these very closest friends require active maintenance (contact and performing activities together) to maintain a high level of emotional closeness, and without this maintenance these relationships are prone to decay" (p. 193). Effective maintenance of the relationship appears to be crucial to the continued health and quality of the friendship.

Relationship maintenance is conceptualized both as the phase in between initiation and termination of the relationship and also as a process. That is, once a relationship has been formed the individuals must engage in behaviors that function to sustain the relationship to the individuals' satisfaction. Although not as exciting as friendship initiation or as distressing as termination, the maintenance phase is, hopefully, the longest phase of the friendship.

## FRIENDSHIP MAINTENANCE BEHAVIORS

Relationship maintenance is generally conceived as behaviors that occur between the initiation and termination of the relationship (e.g., Dindia & Canary, 1993). Although the specific goal of maintenance behaviors can vary, relationship researchers generally conceive of maintenance as behaviors that people engage in to "keep a relationship in existence, to keep a relationship at a specific state or condition, to keep a relationship in satisfactory condition, and to keep a relationship in repair" (Dindia & Canary, 1993, p. 163). This variation in the goal of relationship maintenance is interesting to note as people may vary in the desired degree of closeness or intimacy that they want from that friendship. Thus, friendship maintenance behaviors might be used in different ways depending on the underlying motivations of the person in the friendship. Furthermore, these behaviors can occur routinely or be used strategically (Dainton & Aylor, 2002; Dainton & Stafford, 1993). For example, someone might strategically engage in a behavior when one realizes that the relationship is in deterioration and in need of specific intervention. Alternatively, many of these behaviors might routinely occur throughout the relationship and without any specific intention or motivation. This routine use of maintenance behaviors reflect reasons such as internalization of relationship importance or prosocial values, and also serve to promote the successful continuation of the friendship.

In the initial research identifying friendship maintenance behaviors, Oswald, Clark, and Kelly (2004) conducted an exploratory factor analysis of 45 types of possible maintenance activities. These activities were identified in research based on romantic maintenance (e.g., Dainton & Staford, 1993; Stafford & Canary, 1991) as well as behaviors identified as important for friendships (e.g., Fehr, 1996; Hays, 1984). Based on exploratory factor analysis, Oswald and colleagues found four key maintenance behaviors for friendships: supportiveness, positivity, openness, and interaction. The first factor identified in the exploratory factor analysis was labeled "positivity" (accounting for 30.70% of the variance) and included behaviors that make the relationship rewarding (e.g., *express thanks when one friend does something nice for the other* and *try to be upbeat and cheerful when together)* as well as *not* engaging in antisocial behaviors that would negatively affect the friendship (e.g., *not returning each other's messages)*. The second factor identified was "supportiveness" (accounting for 18.51% of the variance) and included behaviors that involved providing assurance and supporting the friend (e.g., *try to make the other person feel good about who they are* and *support each other when one of you is going through a tough time)* and the friendship (e.g., *let each other know you want the relationship to last in the future)*. The third factor included behaviors related to "openness" (accounting for 6.63% of the variance) and included behaviors related to self-disclosure (e.g., *share your private thoughts)* and general conversation (e.g., *have intellectually stimulating conversations)*. The final factor was labeled interaction (accounting for 4.61% of the variance) and included behaviors and activities that the friends engaged in jointly (e.g., *visit each other's homes* and *celebrate special occasions together)*. This factor structure was similar for both males and females and was subsequently revalidated with confirmatory factor analyses and shortened to 20 items (5 items per scale). The factors on the shorter scale demonstrated adequate scale structure in the confirmatory factor analysis and also acceptable internal reliability (Cronbach alphas ranging from .75 to .95). The subscales are also positively intercorrelated (*r*'s ranging from .12 to .61).

These four key friendship behaviors are theoretically consistent with the maintenance typologies that Fehr (1996) identified based on a literature review of friendships. In that review Fehr suggested key strategies of self-disclosure, providing support and assurance, maintaining levels of rewards, and shared time as central for maintaining friendships. These behaviors also share similarities to the types of behaviors that are used to maintain romantic relationships. Based on exploratory factor analysis, Stafford and Canary (1991) identified five relationship maintenance strategies that were important for maintaining romantic relationships. These behaviors included positivity, assurances, openness, shared tasks, and social networks. This suggests that being positive, providing assurances, and support as well as self-disclosure are important for maintaining a variety of types of relationships. In contrast, while socially interacting is important for maintaining the friendships, romantic relationships also focus on interactions that involved shared tasks and social networks. Thus, while there are similarities of maintenance behaviors across relationship types, it is also important to realize that different types of relationships will require different maintenance behaviors.

Use of maintenance behaviors depends on a number of characteristics including the sex of the individuals in the relationship and the status of the relationship. In regard to friendship status, Oswald and colleagues (2004) found that people reported engaging in more of all of the maintenance behaviors in best friendships than in close or casual friendships. People also reported engaging in more maintenance behaviors for close friendships than for casual friend-ships. Consistent results have been found across numerous studies. For example, among newly formed college friendships, close friends engaged in more maintenance behaviors of positivity, assurances, task sharing, social networking, banter, routine contact, and computer-mediated communication than casual friendships (McEwan & Guerrero, 2012). Binder and colleagues (2012) compared "core friendships" with "significant friendships," where core friendships were defined as having a closer level of emotional intimacy than significant friendships. They found that people engaged in more of each of the maintenance behaviors with "core friends" than "significant friends." Interestingly, the difference in maintenance behaviors between the friend types was most profound for openness, suggesting that intimate self-disclosure was more pronounced in the core friendships. Extending this line of research, Hall, Larson, and Watts (2011) found that best friends were perceived as being more capable of fulfilling ideal relationship maintenance expectations than were close or casual friendships. Taken together, these various findings suggest that friends expect, and receive, more maintenance behaviors from their friendships as they become more intimate.

Consistent with a body of research looking at sex differences in friendships (e.g., Hall, 2011), there are also substantial differences in use of maintenance strategies depending on the sex of the friends. Oswald and colleagues (2004) found that participants reporting on their female same-sex friendship were more likely to engage in supportiveness than those individuals reporting on same-sex male friendship or cross-sex friendships. In contrast, individuals reporting on a cross-sex friendship reported engaging in more supportive behaviors than people reporting on male same-sex friendships. People reporting on cross-sex and female same-sex friendships reported engaging in more openness than those reporting on male friendships. Interestingly, positivity did not vary by gender of friendship. In their research on expectations for friendship maintenance, Hall and colleagues (2011) found that women, compared with men, reported having had higher ideal standards of maintenance behaviors that they expected from their friends. For women, these higher friendship maintenance standards were positively associated with having same-sex friends who actually met the friendship maintenance standard. In contrast, they found for men that having increasingly higher friendship maintenance standards was actually associated with decreased perception that these standards were being fulfilled by their same-sex friends. For both men and women, Hall and colleagues (2011) found that maintenance standards and fulfillment of expectations were positively associated with friendship satisfaction. Taken together, these findings might suggest that male friendships, and to some extent cross-sex friendships, may not be as effective at engaging in maintenance behaviors and may be more vulnerable to deterioration and termination.

The maintenance of cross-sex friendships is especially interesting given that there is the potential for differing relational goals. One friend might want to maintain the relationship as a platonic friendship or alternatively one might want to transition the friendship to a romantic relationship. In investigating cross-sex friendships, Weger and Emmett (2009) found that both men and women who desired a romantic relationship with their friend were more likely to engage in routine maintenance activities. Women who desired a romantic relationship with their male friend also engaged in more of the support and positivity maintenance behaviors. These findings suggest not only that increased use of maintenance behaviors might be associated with increasing the friendship status from casual to close or best friends but also that in the context of cross-sex friendships the individuals may be using maintenance behaviors to escalate the platonic friendship to a romantic relationship.

In sum, this body of research on friendships suggests that the sex of the friends involved in the relationship may play an interesting role in determining the type, frequency, and goal of the maintenance behaviors used to maintain the friendship. However, this research is still in the beginning stages of fully exploring the role of the friends' sex. For example, research has largely ignored how factors such as sexual orientation or transgendered status might be related to engaging in friendship maintenance behaviors [...]. Likewise, most of this research has looked at gender as a binary construct and simply measured sex classification. However, gender roles might play an important role. For example, Aylor and Dainton (2004) found that for romantic relationship maintenance it was the individuals' gender roles (measured as masculinity and femininity), rather than sex, that were a better predictor of their use of maintenance behaviors. Thus, this is an area where additional research could be useful to fully understand the role of sex, gender roles, and sexual orientation in friendship maintenance.

## FRIENDSHIP MAINTENANCE AND RELATIONSHIP SATISFACTION

Friendship maintenance behaviors should function to contribute to mutual intimacy, closeness, and commitment, which have been identified as essential aspects of a friendship (Wiseman, 1986). The four friendship maintenance behaviors (supportiveness, positivity, openness, and interaction) have been found to correlate with, and statistically predict, an individual's satisfaction with the friendship (Oswald et al., 2004). However, friendship commitment was predicted by supportiveness and interaction but not by one's use of openness or positivity. This suggests that while positivity and openness may play a role in making the friendship satisfying, they do not have the same predictive strength with commitment to the friendship. It may be that supportiveness and interaction allow the friendships to develop a deeper level of emotional intimacy that promotes long-term commitment.

If maintenance behaviors are enacted to keep a relationship at the desired level of satisfaction, then usage of maintenance behaviors should also be associated with friendship longevity. To examine the predictive ability of maintenance behaviors over time and distance, Oswald and Clark (2003) examined the maintenance of best friendships during the first year of college. Best friendships during adolescence and young adulthood provide an interesting opportunity to understand the function of friendship maintenance during times of transition. For young adults, close friendships are beginning to become more stable, compared with childhood friendships, yet fewer than half of adolescents' best friendship last longer than 1 year (e.g., Branje, Frijns, Finkenauer, Engels, & Meeus, 2007). Best friends play an especially crucial role for adolescents as they provide acceptance, respect, trust, intimacy and opportunities for self-disclosure (e.g., Cole & Bradac, 1996, [...]). However, these friendships, compared with other types of relationships, appear to be especially vulnerable to deterioration when there is a decrease in contact and time spent in shared activities (Roberts & Dunbar, 2011). Thus, it is essential to understand how these close relationships are maintained, especially during periods of transitions when relationships might be especially vulnerable to deterioration or termination.

In a longitudinal study examining what happens to high school best friendships during the first year of college, nearly half of all of high school best friendships transitioned to close or casual friendships (Oswald & Clark, 2003). However, use of the maintenance behaviors of self-disclosure, positivity, supportiveness, and interaction were predictive of maintaining the friendship during the first year of college. Communication-based maintenance seemed to be of central importance and was associated with not only maintaining the best friendship but also sustaining high levels of friendship satisfaction and commitment. Importantly, maintaining the best friendship was associated with less loneliness, further suggesting the importance of maintaining close friendships for social and mental well-being.

There is growing evidence that use of maintenance behaviors may be associated with a wide range of relationship-related behaviors and individual differences. For example, when conflict in a relationship occurs, the friends might engage in maintenance behaviors to sustain the relationship through tough times and simultaneously engage in problem-solving behaviors. Oswald and Clark (2006) found that maintenance behaviors positively correlated with constructive problem-solving styles of voice (actively and positively working toward solving a problem) and loyalty (constructively but passively solving a problem). In contrast, maintenance behaviors were negatively correlated with destructive problem styles of neglect (a passive, destructive way to solve problems) and exit (destructive active way to solve problems).

Friendship maintenance behaviors are also associated with perception of available resources from newly formed social networks (McEwan & Guerrero, 2012). McEwan and Guerreo note that friendship maintenance behaviors not only are used to sustain developed friendships but also can be used to increase closeness in newly formed friendships. In a study of first-year college students, it was found that maintenance of casual and close friendships was associated with friendship quality. Furthermore, friendship quality and close friendship maintenance were directly related to perceived availability of resources from the network.

Engaging in friendship maintenance behaviors appears to have even broader benefits on psychological well-being. Across four studies, Demir and colleagues (2011) found that engaging in friendship maintenance behaviors was strongly predictive of happiness. Furthermore, while previous research has found that autonomy support from a friend (perception that the friend is supportive of their autonomous actions, perspective, and choices) is predictive of happiness, Demir and colleagues found that this association is fully mediated by use of friendship maintenance behaviors. They argue that perceiving one's friend as supportive of their autonomy is associated with increased engagement of friendship maintenance behaviors to maintain the supportive bond, which in turn contributes to overall happiness.

Together these lines of research suggest interesting implications for friendship maintenance behaviors. Not only does engaging in maintenance behaviors support continuation of a satisfying friendship but also it appears to be part of a broader set of relationship behaviors that help people to resolve relationship conflicts, strengthen friendships that provide autonomy support, and contribute ultimately to a satisfying life and happiness.

## MAINTAINING FRIENDS WITH MODERN TECHNOLOGY

With the development of technology, friends now have a variety of mediums in which they can maintain friendships, even if not in immediate proximity. Online social networking sites are frequently highlighted as being used to maintain long-distance friendships as they allow for frequent "online" interactions and communications (such as instant messaging and active communication exchanges) as well as the ability to stay informed of friends' lives and activities by sharing information via more passive information exchanges such as viewing posts and photos. Given the popularity of online social networking and other computer-mediated communication (CMC) options, it is not surprising that they are becoming an increasingly important part of friendships [...] with an increasing number of people reporting that they use CMC to maintain current friendships (e.g., Craig & Wright, 2012; McEwan, 2013) and to escalate the friendships to more intimate levels (e.g., Sosik & Bazarova, 2014).

In an examination of friendship-maintenance strategies specific to Facebook, it was found that people use Facebook to maintain the relationship via "sharing" (self-disclosure by sharing news, updating one's profile, and commenting on a friend's profile, etc.) behaviors and "caring" (indicating care and interaction with the friend by posting special notes on friends wall, offering support following bad news, congratulating a friend on good news posted, posting photos to share experiences with friends, etc.; McEwan, 2013). Facebook also allows people to passively follow their friends' lives via "surveillance" of the friend's posts and sharing pictures. In McEwan's study of 112 young adult friendship dyads, both of the friends' engaging in the maintenance behaviors that were classified as "caring" were positively correlated with own and friend's report of friendship satisfaction, liking of the friend, and perceived closeness. Similarly, using Facebook as a method of "surveillance" was positively associated with friendship satisfaction, liking, and closeness. However, a different pattern was found for using Facebook "sharing." Interestingly, Facebook "sharing" was negatively associated with friendship satisfaction, liking of the friend, and closeness of the friendship. Both one's own sharing behaviors and their friend's sharing on Facebook behaviors were negatively associated with satisfaction and liking in the friendship. This is inconsistent with research that finds self-disclosure as an important part of friendship maintenance (e.g., Oswald et al., 2004).

The differential findings for McEwan's (2013) caring and sharing Facebook maintenance strategies suggest that self-disclosure on Facebook may function differently than face-to-face self-disclosures. The Facebook self-disclosures measured by McEwan's "sharing" maintenance strategy reflected impersonal mass broadcast of information rather than an interpersonal, intimate exchange. However, the "caring" maintenance dimension included a number of items that reflected personal and intimate exchanges such as congratulating people on their posts of good news and sending condolences upon reading posts of bad news. Thus, the caring dimension included aspects of intimate self-disclosure. These findings together suggest that self-disclosure on Facebook that is intimate and person specific, rather than general mass communication, is predictive of positive friendship outcomes and promotes friendship closeness. Similar results were found by Valkenburg and Peter (2009), whereby instant messaging between adolescent-aged friends was predictive of intimate self-disclosure and friendship quality. Other research has found that Facebook communication strategies that allow for deeper communication that includes self-disclosure and supportiveness, such as private exchanges, rather than mass announcements, not only serve to maintain the relationship but also promote escalation of the friendship to more intimate levels (Sosik & Bazarova, 2014).

The usage of these types of electronic mediums for maintenance may depend on the closeness of the friendship. Yang, Brown, and Braun (2014) found that in newly forming friendships, college students preferred using Facebook posts or text messages that were less intimate. However as the friendship closeness increased, then instant messaging, phone calls, or Skype (computer programs that allow for video conversations) that allowed for intimate self-disclosure became more prevalent. McEwan and Guerrero (2012) had similar conclusions about CMC as a friendship maintenance strategy. They found CMC as a form of maintenance was especially prevalent in the more casual, newly developing friendships, rather than close relationships, where intimate self-disclosure might be more relationship appropriate.

While social networking sites such as Facebook are the most frequently highlighted as CMC mechanisms for maintaining friendships, there are a number of other media that allow friends to engage in maintenance behaviors even when they are not in physical proximity. For example, electronic communication via text and voice messaging (Hall & Baym, 2012) and online gaming programs that allow friends to mutually interact and compete against each other on a game while in different locations (Ledbetter & Kuznekoff, 2012) have been suggested as electronic opportunities for friendship maintenance. For example, Hall and Baym (2012) argued that phone text and voice messaging is one type of friendship maintenance strategy. They found that use of text and mobile phone messaging contributed to relationship interdependence, which was positively associated with friendship satisfaction. However, there appear to be limits on the effectiveness of mediated communications for maintaining friendships. Paradoxically, mobile phone maintenance expectations also contributed to an overdependence between friends that was negatively associated with friendship quality. This suggests an implication for mobile phone messaging as well as CMC more generally. While these methods may be useful for maintaining friendships, everything must be done in a balance that is mutually appreciated by both friends.

When used to maintain friendship over long distances, CMC has also been shown to have psychological benefits (e.g., Baker & Oswald, 2010; Ranney & Tropp-Gordon, 2012). The use of CMC by first-year students who have low-quality face-to-face friendships was associated with decreased psychological anxiety and depression (Ranney & Tropp-Gordon, 2012). However, this benefit of CMC was not found for individuals with higher quality face-to-face relationships, presumably because they were already getting sufficient social support from their proximal friendships. Other research has suggested that shy individuals appear to benefit more from using online social networks in terms of reducing their loneliness and having higher perceived friendship quality (Baker & Oswald, 2010).

In sum, as technology develops, the opportunities and methods of maintaining friendships also advance. While online social networking sites, CMC, and easy access to cellular phones offer increased opportunities for communicating, it is important to note that not all maintenance across these different media is equivalent. These technologically based maintenance behaviors appear to be most effective when they promote more intimate self-disclosures and opportunities for supporting the friendship. In contrast, frequent but impersonal communication appears to be ineffective at successfully maintaining friendships and promoting the support that comes from those types of friendships.

## REFERENCES

Aron, A., Aron, E. N., Tudor, M., & Nelson, G. (1991). Close relationships as including other in the self. *Journal of Personality and Social Psychology, 60,* 241–253.

Aylor, B., & Dainton, M. (2004). Biological sex and psychological gender as predictors of routine and strategic relational maintenance. *Sex Roles, 50,* 689–697.

Baker, L. R., & Oswald, D. L. (2010). Shyness and online social networking services. *Journal of Social and Personal Relationships, 27,* 873–889.

Baumeister, R. F., & Leary, M. (1995). The need to belong: Desire for interpersonal attachments as a fundamental human motivation. *Psychological Bulletin, 117,* 497–529.

Binder, J. F., Roberts, S. G. B., & Sutcliffe, A. G. (2012). Closeness, loneliness, support: Close ties and significant ties in personal communities. *Social Networks, 34,* 206–214.

Branje, S. J., Frijns, R., Finkenauer, C., Engels, R., & Meeus, W. (2007). You are my best friend: Commitment and stability in adolescents' same-sex friendships. *Personal Relationships, 14,* 587–603.

Brehm, S. S., Miller, R. S., Perlman, D., & Campbell, S. M. (2002). *Intimate relationships* (3rd ed.). Boston: McGraw-Hill.

Cole, T., & Bradac, J. (1996). A lay theory of relational satisfaction with best friends. *Journal of Social and Personal Relationships, 13,* 57–83.

Craig, E., & Wright, K. B. (2012). Computer-mediated relational development and maintenance on Facebook. *Communication Research Reports, 29,* 119–129.

Cross, S. E., Bacon, P. L., & Morris, M. L. (2000). The relational-interdependent self-construal and relationships. *Journal of Personality and Social Psychology, 78,* 791–808.

Cross, S. E., Morris, M. L., & Gore, J. S. (2002). Thinking about oneself and others: The relational-interdependent self-construal and social cognition. *Journal of Personality and Social Psychology, 82,* 399–418.

Dainton, M., & Aylor, B. (2002). Routine and strategic maintenance efforts: Behavioral patterns, variations associated with relational length, and the prediction of relational characteristics. *Communication Monographs, 69,* 52–66.

Dainton, M., & Stafford, L. (1993). Routine maintenance behaviors: A comparison of relationship type, partner similarity, and sex differences. *Journal of Social and Personal Relationships, 10,* 255–272.

Demir, M., Ozdemir, M., & Marum, K. P. (2011). Perceived autonomy support, friendship maintenance, and happiness. *Journal of Psychology, 145,* 537–571.

Dindia, K., & Canary, D.J. (1993). Definitions and theoretical perspectives on maintaining relationships. *Journal of Social and Personal Relationships, 10,* 163–173.

Fehr, B. (1996). *Friendship processes.* Thousand Oaks, CA: Sage.

Hall, J. A. (2011) Sex differences in friendship expectations: A meta-analysis. *Journal of Social and Personal Relationships, 28,* 723–747.

Hall, J. A., & Bayn, N. K. (2011). Calling and texting (too much); Mobile maintenance expectations, (over) dependence, entrapment and friendship satisfaction. New *Media and Society, 14,* 312–331.

Hall, J. A., Larson, K. A., & Watts, A. (2011). Satisfying friendship maintenance expectations: The role of friendship standards and biological sex. *Human Communication Research, 37,* 529–552.

Hays, R. B. (1984). The development and maintenance of friendship. *Journal of Social and Personal Relationships, 1,* 75–98.

Ledbetter, A. M. (2013). Relational maintenance and inclusion of the other in the self: Measure development and dyadic test of a self-expansion theory approach. *Southern Communication Journal, 78,* 289–310.

Ledbetter, A. M., & Kuznekoff, J. H. (2012). More than a game: Friendship relational maintenance and attitudes toward Xbox LIVE communication. *Communication Research, 39*, 269–290.

Ledbetter, A. M., Stassen, H., Muhammad, A., & Kotey, E. N. (2010). Relational maintenance as including the other in the self. *Qualitative Research Reports in Communication, 11*, 21–28.

Mattingly, B. A., Oswald, D. L., & Clark, E. M. (2011). An examination of relational-interdependent self-construal, communal strength, and pro-relationship behaviors in friendships. *Personality and Individual Differences, 50*, 1243–1248.

Mattingly, B. A., Oswald, D. L., & Clark, E. M. (2015). *Routine and strategic friendship maintenance and friendship quality: A dyadic examination.* Unpublished manuscript.

McEwan, B. (2013). Sharing, caring and surveilling: An actor-partner interdependence model examination of Facebook relational maintenance strategies. *Cyberpsychology, Behavior and Social Networking, 12*, 863–869.

McEwan, B., & Guerrero, L. K. (2012). Maintenance behavior and relationship quality as predictors of perceived availability of resources in newly formed college friendship networks. *Communication Studies, 63*, 421–440.

Morry, M. M., & Kito, M. (2009). Relational-interdependent self-construal as a predictor of relationship quality: The mediating roles of one's own behaviors and the perceptions of the fulfillment of friendship functions. *Journal of Social Psychology, 149*, 205–222.

Oswald, D. L., & Clark, E. M. (2003). Best friends forever? High school best friendships and the transition to college. *Personal Relationships, 10*, 187–196.

Oswald, D. L., & Clark, E. M. (2006). How do friendship maintenance behaviors and problem-solving styles function at the individual and dyadic levels? *Personal Relationships, 13*, 333–348.

Oswald, D. L., Clark, E. M., & Kelly, C. M. (2004). Friendship maintenance: An analysis of individual and dyad behaviors. *Journal of Social and Clinical Psychology, 23*, 413–441.

Ranney, J. D., & Tropp-Gordon, W. (2012). Computer-mediated communication with distant friends: Relations with adjustment during students' first semester in college. *Journal of Educational Psychology, 104*, 848–861.

Roberts, S. G. B., & Dunbar, R. I. M. (2011). The costs of family and friends: An 18-month longitudinal study of relationship maintenance and decay. *Evolution and Human Behavior, 32*, 186–197.

Rusbult, C. E. (1980). Satisfaction and commitment in friendships. *Representative Research in Social Psychology, 11*, 96–105.

Rusbult, C. (1983). A longitudinal test of the investment model: The development (and deterioration) of satisfaction and commitment in heterosexual involvements. *Journal of Personality and Social Psychology, 45*, 101–117.

Sosik, V. S., & Bazarova, N. N. (2014). Relational maintenance on social network sites: How Facebook communication predicts relational escalation. *Computers in Human Behavior, 35*, 124–131.

Stafford, L., & Canary, D. J. (1991). Maintenance strategies and romantic relationship type, gender and relational characteristics. *Journal of Social and Personal Relationships, 8,* 217–242.

Valkenburg, P. M., & Peter, J. (2009). The effects of instant messaging on the quality of adolescents' existing friendships: A longitudinal study. *Journal of Communication, 59,* 79–97.

Weger, H., & Emmett, M. C. (2009). Romantic intent, relationship uncertainty, and relationship maintenance in young adults' cross-sex friendships. *Journal of Social and Personal Relationships, 26,* 964–988.

Wiseman, J. P. (1986). Friendships: Bonds and binds in voluntary relationship. *Journal of Social and Personal Relationships, 3,* 191–211.

Yang, C., Brown, B. B, & Braun, M. T. (2014). From Facebook to cell calls: Layers of electronic intimacy in college students' interpersonal relationships. *New Media and Society, 15,* 5–23.

# TIPS FOR MAKING FRIENDS

Perhaps you've examined your current social circle and believe you'd like to expand your list of friends. Again, some of you can make that decision and, even in the midst of a pandemic, figure out a way to make that happen. For the rest of us (that would include Sara, Roni, and Kim), we need to put some effort into the endeavor. The following are some tips that we hope will help you get started:

1. *Show up.* Sometimes, even when (or, paradoxically, especially when) we are feeling lonely, it's difficult to imagine joining a volleyball league, signing up for an art class, signing on to the neighborhood social hour via Zoom (eww, we get it), or joining in the group discussion that is starting to take shape after your biology class. However, showing up is a must! Gone are the days when friendships organically emerge over a shared dislike of your ninth-grade PE class. Once you reach young adulthood, new friendships usually require some degree of initiation on your part.

2. *Keep showing up.* Several studies have shown that the phenomenon in social science known as *proximity* will work in your favor, but it means that you need to attend that awkward networking event multiple times. One study (Moreland & Beach, 1990) placed four volunteers in a classroom and asked them not to interact with anyone. At the end of the term, students in the class were asked who (of the four volunteers) they liked the most, and consistently, they chose the individual who had shown up the most, even though they never spoke! (P.S., Proximity also works when you are trying to create a spark on a romantic level; make sure your paths cross [obviously in a safe and noncreepy way] often, and you will tip the odds in your favor.)

3. *Assume people will like you.* Of course, this is easier said than done, but having (and faking) a gentle bit of confidence will create a change in the way you interact with others that may in turn lead to a self-fulfilling prophecy. One study found that when volunteers were led to believe they would be liked by a group of strangers, they were more upbeat and more positive, which led to better connections (Curtis & Miller, 1986).

4. *Remember the basics.* In 1936, Dale Carnegie proposed six rules for getting others to like us, and his words have stood the test of time: (a) become genuinely interested in other people, (b) smile, (c) remember that a person's name is the sweetest and most important sound in any language, (d) be a good listener (refer to Chapter 7 for pointers), (e) encourage others to talk about themselves, and (f) talk in terms of the other person's interests.

5. *Seek help.* If the mere thought of doing the above causes distress, consider talking to a counselor. Granted, the three of us (Sara, Roni, and Kim) are counselors, and we like

to recommend it quite often. That said, social anxiety is an excellent problem to address with a professional. In addition to helping with anxiety, the right counselor can give you feedback (if you ask) on the ways you present yourself to the world that might be hindering or supporting your friendship-acquiring efforts. Seeking help in this way would be a wise investment in your physical and mental health and your overall sense of well-being.

## END-OF-CHAPTER REFLECTIONS

You now know that friendships are a fragile, yet highly significant type of relationship, and the good friends we have are worthy of our energy and attention, and the friends we'd like to have are worthy of our efforts, however uncomfortable they may be. Most of us have felt the strain that the pandemic has had on our friendships, and as you've read here, a decrease in contact with our friends is consistently shown to lead to a reduction in satisfaction and leaves our friendships vulnerable to decay. What steps can you take right away to start resurrecting any friendships that have faded over the course of the pandemic? How can you prepare yourself to meet new people once the social distancing rules are removed? Committing to positivity (as you read in the final excerpt) and putting in effort to meet new people will serve you well and will improve your odds of enjoying greater emotional and physical health long into your future.

## REFERENCES

Curtis, R. C., & Miller, K. (1986). Believing another likes or dislikes you: Behaviors making the beliefs come true. *Journal of Personality and Social Psychology, 51*(2), 284–290.

Moreland, R. L., & Beach, S. R. (1992). Exposure effects in the classroom: The development of affinity among students. *Journal of Experimental Social Psychology, 28*(3), 255–276.

## RECOMMENDATIONS FOR FURTHER READING

Dale Carnegie & Associates. (2014). *How to win friends and influence people in the digital age*. Simon & Schuster.

King, P. (2020). *Better small talk: Talk to anyone, avoid awkwardness, generate deep conversations, and make real friends*. PKCS Media.

# Chapter 10

# Love, Intimacy, and Commitment

*"Love is our supreme emotion: Its presence or absence in our lives influence everything we feel, think, do, and become. It's that recurrent state that ties you in—your body and brain alike—to the social fabric, to the bodies and brains of those in your midst. When you experience love—true heart/mind/soul-expanding love—you not only become better able to see the larger tapestry of life and better able to breathe life into the connections that matter to you, but you also set yourself on a pathway that leads to more health, happiness, and wisdom."*
—(Barbara Fredrickson, 2013, p. 14)

## EDITORS' INTRODUCTION

Anthropologist Helen Fisher has studied love for decades and has found that love exists in every species, dating back thousands of years. Love is considered the ultimate prize. Love is a drug—the same brain centers that respond to drugs like cocaine are activated when we are in love, except we don't come down. The more we are denied love, the more we want it (Fisher, 2008). Barbara Fredrickson (2013), emotion scientist, broadens our understanding of love beyond a feeling experienced between two people. She proposes that we grow and nurture love inside of us, and from within we strengthen our connection with others and the world and ultimately improve the health of our bodies and minds.

So far we've discussed some essential relationship skills that can facilitate satisfaction and success in many kinds of relationships: familial relationships, friendships, dating/romantic relationships, sexual relationships, and committed relationships. In this chapter, we shift our focus to love—the kind that can lead to commitment and longevity. A recent Pew research study (the Pew Research Center is a nonpartisan fact tank located in Washington, DC) found that love, companionship, and commitment were the top three reasons people in a relationship chose to either cohabitate or marry (Horowitz et al., 2019). While commitment is not for everyone, we will offer some perspectives on love, commitment, and relationship stability that will hopefully help you in your relationships, whether you choose commitment or not.

We've chosen to refer to commitment in its many forms as opposed to addressing marriage specifically. There is a ritual around marriage that occupies our culture and many cultures around the world. That said, for many, marriage is not the ultimate goal of a relationship. Marriage is important for some, but for some, commitment, without the legal aspect of marriage, is equally important. Furthermore, we experience equal physiological and emotional benefits in a committed relationship as we might in marriage. Commitment is a general term that implies the intent to stay in a relationship with a partner long-term and acknowledges couples who choose not to enter the legal agreement that is marriage, and also same-sex partners, who until recently could not legally marry. Prior to commitment, we tend to follow a common love trajectory in our initiation and establishment of intimate relationships.

There are distinct differences between what we might experience as love in the beginning stages of a relationship, most commonly understood as infatuation, and mature love that grows over time. In the beginning stages of a romantic relationship, we may feel obsessed with our partners, think about them all the time, require less sleep, eat less, and want nothing more than to be with, touch, and hold the one we desire. During this initial stage of a relationship, which usually lasts between 6 and 18 months, dopamine is the primary neurotransmitter activated in the brain when we think about, talk to, and touch our partners. Dopamine brings us the experience of immense pleasure, *and we just want more*.

Like any drug, we build up a tolerance to our infatuation with our partners, and if the relationship is to endure, we transition the intense passion and obsession we experience to an attachment bond. This is not to say that passion is gone. In fact, happily married couples who have been together for years report more sexual satisfaction than couples in a new relationship. Oxytocin (the cuddle hormone) and vasopressin (the bonding hormone) replace dopamine when we're with our partners, as you'll recall from Chapter 6. What we experience as mature love can be just as wonderful (and much longer lasting) than infatuation. That said, some people "lose that loving feeling" and move on to look for it elsewhere. We call this ongoing search for infatuation (and the associated dopamine high) serial monogamy.

There are endless definitions of love, and we don't endorse any one over others. That said, there are theories of love that help us to understand its components better and achieve the kind of balance that we hope for in our intimate relationships. We'll review two theories of love here: **Sternberg's triangular theory of love** and **Reiss's wheel theory of love**.

Sternberg (1986) proposed a triangular theory of love that we find useful in assessing couple relationship quality and value. The three sides of the triangle (Figure 10.1), are *intimacy, passion, and commitment.* When a couple's relationship possesses components of all three elements (a balanced or equilateral triangle), their love is labeled *consummate.* You will notice a label on each side of the triangle that indicates the presence of two components and then another label at each point indicating that only one element of love exists. You might be thinking at this point that consummate love is the best kind and the kind of love we should all strive for. While ideal in committed relationships, consummate love is not the only kind of love that leads to stability and relationship satisfaction. Relationships are dynamic, and at any point in time, the triangle might be skewed in any of the three directional points. What we hope you take from this theory is that all three components of the triangle are important, and it's up to the couple to negotiate and work toward achieving the shape of triangle that they want and need.

## STERNBERG'S TRIANGULAR THEORY OF LOVE

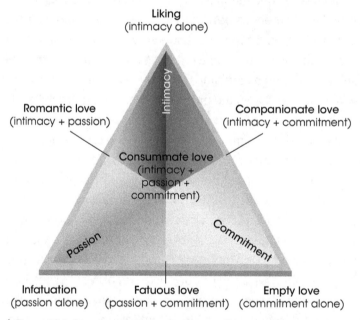

Figure 10.1 Sternberg's triangular theory of love.
Source: From Sternberg, R.J. (1986). A triangular theory of love. *Psychological Review, 93*, 119–135. Copyright© 1986 by the American Psychological Association.

Reiss (1960) offers us a dated, yet still relevant wheel theory of love (Figure 10.2). The elements of rapport (how we get along), self-revelation (how much we share), mutual dependency (counting on your partner and being responsive to their needs), and intimacy need fulfilment (closeness and feeling known) fill each quadrant of the circle and ideally grow as a relationship develops. Also relevant to the theory, and surrounding the wheel, are the roles that we fill in our relationships (equality and equanimity) and sociocultural background.

## REISS'S WHEEL THEORY OF LOVE

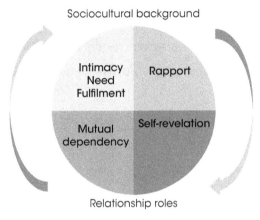

Sociocultural background

Intimacy Need Fulfilment

Rapport

Mutual dependency

Self-revelation

Relationship roles

| Figure 10.2  Reiss's wheel theory of love.

If you imagine superimposing the wheel theory of love over the triangle theory of love, you might see how each theory has its relevant components, and when combined offer us an idea of the many facets and definitions of love. Now imagine, as Fredrickson (2013) purports, that love comes from within us, and until we access the deeper parts of ourselves that create and share love with the world, we cannot enter into either the triangular or the wheel theories of love. In short, no theory alone is a comprehensive theory of love.

We have come to believe many things about love and intimacy: love at first sight; there is a soul mate for everyone; the concept of happily ever after; and thanks to the Beatles, "all we need is love." Most of these clichés are myths—widely held yet false beliefs. Still, they endure. Love and intimacy myths can influence many decisions we make in relationships. In the following reading, "Intimacy, Love, and Commitment," Jerrold Shapiro and Terence Patterson bring our attention to some common myths that couples might face in their relationships. If unaltered, myths about love and intimacy can erode our relationships when they prove themselves untrue. We encourage you to think about your own endorsement of love and intimacy myths and how they affect your thoughts and behaviors in your relationship. They may even affect who you choose as a partner. Shapiro and Patterson write to couples therapists, but we encourage you to consider your own perspectives on intimacy, love, and commitment and how the information presented pertains to your own relationships.

As you read, keep in mind the following primer questions for reflection. If you feel so inclined, take a few minutes and consider your responses to the following questions before you read, and then again after you've read the chapter.

## PRIMERS

1. What is your personal definition of love?
2. What are your most valued qualities in a potential partner? Write them down.
3. What are some values that must be shared in a relationship? Write them down.
4. What are your deal breakers?

## CREDIT

Fig. 10.1: Copyright © 1986 by American Psychological Association.

# Intimacy, Love, and Commitment

*By Jerrold Lee Shapiro and Terence Patterson*

> *"Let there be spaces in your togetherness, and let the winds of the heavens dance between you."*
> —Kahlil Gibran, *The Prophet*

> *"Love is a many-splendored thing."*
> —Sonnet 73 (Shakespeare) and 1955 film

L ove, sex, intimacy, commitment, attachment, connection, living together, partners, paramours, affection, roommates, monogamy, polyamory, adultery, polygamy, etc.

What do these words evoke in you? What do you believe characterizes a close relationship? Emotional attachment, contiguity, sex, intellectual resonance, social compatibility, time together, shared values, similar backgrounds? All of these, or just one? We don't pretend to know; many will say that it's in the eyes and hearts of the beholders—how we define our relationship is all that matters. There is little solid evidence to take a firm stance on what elements a close relationship should include, but there are certainly societal structures, cultural values, and personal and moral standards that may determine whether a relationship is close. Some would say, "I can't define it, but I know one when I see one." In order to avoid such ambiguity, we will attempt to provide some evidence and guidance for understanding intimacy, sex, love, and stability in close relationships. This is a major component of the work of couple therapists: aiding couples struggling with these key issues.

Is this what you would consider true love? It is certainly stable. Their relationship has established them in their community and provided a home, children, and security, but is there intimacy, sex, and romance? If you interviewed Tevye and Golde, would they say they care about these matters? And if they said yes, do you think they repress their desires or harbor resentments over their absence? This situation is similar to many you will find in treating couples. Clinical exploration about the level of intimacy in a relationship can uncover reasons for alienation and hostility, diminish persistent negative interactions and arguments over trivia, and enable couples to acknowledge their feelings and move toward greater connection with their partner.

As always, we cannot ignore how a therapist's personal views enter into the type of intimacy couples engage in (or not). Do we hold to the notion of the Drifters classic song that you can do what you will during the evening, as long as you "save the last dance for me" (Pomas & Shulman, 1960)? Do we believe with Jankowiak, (2008), "I have her/his heart, swinging is just sex?" or do we have a more integrated view of sex, love, and intimacy? Do you believe the Beatles' notion that "all you need is love" or does one's view of intimacy reflect a stronger all-or-none value system?

## DEFINITIONS: INTIMACY AND COMMITMENT

Throughout this text, we will be referring to committed intimate partner relationships involving sharing of affection and common responsibilities. The word *intimate* will be used in the sense of an emotional and physical closeness in a relationship that is primary for each partner and more frequent and intense than others. The intimacy may or may not be overtly sexual but involves emotional and perhaps intellectual attachment and physical touch in some manner that is reinforced by chemical and neurological effects that induce pleasure, comfort, and a sense of belonging. Each of these aspects exists along a continuum and can be freely defined by each couple, regardless of culture and ethnicity, sexual orientation, or gender identification.

The nature of the bond is socially constructed (Beall & Sternberg, 1995) and unique in relation to other relationships each partner has.

The intimacy and commitment that are defined by each partner is significant in assessing and treating couples, while the impact of these concepts is often unclear to partners in a relationship. For example, the word *intimacy* is often considered a euphemism for sex, and disordered couples frequently report an absence or lack of satisfaction with intercourse, and ask, "What's normal?" We can't answer this question because each couple needs to determine what works for them. When we explore the range of intimacy—from warm touch, to kissing, to sexual contact—we often find that these are missing as well. If partners are not extremely alienated from each other, we can strengthen their connection by using approximations at the lower end of the intimacy spectrum (e.g., frequent hugs). Some people need to rediscover an awareness of pleasure in their bodies, and for this we recommend a guide such as *Our Bodies, Ourselves* (Norsigian, 2011). Referral to a credentialed sex therapist may be helpful for some couples, although we generally find that couples have little trouble reinitiating sex when their resentment and hostility are reduced and they become open to intimacy.

## Intimacy and Couple Therapy

For the philosopher and Jewish mystical theologian, Martin Buber (1937/1970), the most essential form of life (and spirituality) was the I-thou encounter. Protestant theologian Paul Tillich (1952) focused on the phenomenon when he asserted that fully becoming a person may only occur in encounters with another person. Rogers (1951) frequently set the center of personal growth on relationship: between partners and between therapist and clients.

For Frankl (1959), love was described as the highest aspirational goal for human beings. He describes how his personal love for his wife and fellow human beings helped him survive the horrible suffering and personal losses in the Nazi death camps.

For all these authors, love (I-thou) was viewed as essential to living fully and the path to salvation or being versus non-being. It is the direct antidote to feelings of meaninglessness. This aspiration can be prominent in all forms of counseling and psychotherapy, particularly as both goal and method in couple therapy. Love and intimacy between equal primary partners are considered the most salient for relationship in life (Shapiro, 2016).

This makes intimacy a prime factor in working with couples. Crowe and Ridley (1990) specifically explored four aspects of intimacy in couple therapy: (a) sexual intimacy, (b) emotional intimacy, (c) physical and nonverbal intimacy, and (d) operational (daily life) closeness.

Crowe (1997) noted that many of the typical relationship difficulties commonly occur in any of these arenas of intimacy, ultimately involving underlying fears of suffocation and abandonment, and more conscious, daily life power conflicts, general bickering, and disagreements about sexuality.

Intimacy-based problems may be seen as foundational in triangulated (Bowen, 1974) situations such as affairs, extended family commitments, and parenting. Crowe (1997) also indicates that these intimacy-based conflicts may also underlie other more significant individual pathology such as in clinical levels of depression, anxiety, and unrelenting jealousy.

## Attachment and Intimacy

The *attachment* history and style of each partner is fundamental in the type and level of intimacy each partner is capable of and desires; those who have faulty attachment in childhood may have lifelong struggles connecting to others emotionally and physically. From a systems viewpoint, this can be addressed conjointly with the couple, but a partner may need individual therapy to address this obstacle fully. Attachment repair may also be essential for those who have been abused emotionally, sexually, or physically, and for those with physical limitations. While we do not advocate a full analytic approach to repairing faulty attachment, an effective means of exploring this issue is through the lens of emotion-focused therapy (EFT) (Johnson, 2019).

## Intimacy as a Necessary Aspect of Commitment

The authors take the position that however defined by the couple, some level of intimacy is essential for couples; resentment accumulates when it is completely absent. If we find that the relationship is devoid of intimacy and commitment is questionable, we may pose paradoxically the option of living together as roommates in order to elicit their motivation to repair the relationship or discuss whether separation is a better option for them. They are often astonished by this suggestion, and only those who decide to remain together for financial reasons or until the children are grown have decided on a solely roommate arrangement. Such an arrangement can become an uneasy truce, but one that breaks repetitive conflictual patterns and provides some relief from conflict.

## Short-Term Intimacy and Long-Term Intimacy

Although intimacy for any couple is best understood by their subjective experiences and definitions, one assessment that couple counselors and therapists are wise to make is the extent that the commitment involves *short-term* or *long-term* intimacy. The definition of short-term intimacy is that the couple "will stay together as long as on the whole there are more pluses than minuses and neither breaks a basic trust (as in betrayal)." By contrast, long-term intimacy is defined by the statement, "Whatever comes up we will deal with together."

Therapists cannot make assumptions about these basic definitions. The long-term commitment is, of course, more stable and more likely to be able to withstand the increased anxiety that therapy (like the potential for any change) may engender.

## CASE BOX 10.1.2 LIVING AS ROOMMATES?

When they began therapy, Mona and Robby, married for 5 years and exclusive for 8 years, reported that they had been "living as roommates for most of the 8 years [they] have been together." Mona described herself as a person with a very low libido and no interest in having children. Robbie reported that he'd like to be more sexual, but his requests had "mostly fallen on deaf ears." He claimed that their companionship and faith-based work together was what mattered most and that "Mona usually agreed about three to four times a year." Both of them reported that although it was troubling that they had such little interest by comparison to others, it was not a deal breaker. One of their therapeutic goals was to be more comfortable physically. This interaction occurred in the fifth session:

M: I think sometimes he doesn't hug me or kiss me, because then he'll want sex and I'll say no.

R: No. I don't hug you because you tense up and I just think that you find me unattractive.

M: You now that's not true. It's just that when you hug me, your hands roam and ...

This interaction progressed for about 10 minutes when the therapist interrupted.

T: Let's try an experiment for the next 2 weeks. You probably won't be giving up a sexual time during that period, so let's make a pact that Mona will approach Robby once a week and hug him. Robby will hug her back in the same way she hugs him. Second, Robby will take the lead twice and Mona will hug him back. Here's the important agreement. This will be done while you are both clothed and agree that it will not go any further than the hugs.

The therapist asked them to not have sex, something they were likely to avoid during the time period. Second, he asked for an agreement that would reduce the potential threat of physical touching going further. Although they agreed, they found ways to avoid the homework during the ensuing week. This was discussed and the therapist instructed them to double up so that they could complete the exercise in the second week.

When they returned, they embarrassingly told the therapist that Robby had touched Mona's breast during one hug and then "pulled his hand away like he was touching a hot stove!"

Mona placed his hand back on her breast and told him that was okay. Two sessions later, they confessed that they had violated the agreement and had atypically satisfying intercourse later that night.

*Commitment* means that time and energy are consistently devoted to maintaining and increasing the connection and developing the relationship, and to upholding whatever agreements partners have with each other. Commitment also involves sharing tasks that are necessary to maintain the bond, which may include household, social, financial, child care, and other responsibilities. Commitment does not necessarily mean "until death do us part," but rather an openness to strengthening the positive aspects of the relationship and working to resolve conflicts as long as the relationship remains functional. Those who engage in polyamory or polyandry may have other partners, but the total emotional and physical attachment and commitment may be the same (to the group) as with the primary partner.[1] Similarly, those in monogamous relationships may have close emotional ties to others of either gender, but the primary attachment and commitment remains with the partner.

Consider the nature of commitment in the following situation.

---

**DECISION BOX 10.1.3  IS THIS A SOLID COMMITMENT?**

Keesha and Kevin, a 30-year-old couple, decide they have a solid relationship and move in together after 2 years together. They buy furniture, decorate, visit each other's parents, adopt a pet, and save together to buy a house. After a year of settling into a comfortable life together, Kevin becomes uncomfortable with Keesha's going on frequent business trips with male colleagues and having lunch on her day off with Elvin, a male colleague, with whom she has become friends. Keesha maintains contact with Elvin on a level similar to her contact and tone as with her women friends. Kevin does not travel for business and does not have close women friends, and although he does not suspect Keesha is having an affair, he tells her that he feels her relationship with Elvin is inappropriate and asks her to stop. Keesha feels her autonomy is being infringed upon and Kevin insists that this is a "deal breaker" for him if she continues her friendship with Elvin. What is your view of Keesha and Kevin's level of commitment after the relationship has been solid for 3 years and no breach of trust has occurred?

---

Keesha and Kevin appear committed from their 3 years together, but now Kevin feels that Keesha's views and behavior are unacceptable in their relationship. If there were an affair or abuse, it would be easy to view Kevin's stance on Keesha's intolerable behavior as weighty, but she believes as an individual she has a right engage in a valued friendship with a man.

Kevin and Keesha's disagreement developed because of a discrepancy in what each expected and what was occurring. Those expectations are often long standing, culturally influenced, and based in some core values. One of the determinants of such strong beliefs and feelings are the myths with which each partner grew up.

---

1   It is important to note that those in polyamorous "group marriages" may define the primary relationship as having three or more members, who are committed equally and exclusively to the marital group.

## SOME MYTHS OF INTIMACY

Because intimacy stands out as a particularly important part of relationships, within each culture there is considerable folklore and myths about the nature of appropriate intimacy for a couple. It is essential that we view these myths as values and beliefs that guide significant portions of couple behavior. Thus, we explore here the idea that they should not be viewed through the common American lens of myths as falsehoods, but rather in the form of the Ancient Greek myths (guidelines for living).

Myths have two essential components: (a) a well-formed belief and (b) emotion. That combination makes them particularly resistant to being altered. Thus, the job of the couple therapist is to use these myths to diagnose and assist the couple from within their system. It is not to debunk a myth.

A brief selection of popular Western myths was presented by Diamond and Shapiro (1983) and these are briefly summarized here.

### Myths Regarding the Nature of Intimacy

There are many beliefs, emotions and concerns that impact the manner of relationships. Understanding those unique influences and personal expectations can make therapy particularly effective. A number of these common myths are described here. It is not an exhaustive list. Each couple and each individual may be motivated by internalized values contained in these myths.

#### Myth #1: The Sexual Myth

Many consider intimacy and sexuality to be one and the same. This myth explores those relational aspects in which close physical connection defines intimacy. Many clients will hem and haw around the question early in therapy. "We are having some problems in ah, er, uh, intimacy relations." Examples of a general belief in this myth are almost ubiquitous in our culture, from advertising any nature of products with sexuality, to popular books that claim that better sex means a better relationship (and of course the book describes how we can enhance our sexuality), and the rapidly growing use of chemical and surgical means to aid sexual performance and satisfaction.

## Myth #2: The Absence of Strife Myth

Partially influenced by the "got married and lived happily ever after" storybook and Hollywood endings, there can be an expectation among many partners that after marriage, strife will be absent. As one client noted, "When she called me a SOB, I thought the marriage was over!" An important diagnostic value of uncovering this particular myth is to help couples anticipate some strife in any partnership, find methods to recognize those situations, and identify ways of recovering. This myth may be held by either partner or both. Couple therapists need to help them realize that even in a bed of roses, there are inevitable thorns.

## Myth #3: The Enchanting Fairytale Myth ("Love Conquers All")

A myth closely related to happily ever after is the notion that if I love someone enough and if they love me truly, all things shall be vouchsafed. Love is the answer, the magic potion, and the desired beginning of a relationship. In this formulation, the love between Tevye and Golda is but one form. The hot passion and shared delusion demonstrated by George and Martha in Albee's (2001) play, *Who's Afraid of Virginia Woolf*, is another example, albeit substantially darker.

One interesting offshoot of the enchanting fairy tale is the recent sense that a partner should get and give unconditional positive regard. That is something possible and derived from an idealistic therapist–client or parent–child relationship, but problematic as an expectation in a relationship of equals.

# Myths Regarding Finding and Beginning Intimacy

Two of the most important and difficult tasks in modern life involves finding a compatible partner and beginning a relationship. Because the process is in some ways so mysterious, there are endless beliefs about the proper ways to pursue the goals and about the definition of a good relationship.

## Myth #4: The Soul Mate Myth

Among many couples is a deeply held belief that there is one and only person for each of us. Once we find that person we can never let him or her go without tragic lifelong loneliness. There is a deep belief in a "Mr. or Ms. Right." We expect the fictional Prince Charming to ride in on his white horse and take us away from whatever drudgery we experience. It is interesting in how cross-cultural this belief in star-crossed lovers seems to be, from Shakespeare's *Romeo and Juliet*, "Running Bear and Little White Dove" (Richardson, 1959), the Bing Crosby and Ingrid Bergman film *The Bells of St. Mary's* (Nichols, 1945), and the story told in *Tiger Balm Gardens* in Hong Kong. Each depict the tragic consequences of such love being blocked by death, religious commitment, or distance. To the extent that each partner views the other through this lens, the more vulnerable she or he may feel. For a therapist, understanding that this is believed to

Victor and Bette were newlyweds in their 60s. They met 4 years ago in a grief support group after their partners of many years passed away. After 2 years of dating, they married. In the first session, she complained that she could not "live up to the memory of Sally, Victor's first wife." For his part, Victor complained that lovemaking was "just not the same." He in particular, deeply ascribed to the "soul mate myth."

Instead of trying to talk them out of this belief of one and only one true love, the therapist explored with them, their survivors' guilt, the realities of being newlyweds some 40 years after they were courting their former partners, the meaning of being in this new relationship, and what they could do to make it work.

T: Bette, what if you cannot ever live up to the memory of Sally?

B: I don't know. Maybe I am not good enough for Victor!

V: That's not true. I just need to let go of Sally more to be with you.

T: And if you don't let her memory go?

V: I just want Bette to know that I love her too, but I don't want to lose my memories and we had three kids and now a grandson.

T: Tell Bette more about how you want to have both the memory and history and your new love for her.

B: If you told me how much you love me and desire me …

T: What would that take?

V: Don't try to take Sal's memory away. Just be with me as Bette.

B: When we are in bed, can you focus all your attention on me and have the split love at other times?

be the only chance for true intimacy and love informs the sensitivity in which the couple may be successfully addressed.

## Myth #5: All the Eggs in One Basket Myth

Another variant of the one and only is the sense that we get one and only one true intimate partner in life. Once that partner is gone by death or desertion, there is no other recourse. This may be particularly strong in some traditional cultures. Indeed, it is not unusual for a widow to eschew further relationships after a long-term marriage ends, even if she outlives her late husband for 40 years.

## Myth #6: The All-or-None Myth (You've Either Got It or You Don't)

There is in Western culture a popular myth that there are "haves" and "have nots" when it comes to intimacy and love. Certain segments of the population are afforded a "right" to almost unlimited intimacy. This was underscored in 2016 when then-presidential candidate Donald Trump was heard on a recording (the famous Access Hollywood video) affirming that as a celebrity, he had the right to walk up to, kiss, and grab women as he desired. Although his depiction may seem outlandish, it did reflect a sense that fame, certain body types, and financial success privileged certain folks to have more rights to intimacy that they desired.

Beyond that image is a deep-rooted phenomenon we call the "reproductive bias." This belief is that the only people who have rights to intimacy are those who could produce a socially acceptable pregnancy. In part, the furor some feel about hetero-non-normative relationships is rooted in this myth. The clinically relevant part of this myth is when people remove themselves from relationships because of it and suffer from it. Groups that this impacts include the young and old, people with disabilities, minorities, people with lower socioeconomic strata of society, and those attracted to others of the same sex.

## Myth #7: The Beauty Myth

Similar to the reproductive bias is the myth that beauty (culturally defined) begets intimacy. In the Dolly Parton (1974) country classic song "Jolene," a woman is pleading with a potential rival to not take her man. Her argument is that Jolene can have any man she desires with her "flaming locks of auburn hair" and other physical attributes.

We are bombarded constantly about beauty and desirability. A quick look at women's magazines such as *Cosmopolitan* indicates that before the articles of improving one's love life begin, there are manifold pages advertising products that presumably make women appear more attractive. Virtually no part of a woman's body eludes the need for some product to "improve" her chances of pleasing a potential mate. It is interesting that a men's magazine like *Playboy* focuses on gear and possessions for seduction. In our culture, it seems that a woman's appeal is about changes to physical self and enhanced beauty and men's is about his possessions or financial wherewithal.

It is clear that this myth will inevitably promote lower self-esteem and that therapy may have to be focused around being attractive enough.

## Myths About Responsibility, Freedom, and Security

What is the nature of relationships? Are they exercises in wins, losses, and endless compromises? Do relationships represent a zero-sum game in which there is a winner and a loser? Does an intimate relationship thrive with teamwork? What deeper psychological needs emerge when committing to another person? Several concerns are evident in myths about the ever-present balance of security and freedom.

### Myth #8: The Myth of Engulfment

Snide comments regarding loss of freedom ("whipped," "ball and chain," "I'm with stupid," "A prisoner of love," "under control," "suffocated") all describe a general sense that once one commits to an intimate relationship, there is an increase of security so powerful that it eliminates a sense of independence and freedom. The dark side of the goal of catching a mate will be a loss of self, restriction of freedom, and potential emotional suffocation.

### Myth #9: The Myth of Abandonment

A corollary to the myth of engulfment is the opposite myth that intimacy and/or marriage will cure feelings of isolation, meaningless, and loneliness: "If only I could get a person to love me, I would be safe from abandonment and rejection." One version of this is the oft-stated belief by couples that they "complete" each other, suggesting a sense that they are incomplete persons without a partner. A downside risk here is that fear of abandonment may lead to avoidance of commitment. As Joey, a client in a men's group opined, "I am not scared of committing; I am scared of committing and being dumped."

## The Intimate Paradox

True intimacy is both desirable and scary. Joey's anxiety is only one aspect of intimacy that may seem paradoxical. Intimacy requires both closeness and distance, connection and separateness. The French have a poignant term for this when they describe sexual connection (orgasm) as *la petite mort* (the little death). It involves a significantly deep connecting between two individuals that they temporarily become as one, followed by the needs to separate and reestablish personal boundaries.

If we were to describe this graphically, it might look similar to the figure that follows.

Intimacy is depicted here as the hard relationship boundary that must not be crossed. However, within such boundaries there are times of intense connection (middle), moderate connection (left), and distant connection (right).

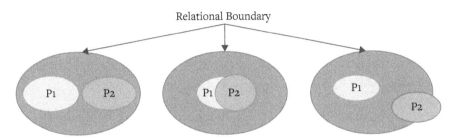

| Figure 10.1.1  Variety of intimate contact.

### Myth #10: Responsibility as Burden Myth

This belief involves a sense of obligation that comes with intimacy. Probably tracing from childhood experiences of demanding chores, many individuals see connection with another as an open path for demands: "If I love you, I have to do whatever you want, with or without being asked, or else there will be 'hell to pay.'"

## Myths Regarding Differences in Intimacy

Is there a belief that the more similarities a couple shares the stronger the relationship or do opposites attract and add vitality to a relationship? Myths abound regarding how much difference or similarity is beneficial.

### Myth #11: Myth of Sameness

This "birds of a feather flock together" notion involves a sense of the importance of similarity. The closer we become, the better our world. In fact, this feeling of identity is an important stage in relationship development [...]. Many computer-assisted mate selection and early dates are predicated on this notion. This myth works toward being connected at the hip and against identifying disagreements or differences in a relationship.

The flip side of this myth—that opposites attract and that "absence makes the heart grow fonder"—is also held generally in the culture. In this myth, we are attracted to things that are unusual in our lives, the exotic, the novel. The basic notion here is that we do not experience the familiar with as much romantic excitement as the different. It is interesting that this myth also reflects an important (wow) stage in a normal relationship.

## Maintenance and Development of Intimacy

It is one thing to be attracted to a new person and to form a relationship, but what does it take to maintain and grow an intimate relationship? Do both parties have to grow together in similar ways? How important is equity and what does that entail? How important is longevity? Many deeply held beliefs may govern the way individuals evaluate their relationships.

### Myth #12: Myth of Parallel Development

A more modern myth is that members of a couple will grow in tandem. Each will grow in similar ways and mostly together. This myth may promote certain forms of togetherness. At the same time, it restricts individuation and personal separate growth. It is increasingly becoming a widely held belief as sex roles become less oriented to division of labor and more to equality.

Tomio and Yoko were assiduous in doing everything in equal measure. When they came into therapy, they described a pattern based on this myth of equality. Tomio was a terrific chef and he loved to cook, but he was a very poor kitchen cleaner. Yoko was very good at cleaning but described herself as a "terrible cook." Because of their shared myth of equality, they each cooked three evenings a week and each cleaned three different evenings.

They confessed that this made for an uncomfortably messy kitchen half the time and poor meals half the time. The therapy consultation involved them redefining what equality meant. Each was most pleased with a division of labor.

That equality in which fairness is central may also fall into this myth. At its core, this myth—when held by couples—promotes valuing each person and each relational task. However, when taken to extreme, this myth can lead to some interesting relational problems.

## Myth #13: Every Problem Has a Solution

Also known as the great American myth, this involves a deep conviction that every discomfort or problem in life can be fixed by finding the right solution. If we can only find the right tool, school, religion, drug, credential, or therapist, our problems will dissolve. Of course, the upside of this myth is that couples can engage in creativity and problem solving that can be quite helpful. However, problems may ensue when nothing works and the problem persists. They can become disheartened and feel like failures.

## Myth #14: Myth of Endurance (More Is Better)

This myth is sense that the more we go through together, the stronger our bond. It also honors a longer relationship more than a shorter one. It is commonplace at wedding receptions to identify (and invite to the dance floor) couples who have been married the longest.

## A FINAL REMINDER ABOUT MYTHS

These myths have great potential for a therapist to discern basic values held by partners in a couple. Although some beliefs—especially those that clash—may become problematic, awareness of one's myths is far more valuable in promoting effective therapy than is an exploration about the dangers of such myths. Such awareness can be used to promote shifts in thoughts, feelings, and behaviors in couples, often within their core belief systems. They also point us to how a particular couple finds and maintains intimacy.

## CULTURAL DETERMINANTS OF LOVE, INTIMACY, AND SEX

It is not our intent in this [reading] to survey the anthropological factors involved in pair bonding throughout the world. For two excellent resources on this topic, please see Jankowiak (2008) and Beall and Sternberg (1995). Let's examine here some issues that vary widely across cultures and play a part in our personal views and how we assess and prioritize clients' relationships:

- Attraction—Is "Love at first sight" a solid basis for developing a relationship? Is it essential for a "spark" to be present or to be "moonstruck" (which translates into Italian as "lunatic")?

- Personality types—Are similarities or opposites more enduring traits in partners?

- Love—Is it important to feel love emotionally and viscerally, express verbally, or demonstrate behaviorally?

- Commitment—Does commitment require a lifetime together, and does a breach of trust and separation indicate lack of commitment?

Attraction in Western societies, and increasingly throughout the world, is based largely on appearance (Hatfield & Sprecher, 1985). Physical beauty is a natural aspect that attracts attention, interest, and often passion. It is, however, culturally defined, and some physical characteristics may be attractive to partners in Bali but not in Beirut, Barcelona, or Boston. Globalization through print, visual, and virtual media has homogenized and idealized beauty, and dating apps and websites have reinforced appearance as an essential element of attraction.

Without an initial attraction, is it possible to develop enduring intimacy with those whom we started out with as friends? Those whose lives are based on agricultural production, such as in central Africa, view attraction and love as being integrated into their connection to the seasons and the ability to feed their tribes (though we will likely find some using *Tinder* today).

Upon inquiring "What attracted you to your partner?" many will say, "We found we had so much in common," and indeed, initial familiarity with similar values, people, places, and experiences can initiate lasting friendships and romance. But the experience of most couples is that extreme commonality (enmeshment) becomes boring, and those whose only friends are their common ones, who do the same things for recreation, who like the same movies, books, travel, and so on, and can finish each other's sentences, have little curiosity about their partner and argue frequently over trivial and large differences. The opposite pattern (complementary) applies to those who have interests and activities apart from each other and who enjoy common ones and take pleasure in hearing their partner's separate experiences

(Werner, Green, Greenberg, Browne, & McKenna, 2001). As in most interpersonal dynamics, neither extreme is viable in all situations, and our perspective follows the general guideline, "Similarities attract and differences keep it interesting."

We may ask, "Is this couple in love? Does it really matter?" Love may follow the Tevye and Golde model, or the more expressive model such as saying "I love you" every day and with frequent endearing acts, including hearts and flowers. One client in a lesbian relationship stated, "I feel she cares about me because she remembers to change the oil in my car." It is difficult to describe patterns of expression throughout cultures in light of socioeconomic, geographic, developmental, ethnic, racial, and immigration factors, and globalization. One aphorism is that Asian or Scandinavian couples are not verbally romantic, but many of the aforementioned factors can disprove that stereotype. Indonesian couples, for instance, place great value on particular types of verbalized expression of love while other cultures do not use the word "love" to denote lasting relationships. Of course, all cultures place value on behavioral demonstrations of attachment, whether it is by providing resources, sharing common tasks, or merely spending time together.

Commitment can be characterized by remaining together for a lifetime regardless of the normal peaks, valleys, and serious breaches of trust (long-term), or by the example of Kevin and Keesha, who may be on the brink of separating after 3 happy years, saying, "I'm with you until our values drift apart." Kevin and Keesha may view their relationship as committed (short-term) but not permanent due to emerging value differences, but the couple who remained together for 50 years despite irreconcilable differences may hardly see themselves as committed. Conversely, if Keesha were having an affair with Elvin, would that indicate a lack of commitment? Perhaps not, but Kevin would need to be able to view the affair as an event that did not shatter Keesha's commitment to him. We do know that in some countries (notably the Middle East), a woman who looks at a man, let alone has a sexual liaison, is seen as breaking the marital bond and is subject to excommunication or death.

## INTIMACY THROUGHOUT THE LIFE SPAN

Returning to our earlier definition of intimacy—which involves emotional and perhaps intellectual attachment and physical touch in some manner and is reinforced by chemical and neurological effects that induce pleasure, comfort, and a sense of belonging—we realize that as with all human processes, changes occur over time. [T]he "moonstruck" (wow) attraction and physical rush that strikes when partners first meet may occur during their teens or in their 80s, but inevitably waxes and wanes as normal transitions occur, physical changes take place, and normal interactions ensue. Intellectual vitality may be constant while physical passion wanes, or social interactions and everyday tasks may be smooth and satisfying at the same time as emotional attachment declines. These are the peaks and valleys that all relationships experience; the essential features in maintaining commitment and a feeling of being in love are

1. understanding that change is a common trajectory and
2. continuing activities on a daily basis to remain connected in a respectful manner that demonstrates that one's partner *is* his or her primary relationship, above all others. Maintaining a healthy sense of separateness (as Gibran says) provides equanimity when struggles emerge.

## LIFE CYCLE ISSUES AFFECTING INTIMACY

Normal couple processes that challenge intimacy at various stages of life may occur at any stage of life. Extraordinary circumstances and losses, such as injuries, immigration, unemployment, trauma, chronic poverty and illness, and racial, ethnic, and other forms of discrimination, can be traumatic and enduring, diminishing an individual's ability to connect with a partner in a satisfying, intimate way. Normal transitions include the following:

- Distance relationships and career pressures in early adulthood
- The transition to family
- Child care, travel, career, and extended family responsibilities—the "sandwich" generation
- Financial pressures, health issues, and the search for meaning in later life

For example, in midlife, work and career factors may necessitate frequent travel for one partner, less time to share household or child care responsibilities, and less couple time. It's easy to become distanced from each other during these times. Clinicians are challenged to help couples understand normal developmental processes and at the same time to show empathy and guide couples to use coping and problem-solving skills. Consider the issues facing the following couple and how you would assess their presenting issues and develop a treatment plan.

To what extent do you view this couple's struggles as part of a normal family developmental cycle and how much do you see it as dysfunctional? Would your treatment plan involve one or more of the following?

- Short-term problem-solving therapy
- Long-term in-depth treatment
- A brief consultation to assist them in recognizing and increasing their connection
- A couple's workshop
- Reading on the "sandwich" generation

Omar is a 45-year-old entrepreneur from a Muslim family that immigrated from the Middle East. He has started his own company, requiring him to be out of the country half of each month. Leticia, his wife, a second-generation Mexican-American, is 39. They have two children, one with special needs. They have recently taken on a large mortgage, and Omar has asked Leticia to take a part-time job to earn extra income. Omar's parents both have health problems and live near the couple, and Leticia does errands for them and helps in other ways while Omar is away.

Omar is generally attentive to sharing child care and other responsibilities when he is home, but his schedule makes it increasingly difficult, and Leticia is becoming resentful of the increased burden she has taken on. They rarely have couple time together and their arguments and bickering are creating distance between them.

- Extended family therapy to increase family cohesion

Whether you think one or more of these or other approaches might be best, a perspective based on the life cycle of this couple is a vital part of the help you provide them. They may not be dysfunctional, but their cultural expectations, responsibilities, foundations of their relationship, and their desire and quality of intimacy at mid-life are often different from when they first met and from where they will be as empty nesters, assuming they are able to maintain their marriage.

Fan-Chi and Lyssa are a couple in their late 70s who have been together 45 years and married for 5, since same sex marriage became legal in their state. They are members of the "free love" generation, had many partners, and considered themselves polyamorous for the first few years they were together. They have maintained a solid foundation and an active sexual relationship through their 60s.

Now they are loving, emotional, intellectual, and fun social partners in retirement and even though Fan-Chi feels she does not need sexual contact, she is resentful because Lyssa no longer expresses her affection through hugs, kisses, or cuddling.

Consider the following couple from a developmental perspective in terms of their intimacy.

How do you see their lack of physical intimacy in view of their life stage, and what approach would you take in treating them?

- Understand the situation as normal and assist Fan-Chi in understanding and accepting Lyssa's actions and look at other indications of commitment and affection

- View Lyssa's lack of physical affection as a rejection of Fan-Chi or perhaps an indication of depression

- See that each person is not taking responsibility for meeting her own needs and explore individually with each partner what her desires and needs are at this time and how they can be met

If this couple were in their early 20s and in the early phases of their relationship, we might not view their lack of physical affection as normal. We would then work to help them restore passion or refer them to a sex therapist. On the other hand, if we view relational dysfunction as "if one partner is dissatisfied, the relationship is unsatisfactory," a suitable agreement on expressing intimacy might be the goal in light of their current life stage as a couple.

## THE ESSENCE OF STABLE RELATIONSHIPS

At this point we have described intimacy and commitment and some of the key cultural, demographic, relational, and developmental factors that determine what is satisfying for each couple in terms that can be used in couple therapy.

Yet, it is precarious to state definitively and succinctly what is essential in creating and sustaining stability, a quality that requires intimacy and is akin to commitment. The term *stability* will be used in this section to denote the skills and processes that create functionality and reduce conflict—or in systems terms, *negentropy,* a lack of predictability and disorder over time. In other words, if love, intimacy, and commitment are present, hostility, contempt, meltdowns, violence, and separation do not need to take place. Arguments will (and should) happen, but "fair fighting" that embodies respect, self-appraisal, and control can prevent escalation (Bach & Wyden, 1970; Lloyd, 1987). Partners who have a solid foundation do not see every dispute as a competition or a zero-sum game in that only one point of view or preference can prevail, nor will they always question different views as relationship-level incompatibility. Even some breaches of trust, such as breaking the hard, outer relational boundary, may not be experienced as lack of commitment and threaten separation.

# INITIAL ASSESSMENT OF STABILITY

Although there are many models from sociology, family studies, research, and theoretical orientations with elaborate constructs, we begin with approaches that are the simplest and most consistent in assessment, treatment planning, and intervention.

Although we approach couples from different perspectives, we are pluralistic and integrative in our approach. Our initial assessment may involve both the "first wave" (Jacobson & Margolin, 1979) and the "second wave" of behavior therapy (Jacobson, Christensen, Prince, Cordova, & Eldridge, 2000), including acceptance and commitment strategies. In addition, we include methods of cognitive reconstruction (Baucom et al., 1990), the importance of emotional expressiveness in couple therapy (e.g., Greenberg & Goldman, 2018; Johnson, 2019), and of meaning making in therapy (Shapiro, 2016). There is more clinical than experimental outcome literature supporting this integration (Halford, 2003).

Hayes, Strosahl, and Wilson (2009) begin with the foundation of a couple's *commitment*. Are they having a fling or a trial relationship, or are they questioning their connection with every argument? Basically, are partners open to strengthening the positive aspects of their relationship and working to resolve conflicts as long as the relationship remains functional?

*Acceptance* of one's partner can be difficult to develop but relates to one simple thing: Can I accept my partner's *basic* traits and behaviors without trying to change him or her? This does

---

## EXERCISE BOX 10.1.9 WHAT ARE YOUR "RED FLAGS?"

Are there certain traits that are the *sine qua non* for you in a relationship? Are there certain traits that you would personally try to change in your partner (usually an exercise in futility)?

We commonly ask this question in our graduate classes in couple therapy. Here are some of their answers:

Addictions (including smoking)

Regular use of pornography

Other relationships (particularly secret ones)

Hygiene

Religious differences

Dishonesty

Serious crippling debt

Cultural differences

Problematic intrusive in-laws

Serious mental illness

Physical infirmities

not mean we need to accept "deal breakers" or the fundamental issues that are incompatible with our own values or behaviors, which can include severe substance abuse, interpersonal violence, repeated breaches of trust, and other issues that need to be examined as "red flags."

We always inquire about such issues in premarital work. For some individuals (often in the helping professions), there is a tendency to take a partner on as a project to save or reform him or her or because of personal low self-esteem ("I will only be able to attract someone who needs help," or "If I save someone, he or she will love me").

As couple therapists, we need to help clients remain assertive, state their preferences, and fairly share chores, daily needs around the home, and connections with in-laws. Acceptance requires prioritizing differences and "choosing our battles" so that minor annoyances do not elicit incessant arguments. Acceptance covers many flaws and prevents nagging, resentment, and hostility.

If we are able to accurately assess a couple's levels of acceptance and commitment early in the process of therapy, we can also determine which interactions to focus on and the tools needed to either develop or strengthen skills. For behavioral couple therapists like Jacobson and Margolin (1979), these include *communication, problem solving,* and *behavior exchange.* Our purpose here is not to provide a primer on behavioral couple therapy, but to elucidate some foundational constructs and processes that are essential to maintaining intimacy, love, and commitment in a stable relationship.

*Communication* is the ability to express thoughts and emotions and to negotiate practical matters that are essential to functioning. Dysfunctional couples will often state that they rarely talk about anything beyond what to have for dinner or when to pick up the kids, and even when they do, a true speaker-listener transaction with clarity does not occur. Discussions between highly dysfunctional clinical couples often reveal wildly disparate descriptions of the same event, with each partner competing to insist his or her version is correct. Therapists begin to scratch their heads at this and wonder if both were at the same event.

---

**BOX 10.1.10  THE AUTHORS AGREE ON OUTCOME, DISAGREE ON APPROACH**

Patterson begins with a deductive approach, closely following more behavioral and cognitive models. This approach begins with a model for problem solving and develops methods of addressing the concerns from within that model.

Shapiro's (existential) approach is more inductive, beginning with the client's frames of reference and moving to an overall theory. The clients' subjective experiences are considered more primary and the problem solving is more an act of creation than deduction.

---

Rather than trying to sort out the details, it becomes necessary at this point to step back and ask, "What is going on between you that your stories are so far apart?" The tried-and-true method of "I messages" (Gordon, 1970) is another useful vehicle for getting communication back on track, so long as partners have a true interest in understanding and listening to each other. [...].

For partners who have difficulty solving basic or complex issues, a valuable method is the *problem-solving* method, beginning with clear communication, openness to each other's preferences, and brainstorming potential solutions. Our approach is an amalgam of diverse approaches that draws from an extensive and diverse body of clinical and research evidence.

In problem solving, each partner is asked to do the following:

- State his or her basic goal on the matter
- Express whatever fantasy or realistic approach might be taken
- Describe in detail what steps have already been taken and how he or she succeeded or failed
- Listen without comment to his or her partner's goals and solutions
- Take time to prioritize his or her preferred, realistic solutions
- Present to his or her partner
- Evaluate each solution together without criticism

One process, *motivational interviewing* (Miller & Rollnick, 2013), offers a client-focused basis for helping partners discover their true desires that lead to solutions. It draws heavily on Rogers's (1986) *person-centered therapy* in that the process begins with the client's self-defined objectives and carefully tracks solutions from a problem-solving perspective that are most feasible for the client to employ.

*Behavior exchange*, or equity, is a critical dimension of stable relationships and is often referred to as the *quid pro quo*, or "this for that" (Lederer & Jackson, 1968). No matter how much passion, love, generosity, and commitment exists in a relationship, partners expect that over time each will receive from each other responses that are commensurate with what they give to their partner. This balance changes over the life cycle and relies in part on the complementary nature of the relationship. One person may be happy handling finances, child care, and social planning, while the other is content to have a busy career and earn most of the income. Emotional nurturing and anticipating needs can be exchanged for doing yard work, if that arrangement is a satisfactory *quid pro quo* for a particular couple. It can also be that a partner provides financial support and does all of the housework while a partner completes a graduate degree, but that arrangement needs to become more equitable after graduation. It's never 50/50 in a given moment, but an imbalance can be accommodated with commitment over time, and each partner's *perception*—more than the actual act or item that is exchanged—is what matters.

## STRUCTURES THAT ENABLE STABILITY

As mentioned earlier, two fundamental structural arrangements that couples tend to follow factor strongly in creating stability: *complementarity* and *symmetry* (Rovers et al., 2011; Werner et al., 2001). Complementarity is a relationship in which differences between partners are attractive to each other and improve the relationship. Complementarity is enhanced by the Bowenian concept of *differentiation* (Jankowski & Hooper, 2012). Symmetry denotes a form of relating in which couples conform to each other's behaviors, values, and personalities in aspects, and similar characteristics and behaviors are more prominent than differences. Bowen's (1966) original formulation was that partners tend to bond at similar levels of psychological and emotional differentiation, although this notion is challenged by our clinical experience, in which partners frequently display considerably different levels of differentiation. Undifferentiated individuals typically have difficulty with boundaries ("He's always so needy and intrusive!"), and those who are extremely differentiated (possibly with poor attachment histories) may have trouble with intimacy ("She's commitment phobic!" or "He needs so much alone time!"). Both symmetry and complementarity are best viewed on a continuum, with neither extreme being functional for most couples. Consider the following couple.

In this situation, we can see how opposites attracted and there appeared to be a high degree of complementarity, but they eventually tried to become more symmetrical and enmeshed; in

---

### CASE BOX 10.1.11 ELOY AND BEN

Eloy and Ben are a late 30s couple who have been together 10 years, and although they have not taken advantage of legal gay marriage in their state, they consider themselves highly committed and have adopted twin 4-year-old girls. Ben is a musician and Eloy is a nonprofit executive, and, upon meeting, their different careers, personalities (outgoing/reclusive), family backgrounds (oldest of six/only child), and personal styles (fashionable/stodgy) were interesting to each other.

After a while Ben became somewhat critical of Eloy's reclusive style and stodgy dress, and Eloy began to emulate Ben by dressing stylishly and speaking up more at parties. They eventually began to bicker more, not over their initial differences, but in a competitive fashion due to each not measuring up to their perceived standards or due to the discrepancy between their internalized fantasy of the partner and the person in reality.

their words, they were "too much in each other's faces" and were constantly annoyed with each other. Neither extreme complementarity nor symmetry worked well for them. The very factors that attracted them to one another were redefined in each person's mind. Thus, "safe, solid, predictable, and conservative" can be later seen as "boring." Similarly, "adventurous" can be redefined as "unpredictable, inconsiderate, and out of control."

The antidote: a return to more complementarity to help them rediscover their individual identities and restore their appreciation of each other's differences and how each contributes to the relational team. Paradoxically, when partners become too much like each other, the intrigue is lost and boredom and bickering ensue.

## RECENT TRENDS IN PAIR BONDING

As it is obvious through popular media and observing friends, relatives, acquaintances, and others, the structures and processes that couples initiate and sustain are far different today than in the mid-20th century (Julian, 2018; Pinsof, 2002; Smock, 2004).

Since the sexual revolution in the 1960s and 1970s, experimentation with alternative relational structures, and the increase in divorce rates—following the legalization of no-fault divorce in Canada in 1968 and the United States (California) in 1969—there has been an increasing liberalization in the acceptability and popularity of serial monogamy, serial exclusivity, and unmarried cohabitation, often considered a "trial marriage" to see how partners might be compatible in sharing daily routines and space. Today, more adults are cohabiting or single than are married. This may have an unpredictable effect on the nature of commitment and couple therapy in the 21st century.

Although quietly at first, gay and lesbian couples formed committed relationships and then married, and transgender, queer, and gender-fluid individuals increasingly formed bonds involving new structures and processes that were self-defined. In other cases, they emulated more traditional patterns of their parents from earlier decades.

Many asked, "Why can't we love whoever we want?" echoing the reality that despite new forms and patterns, couples today basically engage in the same routines, seek the same stability, and struggle with defining their own patterns of love, intimacy, commitment, and sex as other couples throughout the world.

## EXAMPLES OF COMMITTED RELATIONSHIPS ON THE BRINK

While evidence from the professional literature (Roberts & Prager, 2004; Rovers et al., 2011) and our own clinical and personal experience point strongly to elements that are vital to a functional, committed, enduring relationship, too many variables exist to discern a single pattern that works for all couples. In this final section, we will pose some brief vignettes and ask that you review them with some simple questions:

- Can you identify the level and type of intimacy in this couple?
- Are they in love?
- Are they committed to each other?
- Will they endure?

---

### CASE BOX 10.1.12  SANJAY AND UMA

Sanjay and Uma are second-generation Indian-Americans (South Asian) who have met through friends and are conflicted because their parents want to arrange a traditional Indian marriage for them. They have secretly lived together for 4 years far from their parents, who remain in India. They are mostly complementary in their styles and enjoy good friends and activities together.

After 2 years Uma becomes increasingly distressed over being estranged from her parents and feels generally irritated. She withholds sex from Sanjay and argues over minor details of their lives together. Sanjay understands her feelings and in the same time frame has become closer to his parents and visits them frequently.

---

### CASE BOX 10.1.13  ELIZA AND WALTER

Eliza and Walter have been married for 50 years and by all measures had a successful marriage, including grandchildren, shared activities, and a warm, intimate connection. Walter remains strongly interested in maintaining an active sex life while Eliza's sexual interest has waned since menopause. He has an affair with a neighbor and Eliza senses a diminished connection between them.

---

### CASE BOX 10.1.14  TAMAR AND TODD

Tamar has recently undergone surgery to conform to her female identity and Todd, her partner of 20 years, has patiently and lovingly supported her in every way. They find after a year or so that sexual contact is uncomfortable physically and emotionally. They have always had an active sex life and now wonder if their interest in each other will endure.

These three vignettes exemplify common situations the authors have gleaned from treating couples. Each couple considers themselves to be committed and they all are faced with choices that could potentially either end their relationship or open opportunities to work through an impasse, and in the process, make their relationships stronger. Presumably they are in love and have a form of intimacy that will allow them to survive their crises, but is that love and intimacy sufficient to help them weather the storms they face?

As a therapist, you will bring your own views of these dilemmas to the situation and attempt to remain neutral. Of course, you will strive to help them decide if they have the resources individually and conjointly to make the effort to stay together.

Other factors such as culture, finances, morality and religion, health, family loyalty, and each person's sexual interest will also have a significant impact. As we assess their ability and motivation, the emerging question involves how much effort we will urge them to make to work things out. Should they reach an unspecified point where they are unable or unwilling to remain together, we will be able to assist them in making plans to separate. Because both paths respect their autonomy, they are worth pursuing therapeutically.

## SUMMARY

At this point, we hope that readers have developed a viewpoint on the question "Does love conquer all?" The ambiguity of love has considered the aspects of intimacy, sex, romance, and other factors. Although we believe love is a necessary component of a committed relationship, it is not sufficient. Such aspects as clear communication, the ability to effectively solve problems, sharing of responsibilities, agreement on core values, and a sense of enjoyment and friendship also contribute to a lasting relationship. But when love and intimacy fade or are disrupted by time, breaches of trust, or other life circumstances, the absence of intimacy can be pervasive and erode the partners' ability to maintain clear communication, or even to engage with each other in a civil manner as they would a friend. When we hear that emotional abuse is occurring through name-calling and use of four-letter words, we ask "Would you treat a friend that way?" On the other hand, we have seen that even in some highly conflictual couples, intimacy may endure through emotional sharing and frequent sexual congress, even as other aspects of the relationship deteriorate. We strongly recommend that the presence or absence of intimacy and its quality and depth be viewed as a critical factor and a focal point to indicate the likelihood of successful couple therapy. Long-term intimacy and commitment—to work together as a team to deal with whatever vagaries life throws at a couple—is an impressively positive sign for relational endurance and growth.

# REFERENCES

Albee, E. (2001). *Who's afraid of Virginia Woolf?* New York, NY: Signet.

Bach, G. R., & Wyden, P. (1970). *The intimate enemy: How to fight fair in love and marriage.* New York, NY: Avon.

Baucom, D. H., Sayers, S. L., & Sher, T. G. (1990). Supplementing behavioral marital therapy with cognitive restructuring and emotional expressiveness training: An outcome investigation. *Journal of Consulting and Clinical Psychology, 58*(5), 636–644.

Beall, A. E., & Sternberg, R. J. (1995). The social construction of love. *Journal of Social and Personal Relationships, 12*(3), 417–438.

Bowen, M. (1966). *Family theory in clinical practice.* Lanham, MD: Rowman & Littlefield.

Bowen, M. (1974/2004). Toward the differentiation of self in one's family of origin. In M. Bowen (Ed.) *Family therapy in clinical practice* (reprint ed.) (pp. 529–547). Lanham, MD: Rowman & Littlefield.

Buber, M. (1937/1970). *I and thou* (W. Kaufmann, Trans.). New York, NY: Scribner.

Crowe, M. (1997). Intimacy in relation to couple therapy, *Sexual and Marital Therapy, 12*(3), 225–236.

Crowe, M., & Ridley, J. (1990). *Therapy with couples: A behavioural-systems approach.* Oxford, UK: Blackwell Scientific.

Diamond, M. J., & Shapiro, J. L. (1983). *Introduction and the paradoxes of intimacy* [Audiotape]. San Francisco, CA: Proseminar.

Frankl, V. E. (1959). *Man's search for meaning: An introduction to logotherapy.* New York, NY: Washington Square Press.

Gordon, T. (1970). *PET: Parent effectiveness training: the tested new way to raise responsible children.* New York, NY: PH Wyden.

Greenberg, L. S. & Goldman, R. N. (2018). *Clinical handbook of emotion-focused therapy.* Washington, DC: American Psychological Association.

Halford, W. K. (2003). *Brief therapy for couples.* New York, NY: Guilford.

Hatfield, E. & Sprecher, S. (1985). *Mirror, mirror: The importance of looks in everyday life.* New York, NY: SUNY.

Hayes, S. C., Strosahl, K. D., & Wilson, K. G. (2009). *Acceptance and commitment therapy.* Washington, DC: American Psychological Association.

Jacobson, N. S., Christensen, A., Prince, S. E., Cordova, J., & Eldridge, K. (2000). Integrative behavioral couple therapy: An acceptance-based, promising new treatment for couple discord. *Journal of consulting and clinical psychology, 68*(2), 351–355.

Jacobson, N. S., & Margolin, G. (1979). *Marital therapy: Strategies based on social learning and behavior exchange principles.* New York, NY: Brunner/Mazel.

Jankowiak, W. R. (Ed.). (2008). *Intimacies: Love and sex across cultures.* New York, NY: Columbia University Press.

Jankowski, P. J., & Hooper, L. M. (2012). Differentiation of self: A validation study of the Bowen theory construct. *Couple and Family Psychology: Research and Practice, 1*(3), 226–234.

Johnson, S. M. (2019). *Attachment theory in practice: Emotionally focused therapy (EFT) with individuals, couples, and families*. New York, NY: Guilford.

Julian, K. (2018). The sex recession. *The Atlantic*. Retrieved from https://www.theatlantic.com/magazine/archive/2018/12/the-sex-recession/573949/

Lederer, W. J. & Jackson, D. D. (1968). *Mirages of marriage*. New York, NY: Norton.

Lloyd, S. A. (1987). Conflict in premarital relationships: Differential perceptions of males and females. *Family Relations, 36*(3), 290–294.

Miller, W. R., & Rollnick, S. (2013). *Motivational interviewing: Helping people change* (3rd ed.). New York, NY: Guilford.

Nichols, D. (1945). The bells of St. Mary's. *Wikipedia*. https://en.wikipedia.org/wiki/TheBellsof_St._Mary%27s

Norsigian, J. and Boston Women's Health Care Collective (2011) *Our Bodies, ourselves*. New York: Atria Books.

Parton, D. (1974) *Jolene*. https://www.youtube.com/watch?v=IW25foOMkwI

Pinsof, W. M. (2002). The death of "till death us do part": The transformation of pair-bonding in the 20th century. *Family Process, 41*(2), 135–157.

Pomus, D. & Shulman, M. (1960) *Save the last dance for me* [Video file]. Retrieved from Pomus, D. & Shulman, M. (1960) *Save the last dance for me*. New York: Atlantic records https://www.youtube.com/watch?v=n-XQ26KePUQ.

Richardson, J. P. (1959) *Running Bear*. Retrieved from https://www.songfacts.com/lyrics/johnny-preston/running-bear

Roberts, L. J., & Prager, K. J. (2004). Deep intimate connection: Self and intimacy in couple relationships. In D. J. Mashek & A. Aron (Eds.), *Handbook of closeness and intimacy* (pp. 43–61). New York, NY: Routledge.

Rogers, C. R. (1986). Person-centered Rogers on the development of the person-centered approach. *Person-Centered Review, 1*(3), 257–259.

Rovers, M., Kocum, L., Briscoe-Dimock, S., Myers, P. C., Cotnam, S., Henry, T., ... & Sheppard, D. (2011). Choosing a partner of equal differentiation: A new paradigm utilizing similarity and complementarity measures. *Journal of Couple & Relationship Therapy, 6*(3), 1–23.

Shapiro, J. L. (2016). *Pragmatic existential counseling and psychotherapy: Intimacy, intuition and the search for meaning*. Thousand Oaks, CA: SAGE.

Smock, P. J. (2004). The wax and wane of marriage: Prospects for marriage in the 21st century. *Journal of Marriage and Family, 66*(4), 966–973.

Tillich, P. (1952). *The courage to be*. New Haven, CT: Yale University Press.

Werner, P. D., Green, R. J., Greenberg, J., Browne, T. L., & McKenna, T. E. (2001). Beyond enmeshment: Evidence for the independence of intrusiveness and closeness—caregiving in married couples. *Journal of Marital and Family Therapy, 27*(4), 459–471.

# EDITORS' INTRODUCTION

After reading about and pondering some common love and intimacy myths, you might be wondering where they come from. Myths about many things can come from many different places—our families of origin, our faith base, friends, our own relationship experience and observations, and so on. One source of relationship myths that can often go unnoticed is the media. Television, advertising, and especially the internet have grown exponentially in the past few decades. The images that we see every day might be outside of our conscious awareness, but they influence us in important, and sometimes negative ways. In the following reading, "Unrealistic Portrayals of Sex, Love, and Romance in Popular Wedding Films," Kevin Johnson takes off the blinders and challenges some of the images, depictions, and beliefs that are embedded in popular media about love, sex, romance, and specifically marriage. These images can create unrealistic expectations for perfection, unbridled happiness, and the idea that it takes little effort to maintain satisfying committed relationships.

There are two things we know about relationship expectations that we hope you'll remember: (a) Idealized expectations about relationships can lead to disappointment if not adjusted—relationships can be amazing, *and* they take work. (b) Sometimes those who have a difficult family history enter intimate relationships with little optimism that their relationships will be successful; this can serve as a self-fulfilling prophecy (Johnson, 2011). Whether you are someone who believes in happily ever after, someone who suspects they are doomed to fail, or somewhere in between, we encourage you to examine your expectations and beliefs about relationships, know what you have control over and what you don't, and embody the necessary skills to create the best chance at success in your intimate relationships.

## PRIMERS

1. What messages do you think the media wants us to believe about sex, love, and romance?
2. Why might the media target us to develop the beliefs you identified?

# Unrealistic Portrayals of Sex, Love, and Romance in Popular Wedding Films

*By Kevin A. Johnson*

W hat do you think about when you see or hear the word *marriage?* Undoubtedly, you have developed an image and/or relationship to this concept. The reason we have such deeply embedded beliefs about marriage is that it is a central institution in our society. As such, views of marriage are political. For example, U.S. President George W Bush (2003) declared, "Marriage is a sacred institution, and its protection is essential to the continued strength of our society" (n.p.). Whereas Bush has visualized marriage as a heterosexual union, Sullivan (1997) advocated same-sex marriage by arguing that "the right to marry is, in many ways, more fundamental than the right to vote" (n.p.). On the other hand, gay/lesbian/bisexual/transgender activist Ettelbrick (1997) asked, "Since when is marriage a path to liberation?" If the debate over same-sex marriage demonstrates anything, it is that people have a passionate attachment to the idea of this seemingly simple word. The word marriage might be small, but stories continue to get built around it every day.

What are some of the stories told about marriage? Aside from our experiences associated with actually attending weddings, we are bombarded by stories of weddings and marriages all the time in the mass media. Thus, this selection utilizes Galician's (2004) 12 myths of sex, love, and romance in the mass media as a framework for analyzing portrayals of weddings and marriages. On television, we see weddings as pivotal moments in plot lines for shows such as *Friends, Dharrna & Greg, Spin City, Baywatch, Suddenly Susan, Everybody Loves Raymond,* and *NYPD Blue.* We hear about weddings in the music industry, including those of Britney Spears, Jennifer Lopez, Jessica Simpson, Michael Jackson, and Madonna. Then, there are the "reality" shows, including *The Bachelor, The Bachelorette, Joe Millionaire,* and *The Wedding Story.* In sports, radio, and television we hear talk about Tiger Woods and Elin Nordgren, Anna Kournikova and Sergei Federov, Nomar Garciaparra and Mia Hamm, and Andre Agassi and Steffi Graf. On the radio we hear about Howard Stern's marriage and the weddings of numerous local hosts. In the cinema we see movies such as *Father of the Bride, My Big Fat Greek Wedding, Four Weddings and a Funeral, Runaway Bride,* and *The Wedding Singer.* In short, weddings are everywhere in mass media. Ingraham (1999) provided a compelling case that "the visual stimulation of the wedding story is a powerful means for suturing an audience to the interests represented in a film or television show" (p. 126).

Mass media play an influential role in the way people view sex, love, and romance in their own lives. Galician (2004) found, "Higher usage of certain mass media is related to unrealistic expectations about coupleship, and these unrealistic expectations are also related to dissatisfaction in real-life romantic relationships" (p. 5). The primary implication of unrealistic expectations of weddings and marriage is an increased likelihood of divorce (Dreyfus, 2005). Thus, an examination of weddings and marriage as they appear in mass media is important. The purpose of this selection is to trace Galician's (2004, p. 225) myths of unrealistic portrayals of sex, love, and romance as they appear in popular films that feature wedding events, including the engagement, planning, wedding, and honeymoon. In addition to exploring sites of Galician's myths as they appear in wedding films, I also suggest two additional myths specific to these mediated wedding depictions.

I have divided this selection into four sections. In the first section I describe the methodology, including a list of the analyzed films. In the second section I report some of the occurrences of Galician's (2004) myths in these popular wedding films. In the third section, I provide two additional myths that might be added in relation to weddings and marriage that are not included in Galician's 12. Finally, I provide some suggestions for future research of mass media portrayals of weddings and marriage.

## METHOD

To determine precisely what a "popular" film featuring a "wedding event" is, I examined a combination of both the top-grossing wedding films and the results of a Google search to find the most commonly recurring wedding films that appeared on "top wedding picks" (different lists found Web sites as favorite films about weddings).

From this search, the movies selected for this study were *American Wedding* (2003), *Father of the Bride* (1991), *Fools Rush In* (1997), *Four Weddings and a Funeral* (1994) *Just Married* (2003), *Meet the Parents* (2000), Mr. *Wrong* (1996), *Muriel's Wedding* (1995), My *Best Friend's Wedding* (1997), My *Big Fat Greek Wedding* (2002), *Runaway Bride* (1999), *The Wedding Planner* (2001), and *The Wedding Singer* (1998). Although all of these films were analyzed to determine the presence of myths, not all of the films are included in the discussion of the portrayals of the myths.

# MYTHS IN WEDDING FILMS

Because "love and marriage go together like a horse and carriage," it is not surprising to find unrealistic portrayals of sex, love, and romance appearing in wedding films. I found that 11 of the 12 myths were present in the studied films. The only myth that was not in the films was Myth #12, which says that since mass media portrayals of romance aren't real, they don't really affect you (Galician, 2004, p. 225). The reason for its nonappearance is that in this study I do not examine the link between media effects and people. Rather, I examine the messages that movies display. Thus, in this section I analyze each of the other 11 myths as they appear in the films.

## Myth #1: "Your Perfect Partner is Cosmically Pre-destined, So Nothing/Nobody Can Ultimately Separate You"

Galician (2004) traced this myth to ancient Athens and the Platonic ideal that your missing half is somewhere out there because the gods of antiquity were jealous and separated your true love from you. She also noted, "But you know you're living in the 21st century. And you're a human capable of changing and improving your 'destiny' rather than irrationally letting it enslave you" (p. 120). This myth of the cosmically predestined "one" is present in nearly all of the wedding films.

In *American Wedding,* old high school classmates and best friends reunite in the third movie of the *American Pie* trilogy for a wedding of one of the best friends. In this movie, Kevin (Thomas Ian Nichols) says to Finch (Eddie Kay Thomas) regarding Jim's (Jason Biggs) choice to get married: "You don't think there's one girl that you're destined to spend your entire life with?" Finch says, "They're all for me, Kevin." Leaving aside issues of Kevin's choice of the word *girl* and the heterocentric nature of this conversation, this dialogue displays several views about marriage: Kevin's view of marriage is that there is one cosmically destined woman with whom to spend the rest of his life; Finch's view of marriage is that of an institution that ought to be avoided at all costs and replaced with "having" all women. So the message here is that you should only marry someone if you are cosmically predestined or else you should "have" multiple partners if you are male and never get married.

The myth can also be present in the language of "the one" or "doomed" that evidences a logic of destiny and helplessness. In *The Wedding Singer,* a wedding singer meets a poor woman, they fall in love, and despite seemingly insurmountable odds, they end up together when the movie ends. In the movie, Julia (Drew Barrymore) says, "Actually, I am not sure how serious the guy is that gave this [engagement ring] to me. Right now I feel like I'm *doomed* to walk the planet alone forever."

In *My Best Friend's Wedding,* Julianne (Julia Roberts) steals a truck to chase Michael (Dermont Mulroney), whom she wants to marry. However, Michael is chasing Kimmy (Cameron Diaz), whom he wants to marry. During the chase, Julianne calls George (Rupert Everett) on her cell phone, and he tells her "Michael's chasing Kimmy. You're chasing Michael. Who's chasing you? Get it? There's your answer—Kimmy. Jules, you're not *the one.*"

In *The Wedding Planner,* Maria (Jennifer Lopez) is a successful wedding planner who is rescued by Dr. Steve Edison (A.K.A. "Eddie," played by Matthew McConaughey) from what could have been a fatal accident. The two then spend a wonderful night together. Soon after, however, Maria finds out that Eddie is the groom in a wedding she is hired to plan. Complicating the matter is that Massimo (Justin Chambers) wants to marry Maria but tells Eddie, "I could never forgive myself if I got in the way of true love. I am not *the one* ... you are *the one*" By referring to these individuals as "the ones" for each other and thinking about love in terms of destiny (being "doomed"), these films demonstrate that this myth is active in reinforcing the ancient Platonic ideal that you will find your fated mate.

## Myth #2: "There's Such Thing as 'Love at First Sight'"

In discussing Myth #2, Galician (2004) referred to the concept of "Cupid's arrow," which fosters the belief that you will be "struck" by love. She explained that in media portrayals of this myth, "love is maneuvered beyond reason and choice—and beyond our own responsibility" (p. 128). The most glaring example of the Cupid's arrow myth appears in *Just Married,* when Tom (Ashton Kutcher)—upset about his honeymoon with Sarah (Brittany Murphy)—tells his friend Fred (Alex Thomas): "We had the perfect relationship that was ruined by marriage. I mean, you saw us, right? We were perfect from the minute we met, right?" Fred answers, "Yeah, in fact, it was nauseating." Fred confirms what Tom already knew—he loved Sarah at first sight. After this short dialogue, the scene shifts to a flashback fantasy of Tom, where he first meets Sarah on the beach while playing football. Sarah gets hit in the head with the football, Tom comes over to help her, and they are struck by love (or was it the football?). We will later find that *Just Married* combines this myth with Myth #8 (that bickering and fighting a lot shows a loving relationship) to create a supposedly humorous portrayal of being married.

## "Myth #3: "Your True 'Soul Mate' Should KNOW What You're Thinking or Feeling (Without Your Having to Tell)"

In this myth, those who are true soul mates should know what the other is thinking. Galician (2004) cautioned, "The mind-reading dysfunction is one of the most destructive in love relationships (and indeed in any interpersonal relationships). Fortunately, it's one of the easiest to replace" (p. 137). She did admit, however, that it takes a partner who *"wants* to hear what you really mean" for this unhealthy behavior to be remedied (p. 137). This myth, which is demonstrated in many movies, is notable in *Fools Rush In,* the story of a nightclub promoter and a Las Vegas showgirl's one night stand that leads to marriage after she discovers that she is pregnant. A consistent theme throughout the film is that Alex Whitman (Matthew Perry) and Isabel Fuentes (Salma Hayek) are destined to be together (Myth #1). This theme is reinforced by the repeated mantra, "There are signs everywhere." However, as the plot develops, Alex gives Isabel many mixed signals, which come to a head when she shouts, "I'm not a mind reader, Alex!" Ironically, at the end, it turns out that Isabel actually is a mind reader: She fulfills his unspoken desire by agreeing to move to New York with him as long as they stay in Las Vegas until their baby is born. Aside from the whole issue of the woman's making sacrifices for the man, this scene demonstrates that if two people are des tined to be together, they should be able not only to read the other person's mind but also to act in a way that accommodates what is in the other's mind.

## Myth #4: "If Your Partner Is Truly Meant for You, Sex Is Easy and Wonderful"

In identifying this myth, Galician (2004) noted that "making sex easy and wonderful enough equates to a meant-to-be relationship" and that focusing "on sex suggests that sex is the most important and affirming aspect of a relationship, yet it is only one of the three key elements of Sternberg's Triangular Theory of Love" (p. 148). The other factors are *intimacy,* which is the emotional component, and *decision/commitment,* which is the intellectual or cognitive component (Sternberg, as cited in Galician, 2004). In short, this myth suggests that if sex is good, the relationship will work. This myth is present throughout *American Wedding,* in which Jim (Jason Biggs) and Michelle (Alyson Hannigan) are the groom and bride of the movie's title. In the opening scene, Jim, who is trying to propose to Michelle in a restaurant, suggests that she look behind her napkin (where he has hidden the engagement ring). However, she attempts to read Jim's mind, so she goes under the table and starts to perform oral sex on him in the middle of the restaurant. This is not surprising because there are very few scenes in which Jim and Michelle's relationship is not sexualized (including in *American Pie,* the first film in the trilogy—*American Wedding* being the third). This wedding film reifies the myth that if sex is wonderful, then your partner is "the one" for you to marry.

## Myth #5: "To Attract and Keep a Man, a Woman Should Look Like a Model or a Centerfold"

We are exposed to many images of the "idealized" man and woman in the mass media. Galician (2004) commented, "Countless normal males and females irrationally attempt to ape models who are 20% under normal healthy weight, who devote full time to their appearance, and who appear in digitally enhanced specially lit settings in which all imperfections are artificially removed" (p. 155).

The images of the ideal male and female forms are advanced in numerous popular wedding films. *Muriel's Wedding* is a classic ugly-duckling tale mixed with romance. For example, in *Muriel's Wedding*, friends of Muriel (Toni Collette) criticize the way she looks by telling her that her hair is terrible and she is a bit overweight, so she will never attract a husband to marry her. She does appear a bit overweight and her hair is not the same as hair of those who are considered stylish, but the conclusion of never finding a husband does not logically follow from such a description. Although Muriel does find someone to marry her, the groom's motivation is purely financial (to advance his swimming career); thus, in the end, this myth is reinforced as she does not end happily married. Rather, she ends back where she started—living with her girlfriend.

## Myth #6: "The Man Should NOT Be Shorter, Weaker, Younger, Poorer, or Less Successful Than the Woman"

Galician (2004) argued that this myth is invalidating and equally unfair to both men and women:

> Just as it's dehumanizing for women to be objectified as attractive body parts, so is it inhumane to view men as a meal-ticket or security guard. Women who are looking for a knight-in-shining-armor should ask themselves what they think they need to be rescued from! (p. 165).

In *American Wedding*, Jim is taller, but Michelle frequently dominates him with her strength. Interestingly, we never find out who is richer because we do not know what they do for a living. Both of their families appear to be well off, and both are in the same year of school (near the same age). In *Just Married*, Tom comes from a poor family with lower social status; Sarah's parents are wealthy and upper class. However, he is definitely taller and stronger. In *The Wedding Singer*, both Julia (Drew Barrymore), a waitress, and Robbie (Adam Sandler), the wedding singer, appear to make the same amount of money, but Robbie does buy into this myth earlier in the movie, when Julia is engaged to another man who is wealthy: Robbie tries to win her heart by applying for a job in a bank. In response to the interviewer's question about whether he has any experience with money, Robbie admits: "Actually sir, I really need this job to impress a girl. ... You don't even have to give me a job. If you could just give me some business cards with my name on, I think that might help." (Although he buys into this myth in the middle of the movie, it is overshadowed by Myth #1 at the end of the movie, when Robbie and Julia are shown to be cosmically meant for each other.)

## Myth #7: "The Love of a Good and Faithful True Woman Can Change a Man from a 'Beast' into a 'Prince'"

The "beast" in this myth is rarely a person who is physically less than appealing. Galician (2004) cautioned:

> A troubling aspect of most media portrayals of this myth is that the "beast" (male or female) is always depicted as a particularly mean and abusive character who should be loved because there's a tiny morsel of goodness buried somewhere in there that the "good" partner should be perceptive and patient enough to discover and tease out. (p. 179)

She argued that portrayals of this myth might best be understood metaphorically "as archetypal depictions of the struggle of good and evil *within* oneself, with the hope that our own good side will ultimately triumph over the baser side" (p. 179).

This myth was not found in many wedding films in this study. However, one glaring example is *American Wedding*, in which Stifler (Sean William Scott), the obnoxious party/fraternity type guy, goes from talking about sex most of the time, losing the wedding ring, throwing massive parties, and arguing loudly with people, to being a "prince" in the end by giving a flower and being nice to a woman for whom he has "fallen."

## Myth #8: "Bickering and Fighting a Lot Mean that a Man and a Woman Really Love Each Other Passionately"

This is perhaps one of the most difficult myths to judge. Galician (2004) explained the delicate balance by reminding us not to confuse "unhealthy dramatic bickering and fighting with healthy respectful disagreement" (p. 187). If a couple has constant conflicts, then there is a greater likelihood that the conflicts are not a sign of passion. Rather, the constant bickering should be interpreted as "a danger signal that accurately predicts the high likelihood of the failure of a coupleship" (Galician, 2004, p. 187). This myth is most prevalent in *Just Married*. For example, on the honeymoon in the French Alps, Tom is driving to the hotel and Sarah is navigating. Sarah is a bit late in telling Tom to turn, so he turns quickly and nearly hits a truck. After the quick turn, he gets out of the car and yells, "If you would have told me about the turn maybe before we passed it, I wouldn't have had to pull such a NASCAR evasive maneuver!" Sarah yells back "I was looking at the map. Someone has to navigate!" After a short pause, she says, "Listen to us. We sound like an old married couple." Tom then replies "Never again." Then they make up by hugging and kissing. This scene is one of many scenes where they continue bickering and even becoming physically abusive and violent. I chose this scene because Sarah's choice of comparison to an "old married couple" displays a view of marriage that those who are together the longest show their love by bickering more frequently. Despite this unhealthy behavior, the couple stays together at the end of the movie.

## Myth #9: "All You Really Need Is Love, So It Doesn't Matter if You and Your Lover Have Very Different Values"

This myth can destroy the notion of mutual respect. When values conflict, it becomes difficult for one or both of the partners to respect where the other one is spending time and money. Galician (2004) noted, "It's confusing and hurtful when what's important to one isn't to the other. Resentments can build—as one partner or the other begins to wear masks and play roles that are inauthentic" (p. 194). This myth is demonstrated in *My Best Friend's Wedding* by Kimmy's willingness to change what she values to marry Michael. After a fight with Michael, Kimmy tells Julianne (Michael's "best friend"):

> No matter if he wants crème brulée or Jell-O, I love him. And whatever delusions I drove Michael to, there is truth at the heart of it. You see, I want him to work for my father. I want to stay in school, and I want a life of my own. Please tell him that it's my fault and that I love him.

This is exactly what Galician (2004) cautioned against. Kimmy is willing to forsake her values (going to school and having a life of her own), as if her true values are not important to her anymore. The truth at the heart of all of it is that there is a conflict in values, but she specifically says that love will be able to overcome that truth.

In most of the wedding films, there is no mention of such multiple points of potential conflicts. More simply, in some movies values do not conflict because certain values are not discussed. Most of these conflicting values that can produce strains on a relationship could be discussed in real life through premarital counseling sessions, but there was not a single film that showed couples receiving such counseling. Instead, the films advanced the myth that because two people love each other, they can get married and everything will work itself out. However, there are many questions that are unanswered by both the woman and the man before they get married in films, such as: What are their expectations of marriage? What is the role of religion in their life? What do they expect of their spouse religiously? What is the role of a husband? What is the role of a wife? How do they express anger? How should conflicts be resolved in marriage? Do they want to have children? These questions could help eliminate myths in a marriage, which might explain the absence of them in these movies.

## Myth #10: "The Right Mate 'Completes You'—Filling Your Needs and Making Your Dreams Come True"

To illustrate this myth, Galician (2004) used a banking metaphor to explaining the problem in believing that you need someone to complete you:

> Your condition is like that of an applicant for a bank loan. Strange as it seems, lending institutions tend to give money to people who "don't need it"—that is, to people with appropriate collateral who represent "good risks" for repayment. People who desperately "need" the money are not considered good risks to pay back. (p. 203)

Because all of the films in this study are centered around marriage, they all exemplify Myth #10, whether or not the unions are between couples who have—per Galician's Rx #10—cultivated their own completeness.

## Myth #11: "In Real Life, Actors and Actresses Are Often Very Much Like the Romantic Characters They Portray"

Because actors and actresses often play similar characters in different films, many people confuse these performers' roles with their real lives. Galician (2004) explained the danger of this myth:

> It's one thing to appreciate talented artists for their professional work, but it's quite another to confuse reality with fiction. It's actually the ultimate *dis*service to these stars, who are idealized and thus objectified and dehumanized not only by the unfeeling corporate interests that benefit from their popularity but also by the so-called loving worshipers who—lacking any genuine intimacy with their favorites—are engaged in what we can only describe as infatuated or possibly fatuous (foolish) relationships (to extrapolate from Steinberg's model), (p. 211)

Julia Roberts *(Runaway Bride* and *My Best Friend's Wedding)* and Hugh Grant *(Four Weddings and a Funeral)* both star in films in this study. Galician (2004) identified fans of these stars as being particularly susceptible to this myth.

## ADDITIONAL MYTHS SPECIFIC TO WEDDING FILMS

I also found evidence for two additional myths that pertain specifically to wedding films.

The first additional myth is "You can have the wedding of your dreams and afford it, too." The ritual performance of weddings in films is much more costly than the average wedding in real life, and the cost of a wedding in real life is arguably too high. Ingraham (1999) noted that weddings such as those that appear in *Four Weddings and a Funeral* and *My Best Friend's Wedding* "easily equal or exceed the $45,000 model in *Father of the Bride*" (p. 135). In *My Big Fat Greek Wedding,* the bride's parents are able to give a house as a wedding gift! In *Just Married,* the honeymoon was in the French Alps at the nicest hotel. The honeymoon in *Muriel's Wedding* was in the Caribbean. In *My Best Friend's Wedding* there was mention of the honeymoon being in Florence, Italy. All of these glamorous locations involve expenses that are much higher than those for the average wedding, which is between $20,000 and $25,000 ("Statistics on," 2004; "Wedding Facts," 2004; "Wedding Facts & Trends," 2004). The average annual joint income of those getting married is just over twice that, and it is not uncommon for people to go into debt to pay for their wedding (Bayot, 2003; Valhouli, 2004). Therefore, wedding films are unrealistic in their portrayals of weddings as being affordable at more than $45,000.

A second wedding movie myth is "Financial struggles have nothing to with the success of a relationship." In nearly every wedding film studied, love is stripped of any financial difficulties or considerations. There are no discussions of how the bills will get paid, who will pay the bills, how the married couple will make buying decisions, how much debt each person brings into the marriage, what their spending habits are, and whether they are spenders or savers. Some studies rank disagreements over money as a major strain on relationships (Dye, 2004; Zagorsky, 2003). However, even if financial strains are not widespread, they are still a major part of a marriage that is left unexamined in wedding films.

## CONCLUSION

In my analysis of popular wedding films, I found that myths about sex, love, and romance abound. I do not mean to imply that there are not potentially challenging portrayals in these movies. To the contrary, many of these films might provide glimpses of myths while also challenging them. In the end, the goal is to enrich our own sexual, loving, and romantic relationships by avoiding and debunking destructive myths and substituting the rarely portrayed prescriptions (Galician, 2004, p. 225).

## STUDY QUESTIONS/RECOMMENDED EXERCISES

1.  Which of the myths in wedding films did you find the most interesting? Why?

2.  In what way are portrayals of weddings in movies "political"?

3. Which of the movies in this selection appeared in the most myths?

4. What are some of the ways that some movies discussed in this selection might debunk myths about marriage? Which prescriptions do they support?

5. Do you encounter unrealistic expectations of weddings in your own life that correspond to the myths portrayed by wedding films? If so, what are these expectations?

6. Alone or with others in a group, choose a wedding movie that is not covered in this selection. Analyze the myths that are portrayed, debunked, and absent in the movie. Remember to include the additional two myths that pertain solely to wedding movies.

## REFERENCES

Bayot, J. (2003, July 13). For richer or poorer, to our Visa card limit. *New York Times.* Retrieved September 18, 2004, from http://www.nytimes.com/2003/07/13/business/13WED.html

Bush, G. W. (2003). Marriage protection week, 2003. *White House* Web site. Retrieved September 30, 2004, from http://www.whitehouse.gov/news/releases/2003/10/20031003-12.html

Castle, N. (Director). (1996). *Mr. Wrong* [Motion picture]. United States: Buena Vista.

Coraci, F (Director). (1998). *The wedding singer* [Motion picture]. United States: New Line.

Dreyfus, E. A. (2005). *Divorce: What went wrong?* Retrieved January 20, 2005, from http://www.planetpsych.com/zPsychology_101/relationships/divorce.htm

Dye, L. (2004, October 1). Study explains money problems in marriages: Surprise, surprise: Study finds men and women see finances differently. *ABC News.* Retrieved July 24, 2006, from http://abcnews.go.com/Technology/story?id=97626&page= 1

Dylan, J. (Director). (2003). *American Wedding* [Motion picture]. United States: Universal.

Ettelbrick, E (1997). Since when is marriage a path to liberation? In R. M. Baird & S. E. Rosenbaum (Eds.), *Same-sex marriage: The moral and legal debate.* New York: Prometheus.

Galician, M.-L. (2004). *Sex, love, and romance in the mass media: Analysis and criticism of unrealistic portrayals and their influence.* Mahwah, NJ: Lawrence Erlbaum Associates.

Hogan, P. J. (Director). (1995). *Muriel's wedding* [Motion picture]. United States: Miramax.

Hogan, P. J. (Director). (1997). My *best friend's wedding* [Motion picture]. United States: Columbia/Tristar.

Ingraham, C. (1999). *White weddings: Romancing heterosexuality in popular culture.* New York: Routledge.

Levy, S. (Director). (2003). *Just married* [Motion picture]. United States: Fox.

Marshall, G. (Director). (1999). *Runaway bride* [Motion picture]. United States: Paramount.

Newell, M. (Director). (1994). *Four weddings and a funeral* [Motion picture]. United States: MGM/UA.

Roach, J. (Director). (2000). *Meet the parents* [Motion picture]. United States: Universal

Shankman, A. (Director). (2001). *The wedding planner* [Motion picture]. United States: Columbia Tri-Star.

Shyler, C. (Director). (1991). *Father of the bride* [Motion picture]. United States: Touchstone.

Statistics on weddings in the United States. (2004, September 27). *Soundvision* Web site. Retrieved September 27, 2004, from http://soundvision.com/info/weddings/statistics.asp

Sullivan, A. (1997, April 4). Gay marriage. *Slate.* Retrieved April 8, 2000, from http://slate.msn.com/id/3 642

Tennant, A. (Director). (1997). *Fools rush in* [Motion picture]. United States: Columbia/Tristar.

Valhouli, C. (2004, April 22). What your honeymoon will cost: Prices for the $7 billion-a-year industry are on the rise. *Forbes.com.* Retrieved September 15, 2004, from http://msnbc.msn.com/id/4806540

Wedding facts. (2004). *American Greetings* Web site. Retrieved September 27, 2004, from http://press-room.americangreetings.com/Summer04/WeddingFacts04.html

Weddings facts & trends. (2004). *Hallmark* Web site. Retrieved September 27, 2004, from http://press-room.hallmark.com/wedding_facts.html

Zagorsky, J. L. (2003). Husbands' and wives' view of the family finances. *Journal of Socio-Economics, 32,* 127–147.

Zwick, J. (Director). (2002). *My big fat Greek wedding* [Motion picture]. United States: HBO.

# END-OF-CHAPTER REFLECTIONS

This chapter has addressed many myths associated with love and romance, and perhaps you are left wondering what love actually is. We encourage you to develop your own definition of love and allow it to change and grow as you do. In order to keep your definition dynamic, we encourage you to keep a journal of what myths you notice in the media you watch/consume and what messages they communicate about love and intimacy. How might you bring awareness to unrealistic portrayals of love, romance, and commitment?

Another lingering question that we are always asked is "How can I make love last?" We offer some suggestions to build connection and closeness in your romantic relationships. Of course, this is not an exhaustive list, and we encourage you to add to it!

1. John Gottman would probably say that step 1 to a lasting relationship is building love maps. Love maps are the foundation of knowledge you have about your partner. We can't ever know it all, even in long-term relationships. The Gottman Institute offers a free card deck application for Apple and Android users that includes hundreds of questions you can ask your partner to spark lively conversation, and you may even learn something you didn't know. Visit the Apple Store or Google Play and search "Gottman Card Decks."

2. Turn toward your partner—respond to small moments for connection each day.

3. Accept influence. We all want to feel a sense of power in our relationships; equality is important. The happiest couples report accepting influence from their partners and listening (one way of turning toward) when their partners have something important to share.

4. Touch often. Touch is not just something we do when we want to initiate sex. Touch is vital to human connection, and just 6 seconds will trigger a release of oxytocin in the brain that makes you feel more connected. Remember Virginia Satir's words from Chapter 6: We need 12 hugs a day for growth!

5. Infuse lots of positivity in your relationship. Gottman says that you need at least five positive interactions to counteract every negative interaction. This is the magic 5:1 ratio! The more positivity you have in your relationship, the more you build your emotional bank account, as Gottman says, which provides a solid buffer when your relationship is challenged.

While definitions of love abound, we feel particularly attached to the following quote from Barbara Fredrickson (2013), and share it with you in closing:

> Love is far more ubiquitous than you ever thought possible for the simple fact that love is connection. *It's that poignant stretching of your heart that you feel when you gaze into a newborn's eyes for the first time or a shared farewell hug with a dear friend. It's even the fondness and sense of shared purpose you might unexpectedly feel with a group of strangers who've come together to marvel at a hatching of sea turtles or cheer at a football game. The new take on love that I want to share with you is this: Love blossoms virtually anytime two or more people—even strangers—connect over a shared positive emotion, be it mild or strong. (p. 17)*

## REFERENCES

Fisher, H. (2008). *The brain in love* [TED Talk]. TED.

Fredrickson, B. L. (2013). *Love 2.0.* Plume.

Johnson, V. I. (2011). Adult children of divorce and relationship education: Implications for counselors and counselor educators. *The Family Journal, 19*(1), 22–29.

Horowitz, J., Graf, N., & Livingston, G. (2019, November 6). *Marriage and cohabitation in the US.* Pew Research Center. https://www.pewresearch.org/social-trends/2019/11/06/marriage-and-cohabitation-in-the-u-s/

Reiss, I. L. (1960). Toward a sociology of the heterosexual love relationship. *Marriage and Family Living, 22*(2). 139–145.

Sternberg, R. J. (1986). A triangular theory of love. *Psychological Review, 93*(2). 119–135.

## RECOMMENDATIONS FOR FURTHER READING

Fisher, H. (2004). *Why we love: The nature and chemistry of romantic love.* Henry Holt.

Fredrickson, B. L. (2013). *Love 2.0.* Plume.

---

*Chapter 11*

# Becoming Parents

## EDITORS' INTRODUCTION

The transition to parenthood is a special gift with many rewards. Babies are juicy and adorable, and they grow up to be children that amaze us and bring us joy. However, having a baby also creates a tremendous strain on the majority of relationships and decreases relationship satisfaction. In the readings from the book, *And Baby Makes Three*, by John Gottman and Julie Schwartz Gottman, you will be introduced to the slippery slope that is parenting. The Gottmans reference myriad variables that contribute to the decline in relationship satisfaction. Deserving of extra attention are sleep, societal expectations, and postpartum depression, and we are highlighting those topics here.

## SLEEP

Sufficient sleep undergirds the way we manage ourselves. When we get enough sleep we are able to regulate our own emotions with greater skill, solve problems more effectively, and are buffered against developing mental health disorders. In fact, a metanalysis from Baglioni et al. (2011) found that when participants were deprived of sleep, there was a twofold risk of developing depression. Most sleep scientists assert that a minimum of 7 to 8 hours are needed for optimal functioning, so let's see what happens when we add a new baby to the mix.

According to Sleep Junkie (n.d.), over 90% of new parents (and we aren't sure who the other 10% could be) report sleeping 2 to 3 hours less than the 7 to 8 hours prescribed for optimal well-being. Some of you may be thinking that the consequences of getting 5 to 6 hours of sleep are manageable and perhaps not a big deal in the overall scheme. We invite you to think again and consider the following brief review of sleep hygiene, because the real problems begin when we compound reduced sleep quantity with fragmented sleep, a term used to describe when happens when sleep cycles are disrupted.

Babies tend to have wildly erratic sleep patterns in the beginning, and although some might start out sleeping for 2 to 3 hours at a time, many others go through episodes where they sleep for only an hour or so. Conversely, we (adults) move through four stages of non-REM sleep, plus a stage of REM sleep every 90 minutes or so, and we (ideally) repeat this cycle four to six times per night. The final REM stage (otherwise known as our dream state) lasts for about 10 minutes at the beginning of the night and gets progressively longer as we move through the cycles, with the longest phase of REM occurring in the early morning hours. When we are awakened to feed our baby and provide the comfort that they need, we miss out on the critical restorative benefits that sleep cycles provide. Unfortunately, our bodies aren't able to bookmark where we left off in our last sleep cycle, which means that we are continually restarting from square one. Fragmented sleep might need to be endured for weeks, and mostly likely months, before babies are developmentally ready to skip some of their less than convenient feedings.

What happens if these cycles get interrupted? The oversimplified response is that without a series of progressive sleep cycles, our ability to complete simple tasks and stay focused becomes challenged, and, devastating to a healthy relationship, our ability to regulate emotions can be seriously compromised. The good news is that babies do (usually) learn to sleep, so in most cases the difficult effects of sleep deprivation are not permanent.

## SOCIETAL EXPECTATIONS

Societal expectations are tough on parents, and they differ according to a person's ascribed gender role. The variances in these expectations can become quite profound when a couple moves from no kids to new baby and can emerge in ways that a couple without children might not be able to imagine. In recent decades, it's true that when referring to heterosexual couples, there is movement toward more gender equality in childcare, household, and outside work responsibilities. However, even the most well-intentioned couples commonly revert toward traditional gender roles after transitioning to parenthood (Grinza et al., 2017; White et al., 1986).

Traditional gender roles in modern society mean that moms take on a disproportionate share of the household maintenance and childcare, in addition to working outside the home (64% of parents are considered dual income; U.S. Bureau of Labor Statistics, 2020). Explanations for this regression are vast, but the most common are rooted in all the ways children are socialized. Young girls (in comparison to young boys) have been, and continue to be, more socialized to be caregivers. We see this in play when young girls are directly or covertly rewarded for more nurturing behaviors and young boys are similarly rewarded for more physical play, especially play that displays assertiveness and strength, traits that don't typically generate a nurturing skill set. One unfortunate byproduct of this socialization is that many dads report having parenting skill deficits that leave them feeling insecure and overwhelmed. Further, a mother who returns to work and wishes to shift childrearing responsibilities to her coparent continues to be much more vulnerable to admonishment than is a father who wishes to do the same. Similarly, a father who wishes to eschew his career in favor of childrearing is likely to experience his own dose of social reproach. Breaking away from these prescribed roles is no easy task, and the resulting inequities are fertile ground for resentment and disconnection inside the relationship.

Same-sex couples tend to fare slightly better with regard to the decline in relationship satisfaction. The assumptive explanation for these findings is that the distribution of household tasks, childcare, and work responsibility outside the home can be negotiated without the complications created by prescribed gender roles put forth by society.

## POSTPARTUM DEPRESSION

Postpartum depression (PPD) exacerbates the negative impact that parenthood often has on relationship satisfaction. Although both parents are vulnerable to developing PPD (a slight majority of new moms experience some type of depression), hormones, exhaustion, and interpersonal factors place the parent who gave birth at much greater risk. Interestingly, emotional and physical support from a partner are such powerful antidotes that couples who report high relationship satisfaction experience a protective factor against the development of PPD. Specifically, a new mom benefits when her partner possesses traits such as compassion, patience, and low levels of excessive anger (Mickelson & Biehle, 2017). The trick here is that traditionally socialized men often have a dearth of emotional resources outside the relationship and tend to lean on their partners for their emotional needs. If their partner (the new mom) is experiencing depression, they will have a limited capacity to be a resource, thus leaving the traditionally socialized man vulnerable to his own depression. You can see that PPD is complex and highlights interdependence between coparents right out of the gate. By the way, this interdependence between coparents lasts forever because, in some form or fashion, you will always be connected to the other parent of your child.

As you read the excerpts from *Baby Makes Three*, by John Gottman and Julie Schwartz Gottman, keep in mind the following primer questions for reflection. If you feel so inclined, take a few minutes and consider your responses to the following questions before you read, and then again after you've finished each reading.

## PRIMERS

1. Assuming you aren't already a parent (and if you are, try to imagine what it might have been like to contemplate these questions before you were), how would you rate your motivation to have kids at some point in the future?

2. Perhaps you've already spent some time contemplating what qualities you want in a life partner. Now, think about your imaginary future children and list five qualities that you want in a coparent.

3. How do you imagine your parenting style? How important is it to coparent with someone who has a similar style? What if their styles are very different from yours?

# And Baby Makes Three

*By John M. Gottman and Julie Schwartz Gottman*

[...]

## WHAT HAPPENS TO A COUPLE WHEN A BABY ARRIVES? THE BARE FACTS

We know that approximately 3.6 million babies are born to couples every year in the United States of America. This should be a time of great joy, right? Unfortunately, research from many laboratories, including our own, has shown that for many couples these joys are fleeting moments at best.

Our research study found that after the first baby was born, relationship satisfaction dropped significantly for two-thirds of the couples. Conflict within the relationship and hostility toward each other dramatically increased. They found themselves fighting much more. Their emotional intimacy deteriorated. They became bewildered and exhausted. Not surprisingly, their passion, sex, and romance plummeted.

Like many other researchers who had studied new mothers, we also found that postpartum depression in our mothers (and some fathers) occurred more commonly than we anticipated. After a baby's arrival, parents often became fatigued, sleepless, and irritable. In many cases, exhaustion deepened into depression. In addition, parents who were disasters failed to realize the mountain of work they'd face once their baby arrived. Afterward, they battled repeatedly in the house about who should do what. Finally, both parents ended up feeling unappreciated, neglected, and lonely.

Over the course of the next months, as Baby took center stage, the romance between these parents dissolved. Some of them became so isolated that an affair ruptured their connection altogether. Others slowly slid down a cascade toward miserable coexistence and eventual separation. Sadly, it was the majority of our parents who made this descent after the birth of their first baby.

What happened to the babies in the meantime? There was a severe strain on their intellectual and emotional development that put the babies' normal development in jeopardy.

Babies need parents who respond when they have a need, who soothe them when they're upset, calm them when they're frightened, and play enthusiastically with them when they're ready for fun. But when parents are distressed and lonely or depressed, they are less responsive to their babies. Babies' crying only irritates them, babies' fears annoy them, and babies' playfulness feels too demanding. This is especially true when parents are at war with each other.

Babies are also amazingly attuned to orient and respond to their parents' faces and voices. But when babies cry with fear at the hostility they hear in those voices, their cries become a distraction from the parental business at hand—fighting. Distressed parents often want their babies to be quiet and not need them so much, like dolls in a crib. This creates a withdrawn parent-child emotional relationship. Unhappily married parents may also be intrusive to force their babies into preferable behavior—like shutting up.

In our study, babies raised by unhappy parents suffered developmentally. They lagged behind the babies of contented parents both intellectually and emotionally. Speech occurred later, potty training was delayed, and the ability to self-soothe was slow in coming. Studies by psychologist Tiffany Field with depressed parents suggest that some of these delays would last. The children would probably be lagging behind for years to come.

[...]

## PARENTS ARE VERY STRESSED

As early as 1957, a landmark study by E. E. LeMasters claimed that an astounding 83 percent of new parents went through moderate to severe crisis in the transition to parenthood. Unfortunately, no one believed LeMasters. His claims were initially dismissed—or, at best, strongly debated—because no one could believe such high-percentage numbers could be real. But later, in the 1980s, other studies began to appear, and they confirmed LeMasters's findings. Now, after more than sixteen long-term studies, we know that he was right.

## BOTH PARENTS ARE IRRITABLE, OVERLY EMOTIONAL, AND THEY FIGHT A LOT

There is so much to do when a new baby arrives. Babies need to be fed every two hours, including at night. So most babies don't sleep through the night, at least for a while. Also, babies signal their needs by crying. This means that babies cry a lot. Babies cry when they are wet, when they are in pain, when they have gas, when they are scared, when they are lonely, when they need to be held, and when they are hungry.

We parents spend many nights at 3 a.m. walking around the house with our babies trying to help them go to sleep. We dance with our babies, sing to our babies, count to a hundred with our babies, reason with our babies, rock our babies, and bathe our babies. We wipe up baby drool, baby pee, baby poop, and baby spit. We look in mirrors with our babies, go for drives with our babies, play the saxophone to our babies, and take our babies into our parental beds. We sleep with our babies next to us, and we sleep with our babies on top of us. Then we change our babies, feed our babies, take our babies to the park and to the pediatrician. And we buy things for our babies—cribs, playpens, rattles, toys, mobiles, baby music, car seats, diapers, baby food, more diapers, and more baby food. We parents love our babies so much, yet there's so much to do!

It is possible to not answer the phone, to avoid returning messages, to ignore someone knocking at the door, and to avoid doing our e-mail, but most of us *cannot ignore our crying babies*. Baby cries awaken an archetypal drive in us to nurture, protect, and sustain our own. So, of course, with responding around the clock, we get sleep deprived, tired, and crabby. This is totally natural. It happens to all of us.

But what happens when we are sleep deprived and stressed for a long time? We can get mildly depressed. Apparently, sleep deprivation sometimes biologically results in depression even when there's nothing to be depressed about. For example, one study took healthy young childless volunteers and deprived them of deep sleep (found during delta-wave and dream stages) every night for a month. At the end of the month, they were evaluated. Every single one of them had become clinically and biologically depressed! And these young volunteers had no baby in the picture, no one crying to wake them up, and no one saying, "You get the baby, I'm tired."

Sleep deprivation also makes our daily hassles seem more intense. We feel worse, and we take things harder—like encountering rude people, waiting at red lights, or enduring long lines at the grocery store. When we're exhausted, we lose our sense of humor. We just can't cope as well.

In our relationships, we also feel more emotionally out of control. We think we hear something mean and snap! We crack back with something hostile. One minute we're laughing, and the next one, crying. And the fuse on our temper is only a millimeter long. Astoundingly, all of this is normal, given a few months of sleep deprivation and so much to do. It doesn't mean that our relationships are bad. It simply means that we're tired and going through a tremendous transition in our lives.

Then there's who-does-what to consider. For example, here are some of the tasks we new parents must divvy up and do.

- *The breakfast dishes*
- *The dinner dishes*
- *Setting the table*

- *Cleaning the counters*
- *Mopping the kitchen floor*
- *Dusting the house*
- *Vacuuming the house*
- *Cleaning the floors*
- *Cleaning the bathroom*
- *Cleaning out the garage*
- *Cleaning out the basement*
- *Shopping for Baby's needs*
- *Figuring out the other things we need to get*
- *Cooking dinner*
- *Making the other kids' lunches*
- *Making breakfast*
- *Taking out the garbage*
- *Sweeping outside*
- *Putting gas in the car*
- *Changing the oil in the car*
- *Changing lightbulbs in the house*
- *Washing the car*
- *Repairing the car*
- *Changing the baby's diapers*
- *Feeding the baby*
- *Getting up with the baby at night*
- *Getting the baby dressed in the morning*
- *Bathing the baby*
- *Playing with the baby*
- *Dealing with a crying baby*
- *Taking the children to their doctors' appointments*
- *Taking the children to school*
- *Making sure the kids have everything they need when they leave for the day*
- *Getting the baby or kids to sleep at night*

- *Making the bed(s)*
- *Doing the laundry*
- *Putting away the laundry*
- *Doing the grocery shopping*
- *Picking up medicines we need*
- *Cleaning up the yard*
- *Doing the weeding*
- *Taking the dog for a walk*
- *Changing the cat's litter box*
- *Making sure the doors and windows are locked at night*
- *Turning off all the lights when not needed*
- *Doing repair work around the house*
- *Helping the kids with homework*
- *Cleaning out the refrigerator*
- *Watering the plants*
- *Tidying up the common living areas*
- *Putting away the toys*
- *Calming the baby when he or she is upset*

Of course, this isn't everything. We once created a more complete list in order to help couples having a baby, but we found that our list of over six hundred items just depressed everybody even more. Not to mention the fact that most of us handle these chores while having to work part- or full-time, too. So it's no wonder that after our baby has come, we feel overwhelmed.

What else do we know? From sixteen studies that followed parents before and after babies arrived, we learned more.

- Even though both parents are working much harder, they both feel unappreciated.
- During the first year after babies arrive, the frequency and intensity of relationship conflicts increase.
- It is normal for a mom's sexual desire to drop precipitously after birth and even stay low for the first year, especially if she is nursing. Consequently, sex declines dramatically.
- Moms usually become very involved with their babies. But due to their fatigue, they have less to offer their partners emotionally.

- Both moms and dads undergo major changes in their own identities—for example, how they think of themselves not only as parents and partners, but also as friends, brothers, sisters, sons, and daughters. Their values may change, and their goals in life, too.

- Moms and dads often want to be better at parenting than their own parents were with them.

- Many couples change their relationship with time. They start to date events as "Before Baby" and "After Baby." Most important is when Baby did something for the first time.

- Right after the baby is born, many women close to new moms arrive to help out. But this society of women can crowd out the new dads. Dads often respond by withdrawing from their babies and working more, especially if there's more conflict at home.

- Babies withdraw emotionally from fathers who are unhappy with their relationship with their partners. But babies don't withdraw from unhappy moms. This withdrawal from dads can be tragic for babies.

If this is all that happened after we had babies, our birth-rate might also precipitously decline. Fortunately, this isn't the whole story. Having a baby means experiencing those moments when our baby grabs our thumb and holds on for dear life. When we look at our baby's toes and they look like peas. And a month later, the toes grow and they look like string beans. Those moments when our baby's mouth curls up and she gives us her first smile. Or when he gurgles and laughs. Or when we gaze at each other as Baby falls softly asleep between us. Or when Baby flashes the world a grin from atop our shoulders. There's nothing better than taking our baby for a stroll on a warm summer's day. Or playing with a toy and watching our baby laugh.

Maybe the problem is that we have unrealistic expectations about what will happen after baby arrives. Dads expect that when babies come, moms will finally be happy, especially with them. New moms will feel fulfilled as women and see their husbands as manly and potent. They'll get turned on more easily and want to make love all the time. Meanwhile, moms expect that their men will finally open up emotionally and be more sensitive and loving. Their husbands will want to spend hours and hours just cuddling and listening to them. And they'll want to play with their babies, take care of their babies, and be close as a family all the time. So the first straw may look like this: She'll want to be held, but he'll want to put on the game; and later on, when he wants sex, she'll be tired and want to sleep. But there must be some way to navigate this transition into parenthood smoothly.

## MANAGING CONFLICT

Most couples fight, especially when they're stressed and tired. It's natural. The secret to managing conflicts for new parents is to make the fights constructive, not destructive. Constructive means respectful, not disrespectful; gentle and not critical; and taking responsibility for our part and not being defensive. It means listening, not just broadcasting, and acknowledging our partner's point of view, not just repeating our own. Conflict can help us understand our partner better, but we have to be open to accepting our partner's influence and not insisting on getting our way.

If we disrespect each other during conflicts, conflicts become destructive; relationships are marked by criticism, defensiveness, the silent treatment, no compromise, no warmth, and no humor. Closeness spirals downhill fast. We wind up walking on eggshells, fighting louder, or withdrawing and avoiding one another. None of us wants that.

However, conflict managed well can lead us to deeper corn-passion for one another. Then we can be more of a team, cope better with our stress, and navigate this transition to parenthood with ease.

## WHAT ABOUT INTIMACY?

Having a new baby means there's new sweetness in life—and more work to do. But when we're so busy, we forget to say "Thank you." Appreciation seems unnecessary. And we forget to ask, "How was your day?" Time for conversation disappears. If we get a chance to talk, we try—and get interrupted—in midsentence.

We don't experience each other's lives in the same consistent, close way that we did before the baby was born. Not being fully engaged makes intimacy so much more difficult. The increasing emotional demands that hamper intimacy are matched by the often different expectations that couples have about physical contact after the baby is born. Men may want and need physical intimacy to help feel close to their partners, while all women can think about is that they feel about as attractive as a potato.

Ellen Kreidman, in her book *Is There Sex After Kids?* tells the story of going to her obstetrician for her nine-month postpartum. checkup. She asked her doctor about sex. She didn't tell him that she had been lacking sexual desire since the birth of the baby. She expected the doctor to tell her, "Sorry. No sex for the next two years." He examined her. Then he said, "You can resume sexual relations now." She was stunned. When she drove home with her husband, he asked her what her doctor had said. She replied, "The doctor said no sex for two years." He blanched. Then she said, "Not really ...," relieving him. But the reality was she wished that had been the doctor's assessment.

Ellen's story is not unusual. Sexual desire for many new moms seems to dry up, and they become much less emotionally available to their men. Faced with this lack of intimacy from their partners, men may withdraw from both their women and their babies. But during this transition time, it's crucial for husbands and wives to find the time to talk, to stay attuned to one another, and to reach out to one another. Sexual intimacy arises from emotional intimacy. And emotional intimacy comes from partners making the effort to find each other through the maze of duties to perform. When partners feel cherished and appreciated, affection comes naturally. It's no longer the last chore of the day. Then romance and passion can reawaken.

## WE'RE BUILDING A LEGACY

The master couples in our studies sense that they are building something beyond their relationships, something bigger than themselves. With the arrival of their new babies, they are joining the flow of the generations. Now there are children to carry into the world their values, their visions, and their legacies. They ask themselves and each other, what do we want our legacies to be?

They examine everything with new eyes. What does it mean to have a home? Should we have mealtimes together, or apart? If one of us gets sick, how should we care for each other? And if we triumph, should we celebrate? What if we fail? Should we honor birthdays? What about the holidays? Should it be Christmas or Hanukkah? Kwanzaa or Ramadan? And our extended families? When should we include them? What about TV? Do we want it limited1 or not? How about church? And when we vacation, should we do trips in the country, or in the city? What about our philosophy regarding emotions? Should we stay silent about our feelings, or say them out loud? There are so many ways for babies to learn what matters, and every family values thoughts, emotions, and experiences differently.

Each of us represents the family we've come from. And each of our families embodies a culture, that unique set of symbols, values, and rituals. When we become partners and new parents together, we merge not only our families but those cultures as well, and so we create a new culture together.

With our baby's arrival, we face a profound decision: From the cultures we've inherited and the new one we've created, what should we keep and transmit to our offspring, and what should we leave behind?

We can think about this decision and control what our babies absorb. Or we can avoid thinking about it, and let it just happen outside our awareness. Then we "vote with our feet"; in other words, we let our babies learn by what we do, regardless of whether we've thought about the consequences of our actions on our babies. Either way, by the daily choices we make we create a legacy for our children. Our master couples have shown us that by making these choices with purposeful awareness and intention, our children inherit the best from us.

Above all, there's the baby.

Our most important message is this:

> The greatest gift you can give your baby is a happy and
> strong relationship between the two of you

Here's why.

Most babies suffer when there is relationship conflict between parents. Our studies and those of others have shown that parental irritability, hostility, and fighting lead to poor parent-child interaction. This in turn creates a dangerous emotional climate for babies. For example, the blood pressures of babies rise when they witness or overhear their parents fighting. With parental alienation or depression, parents poorly coordinate face-to-face play with their babies and thereby confuse them. Unhappy parents also misread their babies' emotional cues and more often make wrong responses to them. Sometimes, they stop responding to their babies altogether. Overall, their interactions with their babies become more negative and less positive.

Just how serious is this? If babies can't talk, how do they know we're being hostile? Even if they do, can't they adapt to it? When they're so young, aren't they more resilient?

The answers are all no. We now know that even minor signs of untreated depression in parents have profound effects on babies. Infants of these parents often withdraw, at first just from fathers and later from mothers. They can also become depressed themselves, and less physically healthy. They are at greater long-term risk for developing emotional, cognitive, and behavioral problems.

The most troubling research finding we've learned is that parenting compromised by poor partner relationships nearly always has one effect. Compromised parenting will interfere with an infant's ability to self-regulate and to stay calm. Suppose an infant looks away because it is overstimulated and upset, and the baby's attempt to look away and calm down is not understood or respected by the parents. Some parents think that when the baby looks away from them, the baby doesn't like them. We've even seen parents in our lab forcibly move their infant's head so that the baby has to maintain eye contact with the parents. Then the infant is robbed of one of its main methods for self-soothing and adapting to the level of stimulation-looking away. The baby is forced to try a more extreme method of regulating the world, such as escalating his protests, or withdrawing.

During that instant, the baby has lost an opportunity to learn that with his behavior, he can affect his world. If that moment becomes characteristic of the parent-infant relationship, the baby will also learn that he can't communicate his emotions successfully and his emotions don't count. Doesn't that sound like what an unhappy couple might feel?

This issue is momentous because of what might fail to develop in the baby. In the first three years of life, fundamental neural processes are being laid down that have to do with the infant's ability to self-soothe, focus attention, trust in the love and nurturance of his parents, and emotionally attach to his mother and father. This means that a baby born to parents in an unhappy relationship might not develop the neural networks needed for school achievement, healthy peer relationships, and a future happy life.

These findings yell out to us that our babies need us to maintain healthy relationships with each other. When we savor each other, our babies rest in the cradle of our contentment.

## LET'S SHINE A LIGHT ON FATHERS

Utilizing modern advances in science, a mom can get pregnant, have a baby, and parent that baby through adulthood without there ever having been a father in the picture. This begs the question: Do fathers matter? The resounding answer from many studies is that they absolutely do. A longitudinal study from the 1950s found that over a quarter century later kids who had the best relationships with their partners, friends, and community were those whose fathers expressed warmth and caring to them when they were young children (Gottman & Gottman, 2007). Warmth from the father to the child seems to be the characteristic most highly correlated with the development of prosocial behavior later in life. The good news is that fathers in heterosexual relationships who experience lower levels of conflict with moms tend to stay more involved with their children. Conversely, fathers who experience higher levels of conflict with moms tend to withdraw from all members of the nuclear family (Krishnakumar & Buehler, 2000).

## END-OF-CHAPTER REFLECTIONS

Now that you've read about some of the pitfalls of parenthood, you might be wondering if it's possible for a couple to maintain satisfaction with their relationship after they've welcomed home a new baby. We would say, YES, you most certainly can! Taking heed of all that you've learned in this anthology will help, especially if you focus on the words of advice from Chapters 6 and 7. We believe that planning for your baby in the emotional sense as well as the physical will be key for you as you transition your relationship from "we to three." One mistake many parents make is an overfocus on having the necessary items in place (stroller, diapers, toys, etc.) and perhaps an underfocus on the emotional components that are equally necessary. Also, be aware that all stages of parenthood can lead to strain on a relationship, not just the beginning. In fact, some research points to the raising of teenagers as the most stressful time of all. We advocate that couples who have the resources to do so participate in some sort of couples work to assess the strengths and potential weaknesses of the relationship before having kids and at any other time during parenthood when the stresses of the childrearing are compromising the strength of the relationship. At the very least, spending time discussing poignant topics in advance of (or throughout) parenthood is a must. See the following examples:

1. Who do we trust to help us out in the beginning?

2. How will we share household responsibilities? Are we okay with traditional roles? What does "shared responsibility" look like in our relationship?

3. What are some of the ways you want to parent our kids that will be similar to how you were parented? What do you want to do with our kids that differs from the way you were parented?

4. _____

   _____

5. _____

   _____

We hope we haven't scared you away from having kids. We all (Roni, Kim, and Sara) have children, and none of us would trade them in for anything; however, some of us wish we'd had the benefit of a resource like this one to guide us through some tricky periods.

## REFERENCES

Baglioni, C. Battagliese, G., Feige, B. Spiegelhalder, K., Nissen, C., Voderholzer, U., Lombardo, C., & Riemann, D. (2011). Insomnia as a predictor of depression: A meta-analytic evaluation of longitudinal epidemiological studies. *Journal of Affective Disorders, 135*(1–3), 10–19.

Gottman, J., & Gottman, J. S. (2007). *And baby makes three: The six-step plan for preserving marital intimacy and rekindling romance after baby arrives*. Three Rivers Press.

Grinza, E., Devicienti, F., Rossi, M. C., & Vannoni, D. (2017). How entry into parenthood shapes gender role attitudes: New evidence from longitudinal UK data. *IZA Institute of Labor Economics, 11088.* https://ssrn.com/abstract=3056626

Krishnakumar, A., & Buehler, C. (2000). Interparental conflict and parenting behaviors: A meta-analytic review. *Family Relations, 49*(1), 25–44.

Mickelson, K. D., & Biehle, S. N. (2017). Gender and the transition to parenthood: introduction to the special issue. *Sex Roles, 76*(5–6), 271–275.

Sleepjunkie. (n.d.). *Sleep research: What's new in the sleep industry*. https://www.sleepjunkie.com/sleep-research/

U.S. Bureau of Labor Statistics. (2020). *Employment characteristics of families summary*. https://www.bls.gov/news.release/famee.nr0.htm

Watson, N. F., Badr M. S, Belenky G, Bliwise, D., Buxton, O. M., Buysse, D., Dinges, D. F., Gangwisch, J., Malhorta, R. K., Martin, J. L., Patel, S. R., Quan, S. F., & Tasali, E. (2015). Recommended amount of sleep for a healthy adult: A joint consensus statement of the American Academy of Sleep Medicine and Sleep Research Society. *Sleep, 38*(6), 843– 844.

White, L. K., Booth, A., & Edwards, J. N. (1986). Children and marital happiness: Why the negative correlation? *Journal of Family Issues, 7*(2), 131–147.

## RECOMMENDATIONS FOR FURTHER READING

Dueger, S. (2020). *Preparing for parenthood: 55 essential conversations for couples becoming families.* Author Academy Elite.

Pickhardt, C. (2013). *Surviving your child's adolescence.* Jossey-Bass.

Siegel, J. (2000). *What children learn from their parents' marriage.* Harper Collins.

# Chapter 12

# Power and Violence

## EDITORS' INTRODUCTION

Just in case you haven't noticed, relationships are hard. There are so many things that we gain from healthy relationships: love, companionship, intimacy, connection, and overall better mental and physical health. In order to reap these rewards, as we've expressed in each chapter up to this point, you need some essential skills, an open mind and heart, and a strong will. Not every relationship is meant to last a lifetime. As you read, you may even reflect on some relationships gone by that you miss, or perhaps that you're glad to not be a part of anymore! In this chapter, our goals are twofold: (a) We want you to understand the importance of equality, shared power, and mutual respect to the success of relationships; and (b) we want you to know what some characteristics—we refer to them as red flags, or warning signs—of unhealthy relationships are so that if you find yourself in one, you can recognize them and move along. We'll address breaking up in Chapter 13, but for now, we emphasize the following:

1. We need a sense of power in our relationships in order to be our authentic selves.

2. When one person exerts too much power and control over their partner, this is a sign of an unhealthy and perhaps abusive relationship.

3. There are important reasons people stay in unhealthy relationships, and addressing some of the barriers that prevent an abused partner from leaving are important to understand.

4. In order to promote change in our culture regarding sexual assault and rape, consent needs to be at the forefront of our relationships.

In "Love and Power," Hara Estroff Marano emphasizes the necessity of shared power in an intimate relationship. Marano (2014) even goes as far as to say that "Equality ... is the world's best antidote to isolation" (p. 57). At first glance you might think that power and love are opposite sides of a coin, but in fact, "years of research suggests that empathy and social intelligence are vastly more important to acquiring and exercising power than are force, deception, and terror" (Keltner, 2007).

As you read, keep in mind the following primer questions for reflection. If you feel so inclined, take a few minutes and consider your responses to the following questions before you read, and then again after you've read the chapter.

## PRIMERS

1.  What does the word *power* mean to you?
2.  How do you think power is important to intimate relationships?

# Love and Power

*By Hara Estroff Marano*

Power infuses all relationships, but today there's a new paradigm: only equally shared power creates happy individuals and satisfying marriages. increasingly, it is the passport to intimacy.

As water is to fish, power is to people: It is the medium we swim in. And it is typically just as invisible to us.

Power is not limited to leaders or organizations; it doesn't require outright acts of domination. It's a basic force in every social interaction. Power defines the way we relate to each other. It dictates whether you get listened to. It determines whether your needs take priority or get any attention at all.

The problem for romantic partners is that power as normally exercised is a barrier to intimacy. It blunts sensitivity to a partner and precludes emotional connectivity. Yet this connection is what human beings all crave, and need. It satisfies deeply.

But there's only one path to intimacy. It runs straight through shared power in relationships. Equality is not just ideologically desirable, it has enormous practical consequences. It affects individual and relationship well-being. It fosters mutual responsiveness and attunement. It determines whether you'll be satisfied or have days (and nights) spiked with resentment and depression. "The ability of couples to withstand stress, respond to change, and enhance each other's health and well-being depends on their having a relatively equal power balance," reports Carmen Knudson-Martin of Loma Linda University. Equality, psychologists agree, is the world's best antidote to isolation. It's just not easy to attain or to sustain.

# THE ASCENT OF INTIMACY

Intimacy is nothing new. Seeking support, feeling close, forming strong emotional bonds, and expressing feelings are essential to the human experience. Both physical and psychological wellbeing, in fact, depend on the ability to do so.

But where we place intimacy in our lives certainly is new. The intensification of individualism and the development of the love match—ultra recent phenomena on the human timeline—concentrate intimacy in couple hood. Until the 20th century, says social historian Stephanie Coontz of Evergreen State College in Olympia, Washington, intimacy was dispersed among wide family and social circles. The closeness mothers and daughters and even mothers and sons enjoyed, as well as siblings and cousins, would be considered enmeshment today. Saying "I love you" to a cousin or even a neighbor was commonplace. So was displacing a husband to spend a night in bed sharing secrets with an old friend come to town. "We have upped our expectations of intimacy but downgraded our definition of from whom it is expected and to whom it is owed," says Coontz. "We've taken all the personal feelings and expectations from other relationships and put them onto the couple relationship."

So much have social lives shrunk that men today tend to have only one confidante—their wife. That makes men especially reactive to their wives' emotions—notably their negative emotions. That's not to say that wives are not reactive to men's feelings, but having a wider social network allows women more opportunities to calibrate their emotional lives.

The place of intimacy is not all that's changing. For a long time, the prevailing definition of intimacy has revolved around the sharing of feelings and insecurities. Necessary as it is, it is no longer sufficient; confiding can be confining. It makes little allowance for individual growth, a requirement in long-term relationships. And individual growth fuels not only the expansion of love but the sexual desire and eroticism increasingly expected if relationships are to satisfy for a lifetime.

"Intimacy rests on two people who have a capacity to both listen and speak up, who have the courage to bring more and more of their full selves into the relationship," says psychologist Harriet Lerner. "Both need equal power in defining what they want and what they really think and believe. But you have to know you can leave a relationship. If you truly believe you can't survive without a relationship, you have no power to really be yourself within it."

Too often, one partner gives up too much self—core values and priorities become compromised under relationship pressures; one person does more than a fair share of giving in around decision making or gives the other's goals priority. "Historically speaking, that person has been the woman," says Lerner. "I see it more both ways now that women are more economically independent. It takes courage to act on your own behalf." What often happens, she says, is that people accommodate, accommodate, accommodate, grow to resent it, and then fly out of the relationship when they needed to reclaim their power much earlier. "They needed to say much earlier, 'I don't want you to treat me this way and I won't be in the conversation when you talk to me this way.'"

Because intimacy is more important than ever, relationship equality is more necessary than ever.

## SHARED POWER IS THE ONLY POWER

Although many people associate power with manipulation and coercion, contemporary psychologists and philosophers have forged a new power paradigm: They view power as the capacity of an individual to influence others' states, even to advance the goals of others while developing their full self. It doesn't require observable behavior, let alone force.

If a woman is as influential as her partner is, then a relationship lasts, says John Gottman. But if he's much more influential than she is, the relationship doesn't last. For the dean of relationship researchers, an "interlocking influence process" is at the heart of a balance of power. "It's really about responsiveness to your partner's emotions. If you have power in a relationship, you have an effect on your partner with your emotions. That's a good sign for the long-term stability of the relationship and the happiness of the partners. But some people have very high emotional inertia; they weigh a lot emotionally; it's hard to move them."

> "You have to know you can survive without a relationship, if need be, to really be empowered within it".

And responsiveness to a partner is what makes a relationship feel fair, says Gottman, professor emeritus in psychology at the University of Washington and head of Seattle's Relationship Research Institute. Housework and childcare chores don't even have to be divided 50/50 to establish equality in a relationship. "A relationship has to feel fair. And that requires flexibility and responsiveness to emotions. People try to get their partner's attention or interest, or open a conversation or share humor or affection. We look at what proportion of the time a partner turns toward such a bid or a need. The turning towards needs to be at a very high level."

> "If one partner wins and the other loses, both lose—because the loser always makes the winner pay."

Fairness has one critical element, says University of Washington sociologist Pepper Schwartz— respect. In interviewing thousands of couples around the world she found that the American definition of a good relationship is "best friend." (Europeans prefer "passionate lover.") Best friends are egalitarian, and what most characterizes good friendship is respect—equal dignity.

In marriage, Schwartz says, it applies to division of labor, joint decision making, and especially license to speak up. "Respect means that someone takes my humanity into consideration and sees me as worthy in my own right of a positive and collaborative relationship. I'm understood as a human being worthy of occupying the same kind of space in the world as you. Why is cleaning toilets good only for me but not for you? OK, I'll clean the toilets and you'll throw out the dog poop; then we both know we have dirty jobs we do for the collective wellbeing of the relationship."

There's no single objective measure of fairness. People can accept unequal division of labor—as long as they have influence and are appreciated and not demeaned. "Unfairness does not always equal unhappiness," she says.

By contrast, power differences afflict almost all distressed heterosexual couples, and most occur along gender lines, at least in the United States, reports Knudson-Martin. It's not that it results from outright acts of domination. In the press of daily life, couples slip into society based

| Figure 12.1.1

patterns that favor men's needs and desires in ways that seem unquestionable. "Distressed relationships tend to be organized around the interests of the more powerful, often without conscious intention," Knudson-Martin reports in Family Process. Or partners are caught in a power struggle in which one tries in vain to influence the other, and so they are locked in argument, often about one issue over and over again—a positive sign, some experts believe, that a partner hasn't completely sacrificed identity.

For Knudson-Martin, the mutuality of influence that is so central to equality hinges on reciprocal engagement. In her studies of the process, she has found that each partner, by being aware of and interested in the needs of the other, allows the other to feel not only important but supported in the relationship.

With identity and worth affirmed, partners then can open themselves to being changed by the other, to accept influence. They also feel safe enough to reveal their innermost thoughts, express concerns, even admit weakness, uncertainty, or mistakes in a partner's presence. Mutual vulnerability becomes a high-water mark of bringing one's whole self into a relationship.

Knudson-Martin finds that when power is equal, partners also engage in direct communication strategies. They can ask straight-forwardly for what they want. They don't use the children as their mouthpieces. They don't devote hours to doping out the mood of their partner before broaching a topic.

## BEYOND MANIPULATION

Straight talk is essential to shared power, insists relational therapist Terry Real, who is based in Boston. But for some females, that can be dicey at first—it requires giving up the only form of power they have long been confined to practice. "The indirect exertion of power through manipulation is part of the traditional female role," says Real. "Men don't like being manipulated, and it's one of the few legitimate reasons they don't trust women. That women exert indirect power because direct power has historically been blocked doesn't make it any less ugly." There's a significant reward for direct communication, Knudson-Martin finds—the intensification of intimacy, leading to increased relationship satisfaction.

Equal partnership has another critical feature—shared responsibilities for the relationship itself. The more equal the relationship, the more responsibility both partners feel to make it work or get it on track if it is off. Most commonly, Knudson-Martin says, distressed heterosexual couples walk through her door and only one partner—guess which one—is making the effort to understand what is going on. "The men say they want the relationship to work, but they haven't internalized the idea that part of their job is to figure out how to preserve it."

To create a truly shared relationship, Stephanie Coontz notes, women have to loosen their hold on a cherished psychological tradition—emotional sharing. A demand for the constant

| Figure 12.1.2 William James.

confiding of feelings as the mark of closeness, she contends, is a strictly female view of intimacy.

Centering intimate relations around the sharing of feelings is a legacy from the gendered division of labor that prevailed in the 19th century, when men ventured into the new, impersonal world of commerce and women stayed home, says Coontz. "We don't recognize how much of the exploration of feelings arose from female powerlessness. As women, we became skilled in reading the emotions of others in our lives as a way to anticipate them or move them in other directions. And now we demand that kind of intimacy of men without realizing that we took up such emotional specialization precisely because we didn't have any power to just say, 'Hey, this is what I'd like to do.'"

Not only can the demand for too much understanding overburden couple relationships, but every little problem does *not* need to be talked out right now, Coontz adds. "We have underestimated the intimacy of unspoken, practical acts," more the male approach to love.

## AFFAIRS: A COST OF INEQUALITY

He who wields excess power in a relationship wins the battle—but loses the war, says Terry Real, who aims to nudge the world into thinking about relationships ecologically. "You're not above the system. You're in it. If you throw out pollution over there, it winds up in your lungs over here. Relationally, if one partner wins and the other loses, both lose—because the loser always makes the winner pay."

Bullying doesn't engender love, observes Real. It engenders resentment and hatred, which tend to show up in passive-aggressive behavior—withdrawal of generosity, of sexuality, of passion, and, ultimately, of love itself. "People don't like being controlled," Real explains. "The exercise of power is really an illusion, but it's an enormously destructive illusion."

Unless a partner is willing to risk the relationship, power imbalances can lead directly to affairs or the kind of exits that leave a powerful partner in head-scratching surprise. Real calls it "the paradox of intimacy. In order to sustain healthy intimacy you have to be willing to risk the relationship. The powerless person needs to acquire enough self-esteem to stand up to the bully: 'I don't want to make love to you while you're treating me this way.' Or 'I don't want to perform services for you while you're treating me this way. Pick up your own dry cleaning.' It's necessary to be congruent with one's own displeasure, which predictably gets the other person's attention."

Much as power feeds grandiosity, the state of emotional disconnection that the powerful inhabit is awfully lonely. And therein lies trouble. Sometimes the powerful person will say, "This marriage has been dead for years," Real reports. And they're right. "They themselves have built up such a bill of resentment the partner has withdrawn to the point where there is no juice in the relationship. What they don't get is their own culpability."

More often, the powerful slip into outside relationships—and feel fully justified in doing so. The lonelier they feel, says Real, the more they blame their partner. That enables them to feel entitled to find someone else, either by leaving the relationship for a different a partner or by having affairs.

Subordinate partners are no strangers to loneliness, but the cascade of events may be slightly different, less an entitlement than a quest for attention. There's a turning away from the relationship to get one's needs met, says Gottman, because often the partner, usually the woman, doesn't want the relationship to end. She begins a search elsewhere for friends, intellectual stimulation, and fun. But such substitution doesn't work well; loneliness seeks a responsive human being. Boundaries get crossed.

However, even if women are having affairs from a one-down position, after vainly trying to get a partner's attention, the affair gives them some power in the relationship. Their partners may suddenly launch into hot pursuit to get them back into the marriage.

## POWER CHANGES EVERYTHING

Denying the dignity of one partner has consequences not only for relationship stability and happiness, but for health.

Power, says Berkeley psychologist Dacher Keltner, has distinct biological correlates. The "new science of power" emerging from his decades-long research shows that "people with power tend to behave like patients with damage to the brain's frontal lobes, a condition that can cause overly impulsive and insensitive behavior."

The possession of power changes powerholders—usually in ways invisible to them—by triggering activation of the behavioral approach system, based in the left frontal cortex and fueled by the neurotransmitter dopamine. It's automatic. Nevertheless, it makes

"In 200 years, heterosexual relationships will be where gay and lesbian relationships are today."

powerful people quick to act on appetites, to detect opportunities for material and social rewards such as food, money, attention, sex, and approval. They think about sex more and flirt more flagrantly. Poorly attuned to others, they pay little attention to others' feelings and assess their attitudes, interests, and needs inaccurately. Politeness be damned, they act rudely, indulging their own whims. "Having power," Keltner reports, "makes people more likely to act as sociopaths."

The biological obverse marks the powerless. Their lack of power activates the brain's inhibitory system, centered in the right frontal cortex, which directs attention to threat and punishment and sets in motion avoidant behavior. It also ushers in negative feelings, notably anxiety and depression, virtually hallmark emotions of those denied power. If the thwarting of identity isn't distressing enough, add in the lack of partner responsiveness.

"Whenever someone gives up her voice," says Harriet Lerner, author of the now-classic *The Dance of Anger* and most recently of *Marriage Rules*, "whenever one person in the relationship sacrifices too much of the self, that partner experiences the greatest loss of power and is most apt to become symptomatic—to develop depression or anxiety or headaches." It isn't always the woman. "It could be the CEO of a company, if he gets home and doesn't speak up, if he tells himself it's not worth the fight. People lose power in different ways and at different times in the relationship."

One of the consequences of powerlessness, says Keltner, is that the reigning fear narrows focus onto threats and makes the powerless keen observers of those who have power over them. They know them better than the powerful know themselves. It's a natural channel for self-preservation.

## WHEN PRESSURE SPARKS POWER STRIFE

Young couples today enter marriage expecting equality. Both partners assume they are going to be working, Schwartz reports. Men feel much more permission to be involved in the everyday lives of their children than their fathers did. Beginning during courting, they are likely to be sharing expenses.

But ideology crashes into reality when children arrive. Then the necessity of allocating childcare responsibilities gives rise to power inequalities that surreptitiously erode a sense of self and decision-making power. "The woman usually becomes the only parent who is changing her life for the children," Schwartz points out. "She loses outside influence and an internal as well as external sense of who she is. As she loses power as an individual, her partner may exercise veto power in decision making or become cavalier about when to be home for dinner."

Compounding the problem is income disparity. It tends to give men more decision-making power. "But it's more money-specific than gender-specific," says Schwartz.

Either way, the idea and reality of best friendship are corroded. Enter resentment and anger. "It can undermine the generosity and goodwill—what each person will do for the other—that make a relationship work," says Schwartz. Often, sex becomes an instrument for with holding or rewarding. But most of all, the once-equal partner now has a diminished sense of self—unless she brings an unusual array of personal resources into the relationship. Here's where charm, beauty, social skills, and fitness count, undemocratic as their distribution might be. They confer power precisely because they imply a person can function outside the relationship.

## Jettisoning Gender Roles

In 200 years, says Gottman, "heterosexual relationships will be where gay and lesbian relationships are today." That's a long time to wait for change, but it reflects his findings that couple interactions are far more direct and kind among same-sex partners than the power struggles that arise among heterosexual ones.

Rather than rely on cultural assignment of gender roles, gay men and women must come up with their own ways to divide labor and share decisions. Having to actively decide who does what pulls for greater consciousness of fairness and equality, even after children arrive. Lesbian parents—family responsibilities among gay men are too new to have undergone similar study—are "dramatically more equal in sharing of child-care tasks and decision making than heterosexual parents," researchers report.

Conflict discussions are most telling. Both gay men and lesbians are far more egalitarian than heterosexuals in resolving differences. They bring up a problem less harshly; they don't come out of the starting gate with an accrual of resentment and attack their partner—a crucial distinction because conflicts tend to end up the way they start out. Same-sex partners are less accusatory and deploy more humor in their disagreements. There's less belligerence, less domineering, less fear, less whining, Gottman reports in the *Journal of Homosexuality*. Same-sex couples show more affection, listen better, and take more turns talking. Their ability to influence each other keeps discussions positive.

Conflict resolution among same-sex partners gets off to a good start also because "there is nothing to decode," observes Mark McKee, a gay male in a long-term relationship. "No one has to devote mental energy to figuring out what the other partner is really thinking. Each understands exactly what the other means." The sad irony is that same-sex partnerships are not as durable as heterosexual ones, likely because they have not had the same kind of social support to promote their staying together—until now.

Nevertheless, Gottman concludes, heterosexual couples may have a great deal to learn from homosexual relationships. Equity is a greater concern in homosexual relationships—and partners behave in accordance with their concerns.

And all relationships could benefit from recognizing that power and love, long cast as emotional matter and antimatter, are in fact convergent forces. "There's a widely held belief that to be loved you have to abandon power, and vice versa," says Adam Kahane, author of *Power and Love*. "Then you choose a partner who provides the missing function."

In fact, when expressed separately, love and power degenerate, he argues. Lack of love turns power into unconstrained self-interest; lack of power makes love sentimental and romantic, demanding fusion and loss of selfhood. A healthy relationship is both two and one at the same time—love enables individual partners to become their full selves. And such growth provides them with the strength to maintain their oneness.

Power, he explains, isn't dominion over others but the drive of every living thing to realize itself. "Nothing in the world would happen without power; it's the life force. Love enables power."

## THE ELEMENTS OF EQUALITY

**ATTENTION.** Both partners are emotionally attuned to and supportive of each other. They listen to each other. And both feel invested in the relationship, responsible for attending to and maintaining the relationship itself.

**INFLUENCE.** Partners are responsive to each other's needs and each other's bids for attention, conversation, and connection. Each has the ability to engage and emotionally affect the other.

**ACCOMMODATION.** Although life may present short periods when one partner's needs take precedence, it occurs by mutual agreement; over the long haul, both partners influence the relationship and make decisions jointly.

**RESPECT.** Each partner has positive regard for the humanity of the other and sees the other as admirable, worthy of kindness in a considerate and collaborative relationship.

**SELFHOOD.** Each partner retains a viable self, capable of functioning without the relationship if necessary, able to be his or her own person with inviolable boundaries that reflect core values.

**STATUS.** Both partners enjoy the same freedom to directly define and assert what is important and to put forth what is the agenda of the relationship. Both feel entitled to have and express their needs and goals and bring their full self into the relationship.

**VULNERABILITY.** Each partner is willing to admit weakness, uncertainty, and mistakes.

**FAIRNESS.** In perception—determined by flexibility and responsiveness—and behavior, both partners feel that chores and responsibilities are divided in ways that support individual and collective well-being.

**REPAIR.** Conflicts may occur and negativity may escalate quickly, but partners make deliberate efforts to de-escalate such discussions and calm each other down by taking time-outs and apologizing for harshness. They follow up by replacing defensiveness with listening to the other's position.

**WELL-BEING.** Both partners foster the well-being of the other physically, emotionally, and financially.

# EDITORS' INTRODUCTION

Next, Brown and LaJambe discuss some of the common sources of conflict that can cause people in a relationship to experience a power imbalance and can lead to relationship dissatisfaction and dissolution in "Building Positive Relationships." They also discuss some key characteristics of violent relationships. We encourage you to take note of these common sources of conflict and also what constitutes intimate partner violence (IPV) so that you recognize warning signs if they ever occur in your relationships.

An important distinction when discussing relationship violence is between the four identified types of IPV: situational couple violence, coercive-controlling violence, violent resistance, and separation-instigated violence (Kelly & Johnson, 2008). **Situational couple violence** typically arises from a specific argument, frustration, or stressor that a couple experiences. Situational couple violence occurs infrequently in relationships, is often not severe enough to cause injury, and is generally initiated equally by men and women. **Coercive-controlling violence** refers to frequent and serious forms of violence and is typically (but not always) perpetrated by men against women. Brown and LaJambe introduce us to the power and control wheel, which characterizes coercive-controlling violent relationships, formerly referred to as patriarchal or intimate terrorism. **Violent resistance** can most easily be understood as self-defense—violence in response to violence, ironically for the purpose of ending the violence. Finally, **separation-instigated violence** is distinct in that it is instigated by a separation where there has been no prior history of relationship violence. The value in distinguishing different types of relationship violence lies in whether the type of IPV is rooted in power and control by a perpetrator over a victim. Coercive-controlling violence is the only type of violence that is characterized by power and control. The reading immediately following "Building Positive Relationships" by Frederick Brown and Cynthia LaJambe offers us testimony to the experience of coercive-controlling violence.

## PRIMERS

1.  What would you consider a warning sign that you're in an unhealthy relationship?
2.  If you've ever noticed a red flag or warning sign in a relationship, how did it come to your attention? How did you address it?

# Building Positive Relationships

*By Frederick Brown and Cynthia LaJambe*

[...]

There is a good chance that across our lifetime we may become involved in some sort of friendship, love relationship, or business relationship that goes bad. These may occur early as we are trying to develop intimate relationships or careers. Unless the issues are very clear, often there are subtle issues that have built up over time. The negative weight of them has strained the relationship to the point that it is difficult for a member to stay in it. Why? It is because one member now feels that the relationship has gone beyond their control. How this can happen will be explored in three destructive relationship forms: 1) *intentional deceit*; 2) *disruption*; *and 3) violence*. As these are described, let us be aware of who is trying to control what aspects of the relationship, what their objectives are, and what means are being used to gain control.

## A. INTENTIONAL DECEPTION

**Deception** is the act of deliberately misinforming or misleading someone into believing something that is just not true, a lie (Russow, 1986). According to "intentional deception theory" (Buller & Burgoon, 1996), a person can engage in intentional conscious or unconscious deception in a face-to-face relationship in three ways:

1. by *deliberately lying* or claiming that something is true that the lying person knows is false. An example would be a person "maxing out" their credit card account, and then claiming that their credit card had been stolen.

2. by *hiding* (not telling) *important information* from someone that causes them to believe something that is not true. An example would be someone selling a car that had been

in an accident and had frame damage, but telling the buyer that the car was in perfect condition and that they just wanted to buy a model.

3. by what is called "*skirting the issue.*" It goes this way. A skirt goes around a person's body to cover them, just as a skirt on a table covers the top and its legs. By not answering a question directly, or by changing the subject, the correct answer remains hidden. For example, consider the "nonanswer" action taken by a person during a job interview after they were asked about having any difficulties in their last job. Instead of a direct answer, the person responds by stating that they have had several jobs, but the current one they are interviewing for fits their talents much better than their former jobs.

This issue of intentional deceit is that one member of the relationship violates the unspoken terms of *openness* and *honesty* in a way that gains them a selfish advantage. Unfortunately, when the deception is uncovered, the advantage that the deceiver might have gained results in a *recency effect* that will make it very difficult to continue the expectation of *openness* and *honesty.* The expected relationship contract is broken.

## B. DIVISIVENESS (DI-VISS-IV-NESS)

**Divisiveness** in a relationship is one in which upset and conflict occur because of unfairness more often than peace and harmony with fairness. It may be the result of all parties in the relationship having a hard time relating to the others with respect, patience, and tolerance. Anyone in any relationship must accept the fact of life that, inevitably, all relationships have some degree of conflict. Conflict may arise simply from the fact that the needs of different persons are, well, different! Those challenges must be resolved like any others for the good of the relationship.

Investigations into the sources of divisiveness go back to the dawn of recorded history. This can be seen in the rise of various codes of conduct, and then systems of local and national laws, and eventually international treaties between countries. What all of these attempt to do is limit what people can do to each other in their relationships. According to psychologists Brett

| TABLE 12.2.1 **EIGHT SOURCES OF CONFLICT** |
| --- |
| Resources |
| Lifestyle |
| Perception |
| Goals |
| Pressure |
| Expected role |
| Values |
| Unpredictable policies |

Hart (2000) and Art Bell (2002), eight common sources of conflict exist among people, both in their personal and work lives. These are listed in the adjacent Table 12.2.1: competition for resources, differences in life and work styles, in perceptions, in goals, in pressure to perform, in expected roles, in values, and in unpredictable policies.

Brief descriptions of these conflicts are as follows.

1. *resources:* Conflicts in resources have to do with the limits that people have with their time, energy, finances, and available supplies. If any of these are lacking, then the relationship suffers. For examples, one person wants to spend money, but the other cannot because they don't have it; one person wants to take off a day to have fun, but the other cannot because they are required to work. Resentment can develop if an understanding of limits is not reached.

2. *life and work styles:* One person may be very organized, the other may be more casual. Toleration is needed for these two different perspectives.

3. *perceptions:* Differences from our cultural and educational experiences determine our viewpoints, like a sense of independence or interdependence, and what our expectations are for ourselves and for others.

4. *goals:* Striving for perfection versus doing things adequately. A level of mutual satisfaction needs to be reached so that all are comfortable with results.

5. *pressure:* Feeling driven by outside forces to perform versus being internally motivated by enjoyment.

6. *roles:* Who does what and whether is it clearly understood so that each person is able to do what they are expected to do without interference by someone else. This is true regardless of the type of relationship, be it a shared partnership, or supervisor and supervised, supplier and customer, or a team project.

7. *values:* What is seen as important, loyalty versus efficiency, creativity versus practicality, orderliness versus comfortableness.

8. *unpredictability:* Not knowing what to expect in a relationship can produce tension between people, whether personally or in a work situation.

In each of these situations, the differences have to be met with agreeable levels of acceptability. Otherwise, they will remain divisive and detract from the satisfaction that the relationship had been intended for originally.

## C. VIOLENCE

When **violence** enters into a relationship, the feelings of mutual *control* are out of control, because either or both partners in the

**Just a Thought**

If you discovered yourself in a divisive relationship, do you think that you now have enough information to help resolve it, either by fixing or by leaving the relationship?

relationship are trying to grab or maintain control or else prevent from being controlled by the other. This is as true in international situations as well as in personal ones. Words used in TV and newspaper reports, such as revolution, rebellion, mutiny, and coup tend to make us picture in our minds images of warfare and bloodshed. If it is bloodless, it becomes very newsworthy because violence apparently did not happen. In a personal relationship, the issue of control becomes a problem when one person feels no longer treated respectfully, fairly, and humanely. When a person cannot leave such a relationship, they may feel trapped and victimized. How a person feels trapped is because of some power they feel the other person has that they cannot overcome. This power can be expressed in a variety of ways, including threats of harm or actual harm itself. The threats or harm can be physical (including sexual), psychological, social, religious, economic, legal, and reproductive.

Unfortunately, probably the greatest frequency of violence is committed in personal relationships in which the victim of the violence feels somehow committed to the other. These include dating and domestic violence. The following several statistics, not all of them taken from the files of federal governmental agencies, have been listed in the Feminist.com Antiviolence Resource Guide (2014) and show how widespread dating, domestic violence, and rape have become: Every 90 seconds, somewhere in America, someone is sexually assaulted. One out of every five American women has been the victim of an attempted or completed rape in their lifetime. Most female victims are raped before the age of 25, and almost half of female victims are under the age of 18. In 2006, 78,000 children were reported as sexually abused, although the real number could be anywhere from 260,000–650,000 a year. Nearly two-thirds of women who reported being raped, physically assaulted, and/or stalked since age 18 were victimized by a non-stranger, that is, a current or former husband, cohabiting partner, boyfriend, or date. In high school, female students (11.8 percent) were significantly more likely than male students (4.5 percent) to have been forced to have sexual intercourse. The Campus Sexual Assault Study estimated that between 1 in 4 and 1 in 5 college women experience completed or attempted rape during their college years. The US Justice Department and FBI estimate that only 26 to 46 percent of rapes and sexual assaults are reported to law enforcement officials. *About 67.9 percent of rape victims are white; 11.9 percent are black; 14 percent are Hispanic, and 6 percent are of other races* (National Crime Victimization Survey, Department of Justice 2010).

There is much more to sexual violence than just the horrible incident, according to Feminist. com (2014):

> *"Sexual violence victims exhibit a variety of psychological symptoms that are similar to those of victims of other types of trauma, such as war and natural disaster (National Research Council 1996). A number of long-lasting symptoms and illnesses*

*have been associated with sexual victimization including chronic pelvic pain; premenstrualsyndrome; gastrointestinal disorders; and a variety of chronic pain disorders, including headache, back pain, and facial pain (Koss 1992). Between 4% and 30% of rape victims contract sexually transmitted diseases as a result of the victimization (Resnick 1997). The costs of intimate partner violence against women exceed an estimated $5.8 billion. These costs include nearly $4.1 billion in the direct costs of medical care and mental health care and nearly $1.8 billion in the indirect costs of lost productivity and present value of lifetime earnings."*

To summarize this topic: If you or someone you know has been sexually assaulted in any way, the attack needs to be reported to law authorities. A toll-free telephone number to call is 1-800-656-HOPE (4673), or you can go to the following website [https://www.rainn.org/get-elp/national-sexual-assault-hotline].

In addition to sexual violence is domestic violence, which can include sexual violence, but also much more. Although poor and black American populations statistically suffer most from domestic violence, it cuts across all levels of social status, cultures, professions, and income brackets. What domestic abusers have in common is power and control over their victims, maintained by threats of harm or actual violence, or by use of strategies or tactics. The relationship of these factors are diagrammed in Figure 12.2.1 in a "Power and Control Wheel" model (Duluth, 2015), showing power and control at the center. Around the center are the strategies used, with bullying, brutality, and violence to maintain the power and control over

the victims. About 85 percent of abused people are women, so for explanation, this diagram assumes the victim to be a woman and the abuser a man. The list of strategies or tactics comes from admissions of abusers themselves and also from women upon whom these tactics have been used.

Tactics used by abusers can be seen around the inside of the wheel. Beginning at top right, these include using:

1. *intimidation*, making the victim fearful for their safety, like showing a gun or knife, hitting the wall, breaking the victim's things or hurting their pets

Figure 12.2.1 Power and control wheel of domestic violence. Domestic Abuse Intervention Programs, "Power and Control Wheel," http://www.theduluth-model.org/pdf/PowerandControl.pdf.

2. *emotional abuse*, putting them down, using insulting and degrading labels

3. *isolation*, by preventing them having other relationships and contact, except with the abuser

4. *denying* their cruelty and harm to the victim, shifting *blame* to the victim as being the cause, and *minimizing* their victim as a person

5. *using victim's own children against them*, or threatening to have them taken away as unfit mothers

6. "*male privilege*" to make all decisions, as if the victim is incompetent or does not have the right to make decisions about their own life

7. *economic poverty* by controlling all money, possibility of a job, and access to all finances

8. *force or threats* like physical harm, or the abuser threatens to kill them self, or forces the victim into illegal activities to blackmail them.

Obviously, such violence is the furthest thing from a positive healthy relationship. No one ever needs to accept such behavior from another person. If you, or someone that you know is suffering from such a brutal situation, a toll-free phone number can be called for help. A safety alert is suggested for not trying to use a computer for contact: Computer use can be monitored and is impossible to completely clear. If you are afraid your Internet usage might be monitored, call the National Domestic Violence Hotline at 1-800-799-7233 or TTY 1-800-787-3224. Remember, these calls are free and will not be recorded or show up on any phone bill.

[...]

## REFERENCES

Bell, A. (2002). Six ways to resolve workplace conflicts. McLaren School of Business, University of San Francisco. Available on the World Wide Web at http://www.usfca.edu/fac-staff/bell/article15.html

Buller, D. B., & Burgoon, J. K. (1996). Interpersonal deception theory. *Communication Theory, 6* (3), 203–242.

Feminist.com (2014). Facts about violence: U.S. statistics/links to statistics. http://www.feminist.com/antiviolence/facts.html

Hart, B. (2000). Conflict in the workplace. Behavioral Consultants, P.C. Available on the World Wide Web at http://www.excelatlife.com/articles/conflict_at_work.htm

Russow, L. M. (1986). Deception: A philosophical perspective. In W. Mitchell & N. S. Thompson (Eds.), *Perspectives on human and non-human deceit.* Albany: SUNY Press, p. 47.

# EDITORS' INTRODUCTION

The warning signs or red flags that Brown and LaJambe alluded to, and that you identified in the primer, may seem so clear and obvious to an onlooker of someone else's relationship, but it can be more difficult to acknowledge them if they're happening to you. Violence and abuse are supposed to be the opposite of love and intimacy, right? Actually, in many coercive-controlling violent and/or abusive relationships, love and intimacy are still present amidst the fear and anticipation of the next violent episode. Victims trapped in an abusive relationship often share a common experience that Lenore Walker coined the cycle of violence in 1980. The cycle of violence includes three phases: (a) the tension-building phase, where there is a gradual escalation of tension that can include several minor arguments, emotional abuse, or the experience of "walking on eggshells," and can last anywhere from days, to months, to years; (b) the acute violence stage, in which a significant violent outburst happens; and finally, (c) the reconciliation/honeymoon phase, in which the abusive partner is remorseful, apologizes, and promises to never do it again. During this phase, the victim may have hope that the abuser will change, as the abuser is loving, calm, and attempts to atone for their actions. The honeymoon phase typically transitions quickly back into the tension-building phase, and the cycle continues (Figure 12.1).

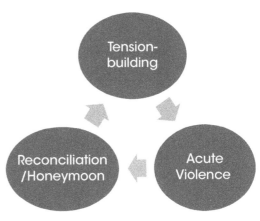

| Figure 12.1 Cycle of violence.

In "Break the Silence, Stop the Violence," Robin Stone addresses the racial disparity between Black and White women who experience IPV, specifically coercive-controlling violence. Some explanations for the racial disparities in IPV include poverty, discrimination, lack of social supports, and traditional gender ideologies, among others (Wright, 2010). That said, relationship violence does not discriminate. You'll recall some of the startling statistics that Brown and LaJambe reported. One statistic worth repeating is that 1 in 4 women and 1 in 10 men will experience sexual violence, physical violence and/or stalking by an intimate partner during their lifetime (National Coalition Against Domestic Violence, 2020), the impact of which includes being concerned for one's safety, PTSD symptoms, injury, or needing victim services (e.g., medical care, counseling, victim advocacy, etc.). Stone shares several women's stories of being abused, why they stayed, and how they ultimately left their violent relationships.

## PRIMERS

1. Why do you think a person would stay in an abusive relationship?
2. Can you think of any barriers that would prevent someone from leaving an abusive partner?

# Break the Silence, Stop the Violence

*By Robin D. Stone*

Rihanna and Chris Brown were our reality check. One in three African-American women *has experienced domestic violence, and nearly 30 percent of us are likely to be in physically abusive relationships at any given time. A recent survey found that 46 percent of people ages 12 to 19 said that Rihanna had provoked her alleged attack. ESSENCE investigates the epidemic of domestic violence in our community and talks to four women who found the courage to walk away.*

Stacey Bishop seemed to have it all: an attractive family, an impressive career as a social worker, a home in a posh Maryland suburb, a Mercedes and a Cadillac in the garage. But behind the facade she lived in terror. She says her husband of six years had threatened and shoved her, and had even hit one of her children. She slept in the living room, keeping her distance from her husband and the gun he stored in their bedroom. The next time she sees him will be in court for his trial for alleged assault in June. Stacey was one of the estimated 1.5 million women who are victims of domestic violence each year. Black women experience abuse at a rate 35 percent higher than that of White women, and women ages 20 to 24 are at greatest risk.

We've all heard the allegations of domestic violence from such celebrities as actress Robin Givens and spiritual leader Juanita Bynum. In both those cases the controversy died down. But the police photo of pop princess Rihanna, her once exquisite face rendered bruised and swollen, gave a new sense of urgency to this issue. When her boyfriend, teen heartthrob Chris Brown, pleaded not guilty to assault charges for her beating, we resumed the conversation with our sisterfriends, with women at the beauty parlor, online with strangers: "Why won't she press charges?" Even more disturbing was the question on the lips of many girls: "What did she do to make him do that to her?"

What isn't usually discussed is how widespread domestic violence is in our community. Is it any wonder? As many as half of domestic violence cases are not reported at all.

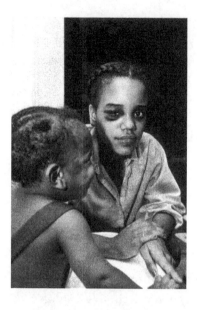

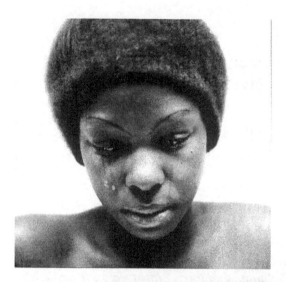

Images from *Living With the Enemy* (Aperture), photographer Donna Ferrate's controversial scenes of domestic violence victims, including (clockwise from above): Yvonne,* who called the police when her abuser attacked her baby; Janice,* who escaped violence then witnessed the murder of her friend, whose husband killed her; police arrest an abuser who was attacking his wife; Jenny* finds security in a shelter after her husband's threats to kill her; on May 25, 1993, Diane Hawkins, mother of six, and her 13-year-old daughter Katrina at their funerals. Hawkins had been disemboweled, her heart cut out; Katrina had been partially decapitated.

*Subjects' names changed.

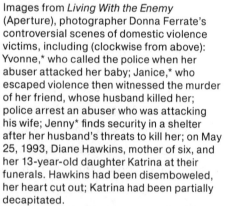

PHOTOGRAPHY BY DONNA FERRATO.ABUSE.AWARE.COM

And 90 percent of all family violence defendants are never prosecuted because victims later recant or dispute their initial report to the police. Which leads us back to another of those beauty parlor questions: "Why won't she just leave?"

There are many reasons why a woman stays. By the time a batterer punches, burns, cuts or shoots her, she's probably isolated from friends and family and feels dependent on him for money, validation, even love. She may be too embarrassed or ashamed to ask for help. She may have mistaken an often-quoted Bible passage—"You wives should be subordinate to your husbands ..." (1 Peter 3:1)—to mean wives should submit to abuse rather than accept nothing less than mutual reverence and respectful love. Or she may be afraid for her life and that of her children.

The truth is, we've been asking the wrong questions. "The issue is more appropriately framed: Why do men continue to use violence against women?" says Rhea V. Almeida, Ph.D., founder and director of the Institute for Family Services in Somerset, New Jersey. For us, one part of the answer may lie in the fact that Black men are often at the bottom of society's pecking order. Black women know the oppression they face, and we may not want them blamed for one more social ill. But we must also understand that nothing a woman does—no disagreement, no argument, no challenge—will ever justify her living in terror of losing her life.

It's a lesson that, because of distorted notions of power and manhood in our culture, some men still need to learn. And we need to enlist other men to help do the teaching.

13% of teen girls report being physically hurt in a relationship.

"The majority of men are not violent, but the majority of men are silent about the violence that men perpetrate against women," says Ted Bunch, cofounder of A Call to Men, a national organization aimed at ending violence against women. "When a man abuses a woman and gets away with it, other men benefit. It reinforces the entitlement and privilege that men have.

## TWISTED TEENAGE LOVE

Kalena Tate was just 14 when she caught the eye of 18-year-old Berthony Vilsaint while walking to school. "He was older," she says. "I thought I was grown." Like many teenagers, she was flattered by his attention. Five years later, she was desperately trying to escape it.

When Vilsaint, a slight, sweet-talking Haitian livery cab driver, scoured her New York City apartment complex looking for her the week after they met in 1992. Kalena took that as a compliment. Vilsaint became a fixture in the neighborhood. "He bought me things, called me all the time. He was like. 'What you doing? Come outside.' I thought that meant he liked me."

Her mother did not allow her to go with Vilsaint, but Kalena found ways to be with him, such as pretending to visit friends. In no time, he was telling her that he loved her. Kalena recalls early signs of trouble, like when he would show up across town where she happened to be. "I now know that he was following me," she says.

Kalena Tate, 31, put her batterer behind bars.

They dated for two years, and at 16, she became pregnant. After she moved into a rented room where he lived, Vilsaint began to isolate her, cutting off ties to her family and friends. "Early on he instilled fear in me," she says. She had never told her mother about this side of Vilsaint. Except for a girlfriend she sometimes saw, she felt alone. Eventually, he became her lifeline. "Being that I was pregnant. I felt like I started to love him," she says.

Once their daughter was born, Kalena says, he tightened his grip on her life—financially, by not allowing her to hold a job for long: emotionally, by demeaning her to his friends: socially, by eavesdropping on her phone calls; and eventually physically, by hitting her. "At one point, if I went to the bathroom, he would pick up my daughter and come in with me," she recalls.

One day when he sent her to the store, she called the police. "They let me pack a few things for me and my daughter," she says. She filed for an order of protection, but before it was served, Vilsaint, concealing two guns, tracked her down at the apartment where her two sisters lived and talked his way in. He fired through the bedroom door where Kalena was hiding, grazing her foot. She says he made her tie up her sisters before taking her and the baby. Over the next two days, he dragged her across New York City on a bleeding, bandaged foot as the police closed in and local TV news documented the pursuit. In April 1997, Vilsaint was arrested and charged with numerous crimes, including first-degree kidnapping and possession and use of a firearm. Convicted and sentenced to 26 years to life, he is eligible for parole in 2024. We found him on a prisoners' dating Web site, smiling, copping a strongman pose, and seeking "voluptuous women of all races."

Outwardly, Kalena says, all that's left of her ordeal is a scar on her right foot, but psychologically and emotionally, she is still healing. She praises her mother and sisters, her best friend and her attorney who supported her though two years of living incognito and in shelters until Vilsaint was off the streets. "I still have work to do," she says. "But I no longer allow anyone to instill any type of fear in me or make me feel afraid to be myself."

What does she tell young women like her daughter, now 14? "Love is not supposed to hurt." she says. "If he hits you or puts you down, that's not love. You're too precious. Love yourself first. Love yourself more. And be free."

## BRUISES, BLACK EYES AND BULLETS

When Bessie Love declined her boyfriend's offer to get married because he had beat her once, he beat her again, she says. She married him anyway, in 1976. She stayed 14 years. She had met the ambitious college-educated James Self in Houston, Texas, in 1974, and thought she had found the perfect catch: "He opened doors, pulled out the seat for you—a gentleman. We had a home, cars; we traveled. I didn't want for anything." Eventually, she says, he showed a different side.

Bessie Love, 58, is a survivor's advocate and speaker.

Bessie remembers him telling her that nobody else would want her because she couldn't bear children. In her statement to the Montgomery County, Texas, district attorney's office, she says he slid a bullet into his revolver, pointed it at her, and played Russian roulette. She also says he once urged her to kill herself because she was wasting air. Still, she stood by her man. "I thought he would eventually realize I was the best thing that happened to him."

Bessie tried to camouflage the bruises and black eyes. Yet it wasn't the beatings that led Bessie to consider leaving for good. It was her husband's words. They were in a honeymoon phase when they started arguing. "I said, 'I thought we were doing okay,'" Bessie recalls. "He said. 'All we've been doing is [having sex].' That shocked me to my core. I knew he didn't love me."

35% of female victims said they did not report the abuse to police because it was a private matter.

She started sneaking off to counseling sessions through the employee assistance program at her job. She packed an emergency escape bag and wrote letters to friends with messages to open them if something happened to her. The next time he hit her. March 4, 1990, was the last, she says.

Bessie took her escape bag and fled to a brother who agreed to take her in only if she promised to have no further contact with her husband. Bessie said yes and, for the first time in almost two decades, began to live a violence-free life.

Bessie did not consider legal action against her husband until a month later. In a statement to the district attorney's office, she describes how she and Self met with an accountant that April to resolve an IRS audit. After the meeting, according to the statement. Self claimed his car had been stolen and asked her to take him to file a report. Once in the car, he threatened her with a gun. She managed to escape and flag down another driver. Soon after, she filed a police report and got a restraining order. James Self was charged with aggravated assault, which was reduced in a plea bargain to a misdemeanor. He was fined $1,000 and put on probation for one year. Bessie divorced him the following year and started telling her story. (Attempts to contact James Self for this article were unsuccessful.)

'Bessie Love, 58, is a survivor's advocate and speaker.

"I realized it was his shame, not my shame." she says. "I use my voice to speak about the more important issue—survival—not the crime."

## HOW TO TALK TO OUR TEENS AND GIRLS ABOUT DATING ABUSE AND VIOLENCE

"The very first thing that any mother or caring adult in a girl's life can do is to let her know it is never ever acceptable for someone to abuse you physically, emotionally, mentally," says Joyce Roché, president and CEO of Girls Incorporated, an organization dedicated to empowering girls.

Girls need to know that if a partner hits, cuts, chokes, intimidates or belittles you, or tries to control when and where you come and go and with whom you talk, he is abusing you, and it needs to stop.

Here are a few ways to help teens understand what a healthy dating relationship looks like:

- Make sure she knows that nothing she does or says justifies her being abused. "There's no such thing as causing this to happen," Roché says. "Abuse is never called for in any kind of situation."

- Reinforce that she has the right to refuse sex, affection or attention at any time.

- Advise her to create a "safe space" from technology's reach. Let her know that constant calls, texts and messages are attempts to control her and are not okay.

- Encourage her to talk. "Foster communication beforehand," Roché says. "Talk about situations like Rihanna and Chris Brown. Use it as an opportunity to hear what she's thinking and to teach."

- Help her get assistance if she needs it by reaching out to: **Loveisrespect.org** provides such resources as a 24-hour national teen dating abuse help line; call 866-331-9474. **Girls Inc.**

(Girlsinc.org) is an empowerment organization for girls. Check out its girls' Bill of Rights at girlsinc.org/about/girls-bill-of-rights, or call 800-374-4475. —R.D.S.

This has been seen as a women's issue and a human rights issue, but if there's anybody who needs to accept responsibility, it's men."

Fraternities can help bring men into this conversation. Churches, too, can offer guidance and support. Unfortunately, because of misinterpretations of the Scriptures, not every house of worship will welcome dialogue that condemns men's domination of women. If that's the case, says the Reverend Aubra Love, founder of the Black Church and Domestic Violence Institute, seek support elsewhere. "You pray, then you prayerfully proceed in a way that will bring good into your life," she says.

She adds that it's critical that the battered tell their story, which is exactly what survivor Bessie Love chose to do: "Some think when you share something traumatic from your past that you're still holding on to that hurt. But when I use my voice, when I share my story, if I can help one person, then what I lived through for 14 years was not in vain."

Battered Black women who reported that they could rely on others for emotional and practical support were less likely to be abused again.

## SHE GRABBED HER KIDS AND FLED

For six years, as she endured the temper and fists of her boyfriend, Courtney Sanchez had friends and family standing by to help. But first, she had to help herself.

Courtney, an Austin, Texas, jazz and blues singer, fell hard and fast for Ishmael Ramirez in the spring of 1996. By the end of the summer, Courtney says he was beating her. The first time it happened, she says she told him they should take a break. Ramirez apologized, and she reconsidered. "I'd never seen him cry before," she says. "I said, 'Okay, as long as it doesn't happen again.' "

Half of the homeless women and children in the U.S. are fleeing domestic violence.

According to her application for a protective order to the district court of Williamson County, Texas, once, when she was five months pregnant, she woke up in the hospital after being beaten unconscious. Doctors told her the baby was not hurt. Courtney says the police took a report but she did not press charges. "I needed the baby to come into the world with a mother and a father," she says. The baby girl came, followed by a boy a year and a half later. On another trip to the hospital—battered and in pain—Courtney learned she had miscarried. This time she pressed charges. In May 2002, she went to SafePlace, a local women's shelter, with nothing more than her two children and her purse. She finally called her mother. In two weeks, she had legal aid, a restraining order, a petition for child support and a deposit for an apartment. "As soon as I started to help myself, people started to help me," she recalls. Ramirez ultimately pleaded guilty in two assault family-violence cases and was sentenced to two years probation. (Attempts to contact Ramirez were unsuccessful.)

Courtney Sanchez, 35, cofounded a charity to aid victims.

Courtney later left Ramirez and married opera singer Paul Sanchez, who is adopting her children. They founded Jonah Ministry (jonahministry.org), a faith-based charity to aid victims of violence. Their first project: securing a donation of five computers so clients can search for jobs and plan for the future.

## SLEEPING WITH THE ENEMY

Stacey Bishop, 38, entered counseling with her children.

By day, Stacey Bishop healed others as a clinical social worker. By night, she was overwhelmed and distressed as she struggled to keep the laundry fresh, the children fed and every crumb off the floor in her suburban Maryland home, as she said her husband, Michael Gooding, demanded.

"Being in my profession makes my going through this seem crazy," Stacey says. "Before him, I had my own house, my own car. I wasn't looking for somebody to take care of me. I went to private schools. I'm working on my Ph.D. You'd think I'd be okay. I'm proof that this can happen to anybody. He made me think I was something less than myself."

Stacey had already escaped an abusive relationship and thought she knew the signs. But the mother of three was charmed by Gooding, a soft-spoken electrician at the hospital where she worked, who invited her to his church for their first date. "It seemed as if he had a relationship with God," she says. "I thought. *What a wonderful man.*"

A few months later, Gooding proposed. They married August 24, 2002, blending their families. On their honeymoon cruise, she saw the signs.

"It started verbally," Stacey says. "He would say stuff like, 'You're so fat, you need to exercise.' Everything I did displeased him."

Like many women in abusive relationships, she says she weathered a storm of debasing words and escalating violence, and she believed Gooding each time he apologized or gave her gifts to make up. "In spite of my accomplishments, I felt as if this man could validate who I was," she says. "He would say things like 'Nobody's going to want you with all these kids.' I had made a vow before God. I had already divorced, and I worried about what people would think."

She convinced him to turn to their pastor for support. "In the church, the thing you hear is you get married for better or for worse," she says. An e-mail from a friend confirmed that sentiment. It told her to be a good Christian wife: pray and trust that the Lord would take care of her. Feeling as if she had little support from her church family, Stacey found outside counseling and went on her own.

As she described in her petition for a protective order in the district court of Maryland for Anne Arundel County, even when he hit one of her children in July 2007, Stacey says she did not call for help: "I did not want to see my children's father taken away in handcuffs." But she did get a protective order to force him out of the house soon after. Gooding left but violated the order not to contact her, she says, sometimes leaving as many as 30 voice messages a day.

Stacey divorced him in August 2008, six years and a set of twins after they met. She remarried in October 2008, to a widower who she says adores her.

But the court ordered visitation for her two youngest children, whom she shared with Gooding. The twins had grown afraid of their father, and often begged not to go. During a custody exchange in the parking lot of a Maryland shopping mall on January 10, 2009, an Anne Arundel County police report states, Gooding attacked Stacey when she tried to stop him from forcing their daughter into his car. The children were witnesses. "He choked Mommy." the girl told officers. Stacey suffered a strained neck.

Gooding, charged with second-degree assault, denied all allegations of abuse when contacted by Essence. He is set to stand trial in June.

Stacey and the children are in counseling now. Looking back, she can see how far she's come. "Nobody should have to suffer in silence, to live in torment," she says. "There are ways out. Maybe if I had gone to a shelter … If I had not worried about what people thought, I could have avoided what I experienced. My kids could be seeing their mother at a cemetery. At least I'm here to tell about it."

# EDITORS' INTRODUCTION

The fact is that physical and sexual violence don't just happen in established relationships. The National Sexual Violence Resource Center (NSVRC, 2010) reports that approximately 40% of women and 67% of men who have been sexually assaulted were assaulted by an acquaintance or stranger. The United States as a whole has endorsed a "rape culture," with a high prevalence of sexual assault and low reporting rate. Rape culture is a combination of rape-supportive attitudes, such as traditional gender roles, hostility toward women, and acceptance of violence (Johnson & Johnson, 2021). Until our collective culture breaks the silence, validates victims' experience, and holds perpetrators accountable for rape and sexual assault, we will continue to perpetuate the "silent epidemic."

In 2006, Tarana Burke founded the MeToo movement, and in 2017, the #metoo hashtag went viral and engaged the world in discussions about sexual violence. #Metoo has given voice to many victims of sexual assault, harassment, and discrimination who had been too afraid, ashamed, and traumatized to come forward. Many public figures have been called out for their actions, and while some would argue that justice has been and continues to be served, others would counter that we have a long way to go before we achieve gender equity and justice for the many victims of sexual assault. The takeaway message when it comes to sex (and most things, actually), is that only an enthusiastic "YES!" means "yes."

In the final reading of this chapter, Mandy Van Deven introduces us to modern feminism as it relates to empowerment, intersectionality, and individualism. In "Just Say Yes," Van Deven offers her critique and perspective on the book *Yes Means Yes: Visions of Female Sexual Power and A World Without Rape*, an anthology edited by Jessica Valenti and Jaclyn Friedman (2008). Van Deven discusses social justice and gender equality, bringing our discussion of power and violence full circle.

As you read, keep in mind the following primer questions for reflection. If you feel so inclined, take a few minutes and consider your responses to the following questions before you read, and then again after you've finished each reading.

## PRIMERS

1. Reflect a bit, and maybe talk with a partner or friend, about ways that you've noticed our society supporting rape culture.

2. Think back to some of the myths we discussed in Chapter 10. Do any of these myths about love perpetuate rape culture?

# Just Say Yes

*By Mandy Van Deven*

The brand of feminism that is generally referred to as the third wave popularized the use of two terms: intersectionality and individualism. The first term emerged largely from the writings of women of colour, working-class women and queers who were left out of a dominant feminist discourse that reflected the experience of women who were predominantly white, middle-class, and heterosexual. Theorists such as bell hooks and Gloria Anzaldua challenged the idea that woman is a homogenous category and complicated the concept by declaring the myriad ways in which their own female identity is coloured by race, class and sexual orientation. Soon, others followed suit, shifting the conversation to allow for a more fluid identity and toward a multi-issue approach to feminism.

At the same time, the oft-repeated second wave mantra, "The personal is political," began to shift. Instead of being used to identify collective women's issues, feminists began to use it to explain how individual acts can empower women as a group. Using this analysis, then, behaviour that might previously have been seen as a perpetuation of what hooks calls "white-supremacist capitalist patriarchy"—for example, wearing makeup or using sexuality for personal gain—could be considered tools of resistance. That is, so long as you had the right analysis.

There are some aspects of modern feminism where these philosophical shifts are now commonplace. We see intersectionality, for example, in the reproductive justice framework developed by organizations like SisterSong. The group published a reproductive justice paper that asserts an understanding that "the impact on women of colour of race, class and gender are not additive but integrative." This approach has now been adopted throughout women's health organizing. Conversely, the popularity of individualism can be seen in the attitude and demographic of *BUST* magazine and *Sex and the City*. Positioned side-by-side, one might wonder which of these ideologies is the real feminism. The answer is both, though we don't often see them overlap.

What did not exist until recently is a place where intersectionality and individualism intersect. One place they do is in Jessica Valenti and Jaclyn Friedman's *Yes Means Yes: Visions of Female Sexual Power and A World Without Rape*. The book is a collection of essays by American and Canadian writers and activists. The contributors to *Yes Means Yes* represent the many faces of feminism, albeit faces that tend to have prominence in the feminist blogosphere: Jill Filipovic and Cara Kulwicki from *Feministe*, LaToya Peterson from *Racialicious*, Kate Harding from *Shapely Prose*, and Samhita Mukhopadhyay from Valenti's own *Feministing*. This variety is necessary if, like Valenti and Freidman, you've set out to tackle the lofty goal of exploring "how creating a culture which values genuine female sexual pleasure can help stop rape, and how the cultures and systems that support rape in the U.S. rob us of our right to sexual power."

> These dichotomies still deny a woman sexual agency, and mens choices remain dichotomous, too, as the nice guy or the asshole.

To help the reader navigate such vast and complex waters, the anthology is set up in a style similar to the choose-your-own-adventure novels that you may have read as a child. It is a style that facilitates making connections between the issues and themes that emerge while reading. In the introduction, the editors lay out themes they believe are useful, but I've identified some themes of my own that help to place the book itself in a historical and political context.

One can't espouse something new without explaining what came before it, and many essays in *Yes Means Yes* recount the breakthroughs of previous feminist anti-violence work. So that's theme number one: Some things have stayed the same. We still live in a patriarchal world where men and women are socialized to conform to particular gender roles and to sexual scripts that define women as passive gatekeepers of their sexual purity and men as aggressive conquistadors seeking to rid a woman of her chastity.

The virgin/whore (or, for black women, mammy/Jezebel) complex is still in full effect. These dichotomies still deny a woman sexual agency, and men's choices remain dichotomous, too, as the nice guy or the asshole. Sex is still a commodity a woman owns, which increases in value the less it has been used—as opposed to an act that is performed. And men still attempt to buy this thing from women in exchange for their own commodities: safety, money, marriage.

Both the sexual objectification of women's bodies and the unattainable beauty standards women are faced with continue to be determined by male desire and to negatively affect women's self-image and sexuality. Women should learn to assert themselves, and men should learn to respect women. Rape is still a weapon of power and punishment for nonconformity, no still means no and blaming women for being raped is still wrong. While I am generalizing here, the book tackles these topics with more depth, providing current examples, including the former U.S. Bush administration's emphasis on abstinence and purity balls as ways for women to earn men's respect. And one of those entrenched ideas, actually, is theme number two: Language and communication are important.

The nature of language is that its meaning is constantly changing, while new terminology is always cropping up. The questions of how to define consent and what constitutes rape are answered over and over again in this book, though the answers provided are in no way uniform. From the vantage point of our previously mentioned sexual script, consent is the absence of no (except if you're a slut, which means you consent by default).

And yet, our thinking about rape is still complicated. As Lisa Jervis tells us in "An Old Enemy in a New Outfit," an August 2007 article in *Cosmopolitan* magazine, restyled "date rape" is nearly indistinguishable doppelganger "grey rape," except for its more covert penchant for blaming the victim. Since victim blaming seems to be a favourite pastime of anti-feminist politicians, journalists and judges, it seems that we need to start rewriting the script entirely and propagating new terms that clarify what seems to be confusing. The writers in this collection do just that.

Enthusiastic consent, also called enthusiastic participation, requires the presence of yes and decreases the possibility of misreading someone's body language or other cues during sex play. It situates women and men as agents of their own sexual desire and takes a lot of the guesswork out of the actual act of having sex. Most people want to have sex, and ideally they want to have good sex, but the sad truth is that sex isn't always good. One reason for this is that darned sexual script, so in "Queering Black Female Sexuality" Kimberly Springer says women should throw out the heterosexual model—you know, the one where women are plundered and men are plunderers—and reclaim their sexuality by following a queer one instead: "A queer black female heterosexuality isn't about being a freak in the bedroom, but about being a sexual person whose wants and needs are self-defined."

To stretch your conceptualization a little further, a handful of the authors advocate looking to BDSM or kink for guidance. In her contribution "A Love Letter from an Anti-rape Activist to her Feminist Sex Toy Store," Lee Jacob Riggs writes that "kink, in many ways, may be the most responsible form of sex because you have to talk about it. You have to articulate exactly what you do and do not want to happen before anything starts happening." It is in such essays that we see the influence of intersectionality.

Rape is painted as just one speck in the larger picture of gendered violence, a speck in which we see theme number three: Everything is connected. As the 27 essays in this important book underline, the backlash against the movement to end sexual violence takes many forms. Among them are attacks on abortion rights (control of a woman's body); immigration policy (border rapes); transphobia (complication of gender roles and sexual scripts); the prison-industrial complex (racist and classisi execution of justice); population control ( forced sterilization of women of colour); sex workers' rights (sexual assault of prostitutes by police officers); and

When a military interrogator at Abu Ghraib suggestively taunts a prisoner in order to procure information, she is enacting an institutionalized exploitation of femininity, as well as state-sanctioned racism and religious bias.

torture (femininity and female sexuality utilized as a military interrogation technique). And so, when a military interrogator at Abu Ghraib suggestively taunts a prisoner in order to procure information, she is enacting an institutionalized exploitation of femininity, as well as state sanctioned (even encouraged) racism and religious bias.

The trouble with intersectionality is that that it can make the problems seem insurmountable, and this may be one reason why the third wave is so fond of individualism. If we can boil activism down to the point where each person's singular actions add up to empowerment for the whole, then we might not feel so overwhelmed. And though it's difficult to know where to start, the fourth and final theme of the book is that, while it is multifaceted, change is attainable.

Sometimes, identifying a large problem can be accompanied by a lot of positing about what the world *should look like*; figuring out a solution to interlocking oppressions can seem impossible. The good news is that there is no single right answer and there are just two options: You can try to change what already exists, or you can create an alternative.

In the category of changing what exists, a classic community-organizing strategy many of the authors suggest is coalition-building between movements. Rape crisis advocates must team up with activists for non-punitive prison reform and public defenders to create strategies for rapists to be held accountable and then rehabilitated in a justice framework. Comprehensive sex education programs must link with transgendered rights and sexual-violence-prevention groups to strategize about ways to dismantle gender roles and sexual scripts, re-envision consent and foster female sexual autonomy. We have to find the commonalities among us and work together despite our disagreements, instead of continually butting heads in a competition-heavy non-profit industrialized complex.

In creating an alternative to our present system, we must recognize that women are the experts in their own experience. And we must ask ourselves what it is that we will need to heal—individually and collectively—from past sexual violence. Whether it is through critical political analysis, awareness of our place in intergenerational violence, mutual aid groups, social justice work, music and art, or selfcare to address secondary trauma, we can create spaces that facilitate healing for ourselves and for others.

Change is never instantaneous; it is always a process. *Yes Means Yes* is an outgrowth of the dynamic work that came before it, and we are the ones who will determine what comes next.

# END-OF-CHAPTER REFLECTIONS

This chapter is heavy. Our goal throughout this book has been to teach you the skills you need to establish and maintain healthy relationships, but the truth is that not all relationships are healthy. We hope that you never find yourself in an unhealthy or abusive relationship, but if you do, hopefully you'll notice some of the warning signs and do what you need to do to keep yourself safe and healthy. We close with the antithesis to the power and control wheel: the equality wheel. Above all else, knowing what you want in a relationship is an essential complement to knowing what you don't want. Many of the relationships characteristics that make up the equality wheel should seem familiar; you've already learned about them in

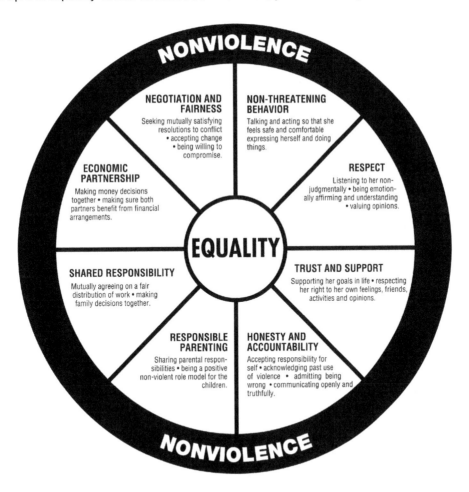

| Figure 12.2  The equality wheel (Domestic Abuse Intervention Programs, 2017).

other parts of this anthology: negotiation and fairness, nonthreatening behavior (making your partner feel safe), mutual respect, trust and support, honesty and accountability, responsible parenting, shared household responsibilities, and an economic partnership (Domestic Abuse Intervention Programs, 2017). We find that while it's helpful to know what doesn't work, and what is unhealthy in a relationship, it's even more important to know what to strive for and what to notice in a healthy and balanced partnership. One thing to take note of when engaging with the equality wheel is that many of the characteristic descriptions refer to "her," implying that women are the only victims of intimate partner violence. We know that the majority of intimate partner violence survivors are women; however, we need to remind ourselves that violence affects all genders, can and does occur in same-sex relationships, and is sometimes perpetrated by women against men.

We asked you in Chapter 10 to reflect on your most valued qualities in a potential partner, values that must be shared in a relationship, and your deal breakers. Look back on what you reflected on and revise your list based on what you've learned in this chapter. How are they similar? How are they different?

## REFERENCES

Domestic Abuse Intervention Programs. (2017). *The equality wheel.* https://www.theduluthmodel.org/

Kelly, J. B., & Johnson, M. P. (2008). Differentiation among types of intimate partner violence: Research update and implications for interventions. *Family Court Review, 46*(3), 476–499. https://doi.org/10.1111/j.1744-1617.2008.00215.x

Keltner, D. (2007, December 1). The power paradox. *Greater Good Magazine.* https://greatergood.berkeley.edu/article/item/power_paradox

Johnson, N. L., & Johnson, D. M. (2021). An empirical exploration into the measurement of rape culture. *Journal of Interpersonal Violence, 36*(1–2). NP70–NP95. https://doi.org/10.1177%2F0886260517732347

Marano, H. E. (2014). Love and power. *Psychology Today 47*(1). 54.

National Coalition Against Domestic Violence. (2020). *Domestic violence.* https://assets.speakcdn.com/assets/2497/domestic_violence-2020080709350855.pdf?1596811079991.

National Sexual Violence Resource Center. (2010). *NISVS 2010 summary report—Sexual assault by a perpetrator.* https://www.nsvrc.org/statistics.

Valenti, J., & Friedman, J. (Eds.). (2008). *Yes means yes: Visions of female sexual power and a world without rape.* Perseus.

Walker, L. E. (1980). *The battered woman.* Harper & Row.

Wright, E. M. (2010). *Neighborhoods and intimate partner violence.* LFB Scholarly.

# RECOMMENDATIONS FOR FURTHER READING

Kahane, A. (2010). *Power and love: A theory and practice of social change.* Berrett-Koehler.

Stiener, L. M. (2014, September 12). He held a gun to my head. I loved him. *The Washington Post.* https://www .washingtonpost.com/opinions/he-held-a-gun-to-my-head-i-loved-him/2014/09/12/31fb5720-39c3-11e4-8601-97ba88884ffd_story.html

## CREDIT

# Chapter 13

# Breakups

## EDITORS' INTRODUCTION

Throughout the text so far, our primary focus has been on building relationship skills and engaging with them in the process of developing a healthy intimate relationship. We continue this theme of building relationship skills, only this time for the purpose of ending an intimate relationship well—for both partners. In the same way good relationships do not "just happen," good breakups do not "just happen."

Some of you may be surprised at the idea of a good breakup and wonder, "What is a good breakup?" Before we explore what constitutes a good breakup, it may be helpful to know what it is not.

- A good breakup is not painless. Breaking up hurts and the pain caused by the broken attachment *is real*. Mental health professionals have found that the pain associated with social rejection and the pain caused by physical injury register in the same part of the brain and that acetaminophen can help both. "We have shown for the first time that acetaminophen, an over-the-counter medication commonly used to reduce physical pain, also reduces the pain of social rejection, at both neural and behavioral levels" (Dewall et al., 2010, p. 936). Always use as directed.

- A good breakup does not require a villain. Neither partner has to be "bad" (unless a partner is abusive). Sometimes people are not a good match despite the best personality traits, communication skills, commitment, and effort. In the United States, we have been socialized to think that if it doesn't work out there must be a fatal flaw in our partner or ourselves—not true. Furthermore, if children are involved, the villain schema can be particularly damaging.

- A good breakup is not easy; it requires self-control and a willingness to engage in difficult conversations. Many of the communication skills we have explored in prior chapters will come in handy as you navigate the emotionally taxing conversations and practical exchanges (i.e., returning personal items, moving out, talking to family and friends) that occur as you navigate disentangling from your former partner.

- A good breakup is not vague or ambiguous; it has a clear ending. Avoiding a direct breaking up conversation can seem like a good plan. However, stringing people along under the guise that you don't want to hurt them can become more hurtful. It is far better to end a relationship so both partners can move on with their lives.

Let's continue our exploration of what makes a good breakup with two readings about breaking up in the digital age. The first article, "The Endless Breakup" by Lisa Phillips, features a number of ways technology can get in the way of a good breakup (e.g., ghosting, orbiting, breadcrumbing, submarining) by perpetuating a relationship that is really going nowhere. Indirect communication modes like texting, social media, and email introduce ambiguity into the relationship by allowing partners to avoid clear communication—especially when the relationship is one-sided or one partner wishes to end it.

As you read, keep in mind the following primer questions for reflection. If you feel so inclined, take a few minutes and consider your responses to the following questions before you read, and then again after you've finished each reading.

## PRIMERS

1. How has technology (e.g., texting, social media) played a part in your breakups?

2. Have you ever ghosted, orbited, bread-crumbed, or submarined a former partner? Has it ever happened to you? How did it feel?

# The Endless Breakup

*By Lisa A. Phillips*

From ghosting to orbiting and submarining, technology keeps elaborating new ways for people to avoid the emotional labor of breakups. But that only keeps them stuck in anxiety and self-doubt.

"I want someone i can talk to, create art with, and bounce ideas off," Alice, an active member of the New Orleans arts community, told a friend one day. "I want us to be each other's critic and support. I want somebody I love to dance with, someone I love to touch and be around." "That's a tall order," the friend replied.

Within days, at a meeting about a new theater project, Alice was introduced to Jonah, who had just moved to town and was looking to join the arts scene. That very night, she took him to the closing party of a film festival, the first event of many they attended together. Not long out of a rough divorce, Jonah feared he would fall into a recent pattern of getting quickly obsessed, then putting up walls. "This doesn't seem to be happening with you," he confided.

Months later, a potential pregnancy prompted Alice to announce that if it were true, she would have the baby: At 40, she felt it might be her only chance. A pregnancy test proved negative, and when, the next morning, she reached for Jonah, he turned decisively away. Long, wrought emails followed. He wanted to cut the intensity without cutting her out but didn't know how. Then they literally danced into each other at Mardi Gras and were a couple again by morning. But she always felt that he held her off. They broke up again, but he kept reaching out to her online, for advice, for perspective. She felt she was the most important woman in his life.

The gravitational pull of the relationship moved to Alice's Facebook feed. Jonah tagged her on Game of Thrones updates; he shared articles about theater and social justice and others that tapped private jokes. He "made me feel that everything was all right, that he still needed me," she recalls. When she tried to break off contact, he boosted the bytes of affection. She curated her own online presence around him. "Everything I posted, I thought, What would he think of this?" she says. "A picture of me looking fabulous, climbing a mountain, on some adventure." She wanted him to see her moving on—the one thing she wasn't doing.

Alice and Jonah were lovers for just a few months, but the long half-life of digital attention from a distance—"orbiting," in today's parlance—kept her hanging onto the hope of rekindling the romance for four years. She finally blocked him to purge him from her psyche and begin the search for a more palpable relationship.

> A generation pushing to banish ambiguity from sexual relations clings to it in romantic relationships, even when it begets paralyzing self-doubt

Alice is scarcely unique. Increasingly, men and women find themselves stuck in a virtual spiderweb of contact, connected by keystroke, with exes lingering electronically, not merely visible through intertwined networks of friends but monitoring their online presence, sending off pale signals through likes and tags on social media posts—but not engaging directly. In this newest iteration of interest, rejection is both more continuous and more amorphous, difficult to define, difficult to get beyond.

Because contact takes place on an electronic landscape where communication demands little investment of effort, gauging a might-be-partner's true level of interest is now a nerve-wracking enterprise from start to finish, fueling soaring levels of anxiety. Reports from the clinic as well as the street leave little doubt that ambiguity is the new norm of relationships. How can a generation pushing to banish ambiguity from sexual relations cling to it in romantic relationships, even when it begets paralyzing rumination and self-doubt?

## THE END IS A BEGINNING

Endings matter. They shape our memory of the entire experience and even determine whether we can think about the experience, whether we find it pleasant enough to mentally revisit for any reason. Nobelist Daniel Kahneman has spent a lifetime exploring the quirks of human judgment. He's found that memories of experiences are disproportionately colored by how they felt at the end. His peak-end rule establishes that the way an experience ends dictates what we take away from the entire thing.

Breakups are by nature emotionally difficult, but a neatly wrapped up breakup—how two people communicate, how they act as they disentangle—doesn't just make a contribution to happiness, it allows exes to grow and move on toward the goal of finding lasting love and emotional fulfillment. If dating is essentially a series of experiments to find a good partner, a good ending makes it pleasurable enough to cognitively appraise the experience and learn from it. To make positive meaning from loss, the breakup itself is as important as the best times a couple shared.

There's hard biological evidence that breakups present an opportunity for growth. Rejection ricochets through a number of neural systems, and at the same time that it stirs the emotional chaos of pain and loss and longing—resembling addiction—it also turns on higher-order brain networks that facilitate learning. The activity prepares people to adapt to the loss.

Anthropologist Helen Fisher and colleagues conducted a pilot brain-imaging study of men and women who had so recently experienced rejection that the sting of unrequited love could be switched on by seeing a photograph of their rejector. In the wake of getting dumped, the research shows, people experience increased activity in the forebrain area associated with processing gains and losses—an indication the rejected lover is trying to figure out what went wrong, likely evaluating the partner choice made. It's not surprising such a process is deeply embedded in the brain. Rejection, Fisher observes, is a common, even inevitable experience in the search for a suitable mate; the ability to learn from it has direct value for our ability to survive and reproduce.

Deep difficulty is a great teacher if at some point it can be seen as a learning experience. In a study that examined hundreds of personal stories about the end of relationships, Stanford University postdoctoral fellow Lauren Howe, working with psychology professor Carol Dweck, identified a common redemption narrative. Among the respondents who suffered the least emotional damage from a breakup were those who viewed the split as a chance for self-improvement.

In some cases, the breakup helped them accept that they couldn't control what their partner did, or it taught them how to be forgiving. "By seeing breakups as opportunities, people can harness them for self-improvement," says Howe. If you learn something new about your priorities and values in a relationship, you can use the experience to move on to a brighter romantic future, she explains.

> Rejection ricochets through a number of neural systems, and as it stirs the emotional chaos of loss and longing, it also turns on networks that facilitate learning.

## THE UNENDING DIGITAL DUMP

Relationship dissolution has always been an anxiety-provoking process. The partner pulling away is anxious about making the right decision, navigating what psychologist Roy F. Baumeister calls the moral dilemma of the rejector—having to decide between hurting another person and staying in the relationship, which would entail pretending to feel something one doesn't. Is the relationship too bad to stay in or too good to leave? Is there something better out there? There is no guilt-free option. Only now, thanks to technology, there's the constant sense that something better maybe out there.

People are far more reluctant to share bad news than good news—what psychologists know as the "mum effect." And with another nod to technology, the digital era is constantly elaborating new ways for rejectors to avoid the emotional labor of a definitive breakup.

Electronic rejections can be unstintingly pithy, delivered in a one-line text message. They can also, gradually and agonizingly, be inferred through silence, in a phenomenon known as "ghosting": You figure out the relationship is over because your partner doesn't answer your texts, calls, and Snapchats for two weeks. "Silence is the new no, and I really hate that people don't have the courage or integrity to say no," observes Andrew, 61, recalling his relationship with a younger man who suddenly stopped responding to messages.

If ghosting is the inevitable price to pay for the ease of digital communication and online dating, its targets still struggle to accept it, says Leah LeFebvre, a University of Alabama communications professor. They may play it cool, she finds, but ghosting changes them. It makes them more cautious about reaching out to explore new possibilities. "They become less invested in communicating with potential partners and starting relationships; they become guarded, careful, and scared to be truthful to others."

Adding to the torment of ghosting are all the ways an ex can continue to haunt. Being orbited—a photo liked, a tweet favorited—may offer the impression that an ex is still paying attention, still emotionally attached, but that feeling can quickly give way to wishing things were different. "We all want to feel seen and heard," says Los Angeles psychologist Jennifer Taitz, author of *How to Be Single and Happy: Science Based Strategies for Keeping Your Sanity While Looking for a Soul Mate*. "We all want to feel that we matter. Orbiting is a tiny dose of feeling that way." In the long term, an insufficient one.

The emotional cost of watching a former partner through social media is high, Taitz observes. It's scarcely mitigated by breadcrumbing, an active if frustratingly minor sign of interest, such as an occasional Snapchat message or text. Inevitably it leads to sadness. People also struggle with feelings of invalidation. If they still long for their partner, seeing a photo of the person having a great time without them may make them feel they no longer matter. "Keeping up with someone can very easily keep you ruminating, obsessing, and feeling regret," says Taitz.

## A CHANGED LANDSCAPE OF LOVE

Relationships today play out on a radically new landscape of love. Electronic contact is cheap; it requires little effort. Emojis can even talk for you, if you wish. Tapping a heart takes only a split second on a free app. Technology has not only lowered the personal investment required for communication, it has vastly extended the reach of communication. People have more connections, but those connections are very thin. Yet connections live on electronically long after they evaporate in the flesh.

| Figure 13.1.1

## How to do a relationship exit interview—and why you should.

The search for human connection is always a trial-and-error process. That doesn't make breaking up easy to do. But it can be done in ways that preserve the dignity of both partners, prepare both for their next relationship, and mitigate the pain of loss with understanding. Two people who once cared for each other owe each other—and themselves—an honest and kind explanation of what became unsatisfying. "The greatest problem people have in breakups is lack of closure—the need to fully understand what happened," says psychologist Barry Lubetkin. That frees them to move on and grow. Simply disappearing may look like the easy way out. but it corrodes self-respect. A good exit talk takes both a degree of maturity and some planning.

### THINK AHEAD

Before initiating a conversation, deeply reflect on why you want to break up. Does your partner have habits or values that are inconsistent with your own? Think carefully how you will express the unresolvable problems in the relationship.

## BE BRAVE

From start to finish, intimacy is a risky business. There's always the possibility that the person you're getting closer to won't return the feeling or that you'll have a change of heart. Don't expect the conversation to be easy. But it will bring relief.

## PLAN AHEAD

Set a reasonable time and place to meet face to face. Having a breakup interview in a public setting helps individuals manage their emotions, says Lubetkin. If possible, ask your partner's friends to intercede to make sure your partner comes to the meeting and has support afterward.

## ENGAGE WITH EMPATHY

Empathy—the ability to understand someone else's feelings—is essential whether you're saying or hearing that the relationship can't continue. Being mindful of the partner's humanity helps the person take in what is always heard as something deeply wrong with oneself that caused the other to stop loving: "I know this is not what you want to hear." "Maybe you've been feeling the same weakening of our relationship: we don't have the same warmth." "I want both of us to have the chance to find the closeness we no longer share."

## GRANT THE GOOD

Let the other person know all the things you've respected and admired. Then point out that while those things remain true, the feelings you once had have come apart.

## EXPLAIN WHY

Be honest, calm, and compassionate as you explain your view of what no longer works for you—"I'm not ready to make a long-term commitment." "Something happened that I can't get out of my mind"—and mention any efforts you've made to get your partner to modify bothersome behavior. Listen carefully when it's your partner's turn to speak.

## AVOID PUT-DOWNS

Breakup talks do not benefit from all-encompassing judgments, either of the person you're leaving or of yourself. They hurt, and they stir defensiveness, prolonging discussion. Don't resort to "I'm not a good person. It's all my fault." If there's someone else in your life, say so.

## EVEN CASUAL RELATIONSHIPS HAVE STRINGS

If you've been friends with benefits, remember the friends part. There is some kind of mutual regard and attachment.

### ASK FOR FEEDBACK

Exit interviews are most valuable when they provide information about what you could do better. Ask how your behavior and attitude contributed to the ruin of the relationship, Lubetkin urges. "Was I too demanding? Too clingy? Too distant?"

### SHOW GENEROSITY OF SPIRIT

Once you've discussed what wasn't working for you and why, "end with a wish or a ritual, something that says, 'I release you to the world with love and light. I hope you find somebody who's good for you,'" advises psychologist Alexandra Solomon.

### IF YOU CAN'T GET THE FULL STORY, WRITE IT.

If a breakup convo doesn't go well or happen at all, you don't have to struggle with feeling worthless and humiliated. You can work through what happened on your own. Recount the breakup story in writing, including the failure to get an explanation—a sign the other lacks emotional maturity and that you need someone who can talk through hard things with you.

### DISCONNECT

Unfriend and block each other on social media and take each other's contact information out of your phones. It's not mean. It's enforcing a healthy boundary to permit healing.

---

Social networks and dating apps open worlds of possible partners. The upshot is that, by its very nature, by creating the sense of options—and especially the illusion that the perfect partner is one click away—digital romance undermines commitment and fosters ambiguity in relationships.

There are no longer clear signals of interest. With cheapened communication, technology itself makes discrimination of interest difficult. Rejectors who feel morally ambivalent about letting a partner go have the means at their fingertips to string along the partner with a two-word text reply or an emoji, while the partner is left to decoding every micro-move and upturned thumb. A prepackaged flirt message, available on most dating apps, can be sent to hundreds. "The goal is to put out feelers to see if someone else is interested without having to fully lay one's own interest on the table," says Carin Perilloux, a psychology professor at Southwestern University. "That way, if we're rejected, it won't be as costly since we can plausibly deny we were showing interest in the first place."

| Figure 13.1.2

There's much to be said for expanded options in life. Having choices is critical to well-being and personal freedom. But as psychologist Barry Schwartz has famously enunciated in *The Paradox of Choice: Why More Is Less*, people have trouble deciding when faced with too many choices. They end up less satisfied. For relationships to work, partners have to commit to each other, an act that requires giving up options. It's also the antidote to ambiguity. Social media serve as a constant reminder of all the partner options out there, ready for exploration the second a conversation sours. And the web of interconnection through social media enables people to monitor former partners even if they don't set out to.

As a result, everyone's on a back burner, hovering on some link in cyberspace, ready to be reactivated with a click. Nicole, 31, thought she was done with her on-again, off-again casual romance with Howard. When she last saw him, she wanted to let him know their sexual relationship was over, but he unexpectedly brought along another woman, "the person he said he wanted to spend his life with." Nicole broke off all contact with him.

Four years later, Howard, newly single, popped up via Hinge, a dating app linked to networks of Facebook friends, by liking a photo she posted—a digital move known as submarining, when someone out of contact for a long time suddenly resurfaces. She decided to see what would happen. The old chemistry was there. But rehashing the past proved upsetting all over again, and Nicole wondered why she'd let him back into her life. "It wasn't like he broke my heart, but still I'm feeling the weight of it."

## AMBIGUITY IS EVERYWHERE

Ambiguity is not just an unpleasant feature of breakups. It suffuses modern relationships from beginning to end. "Ambiguity is pervasive," says Scott Stanley, a professor of psychology at the University of Colorado who researches commitment in romantic relationships. "It's at every stage of mate seeking. People wonder, Are we in a relationship? Is this a date or just a hookup? Do we have a future?"

As a result, it's easier than ever to be in an asymmetrical relationship, where one partner is more interested in maintaining the relationship than the other. A less committed partner has more incentive and more power to keep things ambiguous—the very heart of what makes people so distressed. Despite having less to lose if a relationship folds, less committed partners don't necessarily want the relationship to end immediately. If they avoid defining what's happening, they can string the more invested partner along as long as they want, prolonging ambiguity.

A rejector who feels morally ambivalent about letting a partner go has the means to string along the person, left to decode every micro-move and emoji.

Pushing for clarity in a relationship potentially leads to conflict about the status of the relationship—which may blow the whole thing up and force the more committed partner to leave. "The current conditions are hardest on people who are seriously seeking a partner," Stanley says. "They're going to have a hard time getting a clear read on the potential for a future."

By its nature, electronic communication does not favor getting a clear read on relationships. And it often replaces interaction that could. Because so much relationship building now takes place through texting and interacting via social media, observes psychologist Barry Lubetkin, founder of the Institute for Behavior Therapy in New York City, people lose out on important social cues that would otherwise let them know exactly where they stand with a partner. Body language, eye contact, facial expressions, pauses, sounds of sarcasm: Is the other person leaning toward you or away—or checking out other attractive people on an iPhone?

"Cues such as these are crucial in understanding a person's interest in relating lovingly to a partner," says Lubetkin. "None of this can be accomplished through texting." The resulting impersonality, he notes, encourages a rejector to take the easy, no-feedback way out when the relationship breaks down.

Previous generations faced far less ambiguity, because the culture scaffolded relationships more. Dating took place largely in the context of looking for a mate to settle down with, and it roughly progressed in stages from casual to serious. There were road signs and markers of partner interest all along the way, because decisions to move forward had to be made at every point. You dated different people, you became exclusive when you found someone special, and, if all went well, you got engaged, then married, perhaps with a stage of living together beforehand. The same framework made it possible to talk about what was happening if moving from one stage to another didn't seem possible or desirable.

Most people still want to find a loving partner, but marriage is no longer the majority experience; and those who do marry are older than ever: The average age of first marriage is now 29.8 for men and 27.8 for women, according to the U.S. Census Bureau. One effect of what Stanley calls The Big Delay is that people are having consequential relationships in a "zone of ambiguity"—without the assumption they'll lead anywhere. All that relationship practice does not make perfect.

In most areas of human endeavor, experience is an advantage. But a long history of romantic partnerships doesn't necessarily make people better at relationships. In fact, research Stanley has conducted with University of Denver colleague Galena K. Rhoades shows that people with more sexual encounters or more experience living with a partner are less likely to have quality marriages later on. One reason is that they are especially aware of alternatives in a way that makes it harder for them to dive all the way into a relationship.

> "People get scared about the hurt they're going to cause by breaking up with someone. But people are hurt most when they don't understand."

There is a group of people, generally under age 25, who actually seek ambiguity because they do not feel ready to settle down; the general delaying of adulthood, to say nothing of the widespread burden of student debt, has contributed to their ranks. Stanley calls them Determined Delayers. Their attitude can be summed up as She'll (or He'll) do for now, and moving in together is not a reliable signal of commitment. The ambiguity creates few problems if both enter, maintain, and end the relationship with the same attitude—and with mutual appreciation for its having lived out its purpose.

There are others, says Stanley, who have deeper reasons for preferring ambiguity, reasons that may drive behavior from below the level of conscious awareness. The decades-long run of family instability may have produced a generation among whom many think that ambiguity offers protection against hurt and loss. At the same time, he sees some evidence that family instability has generated a greater number of people than ever with a skittish attachment style. The anxiously attached may be especially reluctant to press for clarity of commitment, even if they want it.

That doesn't mean uncertainty hurts any less. Both seekers and delayers inhabit the same mating markets. Seekers face a hard time getting a clear read on the potential with some people, says Stanley. And any relationship between a seeker and a delayer is asymmetrical from the start: Only one of them may benefit from ambiguity. The other typically gets burned by investing emotionally before having figured out exactly how invested the other is.

A growing body of research shows that uncertainty can lower wellbeing when a relationship really matters to a person. Among many other things, strong relationships provide self-validation, contribute to self-enhancement and personal growth, and deliver support. Ambiguous relationships breed uncertainty and anxiety. "Once people want things to be clearer," Stanley says, "they will not do well with uncertainty."

## THE SOFT BREAKUP HITS HARD

The weakening of relationship scaffolding has taken down whatever social scripts existed for talking about breaking up. If the possibility of a shared future isn't on the table in the first place, it's hard to discuss where a relationship is going. With fewer shared assumptions about the goals of dating and sex, individuals have to be far more skillful at communication in relationships, especially when breaking up. "These are high-skill moments," says Stanley, "and most people don't have those skills."

| Figure 13.1.3

Instead, people resort to what Stanley calls the "soft breakup," leaving with much unsaid about the real reason for the split and how final it truly is. That silence allows the partner who wants the relationship to continue room for hope that things will change. The withdrawing partner may be more certain that the relationship is over, but doesn't say so, often out of a desire to avoid causing harm, or the messiness of conflict.

"The nature of anxiety is not knowing," says Alexandra Solomon, a psychology professor at Northwestern University and the author of *Loving Bravely: 20 Lessons of Self-Discovery to Help You Get the Love You Want.* "It's not knowing what's next. Are we in or are we out? Everyone's walking on eggshells. Everyone feels like they're doing it wrong."

When people get dumped without learning why, explains Solomon, they are at risk of interpreting the rejection as a reflection on who they really are, at risk of thinking: They must have done that to me because of the kind of person I am. That person walked away with no explanation because I am weak/ugly/worthless.

Absent a clear explanation, they are subject to seeing rejection as the diagnostic sign of something deeply negative about them. This, Stanford's Howe finds, is how people acquire the "heavy baggage" that they carry into future relationships. Haunted by a rejection, they fear recurrence and do everything to avoid it. They "put up walls" to protect themselves.

Everyone knows that rejection delivers an immediate sting. But Howe could detect enduring pain five years later among those who responded to rejection by questioning their true self. The more material people have for their breakup survival/redemption/I-learned-from-something-difficult, the better, Howe concludes. "In making sense of a breakup, we start to tell ourselves stories about the relationship and our role in its end. These stories are powerful and can influence both how we feel about ourselves—whether we feel ashamed or empowered—and how we feel about our future."

Even casual pairings suffer from ambiguity, and hazy endings can be just as anxiety-inducing as in more serious relationships. In interviews with college students, Kendra Knight, a professor of communication studies at DePaul University in Chicago, found that partners in "friends with benefits" pairings often avoid discussing what they want from each other. Talking honestly about emotions or conflict is part of what defines a real relationship—exactly what participants feel they're not supposed to be having.

Yet, the habit of reticence in casual relationships deters development of the ability to express oneself in more prized relationships. "It's an acquired skill," says Knight. "If you can't talk about being sex buddies," you can't expect to communicate about the difficulties even good relationships face.

In a world marked by declining empathy, documented especially among the young, text breakups happen because they're easier. If you can't recognize the humanity of others, you can't act with respect for their feelings.

The cost is blindness to the brutality of sparse information. "The [rejectees] have questions: Am I good enough? Why don't they want to be with me anymore?" says D. Scott Sibley, a professor of psychology at Northern Illinois University. "People get scared about facing the hurt they're going to cause by breaking up with someone. But people are hurt most when they don't understand."

Empathy and openness, then, are the essence of The Good End. Moving through partings mindful of the other's humanity gives both individuals the cleanest shot at finding new love.

# EDITORS' INTRODUCTION

In the next reading, "The Thoroughly Modern Guide to Breakups," Elizabeth Svoboda expands on how the digital age has opened the door to a bad breakup culture. She explains the interplay between human biology and attachment style and how indirect endings negatively impact the experience of breaking up and can impede our ability to make meaning of and learn from the experience. Svoboda's article also includes a helpful list of 12 guidelines for constructing a good breakup.

As you read, keep in mind the following primer questions for reflection. If you feel so inclined, take a few minutes and consider your responses to the following questions before you read, and then again after you've finished each reading.

## PRIMER

1. Dr. Helen Fisher proposed that when people break up they long for their partners and feel physical pain and emotional distress. What kinds of (healthy) self-care might ease the discomfort a breakup might bring?

# The Thoroughly Modern Guide to Breakups

*By Elizabeth Svoboda*

Yes, breaking up is hard to do, and we're primed to avoid delivering or digesting such deeply threatening news. Still, it's possible to end affairs with dignity and minimal distress.

Julie Spira isn't just any writer. She bills herself as an expert on Internet dating, and wrote a book called *The Perils of Cyber-Dating*. When, in 2005, she met The Doctor on an online dating site, Spira was positive she'd finally found The One. "He seemed very solid and close to his family," Spira recalls. He made it clear on their first date that, after the end of a lengthy marriage and a year of serial dating, he was looking for an enduring relationship. "That was very appealing to me."

She took it as a sign of his integrity. It didn't hurt that he was handsome, too. Eight months of exclusive dating later, The Doctor asked her to marry him.

They planned a simple wedding. But first, they put their individual homes up for sale so they could buy a place together. They went house-hunting together nearly every weekend. When her father got sick, The Doctor saved his life.

Fourteen months into their engagement, Spira received an email from her fiancé titled, simply, "Please Read This." She put the message aside to savor after work and other commitments. When she finally clicked on it, she wished she hadn't "The email had an attached document. It said I was not the woman for him, that the relationship was over, and to please send back the ring. It said my belongings would be delivered tomorrow," Spira says. "I sat there and my whole body started to shake."

Spira had to plaster on a happy face for a few days—her parents were renewing their marriage vows at a family party on the other side of the country and she wasn't yet ready to tell anyone about the broken engagement. "I wore my ring. I pretended my fiancé had an emergency and couldn't make it. Then I went to my room and sobbed in secret." Once home, she cried every day for a month. Then another electronic communiqué arrived from The Doctor. It said, in its entirety, "Are you OK?"

That was all she ever heard from him.

The breakup left her socially paralyzed. She didn't, couldn't, date,even after many months.She remains single today, three years later. Disappointment ignites anger when she thinks about what happened. "It was cowardly and cruel. Where's the human side of it? Where's the respect from someone who was devoted to you for two years?" It's scant comfort when people tell her that Berger dumped Carrie by Post-it note on *Sex and the City*. "With email, you don't even have a guarantee fhat the person got your message."

Saying good-bye is heartbreaking, and most of us are total jerks about it. Bad dumping behavior is booming, especially among the young. In one recent survey, 24 percent of respondents aged 13 to 17 said it was completely OK to break up with someone by texting, and 26 percent of them admitted to doing so. "It's always been hard to break up with someone face to face," says Stanford University sociologist Clifford Nass, author of *The Man Who Lied to His Laptop*, "but lack of social skills makes it harder. And we're learning fewer and fewer social skills."

As a result, remote shortcuts like electronic endings look deceptively appealing—although, at the very least, they chip away at the self-respect of the dumpers and deprive dumpees of a needed shot at closure. Little wonder that hypersensitivity to rejection is on the rise, and it's contributing to large increases in stalking behavior, especially on college campuses. More than 3 million people report being stalking victims each year, the ultimate measure of collective cluelessness about ending love affairs well.

As drive-by breakups like Spira's become more common, mastering the art of the ending is more necessary than ever. The average age of first marriage now hovers around 27, five years later than in 1970. Most people are having more and more serious relationships before they find the one that works. The emerging social reality demands some preparation for romantic rejection, given its potential to shatter one's sense of self. For both parties, the experience influences how—or even whether—one moves on with life and love.

The best breakups, if there is such a thing, enable acceptance and minimize psychic wreckage, so that the pain of the ending doesn't overwhelm the positive trace of the relationship. For the partnership will take up permanent residence in memory, likely to be revisited many times over the years. The challenge of breaking up is to close the relationship definitively and honorably, without devaluing oneself or the person who previously met one's deepest needs.

> Hypersensitivity to rejection is on the rise, and it's contributing to large increases in stalking behavior.

> Initially, everyone reacts to rejection like a drug user going through withdrawal.

Yes, Virginia, people can fall out of love with grace and dignity—if only they learn how to give breakups a chance.

## Battered by Biology

Because our brains are wired from the beginning for bonding, breakups batter us biologically. Initially, says Rutgers University anthropologist Helen Fisher, everyone reacts to rejection like a drug user going through withdrawal. In the early days and weeks after a breakup, she has found, just thinking about the lover who dumped us activates several key are as of the brain—the ventral tegmental area of the midbrain, which controls motivation and reward and is known to be involved in romantic love; the nucleus accumbens and the orbitofrontal/prefrontal cortex, part of the dopamine reward system and associated with craving and addiction; and the insular cortex and anterior cingulate, associated with physical pain and distress.

As reported in a recent issue of the *Journal of Neurophysiology*, Fisher rounded up 15 people who had just experienced romantic rejection, put them in an fMRI machine, and had them look at two large photographs: an image of the person who had just dumped them and an image of a neutral person to whom they had no attachment. When the participants looked at the images of their rejecters, their brains shimmered like those of addicts deprived of their substance of choice. "We found activity in regions of the brain associated with cocaine and nicotine addiction," Fisher says. "We also found activity in a region associated with feelings of deep attachment, and activity in a region that's associated with pain."

Fisher's work corroborates the findings of UCLA psychologist Naomi Eisenberger, who discovered that social rejection activates the same brain area—the anterior cingulate—that generates an adverse reaction to physical pain. Breakups likely stimulate pain to notify us how important social ties are to human survival and to warn us not to sever them lightly.

Although Eisenberger didn't study romantic rejection, she expects that it actually feels much worse than the social rejection she did document. "If you're getting pain-related activity from someone you don't care about, it would presumably be a lot more painful from someone you share memories with," she points out.

The intensity of the pain maybe what compels some spurned lovers to stalk their ex-partners; they're willing to do just about anything to make the hurt go away. Fisher believes that activation of addictive centers in response to breakups also fuels stalking behavior, explaining "why the beloved is so difficult to give up."

## A Time of Broken Dreams

Biology is nowhere near the whole story. Attachment styles that emerge early in life also influence how people handle breakups later on—and how they react to them. Those with a secure attachment style—whose caregivers, by being generally responsive, instilled a sense of trust that they would always be around when needed—are most likely to approach breakups with psychological integrity. Typically, they clue their partners in about any changes in their feelings while taking care not to be hurtful.

On the receiving end of a breakup, "the secure person acknowledges that the loss hurts, but is sensible about it," says Phillip Shaver, a University of California, Davis psychologist who has long studied attachment behavior. "They're going to have an undeniable period of broken dreams, but they express that to a reasonable degree and then heal and move on."

By contrast, people who develop an anxious or insecure attachment style—typically due to inconsistent parental attention during the first years of life—are apt to try to keep a defunct relationship going rather than suffer the pain of dissolving it. "The anxious person is less often the one who takes the initiative in breaking up," Shaver says. "More commonly, they hang on and get more angry and intrusive."

On the receiving end of a breakup, the insecurely attached react poorly. "*They don't let go,*" says Shaver. "They're more likely to be stalkers, and they're more likely to end up sleeping with the old partner." Their defense against pain—refusing to acknowledge that the relationship is over—precludes healing. They pine on for the lost love with little hope of relief.

Whether we bounce back from abreakup or wallow in unhappiness also depends on our general self-regard. In a University of California, Santa Barbara study where participants experienced rejection in an online dating exchange, people with low self-esteem took rejection the worst: They were most likely to blame themselves for what had happened and to rail against the rejecter. Their levels of the stress hormone Cortisol ran particularly high. Such reactivity to romantic rejection often creates unhealthy coping strategies—staying home alone night after night, for example, or remaining emotionally closed off from new partners.

People with high self-esteem were not immune to distress in the face of romantic rejection, whether they were rejecter or rejectee, but they were less inclined to assume a lion's share of the blame for the split. Best of all, they continued to see themselves in a positive light despite a brush-off.

# THE CLEAN DOZEN: 12 RULES OF BETTER BREAKUPS

No question, breaking up is incredibly difficult because it involves giving, or receiving, bad news that engages our deepest vulnerability—the fear that we are unlovable. Most of us are designed not only to minimize discomfort but to dislike rupturing attachments, priming us for sleights of avoidance in delivering or digesting such deeply threatening information. It takes courage to recognize we have a moral obligation to put aside personal discomfort in approaching someone we cared for and who loved us—especially when means of ducking that responsibility are so readily available. But courage pays dividends in self-respect and accelerated recovery.

Not only do our biology, psychology, and morality influence how we weather breakups, but so do the circumstances of the act. There may be little anyone can do to alter biological responsiveness, but everyone can control the way breaking up is conducted. Here, say the experts, is how to do it so that both parties remain emotionally intact, capable of weathering the inevitable pain and sadness.

1. Take full responsibility for initiating the breakup.

   If your feelings or needs have changed, your dreams diverged, or your lives are going in opposite directions, don't provoke your partner into doing the breakup. Shifting responsibility is not only a weasel tactic that diminishes the doer, says Paul Falzone, CEO of the online dating service eLove, it's confusing. Adds Russell Friedman, executive director of the California-based Grief Recovery Institute and author of *Moving On*, "Trying to manipulate your partner into breaking up, like suddenly giving one-word answers in an attempt to make them say, 'The heck with it,' creates a sense of real distortion." The partner may not initially get the message that you want to break up, but "will start to question themselves: 'Am I not a valuable human being? Am I unattractive?'" The target may also question their own instincts and intuition. "You're setting up the sense that the other person is to blame. You have bypassed their intuition—they can't trust what they felt, saw, heard in the relationship." That kind of uncertainty can cripple them in future relationships; they may not be willing to trust a new partner's devotion or suitability.

2. Do it *only* face to face.

   Humans evolved to communicate face to face, which provides some built-in consolations. We may experience many nonverbal cues that reassure us of our essential lovability—the quick touch on the arm that says you're still valued even as the relationship ends. Anything less than face-to-face sends a distressing message: "You don't matter."

Some dumpers might think that delivering the news by email, text, or even a Facebook statement is less cruel than directly speaking the truth. But remote modes of delivery actually inflict psychic scars on the dumpee that can impede future partnerships. "When you don't get any explanation, you spend a huge amount of time trying to figure out what's wrong with you," says eLove's Paul Falzone. "And you'll be hesitant about entering another relationship."

Being on the receiving end of remote dumping can leave us stuck in emotional limbo, says University of Chicago neuroscientist John Cacioppo. "The pain of losing a meaningful relationship can be especially searing in the absence of direct social contact." With no definitive closure, we're left wondering what the heck happened, which can lead to the kind of endless rumination that often leads to depression.

"Situations where you have an incomplete picture of what's going on are perfect ground for the development of rumination," says Yale University psychologist Susan Nolen-Hoeksema. "It can send people into a tailspin." Many dumpees emerge from the tailspin distrustful of others, making it difficult for them to establish closeness with future partners. "When you begin to distrust others, you make less of an investment in them," adds Bernardo Carducci, professor of psychology at Indiana University Southeast. "So the person you meet next is going to suffer for the sins of a stranger."

Dumpers themselves may come to regret surrogate sayonaras once they realize how badly their vanishing act hurt their former partners—and how little concern they showed. "Five years on, you don't want to be ashamed of how you handled this," says John Portmann, a moral philosopher at the University of Virginia. Guilt and shame encumber future interactions.

3. Act with dignity.

Since a breakup is a potentially explosive scenario, resolve in advance to bite back any insults that are poised to fly out of your mouth. Preserving your partner's self-respect has the compound effect of salvaging your own.

4. Be honest.

"The message to get across is, 'You're not what I'm looking for,'" adds Florida State University psychologist Roy Baumeister. "That doesn't imply that there's something wrong or deficient about your partner." It's simply straightforward.

"I'm not in love with you anymore" is actually OK. But honesty need not be a bludgeon, nor does it demand total disclosure. If you secretly think your partner is a complete snooze in bed, you're probably better off keeping that opinion to yourself. "You have an obligation to watch out for the other person's self-esteem," Virginia's Portmann says. "Do not cut them down in such a way that it's impossible for them to have another successful relationship. Why rub salt in their wounds? That's torture."

5. Avoid big, bad clichés like "It's not you, it's me."

Such generic explanations ring false and communicate a lack of respect. You owe your partner a genuine explanation, however brief, of why things aren't working. One big caveat: If you suspect that your partner might react violently to your decision to end the relationship, don't stick around to justify your reasoning; safety comes first.

6. Avoid a point-by-point dissection of where things fell apart.

"It's not a good idea because there's never going to be agreement," says Russell Friedman. "I'll say, 'This is what happened,' and you'll say, 'No, no'" Prolonged back-and forth often degenerates into a fight—or worse: If your partner gains the upper hand, he or she may succeed in luring you back into a dysfunctional relationship you've decided you want to end.

7. Make it a clean break.

Do not try to cushion the blow by suggesting future friendly meetups. "Saying 'Let's be friends' might be a way for the rejecter to try to handle their own guilt, but it's not always good for the person being rejected," Baumeister observes. Such a misguided attempt to spare a partner pain can leave him or her hopeful there might be a chance at future reconciliation, which can hinder the efforts of both parties to move on.

8. Communicate ongoing appreciation of the good times you shared.

In exchanging good-byes, it's even desirable, says Friedman. It's equally fine to confide disappointment that the hopes you shared for a future together won't be realized. Such statements convey a continued belief in your partner's inherent value.

9. Don't protest a partner's decision.

And don't beg him or her to reconsider later on. The best thing a dumpee can do to speed emotional healing is to accept that the relationship has come to an unequivocal end. In her neuroimaging studies, Helen Fisher found that the withdrawal-like reaction afflicting romantic rejectees diminished with time, indicating that they were well on their way to healing. But the recovery process is fragile, says Fisher, and last-ditch attempts to make contact or win back an ex can scuttle it. "If you suddenly get an email from the person, you can get right into the craving for them again." To expedite moving on, she recommends abstaining from any kind of contact with the rejecter: "Throw out the cards and letters. Don't call. And don't try to be friends."

10. Don't demonize your ex-partner.

It's a waste of your energy. And avoid plotting revenge; it will backfire by making him or her loom ever larger in your thoughts and postpone your recovery.

11. Don't try to blot out the pain you're feeling, either.

Short of the death of a loved one, the end of a long-term relationship is one of the most severe emotional blows you'll ever experience. It's perfectly normal—in fact, necessary—to spend time grieving the loss. "Love makes you terribly vulnerable," Portmann says. "If you allow yourself to fall in love, you can get hurt really badly." The sooner you face the pain, the sooner it passes.

12. Resist thinking you've lost your one true soul mate.

Don't tell yourself you've lost the one person you were destined to be with forever, says Baumeister. "There's something about love that makes you think there's only one person for you, and there's a mythology surrounding that. But there's nothing magical about one person." In reality, there are plenty of people with whom each of us is potentially compatible. It might be difficult to fathom in the aftermath of a breakup, but chances are you'll find someone else.

# EDITORS' INTRODUCTION

Now that we have explored breaking up in the digital age, we turn to what is known about ending romantic relationships (relationship dissolution and divorce) across time. As a reminder, in this text we use commitment as a general term that implies the intent to stay in a relationship with a partner long-term and acknowledges couples who choose not to enter the legal agreement that is marriage, and also same-sex partners, who until recently could not legally marry.

We recognize that intimate relationships can be viewed along a spectrum from dating to committed life partners. Typically, the greater the levels of interdependence and commitment the more complex the breakup will become. For example, if a couple is living together and/ or is committed or legally married and/or have children the breakup becomes exponentially more complicated. Nonmarital or precommitment breakups are more casual and less stressful than marital or committed breakups (Rollie & Duck, 2006) and are typically easier and less costly (Weber, 1998). Still, most couples follow similar patterns in the process of ending their relationships (Rollie & Duck, 2006; Weber, 1998).

In the final reading for this chapter "Losing, Leaving, and Letting Go: Coping With Nonmarital Breakups" Ann Weber provides some insight into common trajectories and processes of how nonmarried couples navigate relationship dissolution. We learn why breaking up can be difficult for both partners and how the lure of indirect communication can increase the hurt a breakup can cause. Weber provides us with ideas for communicating well during the breakup as well as strategies for healing in the aftermath. Although the research is somewhat dated, relationship scholars like Weber continue to cite the works of Duck (1982) and other early researchers when describing relationship dissolution. Notably, recent research is expanding to include the concept of change rather than endings to accommodate the reality that nonmarital or precommitted and marital or committed relationships often continue in a different form (e.g., just friends, coparenting) after the romantic relationship has ended (Rollie & Duck, 2006).

As you read, keep in mind the following primer questions for reflection. If you feel so inclined, take a few minutes and consider your responses to the following questions before you read, and then again after you've finished each reading.

## PRIMERS

1.  If you have ever been a part of a relationship that ended, how did you come to know the relationship was over?

2.  How did your role (leaver or leavee) affect your perspective and behavior?

3.  Can you identify what made the process more or less difficult?

# Losing Leaving and Letting Go

Coping With Nonmarital Breakups

*By Anne L. Weber*

[...]

## DUCK'S TOPOGRAPHICAL MODEL

The fact that breaking up is a process and not a state or event is central to Duck's (1982) proposed topographical model of relationship disengagement and dissolution. After reviewing the literature on dissolved or terminated relationships (somewhat irrespective of marital status), Duck identified four latent models of dissolution: pre-existing doom, mechanical failure, process loss, and sudden death. *Pre-existing doom* describes the fate of those couples who, among Hill, Rubin, and Peplau's (1976) respondents, were badly matched from the start, so that whatever their attraction might be, it could not overcome inevitable clashes of background, goals, and values. *Mechanical failure* occurs when things break—when communication is poor, or interactions go badly. Some mechanical failures may be the result of unique, *emergent properties* of the relationship—qualities and processes produced by the partners' distinctive blend of styles and motives. Other mechanical failures, however, harken back to pre-dooming problems and mismatches, the symptoms of which only showed up after some wear and tear and time. *Process loss* refers to the slow death some relationships die when they never reach their potential—for example, their potential satisfaction or pleasure for both partners—because of fault and poor productivity on the part of one or both members of the dyad. Process loss leads to dissatisfaction in at least one partner's estimation—the first step, as we see in the next section, that sets in motion the four phases of dissolution.

Finally, Duck (1982) described how new information about one partner—proof of deception or betrayal, for example—can produce the *sudden death* of the developing relationship. Trust is slow-growing but fragile and easily broken. Davis (1973) also used this term and described three conditions that produce what he called "sudden death": *two-sided subsidence*. In which both partners maintain, for diverse reasons, a formal association that is no longer truly intimate, *one-sided subsidence, i*n which one partner hangs on, dependently, while the other actively seeks to end the relationship, and *zero-sided subsidence—an* abrupt ending caused primarily by outside factors, such as an out-of-control argument that ends in an ultimatum or a rash choice in speech or action (uttering an insult or being unfaithful) that goes too far and makes retreat or repair impossible.

In contrast with Davis, Duck (1982) proposed that despite vicious or extreme circumstances, "there is no *psychological* necessity that such things do indeed cause the sudden death of the relationship: if they do, then they have to be allowed to do so, or identified as causes, but they may simply cause the intimacy or relationship level to be cranked back a notch, as when partners remain friends after divorce." (p. 7).

Duck also pointed out that not all rash acts precede dissolution, but sometimes follow it in fatalistic response to a *fait accompli* or in a wrong-headed scheme to redress imagined wrongs that have driven him or her to this pass. For example, if your partner believes that you cheated and has been punishing you for this until now imaginary infraction, perhaps you might as well pursue that affair you have been fantasizing about—right?

***Phases of Dissolution.*** Most interesting in Duck's (1982) description of the breakup process is his proposed topographical model or map of the phases of dissolution. The reference to topography is especially apt considering that, in several respondents' accounts, references are made to feeling "lost" and trying to "find their way" from the beginning to the end of some fixed space. Any discussion of loss lends itself to map-like metaphors of place: Heartbreak Hotel, the land of the living dead, graveyards, bleak terrain and wasteland, swamps and quagmires, and murky and bog-like conditions—even "Been there, done that," and "I've been through that myself" both allude to a "thereness" of loss. The walking wounded and other veterans of relationship loss are essentially travelers without a clear destination—wander in the dark, adrift in the cosmos, lost and abandoned, keenly aware of being in transition in a way their stable (stationary) acquaintances are not. We did not see the signs, never saw what hit us, and cannot find the light at the end of the tunnel ... (excuse me while I extricate myself from this appealing but murky metaphor and return to dry land and dry humor).

Duck (1982) identified four phases of relationship dissolution, each entered after one or both partners cross a cognitive threshold, each with distinctive tasks and possibilities:

1. The *intrapsychic phase* begins when one partner, feeling dissatisfied, realizes, "I can't stand this any more." A secret search is begun to understand what is wrong with the partner, whether and how, it can be fixed, and what it would take to feel satisfied. Vaughan (1986) began her book *Uncoupling* with the assertion that "Uncoupling begins with a secret"

(p. 11). In Duck's model, this secret is "I am unhappy" or some variation thereon, festering and intensifying as it is kept secret throughout one's intrapsychic ruminations.

2. A threshold—"I'd be justified in withdrawing"—is crossed when the dissatisfied partner resolves to confront the other person, beginning the *dyadic phase*. This takes one into dreaded and uncharted territory: How will the other react? What if we can still work it out—do I want that? Issues may be negotiated, the relationship itself redefined and even repaired. There may be fights, certainly arguments—this will not be a fun time for either partner. No wonder the intrapsychic partner may put off confrontation, even put off privately acknowledging critical dissatisfaction. Thus, misery can be tolerated and the intrapsychic phase drags on and on. Even the *dyadic phase* is only concluded when both partners resolve either to dissolve or repair the relationship. With two ambivalent people and the distractions of modem life, a couple might conceivably exist in this struggle indefinitely. If one of them gets so fed up as to conclude "I mean it" and determine to depart, he or she enters the next phase.

3. If the resolution is reached to dissolve the relationship, both soon-to-be-ex-partners enter the *social phase,* in which they figure out what happened, how to explain it to their respective social circles (including placing blame and saving face), and what to do next. For these many tasks, they rely on account making, mourning, gossip mongering, and even oscillating between reconciliation and total withdrawal. Yet, if "It's now inevitable," they both cross the threshold into the last phase of relationship dissolution.

4. The picturesquely-named *grave-dressing* phase captures the deceptively simple business of trying "To get over it all and put it behind one" (Duck, 1982, p. 25, Figure 5). Much must be done, and it can take a lifetime (Harvey et al., 1990). Yet, the immediate, pragmatic focus of now ex-partners is to create an acceptable story about their love and loss, to tidy up their memories, and to do whatever cognitive work is necessary—reflection, attribution, rationalization, reassessment of Self and Other—in order to get over the now deceased relationship. The relationship is dead and buried, but the grave marker can still be carved, and revised, and the whole legend prettified in order to glean some personal and/or social value from the loss.

In our work with accounts of loss (Harvey, 1996; Harvey et ah, 1989; Harvey, Weber, & Orbuck 1990), we found that, over time, accounts of past relationships are modified, both in the mind and the delivery of the account maker. This modification is not unlike what happens when a rumor is repeated and reiterated. First, the version related (both to others and to oneself) is shortened and condensed ("Basically there were just a couple of things wrong with my last relationship ... "); the highlights are exaggerated, while contextual detail is omitted ("My partner was basically very self-centered, and I was too eager to please"); and finally, the story is adapted to assimilate the storyteller's own value system or self-biases ("We finally agreed to part amicably rather than continue to struggle with something that wasn't meant to be"). When relating the account to a confidant, or to one's social audience for social or entertainment value, the account maker also adjusts the rendition, á la self-monitoring, to suit the listener's preferences or status. For example, if your boyfriend dumps you, you might whine to your girlfriend "He just dropped this bombshell on me, at the worst possible time, and I'm a basket case!" whereas, in the same evening, you confide to your mother by phone that "He and I have agreed to see other people for a while, and I think it's really for the best."

## EXPERIENCING GRIEF

> In late October, Roddy was lying on the table in the finch room. His eyes were open, and he was looking at a half-opened window in the skylight. A bird flew across it. He heard the door open, but didn't look up ... Mary walked into the finch room, and Roddy sat up on the table. He looked at her through an opening in the cages, and she stared back like a startled animal. He could not imagine what she was reading on his face, but when he focused he could see what was on hers. It was pure grief...
> —Laurie Colwin, "Animal Behavior," in *Passion and Affect*, (1976), p. 33

The legacies of Weiss, Hill et al., and Duck all provide a growing precision and confidence about examining breakups through the eyes of the broken, developing sound strategies for collecting data on breakup processes, difficult as it is to document the events, and a theoretical logic for assembling different levels and genres of experiences into a discernible road map of relationship dissolution. A somewhat different—but still complementary—tactic is taken by scholars who focus more on tasks than on their predictable order or sequence. Here, three task-oriented perspectives are reviewed: a general discussion of the *tasks of grief*, especially from the point of view of counselors, a focus on how partners *communicate* about disengagement, and a *script* of common, even essential, disengagement interactions.

## THE TASKS OF GRIEF

Two Danish practitioners, Leick and Davidsen-Nielsen (1991), synthesized their findings in their clinical work with bereaved clients in *Healing pain: Attachment, Loss and Grief Therapy*. For Leick and Davidsen-Nielsen, grieving could not be described by any sequential or linear model, They found that grieving persons often cycled and recycled—some in seemingly endless loops—through once-covered terrain, until at last they accomplished some task necessary for psychological recovery. In interviews and in content-analyses of clients' accounts, Leick and Davidsen-Nielsen identified the tasks central to this process:

1. The individual must *recognize* the fact of the loss.

2. He or she must *release the emotions* of grief.

3. The bereaved person must not only pick up the pieces and develop face-saving attributions, but must *develop new skills* for the new life that lies ahead.

4. Finally, he or she must cease expectations of reconciliation or relinquish fantasies that block realistic thinking, and instead *reinvest emotional energy* in new interactions and relationships.

This task model of grieving honors the process-orientation of reacting to loss, as opposed to the state or event characterization. Furthermore, Leick and Davidsen-Nielsen focused on grief not only attendant to death or relationship dissolution, but also other kinds of losses such as depression, developmental crises (such as retirement), physical handicaps trauma, and illness. This model does not try to be an "all-purpose theory of grief," but rather a review of what grieving individuals must accomplish in order to deal with their losses and move on.

Applying the task model to nonmarital breakups, we encourage our clients, students, respondents, and ourselves to recognize that, after a loss, subjective as it may be in its import and impact, we must consider how and when we are to accomplish these tasks. We must expect them to interweave and we must tolerate some "unfinishedness" at any given point in the process. According to Leick and Davidsen-Nielson, the order of processes is not as important as the completion of the tasks.

## COMMUNICATING AND DISENGAGEMENT

Duck (1982) and Vaughan (1986) both acknowledged that a breakup begins in the mind of one dissatisfied partner, who must determine whether and how to proceed. Yet, both also agreed that proceeding absolutely requires communicating with the other person. The longer the unhappy partner postpones the confrontation, the more matters between the two are likely to deteriorate—unless he or she has a change of heart. Yet, in this case, silence on the part of the dissatisfied and intrapsychically consternated partner creates not only exclusion (leaving the other out of decisions that are highly consequential for both) but also illusion (allowing the other to go on believing that things, however imperfect, are fine between them).

The departing partner's silence, prior to entering the sudden death phase/causes the shock and dismay that many of my respondents reported when they were the breakees because they did not see it coming:

> I was destroyed. I did not expect a breakup at all. She broke up with me the day after Christmas. I was in literal shock for a week. I couldn't eat, sleep, or function normally in school. My grades dropped a little … I never found out why we broke up. I was left to only guess …. I was devastated. I couldn't let her go. I never accepted for a long while [afterward] that she was gone, never to be in my arms again. (18-year-old heterosexual male)

As important as it is to both parties' mental health to experience clarity and honesty about the end of their relationship, such discourse is oddly easier said than done. No one wants to be the bad guy by admitting his or her loss of interest, we further tell ourselves it would be cruel to reject the other outright and much kinder to let things drift, or even to provoke the other person into being the rejector: "I knew that if I told her that I did not want to continue the relationship it would really hurt her, so I thought I would be an 'asshole' for a while to make her like me less and then I would tell her" (Baxter, 1984, p. 37).

***Trajectories of Disengagement.*** Communication scholars contributed a unique perspective to the literature on breakups by examining the ways partners do—or do not—talk to each other about their dissatisfaction or intentions to leave. Baxter (1984) analyzed 97 heterosexual breakup accounts, identifying six distinctive features of the breakup process that might be traced through a flowchart, a series of choices or trajectories in discourse between parting partners.

1. Gradual versus sudden onset of relationship problems.
2. Unilateral versus bilateral desire to exit the relationship.
3. Direct versus indirect actions used to effect dissolution.
4. Rapid versus protracted negotiation of the breakup.
5. Presence or absence of efforts to repair the relationship.
6. Termination versus continuation as the final outcome.

Most germane to this discussion is Baxter's (1984) finding that most decisions to exit a relationship were unilateral, and most unilateral disengagement talk is *indirect,* consisting of hints or general complaints rather than a direct expression of a desire to breakup. By withholding any clear, explicit declaration of intention to leave—whether out of scriptlessness, confusion, or a concern that the left partner "can't take it"—the leaver allows the left partner to wallow in ambiguity, unsure whether the relationship is on or off, and what his or her response options might be. It is then that we are most likely to make fools of ourselves (or most fearful of doing so). The solution to this misery cannot lie in making dissatisfied partners stay, but rather equipping both partners with strategies to communicate information *and* feelings assertively and clearly. It is not enough to "just say 'go'", we need scripts.

***Separation Scripts***. Did someone say we needed a script? Lee (1984) proposed five possible stages in dissolution: discovery of dissatisfaction, *exposure* (bringing the problem out into the open), *negotiation* (serious discussion about what to do), *resolution* (a decision by one or both partners), and, *transformation* (an actual change in the nature of the relationship). Lee argued that either partner can be the agent of change (or operator) at various stages of the breakup. Breakups vary in the content of the issues that have brought them into conflict or dissatisfaction, and in the latency or duration of each of the stages. Finally, Lee pointed out that not every breakup explicitly cover all five stages, breakups with missing stages are described as *omission formats*. Other formats extend the ordeal or mix the formats, combining and re-ordering tasks to produce convoluted termination scenarios. Thus, Lee suggested, we have scripts of a sort—or perhaps cognitive scenes and vignettes—for possible confrontations, dialogues, and outcomes in our breakups. It is easy to see how popular culture, song lyrics, and film and video images contribute to a rich lore of such script elements without sufficient connective logic or reality to make them work. However, ideas and ideals are no substitute for practiced, careful communication.

## "TELL ME SOMETHING"

If we are lucky enough to have communication, even during otherwise painful disengagement, we might at least piece together the nature and meaning of the loss, and the moral of the story for our own lives and futures. If we were "taken in", we can resolve to be more cautious next time, if we were betrayed, perhaps we can learn to recognize the signs so that future deceptions are less life-disrupting and recovering is easier.

How awful will it be after a breakup? Clearly, it depends—but depends on what? Simpson (1987) surveyed over 200 undergraduates involved in a steady dating relationship, but who were not engaged or married. Three months after the initial survey, almost 95% of the original respondents completed follow-up measures of their relationships' status, intensity, and duration. Among 10 predictor variables, Simpson found three in particular that predicted the intensity and duration of emotional distress in the case of breakup: (a) how close the dating partners were reported to have been, (b) how long the pair had been dating at the time of the initial survey, and (c) respondents' expected ease of finding an alternative partner. Applying these findings to breakups in general, we conclude that we are more likely to suffer and grieve if we were close to the lost partner (Weiss' concept of emotional loneliness), if we were a couple for a relatively long time (dyadic crystallization, as well as integration of couplehood into one's social identity), and if postbreakup social prospects are bleak or difficult (social isolation, bruised esteem, and loss of hope).

If these circumstances—closeness, duration, and belief in available alternatives—are predictors of post-breakup distress, why do we not take preventive measures? For one thing, preventing distress would also prevent commitment, which is arguably a major goal of many nonmarital relationships. In other words, applying Simpson's conclusions, we might anticipate and prevent post-breakup distress by reducing closeness—by keeping our partner at arm's length, at least psychologically. Furthermore, keep it short—do not see each other too long, or you 11 get hung up and expect too much. Finally, keep your options open, diversify your relationship investment portfolio, and you will not be disproportionately wounded when any one partner leaves. So what have you got when you are not close to your partner, have been seeing this person only briefly, and see other people? Well, it is not intimacy. Simpson's ingenious survey highlights the chicken-and-egg problem or more specifically, the "we-need-the-eggs" problem. The very qualities and experiences we seek from another are at risk as intimacy develops. We can only protect ourselves from loss by doing without them in the first place.

*Left Hanging.* When I was a sophomore in college, I met and fell for "Geoff," a Big Man on Campus who was popular, attractive, an officer in the "best" fraternity, and a known heartbreaker. Despite warnings from friends not to get "hung up," I found him engaging and easy to like. I looked forward to our times together, and saw no dark clouds in our future. Geoff, a senior, graduated at the end of the semester and went to work in a town some distance away, but I lived only 1 hour away and we continued to date during the summer. We wrote almost daily (this was long before e-mail and long-distance calls were prohibitively expensive for us). Although we were not emotionally close, we dated steadily and, I believed, exclusively, I thought our best days lay ahead. One weekday, Geoff called me at my job from his, to tell me excitedly that he had just been notified of acceptance for postgraduate study. He promised before he hung up, "I'll drive home on Saturday and call you from my Mom's. Well go out and celebrate on Saturday night." Happy for him, and excited about our weekend, I waited for his call, but I never heard from Geoff again.

Thus, began one of the most anguishing and baffling periods of post-breakup grief in my life. For weeks, I did not know what happened. Had he deliberately lied before disappearing from my life or was he in some sort of trouble? His mother never returned my calls, and our few mutual friends did not know or were not talking. I felt anguished, was an insomniac, and became obsessed. I pretended all was well, continued to write letters with carefully worded "curiosity" about what became of him. I suspected the worst—"dumped again"—but could not understand why it had happened or why he would not just level with me. Did he fear a scene, or dread having to account for his actions? The rest of the summer I wondered, pined, wrote (less and less often), and finally resigned myself to being a victim of the very "hung-upness" I'd been warned about. Summer ended, I wrapped up work at my job, and returned to the campus that had been the scene of so many good times. I played and replayed albums of maudlin love and heartbreak.

I had dreams—of running into him, or finding he had returned with apologies or explanations. Yet, Geoff, the one person who could give me actual information, never showed up or even bothered to write me a Dear Jane letter—not during the time I was dealing with my confusion and bereavement. (A few years later, I actually did run into him at an alumni affair. We had a pleasant conversation, chatted about our lives since graduation, and I met his new wife. A model of restraint, I never once said, "So what the hell happened that summer?!")

During the autumn of my Geoff grief, my old friend Kathy helped get me through the craziness with humor and perspective. A rueful, funny veteran of such kiss-offs, she grasped my need to understand, to label this disappointment as a. "noncatastrophe," in order to get over it, Kathy reminded me of humor, of relevant lyrics in favorite songs from our high school years, and gently suggested that my disappointment in this deception was sad but not tragic. I would not only get over it, but I would learn from it. Together we speculated on what really happened, finally agreeing it was most likely not a bang, but a whimper: Geoff had probably met someone, put off telling me, and found it harder with every passing day to do the right thing, especially as I kept writing letters full of confusion and forgiveness. We were apart anyway, so we were not likely to run into each other and have awkward moments. We only dated a few months, so our circle of mutual friends was small and not much affected by whether or not we broke up. Perhaps he did not mean to break off all contact with me, but doing so certainly put off an unpleasant chore. We just were not that close after all, so it was not that hard for him to rationalize the breakup. End of story—probably.

Eventually I forgot my pain, healed, and moved on—with social support from Kathy and the involvement of work once my college studies resumed. Yet, I never forgot the strange obsession and sorrow that were caused more by not knowing than by the loss of a relationship, which had, after all, been neither central nor close. What I had lost was potential, the promise of a better relationship to come, and the sense that I had some control over my social fate, an equal contribution to make in a romantic partnership. Geoff's silence, which to this day I have never been able to explain, left me with a hole in my social confidence and self-esteem. Bad news would have been welcome—I expected it. Yet, endlessly not knowing, despite good guesses about why he disappeared, left me confused, hurt, and mistrustful.

***The Need for Meaning.*** Cognitively and emotionally, one of the most painful consequences of a breakup is the confusion and doubt it creates, especially if one was clearly rejected or abandoned. Several years ago, I surveyed my classes about various reasons for breakups and assembled their offerings into a checklist: note enough in common, frequent arguments, partner cheats, intolerable jealousy, and so on. I then asked all my students to rank the "top five worst reasons" for a breakup, and scanned their results to discern a pattern. I found no obvious gender or other effects (this was a class exercise, not a formal analysis), but I discovered a consistent, glaring trend: The number one "worst reason" was *partner leaves without explanation* (or, as I still thought of it, the Geoff effect). In class discussions, students agreed that this scenario was the most painful, even among other reasons (such as being cheated on or left for a former love) that entailed considerable humiliation and anguish. What makes no explanation so horrible?

Humans need input, information, explanations, sometimes so desperately that we settle for rumor or fantasy in the absence of empirical data. Thus, we might happily accept bad news rather than no news at all: Your ex-partner is not sparing your feelings by avoiding contact and refusing to tell you directly that the relationship is over, but rather initiating a frustrating and tenacious search for meaning. How can you move on, if you do not know where you have been or how exactly you ended up there?

**The Need for Closure.** In the event of a breakup, one is not satisfied with information, one also needs justification and closure. If you are lucky enough to get reasons from your ex, are those reasons good enough in your opinion? Do they justify the expense to you in pain, sorrow, and social discomfort? An ample literature on self-justification and cognitive dissonance attests to our desire for getting things right, or at least making them look or feel right. Furthermore, do the reasons offered by your former partner make sense—are they valid explanations or excuses for the trauma that ended your relationship with the other? This need for closure is a conscious desire to save face and repair damaged pride and self-esteem: "At least she admitted she took the coward's way out, leaving me like that with a note and some lame complaint about having to 'find herself,'" one friend told me.

Our need for closure also comes from a less conscious, more basic cognitive agenda (Weber, 1992b). In 1938, Kurt Lewin's student Bluma Zeigarnik published a now classic study showing that subjects who were interrupted and prevented from finishing various tasks (such as reading short selections or working puzzles) retained more details of the unfinished tasks in memory than did subjects who were permitted to complete (and presumably, file away) the same tasks. In short, unfinished business is likely to nag us, whether it be the suspended farewell address that would finally terminate the relationship (Davis, 1973), an accounting of the dissatisfied partner's arguments (Duck, 1982), or the opportunity for the wronged party to make some sort of response or rebuttal. Without a final act or interaction, the relationship lacks finishedness, it may even seem to continue in some eerie, surreal *sense* as long as the leavee remains loyal to the memory of the other or holds on to the hope that he or she will return. In Thomas Hardy's *Far from the Maddening Crowd,* Bathsheba gets as far as her wedding day before her long-lost legal husband suddenly returns—with tragic consequences. The effect of such stories, fictional or true, on those who are left and bereft can only be to support continued wonder and confusion:

"Is it really over? I haven't heard anything. For all I know, everything is fine …" except the mail (or whatever is preventing the other person from getting in touch). Without receiving word, one cannot begin to comprehend what happened or even to rationalize it convincingly to oneself.

## COMPREHENSION AND CONTROL

> "Geese mate for life," my mother said, just out of the blue, as we were driving.
> "I hope you know that. They're special birds."
> "I know that," Glen said in the front seat. "I have every respect for them."
> "So where were you for three months?" she said. "I'm only curious."
> —Ford, 1987, p. 219

In Ford's short story "Communist," the narrator, Les, remembers a day when he was 16-years-old and his mother's ex-boyfriend showed up to take him geese hunting. When Glen first arrives, Les's mother Aileen displays pent-up anger and bitterness, and initially refuses to accompany them. Yet, her curiosity about why Glen disappeared for some time and what the day together might be like leads her to join the excursion. Despite her silence and disapproval, she manages to ask the question many abandoned lovers anguish over: Where were you? Why did you leave? For that matter, why have you come back?

Ford's story is compelling and complex, but it is fiction, and therefore, Aileen gets the chance, rare in real life, not only to ask her question (and get a predictably unsatisfying reply), but also to confront something about Glen and herself that makes it easier to let go of her ideals about that relationship. In real life, such confrontations are dreamed of—they would answer so much—but they are difficult to engineer. When someone does not call you, you may not have the social power to initiate the call. You may fear losing face or overreacting and ruining a fragile connection. To this day, I think of the Geoff period I described earlier as a time of odd sadness, nagging insecurity, and important lessons. Part of its poignancy for me is that I was young then and things hit me harder. Yet, I still wish I knew why Geoff disappeared. I had been through what Harvey (1996) called a *haunting loss,* one that caused distress that lingered over time. Typical of losses that haunt are feelings of regret, plaguing bouts of "what if is" and other obsessive thoughts, and memories that recur in ways that seem beyond one's control. To be sure, Harvey described haunting mainly in the context of loss caused by the death of loved ones. To apply it to nonmarital breakups, seems to trivialize or diminish the real anguish suffered by the survivors of trauma.

My point is really to reflect on the niggling, demoralizing effects of any failure or rejection that seems inexplicable. If we do not know what happened, we do not know how to prevent it from happening again. We may be tempted to blame ourselves for the sheer sense of familiarity that comes from self-accusation. If I think it was my fault he left me, then even if it was not, at least I can make plans—including paying more attention to the "telltale signs" of my partner's dissatisfaction or to being less of a chump and demanding to know what happened—next time around.

***Confrontation***. Armed with past self-blame and the resolution to find out reasons if I ever got the chance, years ago I finally confronted one man, call him "Mark," and demanded an explanation for his disappearance. Months earlier we dated exclusively and happily. One day, he returned from a weekend trip out of town and was different. He did not call for days, he was icily remote on the phone when I finally called him, and by now, I knew the drill: He changed his mind about us somehow during the 48 hours he visited old friends and it was clearly over. I recovered fairly quickly but was sad and baffled, why, I asked my close friends, didn't he just 'fess up and tell me it was over, and explain why? Why seemed to be so elusive to so many breakup veterans, it became the Holy Grail of the dating game—a noble but vain quest. The change in Mark was so sudden and complete, I likened it to what the aliens did to their victims in the 1956 film *Invasion of the Body Snatchers:* "The pods got him," I concluded to one friend. For all intents and purposes, the Mark I knew and cared for no longer existed—though a shell of his appearance was still to be seen out and about.

One evening our paths crossed in a restaurant where I had dinner with some co-workers. I greeted Mark and, ever polite, he invited me to join his safely crowded table. Then, a weird thing happened: All his friends finished their drinks and "had to go," not all at once, but very soon he and I were *alone* (in public) together for the first time in 1 year. I was very nice, but I seized my knightly opportunity: "So what happened to you that weekend?" I asked, still smiling. To his credit, he did not feign ignorance about "happened" or ask, "weekend?," but did hem and haw. I played a sort of 20 Questions and eventually extracted enough data to confirm the hypothesis I formulated long before: Call it commitment-phobia, or fear of intimacy, paranoia, or a healthy cynicism about entrapment, but he just did not want to be in a twosome. While he was away, his out-of-town friends asked about me, and his realization that others saw us as a couple made him uncomfortable. When he returned, he postponed seeing me until he knew what to say, allowing the days to drag on while he said nothing at all. Unavailable and remote, he believed he allowed our relationship to pass away (Davis, 1973), although for me the breakup was obvious and abrupt, just what Davis described as *sudden death*. After we talked, we parted on friendly terms, he was surprised, I think, that I did not argue with him or assail him, although I explained how angry I was, and how stupid it was to keep avoiding each other. A whimper instead of a bang, his confession nonetheless, gave me closure, and something more: the comfort of knowing that, because we talked, it was not necessary to wonder how he might react if and when we next ran into each other. Even though I had to drag it out of him, his explanation was a gift, and it made life easier for me afterward.

## STRATEGIES FOR HEALING

A major challenge to recovering after a nonmarital breakup is the prior relationship's lack of definition or public commitment. The survivor of such breakup may find that he or she is not taken seriously by friends, who point out that "At least you weren't married!"—as though the bereft person should be relieved, even happy, that it never got that far. Orbuch (1988) put nonmarital breakups in the category of *disenfranchised grief* a mourning process that is psychologically real but not socially validated. Harvey (1996) explained: "As a society, we do not typically provide the same types of social supports for people who experience dissolution [of a nonmarital relationship]. ... In a certain sense, loss is loss, and each loss deserves due consideration of its meaning in the life of the survivor and requires a time for healing" (p. 40).

## DEALING WITH DISENFRANCHISEMENT

The hard lesson of this for the survivor of a nonmarital breakup is that he or she cannot expect to find ready understanding, sympathy, or practical support during grief. When marriages break up, entire social and professional networks seem to be activated by the event: friends console, former in-laws choose sides, and lawyers open files, list assets, and make adversarial plans for the passive victims to follow. My lawyer, for example, did so much domestic and divorce work that he finally had his business cards printed up on black stock: "I want prospective clients to know," he explained to me, "just how dark this business is-likely to get if they want me to proceed as their advocate in a divorce" (Marvin Pope, personal communication).

The nonmarital breakee may indeed be relieved not to be caught up in the divorce industry or railroaded by a plot to make an enemy of someone whom he or she once loved. Yet, the other extreme—feeling clueless, abandoned by society, embarrassed by failure or betrayal, perhaps guilty about breaking another's heart—leaves one in a bleak, queasy limbo, unsure what to do, aware that everyone says "you'll get over it," but painfully unaware of how to accomplish just that.

We must take matters into our own hands. Because we are disenfranchised, we must chart our own course. Ironically, the pathways open to nonmarital breakees are well-worn, though they may not be the superhighways of divorce proceedings. There have been so many nonmarital breakups in almost any culture studied that we should not find a lack of advice and road maps for this experience. How, then, do we face nonmarital relationship loss, grieve through it, ultimately, to reach—and actively construct—the new sense of self at the end of the healing process?

# RETROSPECTION, REMEMBERING—AND BEING REMEMBERED

So much of the cognitive work of the breakup process is focused on obsession, attribution, and explanation of what happened that it seems clear we must establish some sense of meaning in order to grieve and move on. I essentially began this [reading] by arguing for our need for meaning, and now come full circle. Meaning can be constructed, but such fabrications cannot provide the closure and consolation of the "real thing." For example, I wish I had the truth from old Geoff, my college boyfriend, rather than having to wonder and speculate for months after he ended all contact between us. I figured it out and am 99% sure today that he met someone else and found it more difficult over time to level with me. So I was able to garner meaning in that loss, but not with any expedience or dignity. In contrast, my confrontation years later with Mark, the man who seemed to have been snatched by the Pod people one weekend before breaking off our relationship, had a much more satisfying result emotionally, although the information I collected in that conversation was minimal. The difference was that I got meaningful closure and conclusion. I felt he, however reluctantly, leveled with me, this enabled me to regard myself as someone worth leveling with, and it genuinely eased my sadness over the lost relationship and my transition into a new social life.

Is the missing element dignity or honor? It certainly seems that, in interpersonal relations as well as international ones, a fair policy is to allow your opponent the opportunity to save face after defeat. When one partner leaves the other, does not the leaver owe the leavee an explanation, literally, an accounting? As suggested earlier, even bad news is better than no news at all. Furthermore, if the leaver lacks finesse and cannot depart without a few shots or insults, the pain this causes can eventually lead the rejected person to conclude, "Well, would I really want this person after all, knowing that?" (Work on unrequited love and limerence suggests that there are a few souls out there who say they do still want the abusive, uncaring ex-partner back, (Baumeister & Wotman, 1992, Tennov, 1979). However, I leave discussions of such dynamics to the authors of works on disordered personalities and dysfunctional relationships. For my part here, I am interested in the normal nonmarital breakup and what might be done to better understand it and cope.

***Remember Me.*** A central part of accepting defeat with dignity is understanding whether and how the relationship is viewed and remembered by one's former partner. To be forgotten would mean my own memories were false and my value nill. At least acknowledge that it was once mutual or that I had some reason to be happy, even hopeful, when we were together. Mourning rituals are cultural universals, all humans engage in some act or construction of memorializing those who were dear to them. No non-marital breakup warrants a notation in a county clerk's office, much less a tombstone or official monument. Yet, we keep souvenirs—or perhaps we dramatically destroy them, ripping up photographs, tossing letters on the fire. (One reason to mourn the passing of the fireplace as a form of central heating, frankly, is that now it is impossible to make a symbolic gesture by dropping love letters on a non-incendiary heating vent). We buy books, write poems, play sad songs, some people send dead flowers or spread rumors of social disease as a type of revenge against a former lover. All these acts, whether nostalgic or retaliatory, are types of mental and emotional remembrance. What we seek in return—in some form we can hardly request—is to know we too are remembered, whether as a great love or a bad time, as being real. The first step toward establishing one's new identity is learning about one's old identity, as seen and remembered by those most important to us.

## HUMOR AND HOPE

As indicated earlier, Harvey, Orbuch, and I (1990) proposed that the goal of account making in the wake of loss is ultimately to forge a new identity. This sense of self, figuratively baptized by the fire or blood of loss and pain, must be firmly planted in the new reality of life after the loss, a different world from that which one originally inhabited or wished for. We approach this identity—itself, like breaking up, a process or work in progress rather than a finished state—with a number of resources, despite our bleak beginnings. We take stock of our material resources—the income we might still spend on rent if we must now find a new home or school if the partner who once promised to support us is now gone. We also call on social support, friends who stick by us and survive the odd custodial dispute with our ex-partner and strangers—new friends?—with whom we feel safe disclosing some of the humiliation attendant on our failure or rejection.

In the course of grieving, we also discover inner resources, including strength and endurance, even optimism and hope. Cartoonist Matt Groening (1984), creator of *The Simpsons* and the *Life in Hell* cartoon series, offered his own view of the stages of heartbreak: After the worst times (including "pain" and "pain pain pain"), eventually Binky the heartbroken rabbit experiences "occasional perkiness" and is, at last, "ready for further punishment" (p. 12). This readiness is not a replay of the neediness that preceded the now broken relationship, but rather a sadder but wiser version, a recognition that we need inclusion and desire intimacy, but are not infinitely self-sacrificing or telepathically gifted. We learn, in short, that it takes work, we are not good at all types of work but can do many things, it is reasonable to seek a partner to complement us in this noble work, and we will survive and even thrive. It may be a long journey to this point, but we can get there.

# STRATEGIES FOR GETTING OVER BREAKUP GRIEF

> I am missing you
> far better than
> I ever loved you.
> —Colgrove et al., 1991, p. 121

How do we get there? Pop psychology and self-help books, as well as regular magazine articles (often timed for publication around Valentine's Day), offer ample relationship and breakup advice, some of it sound. As the short poem above hints, reflection during grief can sometimes lead us to realize that the loss and its attendant grief are far more central to us emotionally than the relationship ever was. Some years ago, after being left by a man I dated only a few months, I expressed both misery to my friends and bafflement about just why I should be so miserable. We had not been that close, really, and I was surprised by how hard it hit me when he told me (yes, he told me, so that was some improvement) that he had fallen in love with someone else I did not even know he had been seeing. My friend Diane responded by asking me what I would most miss now that "Ralph" was out of my life. "The fun we had," I replied, "and the intelligent conversations and laughs we shared, among other things." "Well," replied Diane (too wisely, but she was right), "those are things you still have. You haven't lost them! You're still fun, you offer everyone you know intelligence and a sense of humor. Ralph had nothing to do with those qualities. So don't worry about losing something he never gave you."

Coping with grief involves taking stock, making a sort of inventory of one's assets in the wake of loss or trauma. Recall Harvey's (1996) earlier definition of *loss* as a depletion of resources, when you suffer loss, you may have to take some time to sort out what you had to start with, what was sacrificed in the breakup, and what remains for you to cherish, use, or depend on. In addition to these products, coping also requires that we respect the process of loss and grief. Neeld (1990) argued that grief after loss is not a passive experience of suffering setbacks and disappointments in the wake of tragedy, but rather a series of active choices the grieving person must confront and resolve, either in the direction of healing or prolonged suffering. Like many impassioned scholars of loss, Neeld herself was inspired by a terrible tragedy: Her husband died while jogging during a visit to a vacation cabin in Tennessee. With no warning about heart condition and no expectation that their life together could be cut short, Neeld found herself living in and observing her own shock and agony. In later analyzing her own experience and interviewing other survivors of all types of loss, she identified seven choices mourners must face and the many forms these crises can take. In her prologue, Neeld concluded that "those of us who have experienced traumatic loss do not have to be doomed" to pain, passivity, and hopelessness (p. 8). In this spirit, then, here is some of the wisdom I culled from writers who sought to speak to those whose hearts were broken but are determined to grieve actively, to learn from loss, and to get on with it.

**Express Your Emotions.** As Leick & Davidsen-Nielsen (1990) emphasize, expressing sorrow and rage is one of the four central tasks of grief. Perhaps you can vent your emotions at your ex-partner, but chances are he or she will not be available to "receive" this message. In that case, a confidant will do, a sympathetic listener who lets you think out loud without offering clichéd or advice. But, when even a friend cannot be found, how do you express your grief? Work by James Pennebaker (1990) indicates that an audience might not be required for effective expressing and confiding. Instead of talking to someone, keeping a journal or writing out your thoughts and feelings can bring long-term benefits, such as greater physical well-being and emotional recovery.

**Figure Out What Happened.** In *Coming Apart,* Kingma (1987) urged the survivor of a broken relationship to formulate his or her story—what we would call the account—and write it down. This provides some emotional release as well as a record, perhaps an ongoing diary, of one's memories and progress in coping. Do the cognitive work of assembling the souvenirs and reviewing the memories, as well as accepting the reasons. Identify what you need for closure and figure out how to get it on your own if necessary.

**Realize, Don't Idealize.** In *How to Fall Out of Love* (1978), Phillips and Judd recommended several strategies to lessen the pain of a failed or impossible love. One strategy is *silent ridicule,* in which the client mentally pictures some real flaw in the former lover and then mentally exaggerates it in a humorous way. For example, I was once dumped by a man who had a fastidious streak, for example, he would overreact with dismay to a food stain on his tie, to the point of ruining the evening by obsessing about how to get it cleaned. In applying Phillips' advice to my own post-breakup disappointment, I readily conjured up an image of neatly attired "Ralph" with potato salad dumped on his head. It was a bit vengeful, but mainly I knew his reaction to such a silly experience would be self-imposed misery rather than annoyance. (Those of us who have survived food spills know the difference between real tragedy and mere embarrassed annoyance). By vividly imagining Ralph's neurotic neatnik fetish, I was able to chip away at my ideal image of him and so, miss him a bit less. Once I got him back down to human proportions in my mind, I was able to deal with realistic sadness rather than the death of a dream. The real is more mundane than the ideal and much easier to get over.

**Prepare to Feel Better.** In his work with the recently separated, Weiss found that many survivors of breakup are surprised to feel euphoric, even a little embarrassed that they are not prostrate with grief or guilt. Yet, relief and even joy can make sense, especially if you are the leaver or if you have been waiting for the other shoe to drop for some time. This positive feeling may overtake you rather abruptly. In *The Heartbreak Handbook,* Frankel and Tien (1993) told the story of a woman who suddenly snapped out of her post breakup malaise one day in the middle of an aerobics class workout: "I was in full swing, ... when it suddenly popped into my head: 'I'm fine! I'm really doing okay. I have things to do; I can enjoy myself—I don't want to stay mired in the past. I want to go on with my life.' It was weird; it was kind of like an epiphany or something ..." (p. 187). A common theme in respondents' reports is that they feel like laughing or experience the epiphany while talking and joking with friends. Humor breaks the bonds of misery, it is incompatible with self-imposed mourning. By considering the possibility of healing and looking for what is funny—or at least ironic—in your experience, you may find you are better able to process the feelings and lessons of grief.

***Expect to Heal.*** How is it possible to recover after going through a period of intense pain and despair? A break is an injury, and most injuries heal. Spontaneous-healing expert Weil (1997) advised, as a key step in self-promotion of health, make a list of all past illnesses and injuries from which you healed. The point of the listing is to recognize that you normally heal after you are hurt—your mind and body work together to restore you to health. This is true even when some changes have to be made, in order to get well. In the wake of loss and pain, we can change, adapt, and grow. To do this, it helps to remember that we have done so many times before.

***Talk to Others.*** Tell those close to you about your situation, and be honest with them about what they can and cannot expect from you in days and weeks to come. If you do not know what they can expect, tell them that1. Seek out those who have been there, not only to pour out your own tale to sympathetic ears, but also to listen to theirs and look for common themes. Resist the temptation to shut yourself away from others. This is one of those awful periods when you will not be charming or socially skilled but you will need and will appreciate the company of others. In *Love Stinks,* Overbeck (1990) warned that different people react differently—and not always constructively—to your loss. Some say, "I told you so," "I never liked her," or "Too bad, he seemed like a great guy," when it should seem obvious that these are not consoling responses, and may not even be true. Anticipate diversity, make bets with yourself about how others might react, and set yourself the reasonable goal of communicating with others and asking reasonably for what you need. Do not expect others to read your mind or just know how you feel, even those who have been through breakups themselves. Help those closest to you to stay that way—give them hints, even instructions, and encourage new bonds (not rebounds) with a few people you have not really connected with until now.

***Get Some Perspective.*** With loss comes change, and life is so different it may as well be seen as a new start. Prepare yourself as you would for a major wilderness hiking excursion or a new business venture. Learn all you can about this new terrain, become an expert on where you have been and where you might go next. Education can be combined with entertainment. Ask friends to recommend perfect movies to rent or their favorite music to weep to and broaden your cultural horizons with these images and sounds. For example, Sumrall (1994) edited a collection of stories and poems by women, *Breaking Up is Hard to Do,* inspired by her own experience grieving over a breakup. Read poetry, especially if you never tried it before. Years ago, when grieving over yet another breakup, I traveled to visit an old girlfriend who was stationed in the air force in Ohio. We sat in the officer's club as she first listened to my latest tale of woe and then announced, "Ann, I think you are finally ready for country music." Pushing back her chair, she rose and strode over to the juke box in the bar, ceremoniously punching in several tunes selected to be depressing, plaintive, self-pitying, and simply wonderful to hear. To this day, I cannot imagine my life without Willie Nelson's voice in it occasionally, even on very happy days. The art and ideas you are ready for only after a breakup are gifts you have earned by your suffering. They can be lifelong sources of comfort and joy.

***Ready for Further Punishment, or Maybe Reward.*** And so, we take our lessons to heart. We take this heart, this new heart and self, full of hope, humor, and irony, and we face the world—a new world with uncharted possibilities and dangers. Perhaps we try once again, explore a new love, although it will not be the same. Then again, the pain reminds us we do not want it to be exactly the same. We have some memories and fantasies to cherish, some sense of hard-won meaning, the moral of the story. Together these help to forge a sense of promise. Thus, silly to risk it, but crazy not to, we try again, and we take heart.

[...]

# REFERENCES

Baumeister, R. R, & Wotman, S. R. (1992). *Breaking hearts: The two side of unrequited love.* New York: Guilford.

Baxter, L. A. (1984). Trajectories of relationship disengagement. *Journal of Social and Personal Relationships, 1,* 29–48.

Colgrove, M., Bloomfield, H. H., & McWilliams, P (1991). *How to survive the loss of a love.* Los Angeles: Prelude Press.

Colwin, L. (1976). *Passion and affect.* New York: Avon Books.

Davis, M. S. (1973). *Intimate relations.* New York: The Free Press.

Duck, S. (Ed.). (1982). *Personal relationships 4: Dissolving personal relationships.* New York: Academic Press.

Ford, R. (1987). *Rock springs.* New York: Vintage Books.

Frankel, V, & Tien, E. (1993). *The heartbreak handbook.* New York: Fawcett/Columbine. Greene–Pepper, D. (1980). *Hate poems for ex–lovers, or how to breakup laughing.* Secaucus, NJ: Citadel Press.

Groening, M. (1984). Love is hell. New York: Random House.

Harvey, J. H. (1996). *Embracing their memory.* Boston: Allyn & Bacon.

Harvey, J. H., Agostinelli, G., & Weber, A. L. (1989). Account–making and the formation of expectations about close relationships. *Review of Personality and Social Psychology, 10,* 39–62.

Harvey, J. H., Orbuch, T. L, & Weber, A. L. (1990). A social psychological model of account–making in response to severe stress. *Journal of Language and Social Psychology, 9,* 191–207.

Harvey, J. H., Weber, A. L., & Orbuch, T. L. (1990). *Interpersonal accounts: A social–psychological perspective.* Oxford, England: Basil Blackwell.

Kingma, D. R. (1987). *Coming apart: Why relationships end and how to live through the ending of yours.* Berkeley, CA: Conari Press.

Lee, L. (1984). Sequences in separation: A framework for investigating endings of the personal (romantic) relationship. *Journal of Social and Personal Relationships, 1,* 99–73.

Leick, N., & Davidsen–Nielsen, M. (1991). *Healing pain: Attachment, loss, and grief therapy.* (David Stoner, Trans.). New York: Tavistock/Routledge.

Neeld, E. H. (1990). *Seven choices: Taking the steps to new life after losing someone you love.* New York: Dell Publishing.

Orbuch, T. L. (1988). *Responses to and coping with nonmarital relationship terminations.* (Doctoral) dissertation, University of Wisconsin, Madison.

Overbeck, J. (1990). *Love stinks: The romantic's guide to breaking up without breaking down.* New York: Pocket Books.

Pennebaker, J. (1990). *Opening up: The healing power of confiding to others.* New York: Avon Books.

Phillips, D., & Judd, R. (1978). *How to fall out of love.* New York: Fawcett Popular Library.

Simpson, J. A. (1987). The dissolution of romantic relationships: Factors involved in relationship stability and emotional distress. *Journal of Personality and Social Psychology, 53,* 684–692.

Sumrall, A. C. (1994). *Breaking up is hard to do: Stories by women.* Freedom, CA: The Crossing Press.

Tennov, D. (1979). *Love and limerence: The experience of being in love.* New York: Stein and Day.

Vaughan, D. (1986). *Uncoupling: Turning points in intimate relationships.* New York: Oxford University Press.

Weber, A. L. (1992b). A meta–account. In J. H. Harvey, T. L. Orbuch, & A. L. Weber (Eds.), *Attribution, accounts, and close relationships* (pp. 280–287). New York: Springer–Verlag.

Weil, A. (1997). *Eight weeks to optimum health.* New York: Knopf.

# END-OF-CHAPTER REFLECTIONS

1. Now that you have read and thought more about what makes a good breakup, what would you add to our opening list of what a good breakup is not?

2. If you had a do-over for a prior breakup, what would you do differently?

3. Take some time to consider one or two relationships you know of that have ended. You might notice the reasons people break up are sometimes the very same things couples in enduring relationships fight about. What then, is the difference between couples who stay together and couples who end their intimate relationship? If your answer is good communication and conflict management skills you are on the right track.

4. What is a good breakup? "The best breakups, if there is such a thing, enable acceptance and minimize psychic wreckage, so that the pain of the ending doesn't overwhelm the positive trace of the relationship" (Svoboda, 2011, p. 67–68).

We hope that this chapter has offered you some insight into why breakups are difficult and provided you with ideas about what you can do to create a good breakup. Still, breakups hurt, and if you have difficulty managing your emotional reaction to the loss, reach out. Seek support from your family, friends, or a professional counselor.

**WARNING:** Children of divorce or committed relationship dissolution become vulnerable during the time of separation due to numerous changes such as diminished parenting, lowered family finances, and a transition to a two-home family. However, the biggest threat to children's adjustment and mental health is exposure to parental conflict (Golombok & Tasker, 2015; O'Hara et al., 2019). When a parent is villainized, children report increased levels of depression, unhappiness, and hurt. They also report feeling more distant from the villainizing parent(s)—in other words, it backfires (Rowen & Emery, 2018).

In summary, when children are exposed to fighting or put in the middle (e.g., hear parents talk bad about one another, are asked to relay messages, or are asked to report on other parent) they suffer a lot. So DON'T DO IT!

**BONUS WARNING:** The introduction of new potential partners to children can seem like a good thing. However, the introduction of several potential partners as parents reenter the dating scene increases the number of attachment breaks that occur for children. So, it is a good idea to hold off on introductions until parents are pretty sure that the timing is in the best interest of the child(ren).

# REFERENCES

DeWall, C. N., MacDonald, G., Webster, G. D., Masten, C. L., Baumeister, R. F., Powell, C., Eisenberger, N. I. (2010). Acetaminophen reduces social pain: Behavioral and neural evidence. *Psychological Science, 21*(7), 931–937. https://doi.org/10.1177/0956797610374741

Duck, S. W. (1982). A topography of relationship disengagement and dissolution. In S. W. Duck (Ed.), *Personal relationships: Vol. 4. Dissolving personal relationships* (pp. 1–30). Academic Press.

Golombok, S., & Tasker, F. (2015). Socio-emotional development in changing families. In M. E. Lamb (Vol. Ed.), & R. M. Lerner (Series Ed.), *Handbook of child psychology and developmental science* (7th ed., Vol. 3), *Social, emotional and personality development* (pp. 419–463). Wiley.

O'Hara, K. L., Sandler, I. N., Wolchik, S. A., Tein, J., & Rhodes, C. A. (2019). Parenting time, parenting quality, interparental conflict, and mental health problems of children in high-conflict divorce. *Journal of Family Psychology, 33*(6), 690–703.

Rollie, S., & Duck, S. (2006). Divorce and dissolution of romantic relationships: Stage models and their limitations. In M. A. Fine & J. H. Harvey (Eds.) *Handbook of divorce and relationship dissolution* (pp. 223–240). Routledge.

Rowen, J., & Emery, R. (2018). Parental denigration: A form of conflict that typically backfires. *Family Court Review, 56*, 258–268.

Svoboda, E. (2011). The thoroughly modern guide to breakups. *Psychology Today, 44*(1), 64–69.

Weber, A. L. (1998). Losing, leaving, and letting go: Coping with nonmarital breakups. In B. H. Spitzberg & W. R. Cupach (Eds.), *The dark side of close relationships* (pp. 127–143). Routledge.

# RECOMMENDATIONS FOR FURTHER READING

Oprah offers a great list of books that will help heal your broken heart and get your life on track.

Here is a link: https://www.oprahmag.com/entertainment/books/g25894161/best-books-to-read-after-a-breakup/?slide=19

# RECOMMENDED PODCAST

Practically Perfect Parenting Podcast,.hosted by John Sommers-Flannagan and Sara Polanchek

Episode: Divorced and Shared Parenting, https://practicallyperfectparenting.libsyn.com/divorce-and-shared-parenting

# Chapter 14

# Blended Families

## EDITORS' INTRODUCTION

Take a moment and imagine the ideal family. We predict that, in line with the dominant culture, many of you conjured up an image of a traditional nuclear family with a father, mother, and children. Now, think of your family. Odds are your family structure is not the same image. This brief experiment demonstrates our socialization to believe that the traditional family structure is the "ideal" family and may make you think your family is less than ideal. In reality, in the United States, family structures vary widely, leaving the traditional nuclear family outnumbered, by a stretch (Golombok & Tasker, 2015). Regardless of family structure, for children, the best environment is one where positive parenting, the absence of parenting stress, and a harmonious couple relationship come together (Golombok & Tasker, 2015). We believe this is the best environment for adults too!

In this chapter we explore blended (step) family formation and typical challenges family members face. In the United States, about 40% of marriages are remarriages for at least one partner, and half of young adults (younger than 30) are members of a stepfamily (Pew Research Center, 2011). Thus, for some of you, being a part of a blended family is not new. For you, this chapter may offer some new insight into the experiences of the adults (or children) in your family. For others, it is easy to presume that across your life span—even if your first partnership with children remains intact—interacting with blended families is practically inevitable. Our hope here is to break the stigma that blended families are less than ideal and elevate the idea that all families, regardless of structure, can be sources of stability, comfort, love, and relational intimacy.

Typically, a blended family is formed after a couple relationship with children has ended and one or both parents enter a new committed relationship. Blended families are headed by many couple variations (e.g., heterosexual, gay, lesbian). Unfortunately, the research on stepfamilies is skewed, with most studies focusing on heterosexual-led families. Hence, the paltry research of LGBTQ+-led families is fraught with the bias of a heteronormative family structure in data collection and interpretation (Bergeson et al., 2020). Still, as we will see in the first reading, there are many experiences blended families face. We will expand on particular differences between heterosexual-led and LGBTQ+-led families after the first reading.

Now, take a moment and imagine the ideal stepfamily. You thought of the *Brady Bunch*, didn't you? In the same way we have been socialized to see the nuclear family as ideal, we are socialized to believe that the goal of a blended family is to create some version of the *Brady Bunch*. This troublesome ideal leaves stepfamily members holding unrealistic expectations of themselves and one another. In truth, as some of you already know, coming together and forming a blended family is not always smooth sailing. It is one of the few situations where people find themselves engaging in intimate relationships that are not entirely of their choosing.

In the following excerpt from the book chapter "Renegotiating Family Communication: Remarriage and Stepfamilies" Segrin and Flora provide research and insight into the plight of blended family members as they navigate formation, role expectations, and conflicts. As you read about their experiences, we encourage you to think about how healthy communication skills (Chapter 6), mastery of difficult conversations (Chapter 7), conflict management skills (Chapter 8), and quality parenting (Chapter 11) could disrupt the status quo and make a healthy, well-adjusted blended family possible.

As you read, keep in mind the following primer questions for reflection. If you feel so inclined, take a few minutes and consider your responses to the following questions before you read, and then again after you've finished each reading.

## PRIMERS

1. If you are a member of a blended family, what is your role? What is the most challenging aspect of your role? How could you use what you have learned about communication to address this challenge?

2. If you are not a member of a blended family, what do you imagine is the hardest part of being in a blended family? What would you do to address this challenge?

# Renegotiating Family Communication

Remarriage and Stepfamilies

*By Chris Segrin and Jeanne Flora*

[...]

## COMMUNICATION AND STEPFAMILY RELATIONSHIPS

Stepfamilies are quite common in American society. About 30% of all children will live with a stepparent before reaching adulthood (Bumpass, Raley, & Sweet, 1995). It is estimated that one in three Americans is presently a member of a stepfamily and that more than half of all Americans will be a part of a stepfamily at some point in their lives (Larson, 1992). Stepfamilies are also nothing new. American presidents George Washington and Abraham Lincoln each had Stepfamilies. There are a lot of different terms for Stepfamilies including *remarried families, blended families, binuclear families, second families,* and *reconstituted families,* to name but a few (e.g., Bray, 1999; Ganong & Coleman, 1997, 2000). There is something particularly interesting about phenomena that are referenced by multiple terms, such as when two middle-aged people date each other and are described with terms like "partner," "significant other," "boyfriend," "girlfriend," and "lady friend." People often look for different terms when they are somehow uneasy with the concept, or when they feel there is some stigma associated with it. Presumably it is easier to change the label than to change thinking about the concept. Stepfamilies have received a bad reputation in our culture, for reasons that we will get into shortly. However, Stepfamilies are as diverse as families more generally, so broad generalizations about their harm or helpfulness are often difficult to support.

Consider some of the different ways in which Stepfamilies might be formed. People often think of Stepfamilies that are initiated after divorce from a first marriage. That is one of well over a dozen different ways that a stepfamily could be formed. Some people may not find themselves in a stepfamily until they reach their 30s and 40s if an older parent remarries following the death of his or her spouse. Some people may have had children outside marriage and then decide to marry someone other than the biological parent of the children. For both spouses this could be their first marriage, yet one would be a stepparent. The common denominator in all of these cases is that one adult parent has a legal or genetic tie to a child that the other adult does not (Ganong & Coleman, 2000). When these two unite, they form a stepfamily. When only one of the adults has children prior to remarriage, they form what is sometimes referred to as a *simple step-family*. When both have children from previous relationships, they form a *complex stepfamily*. Complex Stepfamilies have a higher likelihood of redivorce (Coleman et al., 2000).

---

### BOX 14.1.1 IMAGES OF STEPFAMILIES IN THE MEDIA

Family scientists Lawrence Ganong and Marilyn Coleman remarked that "cultural beliefs about family life exert a strong influence on the ways in which people conduct themselves, evaluate their situations, and expect to be regarded by others" (Ganong & Coleman, 1997, p. 85). Numerous family scholars have argued that Stepfamilies tend to have a bad reputation, due in part to their portrayal in the media (e.g., Bernstein, 1999; Ganong & Coleman, 1997). Although there has been virtually no scientific study of the effects of stepfamily portrayals in the media, it is worthwhile to at least momentarily consider how Stepfamilies are depicted in stories, movies, and television, and how that might influence both society's and individuals' beliefs, attitudes, and expectations for Stepfamilies.

Without doubt, the dominant media image of stepfamily that is referenced in scholarly essays comes from the story *Cinderella* which was made into a popular film in 1950. It was *Cinderella* that popularized the "wicked stepmother" image. Other fairy tales such as *Sleeping Beauty*, *Snow White*, and *Hansel and Gretel* reinforced this often dim view of stepparents. Negative portrayals of stepfamily life, and stepparents in particular, have continued in earnest since *Cinderella*. Films such as *Table for Five* (1983), *See You in the Morning* (1989), *Radio Flyer* (1992), *This Boy's Life* (1993), *Bastard Out of Carolina* (1996), and *Promise to Caroline* (1996) continue to depict stepparents as mean and sometimes abusive and stepfamily life as dysfunctional. The abundance of such storylines illustrates that there is a long history of negative images of Stepfamilies in American media.

With that said, it would be inaccurate to say that media images of Stepfamilies are uniformly negative. A number of dramatic films such as *The Sound of Music* (1965), *Tender Mercies* (1983), *Sarah Plain and Tall* (1990), and *Stepmom* (1998) depict stepparent-stepchild relationships in a much more positive light, sometimes portraying extraordinary caring and kindness on the part of stepparents. Other films such as *Yours Mine and Ours* (1968), *With 6 You Get Eggroll* (1968), *Seems Like Old Times* (1980), *Murphy's Romance* (1985), and *My Stepmother Is an Alien* (1988) present a comedic view of Stepfamilies. Furthermore, television portrayals of Stepfamilies have been almost exclusively positive, as evidenced by shows such as *The Brady Bunch* (1969–1974), *Eight is Enough* (1977–1981), *Major Dad* (1989–1993), and *Hearts Afire* (1992–1995), although more recent programs such as *Once and Again* (1999–2002) have tackled some of the more difficult issues that face contemporary Stepfamilies. For many Americans under the age of 50, it would be difficult to overstate the potential impact of *The Brady Bunch*. This program was first aired 35 years ago and has continued to be broadcast in syndication virtually without interruption. When family scholars discuss the role of unrealistically positive expectations in stepfamily adjustment (e.g., Jones, 1978), images of *The Brady Bunch* and similarly positive portrayals such as *The Sound of Music* immediately come to mind. However, the general belief of media cultivation theorists is that the media does not cause changes in views of the family but rather reflects and reinforces, or cultivates, already established beliefs (Signorelli & Morgan, 2001).

Despite the presence of both negative and positive images of Stepfamilies in the media, on balance, their depiction on television is relatively rare. Robinson and Skill (2001) content analyzed prime time fictional TV shows with a family configuration. In the 1950s, only 1.2% of these shows featured Stepfamilies. By the period 1990 to 1995 this figure had risen to 6.0%—a considerable increase, but still far below their prevalence in the actual American population.

The media has been blamed for simultaneously depicting overly negative views of stepfamilies and stepparents in particular, as well as portraying unrealistically positive images of stepfamilies. Overall, depictions of stepfamilies on television and in the movies are still relatively rare; but in some cases, very salient and accessible. The exact role of these media images in shaping cultural as well as individual attitudes toward stepfamilies is still largely unknown to family scientists.

## Views of Stepfamilies

In Box 14.1.1, we examine how Stepfamilies are portrayed in the media. Later in this section, we explore portrayals of Stepfamilies in society more generally.

### Societal Views of Stepfamilies

Family scientists have argued that most societal views of stepfamilies are negative in tone and based on an idealization of nuclear families (Ganong & Coleman, 2000). For instance, one image of stepfamilies in society is that of *deviant group*. Because stepfamilies and stepparents are sometimes stigmatized through cultural stereotypes, myths, and media images, Ganong and Coleman argue that many people see them as deviant groups. Consequently, stepfamily members sometimes attempt to conceal their status or engage in deliberate impression management strategies to overcome the stigma and prove that they are a worthwhile family. Another prominent view of stepfamilies is evident in the *incomplete institutionalization hypothesis* (Cherlin, 1978). Cherlin's thesis is essentially that stepfamilies lack guiding norms, principles, and methods of problem solving that are enjoyed by members of nuclear families. Further, there is no institutionalized social support for stepfamilies. In some cases, there are not even any appropriate terms for certain step relationships (e.g., the sibling of a stepparent). For these reasons, stepfamilies do not get adequately incorporated into our institutions and have to function under conditions of unclear or ambiguous expectations. Ganong and Coleman are quick to note that some have criticized Cherlin for overstating the case, but that there is at least a kernel of truth in the incomplete institutionalization hypothesis. Another societal view of stepfamilies is that of the *reformed nuclear family*.

According to this perspective, stepfamilies are just like nuclear families by virtue of having two heterosexual adults and children. People who endorse this view assume that stepfamilies will function as any nuclear family would and that family membership and household membership are one and the same. This societal view of stepfamilies certainly sounds less negative than the incomplete institutionalization hypothesis or the deviant groups perspective, but it is based on a fundamental misunderstanding of stepfamilies. As we reveal later in this selection, stepfamilies face their own unique set of challenges that often distinguish them from nuclear families. And like nuclear families, stepfamilies have diverse forms and functions. For that reason the reformed nuclear family view appears to stem from a whitewashed vision of what stepfamilies are all about. At the same time, we hasten to point out that the deviant groups and incomplete institutionalization perspectives are perhaps equally off base, just in the opposite direction. In any event, the societal views of stepfamilies described by Ganong and Coleman indicate that myths and stereotypes abound when it comes to understanding stepfamilies.

## The Development of Stepfamily Communication and Relationships

Family clinicians such as Papernow (1993) recognize that stepfamilies go through distinct phases in their efforts to form a cohesive "family." At the start of the remarriage, many stepfamilies are in the *fantasy stage*. This stage is represented by hope and perhaps expectation that the new spouse will be a better partner and parent than the previous spouse. The spouse who marries a partner with children will often enter into the relationship with similarly lofty goals and an immediate effort to be a super-parent. The image of stepfamilies portrayed in *The Brady Bunch* is a good illustration of the sort of family communication dynamics that might be hoped for in the fantasy stage. However, as most people are aware, that image of Stepfamily life is just that—a fantasy. Next, stepfamilies enter into the *immersion stage*. In this stage, the stepparent tends to feel like an outsider looking in and their grand expectations are often shattered. Children become more aware of the relationship between their biological parent and stepparent. This can generate feelings of jealousy, resentment, and confusion. The reality of different views toward child rearing, parental roles, and negotiation of new boundaries creates conditions that are ripe for family conflict.

The transformation from the fantasy to immersion stages described by Papernow (1993) is clearly evident in research findings on stepfathers and their stepchildren. Stepfathers often enter the Stepfamily with what appear to be the best of intentions, overtly expressing positivity toward the stepchildren in the hope of developing a good relationship with them. However, research shows that they quickly become disengaged from the stepchildren when their positive overtures are rebuffed (Hetherington & Clingempeel, 1992). Despite the fact that sharing information with the children, paying attention to them, and engaging them in shared activities are all positive rapport-building communication behaviors, Stepfamily relationships like all other relationships cannot be forced or rushed. Children have a knack for putting on the brakes when stepparent–stepchild relationships develop too quickly This regulation of relationship development may be interpreted as rejection by the stepfather, resulting in his disengagement from the relationship. This pattern of early Stepfamily relationship development clearly illustrates the sort of changes in behavior that would be expected as stepfamilies progress from the fantasy into the immersion stage.

The development of Stepfamily relationships is often evident in how the family negotiates and develops family rituals. To explore this issue, communication researchers Dawn Braithwaite, Leslie Baxter, and Anneliese Harper (1998) interviewed 20 stepparents and 33 stepchildren and asked them to focus on family rituals during the first 4 years of the stepfamily's history. They found that families had to balance the dialectical opposition between honoring rituals of the "old" family and developing rituals in the "new" family. This management was accomplished in several ways. First, some rituals from the old family were dropped because they could no longer be performed in the new family, they were no longer appropriate, or the new spouse would not participate in the new ritual. It is sometimes the case that family rituals are built around one person (e.g., going to a certain restaurant on the father's birthday) and when that person is no longer a part of the household the ritual is dropped. In other cases, the new spouse may have different religious beliefs and practices that are at odds with the family's adherence to a former ritual. Second, some rituals were successfully imported unchanged into the new family. Braithwaite and her colleagues explain that the perseverance of such rituals functions to honor both the old and the new family. For example, a family that goes on a camping trip every summer might continue to do so after the remarriage of one of the parents. In this way they keep the "old family" tradition alive, while also incorporating the new family member(s) into that tradition ultimately making it the "new family's" ritual as well. Third, some family rituals are imported into the new family but adapted in some way. A family that always gets together for an afternoon barbeque on the 4th of July might have to modify their ritual when their new stepmother, who is a police officer, has to work on that day. Instead, this family may have a dinner and then go to their local park to watch a fireworks display in the evening. The family still celebrates the ritual of getting together for a big meal on the 4th of July, but they adapted it to meet the needs of the new family member. Finally, stepfamilies will often form new rituals of their own. These can help to create a new and unique identity for the stepfamily so long as everyone in the family is a willing participant in the ritual.

In a further analysis of these same interviews Baxter, Braithwaite, and Nicholson (1999) turned their attention to turning points in the development of these stepfamily relationships. When asked to focus on those keys events in the family's early history that brought them to where they are today, respondents most frequently cited "changes in household/family composition" (mentioned by 94% of all respondents), "conflict or disagreement" (72%), "holidays and special events" (67%), "quality time" (64%), and "family crisis" (55%). It appears that these various turning points are characteristic in the development of most stepfamilies. As part of these interviews, Baxter and her associates asked participants to draw a graph where the horizontal axis is time (0–48 months) and the vertical axis is what percent they "feel like a family" (0–100). Analyses of these revealed five distinct stepfamily development trajectories that are summarized in Table 14.1.1.

There are several notable qualities to Baxter et al.'s (1999) findings on stepfamily development trajectories that are evident from Table 14.1.1. First, it is quite obvious that not all stepfamilies develop in the same way. Some experience a smooth and rapid progression toward feeling like a family, whereas others have a more turbulent development trajectory, or never really develop the sense of being a family. Second, even though the majority of stepfamilies successfully develop a sense of cohesion and unity, it is apparent that some (i.e., "stagnating" and "declining") never successfully achieve that goal. From these data, that appears to be the case for about one in five stepfamilies.

To gain a deeper understanding of what differentiated the stepfamilies, Braithwaite and her associates conducted further analyses of the interviews from these stepfamily members to examine how family processes variables discriminated among the different types (Braithwaite, Olson, Golish, Soukup, & Turman, 2001). They found that *accelerated* stepfamilies rapidly developed traditional family roles, norms, boundaries, and expectations. They seemed to approach stepfamily life expecting traditional nuclear family roles and norms to develop. Their strong solidarity helped them to smoothly work through the conflicts that they experienced

## TABLE 14.1.1 BAXTER ET AL.'S (1999) TAXONOMY OF STEPFAMILY DEVELOPMENT TRAJECTORIES

| Trajectory | Prevalence | Description Type |
|---|---|---|
| Accelerated | 31% | Started out at feeling somewhat like a family and rapidly progressed with an almost 4:1 ratio of positive to negative turning points |
| Prolonged | 27% | Started out not feeling like a family but slowly progressed toward family cohesion with a 3:1 ratio of positive to negative turning points |
| Stagnating | 14% | Started out not feeling like a family and never developed the feeling over the first four years; they experienced a 2:1 ratio of positive to negative turning points but these did not create the feeling of a family |
| Declining | 6% | Started out feeling like a family but that feeling steadily declined over the first four years; they experienced a 2:1 ratio of negative to positive turning points |
| High-Amplitude Turbulent | 22% | Drastic fluctuation in feeling like a family during the first four years; numerous positive and negative turning points that each altered their feeling of being a family |

Note. Adapted from Baxter, Braithwaite, & Nicholson (1999).

early in their development. *Prolonged* families tended to be adaptable, flexible, and generally satisfied with their stepfamily experiences. Even though they started out uncertain, they were willing to negotiate things like family roles and were open to communication about these issues. Unlike the accelerated families, those with a prolonged trajectory did not compare themselves to a nuclear family. Families with the *declining* trajectory seemed to have a lot of trouble from the word go. They started out with great expectations but almost immediately experienced loyalty conflicts, ambiguous and strained family roles, and divisive family boundaries. Their struggles were characterized by eventually developing impermeable and divisive boundaries by bloodline and generation and, ultimately, by avoidance of communication. By the end of their fourth year, these families were around zero on the "feeling like a family" scale. *Stagnating* families experienced awkwardness in their role and felt, as Braithwaite and her associates put it, "thrown together." They wanted a normal or traditional family life, but ironically, the more they tried to create that the more resistance they experienced from within. Obviously, not all members of these families were on the same page when it came to developing a "normal" family life. Loyalty conflicts, resentment, and dissatisfaction were common themes in these families that simply never took off. Finally, the *high-amplitude turbulent* families had a diverse and unstable development in their first 4 years. Like many other newly formed stepfamilies they started off with great expectations and quickly collided with realities that were at odds with these expectations. Feelings of betrayal and a lack of trust were common in these family types. Braithwaite et al. noted that a lack of solidarity between the couple was common in these families and prevented them from communicating a unified front to the children. Conflicts typically culminated in a "fork in the road" that was successfully negotiated in some turbulent families. Those who avoided these conflicts were among the least satisfied of the turbulent families. After carefully examining the development trajectories and experiences, Braithwaite et al. concluded that the three key family processes that varied across the different families were boundary management, solidarity, and adaptation. Even though these conclusions were derived from a small sample of stepfamily members, they are generally consistent with the research literature on stepfamilies that highlights the importance of these same critical issues.

## Diversity Within Stepfamilies

As we mentioned earlier in this selection, there is no single standard or norm for stepfamilies. Like families, more generally, stepfamilies are quite diverse and can take a variety of forms. In this section we consider the variety of different roles that people might occupy in stepfamilies and some of the many different types of relationships that occur in these different stepfamilies. Finally, this section includes an analysis of different types of stepfamilies based on the members' orientation toward stepfamily life.

### Roles in Stepfamilies

Family roles simultaneously shape and are shaped by communication patterns within the family. Although the roles of child and parent are fairly dear in most family contexts, there is considerable ambiguity inherent in being a stepparent. Many stepparents are unsure about assuming the role of parent. After all, in many stepfamilies the children still have two biological parents. What is the ideal role of a stepparent in this family context? Family scientists Mark Fine, Marilyn Coleman, and Lawrence Ganong (1998) investigated this issue by asking parents, stepparents, and children in stepfamilies about what they think the ideal role of a stepparent is. They also asked respondents to describe the actual role of the stepparent in their family. For the ideal role of a stepparent, just over half of the parents and stepparents said "parent." In other words, the stepparent should assume the role of parent just as a biological parent would. In contrast, only 29% of the children offered this response. Evidently, a greater proportion of parents and stepparents, compared to children, think that "parent" is the ideal role for a stepparent. Among these same respondents, 18% of the parents and 18% of the stepparents indicated that "friend" was the ideal role of a stepparent. In contrast, 40% of the children thought that "friend" was the ideal role for a stepparent. So it seems that more children want their stepparent to assume the role of friend, whereas parents and stepparents want the stepparent to assume the role of parent. It is also interesting that 48% of the stepparents said that their actual role in the family was that of parent, whereas only 28% of the children said that their stepparent held the role of parent. Fine et al.'s study illustrates not only how there are different desires within the family for stepparent roles but also how family members do not necessarily agree on what the actual role of the family's stepparent is. For the most part, parents and children have a clearer perception of what the stepparent role is in contrast to stepparents who indicate that their role in the family is not entirely clear (Fine, Coleman, & Ganong, 1999).

The performance of some parental roles in stepfamilies may be specific to the sex of the parent. For example, mothers will often assume a variety of roles to control the development of the relationship between their children and new spouse (Coleman, Ganong, & Weaver, 2001). Mothers will sometimes perform the role of *defender* in which they try to shield their children from unfair discipline, perceived slights, and misunderstanding on the part of the stepfather. In the role of *gatekeeper,* mothers literally control the stepfather's access to their children during both courtship and marriage. For instance, it may take many years before a mother will leave her children alone with their stepfather. Mothers also act as *mediators* between children and their stepfathers. Coleman et al. note that the mediator role is particularly common early in the formation of stepfamilies when disagreements are prevalent. A related role performed by mothers in stepfamilies is that of *interpreter*. Interpreters not only step in and referee conflicts but also explain each family member's perspective to the other. When lines of communication between children and the stepfather may be hindered or nonexistent, the mother's performance of the interpreter role can be vital to salvaging some degree of civility in the family environment.

Remarriage and the formation of a stepfamily often change the interactions between a mother and her children. When mothers remarry, they decrease their use of harsh discipline tactics such as yelling, spanking, and hitting (Thomson, Mosley, Hanson, & McLanahan, 2001). However, remarried mothers supervise their children less than do stable single mothers (Thomson et al.). So remarriage brings not only some obvious improvements to mother–child interactions but also some declines in the form of less supervision.

Stepmothers have a particularly challenging role to fulfill in many remarried families. As mentioned elsewhere in this selection, there is an abundance of negatively toned folklore concerning stepmothers. Stepmothers often feel that they have to go the extra mile to prove that they are not like the wicked stepmother in *Cinderella* (Guisinger, Cowan, & Schuldberg,

1989). In so doing, they often start by forming good relationships with their stepchildren, but their optimistic attitudes toward stepparenting erode noticeably within 3 to 5 years of marriage. Guisinger et al. also found that a quality marriage goes hand in hand with good relationships between stepmothers and their stepchildren. Many stepmothers must also contend with some of the negative emotions that stem from occupying a role that sometimes excludes them or makes them feel less than 100% legitimate. The feminist scholar Elizabeth Church (1999) interviewed 104 stepmothers and found that about half had felt jealous or envious in their role as stepmother. Feelings of jealousy were provoked by three types of circumstances: feeling second best, feeling like an outsider, and feeling like a rival. When stepmothers felt jealous due to a perceived rivalry, it was not the children's biological mother who was the rival. Rather, many felt that they had to compete with their stepchildren for their partner's attention. Church argues that often stepmothers' jealousy is an expression of feeling disconnected from the family and feeling powerless. In many families stepmothers occupy a precarious role. They are expected to form good relationships with the children and get involved in their care—but not too involved. When either biological parent pursues interaction with the children, stepmothers may be expected to step back, never having all of the full rights and privileges of a regular mother.

## Stepfamily Relationships and Stepfamily Types

It is customary to describe different types of stepfamilies by their formal structure (e.g., mother with her biological children and stepfather and both spouses with their own biological children). However, Gross (1986) described different stepfamilies from the perspective of their children. To do so, she interviewed 60 children and asked them to describe and explain who was in their family. The children's responses provide insight into the many different ways that some people might define family relationships, and how communication patterns in stepfamilies can sometimes be almost nonexistent, despite the fact that two people may share the same residence. These family structures, defined by children's subjective impressions, appear in Table 14.1.2 Gross (1986) found that the four different stepfamily structures were about equally common in her sample. In some cases (*retention* and *reduction*) the stepchildren refused to characterize their stepparents as "family." In other cases (*substitution* and *reduction)* the children essentially dropped one of the biological parents from their mental representation of "family." There are also many cases (*substitution* and *augmentation)* where the stepchildren willingly characterized their stepparents as family members. This unique taxonomy developed by Gross is a reminder that children approach stepfamily relationships with vastly differing perspectives. The theory of symbolic interaction would explain these different realities of family life through the children's communication patterns with their parents and stepparents. Where there is little communication at all, as in the case of a noncustodial "deadbeat dad," some children literally revise their mental representation of "family" to exclude that member.

## TABLE 14.1.2 GROSS'S (1986) TYPOLOGY OF CHILDREN'S PERCEPTIONS OF FAMILY MEMBERSHIP

| Stepfamily Structure | Prevalence | Description |
|---|---|---|
| Retention | 33% | Include both biological parents as family |
| | | Do not include stepparent as a family member |
| | | Family identified as prior to divorce |
| | | Nonresidential parent still very involved in child's life |
| | | Stepparents play a more negative role in child's life |
| Substitution | 13% | Exclude at least one biological parent from family, usually the nonresidential parent |
| | | Include at least one stepparent in family |
| | | Views family as child, one biological parent, and stepparent |
| | | Household and family are synonymous |
| | | Children are younger at separation from biological parent and remarriage to stepparent |
| | | Qualified acceptance of stepparent |
| Reduction | 25% | Fewer than the original two parents viewed as family |
| | | Stepparent not viewed as family member |
| | | At least one biological parent (usually nonresidential) not viewed as family member |
| | | Experience family as "one-parent family" |
| | | Negative feelings toward stepparent |

(continued)

| Stepfamily Structure | Prevalence | Description |
| --- | --- | --- |
| Augmentation | 28% | Both biological parents identified as family, as well as at least one stepparent |
| | | Stepparent is not a "replacement" but an "addition" |
| | | Usually involved custodial father and stepmother |
| | | Many had previously lived with their mother |
| | | Maintained contact with nonresidential parent |
| | | Free movement between households, and lack of hostility between biological parents |

*Note. Adapted from Gross (1986).*

On the other hand, where stepparent–stepchild communication patterns reflect issues such as concern, guidance, reasonable discipline, recreation, and so forth, symbolic interactionists would argue that children would more readily incorporate the stepparent into the family's membership.

Much of the research on stepfamily relationships has understandably focused on relationships between children and their stepparents and the marital relationship in stepfamilies. What is sometimes overlooked when people think about stepfamily relationships is the relationship between the two biological parents, only one of whom is currently the custodial parent. Remarriage after a divorce does not represent the end of the relationship between two biological parents. A divorced couple with children often needs to continue some form of relationship to coordinate child care and visitation, even though one or both may have remarried and formed a new family. In such cases, children become part of a *binuclear family*. The communication patterns of formerly married spouses can take on a variety of forms. Ahrons and Rodgers (1987) described these in their taxonomy of postdivorce relationships described in Table 14.1.3 What is most striking from the descriptions of these relationships is the diverse range of interaction patterns maintained by former spouses. Some (e.g., *dissolving duos*) permanently sever their lines of communication. This is probably a much more common communication pattern in divorced couples without any children. At the other end of the spectrum, the *perfect pals* manage to maintain open communication and continue to participate together in family activities and rituals. It is instructive to compare the types of postdivorce relations in this scheme to the children's subjective impressions of family membership described by Gross (1986). Recall that

| TABLE 14.1.3 **AHRONS AND RODGERS' (1987) TYPOLOGY OF POSTDIVORCE RELATIONSHIPS** | |
|---|---|
| **Relationship Type** | **Description** |
| Dissolving Duos | No contact after divorce |
| Perfect Pals | Maintain mutual respect for each other after divorce |
| | Remain good friends |
| | Maintain open communication and family rituals |
| | They often remain single |
| Cooperative Colleagues | No real friendship |
| | Cooperate and coordinate efforts at parenting |
| | Compromise for the children's benefit |
| | Effectively manage conflicts |
| Angry Associates | Harbor resentment and anger toward each other |
| | Both active as parents but in parallel, not collectively |
| | Children experience loyalty conflicts |
| Fiery Foes | Intense anger |
| | No acceptance of other parent's rights |
| | Attempts to separate ex-spouse from children |
| | No cooperation between parents |
| | Children become pawns |
| | Parents still attached to each other as evidenced by their intense emotional reaction to each other |

*Note. Adapted from Ahrons & Rodgers (1987).*

in some cases (*substitution* and *reduction)* Gross found that children would no longer consider one of their biological parents to be a member of the family. It would not be much of stretch to suppose that the biological parents in such families are *dissolving duos* or perhaps fiery *foes*. Gross also found that children would often still consider a non-custodial parent to be a member of the family, in the cases of *retention* and *augmentation*. One might suppose that the divorced biological parents in these cases would be *perfect pals* or *cooperative colleagues*. One could develop additional hypotheses linking these different stepfamily relationships, but the underlying assumption is that the nature of the postdivorce relationship of the biological parents influences to some extent the child's consideration of these parents as members of the family.

Finally, we present a recent summary of some of the distinct types of stepfamilies that have been identified in past research. Family scientists Coleman, Ganong, and Fine (2004) noted that almost every typology of stepfamilies identifies *Brady Bunch Stepfamilies*. The label that scientists use for these families is a testament to the power of the media in influencing our thinking about families. Needless to say, these are stepfamilies that try to set up a situation that is indistinguishable from a first-marriage family. Members of these families relate to each other as if they were parents and children, not stepparents and stepchildren. Their communication is open and abundant, as is their expression of affection. Coleman et al. observe that such families may be ill-prepared, unrealistic, and in denial. Like the Brady Bunch, these families may be striving not to function like a true first-marriage family but rather as a stereotype of a first-marriage family. As Coleman et al. note, often situational demands for communication and problem solving do not fit the Brady Bunch ideal, and this can be cause for dissatisfaction. For some stepfamilies, however, this mentality may work, particularly when children are very young when the stepfamily is formed.

In contrast to the Brady Bunch Stepfamilies, the *detached stepparent–engaged parent stepfamilies* function with nonequivalent parental roles. Generally the mothers in these families are involved in the upbringing of the children and the stepfathers are detached. Stepfathers in these families show little affection toward the stepchildren; they might not get involved in their supervision and engage in limited communication with them. In contrast mothers in these families are prone to engaging in frequent and intense communication with the children. Before condemning these stepfathers, it is important to realize that their detachment sometimes follows the directives of either the mother or her children (Coleman et al., 2004). Stepfathers are sometimes thrown into relationships with stepchildren merely as a function of their marriage to the mother. The stepparent–stepchild relationship is sometimes an incidental one that families manage by keeping a distance between the two and leaving most of the parenting up to the mother.

A related type of stepfamily can be found in the *couple-focused stepfamilies*. Here the marital union is of paramount importance. In these stepfamilies, the communication is largely between the spouses, and the stepparent is detached from the stepchildren. This pattern is perhaps most likely in cases where the children are older and breaking out on their own or when the children do not reside with the married couple. One might expect to see couple-focused stepfamilies, for example, in marriages that follow the death of a spouse later in life.

Finally, some stepfamilies could be characterized as *progressive stepfamilies*. Communication in these stepfamilies is modified to fit the needs to the family's particular situation and demands. Well-established stepfamilies often develop their own unique and creative style of communication to meet the complexities of their family life. One example cited by Coleman et al. (2004) is when mothers interpret the stepfathers to stepchildren and vice versa. As a way of compensating for the lack of shared history in the stepfamily, the mothers may aid their children's and spouse's understanding of each other by enacting this creative communication behavior. Progressive stepfamilies often exhibit excellent family communication and problem solving. Their relationships are sometimes closer than those of first-marriage families. At this time, family scientists and clinicians do not fully understand how such families are developed. However, it appears that a very flexible approach to family communication coupled with a respect for different family forms, devoid of any preconceived notions, are integral elements of progressive stepfamilies.

## Challenges in Stepfamilies

Stepfamilies face a number of challenges in sorting out their relationships that contribute to family stress. Some of the issues that they face, such as conflict, are comparable in kind to those of nuclear families, but perhaps differ in intensity. Other challenges such as negotiating conflicting loyalties to a stepparent and noncustodial parent are unique to stepfamilies. In this section, we examine challenges faced by stepfamilies that include relational communication issues, conflict, adaptability and cohesion, and child adjustment.

### Communication Challenges

Although all developing families face a number of communication challenges as they build relationships, trust, roles, and boundaries, stepfamilies have unique dynamics that make these challenges particularly salient. Furthermore, stepfamilies must face a number of unique challenges that differ from nuclear families with both biological parents. To identify these issues Golish (2003) interviewed 90 people (stepparents, biological parents, and children and stepchildren) from 30 different stepfamilies. They were asked how their communication, feelings, and expectations changed over time and to identify their problem areas and strengths. One of the most common challenges cited by participants was *feeling caught*. This typically involved triangulation in the relationship among a child, his or her custodial parents, and his or her noncustodial parent. This challenge caused children to avoid talking to one parent in front of the other or bringing up certain topics of discussion with one of the parents. Interestingly, it was sometimes the parents who felt caught. For example, sometimes the biological parent was used as a go-between by their child and spouse. Instead of the stepchild and stepparent communicating directly, they would air their grievances through the parent. Some families had problems with *ambiguity of parental roles*. Almost all of the stepfamilies studied by Golish (2003) experienced confusion and uncertainty about the stepparent's role in disciplining children. This sometimes causes a clash between the "friend" and "disciplinarian" role performed by the stepparent. Stepfamilies also had to contend with *regulating boundaries with the noncustodial family*. Many children in stepfamilies are still grieving the loss of their family system. This often took the form of having to renegotiate a different kind of relationship with a now noncustodial father. However, sometimes this challenge in regulating relationships was experienced between former spouses. Where there are issues of joint or shared custody, former spouses cannot simply stop communicating, but rather have to work out arrangements for care of the children.

One particularly unique challenge faced by stepfamilies is *traumatic bonding*. It was often the case that mothers and daughters formed a very close bond as the mother made the transition from divorce to single parenthood. The bond formed during these hard times would often persevere during formation of the stepfamily. At this time, the stepparent would be seen as an intruder in the family. At the same time, the stepparent may feel jealous or excluded by this intense mother–daughter bond. Stepfamilies were also challenged by *vying for resources*. Issues like money, space, and privacy are particularly salient in stepfamilies. The desire for one's own territory could be fueled by the feeling of being invaded by outsiders, which could also increase the desire for privacy. Struggling to secure these resources in an environment where they are often scarce sets the stage for abundant conflicts within the stepfamily. A related challenge faced by stepfamilies is *discrepancies in conflict management styles*. The most common scenario for this challenge was a stepparent's desire to openly confront an issue and the biological parent's and children's desire to avoid the issue. Successfully overcoming this challenge often involved all parties adjusting their communication style. The final communication challenge documented by Golish (2003) was *building solidarity as a family unit*. Particularly strong and successful families accomplished this by spending time together, developing their own family rituals, and displaying affection toward each other. In other cases stepfamilies would incorporate humor into their interactions or naturally and gradually introduce the child and stepparent without trying to force the relationship. Even though most families have to deal with at least some of these issues, they are particularly evident in stepfamilies, and their successful negotiation is vital to developing strong stepfamily relationships. Golish observed that the "meta-theme" underlying many of these communication challenges is the negotiation of boundaries within the family and across families.

In a comparable study, Cissna, Cox, and Bochner (1990) interviewed nine step-families that had at least two school-aged children at home and asked them about issues such as managing relationships with the former spouse, problems in reorganizing their family, and strategies for overcoming these problems. All nine of the families mentioned issues related to balancing the marital versus the parental relationships. Cissna et al. found that there were two dominant tasks that families faced in order to manage this dialectic. First, the family needs to *establish the solidarity of the marriage relationship in the minds of the stepchildren*. Marriages are freely chosen by the spouses, but not by their children. As Golish (2003) observed, sometimes children might view the stepparents as an intruder into a close relationship that was established during tough times. For a stepfamily to develop and function effectively, stepchildren need to see the marital relationship as solid and unified. A second major task that stepfamilies face is *establishing parental authority, particularly the credibility of the stepparent*. Once the children appreciate the substantial nature of the parent-stepparent relationship, the next step is to view the stepparent as something of an authority figure. Without that, boundaries can get blurred and conflicts can arise. Cissna et al. observed that one of the difficult chores for the stepparent is building a friendship relationship with the child while at the same time exercising discipline and developing the role of authority figure. This is an unusually challenging dialectic that must be delicately balanced with acute sensitivity and social skills on the part of the stepparent.

## Conflict

Because of their unique family structure stepfamilies tend to have their own set of stressors and concerns that contribute substantially to interpersonal conflicts (Burrell, 1995). It is often the case in stepfamilies that an "outsider" comes into a long-established physical environment and relational context. Children sometimes have a close relationship with their custodial parent forged during difficult times. They are often accustomed to their custodial parent's undivided attention when they are home together. In addition children may have their own room and space in the house that does not have to be shared with others. The introduction of a stepparent, particularly one with children in tow, can dramatically upset these norms. Obviously the situation is ripe for conflict and may explain why stepfamilies experience more conflict than do intact families (Barber & Lyons, 1994). A lot of the conflicts in stepfamilies occur between the spouses and often concern the children and stepchildren (Ganong & Coleman, 2000). In stepfamilies, it is sometimes the case that the biological parent has far more history and experience raising children than does the stepparent, who may have no child-rearing experience at all. This immediately sets up a situation where the legitimacy of one person's perspective on child rearing is questioned and almost impossible to substantiate. It is no wonder that conflicts over child-rearing issues are so prevalent among spouses in stepfamilies.

Observations of family clinicians indicate that stepfamily households often have to address multiple sources of potential conflict that include outsiders and insiders, boundary disputes, power issues, conflicting loyalties, triangular relationships, and unity versus fragmentation of the new couple relationship (Visher, Visher, & Pasley, 2003). Scientific researchers have reached similar conclusions, noting that the primary sources of conflict in stepfamilies often revolve around boundary issues (Burrell, 1995; Coleman, Fine, Ganong, Downs, & Pauk, 2001). Subsidiary issues included disagreements over resources, loyalty conflicts, individuals having a "guard and protect" mentality, and conflict with extended family (Coleman et al.). Coleman and her associates documented these family conflicts through interviews of adults and children from 17 stepfamilies. Some of the major resources that they frequently argued about were possessions, space, time and attention, and finances. Loyalty conflicts were often felt by children who seemed to be torn between loyalty to their stepparent and their noncustodial parent. What Coleman et al. characterized as a "guard and protect" ideology involved the mother trying to protect an almost peer-like mother–daughter relationship, attempts to protect the children from an overly strict stepfather, or attempts to protect the children from a nonresidential parent. Instances of these interaction patterns highlighted sharp disagreements and conflicts often ensued. Finally, stepfamilies often experienced conflicts with extended family members who did not view the stepfamily as a legitimate family unit. This type of conflict is a good illustration of a dispute that involves an external boundary issue, whereas most other conflicts in the stepfamilies concerned boundaries within the family.

It is sometimes the case in stepfamilies that role ambiguity and boundary issues collectively contribute to conflicts (Burrell, 1995). For example, role ambiguity occurs when people are uncertain about what actions they are expected to take and exactly what their function is in the family. Of course, boundaries represent the often invisible psychological limits of enacted and accepted behaviors within the family and between its members and outsiders. For a new stepparent, role ambiguity and boundary issues may go hand in hand. The role of disciplinarian is often a very uncertain one for the new stepparent. Stepchildren who are unaccustomed to this new role of the stepparent may reject such forms of communication. At the same time, some stepparents may have a hard time communicating in an authoritarian or authoritative fashion toward their stepchildren. This role ambiguity is entwined in boundary issues. How permeable is the stepparent–stepchild relationship? Does the stepparent have the "right" or authority to command the stepchild to do something or to not do something? Does the stepparent have the right or authority to use corporal punishment (involving nonverbal communication)? Should there be as much physical affection in the stepparent–stepchild relationship as might be expected between biological parents and their children? These are all issues that concern both roles and boundaries. They can be very potent catalysts for conflict in most stepfamilies. These conflicts may occur between stepparent and stepchild, between two spouses who disagree on how the stepparents should interact with the stepchild, or between a child and his or her biological parent who disagree on what is acceptable behavior on the part of the stepparent.

There is an interesting power dynamic in stepfamilies that helps to explain the nature of some common conflicts that occur in these contexts. In stepfather families (perhaps the most common form of remarried families with children), family members agree that the mother has most authority and power for major decision making (Giles-Sims & Crosbie-Burnett, 1989). However, for everyday decisions, adolescents appear to have as much influence as the adults, especially early on in the history of the stepfamily. Further, Giles-Sims and Crosbie-Burnett (1989) found that when it comes to making major decisions, adolescents perceived themselves as having more power than their stepfathers—a view that was not necessarily shared by their stepfathers. This potential power struggle between adolescent and stepparent is undoubtedly manifest in conflict interactions until the family is able to establish some norms, or in systems theory terminology, homeostasis. The struggle for power and the quest to establish new family norms may explain why long-term remarried couples with stepchildren experience more conflict than long-term remarried couples with their own biological children (MacDonald & DeMaris, 1995). When children are born into an intact marriage, power, roles, norms and decisionmaking patterns can be gradually and consistently developed throughout childhood. On the other hand, when a remarried couple has stepchildren, where there is no relational history with one of the parents, these same roles, norms, and decision-making patterns must be negotiated and established from scratch. In long-term marriages, where the stepchildren are likely to be older children and adolescents, the potential for interpersonal conflict is extensive.

What are the communication strategies that stepfamilies use to resolve their conflicts? Coleman et al. (2001) found that stepfamilies would often compromise on rules and discipline, present a unified parental front on rules and discipline, talk directly with the person one is in conflict with, or reframe the problem as less serious, perhaps with a joke. Most communication scholars would agree that these are generally effective ways of handling conflict. This suggests, through their often extensive experience with conflict, that stepfamilies often develop and deploy effective means for managing these conflicts.

Having said that "talking directly" is one way stepfamilies resolve conflict, there are some special exceptions. Sometimes stepchildren handle conflict-laden or other sensitive topics is by avoiding the topic in family interactions. Golish and Caughlin (2002) studied this issue by interviewing 115 adolescents and young adults in stepfamilies, using Petronio's (2000) Communication Privacy Management perspective to develop hypotheses about why and when adolescents would avoid various topics with their parents and stepparents. They found that children reported the greatest topic avoidance with stepparents, followed by fathers, and finally by mothers. The most commonly avoided topic across all types of parental relationships was sex. Other commonly avoided topics included talking about the other parent or family and money (e.g., child support payments). When asked why they avoided these topics, the adolescents' and young adults' most typical replies concerned self-protection, protecting the harmony of the relationship with the parent or stepparent, and conflict. Responses that reflected concerns with conflict included the desire to keep conflicts from happening as well and the desire to keep some conflicts from escalating. Even though people often feel that discussing concerns openly is the best way to develop and manage relationships, in an often fragile context of stepfamily relationships, sometimes the avoidance of certain topics is the more sensible and comfortable strategy—at least from the perspective of a child in the stepfamily.

Before leaving the topic of conflict, it bears mentioning that conflict can be a catalyst for positive change in stepfamilies (Coleman, Fine, et al., 2001). As hard as it is for many stepfamilies to sort out their various issues, establish boundaries, and define new roles, the efforts invested in these conflicts may yield dividends so long as they do not consume the stepfamily. Stepfamilies can achieve harmony and happiness, but that may only come after intense negotiation, or conflict, over issues such as space, roles, expectations, discipline, and privacy.

## Adaptability and Cohesion

It is generally the case that stepfamilies have lower family cohesion and adaptability than do first-married families (Pink & Wampler, 1985; Waldren, Bell, Peek, & Sorell, 1990). People in stepfamilies report lower cooperation and greater fragmentation in family relationships than do people in nuclear families (Banker & Gaertner, 1998). Bray and Berger (1993) found not only that newly formed (within 6 months) stepfamilies had lower levels of cohesion than did nuclear families but also that levels of family cohesion dropped even lower in longer established (i.e., 2.5 and 5–7 years) stepfamilies. The fact that stepfamilies have lower cohesion than do first-married families is understandable. After all, the stepparent and any of his or her children often have very little relational history with other family members. Recall that the typical interval between divorce and remarriage is only 3 years. It is therefore plausible to assume that many stepchildren might have only known their stepparent for a year or two prior to sharing a residence with him or her. Therefore, the type of family cohesion that is associated with first marriage families of longer duration may take years to develop, and in a the majority of cases, it may never fully develop. What is perhaps more perplexing is the lower adaptability in stepfamilies. Stepfamilies experience higher levels of stress than do first married families (Waldren et al.). Although extreme adaptability can actually generate stress, some degree of adaptability is necessary to effectively cope with stressors. It is exactly this adaptability that seems to be in short supply in many stepfamilies. It is also worth noting that stepfamilies want levels of cohesion and adaptability similar to those of first-marriage families (Pink & Wampler, 1985), so it is not by design that they have lower adaptability and cohesion.

The lower adaptability and cohesion of stepfamilies is clearly evident in their communication patterns. For example, newly formed stepfamilies rate their family communication more poorly than do newly formed first-marriage families (Bray & Berger, 1993). Also, stepfathers report less positive and more negative communication with family members than do fathers in nuclear families (Pink & Wampler, 1985). Grinwald (1995) asked adolescents aged 12 to 18 to report on various positive (e.g., "my mother or father is always a good listener") and negative (e.g., "my mother or father insults me when he or she is angry with me") aspects of communication with their parent and stepparent. The reports of adolescents from first-marriage families were compared with those of stepfamilies that were formed after divorce and with stepfamilies that were formed after death of a parent. The poorest parent–child communication was reported in the stepfamilies formed after divorce, followed by those formed after death, and the best parent–child communication was reported by adolescents in first marriage families. Grinwald's study points to the fact that at least some of the cohesion and communication problems experienced by stepfamilies may be a continuation of the turmoil experienced in a prior family that ended in divorce. Remarried parents also provide less social support to their children—a level of support that is equivalent to that for divorced parents but less than that for parents in first marriages (White, 1992). White's investigation suggested that the social support deficits from remarried parents can be explained by lower levels of contact with the children and lower quality relationships and solidarity with them.

Elsewhere in this selection we review research findings that show that levels of conflict are often higher in stepfamilies than in first-marriage families. This communication pattern is undoubtedly linked with issues of problematic adaptability and cohesion. One particularly interesting consequent of this higher family conflict and lower cohesion is that children in stepfamilies leave home sooner than do children in nuclear families (White, 1994b). In a very carefully controlled study, 65% of stepchildren were found to leave home before the age of 19, compared to 50% of the children in first-marriage families (Aquilino, 1991). Two compelling explanations for this effect concern weaker relationships or cohesion in stepfamilies, including failure to fully integrate adolescent children into the family system, and children being driven out by or seeking to escape family conflict (Crosbie-Burnett & McClinitic, 2000b; White, 1994b). Obviously, as children depart from stepfamilies, parent–child communication presumably drops as well.

## Child Adjustment in Stepfamilies

Given what is known about the special challenges faced by stepfamilies, the nature of their relationships, and their opportunities for conflict, researchers have been understandably concerned with the social and psychological adjustment of children who live in stepfamilies. Although a thorough review of this research is beyond the scope of this selection, there are several highlights that are worth noting. First, children who live in stepfamilies tend to have slightly more externalizing behavior problems and slightly less social competence than do their counterparts in first-marriage families (Bray, 1999). Why is this the case? Obviously many children in stepfamilies undergo difficult life transitions that might include witnessing their biological parents' marriage deteriorate, experiencing the departure of one parent, perhaps living in financial hardship, moving to a new residence, and having a new adult member of the family move in to their residence (Anderson, Greene, Hetherington, & Clingempeel, 1999). These changes can sometimes all occur in a relatively short period of time.

Aside from the obvious structural and residential stressors that children in stepfamilies might have experienced, there is compelling evidence to show that their adjustment problems are also linked to family communication and relationship issues. In remarried families, parental negativity is significantly and positively correlated with child behavior problems (Anderson et al., 1999). This same research team found that adolescents in remarried families displayed more negativity toward their parent and stepparent than did adolescents in nondivorced families. Research also shows that the amount of conflict in stepfamilies is associated with child adjustment problems (Bray, 1999; Dunn, 2002).

Parents in stepfamilies tend to be less involved in the lives of their children than are parents in two-parent biological or adoptive families (Zill, 1994). This effect is especially pronounced for stepfathers (Fine, Voydanoff, & Donnelly, 1993). This is unfortunate because communication with stepfathers appears to be more vital to child adjustment outcomes than does communication with mothers in stepfather families (Collins, Newman, & McKenry, 1995). On the other hand, communication with the father was a stronger predictor of child adjustment than communication with the stepmother in stepmother families (Collins et al). The Fine et al. investigation additionally revealed that positive parental communication behaviors such as praise, hugs, reading to the child, and private talks with the child were positively associated with child adjustment in step-families, whereas negative parental communication behaviors such as spanking and yelling at the child were negatively associated with child adjustment.

Some of the difficulties that children in stepfamilies experience may be more attributable to the legacy of their original family life. A sophisticated longitudinal study that followed over 1,000 school children from age 6 to age 12 indicates that remarriage per se had no appreciable impact on children's aggressive and oppositional behavior, once the effects of parental divorce were taken into account (Pagani, Boulerice, Tremblay, & Vitaro, 1997). This study shows that many of the behavior problems that are evident in children living in stepfamilies may be a legacy of their biological parents' divorce. Contrary to what some might believe, a fairly rapid transition from the first-marriage family to the stepfamily is associated with fewer relationship problems in the new family (Montgomery, Anderson, Hetherington, & Clingempeel, 1992). Evidently, it is less disruptive to move from one two-parent household to another in rapid succession than it is to get settled into a single-parent household, only to then have to transition back into a two-parent household.

For the most part, research on child adjustment problems in stepfamilies supports the view that children in these contexts have slightly more behavior problems than do children in first-marriage families. Notwithstanding the environmental stress explanations for these effects, several theoretical explanations for these behavior problems focus on family relationship and communication problems in stepfamilies (Coleman et al., 2000). Most prominent among these are the family conflict explanation, which says that conflicts among divorced parents and within the stepfamily incite behavioral problems in children, and the deterioration of parental competencies theory, which explains child behavior problems in stepfamilies as a function of poor-quality parenting, including uninvolved parenting, minimal parental positivity, and more negatively toned communication behaviors from parents and stepparents.

## CONCLUSION

When marriages end because of death or divorce, most people tend to remarry. However, remarriages have a divorce rate even higher than do first marriages. Many of the interpersonal behaviors that might have contributed to deterioration of the first marriage might work similarly in a remarriage. A natural consequent of abundant remarriage is a large number of stepfamilies. There are many negative images and views of stepfamilies in both the media and, more generally, the society. Where there are positive images of stepfamilies in the media, as in *The Brady Bunch*, they are often unrealistic and may engender expectations for relational harmony that simply cannot be met. People in stepfamilies often start out with great expectations, but the sometimes difficult realities of living in a stepfamily quickly become evident and create distance between stepparents and stepchildren. Family scholars have found that not all stepfamilies develop their relationships in the same way. Some develop rapidly, some slowly, and some never really develop a sense of "family." As stepfamilies develop, they often face disagreements about the role of stepparents in the family. Mothers in stepfather families often assume a variety of roles to regulate and referee the relationship between their children and their spouse. Research consistently shows that there are a wide variety of different stepfamily types and forms. However, most stepfamilies face communication challenges such as feeling caught, negotiating ambiguous parental roles, regulating boundaries, and vying for resources. Research findings also indicate that many stepfamilies have to contend with greater conflict, lower adaptability, lower cohesion, and more issues of boundary regulation than do nuclear families. Finally, children in stepfamilies exhibit more behavior problems than do children in nuclear families, and these are associated to some extent with the quality of the stepfamily relationships and communication.

# REFERENCES

Ahrons, C. R., & Rodgers, R. H. (1987). *Divorced families: A multidisciplinary developmental view.* New York: Norton.

Anderson, E. R., Greene, S. M., Hetherington, E. M., & Clingempeel, W. G. (1999). The dynamics of parental remarriage: Adolescent, parent, and sibling influences. In E. M. Hetherington (Ed.), *Coping with divorce, single parenting, and remarriage* (pp. 295–319). Mahwah, NJ: Lawrence Erlbaum Associates.

Aquilino, W. S. (1991). Family structure and home-leaving: A further specification of the relationship. *Journal of Marriage and the Family, 53,* 999–1010.

Banker, B. S., & Gaertner, S. L. (1998). Achieving stepfamily harmony: An intergroup-relations approach. *Journal of Family Psychology, 12,* 310–325.

Barber, B. L., & Lyons, J. M. (1994). Family processes and adolescent adjustment in intact and remarried families. *Journal of Youth and Adolescence, 23,* 421–436.

Baxter, L. A., Braithwaite, D. O., & Nicholson, J. H. (1999). Turning points in the development of blended families. *Journal of Social and Personal Relationships, 16,* 291–313.

Bernstein, A. C. (1999). Reconstructing the Brothers Grimm: New tales for stepfamily life. *Family Processes, 38,* 415–429.

Braithwaite, D. O., Baxter, L., & Harper, A. M. (1998). The role of rituals in the management of the dialectical tension of 'old' and 'new' in blended families. *Communication Studies, 49,* 101–120.

Braithwaite, D. O., Olson, L. N., Golish, T. D., Soukup, C., & Turman, P. (2001). "Becoming a family": Developmental processes represented in blended family discourse. *Journal of Applied Communication Research, 29,* 221–247.

Bray, J. H. (1999). From marriage to remarriage and beyond: Findings from the developmental issues in stepfamilies research project. In E. M. Hetherington (Ed.), *Coping with divorce, single parenting, and remarriage* (pp. 253–271). Mahwah, NJ: Lawrence Erlbaum Associates.

Bray, J. H., & Berger, S. H. (1993). Developmental issues in stepfamilies research project: Family relationships and parent-child interactions. *Journal of Family Psychology, 7,* 76–90.

Bumpass, L. L., Raley, R. K., & Sweet, J. (1995). The changing character of stepfamilies: Implications of cohabitation and nonmarital childbearing. *Demography, 32,* 425–436.

Burrell, N. A. (1995). Communication patterns in stepfamilies. In M. A. Fitzpatrick & A. L. Vangelisti (Eds.), *Explaining family interactions* (pp. 290–309). Thousand Oaks, CA: Sage.

Cherlin, A. (1978). Remarriage as an incomplete institution. *American Journal of Sociology, 84,* 634–650.

Church, E. (1999). The poisoned apple: Stepmothers' experience of envy and jealousy. *Journal of Feminist Therapy, 11,* 1–18.

Cissna, K. N., Cox, D. E., & Bochner, A. P. (1990). The dialectic of marital and parental relationships within the stepfamily. *Communication Monographs, 57,* 44–61.

Coleman, M., Fine, M. A., Ganong, L. H., Downs, K. J. M., & Pauk, N. (2001). When you're not the Brady Bunch: Identifying perceived conflicts and resolution strategies in stepfamilies. *Personal Relationships, 8,* 55–73.

Coleman, M., Ganong, L., & Fine, M. (2000). Reinvestigating remarriage: Another decade of progress. *Journal of Marriage and the Family, 62,* 1288–1307.

Coleman, M., Ganong, L., & Fine, M. (2004). Communication in stepfamilies. In A. L. Vangenisti (Ed.), *Handbook of family communication* (pp. 215–232). Mahwah, NJ: Lawrence Erlbaum Associates.

Coleman, M., Ganong, L., & Weaver, S. (2001). Relationship maintenance and enhancement in remarried families. In J. Harvey & A. Wenzel (Eds.), *Close romantic relationships: Maintenance and enhancement* (pp. 255–276). Mahwah, NJ: Lawrence Erlbaum Associates.

Collins, W. E., Newman, B. M., & McKenry, P. C. (1995). Intrapsychic and interpersonal factors related to adolescent psychological well-being in stepmother and stepfather families. *Journal of Family Psychology, 9,* 433–445.

Crosbie-Burnett, M., & McClintic, K. M. (2000b). Remarried families over the life course. In S. J. Price, P. C. McKenry, & M. J. Murphy (Eds.), *Families across time: A life course perspective* (pp. 37–50). Los Angeles: Roxbury.

Dunn, J. (2002). The adjustment of children in stepfamilies: Lessons from community studies. *Child and Adolescent Mental Health, 7,* 154–161.

Fine, M. A., Coleman, M., & Ganong, L. H. (1998). Consistency in perceptions of the step-parent role among stepparents, parents and stepchildren. *Journal of Social and Personal Relationships, 15,* 810–828.

Fine, M. A., Coleman, M., & Ganong, L. H. (1999). A social constructionist multi-method approach to understanding the stepparent role. In E. M. Hetherington (Ed.), *Coping with divorce, single parenthood, and remarriage* (pp. 273–294). Mahwah, NJ: Lawrence Elrbaum Associates.

Fine, M. A., Voydanoff, P., & Donnelly, B. W. (1993). Relations between parental control and warmth and child well-being in stepfamilies. *Journal of Family Psychology, 7,* 222–232.

Ganong, L. H., & Coleman, M. (1997). How society views stepfamilies. *Marriage and Family Review, 26,* 85–106.

Ganong, L. H., & Coleman, M. (2000). Remarried families. In C. Hendrick & S. S. Hendrick (Eds.), *Close relationships: A sourcebook* (pp. 155–168). Thousand Oaks, CA: Sage.

Giles-Sims, J., & Crosbie-Burnett, M. (1989). Adolescent power in stepfather families: A test of normative-resource theory. *Journal of Marriage and the Family, 51,* 1065–1078.

Golish, T. D. (2003). Stepfamily communication strengths: Understanding the ties that bind. *Human Communication Research, 29,* 41–80.

Golish, T. D., & Caughlin, J. P. (2002). "I'd rather not talk about it": Adolescents' and young adults' use of topic avoidance in stepfamilies. *Journal of Applied Communication Research, 30,* 78–106.

Grinwald, S. (1995). Communication-family characteristics: A comparison between stepfamilies (formed after death and divorce) and biological families. *Journal of Divorce and Remarriage, 24,* 183–196.

Gross, P. (1986). Defining post-divorce remarriage families: A typology based on the subjective perceptions of children. *Journal of Divorce, 10,* 205–217.

Guisinger, S., Cowan, P. A., & Schuldberg, D. (1989). Changing parent and spouse relations in the first years of remarriage of divorced fathers. *Journal of Marriage and the Family, 51,* 445–456.

Hetherington, E. M., & Clingempeel, W. G. (1992). Coping with marital transitions: A family systems perspective. *Monographs of the Society for Research in Child Development, 57*(2-3, Serial No. 227).

Jones, S. M. (1978). Divorce and remarriage: A new beginning, a new set of problems. *Journal of Divorce, 2,* 217–227.

Larson, J. (1992). Understanding stepfamilies. *American Demographics, 14,* 36–39.

MacDonald, W. L., & DeMaris, A. (1995). Remarriage, stepchildren, and marital conflict: Challenges to the incomplete institutionalization hypothesis. *Journal of Marriage and the Family, 57,* 387–398.

Montgomery, M. J., Anderson, E. R., Hetherington, E. M., & Clingempeel, W. G. (1992). Patterns of courtship for remarriage: Implications for child adjustment and parent-child relationships. *Journal of Marriage and the Family, 54,* 686–698.

Pagani, L., Boulerice, B., Tremblay, R. E., & Vitaro, F. (1997). Behavioural development in children of divorce and remarriage. *Journal of Child Psychology and Psychiatry and Allied Disciplines, 38,* 769–781.

Papernow, P. (1993). *Becoming a stepfamily: Patterns of development in remarried families.* New York: Gardner.

Petronio, S. (2000). The boundaries of privacy: Praxis of everyday life. In S. Petronio (Ed.), *Balancing the secrets of private disclosures* (pp. 37–49). Mahwah, NJ: Lawrence Elrbaum Associates.

Pink, J. E.T., & Wampler, K. S. (1985). Cohesion, adaptability, and the stepfather-adolescent relationship. *Family Relations, 34,* 327–335.

Robinson, J. D., & Skill, T. (2001). Five decades of families on television: From the 1950s through the 1990s. In J. Bryant & J. A. Bryant (Eds.), *Television and the American family,* 2nd ed. (pp. 139–162). Mahwah, NJ: Lawrence Erlbaum Associates.

Signorelli, N., & Morgan, M. (2001). Television and the family: The cultivation perspective. In J. Bryant & J. A. Bryant (Eds.), *Television and the American family* 2nd ed., pp. 333–351. Mahwah, NJ: Lawrence Erlbaum Associates.

Thomson, E., Mosley, J., Hanson, T. L., & McLanahan, S. S. (2001). Remarriage, cohabitation, and changes in mothering behavior. *Journal of Marriage and the Family, 63,* 370–380.

Visher, E. B., Visher, J. S., & Pasley, K. (2003). Remarriage families and stepparenting. In F. Walsh (Ed.), *Normal family processes: Growing diversity and complexity* 3rd ed., pp. 153–175. New York: Guilford.

Waldren, T., Bell, N. J., Peek, C. W., & Sorell, G. (1990). Cohesion and adaptability in post-divorce remarried and first married families: Relationships with family stress and coping styles. *Journal of Divorce and Remarriage, 14,* 13–28.

White, L. (1992). The effect of parental divorce and remarriage on parental support for adult children. *Journal of Family Issues, 13,* 234–250.

White, L. (1994b). Stepfamilies over the life course: Social support. In A. Booth & J. Dunn (Eds.), *Stepfamilies: Who benefits? Who does not?* (pp. 109–137). Hillsdale, NJ: Lawrence Erlbaum Associates.

Zill, N. (1994). Understanding why children in stepfamilies have more learning and behavior problems than children in nuclear families. In A. Booth & J. Dunn (Eds.), *Stepfamilies: Who benefits? Who does not?* (pp. 97–106). Hillsdale, NJ: Lawrence Erlbaum Associates.

# EDITORS' INTRODUCTION

While reading Segrin and Flora's writing, you may have noticed the heterosexual normative bias. Unfortunately, this is not uncommon in the literature regarding intimate relationships and blended families. Thus, the research on LGBTQ+-led families is sparse, but what we do know is that LGBTQ+-led families face increased stigmatization beyond the experiences of heterosexual-led blended families. In addition to being considered *incomplete institutions*, there is a lack of terminology for their family relationships. Members often have to resort to using labels like "friend" or "partner's daughter" when referring to their adult–child relationships. LGBTQ+-led families also experience heightened safety concerns, hold few legal obligations and rights, and lack social support in general (Ganong & Coleman, 2017).

In order to compensate, LGBTQ+-led families use resilience strategies to legitimize and protect their members. Oswald (2002) suggested a resilience framework with two processes, intentionality and redefinition. Some of the ways that LGBTQ+-led families are intentional include building their community through friendships and chosen family kinships, managing disclosure, and ritualizing. Redefinition strategies often incorporate naming (what to call each other) and envisioning family (reimagining the construct of family; Oswald, 2002).

As we continue our exploration of the experiences of blended family members, we turn to the lived experiences of two adults in their roles. The readings represent both struggles and successes in navigating blended family relationships. We find that even when family members mean well, communication can break down and spur conflict. Further, the readings reemphasize the need for consistent and regular communication and a willingness to engage in difficult conversations. We first hear from a mother as she discusses her relationship with her biological children's stepmother. Then, we hear from a stepfather who shares how his stepfather's modeling negatively affected his interactions with his stepson and how support from other understanding adults helped him become more comfortable in his role.

As you read, keep in mind the following primer questions for reflection. If you feel so inclined, take a few minutes and consider your responses to the following questions before you read, and then again after you've finished each reading.

## PRIMERS

1. As you read about the experiences of the biological mother, consider how communication has enhanced and diminished the relationship between her and the children's stepmother.

2. As you read about the experiences of the stepfather, consider how his behaviors were affecting his stepson.

3. Think about how the differing values among the adults influences their conflicts.

## READING 14.2

# My Wife-in-Law and Me

Reflections on a Joint-Custody Stepparenting Relationship

*By Sarah Turner*

## INTIMACY AS A REQUIRED COURSE

Ann and I have had to learn how to deal with each other's personalities and particularities on a level that is usually reserved for intimate friends and lovers. We are thrown, for example, into making plans together, as in getting the children ready for a trip. She likes them to be organized and packed a day in advance and I don't care that much about preplanning. Once, we had a misunderstanding about arrangements I had made for a particular weekend, plans involving the vacation house (another joint-custody project), I had intended to use the house, and when my plans fell through I failed to let her know. She would have gone up there had she known it was free, but I didn't know about her anger and disappointment until I called her up on a completely different matter. She had been upset for several days. As I recall, we had an interesting conversation at that point about our different personality styles: my spontaneity and her careful planning. "When I'm upset," I said, "I want to deal with it right away, get it over with. I can't believe you were mad and I didn't know." She said she had been trying to deal with her anger on her own, that she, in turn, could not believe that I had failed to let her know that I wasn't going to use the house.

The point here is twofold; one, the most obvious, is the sudden intimacy of people thrown together by a situation central to both of their lives. The other is that, like many women, I construct relationships with other women quite easily. Particularly in my life as a women's studies teacher and professional, I am accustomed to making the personal political and the private public; I am comfortable and familiar with mutual self-disclosure. Yet, also like many women, I am more comfortable with connection than with conflict, more comfortable with commonalities than with differences. Here, in a closeup situation involving two people with a lot in common, we cannot easily be forthcoming with each other. The things that unite us also divide us. We are never going to be close friends because the situation imposes on us inherently different perspectives on the same events, people, and the situation itself. Whether, without our common situation, we would become friends, is not at issue here. (We have close mutual friends, and some say we would and others say we wouldn't.) What is at issue is the construction of relationships across inherent differences and conflicts. How can we get there from here when, as sometimes happens, I don't get the vacation house precisely because they do? Perhaps the feminist approach is to acknowledge and compare the different perspectives, and allow the resolution to occur over time, and one episode at a time. We cannot usefully either fail to acknowledge the conflict or expect it to be resolved once and for all.

# Tears of a Stepfather

*By Hector V. Lino, Jr.*

'I thought I could enter my wife's and stepson's lives and easily make whatever changes were necessary.'

## TEARS OF A STEPFATHER

After three years of marriage, I found myself in a therapist's office on a Saturday morning holding hands with my wife and stepson. We were crying because our problems had turned our family interactions into tumultuous encounters. Beneath my tears lay the greatest frustration of my adult life: Marriage and stepparenting, to which I had wholeheartedly subscribed, were kicking my ass, and I didn't know how to handle the situation.

I had come home at 8:00 A.M. on the morning of our therapy session, having told myself that hanging out once a week enabled me to handle our problems. But the tension it created in our home only exacerbated our conflict. My wife questioned the future of our relationship and worried about the impact my behavior was having on my stepson. I knew I had to take responsibility for what I was doing, and somehow I had to change and cope more effectively, but I wasn't sure of what to do. I had totally misjudged the reality of becoming a stepparent. Like my own stepfather, I thought that because I am a man, and men have the power to do all things, I could enter the lives of my wife and stepson and easily make whatever changes were necessary to ensure our happiness. Instead I saw how unprepared I was.

I sat my stepson down one afternoon to talk about my hanging out and told him that my actions were poor examples of how to cope. He said he understood, and as we talked he shared with me his frustrations over the absolute authority his mother and I retained over everything in our home. I admitted that I did sometimes assume a dictatorial posture and agreed that I needed to be more understanding and sympathetic toward him. I felt uncomfortable admitting this, and I confided these feelings to my son. He was pleased by my willingness to discuss my insecurities with him openly.

Soon after this conversation I had to pick up my stepson from the police station, where he was being held for painting graffiti on a subway car. I was apprehensive, but when I saw how dejected and helpless he looked, I knew he needed my support. His acceptance of my insecurities and mistakes enabled me to be far less judgmental and more understanding of his. In fact, this was the beginning of my understanding of how much attention he needed and the extent to which he would go to get it.

The biggest hurdle that our family had to overcome was my stepson's attitude toward school. He hated it and refused to go. After several years of fighting with him, trying to get him to do something he absolutely did not want to do, we let him make his own decision. He signed himself out, got a job and later earned his G. E. D. Now he's a college sophomore.

There were times over the years when I was so angry I could have beaten him up. I felt he had to do what I said, as had been the case with me and my stepfather. But my wife made it clear that hitting him would satisfy my own frustrations but change nothing. I could not deal with that kind of impotence.

Eventually I found a Black male support group run by a therapist. The members of the group were my age, married and with similar family difficulties. After many sessions I had to come to terms with my own contributions to my family's problems. I learned to let go a little and allow my son to be who he needed to be. I had to accept that my not knowing how to "fix" the problem did not make me less a man. In fact, I found out it provided me with greater avenues and opportunities for personal growth.

The group helped me see that I had not made a full commitment to our marriage and to fathering our son. My disappearing acts had created insecurity and fear in my household. This insight forced me to come to terms with the commitment I needed to make and ultimately made to our family.

My relationship with both my wife and my son improved after I joined the group, and I've stopped hanging out. I have become more of a friend to both my wife and son, and a better husband and father.

We have not overcome all of the difficulties we encounter as a family. I do, however, realize that I can only do the best I can with what I have.

# END-OF-CHAPTER REFLECTIONS

Take a moment and again imagine the ideal family. Our hope is that the image you conjure up this time is less focused on the structure of the family and more focused on the quality of the relationships. Hopefully, your perspective of blended families has changed too, and you understand the complexity of bringing adults and children together to form a blended family. Perhaps you are feeling more empathic toward the other people in your blended family or feeling more empathy toward blended family members in general. In all cases, blended family formation and maintenance is different than in traditional nuclear families. Adult members, in particular, must be deliberate and intentional in developing a cohesive, well-adjusted family. This includes the following:

- Clear, regular communication between the adults and between the adults and children
- Empathy and awareness of the plight of other family members (especially children)
- Acceptance that relationships between stepparents and children (especially adult children) take time to develop and may never become close
- Flexibility in establishing the roles members will play in each other's lives
- Resisting unhealthy stereotypes and schemas for how blended family members "should" behave

# REFERENCES

Bergeson, C., Bermea, A., Bible, J., Matera, K., Van Eeden-Moorefield, B., & Jushak, M. (2020). Pathways to successful queer stepfamily formation. *Journal of GLBT Family Studies, 16*(4), 368–384.

Ganong L., & Coleman M. (2017). *Stepfamily relationships.* Springer. https://doi.org/10.1007/978-1-4899-7702-1_6

Golombok, S., & Tasker, F. (2015). Socio-emotional development in changing families. In M. E. Lamb (Vol. Ed.) & R. M. Lerner (Series Ed.), *Handbook of child psychology and developmental science* (7th ed.; Vol. 3), *Social, emotional and personality development* (pp. 419–463). Wiley

Oswald, R. (2002). Resilience within the family networks of lesbians and gay men: Intentionality and redefinition. *Journal of Marriage and Family, 64*(2), 374–383.

Pew Research Center. (2011). *Pew social & demographic trends survey: A portrait of stepfamilies.* https://www.pewresearch.org/social-trends/2011/01/13/a-portrait-of-stepfamilies/

# RECOMMENDATIONS FOR FURTHER READING

Ahrons, C. (1994). *The good divorce*. HarperCollins.

Einstein, E., & Albert, L. (2005) *Strengthening your stepfamily*. Impact Publishing.

Ricci, I. (1997). *Mom's house, dad's house: Making two homes for your child*. MacMillan.

Thomas, S. (2005). *Two happy homes: A working guide for parents and stepparents after divorce and remarriage*. Springboard Publications.

# Chapter 15

# Dating Later in Life and Growing Old Together

## EDITORS' INTRODUCTION

We hope at this stage in your learning about intimate relationships you're feeling more confident, more self-efficacious, and optimistic about your ability to initiate, establish, and maintain a satisfying intimate relationship. We can't overstate the importance of connection and intimacy at all life stages. To conclude this anthology, we look ahead to relationships in later life, how they sustain, grow, and sometimes die. We may all be in pursuit of "happily ever after," but happily ever after is not a reality for many. Relationships change and individuals within relationships change. If we put in the effort, hopefully those changes serve to grow the relationship, and we're happier and more content as a result. Sometimes forces outside of our control, for example health issues and aging, have a significant impact on relationships later in life. Whether you're partnered, single, or anywhere in between as you age, connection and intimacy can be present and alive in your life. We discuss many perspectives on aging and relationships in this chapter:

- Companionship and dating later in life
- Sexuality in older adulthood
- Staying happy and healthy together as we age
- Retirement
- Declining health
- Losing a partner

In the first reading of this chapter, "The Initiation and Progressions of Late-Life Romantic Relationships," Sue Malta and Karen Farquharson discuss results of a qualitative study they conducted with adults over the age of 60 in Australia. Malta and Farquharson interviewed 45 unmarried adults to learn about their experiences dating, partnering, and committing to romantic relationships later in life. This reading represents a snapshot of a homogenous sample; however, we think it provides valuable perspectives on what some people over 60 value, what they seek, and how they experience romance. At the end of this chapter, we share some of our loved ones' stories and words of wisdom as we contemplate all kinds of relationships as we age.

As you read, keep in mind the following primer questions for reflection. If you feel so inclined, take a few minutes and consider your responses to the following questions before you read, and then again after you've read the chapter.

## PRIMERS

1. Pause for a moment and imagine yourself at age 60, 70, and 80 years old. What do you see? Take some time and document some of the key features of your future autobiography.

2. Now, take a closer look at your future autobiography. What values are apparent in what you wrote (e.g., independence, equality, family, health, adventure, sex, etc.)? How are these values similar and different from some of the values you identified in Chapter 1 (top five most important things in your life)?

# The Initiation and Progression of Late-Life Romantic Relationships

*By Sue Malta and Karen Farquharson*

F ew studies exist which describe the initiation and progression of late-life romantic relationships. This is surprising, as it is likely that the dynamics of romance in later life differ from romance among younger adults (Bulcroft and Bulcroft, 1991: 246; Dickson et al., 2005). Previous research which has looked specifically at heterosexual older adults has largely described their sexual functioning rather than the meaning they give to their loving relationships (see Gott and Hinchliff, 2003: 1618). Much of the research has been quantitative and has largely centred on medical issues, such as decline in sexual activity over time (for example Lindau et al., 2007), although there have been some recent exceptions (see for instance Malta, 2008; Waite et al., 2009). Such research is usually conducted within the context of long-term marriage, rather than among single, dating older adults (Bulcroft and Bulcroft, 1991), who may, arguably, have different sexual profiles.

Although research into older adult romance has tended not to focus on new relationships, a large number of older adults are single. Australian statistics (ABS, 2006) indicate that more than one-third of those over 65 are not married. It is therefore reasonable to expect that older adults are initiating new relationships in later life. Our study aims to contribute to the literature on older adult romance by investigating new late-life relationships among a group of Australian older adults. We looked at what types of relationship these older adults were participating in and how the relationships progressed. We found that very few of the relationships led to cohabitation or marriage, with most older adults in our study preferring to date or live separately, even when their relationship was long-term and committed (Levin and Trost, 1999). Our research indicates that these older adults were looking for and finding relationships based on emotional and sexual equality but not necessarily based on cohabitation or monogamy. In the following sections we outline previous research on love and romance, and on the progression of older adult romantic relationships. We then discuss our research approach and report our findings.

## LOVE AND ROMANCE AMONG OLDER ADULTS

Social changes of the modern and post-modern periods 'have contributed to detaching people from traditional roles and obligations' (Lindsay and Dempsey, 2009: 62). Because society is no longer clearly structured by social institutions such as religion, gender and class, decisions about appropriate ways to live are now made at the individual level (see Beck and Beck-Gernsheim, 1995 for discussion) and, what is more, they have become a point of negotiation. This is undoubtedly the case for romantic love.

The introduction of oral contraception in the middle of the 20th century brought major changes to society. People were now free to express their sexuality without fear of conception. This subsequently led to a rise in personal autonomy (especially for women) and resulted in what Giddens has described as the democratization of sexuality (Giddens 1992: 182). With these changes, love and sexuality were no longer tied to marriage, which Giddens argues brought about a complete restructuring of intimate relationships (1992: 58). In the past, marriages were 'never ... based upon intimacy [or] emotional communication', and it is this intimate communication which Giddens argues provides the 'foundation' for the new 'couple' relationships (1999: [4]). Giddens termed these relationships as 'pure' relationships, based as they are on what he calls 'confluent' love (1992: 61).

For Giddens, today's pure relationship is based on a love that is contingent. Self-reflexivity is also important, as individuals think about what they want in a relationship and also what they bring to a relationship (Giddens, 1992). Such contingency and self-reflection suggests ongoing revision and renegotiation of what the relationship is and what it stands for. This notion of change, of adjustment, in contemporary relationships, is reflected in Giddens' premise that confluent love is 'not necessarily monogamous' and therefore sexuality becomes yet another factor to be negotiated in the relationship (1992: 63). In such relationships, love is 'liquid' (Bauman, 2003) and sexuality itself becomes 'plastic' (Giddens, 1992: 2), meaning it is both changeable and also subject to negotiation (Jamieson, 1999).

This renegotiation involves personal growth, communication and change for the individuals involved and therefore, according to Giddens, the relationship is inherently unstable: unstable to such an extent that if it 'doesn't suit' or if it doesn't provide satisfaction, it can be terminated (1992: 58). Giddens cites the high rates of divorce and the corresponding increasing level of cohabitation as evidence for this view (1999: [3–4]). A US study adds empirical support to Giddens' arguments. It indicates that while less secure than so-called 'romantic love relationships', pure relationships are, nevertheless, happier, more autonomous and egalitarian (Gross and

Simmons, 2002: 547–8). Older adults provide an interesting case to use to explore Giddens' ideas. Are older adults looking to participate in pure-type relationships? Do they find new relationships easy to initiate and/or leave when they no longer suit?

Giddens' view of contemporary relationships has been criticized as being unrealistic (Jamieson, 1999). What is missing from his account is an awareness of the reality of how little relationships have effectively changed—partly because of the ongoing prevalence of what is seen as 'gendered responsibilities' between couples (Jamieson, 1998: 140). Indeed, time-use and qualitative studies of domestic household labour indicate that gender inequality in relationships is remarkably persistent (see Carter, 2007 for an in-depth discussion). Furthermore, the work by Ghazanfareeon Karlsson and Borell (2002) indicates that in older adult, non-cohabiting relationships, the traditional labour division is still the norm, despite the maintenance of separate households. These studies serve to highlight that the democratization of intimate relationships which Giddens champions exists in theory but not necessarily in fact. As Jamieson contends, Giddens' narrative fails to make a distinction between how lives are *actually* lived and his view of 'how they *should* be lived' (1999: 480, emphasis added). That said, Giddens does acknowledge that the principles he espouses are, essentially, ideals and that 'most ordinary relationships don't come even close' (1999: [5]). Very few studies have tested Giddens' theory empirically (see Hughes, 2005 for further discussion).

Like Giddens, Bauman (2003), argues that romantic love has changed. In contrast to Giddens, however, Bauman's view of contemporary romantic relationships is far more pessimistic. He argues that, 'liquid modern life' (Bauman, 2005: 2) encourages a similar form of togetherness: that of virtual relationships which are 'loose and eminently revocable' (Bauman, 2003: 90). According to Bauman, today's society values being connected by belonging to networks rather than to individuals. This connection by, and as, networks encourages people to create ties and links that are very easily formed but just as easily broken. Consequently, we are no longer developing the skills that are necessary to foster and sustain long-term bonds. We are caught up in what Jacobs (2004: 127) describes as a 'commitment to transience', which has 'replaced the value of durability'. In Bauman's (2003: 49) view, individuals still want romantic relationships but do not want the responsibilities that being in them demands—they want relationships that can be easily disposed of when something better and brighter comes along. This argument is very similar to the 'until further notice' aspect of Giddens' pure relationships (1992: 63), in which relationships last only as long as they provide benefit for those involved.

Under Bauman's consumerist scenario, love and sex become, in effect, just other objects that lend themselves to quick usage and equally quick disposal: *viz.* 'liquid love' (Bauman, 2003). Or, as put so succinctly by Blum in her critique of Bauman's treatise, 'in consumer culture, fucking and shopping are pretty much the same thing' (Blum, 2005: 339–40). Likewise Illouz (2007: 110) argues that emotions are now tied to and shaped by market forces. And internet dating, in particular, provides a prime example of the market at work and how people shape themselves to produce (and look for) an ideal product based on 'categories and cognitions' not 'senses' (Illouz, 2007: 104). While the internet effectively provides unparalleled access to others, she claims it removes the 'emotional and bodily resources' essential to conducting personal love relationships (Illouz, 2007: 111).

Subsequently, while Giddens finds much to be optimistic about with regard to pure relationships, for Bauman, like Illouz, the shift towards commodified love as facilitated by the internet is inherently bad for society (see Barraket and Henry-Waring, 2008, for discussion). Like Giddens, Bauman has also been critiqued, in particular for not offering empirical support for his theory (Smart, 2007). Bauman does raise questions for late-life relationships, however, which are of particular relevance to this study: were the older adults experiencing their new romances as disposable, with low entry and exit costs? Or were they looking for something more durable?

Neither of the portrayals of modern relationships by Giddens or Bauman accounts specifically for older adults. This is a significant omission given that there are many older adults potentially looking for and engaging in new late-life romantic relationships. Further, the numbers of older adults who are doing so are likely to increase given the anticipated growth in the older population (United Nations Population Division, 2003: 15). Current research in this area has thus far been extremely limited.

## THE PROGRESSION OF OLDER ADULT RELATIONSHIPS

There is some evidence that older adults partner with a view to companionship and sexual activity (Bulcroft and Bulcroft, 1991; Dickson et al., 2005), but older adult relationships appear less likely to progress to cohabitation or marriage (Bulcroft and Bulcroft, 1991; Bulcroft and O'Connor-Roden, 1986a; Dickson et al., 2005), due to a desire to remain independent and—especially for the women—a desire to avoid the care-giving role (Borell and Ghazanfareeon Karlsson, 2003; Bulcroft and O'Connor-Roden, 1986a; Dickson et al., 2005). For example, when asked why they had not married their partners, 46 per cent of unmarried women and 44 per cent of unmarried men in one study reported that they 'preferred things the way they are' and 43 per cent of women and 16 per cent of men said they could not marry because their partner was married to someone else (Brecher, 1983: 207). Other reasons for not marrying sexual partners included economic factors (not wishing to be responsible for each other's medical bills or not wishing to lose government benefits) and the desire to remain separate (Brecher, 1983: 207). An additional study found that very few couples provided ongoing instrumental support to each other in the way of housekeeping, health care and finances (Bulcroft and O'Connor, 1986b: 400). Although dated, these findings suggest that older adult romance is not necessarily organized around cohabitation and, further, that extramarital relationships are not uncommon, particularly for unmarried older women.

Overall, the research into dating and courtship in late life suggests there is a strong desire among older adults—especially women—to retain their independence and maintain separate lives from their romantic partners. The studies discussed above suggest that late-life couples want to maintain close, romantic and intimate relationships while living separately—a phenomenon which has since become known as living-apart-together (LAT) (Levin and Trost, 1999).

What distinguishes dating in late life from LAT relationships? Dating involves short-term, non-committed interactions, sexual or otherwise (see for instance Aleman, 2003), whereas LAT relationships involve longer-term, committed and, for the most part, sexually intimate relationships. Investigations into LAT relationships indicate that they are popular among older adults (de Jong Gierveld, 2002), particularly women (Borell and Ghazanfareeon Karlsson, 2003), and suggest that senior couples may choose such partnerships for a variety of reasons, including an unwillingness to move away from one's home and belongings and to help maintain relationships with one's family (Levin, 2004).

There is limited data on older adult relationships or LAT relationships in Australia in any age group. One study suggested that nearly 16 per cent of adults over the age of 45 were involved in LAT relationships (Reimondos et al., 2009). The study found that older people were more likely to choose to live-apart-together than younger people, and were also more likely to have no intention to cohabit in the future, although the authors were not able to determine why that may be the case. The analysis suggested that fewer than 10 per cent of older adults (over 60) were in LAT relationships (Reimondos et al., 2009), and even fewer were cohabiting.

## RESEARCH QUESTIONS

Together these findings from the literature provided the impetus for our research project investigating older adults' romantic relationships. In particular we asked: How do these new late-life relationships progress? Are they casual and short-term or long-term relationships leading to something more committed (marriage, cohabitation, LAT)? And what types of relationships are these Australian older adults engaged in? Do they reflect 'pure relationships' (Giddens, 1992)? Do older adults experience their relationships as having low entry and exit costs (Bauman, 2003)?

## METHOD

The exploratory nature of our research necessitated a qualitative approach, and we used semi-structured in-depth interviews to answer our research questions.[1] Such an approach produces data that are both rich and descriptive (Neuman, 2003). In-depth interviews allow people to convey their perspectives on their own particular situations—in other words, how *they* interpret what is happening (Kvale, 1996).

Forty-five Australian participants 60 years of age or older and either currently or recently involved in a romantic relationship that began in late life were interviewed. Participants were recruited by a variety of means including through posts to RSVP.com.au°, articles written about the study in local newspapers and seniors' magazines, radio interviews and by word of mouth. The in-depth interviews were conducted by various means: online by instant messaging ($n = 26$) or email ($n = 4$), by phone ($n = 5$) and face to face ($n = 10$), with participants selecting their preferred interview mode (see Kazmer and Xie 2008). Interview schedules were adjusted to reflect the mode of interview. All interviews lasted between one and two hours, with the exception of the four email interviews. The phone and face-to-face interviews were digitally recorded and later transcribed. Instant messaging and email interviews generated their own transcripts. Transcripts were analysed thematically by means of 'analytic grids' (Miles and Huberman, 1994: 127–32).

To elaborate further, data analysis involved identifying themes based on the research questions. Further themes were identified as the process of analysing the transcripts continued. Once completed, each theme was transferred to its own grid and a further process of identifying sub-themes was undertaken. The analytic grids were printed out and re-checked for anomalies, exceptional examples and so on. Summaries were made of each theme and these were compared and contrasted against each other, in an effort to make sense of the data and as an aid to find the best way to disseminate the information gathered.

Because the study uses a convenience sample we cannot generalize the findings to a broader population of older adults. Advertising for participants online at dating websites might have skewed the sample in favour of participants who were actively 'still looking' for relationships, as opposed to those who had 'found' partners. This was not always the case however, as many online participants who were involved in ongoing relationships still maintained regular contact with dating websites and so still received notices from them. Furthermore, the individuals who participated in the study were those who were currently in or had recently been involved in a late-life romance and *wanted* to talk about their experiences. This means that the views of older adults engaged in long-term relationships or not involved in or uninterested in the subject of late-life romance, or sex, are unrepresented. Neuman has argued, nonetheless, that purposive, non-random sampling is an acceptable method for exploratory research, as it allows researchers to 'identify particular types of cases for in-depth investigation' (2003: 213), based on their relevance to the topic being researched rather than their 'representativeness' per se (Neuman, 2003: 211). Consequently this type of research is useful as it can provide insight into older adults' experiences of their relationships.

All participants are referred to by a pseudonym followed by their age (for example: Mary 76). The age and gender characteristics of the sample are shown in Table 15.1.1 Ages ranged from 60 to 92 years and the mean age was 67 years.

| TABLE 15.1.1 **SAMPLE AGE BY GENDER** | | | |
|---|---|---|---|
| | **Men** | **Women** | **Total** |
| N | 21 | 24 | 45 |
| Age (mean) | 67.6 | 66.9 | 67.2 |
| Age (median) | 69.0 | 65.5 | 66.0 |
| Age range | 60–81 | 60–92 | 60–92 |

In terms of previous relationships, 30 participants were divorced or separated (three divorced twice; one divorced, remarried and then separated), 14 were widowed and one had never married or cohabited out of choice.

## RESULTS

### What Types of Romantic Relationships Were These Older Adults Engaged In?

While all participants desired long-term relationships, 20 reported only making short-term or casual connections; the other 25 developed long-term connections. Interestingly, those who were in long-term relationships were very unlikely to want to live with their partners, preferring instead to maintain separate households. In the following section we discuss the types of relationships these older adults entered into and how they were organized. We note here that two participants, both men, were involved in more than one relationship at the time of their interview. Despite being non-monogamous, both of them sought and engaged in long-term commitments.

*Casual and/or short-term.* In this study relationships that lasted less than 12 months were termed short-term or transitory. Many of our participants who went looking for new partners experienced such short-term and casual connections rather than the long-term connections they desired. In all cases, these relationships were sexually intimate.

The participants attributed the short-term nature of their connections to three main factors: First, the large numbers of people available through online dating sites made it possible to try out relationships before committing to them. Second, because all were seeking long-term relationships, if the people they met were not looking for long-term involvement, these connections were ended. Finally, some attributed the short-term nature of their relationships to a lack of flexibility on the part of their partners. Online dating emerges as an important part of the picture here as it facilitated new relationships, but also made them easy to exit. We discuss each factor in turn.

The first explanation for the transitory, short-term nature of the relationships was the large number of possible partners available through online dating. Participants reported that there were far more potential partners available online via dating websites than in their offline or real world social environments:

> I was just moving through a divorce after 35+ years of marriage and determined
> I was not cut out to be single. I registered on RSVP after researching various
> sites. I was inundated with a dozen or so emails from a range of ladies before
> I could get my own emails out. (Nicholas 63)

This plethora of possible partners gave the participants chances to try out relationships before committing to them, meaning that they could leave partnerships that were not ideal as there were many other potential partners to pursue. For these participants the low entry and exit costs to online dating were an attraction. Such factors meant that the older adults could easily end relationships that did not suit them and just as easily look for ones that might.

Several of our participants commented that that their relationships had been short-term because the people they had met were not interested in commitment. For example, Veronica was divorced and had been involved with a number of men through RSVP.com.au°. None of her relationships had lasted longer than two months, and she held the view that most of the men she met were not after ongoing, committed relationships, although she herself was looking for one:

> [most are after] casual sex. if you say no, you never hear from them again, and
> if you have sex you don't see them again. one guy a week later tried to contact
> me again, he hadn't remembered that he'd already met me. he states in profile
> not after casual sex! [sic] (Veronica 60)

This quote shows that Veronica felt somewhat duped by the men she had met who were interested in sex but not commitment. She did not desire casual relationships but nevertheless found herself participating in them. As there are so many people available online, she continued to date, still hoping for a long-term connection. Other participants echoed Veronica's experiences.

The final reason our participants gave for the short-term nature of their relationships was a lack of flexibility on the part of their lovers. Neil had been involved in a number of romantic relationships, none of which had lasted longer than four to eight months. He described older women as lacking flexibility and used this as a reason for why his relationships had been short-lived:

> Senior women are more fixed in their ways. They also carry a lot of baggage about power and control issues. Some have been badly abused in childhood and in their previous relationships/marriages—several women started out being loving and friendly but after a few months started getting bossy or angry—that's when I walk quietly away. (Neil 71)

For Neil, senior women were 'fixed in their ways' and, implicitly, so was he, making it difficult to come to a compatible situation. Kristen also attributed the demise of one of her short-term relationships to a lack of flexibility, which she described as selfishness:

> The relationship carried on for a few months off and on. ... I felt that he was very selfish and wanted me to fit in with the life he was planning; he wanted me to move and leave my family. (Kristen 66)

Although several found themselves in short-term relationships, none of our participants were seeking them. The three reasons given for failed relationships essentially all involved a lack of compatibility with a potential partner. Also, the large pool of potential partners available through dating websites meant that our participants were less likely to compromise in their search for a long-term partner.

*Long-term: marriage/cohabitation/LAT.* Of our 45 participants, 25 had initiated long-term romantic relationships as older adults (range 12 months–10 years; mean = 3.4 years). Interestingly, only six of these 25 relationships involved cohabitation or marriage (and two of these relationships had ended upon the death of the partner). None of the 19 remaining participants who were currently in long-term relationships were interested in living with or marrying their partners. Moreover, none of the long-term relationships that had ended had taken such a form, indicating that cohabiting was very much the exception for our participants, the majority of whom elected to live-apart-together.

Evie was one of the few who did live with her partner, although they did not marry. She was introduced to her partner Len by a mutual friend at the local dance. Their relationship developed slowly over a 12 month period after which Len moved in to Evie's house. They eventually bought a unit where they lived as co-owners: "he paid half and I paid half... equal share". When asked if they had married, she said:

> He wanted to marry me eventually ... and I said, no, I wouldn't be bothered now, you know. No that's a bit silly now, bothering at my age, bothering at his age. So I just said, no Len, we'll stay the way we are. (Evie 92)

Evie clearly indicated that she was not interested in marriage, even though Len may have been. Among our participants, the women in particular were reluctant to marry. This supports the earlier work by Borell and Ghazanfareeon Karlsson (2003) who argue that women in particular, favour LAT-arrangements in their late-life partnerships. One who did marry was Ursula, but only because her partner insisted:

> but I said ... 'Buy some house close to my house and we can see each other every day'. He said, 'no I don't want a friend, I want a wife' and we marry in 75 days. (Ursula 69)

Ursula's experience was very much the exception. Most of our participants did not wish to cohabit. When asked why they did not live with their partner, three themes emerged: (1) a desire to appease the concerns of children regarding inheritance issues, (2) a strong need for independence, and (3) a desire to maintain separate households and finances. Some of these themes overlapped.

The presence of adult children was important for many participants in the decisions about living together. Edwin had this to say about the attitude of some of his children to his partner of two years:

> [The children] are hostile ... they won't talk. They won't have anything to do with her. They think she's just out to get what I've got ... what's left. So, no, we've decided we just go on with our separate lives ... (Edwin 81)

For Edwin, it was tremendously important that he and his partner appeased his children's concerns and also preserved their separateness by retaining separate households and separate financial arrangements. Despite this they spoke on the phone every day, stayed over at each other's houses at least three nights during the week and every weekend. In this manner they felt they were allaying any fears the children might have about losing any legacy that might come to them upon Edwin's death. For Edwin, being involved in an LAT arrangement rather than a marriage or cohabitation, helped him to preserve his family relationships (see Levin, 2004).

Others, like Abbie, had no such considerations about children or their inheritance. Abbie had, however, always strongly guarded her independence from her much older lover and continued to live in her own home, despite the relationship lasting for nine years. She and her lover had never lived together and never intended to. She said they had never classed themselves as a 'couple' even though they were heavily involved in each other's lives. Although Abbie felt connected to her partner, the relationship was not the kind that involved instrumental support. These anecdotes provide support for previous research which showed that older women in particular resisted partnerships where they would have to provide care-giving (Borell and Ghazanfareeon Karlsson, 2003; Bulcroft and O'Connor-Roden, 1986a; Dickson et al., 2005).

Stewart was in the situation of having two partners at the one time—one for 18 years and the other for 22 months. For him, the possibility of marriage or cohabitation with either of them was not an option that he would ever have considered, even as a young man:

> I had a feeling, a gut feeling, when I was very young you know ... that this marriage bit wasn't for me; and this living together bit wasn't for me at all.... [And] it suits Meg to have that level of independence and you know she loves her own house ... And Una ... is similar ... she's very independent, very career orientated. (Stewart 63)

Stewart's point about his partners valuing their separateness, their 'independence', was repeated throughout this research, particularly by female participants, who said they valued the freedom of not having to care for and look after a male partner, sometimes for the first time in their lives. As in previous research which showed that older female widows were reluctant to remarry because of a fear of being 'locked into traditional marriage roles' (Bulcroft and Bulcroft 1991: 246; see also Brecher 1983; Bulcroft and O'Connor-Roden 1986a), these participants were careful not to put themselves in a position where they might have to relinquish their independence. One key strategy was to live separately.

The following quote from Neville illustrates all three themes: the desire to appease children, be independent and maintain separate households:

> Well, there's separate families, separate dependencies ... oh not dependencies, the kids are independent. But [pause] I'm not keen to relinquish my house. I'm hard to live with because I'm not tidy [laughs] and that's a difficulty I think for most women. And so I can minimise those sorts of difficulties. But apart from that my grandchildren ... now live [nearby] and attend schools

locally and come to me after school and my partner's grandchildren come to her. And so it doesn't disrupt any of their lives. It means that my own financial things remain confidential and [pause] I'm comfortable with this arrangement. (Neville 76)

Although our participants did not call their partnerships living-apart-together, the type of relationships they described certainly fit that term. These participants wanted commitment, companionship and sex, but they did not want to cohabit.

## Late-life Romances: Pure Relationships or Something Else?

According to Giddens (1992), intimate communication forms the basis for today's pure relationships. Our findings indicate that this was the case for our participants who, for the most part, desired egalitarian relationships based on intimate communication and shared ideals.

Joyce expresses this in her discussion of what she was looking for in a partner:

The sort of man I want is an educated, well adjusted man who is capable of sharing an equal relationship where we can enjoy our like interests. (Joyce 66)

Here Joyce clearly expresses a desire for an egalitarian relationship based on shared ideals and values. This desire was also discussed by Dennis, providing some support for the idea that contemporary relationships among older adults are based on mutual satisfaction rather than on obligation or social institutions:

we appear to have similar values, politically, socially, emotionally and, importantly she was financially independent. (Dennis 60)

In seeking, and being attracted to, particular types of partners, our participants reported aiming for sexual and emotional equality in their relationships. Furthermore, that Dennis knows and is able to articulate his desire for someone with similar 'values' and so on, indicates a process of self-reflection which is highlighted as a key aspect of pure relationships (Giddens, 1992).

Veronica (60) had begun a number of short-term, casual relationships through RSVP.com. au*, although she was ultimately looking for a committed, long-term arrangement. She was looking for 'strength, security, companionship' and a 'best friend' who would then become a 'lover'. Veronica's desire for a 'best friend' who would then become a 'lover' underscores Giddens' (1992) idea of intimate communication as the foundation for the pure relationships.

Likewise, Amy's quote about the type of person she was looking for perhaps ideally illustrates the notion of democratic, emotionally and sexually equal relationships:

> I think that I am looking more for companionship, shared values and a person with an equal intelligence to my own.... I definitely want recognition as a person, not as a stereotyped female ... (Amy 64)

For Betty, who met her romantic partner at a social venue where she was a regular, the relationship ended because it did not develop into a long-term commitment:

> The problem was that we never really became a couple. That was why I ended it. It was a wild courtship on his part for two weeks and once we had been to bed together, he became more casual. What I said to him when I broke it off was that where I wanted a relationship, he only wanted an affair! (Betty 69)

This type of relationship epitomizes the pure relationship: it was based on intimate communication and egalitarianism, and it ended when it was no longer satisfying. Betty's desire for a relationship, not just an affair, indicates her expectation that a relationship should be ongoing and committed—not just casual sex. She was willing to try a new relationship out, providing some support for the idea that contemporary relationships have low entry and exit costs (Bauman, 2003), but what she really wanted was a long-term relationship, which, once achieved, would not be something she would want to leave.

Even though the participants in this study were looking for ongoing, long-term connections, not all of them were seeking monogamy, reflecting the notion of 'plastic sexuality' (Giddens, 1992). For example, Nigel (79) had been married twice before and was already involved in four concurrent relationships at the time he met his new partner. He said that although they were both looking for a 'steady' relationship, his partner had wanted an 'exclusive' one, and he had a problem with that. He said:

> Today [people] have their relationships and sow their wild oats, and have all sorts of experiences before they're married. Most people in my vintage ... that didn't happen. Once I was free, I decided it was time that I started to catch up [laugh] and I certainly did [laugh]. (Nigel 79)

Although Nigel was very happy in his committed relationship, he relished his freedom and maintained contact with his other relationships. He said he was 'still attracted to other women' and that he and his partner would 'make a joke of it' but that at times it could be painful for her. Nevertheless, Nigel considered his relationship a 'partnership', albeit one that did not involve cohabiting or even exclusiveness, in effect, a non-monogamous LAT relationship. Like Stewart, despite having multiple partners, Nigel was interested in maintaining ongoing, stable connections; he was not interested in disposable relationships.

The above indicates that our participants were looking for companionship and intimacy on egalitarian terms. Unlike Bauman's (2003) description of liquid love as akin to brief episodes of affection which are then disposed of, our participants were looking for meaningful and lasting love. For those whose relationships were over, there was no indication that they had experienced the relationship as trivial. Nevertheless, relationships appeared to be easy to enter and also easy to exit, and this was especially so for those that were initiated online compared to those that were initiated face to face.

## DISCUSSION AND CONCLUSION

It is clear from our findings that these older adults were looking for meaningful ongoing relationships which were egalitarian and based on shared intimacy, in other words, they desired the idea of the pure relationship. Like Stewart and Nigel and their non-monogamous arrangements, the relationships were negotiated but they did not appear disposable. In fact, all the older adults desired long-term, committed relationships; however, they were not willing to settle for something that was less than ideal. Dating services, in particular online dating, gave these older adults the means to be able to pursue this ideal by allowing them access to many more potential partners than would otherwise be available. In this manner, it appears that while Giddens' (1992) theory describes the type of relationship that these older adults were seeking, their relationships were not experienced as being disposable, as Bauman's (2003) theory would suggest. Giddens' argument that today's pure relationships are 'contingent' and not reliant on idealized, romantic love describes the relationships in our study, as our participants were interested in developing democratic, intellectually and sexually fulfilling partnerships, and were willing to move on when these relationships no longer suited their needs. Also in line with Giddens, the participants were reflexive in their approach to their new relationships, engaging in critical self-reflection about what they wanted and what they brought to the relationships.

Neither of these theories was able to account for the fact that the older adults in this study, despite their openness to ending relationships that were not working, were hoping for long-term, committed relationships, although not ones that were necessarily monogamous nor involved cohabitation. Our finding that the older adults in long-term relationships were likely to live-apart-together (LAT) supports the literature which indicates that older adult romance is not necessarily organized around cohabitation (Borell and Ghazanfareeon Karlsson, 2003; Brecher, 1983; Bulcroft and Bulcroft, 1991; Bulcroft and O'Connor, 1986b; de Jong Gierveld, 2002; Dickson et al., 2005), and that older adult women in particular resist marriage (Borell and Ghazanfareeon Karlsson, 2003; Dickson et al., 2005; Ghazanfareeon Karlsson and Borell, 2002). Unlike Reimondos et al. (2009), who were unable to determine why older people were more likely to choose to LAT than younger people, we found that the specific contexts of older adulthood—particularly the need to maintain cordial relations with their children and to protect their inheritance, as well as the desire for independence and an unwillingness to undertake daily care activities for their partners—were key reasons why these older adults did not elect to either marry or cohabit. This finding suggests that it is very important to consider an individual's stage of life when trying to understand LAT relationships, as older adults have different considerations than those at earlier life stages.

This research provides a starting point for further research in the area of older adult love and sexuality in Australia and, particularly, the role and impact of the internet and online dating on late-life romantic relationships. Our research raises a number of questions that should be investigated: how do older adults negotiate new romantic relationships within the context of their families and friends? Are there qualitative differences between long-term relationships which begin as a consequence of one's daily interactions and those which are deliberately sought and if there are, what are they? We would also invite comparisons with other age groups.

## NOTE

1. For a more detailed description of the interview methods used see Malta's chapter, 'Qualitative Interviewing of Older Adults using Online Methods', in *Researching Later Life and Ageing—Expanding Qualitative Research Agendas and Methods* (to be published by Palgrave, UK, in 2012).

## REFERENCES

ABS (Australian Bureau of Statistics) (2006) 'Registered Marital Status by Age by Sex, Table', 2006 Census of Population and Housing Australia. Canberra: ABS.

Aleman, M.W. (2003) '"You Should Get Yourself a Boyfriend" but "Let's Not Get Serious": Communicating a Code of Romance in a Retirement Community', *Qualitative Research Reports in Communication* 4: 31–7.

Barraket, J. and M.S. Henry-Waring (2008) 'Getting it (On)line: Sociological Perspectives on e-Dating', *Journal of Sociology* 44(2): 149–65.

Bauman, Z. (2003) *Liquid Love: On the Frailty of Human Bonds*. London: Polity Press.

Bauman, Z. (2005) *Liquid Life*. Cambridge: Polity Press.

Beck, U. and E. Beck-Gernsheim (1995) *The Normal Chaos of Love*. Cambridge: Polity Press.

Blum, V.L. (2005) 'Love Studies: Or, Liberating Love', *American Literary History* 17(2): 335–48.

Borell, K. and S. Ghazanfareeon Karlsson (2003) 'Reconceptualizing Intimacy and Ageing: Living Apart Together', in S. Arber, K. Davidson and J. Ginn (eds) *Gender and Ageing: Changing Roles and Relationships*. Maidenhead: Open University Press.

Brecher, E.M. (1983) *Love, Sex and Aging: A Consumers Union Report*. Boston, MA: Little, Brown.

Bulcroft, K. and M. O'Connor-Roden (1986a) 'Never Too Late', *Psychology Today* 20(6): 66–9.

Bulcroft, K. and M. O'Connor (1986b) 'The Importance of Dating Relationships on Quality of Life for Older Persons', *Family Relations* 35: 397–401.

Bulcroft, R.A. and K. Bulcroft (1991) 'The Nature and Functions of Dating in Later Life', *Research on Aging* 13(2): 244–60.

Carter, M. (2007) *Who Cares Anyway? Negotiating Domestic Labour in Families with Teenage Kids*. PhD Thesis, Swinburne University of Technology, Faculty of Life and Social Sciences, Melbourne.

de Jong Gierveld, J. (2002) 'The Dilemma of Repartnering: Considerations of Older Men and Women entering New Intimate Relationships in Later Life', *Ageing International* 27(4): 61–78.

Dickson, F.C., P.C. Hughes and K.L. Walker (2005) 'An Exploratory Investigation into Dating Among Later-life Women', *Western Journal of Communication* 69(1): 67–82.

Ghazanfareeon Karlsson, S. and K. Borell (2002) 'Intimacy and Autonomy, Gender and Ageing: Living Apart Together', *Ageing International* 27(4): 11–26.

Giddens, A. (1992) *The Transformation of Intimacy: Sexuality, Love, and Eroticism in Modern Societies*. Stanford, CA: Stanford University Press.

Giddens, A. (1999) 'Family', Lecture 4: Reith Lectures 1999: Runaway World. London: BBC Radio 4. Available at: http://www.bbc.co.uk/radio4/reith1999/lecture4.shtml (accessed March 2012).

Gott, M. and S. Hinchliff (2003) 'How Important is Sex in Later Life? The Views of Older People', *Social Science & Medicine* 56: 1617–28.

Gross, N. and S. Simmons (2002) 'Intimacy as a Double-edged Phenomenon? An Empirical Test of Giddens', *Social Forces* 81(2): 531–55.

Hughes, K. (2005) 'The Adult Children of Divorce: Pure Relationships and Family Values?', *Journal of Sociology* 41(1): 69–86.

Illouz, E. (2007) *Cold Intimacies: The Making of Emotional Capitalism*. Cambridge: Polity Press.

Jacobs, R.N. (2004) 'Bauman's New World Order', *Thesis Eleven* 79: 124–33.

Jamieson, L. (1998) *Intimacy: Personal Relationships in Modern Societies*. Malden, MA: Polity.

Jamieson, L. (1999) 'Intimacy Transformed? A Critical Look at the "Pure Relationship"', *Sociology* 33(3): 477–94.

Kazmer, M.M. and B. Xie (2008) 'Qualitative Interviewing in Internet Studies: Playing with the Media, Playing with the Method', *Information, Communication & Society* 11(2): 257–78.

Kvale, S. (1996) *InterViews: An Introduction to Qualitative Research Interviewing*. Thousand Oaks, CA: Sage Publications.

Levin, I. (2004) 'Living Apart Together: A New Family Form', *Current Sociology* 52(2): 223–40.

Levin, I. and J. Trost (1999) 'Living Apart Together', *Community, Work & Family* 2: 279–94.

Lindau, S.T., L.P. Schumm, E.O. Laumann, W. Levinson, C.A. O'Muircheartaigh and L.J. Waite (2007) 'A Study of Sexuality and Health among Older Adults in the United States', *New England Journal of Medicine* 357(8): 762–74.

Lindsay, J. and D. Dempsey (2009) *Families, Relationships and Intimate Life*. South Melbourne: Oxford University Press.

Malta, S. (2008) 'Intimacy and Older Adults: A Comparison between Online and Offline Romantic Relationships', in T. Marjoribanks, J. Barraket, J.-S. Chang, A. Dawson, M. Guillemin, M. Henry-Waring et al. (eds) *Re-imagining Sociology*, Proceedings of the Annual Conference of the Australian Sociological Association. Melbourne: TASA.

Miles, M.B. and A.M. Huberman (1994) *Qualitative Data Analysis: An Expanded Sourcebook*. Thousand Oaks, CA: Sage.

Neuman, W.L. (2003) *Social Research Methods: Qualitative and Quantitative Approaches*, 5th edn. Boston: Allyn and Bacon.

Reimondos, A., A. Evans and E. Gray (2009) 'Living-Apart-Together (LAT) Relationships in Australia: An Overview', in S. Lockie, D. Bissell, A. Greig, M. Hynes, D. Marsh, L. Saha et al. (eds) *The Future of Sociology*, Proceedings of the Annual Conference of the Australian Sociological Association. Canberra: TASA.

Smart, C. (2007) *Personal Life: New Directions and Sociological Thinking*. Cambridge: Polity.

United Nations Population Division (2003) *World Population Prospects: The 2002 Revision—Highlights*. New York: UN.

Waite, L., E.O. Laumann, A. Das and L.P. Schumm (2009) 'Sexuality: Measures of Partnerships, Practices, Attitudes and Problems in the National Social Life, Health, and Ageing Study', *Journals of Gerontology Series B: Psychology and Social Sciences* 64B(Supplement 1): i56–i66.

# EDITORS' INTRODUCTION

In Chapter 10, we discussed how love changes as a relationship grows—from infatuation to mature love. In the next reading, "Love in Later Life," Aaron Ben-Ze'ev discusses how love changes as our relationships (and we) mature, love after loss, and love in the case where one partner has dementia. Ben-Ze'ev acknowledges that some of our Western cultural beliefs about love—that it is spontaneous, exciting, and impulsive—perhaps are not the building blocks on which mature love grows. Perhaps mature love lives on the companionship side of Sternberg's triangular theory of love, a combination of intimacy and commitment, with less passion. We propose that with maturity we may lose spontaneity and impulsivity, but that does not equate to a loss of passion. It is perhaps a shift in what one considers passion that changes, as many older adults still desire and report satisfying sex. More on that later. For now, consider the following before reading on.

## PRIMERS

1. How would you define mature love? Think about some relationships that you admire between people you know over 60. What stands out to you?

2. Consider interviewing a couple over 60 who have been together for at least 20 years about their relationship. You may find that their story not only inspires you, but sparks something in them that they haven't thought about in a long time. We asked several of our loved ones to share their relationship wisdom (their words are at the end of this chapter), and we were humbled to hear how meaningful it was to them to be asked about their experiences and share with all of you!

# Love in Later Life

*By Aaron Ben-Ze'ev*

> One is never too old to yearn.
> Italian Proverb

> Mature calmness is exciting. I am so thrilled by the calmness and acceptance of my older lovers who focus on the moment without calculating future prospect.
> A man in his thirties who loves dating women in their fifties

At this bend in the road toward profound love, the issue of time takes center stage as we examine mature love in old age and in times of illness. The belief has been that, along with a decay in physical and mental capacities, happiness and romantic love decline with age. We now know better. Older people, it turns out, are often happier and more satisfied with their lives and their marriages than younger people are. Perhaps when we realize that our years are numbered, we change our perspective and focus on positive present experiences, which are more likely to consist of peacefulness and serenity rather than excitement and joy. Sonja Lyubomirsky summarizes these findings, reporting that for most people the best years are in the second half of life.[1] Needless to say, there is a great deal of diversity here as well, and some older people become depressed and afraid of death. This [reading] also discusses other phenomena characteristic of love in old age, specifically love after the death of a spouse and love when one spouse suffers from dementia.

# MATURITY AND LOVE

> It strikes me that we are "behaving" (actually we are *not* behaving) like teenagers.
> Can't we at least try to behave *as if* we were mature adults?
>
> A married man to his married lover

Maturity seems to run counter to novelty and excitement. No wonder young people are considered more emotional than older people. This of course does not mean that exciting positive as well as negative experiences do not occur at all ages. Intense emotions are typically elicited in the midst of unfinished business and hence are mainly concerned with the future; maturity is focused on the present and requires satisfaction with your current lot. Intense emotions are generated by change, while maturity involves growing accustomed to changes and perceiving them as less significant. Although at all ages we enjoy both familiarity and novelty, the relative weight of familiarity increases in maturity. As we've discussed, the happiness associated with intense love is excitement; the happiness associated with profound mature love is peacefulness (calmness) and serenity. Similar findings indicate that the transition from youth to older age includes a shift in close social relations, involving a change of emphasis from quantity to quality. It has been suggested that the main developmental task for younger couples is managing conflicts, while for older couples it is maintaining mutual support.[2]

People who behave in an immature manner are exceedingly attractive: they are very lively, joyful, and youthful, living in the moment as if there is no tomorrow. However, like children, they are often inconsistent and unstable, making you wonder whether they will love you tomorrow after meeting another exciting person enabling them to fully embrace romantic life from another perspective.

Romantic compromises express a kind of maturity. As in maturity, compromises reflect an acceptance of our limitations and current situation. However, unlike maturity, the acceptance in compromises is mainly a behavioral acceptance rather than an attitudinal one. So long as the situation is still regarded as a compromise, deep down the individual does not actually accept it. The moment people wholeheartedly accept a compromise, it stops being a compromise. Like habituation, maturity and compromise often reduce desire and thus can be deadly to romantic relationships. Maturity lessens both positive and negative emotional experiences, while compromises can reduce positive experiences and increase negative ones. In maturity and compromises, expectations are reduced, though not eliminated, and the desired object is often replaced by the possible and the reasonable. Mature love is often not what passionate romantic love is all about. Hence, many people say that they never want to become mature, because settling for what is possible while ignoring the desirable can be a sign of a decline in enthusiasm and spontaneity. However, this is precisely what people do when they compromise.

We want children to mature and learn to value long-term considerations, while we want older adults to worry less about long-term threats and to give greater expression to their emotions. We do not want to lose our positive child-like aspects. We want to be optimistic and sincere and to love passionately. We want to adore each other despite our obvious flaws. We want to understand each other well, but at the same time we would like our views of each other to be somewhat rosy so that we can harbor some positive illusions. We want to maintain the buoyancy, naturalness, and ardor that we associate with children, while being mature adults who stand by each other through the pain that inevitably arises during long-term romantic relationships. We want to overcome problems, not so much by changing each other but by adapting to each other.

## LOVE IN OLD AGE

> This is the first time that I am getting old. I have no experience in being old.
>
> Naomi Polani

> Love is the word used to label the sexual excitement of the young, the habituation of the middle-aged, and the mutual dependence of the old.
>
> John Ciardi

A common view considers old people to be incapable of experiencing strong love, as their sexual desire and physical abilities are expected to have declined with age. This is a simplistic and distorted idea. It is often the case that love in old age is deeper than love at a young age.

Carstensen informs us that although chronological age is an excellent (albeit imperfect) predictor of cognitive abilities and behavior, it is a poorer predictor in later age. An additional temporal aspect that becomes more important than the time since our birth is the subjective sense of our remaining time until death. The temporal extent of our horizons plays a key role in motivation. Carstensen argues that as people age and increasingly experience time as finite and their horizons as being gradually narrowed, they change their priorities. For example, they attach less importance to goals that expand their horizons and greater importance to goals from which they derive present emotional meaning. When time is seen as short, we tend to focus on short-term goals. Older people have smaller social networks, are less drawn to novelty than younger people, and reduce their spheres of interest. Nevertheless, they appear as happy as (if not happier than) younger people. This makes sense, as in a situation of decreasing horizons, people prioritize deepening existing relationships and developing expertise in already satisfying areas of life.[3]

Carstensen notes a preference for emotionally positive information over emotionally negative information in older adults' memories. This, she contends, is particularly intriguing because it has long been known that younger people find negative information more attention-grabbing and memorable than positive information. In contrast, older people process negative information less deeply than they do positive information, and at the very early stages of processing, older adults also engage in less encoding of negative material. Carstensen concludes that when people, young or old, see time as finite, they attach greater importance to emotional meaning and satisfaction from life and invest fewer resources in gathering information and expanding horizons. Thus, although their social networks grow smaller, older adults grow more satisfied.[4]

Elderly couples indeed more readily take the attitude of being happy with their lot. Consider the following confession of a single mother in her fifties: "I am looking for perfection and I have been mistaken in my choices. I turn down opportunities to be with men because I judge these men as far from perfect. As I get older, I seem to be softening, but I also seem to be getting clearer on what I like and want. I don't want superficiality—but for the first time in my life, I am considering having sex with someone I don't see as partner material!" An apparent exception to shrinking horizons in older ages is the benefit and joy derived from grandchildren that in part come from the expanding new horizons that grandchildren both provide and represent. Many grandparents talk about experiencing a "new lease on life" with their grandkids, and even observe, as the old saying goes, that "if I had known grandchildren were this much fun, I would have had them first!"

We have supporting evidence for these anecdotal comments. Older individuals often experience their spouses as affectionate both when disagreeing and when performing joint tasks, and they report high marital satisfaction. Older married couples have fewer marital conflicts than their younger counterparts do, although they report that erotic bonds are less central in their lives. Companionate love, which is based on friendship, appears to be the cardinal feature of their interactions. Intimate relationships in old age are largely harmonious and satisfying.[5]

Romantic compromises become less of an issue as we age. Over time, people become used to their spouse's negative traits. They learn to live with them, while minimizing their negative impact. When we realize that our time is running out and that our alternatives are decreasing, we are more likely to accept our limitations and not feel compromised by not pursuing an attractive option. Moreover, as older people are more dependent on each other, the marital chains tend to turn into helping hands. Despite feeling as much negativity as younger people, older individuals may be more resilient in the face of tensions in their closest relationships. Older adults are less likely to argue and often let issues go. They are better able to place conflict in perspective and to think that it is not worth fighting over issues.[6]

It seems that in old age, when cognitive and physical capacities tend to decline, the ability to be satisfied with one's own lot increases; this reduces marital conflicts as well as the experience of romantic compromise. Older people are more likely to adopt the constructive attitude of making the most of what they already (or still) have. Their concern is not with having more, but with losing less.

## LOVE AFTER DEATH

> Broken crayons still color.
> Shelley Hitz

While most of us have had romantic predicaments, those of widows and widowers seem particularly poignant. Should they actively search for another lover? And if they find another lover while still loving their late spouse, how can these two loves coexist in their hearts? Is loving again worth the effort of having to adjust to another person? And what is the proper time to fall in love again? (In what follows, when I refer to widows, I mean it to include widowers' experiences too.)

### The End of Love and Death

For many people, romantic love forms an essential aspect of their lives; without love, life may seem worthless. Romantic love is a central expression of a meaningful and flourishing life. Without it, people can feel that an important part of them is dead. The lover is perceived as the sunshine in their life, and for many, without such sunshine, decay and death are all around. Even during one of the darkest periods of history, the Holocaust, people fell in love despite the risks they had to take to express it. People did not relinquish love, and love even enabled some of them to survive the horrors of the death camps.

Love and death are unlikely partners. Romantic breakups, for example, are often described as a kind of death. In the words of Dusty Springfield, after such a breakup, "Love seems dead and so unreal, all that's left is loneliness, there's nothing left to feel." Personal relationships without love are also often associated with death. We speak about "dead marriages," "cold husbands," and "frigid wives." People within a dull relationship often consider their situation to be a kind of death, and having an affair is described as living again. Thus, a married woman, having her first affair after twenty years, describes her relationship with her husband as being that of roommate. While having the affair, she said, "I felt like I had awoken from a coma. I felt connected to life and the people in it. I felt youthful, confident, and brave."

Since love is perceived to be vital to life, the end of love can cause some people to wish to end their lives as well or to kill others for love. In the name of love, there are men who kill their partners and commit suicide when the latter intend to leave them.[7]

Despite the crucial role of love in human flourishing, there are people who give up the search for it, believing that they will never find what they seek. These individuals say that they would not reject profound love if it found its way to them, but that they will not actively pursue it. This attitude is understandable—after all, love is not all you need in life—though people are often much happier with love.

## A Widow's New Romantic Situation

Is the human heart large enough to hold more than one romantic love? This is entirely possible—both loving one person after another and having two lovers at the same time. Let's think for a moment of the complicated case of widows' love. Their love for two people is particularly complex, given the continuing impact of bereavement, even years after the death occurs. Their bond to the deceased can remain a personal defining force. They face the double challenge of loving two people at the same time and a huge practical change: a relationship with a current companion who provides active support and love and with the memory of someone who is no longer alive and cannot be active in their life.

According to romantic ideology, profound love should last forever. The end of love is a sign that it was superficial in the first place. In fact, however, love *can* end for reasons connected to different circumstances, and such changes do not necessarily indicate that the love was superficial. Profound love is less likely to perish, but it can nevertheless. Hence, there is no reason to assume that one's heart is not big enough to include several genuine loves during a single lifetime.

The death of a spouse and the end of love dovetail in different ways. But widowhood is unique. Whether a relationship is average, as most relationships are, or very good or very bad, the ending of any personal relationship changes one's circumstances. In most cases of widowhood, any positive attitude toward the spouse is enhanced. This is due both to the tendency to idealize the past and to our sense of propriety in not speaking ill of the dead. Although the late spouse is physically absent, the widow's love for him can remain—and even grow.

The newly widowed confront different situations when contemplating love. Here I will discuss two situations: (1) adapting to a new love while still loving the late spouse, and (2) falling in love with another person almost immediately.

## Adapting to a New Lover

> A widow's refusal of a lover is seldom so explicit as to exclude hope.
>
> Samuel Richardson

Falling in love again after losing a spouse is not the same as having a new love affair after a previous one has ended. This is especially so if, at the time of the spouse's death, both partners shared a profound love. In this case, the survivor's love does not die. Although a new love might develop, from a psychological viewpoint, the widow will now love two people at the same time. Her experience eloquently expresses the nonexclusive nature of love.

Importantly, love is a shape-changer. Seeking the same love with another partner can be devastating, as no two people are identical. In a sense, the new lover can bring a bereaved partner back to life. One widow told the friend who ignited in her the desire to make love again: "Thank you for bringing me back to life."

The widow faces the challenge of entering a new and meaningful romantic relationship without forgetting or negating the old one. Ofri Bar-Nadav and Simon Rubin compare the issues facing bereaved and nonbereaved women when they enter new relationships after a long-term one has ended. The bereaved experienced themselves as having changed more, but the nonbereaved reported the changes they experienced as more positive. The growth experienced by the nonbereaved at this stage of life is likely to be less conflicted, and while the bereaved experience such growth, it lags behind that of their counterparts. Bar-Nadav and Rubin argue that in the wake of loss and its aftermath, widows feel greater hesitancy than their peers do about engaging in intimacy with new partners. These concerns about intimacy arise from fears of further loss, of opening themselves up to new relationships, and of lack of fidelity to the deceased spouse.[8]

Our minds work wonders in these situations. While the deceased spouse ceases to disappoint and irritate us, the new (and very much alive) partner continues to do so, reminding us of the richness and challenge of ongoing living relationships. Although love for the deceased spouse might increase as time goes by, it may be less of a preoccupation, easing adaptation to the new relationship. A new loving relationship requires both letting go of and holding on to the previous relationship, creating a new equilibrium.[9]

Finding the right partner and learning to live with them can take a lot of time and effort. Some people reach an age at which they doubt whether it is worth the effort, especially when the memory of their late spouse remains ever present as the new relationship develops.

## How Soon Should Widows Fall in Love Again?

Even if all the above obstacles to being with a new lover are resolved, the widow still faces a whole set of dilemmas. These include the proper period for grieving, whether and when to take off their wedding ring, when to begin dating, when to give away the late partner's belongings, how to dress for various occasions, how often to talk about the past, and what loving gestures toward the new lover can be shown in public. As widows tend to be judged critically, sensitivity, careful pacing, and moderation are in order. A widow dating a married man will be subject to greater criticism than a divorced or single woman—after all, she should know better what it is to lose a spouse. It seems that, like Julius Caesar's wife, widows are expected to be "above suspicion."

Consider the following true story. A widow who was dating a widower observed that her beau continued to wear his wedding ring—he had not taken it off when his wife died. In due time, the two became engaged and started to plan their wedding. The wedding ring remained on the widower's finger. Finally, just as the bride-to-be was choosing her new wedding band, her intended turned to her and said: "Would it be okay with you if I wore two wedding rings?" This poignant question (answered, incidentally, in the negative) exposes a deep dilemma—profound love cannot be exclusive in all its aspects. There are things that we cannot, and should not, erase from our partner's heart.

And now we come to a particularly contested point: the waiting period before dating. Different cultures have different norms: in some traditions, people wait at least a year; in others, it can be longer or shorter. Michelle Heidstra's experience is telling. Only four weeks after the death of her husband, Jon, she embarked on a new love affair with his best friend, Adrian, a pallbearer at the funeral. Lost in her grief, she found herself drawn to the man who could comfort her. Adrian was very supportive of both her and her infant. At the end of a day spent with a group of her husband's friends, including Adrian, Michelle found herself in his house. "We were both in turmoil and we needed each other. We made love," says Michelle. "We couldn't help ourselves. It seemed so right." It is, she says, exactly what Jon would have wanted. She was not even embarrassed to tell her friends about it. Michelle understands those who criticized her, but says, "How can you make rules about people's emotions? We all love and grieve differently. I have never stopped grieving for Jon. But that doesn't rule out a new love." After a year of seeing each other, they felt that the relationship was getting too serious too quickly, and they took a break. A year later, they started dating again. This time the pace was slower, and they moved in together only six months later. They are now engaged to be married. Michelle says, "Blame me if you like, but grief hits people in different ways and I have no regrets."[10]

Such stories are far from rare; many people fall in love with their late partner's best friend within a short time after the partner's death. This can be a reasonable response to intense loss, when a supportive friend is the most natural person in the world to be with. The terrible grief can be shared.

To sum up, widows must manage a unique form of romantic breakup, which involves a final physical separation but not a psychological one. The breakup caused by the spouse's death is unwelcome and irreversible, and the surviving partner might still be in love with her late spouse. Different people do different things under such circumstances. Although it is often better to find a new lover than to give up and never search for a new love, this option is not always available. It is possible to fall in love again, but new loving relationships are always well populated: the deceased partner is always in the background.

## LOVE AND DEMENTIA

Love is an act of endless forgiveness, a tender look which becomes a habit.

Peter Ustinov

What is the meaning of love in relationships between couples in which one partner has dementia? This is a question for which the role of time in love is highly relevant, since one of the partners has virtually lost a sense of the past. In such situations, the healthy spouse's sense of the past is a major factor in maintaining love.

In old age, the reduced ability to share various activities presents a challenge to the dialogue model, which is based on spouses' engagement in joint activities and thus creating a meaningful *we*. Dementia, which severely damages the ability to socialize, and especially the capacity to converse and share interests with others, magnifies this problem.

Orit Shavit and colleagues present a nuanced picture of the romantic attitudes of individuals whose spouses are living with Alzheimer's disease. They identify five major types of relationship development following the emergence of the disease: love died, love became weaker, love did not change, love was enhanced, and the healthy spouse fell in love again. These types are also common among the loving relationships of other couples in old age. Participants described their love in a compassionate manner and in the context of their daily routines of caring. Most spouses stated that their intimacy gained a new meaning; they reported greater intimacy with their spouses living with the disease. It seems that the increased romantic intimacy experienced by some is related to an enhanced component of care.[11]

On the face of it, the dialogue approach would seem to have trouble explaining love in relation to dementia, in which the partners' interactions decline in quantity and quality. It is the care model, instead, that leaps to mind as most appropriate. Although in old age and with dementia the shared time and activities are more limited and less diverse, they can still be part of love and intimacy. Thus, even if sick people cannot contribute to the loving relation as much as they did before, their loving relation is the continuation of what was before. This is compatible with the dialogue model.

## CONCLUDING REMARKS

Romantic horizons indeed shrink at an older age; certainly, there are fewer possibilities numerically and emotionally. This makes many people too willing to stay in their comfort zone and not engage in a relationship or expect a relationship to just happen to them without doing anything.

Hara Estroff Marano

Extramarital affairs express the determined refusal to grow older gracefully.

Catherine Hakim

Later life is a patchwork for profound love—it presents some of the best circumstances for it as well as some of its greatest obstacles. Since time nurtures profundity, the deepest point of connection for romantic partners in healthy relationships is sometimes after they have accumulated decades of experiences that they can build upon together in later life. After the loss of a partner in old age, the severing of this bond can be extremely difficult to deal with. It can be tempting to give up on love completely after the death of one's lover. But, as love is so vital to flourishing and well-being, it is important to find a suitable new relationship, though the type and timing of such a relationship differs from person to person.

When one partner passes away and the other is left single, often for the first time in nearly a lifetime, there are unique challenges in achieving new love. Not only do widows tend to idealize their deceased partner, but their profound love might very well be everlasting, so dealing with mixed emotions when establishing new love becomes even more complex. Questions of whether to try to forget or to replace the previous partner further complicate the beginning of a new relationship.

Adding to the hurdles for love in old age, dementia presents a unique set of issues and questions, as the disease often unpredictably influences a crucial aspect of the romantic connection—profound meaningful interactions and experiences, including communication, sex, caring, friendship, reciprocity, and love. While individual experiences differ widely, dementia does consistently mark a change in the way that partners relate to each other and interact. This is not a barrier to profound, though limited, love, but it requires significant adjustments to the new type of relationship.

Emotional experiences in later life are likely to be marked by calmness rather than excitement. As both calmness and excitement are important in a romantic relationship, the issue is not one of either/or, but of choice of focus.

Obstacles to love are scattered throughout the life course. Old age can rebalance partners' ability to engage constructively in the relationship. When dementia figures into the equation, the maintenance of love calls for great sacrifice. Serious consideration must be given to the impact of such sacrifice on the relationship and one's personal flourishing. This is how we honor the wholeness necessary to sustain profound, romantic relationships.

## NOTES

1. Lyubomirsky 2013.

2. Carmichael et al. 2015.

3. Carstensen 2006.

4. Carstensen 2006.

5. Charles and Carstensen 2002.

6. Charles and Carstensen 2010; Birditt et al. 2018.

7. Ben-Ze' ev and Goussinsky 2008.

8. Bar-Nadav and Rubin 2016.

9. Rubin et al. 2012.

10. "How soon is too soon to find love after being widowed?," *Mail Online*, July 10, 2010.

11. Shavit et al. 2017..

# REFERENCES

Bar-Nadav, O., and S. S. Rubin. 2016. Love and bereavement. *OMEGA—Journal of Death and Dying* 74: 62–79.

Ben-Ze'ev, A., and R. Goussinsky. 2008. *In the name of love*. Oxford: Oxford University Press.

Birditt, K. S., C. W. Sherman, C. A. Polenick, L. Becker, N. J. Webster, K. J. Ajrouch, and T. C. Antonucci. 2018. So close and yet so irritating: Negative relations and implications for well-being by age and closeness. *Journals of Gerontology: Series B*: gby038.

Carmichael, C. L., H. T. Reis, and P. R. Duberstein. 2015. In your 20s it's quantity, in your 30s it's quality: The prognostic value of social activity across 30 years of adulthood. *Psychology and Aging* 30:95–105.

Carstensen, L. L. 2006. The influence of a sense of time on human development. *Science* 312 (5782): 1913–15.

Charles, S. T., and L. L. Carstensen. 2002. Marriage in old age. In M. Yalom, L. L. Carstensen, E. Freedman, and B. Gelpi (eds.), *American Couple*, 236–54. Berkeley: University of California Press.

———. 2010. Social and emotional aging. *Annual Review of Psychology* 61:383–409.

Lyubomirsky, S. 2013. *The myths of happiness*. New York: Penguin.

Rubin, S. S., R. Malkinson, and E. Witztum. 2012. *Working with the bereaved*. New York: Routledge.

Shavit, O., A. Ben-Zeev, and I. Doron. 2017. Love between couples living with Alzheimer's disease: Narratives of spouse care-givers, *Ageing & Society*, 1–30.

# EDITORS' INTRODUCTION

Is it weird to think of your parents having sex? How about your grandparents? We get it. You're not alone. Being uncomfortable with the idea of older people being sexual can make it a somewhat taboo topic, even for older people! Our society and culture have influenced us to think about sex only happening between young, beautiful people, when in fact people of all ages, races, religions, sexual orientations, genders, and so on can and do have sexual feelings, enjoy being sexual, and think sex is an important part of a romantic relationship. A recent study showed that partnered adults between the ages of 65 and 75 reported high sexual self-esteem, positive attitudes toward sexuality and aging, satisfaction with their sexual lives, and interest in sex (Santos-Iglesias et al., 2016). In the final reading for this chapter, "The Evolving Concept of Older Adult Sexual Behavior and Its Benefits," Maggie Syme challenges us to consider our beliefs and assumptions about older adult sexuality and open ourselves to consider the importance that sex and intimacy still play as we age. Syme writes to health care providers, but her message is relevant to all.

As you read, keep in mind the following primer question for reflection. If you feel so inclined, take a few minutes and consider your responses to the following questions before you read, and then again after you've finished each reading.

## PRIMER

1. As you know, intimacy means much more than having sex. Try to think of at least five intimate behaviors that couples could practice at any age, regardless of physical ability.

# The Evolving Concept of Older Adult Sexual Behavior and Its Benefits

*By Maggie L. Syme*

Due to prolonged life and health, there are increased numbers of sexually active elders. Practitioners must keep an open attitude and encourage this healthy practice.

A lthough intimate partners can be the most influential source of social support for older adults who have them, the sexual and intimate aspects of their relationships are rarely discussed in practice settings or scientific literature. It is a wasted opportunity to disregard sexuality, as it contributes to health and well-being for many of our older adult clients. Intimacy can impact well-being through the construction of joint beliefs and behaviors, as well as through pooled resources. The expression of intimate and sexual behaviors also directly links to health and quality of life across the lifespan (Waite and Das, 2010). Sexual expression affects both the quality of the relationship and each individual's overall health, making it an integral part of health as we age.

Yet older adult sexuality is often ignored. Healthcare professionals often report stereotypic beliefs, such as thinking older adults are asexual, and express worry about addressing sexuality with older adults because of a lack of knowledge and embarrassment (Hinchliff and Gott, 2011). Consider Joe, a seventy-year-old man who sees his primary care doctor for high blood pressure. Recently, Joe mentioned he feels less "close" to his wife. His doctor nods knowingly and tells Joe it is normal to have ups and downs in a relationship. Even though Joe is at higher risk for sexual concerns due to cardiovascular issues, his doctor does not even think to ask about sex (given Joe's age), ignoring a potentially crucial aspect of emotional intimacy between Joe and his wife and ignoring a potential health risk.

Sex and intimacy cannot be ignored, as older adults are living healthier and longer lives and engaging in a variety of intimate and sexual behaviors—and this is true for those in the oldest cohorts (Lindau and Gavrilova, 2010). Also, sex and intimacy are an important

Maggie L. Syme, "The Evolving Concept of Older Adult Sexual Behavior and Its Benefits," *Generations*, vol. 38, no. 1, pp. 35-41.

part of life, with the majority of older adults indicating sex is "critical for a good relationship" (67 percent of men, 50 percent of women) and an integral part of quality of life (85 percent of men, 61 percent of women) (Fisher, 2010).

Older adults are also becoming increasingly open in their attitudes and beliefs about sexuality, with the majority endorsing the appropriateness of sex outside of marriage and very few endorsing sex as just for procreation (Fisher, 2010). This shift in attitudes and behaviors has combined with medical advances to prolong a sexually active life and change the landscape of aging sexuality. The challenge is for professionals in aging to meet the unique needs of older adults who are staying sexually interested and active. This [reading] will present key issues related to sexuality and intimacy in later life and their importance to older adult health and well-being, and introduce resources to use with older adults to support intimacy and sexuality and promote overall health.

## WHY ADDRESS SEXUALITY AND WHAT DOES IT MEAN?

Quality social connections, including intimate partnerships, have many health benefits, such as increased longevity and positive health behaviors (Cohen and Janicki-Deverts, 2009). Having a sexual partnership, with frequent sexual expression, having a good quality sex life, and being interested in sex have been found to be positively associated with health among middle-aged and older adults in the United States (Lindau and Gavrilova, 2010).

Many health benefits are linked to sexual expression, including the following: increased relaxation, decreased pain sensitivity, improved cardiovascular health, lower levels of depression, increased self-esteem, and better relationship satisfaction (Brody, 2010; Davison et al., 2009; Heiman et al., 2011; Jannini et al., 2009). Perhaps more importantly, older adults remain interested in sex and intimacy within their partnerships and find it an important source of well-being (Fisher, 2010; Waite et al., 2009).

Sexuality is a broad concept, encompassing interest, behaviors, functioning, satisfaction, intimate relationships, and sexual self-esteem. It historically has been perceived more narrowly in a biomedical context, with emphasis placed on the sexual response cycle, hetero-normative behaviors (e.g., penile-vaginal intercourse), and heterosexist and ageist assumptions (Marshall, 2011). In contrast, a holistic view of sexuality incorporates an integration of emotional, social, intellectual, and somatic experiences, represents diverse sexual experiences, reflects the relationship context, and focuses on pleasure as well as on sexual dysfunction.

The holistic view aims to capture the realities of sexuality across the lifespan and is more inclusive of sexuality and intimacy into later life, as many older adults, as they age, shift their concept of sexuality to include intimate and pleasurable behaviors such as hugging, touching, kissing, and emotional intimacy (Metz and McCarthy, 2007; Taylor and Gosney, 2011; Waite and Das, 2010).

> The majority of older adults indicate sex is 'critical for a good relationship.'

In a qualitative study of older adult women who remarried in later life, many women described their marriages as initially having higher levels of sexual passion, which tended to evolve into a stronger emotional intimacy as the relationship progressed, particularly as barriers to sexual activity (such as physical health) emerged. Both phases of marriage were fulfilling for the women, depending upon the quality and expectations of their marital relationships (Clarke, 2006). Redefining sexual relationships as we age is a common theme of older adulthood, which may include changes in typical sexual and intimate behaviors, or a shift away from sexual expression to a more emotional intimacy.

## PATTERNS OF EXPRESSION AND COMMON CONCERNS

Many older adults continue to be interested in sex and engage in a variety of sexual and intimate behaviors, which remain relatively consistent through their early seventies. In fact, the majority of partnered older adults report recent sexual activity through age 74 (62.8 percent of women and 74.7 percent of men), with a more significant decline between the ages of 75 to 84 (41.4 percent of women and 54.2 percent of men) (Waite et al., 2009).

Older adults engage in a spectrum of sexual and physically intimate behaviors, with masturbation, vaginal intercourse, and foreplay (e.g., kissing, caressing) as the most frequently reported activities (Schick et al., 2010; Waite et al., 2009). Typical sexual behaviors may shift in older adulthood as the normal aging process affects physical health and functional capacity of the older adult. In these cases, intimate interactions may focus more on kissing, fondling, cuddling, or the use of assistive devices and medications (Clarke, 2006; DeLamater, 2012; Waite and Das, 2010). In order to build emotional closeness, or keep the "romance" in the relationship, older adults report behaviors such as saying "I love you" and recognizing important days like birthdays and anniversaries (Fisher, 2010).

Sexual functioning concerns are a reality for many sexually active older adults, with approximately half of them reporting at least one sexual problem and one-third reporting two or three sexual problems (Lindau et al., 2007). The most common concerns for older adult men include erectile dysfunction and premature climax, and older adult women most commonly report lack of desire, problems with vaginal lubrication, sexual pain, and inability to reach orgasm.

Despite these concerns, many older adults remain sexually active, with 22 to 34 percent of sexually active older adults indicating they avoid sex because of those problems (Waite et al., 2009). Various medical and psychosocial interventions are available to treat these common concerns (see Hillman, 2011, and Syme et al., forthcoming, for a discussion of assessment and treatment options for sexual concerns among older adults). However, older adults often avoid seeking help for sexual concerns because of a lack of knowledge about their sexual problems, embarrassment or discomfort talking about sex, and stigma-related beliefs about older adults and sexuality in older age being inappropriate (Fisher, 2010; Taylor and Gosney,

| Figure 15.3.1

2011). Think back to Joe's situation, with the doctor ignoring sexual concerns—now we have Joe avoiding bringing them up because he's embarrassed, thus his concerns go undetected and unaddressed.

Older adults face unique challenges as they establish sexually satisfying relationships, such as physical and functional limitations and loss of a partner (Waite and Das, 2010). The good news is the vast majority of older adults enjoy sexual and intimate lives, however they are expressed. In a large international study, 65 to 77 percent of older adult women and men in the United States reported physical and emotional pleasure in their intimate relationships, and more than 80 percent were satisfied with their sexual functioning (Laumann et al., 2006). Also, in a recent survey conducted by AARP, older adults reporting a "happy sexual relationship" tended to have a sexual partner, frequent sexual intercourse, good health for the individual and partner, low levels of stress, and an absence of financial worries (Fisher, 2010). Building satisfying physical and emotional intimacy will help to support relationship quality into older age and the overall health of the dyad.

## FACTORS ASSOCIATED WITH SEXUALITY AND INTIMACY

Sexuality is shaped by several interrelated factors that are biological, psychological, social, and cultural in nature; these interact with each other to influence how sexuality is expressed across the lifespan (Bitzer et al., 2008; Hillman, 2011). Below is a brief overview of the biopsychosocial factors associated with sexuality (for a more comprehensive discussion, see DeLamater, 2012).

## Biological

Changes in physiological functioning through normal aging can influence sexual and intimate expression. Hormonal changes occur in older adult women as a part of menopause—cessation of principal estrogen—and can affect blood flow, atrophy of the vaginal wall, vaginal narrowing, and decreases in lubrication. Men also experience hormonal changes, with a gradual decline in testosterone being associated with decreased orgasm, longer refractory periods, and erectile dysfunction (Bitzer et al., 2008; DeLamater, 2012). For both men and women, one or more chronic diseases and the associated treatments can negatively impact sexual functioning. Common conditions that impact sexual functioning include cardiovascular disease, diabetes, degenerative and rheumatoid arthritis, stroke, cancer, kidney disease, and spinal cord injury (Bach et al., 2013; DeLamater, 2012). Physical health also affects sexual satisfaction in older adulthood, with poorer individual and partner health status associated with decreased satisfaction (Syme et al., 2013). Also, older men's physical health tends to be more predictive of continued sexual activity and satisfaction within the relationship than does older women's health (Lindau et al., 2007).

> Body image and sexual self-esteem are major factors in sexual interest and activity in older adulthood, particularly for women.

## Psychological

At any age, psychological concerns such as depression and anxiety can affect sexual and intimate expression, whether through mental health symptoms, treatments, or subsequent changes in everyday behavior (DeLamater, 2012). For instance, a mental health issue can significantly change the way we interact with others, potentially affecting the intimate relationship and altering feelings of emotional intimacy between partners. Body image and sexual self-esteem are also major factors in sexual interest and activity in older adulthood, particularly for women, and can be negatively impacted by ageist notions of youth and beauty (Montemurro and Gillen, 2013). Sexual health practices are also impacted by attitudes and beliefs commonly held among older adults, such as misconceptions about sexual risk and preventative practices (e.g., using condoms as birth control only, fear of negotiating condom use) (Hillman, 2011).

> Internalized stereotypic ageist beliefs help maintain an ignorance of older adult sexuality.

Additionally, the cognitive status of older adults can influence sexual consent capacity (i.e., sexual decision making). No uniform standards exist for assessing sexual consent capacity in older adults, though a growing body of information is available on the key issues involved in determining sexual consent and supporting older adults who can make their own sexual decisions, while protecting those who may not be able to (e.g., American Bar Association/American Psychological Association, 2008; Connolly et al., 2012; Hillman, 2011). For older adults in long-term-care settings, intimacy is further complicated by the pervasive stigma about sexuality and commonly held ageist attitudes (Hillman, 2011).

## Relationship

For many older adults, marriage provides the social and emotional context for intimate and sexual expression. In fact, having a partner, most often defined as a spouse, is highly predictive of continued sexual interest and activity for both older men and women (DeLamater, 2012; Lindau et al., 2007). Men are more likely than women to be partnered in later life, due to increased longevity of women and the tendency of older men to remarry younger women ("age hypergamy"), which differentially affects older women's opportunities for sexuality and intimacy into older age (Waite and Das, 2010, p. S94). The quality of the marital relationship also affects sex and intimacy, with those reporting higher relationship satisfaction also reporting higher sexual satisfaction and less sexual dysfunction (Heiman et al., 2011).

## Cultural

Older adults are a unique cultural group, growing in diversity and influenced by myriad socio-cultural events, which also shape their beliefs and attitudes toward sexuality. In Western society, older adults learn sex is for the young and beautiful, and sex for older people is shameful, disgusting, or nonexistent (Bitzer et al., 2008; Hillman, 2011); this can lead to internalized stigma and lowered sexual self-esteem. These stereotypic beliefs help maintain an ignorance of older adult sexuality, especially across various settings, which can have detrimental results (e.g., underreporting of sexual concerns, rising sexually transmitted infection rates among older adults) (Hillman, 2011; Hinchliff and Gott, 2011). Also, older lesbian, gay, bisexual, and transgendered (LGBT) adults are less likely to have come out about their sexual orientation and have fewer social connections. They also may experience shame and fear that they will face discrimination in healthcare settings (Hinchliff and Gott, 2011). All of these factors dispose them to negative health effects.

## OPEN ATTITUDES OPTIMAL FOR PROVIDERS

Sexual relationships are crucial for older adult health, and the way these are expressed among older adults is changing, particularly with the aging of the baby boomers. When promoting health, sexuality, and intimacy among older adults, considerations may include increasingly open attitudes toward sexuality, dating and developing new relationships, challenges of facilitating intimacy in residential settings, supporting caregivers in building intimacy within and outside spousal relationships, and promoting sexual health and safe sex practices among older adults.

Research is beginning to tackle these issues (Fisher, 2010; Schick et al., 2010), and more resources related to sexuality in later life are emerging (e.g., the American Psychological Association's Aging and Human Sexuality Resource Guide; http://goo.gl/ogVeFR), with specific information on sex education (Brick et al., 2009), sexuality in long-term care (The National Long-Term Care Ombudsman Resource Center's Sexuality and Intimacy in Long-Term Care Facilities; http://goo.gl/5oLy3g), and LGBT older adults (Services and Advocacy for Gay, Lesbian, Bisexual and Transgender Elders; www.sageusa.org).

## IMPLICATIONS FOR PRACTICE

Sex and intimacy among older adult clients is a reality that professionals in aging need to face. How can we meet this challenge and promote sexual health across the lifespan? First, understand your beliefs and attitudes toward sexuality in later life, and examine any barriers there might be to working supportively with older adults (see Price, 2009). Also, get to know the important sexuality and intimacy issues that are specific to those you serve—community-dwelling, older adults in adult day health, residents with dementia, LGBT older adults—and start with the resources provided here. Increasing your understanding will help you become more aware of and identify intimacy needs and opportunities for discussion as well as give you tools to begin addressing intimacy needs.

It may be especially useful to provide your older adult clients with a safe and supportive climate within which they can discuss sex, and to have basic information to educate them about common sexual concerns and functioning in older adulthood. You can also advocate that sexuality and intimacy be integrated into the services provided at your organization: education for staff, addressing sexual consent policies, activities that allow coupled residents to build intimacy (e.g., dances, date nights), incorporating physical intimacy goals into physical therapy, or providing a confidential space for older adults to discuss sexual health issues.

What will you do when a "Joe" comes to you needing help? Instead of overlooking his concerns or shying away because you're embarrassed, try giving him permission to talk about sex and letting him know you will work with him to support his goals for sex and intimacy.

## REFERENCES

American Bar Association/American Psychological Association. 2008. Assessment of Older Adults with Diminished Capacity: A Handbook for Psychologists. Washington, DC: American Bar Association/American Psychological Association.

Bach, L. E., et al. 2013. "The Association of Physical and Mental Health with Sexual Activity in Older Adults in a Retirement Community." Journal of Sexual Medicine 10(11): 2671–8.

Bitzer, J., et al. 2008. "Sexual Counseling for Elderly Couples." Journal of Sexual Medicine 5(9): 2027–43.

Brick, P., et al. 2009. Older, Wiser, and Sexually Smarter: 30 Sex Ed Lessons for Adults Only. Morristown, NJ: Planned Parenthood of Greater Northern New Jersey.

Brody, S. 2010. "The Relative Health Benefits of Different Sexual Activities." Journal of Sexual Medicine 7(4/Pt1): 1336–61.

Clarke, L. H. 2006. "Older Women and Sexuality: Experiences in Marital Relationships Across the Life Course." Canadian Journal on Aging 25(2): 129–40.

Cohen, S., and Janicki-Deverts, D. 2009. "Can We Improve Our Physical Health by Altering Our Social Networks?" Perspectives on Psychological Science 4(4): 375–8.

Connolly, M. T., et al. 2012. "The Sexual Revolution's Last Frontier: How Silence About Sex Undermines Health, Well-Being, and Safety in Older Adults." Generations 36(3): 43–52.

Davison, S. L., et al. 2009. "The Relationship Between Self-reported Sexual Satisfaction and General Well-being in Women." Journal of Sexual Medicine 6(10): 2690–7.

DeLamater, J. 2012. "Sexual Expression in Later Life: A Review and Synthesis." Journal of Sex Research 49(2–3): 125–41.

Fisher, L. 2010. Sex, Romance, and Relationships: AARP Survey of Midlife and Older Adults. (AARP Pub. No. D19234). Washington, DC: AARP.

Heiman, J. R., et al. 2011. "Sexual Satisfaction and Relationship Happiness in Midlife and Older Couples in Five Countries." Archives of Sexual Behavior 40(4): 741–53.

Hillman, J. 2011. Sexuality and Aging: Clinical Perspectives. New York: Springer.

Hinchliff, S., and Gott, M. 2011. "Seeking Medical Help for Sexual Concerns in Mid- and Later Life: A Review of the Literature." Journal of Sex Research 48(2–3): 106–17.

Jannini, E. A., et al. 2009. "Is Sex Just Fun? How Sexual Activity Improves Health." Journal of Sexual Medicine 6(10): 2640–8.

Laumann, E. O., et al. 2006. "A Cross National Study of Subjective Sexual Well-being among Older Women and Men: Findings from the Global Study of Sexual Attitudes and Behaviors." Archives of Sexual Behavior 35(2): 145–61.

Lindau, S. T., and Gavrilova, N. 2010. "Sex, Health, and Years of Sexually Active Life Gained Due to Good Health: Evidence from Two U.S. Population-based Cross Sectional Surveys of Ageing." British Medical Journal 340: 1–11.

Lindau, S. T., et al. 2007. "A Study of Sexuality and Health among Older Adults in the United States." New England Journal of Medicine 357: 762–74.

Marshall, B. L. 2011. "The Graying of 'Sexual Health': A Critical Research Agenda." Canadian Review of Sociology 48(4): 390–413.

Metz, M. E., and McCarthy, B. W. 2007. "The 'Good-Enough Sex' Model for Couple Sexual Satisfaction." Sexual and Relationship Therapy 22(3): 351–62.

Montemurro, B., and Gillen, M. M. 2013. "Wrinkles and Sagging Flesh: Exploring Transformations in Women's Sexual Body Image." Journal of Women & Aging 25(1): 3–23.

Price, B. 2009. "Exploring Attitudes Towards Older People's Sexuality." Nursing Older People 21(6): 32–9.

Schick, V., et al. 2010. "Sexual Behaviors, Condom Use, and Sexual Health of Americans Over 50: Implications for Sexual Health Promotion for Older Adults." The Journal of Sexual Medicine 7(Suppl 5): 315–29.

Syme, M. L., et al. 2013. "Predicting Sexual Unwellness in Older Adults: The Role of Physical and Mental Health Risk Factors." The Journals of Gerontology, Series B: Psychological Sciences and Social Sciences 68(3): 323–32.

Syme, M. L., et al. Forthcoming. "Sexual Health and Well-being in the Context of Aging." In Lichtenberg, P., and Mast, B., eds., APA Handbook of Clinical Geropsychology. Washington, DC: American Psychological Association.

Taylor, A., and Gosney, M. A. 2011. "Sexuality in Older Age: Essential Considerations for Healthcare Professionals." Age and Ageing 40(5): 538–43.

Waite, L., and Das, A. 2010. "Families, Social Life, and Wellbeing at Older Ages." Demography 47(Suppl): S87–S109.

Waite, L. J., et al. 2009. "Sexuality: Measures of Partnerships, Practices, Attitudes, and Problems in the National Social Life, Health, and Aging Study." The Journals of Gerontology, Series B: Psychological Sciences and Social Sciences 64(Suppl 1): i56–i66.

# END-OF-CHAPTER REFLECTIONS

We bring this anthology to a close with some stories and words of wisdom from some of our favorite people—family members and friends who have significant life and relationship experience. All the words of wisdom come from men and women who are 55 years or older. Some are married, some divorced, some widowed, some partnered, some single. We hope you take their words to heart and integrate them with the many things you've learned about relationships in this anthology.

On maintaining a happy marriage: Walt (67) and Stace (60), married 27 years

> Our #1 rule above everything else is good communication. What helped us for years was having common goals and revisiting those goals often (as to be on the same page and excited for the same things). Be grateful and aware of how great this [marriage] is and talk about it (it is a choice relationship—two-way street). Intimacy is really important while growing old together. Even just holding hands means so much. EQUALITY in everything from chores to financial to doing your part fairly in a relationship. HUMOR for us was key. PATIENCE is probably the most important yet the hardest to practice daily. Something we do every 5 years is check in and see if your partner still wants to do this. It would be so much easier to split up while you still like the other person but we all change as we grow older so back to communication.

On the importance of friendship: Berni (74), divorced, single

> I come from a small family, so my friendships are like sisterhoods. We talk, we travel, we play games, we confide in each other as you would a sister. Most men [at this stage of life] want a nurse and a purse.

On loving, and loving after loss: Mart (71), widowed, in a relationship

I went from wife to widow in a twinkling of an eye. It was July 2005. That morning started with a conversation about how much we meant to each other—him thanking me for sticking with him all these years, through thick and thin; me telling him he was the only man for me and that I loved him more than ever. That evening he was gone—taken by a sudden heart attack. He was 58; I was 55. Our last conversation was filled with love and grace. We didn't realize we were saying goodbye.

The future was confusing. I had never been alone. A couple of years passed before I decided to try to move on. I tried eharmony and Match dating sites. It was disheartening. I worked on being alone. I had a loving family, children, grandchildren, friends, siblings, and a job that fulfilled me. Yet, the intimacy of a partner left a void. It was too quiet going to bed and waking up alone.

Fast forward 12 years. I was 67 years old and retired. I made a life for myself that was satisfying. By chance, though, I discovered that someone I used to date 50 years before had lost his wife 3 years prior. I found him on Facebook and sent a message asking if he'd remembered me. And, oh yes, he did remember me!

We planned to meet at a restaurant for dinner. When we met it was as if all the years melted away. We saw each other as if we were 20 years old again. There was so much to talk about—our children, grandchildren, our lives—so parallel. It was as if we had been together all that time but with a different partner. The synchronicity was miraculous. There were so many connections between our families, yet our paths never crossed. It was all about timing.

I always knew I had capacity for more. My family has literally doubled in size. We now share hopes and dreams. Our only job is to become blessings to one another and to make each day better than the one before. It is an easy task to simply be a joy to another person. Because we both loved and were loved before, we knew how to love again.

On appreciating every moment: Deb (75), in a committed relationship

Resistance fades with increased trust, compassion, and love. Time is precious; listening well and laughing often connects us to what is truly important in our lives: a grown son's unexpected empathy, a granddaughter's growing self-confidence in the world around her, a coiled and sleeping Tuxedo cat, the nocturnal coyote's call, a full moon, handholding, kisses, and bowls of first-rate ice-cream. To see the morning light together is a joyous celebration, and we know our lives have been well lived.

On retirement: Jo (76) and Les (78), married over 20 years

Retirement was probably one of the greatest challenges to our relationship. We were comfortable in our careers and had adjusted to spending time with family and friends and other activities in the context of the free time our work afforded. We had a routine of having to schedule time to be alone together, which worked well for us. When we retired, we found ourselves with a lot of time together with nothing much to distract us. Taking full responsibility for our schedule was a new skill we needed to develop because previously work schedules dictated much of our free time. We had not had that luxury previously and at first found it a difficult adjustment. We were together for breakfast, lunch, and dinner and all the other times in between. We quickly realized we needed to schedule time away from each other in order to make our relationship work. We also noticed it was easy to "just do nothing" for a while but that soon became a problem physically, emotionally, and intellectually. We decided to become more involved in volunteer and community activities, spend more time with individual and couple friends, and involve ourselves with more time in separate hobbies.

Adjusting to extra time in general and extra time together required a major change in our thinking and our doing. We found that when we spent time apart, we had more to talk about when we were together. We also discovered that when we had other things such as volunteer work and hobbies to engage us, we focused less on each other and appreciated each other more.

We moved to another location with a milder climate that was less confining due to cold winters. In the process we downsized, lost our support network and familiar environment, and concentrated on moving and adjusting. This united us in meeting the difficulties of making friends and adjusting to a new location without having jobs, children, and family to bridge the gap. We learned to spend our together time making plans for activities, sharing books we were reading, catching each other up on conversations we had with other people, talking about volunteer activities we were involved in, and taking advantage of the cultural events around us. We talked more about what we appreciated around us as well as what we appreciated about each other.

We needed to take a positive attitude about the changes we made and the changes that were happening around us. We learned to walk away from arguments that became heated but knew we had to return to finish them when we were more calm and less emotional. We have grown into a new phase of our relationship that is different from all the others, and is one of appreciation, and deeper friendship and intimacy.

On trust: Dona (60) and Boomer (57), lesbians together 20 years

The key to a lasting relationship is trust. With trust you can get through the work that all relationships take to be successful. Say what you want, and want what you say. Communication is key. Without it you don't truly know what your partner is thinking.

On dating late in life: E.J. (91), widower at 67, dating

Treat everyone like you want to be treated, regardless of age or whatever; that's the first thing. Other than that, don't get too anxious about anybody; don't let them upset you too much. It's hard to replace the one you were married to, but living by yourself is no fun.

On just being together: Scott (70), widower at 62, single

[The most important things in a relationship are] love, respect and tenderness, a sense of humor, a willingness to argue when needed, and being able to forgive your mate and yourself. Know how to enjoy a boring evening at home.

On slowing down: Teresa (69), married 45 years, retired

> Me: "Did I already kiss you good morning?"
> Him: "I think so . . ."
> We kiss again to make sure.

Our days and nights are so much quieter now, after 45 years together and 44 years of marriage. They are not as fast paced and frantic as they once were with a growing family. And the days and nights are more predictable, unless the kids are home. RC and I visit with each other and talk, and walk and bike a lot. The abject joys and profound sorrows we have experienced together, and the amazing family we have shared, have become one with our souls. As commitment deepens, so does love, friendship, and companionship. Hope we remember if we kiss each other goodnight tonight.

## REFERENCES

Santos-Iglesias, P., Byers, E. S., & Moglia, R. (2016). Sexual well-being of older men and women. *Journal of Human Sexuality, 25*(2), 86–96. https://doi.org/10.3138/cjhs.252-A4

## RECOMMENDATIONS FOR FURTHER READING

Frankowski, A. C. (2015, August). Don't touch! The taboo of intimacy in assisted living. *Aging Today, 36*(4). 3.

Printed in the USA
CPSIA information can be obtained
at www.ICGtesting.com
LVHW081032191223
766811LV00003B/21